READING
THE WORLD

SECOND EDITION

READING THE WORLD

IDEAS THAT MATTER

SECOND EDITION

MICHAEL AUSTIN

W . W . NORTON & COMPANY

NEW YORK   LONDON

W. W. Norton & Company has been independent since its founding in 1923, when William Warder Norton and Mary D. Herter Norton first published lectures delivered at the People's Institute, the adult education division of New York City's Cooper Union. The firm soon expanded its program beyond the Institute, publishing books by celebrated academics from America and abroad. By midcentury, the two major pillars of Norton's publishing program—trade books and college texts—were firmly established. In the 1950s, the Norton family transferred control of the company to its employees, and today—with a staff of four hundred and a comparable number of trade, college, and professional titles published each year—W. W. Norton & Company stands as the largest and oldest publishing house owned wholly by its employees.

Editor: Marilyn Moller
Developmental Editor: Erin Granville
Production Manager: Benjamin Reynolds
Permissions: Nancy Rodwan, Sarah Feider
Text Designer: Margaret Wagner
Art Researcher: Junenoire Mitchell
Managing Editor, College: Marian Johnson

Library of Congress Cataloging-in-Publication Data

Reading the world : ideas that matter / [edited by] Michael Austin.—2nd ed.
    p.   cm.
  Includes bibliographical references and index.

  ISBN 978-0-393-93349-9 (pbk.)

  1. College readers.   2. English language—Rhetoric—Problems, exercises, etc.
  3. Critical thinking—Problems, exercises, etc.   I. Austin, Michael, 1966–

PE1417.R396 2010
808'.0427—dc22   2009047995

  Instructor's Edition ISBN: 978-0-393-93512-7

W. W. Norton & Company, Inc., 500 Fifth Avenue, New York, N.Y. 10110
                          www.wwnorton.com

W. W. Norton & Company, Ltd., Castle House, 75/76 Wells Street, London W1T 3QT

  2 3 4 5 6 7 8 9 0

CONTENTS

PART 1 READING THE WORLD

1 EDUCATION *3*

☐ *Greek Schoolchildren on a Kylix* *5*
This image painted on an ancient Greek *kylix*, or drinking cup, is one of the earliest representations of a dedicated educational setting known in any human culture.

HSÜN TZU *Encouraging Learning* *8*
To pursue [learning] is to be a man, to give it up is to become a beast.

SENECA *On Liberal and Vocational Studies* *16*
I have no respect for any study whatsoever if its end is the making of money. Such studies are to me unworthy ones. They involve the putting out of skills to hire, and are only of value in so far as they may develop the mind without occupying it for long.

AL-GHAZĀLĪ *Manners to Be Observed by Teachers and Students* *24*
A teacher is like a stamp to clay and a student is like clay. If the stamp has no character, there is no impression on clay.

☐ *Image*

☐ *Image*

☐ *Image*

GLORIA ANZALDÚA *How to Tame a Wild Tongue* 527

If you want to really hurt me, talk badly about my language. Ethnic identity is twin skin to linguistic identity—I am my language.

TONI MORRISON *Nobel Lecture* 539

Oppressive language does more than represent violence; it is violence; does more than represent the limits of knowledge; it limits knowledge.

PART 2 A GUIDE TO READING AND WRITING 547

PREFACE

THE FIRST EDITION of *Reading the World: Ideas That Matter* was based on a simple premise: that the great-ideas tradition is fully compatible with the objectives of multiculturalism. To me, this has always seemed obvious. Great ideas are not the exclusive province of any culture, or of any historical epoch. Understanding diversity—really understanding it—requires us to understand the great ideas that have formed diverse societies. And overcoming prejudice requires us to see the essential sameness between our own experiences and those that seem alien to us. By exploring the most important and influential ideas of a variety of human cultures, we can accomplish both objectives.

In the world of contemporary writing instruction, however, these two approaches have come to be seen as, if not quite antithetical, at least incompatible. Multicultural readers largely confine themselves to twentieth- and twenty-first-century issues and readings, while great-ideas readers focus almost exclusively on Western traditions. Those who argue in favor of a multicultural approach to teaching reading and writing often find themselves—in the textbook debates for which English departments are justly famous—on the other side of the table from those who value a rigorous introduction to the great-ideas tradition. *Reading the World places* itself, squarely and unapologetically, on both sides of the table.

I have been extremely gratified by the response to the first edition of *Reading the World: Ideas That Matter*. Since it appeared in 2006, I have heard from many instructors who have used the book and a number of students who have benefitted from its unique approach. What has gratified me the most is the number of readers who have "gotten it," who have understood the power of two approaches that I have tried to combine in this textbook. I believe now more than ever in both the importance and the viability of a meaningfully multicultural, intellectually rigorous introduction to the intellectual traditions of the world's cultures.

The second edition, like the first, groups its readings into seven universal themes: Education, Human Nature; Law and Government; War and Peace; Wealth, Poverty, and Social Class; Science and Nature; and Language and Rhetoric. Several possible chapter groupings are purposely absent. The book does not have, for example, a chapter called "Religion," but not because religion is unimportant in the world's intellectual traditions—quite the opposite. Religion has been so important to the development of ideas that its influence can be seen across the spectrum of human thought. *Reading the World* attempts to show this influence in each chapter by presenting the ideas of the world's great religions and religious leaders on every topic area covered in the book. Likewise, *Reading the World* includes no chapter titled "Women" or "Feminism." To include such a chapter would, in my view, suggest that women writers have limited themselves to a narrow set of issues. Women have written about all the issues covered by this book; therefore, women writers appear in all of its sections. Every chapter in *Reading the World* has been carefully constructed to incorporate multiple perspectives on a particular theme.

English translations of many texts in this volume vary greatly. I have tried to maintain consistency among the different translations while, at the same time, remaining faithful to the original sources. In some cases, however, fidelity seemed more important to the goals of this book than consistency. Thus, the translated texts include some minor variations in spelling, accenting, diacritic marks, and other types of punctuation. Similarly, all British spellings and punctuation have been retained in translated and nontranslated texts.

HIGHLIGHTS

The second edition of *Reading the World* includes a number of new and updated texts. In deciding which texts to add and which to retire, I have been guided by the feedback that I have received from both instructors and students who have used the first edition. Some of this feedback has been very specific—comments about the ways that specific texts have worked in a classroom setting. Much of it, though, fits into several large patterns that I have tried to address in the second edition. Among the changes that readers will find in this new edition are

- **More readings from contemporary authors:** Along with the classical texts and influential ideas from across the spectrum of human cultures, the new edition includes more recent texts from such influential thinkers as Desmond Tutu, Barack Obama, Mohammad Yunus, Toni Morrison, and Al Gore.

- **More attention to rhetoric:** All headnotes have been revised to emphasize the rhetorical strategies that authors use to present their information, structure their thoughts, and convince their audiences.

- **More help with revising and editing:** Part 2, The Guide to Reading and Writing, now includes more information for students on the process of revision.

I believe that these changes will help students get more out of their experience with the challenging yet extremely rewarding texts that they will encounter in *Reading the World*. The essential features of the book remain unchanged from the first edition and include

- **A balance of Western and non-Western texts:** Nearly half of the selections come from Eastern, Islamic, African, and South American sources. These texts highlight both the differences between Western and non-Western thinking and the similarities in the ways that all human cultures have formulated and approached essential problems.

- **A substantial yet flexible guide to reading and writing:** At the end of *Reading the World* is Part 2, The Guide to Reading and Writing, which explores the writing process from reading critically to generating topic ideas to organization and support to evaluating and documenting sources. This substantial segment draws examples largely from the selections in the book.

- **Readings on language and rhetoric:** One full chapter of the reader is devoted to primary sources on language and rhetoric. Here, students involved in the writing process can read accessible selections from writers such as Plato, Aristotle, Gertrude Buck, and Chinua Achebe.

- **Images as texts:** Great Ideas are not always expressed in words; sometimes, they are conveyed through visual texts. Included throughout *Reading the World*, therefore, are the kinds of visual texts that contemporary students need to decode on a daily basis: drawings, paintings, photographs, woodcuts, a film still, and so on. Not merely illustrations or visual aids, these complex texts make substantial arguments in their own right, and they are presented here *as texts*, with headnotes, study questions, and writing suggestions.

- **Mix of longer and shorter readings:** To meet a variety of teaching and assignment styles, the selections in *Reading the World* vary widely in length. Each chapter includes some pieces of only a page or two, which can be read quickly and incorporated into group discussions and in-class writing assignments. Each chapter also includes several medium-length selections, of three to six pages, and one or two lengthy selections, which require in-depth reading and extensive discussion.

- **Cross-textual connections:** The readings work together both within and across chapters. Following each reading, a set of questions titled "Making Connections" prompts students to explore these threads.

Editorial Apparatus

- The detailed editorial apparatus in *Reading the World: Ideas That Matter* will guide students through the process of reading and writing about sophisticated texts and ideas. This apparatus includes the following elements: **Chapter introductions** begin with a single question that all of the selections in a chapter are responding to in some way. These introductions set out the major issues and concerns that each chapter deals with and situate each reading in a bigger overall scheme. **Text headnotes** offer necessary historical contextual information about the authors and texts. **Explanatory footnotes** describe unfamiliar terms, concepts, and references in the selections. **Study questions** prompt students to think about the major ideas in each selection, consider the elements of writing, and think about how texts interact. **Writing suggestions** prompt creative, analytical, and comparative responses.

ACKNOWLEDGMENTS

Reading the World: Ideas That Matter truly has many authors. It owes its existence to the great writers, artists, philosophers, and critics whose works fill its pages. Those pages, in turn, are the product of the attention, support, and creative energy of many people.

After the publication of the first edition, the writing programs at both Shepherd University and the Catholic University of America invited me to speak with instructors using the book. I thank these instructors and their students for the crucial feedback that they provided. My new colleagues at Newman University have also been extremely supportive as I have prepared the new edition. I am especially grateful to Father Joseph Gile and Dr. Susan Crane for their specific—and excellent—suggestions on the manuscript. I am also grateful to President Noreen M. Carrocci for enduring a provost who was occasionally missing in action as deadlines for the new edition approached.

The staff at W. W. Norton provided more support than I ever imagined possible. This support began very early in the process, when John Kelly "discovered" the book during a meeting in my office on other textbook concerns. Marilyn Moller, who believed in the project from the beginning, was enormously helpful in giving the book its current shape and configuration—which is far superior to the shape and configuration that I originally had in mind. Erin Granville, the most competent, attentive, and helpful editor that I have ever had, worked with incredible speed to complete the manuscript and, in the process, held me to the same standards of clarity, concision, and logical consistency that I ask of all students who use *Reading the World*. Nancy Rodwan and Sarah Feider performed the task of clearing permissions for all the readings. Katharine Ings gave careful attention to correcting grammatical and factual errors.

Reading the World has also benefited tremendously from the teachers and scholars who took valuable time to review the first edition: John Gudmundson (Ontario College of Art and Design), Heidi Hanrahan (Shepherd University), Ellen P. Walroth (San Antonio College), and Pam Ward (Catholic University of America).

Finally, *Reading the World* is the result of personal debts that can never be adequately repaid. These include debts to my parents, Roger and Linda Austin, who taught me how to read and who always made sure that I lived in a house full of books and ideas; to my wife, Karen Austin, for her emotional and intellectual nurturing during the entire process of conceiving and executing this book—and for taking a lead role in writing the instructor's manual that accompanies it; and to my children, Porter and Clarissa Austin, who patiently endured more than a year of seeing their daddy always at the computer. My greatest hope is that they will someday understand why.

TIMELINE

15,000–13,000 BCE	**The Shaft of the Dead Man**
ca. 3000–1500 BCE	Indus Valley civilization flourishes in present-day northeast India. Writing present
ca. 3000 BCE	Mesopotamia. Cuneiform writing on clay tablets
ca. 2575–2130 BCE	Old Kingdom in Egypt (Great Pyramids, Sphinx)
ca. 2130–1540 BCE	Middle Kingdom in Egypt
ca. 2070–1600 BCE	Xia Dynasty flourishes in present-day China
1600–1046 BCE	Shang Dynasty in China. Ideograph writing on oracle bones
ca. 1539–1200 BCE	New Kingdom in Egypt
1240 BCE	**The Papyrus of Ani**
ca. 1200 BCE	Moses leads Hebrews out of Egypt to Palestine
1030 BCE	Kingdom of Israel founded
776 BCE	First recorded Olympics held in Greece
753–510 BCE	Roman Kingdom founded
700 BCE	Emergence of kingdoms and republics in northern India
648 BCE	Rise of first Persian state
600–400 BCE	Lao Tzu, **Tao te Ching**
510 BCE	Roman Republic founded with the overthrow of the Roman Kingdom
475–221 BCE	Period of Warring States in China. "Hundred Schools of Thought" flourish
ca. 460 BCE	**Greek Schoolchildren on a Kylix**
431 BCE	Pericles, **The Funeral Oration**
425 BCE	Mo Tzu, **Against Music** · Mo Tzu, **Against Offensive Warfare**
400–320 BCE	Sun Tzu, **The Art of War**

*Many dates, especially ancient ones, are approximate. **Boldface** titles indicate works in the anthology.*

399 BCE	Socrates, tried for impiety and corrupting the youth of Athens, sentenced to death by hemlock
380 BCE	Plato, **Gorgias**
350 BCE	Aristotle, **Rhetoric**
331–330 BCE	Alexander the Great conquers Syria, Mesopotamia, and Iran
330–323 BCE	Alexander the Great conquers Central Asia and Indus Valley, but dies in Babylon. His generals divide his empire and found the Ptolemaic Dynasty in Egypt and Seleucid Empire in Syria, Mesopotamia, and Iran
300 BCE	Mencius, **Man's Nature Is Good** · Hsün Tzu, **Man's Nature Is Evil**
250 BCE	Hsün Tzu, **Encouraging Learning**
221–207 BCE	Qin Dynasty established in China. Rule guided primarily by Legalist philosophy
206 BCE–220 CE	Han Dynasty founded. Rule guided by a mixture of Legalist and Confucian philosophies
2nd–1st centuries BCE	Buddhism spreads to China
49 BCE	Beginning of civil war that ends the Roman Republic and leads to the Roman Empire
30 BCE	Rome conquers Egypt

6?	Birth of Jesus
90	**New Testament**
131–134	Jewish revolt against Roman rule; Jews expelled from Palestine
150	**Cosmological Chart of the Ptolemaic Universe**
200–350	Introduction and spread of Christianity in North Africa
4th–6th centuries	Clans ally to form Yamato, precursor of Japanese state
330	Constantine moves capital of the Roman Empire to Byzantium and renames it Constantinople
367	Final canon of the New Testament of the Bible established
395	Roman Empire divided into the Eastern and Western Empires
476	Last emperor of the Western Empire deposed
500–1495	Rise of the West African savanna empires
550–700	Asuka period in Japan develops around the rule of the Yamato clan. Buddhism introduced to the Japanese archipelago by way of Korea
570 CE	Birth of Mohammed
610–1000	Introduction and spread of Islam in East and West Africa

610–632	Period of Mohammed's prophesy, the growth of his following, his flight to Medina, and his return to Mecca
776	Beatus of Líebana, **Beatus Map**
819–1005	The Samanids, the first Persian Muslim dynasty, become hereditary governors of eastern Iran and central Asia
900	Abu Nasr al-Farabi, **Perfect Associations and Perfect Rulers**
1096	Al-Ghazālī, **Manners to Be Observed by Teachers and Students**
1096–1290	European Crusades to regain Christian control of the Holy Lands
1190	Averröes, **On the Harmony of Religions and Philosophy**
1200	Moses Maimonides, **The Guide for the Perplexed**
1265–1274	St. Thomas Aquinas, **Summa Theologica**
1281–1924	Ottoman rulers gradually establish the last great Islamic dynasty to rule in the Middle East. They dominate the region until World War II
1300–1500	Rise of the Kongo kingdom on the lower Zaire
1338–1453	Hundred Years' War between France and England
1487	Leonardo da Vinci, **Vitruvian Man**
1405	Christine de Pizan, **The Treasure of the City of Ladies**
1453	Constantinople falls to the Turks, increasing dissemination of Greek culture in western Europe
1492	Columbus lands in America
1513	Niccolò Machiavelli, **The Prince**
1517	Luther's Ninety-five Theses denounce abuses of the Roman Church
1534	Henry VIII breaks with Rome and becomes head of the Church of England
1541	**The Progress of an Aztec Warrior**
late 16th–mid 19th centuries	Atlantic slave trade
1620	Colony founded by Pilgrims at Plymouth, Massachusetts
1651	Thomas Hobbes, **Leviathan**
1690	John Locke, **Of Ideas**
1751	William Hogarth, **Gin Lane**
1756–1763	Seven Years' War, involving nine European powers
1768	Joseph Wright of Derby, **An Experiment on a Bird in the Air Pump**
1775–1783	American War of Independence; Declaration of Independence

1777	**New England Primer**
1789	French Revolution begins. French National Assembly adopts the Declaration of the Rights of Man
1792	Mary Wollstonecraft, **On National Education**
1798	Thomas Malthus, **An Essay on the Principle of Population**
1830	Eugène Delacroix, **Liberty Leading the People**
1839	Lin Tse-hsü, **A Letter to Queen Victoria**
1845	Frederick Douglass, **Learning to Read**
1852	John Henry Newman, **Knowledge Its Own End**
1859	Charles Darwin, **Natural Selection; or the Survival of the Fittest**
1861–1865	American Civil War. Lincoln signs the Emancipation Proclamation, freeing the slaves in the Confederate States of America
1868	Meiji restoration in Japan overthrows the Tokugawa Shogunate and results in rapid modernization
1899–1902	Boxer Rebellion in China in response to the European presence. The combined response of the European powers and Japan is something of the world's first international peacekeeping mission
19th or 20th century	**Igbo Mother and Child**
1900	Gertrude Buck, **The Present Status of Rhetorical Theory**
1904–1905	Japan becomes the first Asian power to defeat a Western nation, when it wins the Russo-Japanese War
1911	China is thrown into decades of chaos when the Qing Dynasty is overthrown and the last emperor is deposed
1914–1918	World War I in Europe and the colonies. The United States enters in 1917
1916	Mohandas K. Gandhi, **Economics and Moral Progress**
1917	Russian Revolution overthrows the Romanov Dynasty
1929	American stock market crash heralds beginning of world economic crisis; Great Depression lasts until 1939
1933	Adolf Hitler given dictatorial powers in Germany
1934	Ruth Benedict, **The Individual and the Pattern of Culture**
1935	Leni Riefenstahl, **The Triumph of the Will**
1936–1938	Spanish Civil War. After the Nationalist side prevails against the Republican side, Francisco Franco is installed as dictator
1936	Dorothea Lange, **Migrant Mother**
1937	Pablo Picasso, **Guernica** · Japan invades China

1939	Germany invades Poland, pulling all of Europe into war
1940	Margaret Mead, *Warfare: An Invention—Not a Biological Necessity*
1941	Japan attacks Pearl Harbor. The United States enters World War II
1942	George Orwell, *Pacifism and the War*
1943	Norman Rockwell, *Freedom of Speech*
1945	World War II ends with the United States dropping atomic bombs on Hiroshima and Nagasaki. United Nations founded
1946	Cold War begins with Winston Churchill's "Iron Curtain" speech
1948	State of Israel founded
1949	Mao Zedong's Communists push the Nationalist forces off mainland China and establish the People's Republic of China · Apartheid instituted in South Africa
1950	Octavio Paz, *The Day of the Dead*
1950–1953	Korean War involves North and South Korea, the United Nations, and China
1952	Revolution in Egypt, which becomes a republic in 1953
1960–1962	Independence for Belgian Congo, Uganda, Tanganyika, Nigeria
1961	Yuri Gagarin becomes first human in space
1962–1973	United States engaged in Vietnam War
1962	Rachel Carson, *The Obligation to Endure*
1963	Martin Luther King Jr., *Letter from Birmingham City Jail*
1965	Kenzaburo Oe, *The Unsurrendered People* · Lucy Lameck, *Africans Are Not Poor*
1966–1969	Mao Zedong's Cultural Revolution attacks Confucian tradition and intellectuals in China
1969	Neil Armstrong becomes first human on the moon
1970	Paulo Freire, *The Banking Concept of Education*
1972	Chinua Achebe, *Language and the Destiny of Man*
1973	Arab oil producers cut off shipments to nations supporting Israel. Ensuing energy crisis reshapes global economy
1974	Garrett Hardin, *Lifeboat Ethics: The Case against Helping the Poor*
1980	*Ad for Chinese Population Policy*
1985	Richard Feynman, *O Americano Outra Vez*
1987	Gloria Anzaldúa, *How to Tame a Wild Tongue* · N. Scott Momaday, *Personal Reflections*
1989	Kisautaq Leona Okakok, *Serving the Purpose of Education*

PRONUNCIATION GUIDE

PHONETIC KEY

a as in cat

ah as in father

ai as in light

ay as in day

aw as in raw

e as in pet

ee as in street

ehr as in air

er as in bird

eu as in lurk

g as in good

i as in sit

j as in joke

nh a nasal sound (as in French vin)

o as in pot

oh as in no

oo as in boot

oy as in toy

or as in bore

ow as in now

s as in mess

u as in put

uh as in us

zh as in vision

NAMES, TERMS, AND TITLES

Abu Nasr al-Farabi   ah'-boo' nah-sahr ahl-fah-rah'-bee

Al-Ghazālī   ahl-gah-za'-lee

Ani   ah-nee

Aung San Suu Kyi   owng sahn soo chee

Averroës   a-veer'-uh-weez

Beatus of Liébana   bee-a'-tuhs   lee-ay'-ba-na

Chinua Achebe   chin'-oo-ah ah-chay'-bay

Eugène Delacroix   eu-zhen' duh-lah-krwah'

Hsün Tzu   shinh tsuh

Ibn Khaldūn   i'-ben khahl-doon'

Kenzaburo Oe   ken-zuh-boh'-roh oh-ay'

Kisautaq Leona Okakok   kis'-ah-tok lee oh'-nah ah'-ka-kok

Lao Tzu   low tsuh

Leni Riefenstahl   le'-nee ree'-fen-shtahl

Lin Tse-hsü   lin dze-shu

Matthieu Ricard   mah-ti'-eu rik-ahr'

Mencius   men'-chee-oos

Mo Tzu   mor tsuh

Moses Maimonides   mai-mon'-uh-dees

Paulo Freire   pah-oo-loo frai-ree

Pericles   pehr'-uh-klees

Sun Tzu   shunh tsuh

Sura   soo'-rah

Tao te Ching   dow der jinh

Trinh Xuan Thuan   trin swan thoo'-ahn

READING
THE WORLD

SECOND EDITION

PART 1

READING THE WORLD

1

EDUCATION

WHAT DOES IT MEAN TO BE
AN "EDUCATED PERSON"?

Education is suffering from narration sickness.
—*Paulo Freire*

IN *PEDAGOGY OF THE OPPRESSED*, the Brazilian educator Paulo Freire describes the education process as a narrative. The relationship between students and teachers, he argues, plays out according to a script much like that of a play. In this script, the teachers are narrators holding all the knowledge, and the students are empty receptacles to be filled up with facts. For Freire, the problem with this model is that the script was written by those with political and economic power for the purpose of perpetuating oppressive social systems. The only way to end the oppression is to rewrite the script and construct a new narrative of what it means to engage in education.

The education narrative has, in fact, been rewritten many times. The model that most people today think of when they hear the word "school"—a roomful of students headed by a teacher who has been specifically trained and certified in his or her profession—is less than a century old. The notion that a society should even try to educate all of its citizens, rather than just an elite few, is not much older. And the idea that education can be placed into "secular" and "religious" categories, divided by what Thomas Jefferson called "a wall of separation between church and state," would have been virtually unthinkable for the majority of human beings in world history. This chapter aims to present some of the different narratives about education that have emerged in the history of ideas.

The discussion begins with a visual text from classical antiquity: a painted drinking cup from ancient Greece that depicts a scene from a very early school. Such schools were set up by teachers known as "Sophists," who earned money by teaching wealthy young people subjects such as grammar, logic, and rhetoric. This is followed by two ancient treatises on learning. From China, Hsün Tzu's "Encouraging Learning" argues that education is necessary to shape an inherently evil human nature. From ancient Rome, Seneca's "On Liberal and Vocational Studies" highlights connections between education and the moral development necessary for a citizen.

These ancient texts are followed by two very different religious approaches to education. Al-Ghāzalī's "Manners to Be Observed by Teachers and Students," from the world of medieval Islam, outlines the proper roles of all participants in the education enterprise. A Christian Puritan view of education is given by the chapter's second graphic text: a series of woodcuts from the 1777 edition of the *New England Primer*, a popular schoolbook in colonial America that uses a strict Puritan theology as the basis for teaching the alphabet.

The remainder of the chapter presents a series of early modern and modern texts that, though from similar time periods, give very different perspectives on the function of education. Three of these readings come from theorists and philosophers. John Henry Newman's "Knowledge Its Own End" picks up on Seneca's view of liberal education and argues that the attainment of knowledge is an independent good that needs no further utilitarian justification. Paulo Freire's "The Banking Concept of Education" gives a very different view, but one also influenced by Seneca. Freire, a Brazilian educator, argues that education must be a factor in liberating oppressed people, and that, to do so, it must empower students to do more than simply listen to teachers. Richard Feynman's "O Americano Outra Vez" relates a famous scientist's experience with the Brazilian educational system that Freire criticizes.

A second group of three readings come from the margins of Western society. Mary Wollstonecraft's "On National Education" argues, at a time when women were largely barred from education, for the equal inclusion of women in the nation's schools. A selection from Frederick Douglass's autobiography tells how he, as a slave, learned to read and write in violation of the law and, in the process, discovered the value of freedom. And in the chapter's final reading, Kisautaq Leona Okakok's "Serving the Purpose of Education," an Inupiaq educational reformer from Alaska's extreme North compares her culture's view of the purpose of education with that of the Western school system that employs her.

Greek Schoolchildren on a Kylix
(circa 460 BCE)

ANCIENT GREEK CULTURE placed a high value on the visual arts, and the Greeks were known to paint portraits and scenery on wood panels, interior walls, buildings, and statues. None of these materials, however, can support paint for long periods of time, and as a result, we now have only a few, badly degraded examples of most forms of Greek painting. On the other hand, the heavy pottery of ancient Greece is extremely good at holding paint; consequently, we have hundreds of thousands of vases, jars, cups, and bowls decorated with scenes of Greek life and myth, dating back to the Dark Ages of ancient Greece (1050–900 BCE)—a time when written language had been lost and that we therefore know little about, aside from what can be seen on surviving pieces of pottery. The cup featured here is from around 460 BCE, during the Golden Age of Greek culture, a time that saw the flowering of art, poetry, drama, and music.

Though Greek vases and cups now occupy honored spots in the world's greatest museums, they were not created to be displayed. Greek pottery was designed to be used—much the same way that we uses dishes, cups, and glasses. More often than not, their decorations highlighted this utilitarian nature by depicting scenes from everyday life. Unlike the great epic poems and tragic dramas of the Golden Age—which focused on the lives of gods, heroes, and kings—Greek pottery depicts the lives of farmers, shepherds, craftsmen, and athletes. As a result, it has become the source of much of what we now know about the life of the average men and women of the ancient Greek world.

The image of Greek schoolchildren depicted here comes from a shallow drinking cup, known as a *kylix*. It uses a technique that was state-of-the-art at the time, the "red-figure technique," that allowed much more attention to detail than had been possible with earlier techniques. Until the red-figure technique was developed in or around 530 BCE, images on pottery had to be etched with an engraving tool—a labor-intensive process that, even at its best, yielded images that were vague and poorly defined. This red-figure technique allowed painters to add detail with a brush before the firing process, producing images that were both lively and permanent.

The date of this painting, 460 BCE, places it during the life of the famous Sophist Gorgias, who is the subject of Plato's dialogue of the same name in chapter 7 (p. 478). The image depicts an educational experience consistent with what we know about the schools of the Sophists, the paid tutors who educated the children of the wealthy in schools of their own design. In it, two school boys are standing before an instructor, who is seated and holding a stick. One of the boys is holding a rolled-up scroll, and the other is holding a writing tablet. The instructor is not noticeably older than the boys, but they appear to give him the respect and deference that would be due an honored teacher. 🖎

UNDERSTANDING THE TEXT

1. What does it say about ancient Greek culture that purely functional objects, such as vases and cups, were decorated so carefully and with such attention to detail? How does the decoration on this Greek *kylix* compare to the decorations on similar items in our own culture, such as drinking glasses, plates, and water bottles? Do you believe that the Greeks spent more or less time decorating these items than we do? Why?

2. What can you infer about the relationship between the teacher and the students on this drinking cup, and, by extension, the ideal relationship between teachers and students in ancient Greece? Why is the teacher seated? Why does he carry a staff or walking stick even when seated? Do the positions of the figures suggest any attitudes on the part of the characters?

3. What can we interpret from the items that each of the boys is carrying: a rolled-up scroll and a writing tablet? What kinds of subjects would these kinds of tools have been appropriate for?

4. Why do you think that the teacher is shown as being of roughly the same age as the students? If this image is representative of education at the time, what might it suggest about the qualifications for being a teacher? Compare

this image with other cultural traditions in which teachers are depicted as older (and presumably wiser) than students.

CONNECTING IDEAS

1. How is this image consistent with what we know about the kind of education favored by Gorgias the Sophist (p. 478), who would have been in his late twenties when this cup was made?

2. How do the figures in this painting compare with the ideal student and teacher described in al-Ghazālī's "Manners to Be Observed by Teachers and Students" (p. 24)? Is there anything in the painting that might seem to violate one of the principles laid down by al-Ghazālī?

3. What might Paulo Freire (p. 62) say about the layout of the classroom depicted in this drawing? Does the instructor seem to be portrayed as a dispenser of wisdom, or, in Freire's terms, is he a "banker" charged with depositing knowledge into the minds of his students? Why do you say so?

WRITING ABOUT THE TEXT

1. Write an essay in which you attempt to determine what kind of educational experience the image on the vase depicts. Carefully consider the details of the painting and use them to support an argument about the educational practices of Athens in the fifth century BCE.

2. Look at the decorations on one or more functional objects that you own, such as a T-shirt, a bumper sticker, a cereal box, or your computer desktop. Using an object that you own as an example, write an essay in which you explain why people desire artistic characteristics in objects whose primary purpose is not artistic expression—why, for instance, a cereal box is decorated with images rather than being a plain white box with the name of the cereal on it.

3. Write an essay that compares the instructor in this painting with the bearded instructor in Joseph Wright of Derby's painting *An Experiment on a Bird in the Air Pump* (p. 403). Do the two teachers appear to have the same purpose? What are they trying to do? Do they have the same effect on their students? How can you tell?

Hsün Tzu
Encouraging Learning
(circa 250 BCE)

THE GREAT CHINESE PHILOSOPHER Confucius (551–479 BCE) taught his disciples that human beings must always strive for perfection through strict attention to duty, order, and ritual. He did not, however, clearly state how he viewed human nature. Some time after Confucius's death, his disciples split into two camps. The majority of Confucians followed the teachings of Mencius, who believed that the rites that Confucius advocated could produce virtue and rectitude only because humans inherently possessed these qualities. A second group of Confucians believed exactly the reverse: that the Confucian program of rites and observances was necessary because humans were inherently evil. The most famous advocate of this position was the scholar Hsün Tzu.

Because Hsün Tzu believed that becoming virtuous means altering human nature, he was one of the ancient world's strongest advocates of education. He believed that only rigorous training and devoted study could bring about this change. He compared the process of educating a child to the process of straightening a piece of wood against a board or sharpening a piece of metal with a stone. If done correctly, each process permanently transforms the nature of the thing: the wood becomes straight, the metal becomes sharp, and the child becomes a "gentleman," as Confucius termed a person of moral character.

Confucius's ideas have come down to us only as epigrams recorded by his disciples; Lao Tzu wrote poems and prose pieces marked by paradox; Mencius wrote dialogues, parables, and indirect narratives. Hsün Tzu, the most systematic of the classical Chinese philosophers, developed brief essays that introduce and support clearly labeled, easy-to-follow arguments. In "Encouraging Learning," he employs his straightforward style on a series of metaphors and object lessons, drawn from the natural world, to illustrate his principal point: that education can compensate for natural human defects and make people good.

Long after Hsün Tzu's death, Confucianism became the official state philosophy of China. However, the later, official versions of Confucian doctrine rejected Hsün Tzu's arguments about human nature and instead accepted Mencius's more optimistic theories. Nonetheless, Hsün Tzu, as the first philosopher to create a complete system of Confucian thought, remains an important figure in the development of Chinese philosophy. Unlike his views on human nature, his views on the importance of education became part of the Confucian mainstream and have influenced many people throughout Chinese history to devote their lives to scholarly pursuits.

Hsün Tzu's primary method of supporting arguments in this selection is to give examples, either from the natural world or from figures in Chinese history. Pay close attention to these examples and to the claims that they support.

THE GENTLEMAN[1] SAYS: Learning should never cease. Blue comes from the indigo plant but is bluer than the plant itself. Ice is made of water but is colder than water ever is. A piece of wood as straight as a plumb line may be bent into a circle as true as any drawn with a compass and, even after the wood has dried, it will not straighten out again. The bending process has made it that way. Thus, if wood is pressed against a straightening board, it can be made straight; if metal is put to the grindstone, it can be sharpened; and if the gentleman studies widely and each day examines himself, his wisdom will become clear and his conduct be without fault. If you do not climb a high mountain, you will not comprehend the highness of the heavens; if you do not look down into a deep valley, you will not know the depth of the earth; and if you do not hear the words handed down from the ancient kings, you will not understand the greatness of learning. Children born among the Han or Yüeh people of the south and among the Mo barbarians of the north cry with the same voice at birth, but as they grow older they follow different customs. Education causes them to differ. The *Odes*[2] says:

Oh, you gentlemen,
Do not be constantly at ease and rest!
Quietly respectful in your posts,
Love those who are correct and upright
And the gods will hearken to you
And aid you with great blessing.

There is no greater godliness than to transform yourself with the Way,[3] no greater blessing than to escape misfortune.

I once tried spending the whole day in thought, but I found it of less value than a moment of study. I once tried standing on tiptoe and gazing into the distance, but

Some of the translator's footnotes have been omitted.

1. **Gentleman:** the Confucian term for a person of virtue and breeding—one who always fulfills the appropriate roles for a person of his or her rank.

2. **The Odes:** Chinese poetic writings much older than Confucianism that Confucius and his followers considered sources of ancient wisdom. Confucius is traditionally considered the editor and compiler of the *Shih Ching*, or *Book of Odes*, in which these odes are collected.

3. **The Way:** *Tao*, which can be translated as "the Way" or "the Path," is a vital concept in almost all classical Chinese philosophy; however, its meaning is not the same for Confucians as it is for Taoists. For Lao Tzu (p. 158), the Way means something like "the way of nature" or "the natural order of things." For Confucius, it means something more like "the path to perfection."

I found I could see much farther by climbing to a high place. If you climb to a high place and wave to someone, it is not as though your arm were any longer than usual, and yet people can see you from much farther away. If you shout down the wind, it is not as though your voice were any stronger than usual, and yet people can hear you much more clearly. Those who make use of carriages or horses may not be any faster walkers than anyone else, and yet they are able to travel a thousand *li*.[4] Those who make use of boats may not know how to swim, and yet they manage to get across rivers. The gentleman is by birth no different from any other man; it is just that he is good at making use of things.

In the south there is a bird called the *meng* dove. It makes a nest out of feathers woven together with hair and suspends it from the tips of the reeds. But when the wind comes, the reeds break, the eggs are smashed, and the baby birds killed. It is not that the nest itself is faulty; the fault is in the thing it is attached to. In the west there is a tree called the *yeh-kan*. Its trunk is no more than four inches tall and it grows on top of the high mountains, from whence it looks down into valleys a hundred fathoms deep. It is not a long trunk which affords the tree such a view, but simply the place where it stands. If pigweed grows up in the midst of hemp, it will stand up straight without propping. If white sand is mixed with mud, it too will turn black. The root of a certain orchid is the source of the perfume called *chih*; but if the root were to be soaked in urine, then no gentleman would go near it and no commoner would consent to wear it. It is not that the root itself is of an unpleasant quality; it is the fault of the thing it has been soaked in. Therefore a gentleman will take care in selecting the community he intends to live in, and will choose men of breeding for his companions. In this way he wards off evil and meanness, and draws close to fairness and right.

Every phenomenon that appears must have a cause. The glory or shame that come to a man are no more than the image of his virtue. Meat when it rots breeds worms; fish that is old and dry brings forth maggots. When a man is careless and lazy and forgets himself, that is when disaster occurs. The strong naturally bear up under weight; the weak naturally end up bound. Evil and corruption in oneself invite the anger of others. If you lay sticks of identical shape on a fire, the flames will seek out the driest ones; if you level the ground to an equal smoothness, water will still seek out the dampest spot. Trees of the same species grow together; birds and beasts gather in herds; for all things follow after their own kind. Where a target is hung up, arrows will find their way to it; where the forest trees grow thickest, the axes will enter. When a tree is tall and shady, birds will flock to roost in it; when vinegar turns sour, gnats will collect around it. So there are words that invite disaster and actions that call down shame. A gentleman must be careful where he takes his stand.

---

4. **Li:** a traditional Chinese unit of distance; about one-third of a mile.

Pile up earth to make a mountain and wind and rain will rise up from it. Pile up   5
water to make a deep pool and dragons will appear. Pile up good deeds to create
virtue and godlike understanding will come of itself; there the mind of the sage will
find completion. But unless you pile up little steps, you can never journey a thousand *li*; unless you pile up tiny streams, you can never make a river or a sea. The
finest thoroughbred cannot travel ten paces in one leap, but the sorriest nag can go
a ten days' journey. Achievement consists of never giving up. If you start carving
and then give up, you cannot even cut through a piece of rotten wood; but if you
persist without stopping, you can carve and inlay metal or stone. Earthworms have
no sharp claws or teeth, no strong muscles or bones, and yet above ground they feast
on the mud, and below they drink at the yellow springs. This is because they keep
their minds on one thing. Crabs have six legs and two pincers, but unless they can
find an empty hole dug by a snake or a water serpent, they have no place to lodge.
This is because they allow their minds to go off in all directions. Thus if there is no
dark and dogged will, there will be no shining accomplishment; if there is no dull
and determined effort, there will be no brilliant achievement. He who tries to travel
two roads at once will arrive nowhere; he who serves two masters will please neither. The wingless dragon has no limbs and yet it can soar; the flying squirrel has
many talents but finds itself hard pressed. The *Odes* says:

> Ringdove in the mulberry,
> Its children are seven.
> The good man, the gentleman,
> His forms are one.
> His forms are one,
> His heart is as though bound.

Thus does the gentleman bind himself to oneness.

In ancient times, when Hu Pa played the zither, the fish in the streams came
forth to listen; when Po Ya played the lute, the six horses of the emperor's carriage
looked up from their feed trough. No sound is too faint to be heard, no action too
well concealed to be known. When there are precious stones under the mountain,
the grass and trees have a special sheen; where pearls grow in a pool, the banks are
never parched. Do good and see if it does not pile up. If it does, how can it fail to
be heard of?

Where does learning begin and where does it end? I say that as to program,
learning begins with the recitation of the Classics and ends with the reading of
the ritual texts; and as to objective, it begins with learning to be a man of breeding, and ends with learning to be a sage. If you truly pile up effort over a long
period of time, you will enter into the highest realm. Learning continues until
death and only then does it cease. Therefore we may speak of an end to the program of learning, but the objective of learning must never for an instant be given

up. To pursue it is to be a man, to give it up is to become a beast. The *Book of Documents*[5] is the record of government affairs, the *Odes* the repository of correct sounds, and the rituals are the great basis of law and the foundation of precedents. Therefore learning reaches its completion with the rituals, for they may be said to represent the highest point of the Way and its power. The reverence and order of the rituals, the fitness and harmony of music, the breadth of the *Odes* and *Documents*, the subtlety of the *Spring and Autumn Annals*[6]—these encompass all that is between heaven and earth.

The learning of the gentleman enters his ear, clings to his mind, spreads through his four limbs, and manifests itself in his actions. His smallest word, his slightest movement can serve as a model. The learning of the petty man enters his ear and comes out his mouth. With only four inches between ear and mouth, how can he have possession of it long enough to ennoble a seven-foot body? In old times men studied for their own sake; nowadays men study with an eye to others.[7] The gentleman uses learning to ennoble himself; the petty man uses learning as a bribe to win attention from others. To volunteer information when you have not been asked is called officiousness; to answer two questions when you have been asked only one is garrulity.[8] Both officiousness and garrulity are to be condemned. The gentleman should be like an echo.

In learning, nothing is more profitable than to associate with those who are learned. Ritual and music present us with models but no explanations; the *Odes* and *Documents* deal with ancient matters and are not always pertinent; the *Spring and Autumn Annals* is terse and cannot be quickly understood. But if you make use of the erudition of others and the explanations of gentlemen, then you will become honored and may make your way anywhere in the world. Therefore I say that in learning nothing is more profitable than to associate with those who are learned, and of the roads to learning, none is quicker than to love such men. Second only to this is to honor ritual. If you are first of all unable to love such men and secondly are incapable of honoring ritual, then you will only be learning a mass of jumbled facts, blindly following the *Odes* and *Documents*, and nothing more. In such a case you may study to the end of your days and you will never be anything but a vulgar pedant.[9] If you want to become like the former kings and seek out benevolence and righteousness, then ritual is the very road by which you must travel. It is like picking up a fur coat by the collar: grasp it with all five fingers and the whole coat can

---

5. **Book of Documents:** the *Shu Ching*, a collection of speeches, legal codes, government actions, and other reputedly primary texts from pre-Confucian Chinese dynasties.
6. **Spring and Autumn Annals:** the *Ch'un Ch'iu*, a work of ancient history, traditionally thought to have been compiled by Confucius.
7. This sentence is quoted from *Analects* XIV,

25, where it is attributed to Confucius. [Translator's note]
8. **Garrulity:** talkativeness.
9. **Vulgar pedant:** literally, "vulgar Confucian," but here and below Hsün Tzu uses the word *ju* in the older and broader sense of a scholar. [Translator's note]

easily be lifted. To lay aside the rules of ritual and try to attain your objective with the *Odes* and *Documents* alone is like trying to measure the depth of a river with your finger, to pound millet with a spear point, or to eat a pot of stew with an awl. You will get nowhere. Therefore one who honors ritual, though he may not yet have full understanding, can be called a model man of breeding; while one who does not honor ritual, though he may have keen perception, is no more than a desultory pedant.   *10*

Do not answer a man whose questions are gross. Do not question a man whose answers are gross. Do not listen to a man whose theories are gross. Do not argue with a contentious man. Only if a man has arrived where he is by the proper way should you have dealings with him; if not, avoid him. If he is respectful in his person, then you may discuss with him the approach to the Way. If his words are reasonable, you may discuss with him the principles of the Way. If his looks are gentle, you may discuss with him the highest aspects of the Way. To speak to someone you ought not to is called officiousness; to fail to speak to someone you ought to is called secretiveness; to speak to someone without first observing his temper and looks is called blindness. The gentleman is neither officious, secretive, nor blind, but cautious and circumspect in his manner. This is what the *Odes* means when it says:

Neither overbearing nor lax,
They are rewarded by the Son of Heaven.

He who misses one shot in a hundred cannot be called a really good archer; he who sets out on a thousand-mile journey and breaks down half a pace from his destination cannot be called a really good carriage driver; he who does not comprehend moral relationships and categories and who does not make himself one with benevolence and righteousness cannot be called a good scholar. Learning basically means learning to achieve this oneness. He who starts off in this direction one time and that direction another is only a commoner of the roads and alleys, while he who does a little that is good and much that is not good is no better than the tyrants Chieh and Chou or Robber Chih.[10]

The gentleman knows that what lacks completeness and purity does not deserve to be called beautiful. Therefore he reads and listens to explanations in order to penetrate the Way, ponders in order to understand it, associates with men who embody it in order to make it part of himself, and shuns those who impede it in order to sustain and nourish it. He trains his eye so that they desire only to see what is right, his ears so that they desire to hear only what is right, his mind so that it desires to think only what is right. When he has truly learned to love what is right, his eyes

---

10. **Chieh and Chou or Robber Chih:** traditional figures in Chinese history. Cheih and Chou were tyrannical kings; Robber Chih led a band of nine thousand criminals who terrorized all of China.

will take greater pleasure in it than in the five colors; his ears will take greater pleasure than in the five sounds; his mouth will take greater pleasure than in the five flavors; and his mind will feel keener delight than in the possession of the world. When he has reached this stage, he cannot be subverted by power or the love of profit; he cannot be swayed by the masses; he cannot be moved by the world. He follows this one thing in life; he follows it in death. This is what is called constancy of virtue. He who has such constancy of virtue can order himself, and, having ordered himself, he can then respond to others. He who can order himself and respond to others—this is what is called the complete man. It is the characteristic of heaven to manifest brightness, of earth to manifest breadth, and of the gentleman to value completeness.

UNDERSTANDING THE TEXT

1. What distinction does Hsün Tzu draw between "thought" and "study"? Why does he privilege study over thought in education? How have your teachers emphasized "study" and "thought" differently as you have progressed through school?

2. How would you classify Hsün Tzu's methods of supporting his argument (p. 594)? What kinds of support does he include? What kinds does he omit? How persuasive are his methods?

3. Several of Hsün Tzu's metaphors suggest that hard work and study, rather than natural ability, determine success. How is this assertion important to his overall argument? Do you agree with his assessment? Why or why not?

4. According to Hsün Tzu, what should be part of the education of a gentleman? What, by implication, should *not* be part of such an education?

5. What role do associations with other people play in a good education? Would it be possible to follow Hsün Tzu's educational program by reading in isolation?

6. According to Hsün Tzu, what is the ultimate objective of education? What reward can an educated person expect? In your opinion, is this reward a sufficient motivation to pursue learning? Why or why not?

MAKING CONNECTIONS

1. Consider "Encouraging Learning" in the context of the debate between Hsün Tzu and Mencius about human nature. How do Hsün Tzu's ideas about education flow from the position that he articulates in "Man's Nature Is Evil" (p. 100)?

2. Compare Hsün Tzu's implied definition of "education" with those of Seneca (p. 16) and Paulo Friere (p. 62). For each thinker, what does the best kind of education focus on?

3. How might Hsün Tzu respond to one of Plato's major arguments in *Gorgias* (p. 478), that educating people often increases their ability to act unvirtuously? Would the kind of education that Hsün Tzu advocates be susceptible to abuse by the unscrupulous?

4. Does Hsün Tzu's overall purpose for education accord with the purpose of the *New England Primer* (p. 32)? What assumptions does each text make about moral education and practical education?

5. Compare Hsün Tzu's views on the need to alter human nature with those of Lao Tzu (p. 158). What specific statements in the *Tao te Ching* might apply to education or learning in general?

WRITING ABOUT THE TEXT

1. Write an essay supporting or opposing Hsün Tzu's assumption that education should promote virtue. Do schools have the responsibility to teach people to act ethically? What problems might arise (or have arisen) when schools teach ethics?

2. Respond to Hsün Tzu from the perspective of someone who believes that human beings are inherently good. What kind of education would result from this assumption?

3. Compare the purpose of education that Hsün Tzu describes with the one described by either Frederick Douglass (p. 46) or al-Ghazālī (p. 24). What philosophical assumptions shape one's view of education? How so?

Seneca
On Liberal and Vocational Studies
(circa 55 CE)

LUCIUS ANNAEUS SENECA (4 BCE–65 CE), sometimes called "Seneca the Younger," was a member of the early Roman Empire's most celebrated literary family. His father, Marcus Annaeus Seneca, or Seneca the Elder (circa 54 BCE–circa 39 CE), was a noted orator and writer. His nephew, Lucian (39–65 CE), was a celebrated poet who made important contributions to the development of satire. Seneca the Younger distinguished himself as a scientist, scholar, playwright, and philosopher—as well as a politician whose career rose and fell on the whims of three powerful emperors.

Seneca received a first-rate education and as a young man became a successful politician. But in 37 CE, he came into conflict with the emperor Caligula and barely escaped a death sentence. Four years later, in 41 CE, Seneca was accused of having an improper relationship with the niece of the emperor Claudius, who consequently banished him to the island of Corsica. Seneca remained there until 49 CE, when he was summoned back to Rome to tutor the twelve-year-old Nero, who would become emperor in 54 CE after Claudius's death. Seneca became one of the young Nero's most trusted and powerful advisors, but as the emperor became more corrupt, Seneca became less powerful. He received permission to retire in 62 CE, but three years later, Nero accused Seneca of conspiring against him and ordered Seneca to commit suicide by slitting his own wrists.

Seneca was a well-known member of the Stoic school of philosophy. Stoics held that the people achieved the greatest good by living a life founded on reason and in harmony with nature. Stoics also believed that wealth and social position were ultimately unimportant because reason and virtue were available to everybody. In fact, two of the most famous Roman Stoics were the slave Epictetus (55–153) and the emperor Marcus Aurelius (121–180). As a Stoic, Seneca believed that excessive passions diluted the influence of reason, that the point of living is to live virtuously, and that one could be happy and virtuous in any physical or economic condition.

"On Liberal and Vocational Studies" is the eighty-eighth of 124 letters from Seneca that are collectively known as the "Moral Epistles." In this letter, Seneca attempts to define liberal studies and separate them clearly from vocational training. During Seneca's time, a "liberal" education was the kind of education appropriate for a *liber*, or a free person. Unlike many of his contemporaries, Seneca was unwilling to defend pursuits such as literature, music, geometry, and astronomy by arguing that they made people virtuous. This argument, Seneca believed, reduced the liberal arts to a sort of moral propaganda. They do not convert people to virtue, he insists; rather, they are the raw materials out of which a virtuous life can be built—and as such they are indispensible to the functioning of a free society.

Much of Seneca's philosophical work comes to us in the form of letters to other people. As you read Seneca's argument, consider how his use of the second-person address ("You want to know . . . ", "You teach me") creates a connection with the reader and constructs his own ethos as a writer. ✎

Letter LXXXVIII

You want to know my attitude towards liberal studies. Well, I have no respect for any study whatsoever if its end is the making of money. Such studies are to me unworthy ones. They involve the putting out of skills to hire, and are only of value in so far as they may develop the mind without occupying it for long. Time should be spent on them only so long as one's mental abilities are not up to dealing with higher things. They are our apprenticeship, not our real work. Why 'liberal studies' are so called is obvious: it is because they are the ones considered worthy of a free man.[1] But there is really only one liberal study that deserves the name— because it makes a person free—and that is the pursuit of wisdom. Its high ideals, its steadfastness and spirit make all other studies puerile and puny in comparison. Do you really think there is anything to be said for the others when you find among the people who profess to teach them quite the most reprehensible and worthless characters you could have as teachers? All right to have studied that sort of thing once, but not to be studying them now.

The question has sometimes been posed whether these liberal studies make a man a better person. But in fact they do not aspire to any knowledge of how to do this, let alone claim to do it. Literary scholarship concerns itself with research into language, or history if a rather broader field is preferred, or, extending its range to the very limit, poetry. Which of these paves the way to virtue? Attentiveness of words, analysis of syllables, accounts of myths, laying down the principles of prosody? What is there in all this that dispels fear, roots out desire or reins in passion? Or let us take a look at music, at geometry; you will not find anything in them which tells us not to be afraid of this or desire that—and if anyone lacks this kind of knowledge all his other knowledge is valueless to him. The question is whether or not that sort of scholar is teaching virtue. For if he is not, he will not even be imparting it incidentally. If he is teaching it he is a philosopher. If you really want to know how far these persons are from the position of being moral teachers, observe the absence of connexion between all the things they study; if they were teaching one and the same thing a connexion would be evident. . . .

Turning to the musical scholar I say this. You teach me how bass and treble harmonize, or how strings producing different notes can give rise to concord. I would rather you brought about some harmony in my mind and got my thoughts into tune. You show me which are the plaintive keys. I would rather you showed me how to avoid uttering plaintive notes when things go against me in life.

---

1. . . . **Free man:** The word for "free man" in Latin is *liber*, the root word of *liberal*.

The geometrician teaches me how to work out the size of my estates—rather than how to work out how much a man needs in order to have enough. He teaches me to calculate, putting my fingers into the service of avarice, instead of teaching me that there is no point whatsoever in that sort of computation and that a person is none the happier for having properties which tire accountants out, or to put it another way, how superfluous a man's possessions are when he would be a picture of misery if you forced him to start counting up single-handed how much he possessed. What use is it to me to be able to divide a piece of land into equal areas if I'm unable to divide it with a brother? What use is the ability to measure out a portion of an acre with an accuracy extending even to the bits which elude the measuring rod if I'm upset when some high-handed neighbour encroaches slightly on my property? The geometrician teaches me how I may avoid losing any fraction of my estates, but what I really want to learn is how to lose the lot and still keep smiling. . . . Oh, the marvels of geometry! You geometers can calculate the areas of circles, can reduce any given shape to a square, can state the distances separating stars. Nothing's outside your scope when it comes to measurement. Well, if you're such an expert, measure a man's soul; tell me how large or how small that is. You can define a straight line; what use is that to you if you've no idea what straightness means in life?

I come now to the person who prides himself on his familiarity with the heavenly bodies:

> Towards which quarter chilly Saturn draws,
> The orbits in which burning Mercury roams.[2]

What is to be gained from this sort of knowledge? Am I supposed to feel anxious when Saturn and Mars are in opposition or Mercury sets in the evening in full view of Saturn, instead of coming to learn that bodies like these are equally propitious wherever they are, and incapable of change in any case. They are swept on in a path from which they cannot escape, their motion governed by an uninterrupted sequence of destined events, making their reappearances in cycles that are fixed. They either actuate or signalize all that comes about in the universe. If every event is brought about by them, how is mere familiarity with a process which is unchangeable going to be of any help? If they are pointers to events, what difference does it make to be aware in advance of things you cannot escape? They are going to happen whether you know about them or not. . . .

'So we don't,' you may ask, 'in fact gain anything from the liberal studies?' As far as character is concerned, no, but we gain a good deal from them in other directions—just as even these admittedly inferior arts which we've been talking

---

2. **Mercury roams:** Virgil, *Georgics*, I: 336–7. The person meant is of course the astrologer, not the astronomer. [Translator's note]

about, the ones that are based on use of the hands, make important contributions to the amenities of life although they have nothing to do with character. Why then do we give our sons a liberal education? Not because it can make them morally good but because it prepares the mind for the acquisition of moral values. Just as that grounding in grammar, as they called it in the old days, in which boys are given their elementary schooling, does not teach them the liberal arts but prepares the ground for knowledge of them in due course, so when it comes to character the liberal arts open the way to it rather than carry the personality all the way there. . . .

In this connexion I feel prompted to take a look at individual qualities of character. Bravery is the one which treats with contempt things ordinarily inspiring fear, despising and defying and demolishing all the things that terrify us and set chains on human freedom. Is she in any way fortified by liberal studies? Take loyalty, the most sacred quality that can be found in a human breast, never corrupted by a bribe, never driven to betray by any form of compulsion, crying: 'Beat me, burn me, put me to death, I shall not talk—the more the torture probes my secrets the deeper I'll hide them!' Can liberal studies create that kind of spirit? Take self-control, the quality which takes command of the pleasures; some she dismisses out of hand, unable to tolerate them; others she merely regulates, ensuring that they are brought within healthy limits; never approaching pleasures for their own sake, she realizes that the ideal limit with things you desire is not the amount you would like to but the amount you ought to take. Humanity is the quality which stops one being arrogant towards one's fellows, or being acrimonious. In words, in actions, in emotions she reveals herself as kind and good-natured towards all. To her the troubles of anyone else are her own, and anything that benefits herself she welcomes primarily because it will be of benefit to someone else. Do the liberal studies inculcate these attitudes? No, no more than they do simplicity, or modesty and restraint, or frugality and thrift, or mercy, the mercy that is as sparing with another's blood as though it were its own, knowing that it is not for man to make wasteful use of man.

Someone will ask me how I can say that liberal studies are of no help towards morality when I've just been saying that there's no attaining morality without them. My answer would be this: there's no attaining morality without food either, but there's no connexion between morality and food. The fact that a ship can't begin to exist without the timbers of which it's built doesn't mean that the timbers are of 'help' to it. There's no reason for you to assume that, X being something without which Y could never have come about, Y came about as a result of the assistance of X. And indeed it can actually be argued that the attainment of wisdom is perfectly possible without the liberal studies; although moral values are things which have to be learnt, they are not learnt through these studies. Besides, what grounds could I possible have for supposing that a person who has no acquaintance with books will never be a wise man? For wisdom does not lie in books. Wisdom publishes not words but truths—and I'm not sure that the memory isn't more reliable when it has no external aids to fall back on.

There is nothing small or cramped about wisdom. It is something calling for a lot of room to move. There are questions to be answered concerning physical as well as human matters, questions about the past and about the future, questions about things eternal and things ephemeral, questions about time itself. On this one subject of time just look how many questions there are. To start with, does it have an existence of its own? Next, does anything exist prior to time, independently of it? Did it begin with the universe, or did it exist even before then on the grounds that there was something in existence before the universe? There are countless questions about the soul alone—where it comes from, what its nature is, when it begins to exist, and how long it is in existence; whether it passes from one place to another, moving house, so to speak, on transfer to successive living creatures, taking on a different form with each, or is no more than once in service and is then released to roam the universe; whether it is a corporeal substance or not; what it will do when it ceases to act through us, how it will employ its freedom once it has escaped its cage here; whether it will forget its past and become conscious of its real nature from the actual moment of its parting from the body and departure for its new home on high. Whatever the field of physical or moral sciences you deal with, you will be given no rest by the mass of things to be learnt or investigated. And to enable matters of this range and scale to find unrestricted hospitality in our minds, everything superfluous must be turned out. Virtue will not bring herself to enter the limited space we offer her; something of great size requires plenty of room. Let everything else be evicted, and your heart completely opened to her.

'But it's a nice thing, surely, to be familiar with a lot of subjects.' Well, in that case 10 let us retain just as much of them as we need. Would you consider a person open to criticism for putting superfluous objects on the same level as really useful ones by arranging on display in his house a whole array of costly articles, but not for cluttering himself up with a lot of superfluous furniture in the way of learning? To want to know more than is sufficient is a form of intemperance. Apart from which this kind of obsession with the liberal arts turns people into pedantic, irritating, tactless, self-satisfied bores, not learning what they need simply because they spend their time learning things they will never need. The scholar Didymus wrote four thousand works: I should feel sorry for him if he had merely read so many useless works. In these works he discusses such questions as Homer's origin, who was Aeneas' real mother, whether Anacreon's manner of life was more that of a lecher or that of a drunkard, whether Sappho[3] slept with anyone who asked her, and other things that would be better unlearned if one actually knew them! Don't you go and tell me now that life is long enough for this

3. **Sappho (circa 630–circa 612 BCE):** a Greek poet from the isle of Lesbos who was reputed to have loved both men and women. **Homer's origin:** Very little was known about Homer, the author of the *Iliad* and the *Odyssey*. **Aeneas' real mother:** Aeneas, the hero of Virgil's epic *The Aeneid*, was the son of the goddess Venus, who tried to keep the fact that she had a mortal child a secret. **Anacreon (570–480 BCE):** a lyric poet known for his drinking songs.

sort of thing! When you come to writers in our own school, for that matter, I'll show you plenty of works which could do with some ruthless pruning. It costs a person an enormous amount of time (and other people's ears an enormous amount of boredom) before he earns such compliments as 'What a learned person!' Let's be content with the much less fashionable label, 'What a good man!' . . .

I have been speaking about liberal studies. Yet look at the amount of useless and superfluous matter to be found in the philosophers. Even they have descended to the level of drawing distinctions between the uses of different syllables and discussing the proper meanings of prepositions and conjunctions. They have come to envy the philologist and the mathematician, and they have taken over all the inessential elements in those studies—with the result that they know more about devoting care and attention to their speech than about devoting such attention to their lives. Listen and let me show you the sorry consequences to which subtlety carried too far can lead, and what an enemy it is to truth. Protagoras[4] declares that it is possible to argue either side of any question with equal force, even the question whether or not one can equally argue either side of any question! Nausiphanes[5] declares that of the things which appear to us to exist, none exists any more than it does not exist. Parmenides[6] declares that of all these phenomena none exists except the whole. Zeno of Elea[7] has dismissed all such difficulties by introducing another; he declares that nothing exists. The Pyrrhonean, Megarian, Eretrian and Academic schools[8] pursue more or less similar lines; the last named have introduced a new branch of knowledge, non-knowledge.

Well, all these theories you should just toss on top of that heap of superfluous liberal studies. The people I first mentioned provide me with knowledge which is not going to be of any use to me, while the others snatch away from me any hopes of ever acquiring any knowledge at all. Superfluous knowledge would be preferable to no knowledge. One side offers me no guiding light to direct my vision towards the truth, while the other just gouges my eyes out. If I believe Protagoras there is nothing certain in the universe; if I believe Nausiphanes there is just the one certainty, that nothing is certain; if Parmenides, only one thing exists; if Zeno, not even one. Then what are we? The things that surround us, the things on which we live, what are they? Our whole universe is no more than a semblance of reality, perhaps a deceptive semblance, perhaps one without substance altogether. I should find it difficult to say which of these people annoy me most, those who would have us know nothing or the ones who refuse even to leave us the small satisfaction of knowing that we know nothing.

4. **Protagoras (490–420 BCE)**: an early Sophist philosopher.

5. **Nausiphanes (circa 325 BCE)**: a Greek philosopher and scientist.

6. **Parmenides (fifth century BCE)**: an early Greek philosopher whose belief that truth can be derived only from reason, and not through the senses, was a significant influence on Plato.

7. **Zeno of Elea (circa 490–circa 430 BCE)**: a Greek philosopher noted for his paradoxes.

8. **Pyrrhonean, Megarian, Eretrian, and Academic schools**: philosophical schools in ancient Greece that practiced some form of skepticism, or mistrust of claims to philosophical and scientific truth.

UNDERSTANDING THE TEXT

1. What does Seneca see as the connection between a liberal studies education and the status of a free person? Think of other words based on the Latin word *liber* (liberty, liberate, library) and explain how these concepts might all be connected through Seneca's concept of liberal studies.

2. What does Seneca consider the only subject that deserves to be called "liberal"? Are the other disciplines that he mentions (music, mathematics, etc.) subsets of a larger discipline? If so, how? If not, why not?

3. What Seneca see as the distinguishing feature between liberal and vocational studies? Is this distinction still valid in education today? Explain.

4. Why does Seneca reject the ideal that liberal studies make people virtuous? Given that he is writing in support of liberal studies, why does he spend more than half of the essay demonstrating the inability of liberal studies to produce moral behavior?

5. What, for Seneca, is the difference between studies that make people morally good and studies that lay a foundation that people can use in acquiring moral values?

MAKING CONNECTIONS

1. How does Seneca's view of liberal education compare with John Henry Newman's (p. 53)? How would they compare practical and vocational studies? Do the two philosophers have similar definitions of "liberal education"?

2. What might Seneca say about the *New England Primer* (p. 32)? Would he see it as part of a liberal or vocational education, or as some other kind of education?

3. Compare Seneca's view of useless knowledge with the view implied in Richard Feynman's "O Americano Outra Vez" (p. 68). Does Seneca agree with Feynman's point that even very important subjects can be taught in such a way that they lose their value?

4. Seneca and Mo Tzu (p. 253) both see music as a thing with no practical value. Why, then, does Seneca value music while Mo Tzu opposes it?

5. Compare Seneca's view of the political importance of knowledge with the view that Frederick Douglass advances in "Learning to Read" (p. 46). Would Seneca view Douglass's arguments for literacy education as "liberal" in the sense of befitting a free person? Why or why not?

WRITING ABOUT THE TEXT

1. Write an essay that explores the connection between education and freedom. Explain how you think education should function in a free society and how educational institutions should prepare people to be citizens.

2. Provide a rebuttal to Seneca's view of vocational training as inconsistent with liberal education as he defines it. Consider how training people for careers might be important for "free people."

3. Choose one of the disciplines that Seneca lists—literature, music, geometry, or astronomy—and either agree or disagree with his reasoning that these studies do not directly produce virtue directly in those who study them.

4. Examine a current catalog from your college and write an essay describing one subject that Seneca would consider a liberal art and one that he would not. Support your position with quotations from Seneca's letter.

Al-Ghazālī
Manners to Be Observed by Teachers and Students
(1096)

MANY SCHOLARS BELIEVE THAT, with the exception of Mohammed himself, no one has influenced the development of Islamic thought more than Abū Ḥāmid al-Ghazālī (1058–1111). Al-Ghazālī lived during Islam's golden age of intellectual development, when the spread of Islam from Spain to India opened borders and created an unprecedented flow of people, goods, and ideas across three continents. Arab scientists and mathematicians during this time made discoveries that remain important, and Muslim philosophers rediscovered Plato's and Aristotle's works and translated them into Arabic.

During the eleventh century, Aristotle's philosophy dominated the intellectual climate of the Islamic world. Philosophers and logicians such as al-Farabi (870–950) and Avicenna (980–1037) had already devised complex systems for integrating Aristotelian philosophy with Islamic principles. Al-Ghazālī was trained in this system of thought, and, by all accounts, excelled in it. He was appointed the head of Baghdad's prestigious Nizamiyyah College and became one of Islam's most celebrated thinkers. However, in 1095, al-Ghazālī suffered a spiritual crisis that left him unable to reconcile pagan philosophy with the tenets of his religion. He renounced his academic position and wrote *The Incoherence of the Philosophers*, in which he argued that Islam was fundamentally incompatible with philosophy as his colleagues understood it.

After his spiritual crisis, al-Ghazālī turned toward Sufism, a mystical branch of Islam that focuses on forming a direct relationship with God and holds that all life on Earth is part of God. Sufi beliefs pervade his most important work, *The Revival of Religious Learning* (1096–97), a massive, four-volume treatise that covers nearly every important aspect of life in the medieval Islamic world. In this work, al-Ghazālī aimed to move the discussion of important subjects away from the theoretical abstractions of the philosophers and toward what he considered the unchanging truths of Islam.

For nearly a thousand years, *The Revival of Religious Learning* has been the most frequently read book in the Muslim world after the Quran. "Manners to Be Observed by Teachers and Students" constitutes only a small portion of the first volume, but it provides an excellent introduction to al-Ghazālī's overall argument. In listing the duties of both students and teachers, al-Ghazālī covers a number of important points, some of which are just as applicable to secular instruction as to religious instruction. But he always emphasizes education's spiritual dimension, without which, he believes, neither teaching nor learning can occur meaningfully.

Al-Ghazālī does not attempt to support his argument in this selection with evidence or logical reasoning. Rather, he relies on his ethos as one of the most respected teachers and writers of his day to give credibility to claims of value that he states as simple facts. 🖎

MANNERS TO BE OBSERVED by teachers and students. These manners comprise ten duties.

(1) The first duty of a student is to keep himself free from impure habit and evil matters. Effort to acquire knowledge is the worship of mind. It purifies secret faults and takes to God. Prayer is observed by outward organs and as outward purity is not gained except by outward organs, so worship by mind, the fountain head of acquisition of knowledge, cannot be attained without the removal of bad habits and evil attributes. The Prophet[1] said: Religion is founded on cleanliness. So outward and inward purities are necessary. God says: The polytheists are impure. . . . It is understood from this that purity and impurity are not merely external as the polytheists also keep their dresses clean and bodies clean, but as their mind is impure, so they are generally impure. The inward purity is of greatest importance. The Prophet therefore said: Angels do not enter a house wherein there are dogs. Human mind is a house, the abode of angels, the place of their movements. The blameworthy evils like anger, lust, rancour, envy, pride, conceit and the like are dogs. When dogs reside in a heart, where is the place for the angels? God takes the secrets of knowledge to the hearts through the angels. They do not take it except to the pure souls. Hazrat Ibn Masud[2] said: Knowledge is not acquired through much learning. It is a light cast in heart. A certain sage said: Knowledge is God-fear. As God said: The learned among the people fear God most.

(2) The second duty of a student is to reduce his worldly affairs and keep aloof: from kith and kin as acquisition of knowledge is not possible in these environments. For this reason, a certain sage said: God has not gifted two minds to a man. For this reason, a certain sage said: Knowledge will not give you its full share till you surrender your entire mind to it.

(3) The third duty of a student is not to take pride or exalt himself over the teacher but rather entrust to him the conduct of all his affairs and submit to his advices as a patient submits to his physician. The Prophet said: It is the habit of a believer not to flatter anyone except when he seeks knowledge. Therefore a student should not take pride over his teacher. Knowledge cannot be acquired except through modesty and humility. God said: Herein there is warning for one who has got a heart or sets up ear while he himself being a witness. . . . The meaning of having a heart

---

1. **The Prophet:** Mohammed.
2. **Hazrat Ibn Masud:** "Hazrat" is a Persian title of respect used in the Sufi tradition to designate

great teachers or leaders. Abdullah ibn Mas'ud was an early convert to Islam and a companion of Mohammed.

is to be fit for receiving knowledge and one who is prepared and capable of under-standing knowledge. Whatever the teacher should recommend to the student, the latter should follow it putting aside his own opinion. . . .

(4) The fourth duty of a student is that he should first pay no attention to the difference, whether about worldly sciences or sciences of the hereafter, as it may per-plex his mind and he may lose enthusiasm. He should adopt first what the teacher says and should not argue about the different mazhabs[3] or sects.

(5) The fifth duty is that a student should not miss any branch of knowledge. He should try to become perfect in them as all branches of learning help one another and some branches are allied with others. If a man does not get a thing, it becomes his enemy. God says: When they do not find guidance they say, it is an age-long lie. . . . A poet said: A sweet thing is bitter in the mouth of a patient as sweet water is tasteless to a sick man. Good knowledge is acquired according to one's genius. It leads man to God or helps him in that way. Each branch of knowledge has got its fixed place. He who guards it, is like a guard who patrols the frontiers in jihad.[4] Each has got a rank in it and each has got a reward in the hereafter according to his rank. The only condition required is that the object of acquisition of knowledge should be to please God.

(6) The sixth duty of a student is that he should not take up all branches of knowledge at a time, but should take up the most important one at first as life is not sufficient for all branches of knowledge. A little learning if acquired with enthu-siasm perfects the knowledge of the hereafter or the sciences of the worldly usages and the sciences of revelation. The object of the science of worldly usages is to acquire spiritual knowledge. The goal of the spiritual knowledge is to know God. Our object by this knowledge is not that belief which is handed down from gen-erations to generations. Our object for this knowledge is to acquire light arising out of certain faith which God casts in soul. Such light was acquired by Hazrat Abu Bakr.[5] The Prophet said about Abu Bakr: If the faith of the people of the world is weighed with the faith of Abu Bakr, his faith would be heavy. In short, the highest and the noblest of all science, is to know God. This science is like a sea of which the depth cannot be ascertained. In this science, the highest rank is that of the Prophets, then of the friends of God and finally that of those who fol-

3. **Mazhabs:** the major schools of thought about Islamic law. The four current mazhabs within Sunni Islam have been consolidated from many more that existed in al-Ghazālī's time.

4. **Jihad:** This Islamic concept is much misun-derstood in contemporary political discourse. In traditional Islamic law, *jihad,* or "holy war," can refer to the personal struggle to acquire knowl-edge and live the tenets of Islam. It can also refer to a defensive war necessary to preserve Islam

itself. It cannot, in classical Islamic thought, refer to a war of conquest, a war to punish ene-mies of Islam, or a war designed to bring about religious conversion.

5. **Hazrat Abu Bakr:** A close associate of Mohammed who succeeded him as leader of the Muslim community in Mecca, Abu Bakr is gen-erally considered the first caliph, or non-prophetic Islamic leader.

low them. It has been narrated that the portraits of two ancient wise men were seen on the wall of a mosque. One of them held a piece of paper in which it was written: If you purify everything, don't understand that you have even purified one thing till you know God and know that He is the cause of all Causes and the Creator of everything. In the hand of the second man, there was a scroll in which it was written: I removed thirst before by drinking water and then I have come to know God. But when I have come to know God, my thirst was quenched without any water.

(7) The seventh duty of a student is that he should not take up a new branch of learning till he has learnt fully the previous branch of learning, because it is requisite for the acquisition of knowledge. One branch of knowledge is a guide to another branch. God says: Whoso has been given the Quran recites it with due recitation. . . . In other words, he does not take up one learning till he masters the previous one. Hazrat Ali[6] said: Don't conceal truth from men, rather know the truth, then you will be the masters of truths.

(8) The eighth duty of a student is to know the causes for which noble sciences are known. It can be known from two things, nobility of its fruit and the authenticity of its principles. Take for example the science of religion as medicine. The fruit of the science of religion is to gain an eternal life and the fruit of the other is to gain a temporary life. From these points of view, the science of religion is more noble as its result is more noble. Take up mathematics and astrology; the former is nobler because the former is more authentic in its foundations. From this, it is clear that the science of the knowledge of God, of His angels, of His books and of His prophets is the noblest and also the branches of knowledge which help it.

(9) The ninth duty of a student is to purify mind and action with virtues, to gain   10
proximity to God and His angels and to live in the company of those who live near Him. His aims should not be to gain worldly matters, to acquire riches and properties, to argue with the illiterate and to show pride and haughtiness. He whose object is to gain nearness of God should seek such learning as helps towards that goal, namely the knowledge of the hereafter and the learnings which are auxiliary to it. God said: God will raise herewith in rank who are believers and to whom knowledge have been given. . . . God said: They have got stages, some lower, some higher. The highest rank is that of the Prophets, then of the friends of God and then of the learned who are firm in knowledge and then of the pious who follow them.

(10) The tenth duty of a student is that he should keep attention to the primary object of knowledge. It is not in your power to enjoy bliss of this world and that of the next world together. This world is a temporary abode. Body is a conveyance and the actions run towards the goal. The goal is God and nothing else. All bliss and happiness lie in Him. So give more importance to the sciences which take to that ultimate goal. . . .

6. **Hazrat Ali:** Mohammed's son-in-law and the fourth caliph.

Second Subject-Duties of a Teacher

Whoever takes up the profession of teaching should observe the following duties:—

(1) He will show kindness and sympathy to the students and treat them as his own children. The Prophet said: I am to you like a father to his son. His object should be to protect the student from the fire of Hell. As parents save their children from the fire of this world, so a teacher should save his students or disciples from the fire of Hell. The duties of a teacher are more than those of parents. A father is the immediate cause of this transient life, but a teacher is the cause of immortal life. It is because of the spiritual teacher that the hereafter is much remembered. By teacher, I mean the teacher of the sciences of the hereafter or the sciences of the world with the object of the hereafter. A teacher ruins himself and also his students if he teaches for the sake of the world. For this reason, the people of the hereafter are journeying towards the next world and to God and remain absent from the world. The months and years of this world are so many stations of their journey. There is no miserliness in the fortunes of the next world and so there is no envy among them. They turn to the verse: The believers are brethren. . . .

(2) The second duty of a teacher is to follow the usages and ways of the Prophet. In other words, he should not seek remuneration for teaching but nearness to God. . . . God instructs us to say: I don't want any remuneration for this from you. . . . Wealth and property are the servants of body which is the vehicle of soul of which the essence is knowledge and for which there is honour of soul. He who searches for wealth in lieu of knowledge is like one who has got his face besmeared with impurities but wants to cleanse his body. In that case, the master is made a servant and the servant a master.

(3) The third duty of a teacher is that he should not withhold from his students any advice. After he finishes the outward sciences, he should teach them the inward sciences. He should tell them that the object of education is to gain nearness of God, not power or riches and that God created ambition as a means of perpetuating knowledge which is essential for these sciences.

(4) The fourth duty of a teacher is to dissuade his students from evil ways with care and caution, with sympathy and not with rebuke and harshness, because in that case it destroys the veil of awe and encourages disobedience. The Holy Prophet is the guide of all teachers. He said: If men had been forbidden to make porridge of camel's dung, they would have done it saying that they would not have been forbidden to do it unless there has been some good in it.

(5) The fifth duty of a teacher is that he shall not belittle the value of other sciences before his students. He who teaches grammar naturally thinks of the science of jurisprudence[7] as bad and he who teaches jurisprudence discourages the science of traditions and so on. Such evils are blameworthy. In fact the teacher of one learn-

7. **Jurisprudence:** the study of law or of legal philosophy.

ing should prepare his students for study of other learnings and then he should observe the rules of gradual progress from one stage to another.

(6) The sixth duty that a teacher should do is to teach his students up to the power of their understanding. The students should not be taught such things as are beyond the capacity of their understanding. In this matter, he should follow the Prophet, who said: We prophets form one class. We have been commanded to give every man his rightful place and to speak to men according to their intellect. The Prophet said: When a man speaks such a word to a people who cannot grasp it with their intellect, it becomes a danger to some persons. Hazrat Ali said, pointing to his breast: There is much knowledge in it, but then there should be some people to understand it. The hearts of pious men are graves of secret matter. From this, it is understood that whatever the teacher knows should not all be communicated to the students at the same time. Jesus Christ said: Don't hang pearls around the neck of a swine. Wisdom is better than pearls. He who knows it as bad is worse than swine. Once a learned man was questioned about something but he gave no reply. The questioner said: Have you not heard what the Prophet said?—He who conceals any useful knowledge will on the Resurrection Day be bridled with a bridle of fire. The learned man said: You may place the bridle of fire and go.

If I don't disclose it to one who understands it, then put the bridle of fire upon me. God said: Don't give to the fools your property. . . . There is warning in this verse that it is better to safeguard knowledge from those who might be corrupted by it. To give a thing to one who is not fit for it and not to give a thing to one who is fit for it are equally oppression. A certain poet therefore said:

Should I cast pearls before the illiterate shepherds?
They will not understand, nor know their worth.

If God by His knowledge sends one with knowledge, I will give my goods to him, 20
and gain his love. He wastes his learning who gives it to one unworthy. He commits sin who withholds it from one worthy.

(7) The seventh duty of a teacher is that he should teach his backward students only such things as are clear and suited to their limited understanding. Every man thinks that his wisdom is perfect and the greatest fool is he who rests satisfied with the knowledge that his intellect is perfect. In short, the door of debates should not be opened before the common men.

(8) The eighth duty of a teacher is that he should himself do what he teaches and should not give a lie to his teaching. Knowledge can be grasped by internal eye and actions by external eye. Many people have got external eyes but very few have got internal eyes. So if the actions of a teacher are contrary to what he preaches, it does not help towards guidance, but it is like poison. A teacher is like a stamp to clay and a student is like clay. If the stamp has no character, there is no impression on clay. Or he is like a cane and the student is like the shadow of the cane. How

can the shadow of the cane be straight when the cane itself is crooked? God said: Do you enjoin good to the people and forget it for yourselves . . . ? Hazrat Ali said: Two men have broken my back, the learned man who ruins himself and the fool who adopts asceticism. The learned man misleads the people through his sins and the fool through his evil actions.

UNDERSTANDING THE TEXT

1. How would you summarize, in a few sentences, the most important duties of students and of teachers, according to al-Ghazālī?

2. Why does al-Ghazālī believe that a student must "keep aloof: from kith and kin"? What might be the advantages to learning in isolation from friends and family? What might be the disadvantages?

3. How does al-Ghazālī characterize the relationship between teacher and student? What kind of power dynamic exists between the two? Who is primarily responsible for making sure that learning occurs? How does this arrangement compare with those in contemporary classrooms?

4. What topics does al-Ghazālī believe that students should learn? What topics, if any, would he declare off-limits to students?

5. According to al-Ghazālī, what is the ultimate purpose of education? How do a student's motives affect his or her ability to receive an education?

6. How does al-Ghazālī believe that teachers should treat students who are or seem incapable of learning the subject matter? Do teachers today do the same things? Should they?

7. Is al-Ghazālī right in saying that teachers should always put into practice what they teach? Is it possible to teach something well without practicing it or believing it? Why or why not?

8. What important assumptions (p. 564) about both religion and education does al-Ghazālī leave unstated in the text?

MAKING CONNECTIONS

1. Compare the teacher-student relationship that al-Ghazālī sets up with the "banking concept of education" discussed by Paulo Friere (p. 62). Would al-Ghazālī agree that education deposits knowledge into a student's mind to be withdrawn later?

2. Both al-Ghazālī and Hsün Tzu (p. 8) argue that education should make people more virtuous. Does al-Ghazālī seem to share Hsün Tzu's negative assessment of human nature? How so?

3. How does al-Ghazālī's view of Islam and education compare with the *New England Primer*'s implicit view of Christianity and education (p. 32)? Once

you account for the differences in values and doctrines, how are the overall views of education similar?

4. Situate al-Ghazālī's views in this selection in the context of Averroës's view of the role of science and philosophy in Islam (pp. 391–96).

WRITING ABOUT THE TEXT

1. Compose your own lists of "Duties of a Student" and "Duties of a Teacher," describing each duty in a separate paragraph. Proceed, as al-Ghazālī does, from concrete beliefs about what education should accomplish.

2. How might your college or university change if it adopted al-Ghazālī's principles of education? Consider especially those duties of "learning" and "teaching" that are not primarily religious. Would you want to attend this school?

3. Write an essay supporting or disputing one of the following assertions that al-Ghazālī makes: (1) that education must take place in an environment removed from friends and family; (2) that teachers should teach only up to the limit of students' understanding; or (3) that students should focus on one subject at a time until they have mastered it.

The *New England Primer*
(1777)

THE FIRST EDITION of the *New England Primer* was published in Boston in 1690 by Benjamin Harris, a British printer who had published similar primers in England. For the next two hundred years, the *Primer* went through dozens of editions and revisions and became the best-selling textbook in America. Most Americans who went to school in the eighteenth and nineteenth centuries studied from the primer, and it continued to be used in some schools well into the twentieth century. At least one of its verses is still widely known: "Now I lay me down to take my sleep / I pray the Lord my soul to keep / If I should die before I wake / I pray the Lord my soul to take."

No distinction between religious education and secular education informs the pages of the *New England Primer*. Its original authors could never have imagined such a distinction. The work collects songs and prayers, lessons on spelling and grammar, a lengthy catechism (or series of questions and answers about spiritual matters), and other selections designed to reinforce spiritual values while teaching children to read. With its thoroughly Puritan theology, the *New England Primer* teaches of God's greatness and human depravity, the inevitability of death and the horrors of hell, the ever-present nature of sin, and the promise of eternal salvation for those who scrupulously avoid sin.

One notable feature of every edition of the *New England Primer* was an illustrated alphabet with woodcuts on the left side of the page paired with simple couplets on the right. Though the pictures and the couplets changed somewhat from edition to edition, their basic messages remained consistent from 1690 to the last major edition, published in 1843. The overwhelming majority of the images are religious. Most focus on biblical characters or scenes, but some make moral arguments or point to the consequences of certain actions.

The illustrated alphabet reprinted here is from the 1777 edition of the *New England Primer*. Though this book was published one year after America declared its independence from England, nothing sets it apart from editions published when the American states were still nonrevolutionary colonies (later editions added an illustration of George Washington for the letter "W").

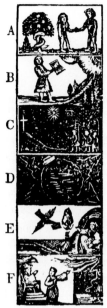

A   In A D A M's Fall
We finned all.

B   Heaven to find,
The Bible Mind.

C   Chrift crucify'd
For finners dy'd.

D   The Deluge drown'd
The Earth around.

E   E L I J A H hid
By Ravens fed.

F   The judgment made
F E L I X afraid.

N   N O A H did view
The old world & new.

O   Young O B A D J A S,
D A V I D, J O S I A S,
All were pious.

P   P E T E R deny'd
His Lord and cry'd.

Q   Queen E S T H E R fues
And faves the *Jews*.

R   Young pious R U T H,
Left all for Truth.

S   Young S A M' L dear,
The Lord did fear.

G   As runs the Glass,
Our Life doth pass.

H   My Book and Heart
Must never part.

I   J O B feels the Rod,—
Yet bleffes GOD.

K   Proud Korah's troop
Was fwallowed up

L   L O T fled to *Zoar*,
Saw fiery Shower
On *Sodom* pour.

M   M O S E S was he
Who *Israel's* Hoft
Led thro' the Sea

T   Young T I M O T H Y
Learnt fin to fly.

U   V A S T H I for Pride,
Was fet afide.

W   Whales in the Sea,
GOD's Voice obey.

X   X E R X E S did die,
And fo muft I.

Y   While youth do chear
Death may be near.

Z   Z A C C H E U S he
Did climb the Tree
Our Lord to fee.

The New England Primer, 1777 edition.

Understanding the Text

1. What overall values do the pictures and the text convey? What kinds of behavior does this text (pictures and text as a whole) promote? What behaviors does it caution against?

2. How do the pictures and the text work together? Do the pictures add to or detract from the text's messages? Why might this have been the only section of the *New England Primer* that routinely was illustrated?

3. What purpose do the biblical references serve? Does the text seem more interested in teaching biblical facts or in applying biblical lessons? What is the purpose of the couplets that do not refer specifically to biblical narratives?

4. Why are several of the pictures accompanied by triplets instead of couplets? Why do these images receive that additional emphasis?

5. Do educational materials today—such as this book—incorporate the values of contemporary America the same way that the *New England Primer* incorporated the values of early America? Will future generations see biases in our textbooks, in the way that most people today see biases in the *New England Primer*?

Making Connections

1. What assumptions about human nature does the *New England Primer*'s alphabet make? Are these assumptions more in line with Hsün Tzu's (p. 100) or with Mencius's (p. 94)? How are these assumptions reflected in the alphabet's educational methodology?

2. How would al-Ghazālī (p. 24) view the *New England Primer*'s moralizing if it were done from a Muslim perspective? Consider, from a religious perspective or a secular one, the advantages and disadvantages of teaching religion and reading at the same time.

3. Compare the way that biblical concepts and images are used in the *New England Primer* with the way they are used in the Beatus Map (p. 388).

Writing about the Text

1. Describe your initial response to this alphabet. How did your thoughts and feelings about the pictures change when you read the texts?

2. Find a modern illustrated alphabet (perhaps in a public library or a bookstore) and see if you can spot cultural values within it, especially behind the combinations of pictures and text. Analyze that alphabet and those values from the perspective of someone from the future or from a different culture.

3. Explore the role of religious values in shaping educational pedagogy, drawing on the *New England Primer* and at least one other work in this chapter.

4. Paraphrase the messages of this alphabet, one sentence per message.

Mary Wollstonecraft
On National Education
(1792)

WHEN THE FRENCH ARISTOCRACY was overthrown by a popular revolution in 1789, radical ideas that had seemed impossible to realize only a generation earlier swept throughout Europe with astounding force. Suddenly, everything that once seemed "natural" was thrown open to investigation and critique: class distinctions, religious ideals, economic practices, and even gender roles. Mary Wollstonecraft (1759–1797), who lived in this radical intellectual environment, was one of the first writers in England to advocate full political, social, and economic equality for women.

Wollstonecraft first came to the reading public's attention with her defense of the French Revolution, *A Vindication of the Rights of Man* (1790). She wrote this work—which argued in favor of abolishing hereditary aristocracy and absolute monarchy—in response to Edmund Burke's attack on the Revolution in *Some Reflections on the Revolution in France* (1790). After defending the equality of social classes in *A Vindication of the Rights of Man*, Wollstonecraft took the ideals of the French Revolution to their logical conclusion. In her most important work, *A Vindication of the Rights of Woman* (1792), she asserted that universal equality applies to women as well as men. Wollstonecraft's insightful social and economic arguments were read and admired by other liberal British writers, including the radical anarchist William Godwin, whom Wollstonecraft married in 1797. (She died the same year while giving birth to their daughter, Mary, who in 1818 would gain literary fame as the author of the novel *Frankenstein*.)

In *A Vindication of the Rights of Woman,* Wollstonecraft adapted the argument that there are no natural differences between aristocrats and commoners, an assertion often made by defenders of the French Revolution, to argue that there are no natural differences in intellect or ability between the sexes. Differences that appear to be natural can be ascribed to discrepancies in educational opportunities. Wollstonecraft's solution was as simple as it was unthinkable to many of her contemporaries: educate men and women in the same schools.

In "On National Education," chapter 12 of *A Vindication of the Rights of Woman,* Wollstonecraft sets forth a proposal for educating boys and girls. They should, she argues, attend school together and receive the same educational opportunities. Education should be based on reason, not superstition, and some kind of education should be available to all children. Few modern readers will be shocked by these proposals, as they have been adopted in most countries in the world. However, at a time when even a basic education was available only to wealthy and middle-class males, these proposals were truly revolutionary, not just in their advocacy of equal opportunities for women but in their crucial underlying assumption: that such opportunities were the only thing standing in the way of women's success.

Wollstonecraft's argument relies on a very strong underlying assumption about the overall value and equality of women. For those who agreed with that premise, her argument proceeds through clear deductive steps to her conclusion about women's education.

I HAVE ALREADY ANIMADVERTED on the bad habits which females acquire when they are shut up together; and, I think, that the observation may fairly be extended to the other sex, till the natural inference is drawn which I have had in view throughout—that to improve both sexes they ought, not only in private families, but in public schools, to be educated together. If marriage be the cement of society, mankind should all be educated after the same model, or the intercourse of the sexes will never deserve the name of fellowship, nor will women ever fulfil the peculiar duties of their sex, till they become enlightened citizens, till they become free by being enabled to earn their own subsistence, independent of men; in the same manner, I mean, to prevent misconstruction, as one man is independent of another. Nay, marriage will never be held sacred till women, by being brought up with men, are prepared to be their companions rather than their mistresses; for the mean doublings of cunning will ever render them contemptible, whilst oppression renders them timid. So convinced am I of this truth, that I will venture to predict that virtue will never prevail in society till the virtues of both sexes are founded on reason; and, till the affections common to both are allowed to gain their due strength by the discharge of mutual duties.

Were boys and girls permitted to pursue the same studies together, those graceful decencies might early be inculcated which produce modesty without those sexual distinctions that taint the mind. Lessons of politeness, and that formulary of decorum, which treads on the heels of falsehood, would be rendered useless by habitual propriety of behaviour. Not, indeed, put on for visitors like the courtly robe of politeness, but the sober effect of cleanliness of mind. Would not this simple elegance of sincerity be a chaste homage paid to domestic affections, far surpassing the meretricious compliments that shine with false lustre in the heartless intercourse of fashionable life? But, till more understanding preponderates in society, there will ever be a want of heart and taste, and the harlot's *rouge* will supply the place of that celestial suffusion which only virtuous affections can give to the face. Gallantry, and what is called love, may subsist without simplicity of character; but the main pillars of friendship, are respect and confidence—esteem is never founded on it cannot tell what!

A taste for the fine arts requires great cultivation; but not more than a taste for the virtuous affections; and both suppose that enlargement of mind which opens so many sources of mental pleasure. Why do people hurry to noisy scenes, and crowded

The author's footnotes have been omitted.

circles? I should answer, because they want activity of mind, because they have not cherished the virtues of the heart. They only, therefore, see and feel in the gross, and continually pine after variety, finding every thing that is simple insipid.

This argument may be carried further than philosophers are aware of, for if nature destined woman, in particular, for the discharge of domestic duties, she made her susceptible of the attached affections in a great degree. Now women are notoriously fond of pleasure; and, naturally must be so according to my definition, because they cannot enter into the minutiae of domestic taste; lacking judgment, the foundation of all taste. For the understanding, in spite of sensual cavillers,[1] reserves to itself the privilege of conveying pure joy to the heart.

With what a languid yawn have I seen an admirable poem thrown down, that a man of true taste returns to, again and again with rapture; and, whilst melody has almost suspended respiration, a lady has asked me where I bought my gown. I have seen also an eye glanced coldly over a most exquisite picture, rest, sparkling with pleasure, on a caricature rudely sketched; and whilst some terrific feature in nature has spread a sublime stillness through my soul, I have been desired to observe the pretty tricks of a lap-dog, that my perverse fate forced me to travel with. Is it surprising that such a tasteless being should rather caress this dog than her children? Or, that she should prefer the rant of flattery to the simple accents of sincerity?

To illustrate this remark I must be allowed to observe, that men of the first genius, and most cultivated minds, have appeared to have the highest relish for the simple beauties of nature; and they must have forcibly felt, what they have so well described, the charm which natural affections, and unsophisticated feelings spread round the human character. It is this power of looking into the heart, and responsively vibrating with each emotion, that enables the poet to personify each passion, and the painter to sketch with a pencil of fire.

True taste is ever the work of the understanding employed in observing natural effects; and till women have more understanding, it is vain to expect them to possess domestic taste. Their lively senses will ever be at work to harden their hearts, and the emotions struck out of them will continue to be vivid and transitory, unless a proper education store their mind with knowledge.

It is the want[2] of domestic taste, and not the acquirement of knowledge, that takes women out of their families, and tears the smiling babe from the breast that ought to afford it nourishment. Women have been allowed to remain in ignorance, and slavish dependence, many, very many years, and still we hear of nothing but their fondness of pleasure and sway, their preference of rakes and soldiers, their childish attachment to toys, and the vanity that makes them value accomplishments more than virtues.

---

1. **Cavillers:** those who *cavil*, or raise trivial, insignificant objections to something.

2. **Want:** lack (not desire).

History brings forward a fearful catalogue of the crimes which their cunning has produced, when the weak slaves have had sufficient address to over-reach their masters. In France, and in how many other countries, have men been the luxurious despots, and women the crafty ministers?—Does this prove that ignorance and dependence domesticate them? Is not their folly the by-word of the libertines,[3] who relax in their society; and do not men of sense continually lament that an immoderate fondness for dress and dissipation carries the mother of a family for ever from home? Their hearts have not been debauched by knowledge, or their minds led astray by scientific pursuits; yet, they do not fulfil the peculiar duties which as women they are called upon by nature to fulfil. On the contrary, the state of warfare which subsists between the sexes, makes them employ those wiles, that often frustrate the more open designs of force.

When, therefore, I call women slaves, I mean in a political and civil sense; for, indirectly they obtain too much power, and are debased by their exertions to obtain illicit sway.

Let an enlightened nation then try what effect reason would have to bring them back to nature, and their duty; and allowing them to share the advantages of education and government with man, see whether they will become better, as they grow wiser and become free. They cannot be injured by the experiment; for it is not in the power of man to render them more insignificant than they are at present.

To render this practicable, day schools, for particular ages, should be established by government, in which boys and girls might be educated together. The school for the younger children, from five to nine years of age, ought to be absolutely free and open to all classes. A sufficient number of masters should also be chosen by a select committee, in each parish, to whom any complaint of negligence, &c. might be made, if signed by six of the children's parents.

Ushers[4] would then be unnecessary; for I believe experience will ever prove that this kind of subordinate authority is particularly injurious to the morals of youth. What, indeed, can tend to deprave the character more than outward submission and inward contempt? Yet how can boys be expected to treat an usher with respect, when the master seems to consider him in the light of a servant, and almost to countenance the ridicule which becomes the chief amusement of the boys during the play hours?

But nothing of this kind could occur in an elementary day-school, where boys and girls, the rich and poor, should meet together. And to prevent any of the distinctions of vanity, they should be dressed alike, and all obliged to submit to the same discipline, or leave the school. The school-room ought to be surrounded by a

3. **The by-word:** the often-used expression. Wollstonecraft means that the foolishness of women is a common theme in the conversations and writings of England's **libertines**, or witty men of taste and fortune.

4. **Ushers:** in the British schools of Wollstonecraft's day, assistant teachers subordinate to the main teachers, or masters.

large piece of ground, in which the children might be usefully exercised, for at this age they should not be confined to any sedentary employment for more than an hour at a time. But these relaxations might all be rendered a part of elementary education, for many things improve and amuse the senses, when introduced as a kind of show, to the principles of which, dryly laid down, children would turn a deaf ear. For instance, botany, mechanics, and astronomy. Reading, writing, arithmetic, natural history, and some simple experiments in natural philosophy, might fill up the day; but these pursuits should never encroach on gymnastic plays in the open air. The elements of religion, history, the history of man, and politics, might also be taught by conversations, in the socratic form.

After the age of nine, girls and boys, intended for domestic employments, or mechanical trades, ought to be removed to other schools, and receive instruction, in some measure appropriated to the destination of each individual, the two sexes being still together in the morning; but in the afternoon, the girls should attend a school, where plain-work, mantua-making, millinery,[5] &c. would be their employment. 15

The young people of superior abilities, or fortune, might now be taught, in another school, the dead and living languages, the elements of science, and continue the study of history and politics, on a more extensive scale, which would not exclude polite literature.

Girls and boys still together? I hear some readers ask: yes. And I should not fear any other consequence than that some early attachment might take place; which, whilst it had the best effect on the moral character of the young people, might not perfectly agree with the views of the parents, for it will be a long time, I fear, before the world will be so far enlightened that parents, only anxious to render their children virtuous, shall allow them to choose companions for life themselves.

Besides, this would be a sure way to promote early marriages,[6] and from early marriages the most salutary physical and moral effects naturally flow. What a different character does a married citizen assume from the selfish coxcomb,[7] who lives, but for himself, and who is often afraid to marry lest he should not be able to live in a certain style. Great emergencies excepted, which would rarely occur in a society of which equality was the basis, a man can only be prepared to discharge the duties of public life, by the habitual practice of those inferiour ones which form the man.

In this plan of education the constitution of boys would not be ruined by the early debaucheries, which now make men so selfish, or girls rendered weak and vain, by indolence, and frivolous pursuits. But, I presuppose, that such a degree of equality should be established between the sexes as would shut out gallantry and coquetry, yet allow friendship and love to temper the heart for the discharge of higher duties.

5. **Millinery:** hatmaking. **Plain-work:** basic sewing. **Mantua-making:** dressmaking (a **mantua** was a kind of gown popular with women in the eighteenth century).

6. In Wollstonecraft's day, **early marriages** were seen as an effective, morally sanctioned way to prevent premarital sex among young people.

7. **Coxscomb:** a foolish, self-absorbed man.

These would be schools of morality—and the happiness of man, allowed to flow 20 from the pure springs of duty and affection, what advances might not the human mind make? Society can only be happy and free in proportion as it is virtuous; but the present distinctions, established in society, corrode all private, and blast all public virtue.

I have already inveighed against the custom of confining girls to their needle, and shutting them out from all political and civil employments; for by thus narrowing their minds they are rendered unfit to fulfil the peculiar duties which nature has assigned them.

Only employed about the little incidents of the day, they necessarily grow up cunning. My very soul has often sickened at observing the sly tricks practised by women to gain some foolish thing on which their silly hearts were set. Not allowed to dispose of money, or call any thing their own, they learn to turn the market penny; or, should a husband offend, by staying from home, or give rise to some emotions of jealousy—a new gown, or any pretty bawble, smooths Juno's[8] angry brow.

But these *littlenesses* would not degrade their character, if women were led to respect themselves, if political and moral subjects were opened to them; and, I will venture to affirm, that this is the only way to make them properly attentive to their domestic duties.—An active mind embraces the whole circle of its duties, and finds time enough for all. It is not, I assert, a bold attempt to emulate masculine virtues; it is not the enchantment of literary pursuits, or the steady investigation of scientific subjects, that leads women astray from duty. No, it is indolence and vanity— the love of pleasure and the love of sway, that will reign paramount in an empty mind. I say empty emphatically, because the education which women now receive scarcely deserves the name. For the little knowledge that they are led to acquire, during the important years of youth, is merely relative to accomplishments; and accomplishments without a bottom, for unless the understanding be cultivated, superficial and monotonous is every grace. Like the charms of a made up face, they only strike the senses in a crowd; but at home, wanting mind, they want variety. The consequence is obvious; in gay scenes of dissipation we meet the artificial mind and face, for those who fly from solitude dread, next to solitude, the domestic circle; not having it in their power to amuse or interest, they feel their own insignificance, or find nothing to amuse or interest themselves.

Besides, what can be more indelicate than a girl's *coming out* in the fashionable world? Which, in other words, is to bring to market a marriageable miss, whose person is taken from one public place to another, richly caparisoned.[9] Yet, mixing in the giddy circle under restraint, these butterflies long to flutter at large, for the first affection of their souls is their own persons, to which their attention has been called

8. **Juno:** in Roman mythology, the famously angry wife of Jupiter; in Greek mythology, she is Hera, angry wife of Zeus.

9. **Caparisoned:** richly dressed. **Coming out:** in Wollstonecraft's day, a young woman's debut into the social world, usually accompanied by a party or a ball.

with the most sedulous care whilst they were preparing for the period that decides their fate for life. Instead of pursuing this idle routine, sighing for tasteless shew, and heartless state, with what dignity would the youths of both sexes form attachments in the schools that I have cursorily pointed out; in which, as life advanced, danc-ing, music, and drawing, might be admitted as relaxations, for at these schools young people of fortune ought to remain, more or less, till they were of age. Those, who were designed for particular professions, might attend, three or four mornings in the week, the schools appropriated for their immediate instruction.

I only drop these observations at present, as hints; rather, indeed, as an outline of the plan I mean, than a digested one; but I must add, that I highly approve of . . . making the children and youths independent of the masters respecting punishments. They should be tried by their peers, which would be an admirable method of fixing sound principles of justice in the mind, and might have the happiest effect on the temper, which is very early soured or irritated by tyranny, till it becomes peevishly cunning, or ferociously overbearing.

My imagination darts forward with benevolent fervour to greet these amiable and respectable groups, in spite of the sneering of cold hearts, who are at liberty to utter, with frigid self-importance, the damning epithet—romantic; the force of which I shall endeavour to blunt by repeating the words of an eloquent moralist.—I know not whether the allusions of a truly humane heart, whose zeal renders every thing easy, be not preferable to that rough and repulsing reason, which always finds in indifference for the public good, the first obstacle to whatever would promote it.

I know that libertines will also exclaim, that woman would be unsexed by acquir-ing strength of body and mind, and that beauty, soft bewitching beauty! would no longer adorn the daughters of men. I am of a very different opinion, for I think that, on the contrary, we should then see dignified beauty, and true grace; to produce which, many powerful physical and moral causes would concur.—Not relaxed beauty, it is true, or the graces of helplessness; but such as appears to make us respect the human body as a majestic pile fit to receive a noble inhabitant, in the relics of antiquity.

I do not forget the popular opinion that the Grecian statues were not modelled after nature. I mean, not according to the proportions of a particular man; but that beautiful limbs and features were selected from various bodies to form an harmonious whole. This might, in some degree, be true. The fine ideal picture of an exalted imag-ination might be superior to the materials which the statuary found in nature, and thus it might with propriety be termed rather the model of mankind than of a man. It was not, however, the mechanical selection of limbs and features; but the ebulli-tion of an heated fancy that burst forth, and the fine senses and enlarged under-standing of the artist selected the solid matter, which he drew into this glowing focus.

I observed that it was not mechanical, because a whole was produced—a model of that grand simplicity, of those concurring energies, which arrest our attention and command our reverence. For only insipid lifeless beauty is produced by a servile copy of even beautiful nature. Yet, independent of these observations, I believe that the human form must have been far more beautiful than it is at present, because extreme indolence, barbarous ligatures, and many causes, which forcibly act on it, in our luxurious state of society, did not retard its expansion, or render it deformed. Exercise and cleanliness appear to be not only the surest means of preserving health, but of promoting beauty, the physical causes only considered; yet, this is not sufficient, moral ones must concur, or beauty will be merely of that rustic kind which blooms on the innocent, wholesome, countenances of some country people, whose minds have not been exercised. To render the person perfect, physical and moral beauty ought to be attained at the same time; each lending and receiving force by the combination. Judgment must reside on the brow, affection and fancy beam in the eye, and humanity curve the cheek, or vain is the sparkling of the finest eye or the elegantly turned finish of the fairest features: whilst in every motion that displays the active limbs and well-knit joints, grace and modesty should appear. But this fair assemblage is not to be brought together by chance; it is the reward of exertions calculated to support each other; for judgment can only be acquired by reflection, affection by the discharge of duties, and humanity by the exercise of compassion to every living creature.   30

Humanity to animals should be particularly inculcated as a part of national education, for it is not at present one of our national virtues. Tenderness for their humble dumb domestics, amongst the lower class, is oftener to be found in a savage than a civilized state. For civilization prevents that intercourse which creates affection in the rude hut, or mud hovel, and leads uncultivated minds who are only depraved by the refinements which prevail in the society, where they are trodden under foot by the rich, to domineer over them to revenge the insults that they are obliged to bear from their superiors.

This habitual cruelty is first caught at school, where it is one of the rare sports of the boys to torment the miserable brutes that fall in their way. The transition, as they grow up, from barbarity to brutes to domestic tyranny over wives, children, and servants, is very easy. Justice, or even benevolence, will not be a powerful spring of action unless it extend to the whole creation; nay, I believe that it may be delivered as an axiom, that those who can see pain, unmoved, will soon learn to inflict it.

The vulgar are swayed by present feelings, and the habits which they have accidentally acquired; but on partial feelings much dependence cannot be placed, though they be just; for, when they are not invigorated by reflection, custom weakens them, till they are scarcely perceptible. The sympathies of our nature are strengthened by pondering cogitations, and deadened by thoughtless use. Macbeth's heart smote him more for one murder, the first, than for a hundred subsequent ones, which were necessary to back it. But, when I used the epithet vulgar, I did not mean to confine my remark to the poor, for partial humanity, founded on present sensations, or whim, is quite as conspicuous, if not more so, amongst the rich.

The lady who sheds tears for the bird starved in a snare, and execrates the devils in the shape of men, who goad to madness the poor ox, or whip the patient ass, tottering under a burden above its strength, will, nevertheless, keep her coachman and horses whole hours waiting for her, when the sharp frost bites, or the rain beats against the well-closed windows which do not admit a breath of air to tell her how roughly the wind blows without. And she who takes her dogs to bed, and nurses them with a parade of sensibility, when sick, will suffer her babes to grow up crooked in a nursery. This illustration of my argument is drawn from a matter of fact. The woman whom I allude to was handsome, reckoned very handsome, by those who do not miss the mind when the face is plump and fair; but her understanding had not been led from female duties by literature, nor her innocence debauched by knowledge. No, she was quite feminine, according to the masculine acceptation of the word; and, so far from loving these spoiled brutes that filled the place which the children ought to have occupied, she only lisped out a pretty mixture of French and English nonsense, to please the men who flocked round her. The wife, mother, and human creature, were all swallowed up by the factitious character which an improper education and the selfish vanity of beauty had produced.

I do not like to make a distinction without a difference, and I own that I have been as much disgusted by the fine lady who took her lap-dog to her bosom instead of her child; as by the ferocity of a man, who, beating his horse, declared, that he knew as well when he did wrong, as a Christian.

This brood of folly shews how mistaken they are who, if they allow women to leave their harams, do not cultivate their understandings, in order to plant virtues in their hearts. For had they sense, they might acquire that domestic taste which would lead them to love with reasonable subordination their whole family, from their husband to the house-dog; nor would they ever insult humanity in the person of the most menial servant by paying more attention to the comfort of a brute, than to that of a fellow-creature.

My observations on national education are obviously hints; but I principally wish to enforce the necessity of educating the sexes together to perfect both, and of making children sleep at home that they may learn to love home; yet to make private support, instead of smothering, public affections, they should be sent to school to mix with a number of equals, for only by the jostlings of equality can we form a just opinion of ourselves.

To render mankind more virtuous, and happier of course, both sexes must act from the same principle; but how can that be expected when only one is allowed to see the reasonableness of it? To render also the social compact truly equitable, and in order to spread those enlightening principles, which alone can meliorate the fate of man, women must be allowed to found their virtue on knowledge, which is scarcely possible unless they be educated by the same pursuits as men. For they are now made so inferiour by ignorance and low desires, as not to deserve to be ranked with them; or, by the serpentine wrigglings of cunning they mount the tree of knowledge, and only acquire sufficient to lead men astray. . . .

Besides, by the exercise of their bodies and minds women would acquire that mental activity so necessary in the maternal character, united with the fortitude that distinguishes steadiness of conduct from the obstinate perverseness of weakness. For it is dangerous to advise the indolent to be steady, because they instantly become rigorous, and to save themselves trouble, punish with severity faults that the patient fortitude of reason might have prevented.

But fortitude presupposes strength of mind; and is strength of mind to be acquired by indolent acquiescence? by asking advice instead of exerting the judgment? by obeying through fear, instead of practising the forbearance, which we all stand in need of ourselves?—The conclusion which I wish to draw, is obvious; make women rational creatures, and free citizens, and they will quickly become good wives, and mothers; that is—if men do not neglect the duties of husbands and fathers.

Discussing the advantages which a public and private education combined, as I have sketched, might rationally be expected to produce, I have dwelt most on such as are particularly relative to the female world, because I think the female world oppressed; yet the gangrene, which the vices engendered by oppression have produced, is not confined to the morbid part, but pervades society at large: so that when I wish to see my sex become more like moral agents, my heart bounds with the anticipation of the general diffusion of that sublime contentment which only morality can diffuse. 40

UNDERSTANDING THE TEXT

1. Why, according to Wollstonecraft, do women develop bad habits? How does this view differ from the prevailing opinions of her day? What solution does she advocate?

2. How does Wollstonecraft believe that taste in things such as art and literature is cultivated? Why, according to her, did the women of her day have bad, overly sentimental taste in the arts?

3. In what sense does Wollstonecraft believe that women are "slaves"? How does she imply that the institution of marriage plays into that slavery?

4. What objections to a coeducational system does Wollstonecraft anticipate? How does she respond to these objections? Do her responses answer these questions persuasively? Why or why not?

5. What does Wollstonecraft see as the connection between education and virtue? Does she believe that all educated people are virtuous?

6. Does Wollstonecraft acknowledge any inherent distinctions between men and women, or does she believe that all differences are socially constructed? Would she accept any gendered view of human nature?

MAKING CONNECTIONS

1. Plato was one of the earliest proponents of equal education for women; in the *Republic*, he argues that male and female guardians should receive the

same education. How else does "On National Education" appear to have been influenced by Plato and, specifically, by the "Speech of Aristophanes" (p. 89) and its view of gender?

2. Compare Wollstonecraft's arguments about the social construction of women's inferiority with Martin Luther King Jr.'s (p. 202) and Frederick Douglass's (p. 46) arguments concerning common assumptions about African Americans. How might Wollstonecraft's arguments about gender be extended to include race?

3. How do Wollstonecraft's proposals for women's education differ from the suggestions about women's learning made by Christine de Pizan in *The Treasure of the City of Ladies* (p. 175)? How well does the term "feminist" apply to each text?

4. Wollstonecraft asserts that Western cultures have, over centuries, come to view women as naturally less intelligent than men. How might the acculturation that Ruth Benedict describes in "The Individual and the Pattern of Culture" (p. 132) explain this process?

WRITING ABOUT THE TEXT

1. Examine the implicit definition of either "taste" or "virtue" that underlies Wollstonecraft's arguments in "On National Education." Discuss how this implicit definition affects her overall argument.

2. Construct an argument in favor of educating women apart from men. Discuss highly successful women's colleges and private girls' schools to support the assertion that women can experience more academic success in segregated schools.

3. Trace the development of "feminist" ideas from Christine de Pizan (p. 175) to Mary Wollstonecraft and from Mary Wollstonecraft to Gloria Anzaldúa (p. 52). How have arguments for women's equality changed over the centuries? What about them has remained constant?

Frederick Douglass
Learning to Read
(1845)

FREDERICK DOUGLASS (1817–1895) was the most famous and respected African-American in the United States for much of the nineteenth century. In 1845, he published his autobiography, *Narrative of the Life of Frederick Douglass, an American Slave*, which tells of his birth as the son of a slave and an unknown white man, his early life as a slave in Maryland, and his escape to freedom in 1837. The book became an international best seller and catapulted him into a prominent position that he maintained for the rest of his life. He became a leader of the abolitionist movement and tirelessly spoke and wrote about the evils of slavery.

The turning point in Douglass's early life, as he presents it in his autobiography, was when he learned to read and write. His master's wife, Mrs. Auld, first taught him the alphabet—illegally, since slaves were forbidden to read or write. However, under pressure from her husband, she soon abandoned the effort, and he was left to learn on his own. His one guide in this effort was the children's schoolbook *The Columbian Orator*, a collection of great speeches, poems, soliloquies, and occasional pieces used to teach rhetoric and public speaking. In *The Columbian Orator*, Douglass learned a perplexing truth: the same country that had enslaved him had fought a revolution in the name of freedom. For the rest of his life, he drew on this tradition to call attention to the hypocrisy of slavery in a nation founded on principles of, in his words, "justice, liberty, prosperity, and independence."

In the excerpt that follows, Douglass describes the strategies that he used to learn to read and write. The passage is important not only because it records Douglass's determination and perseverance but also because it reveals his keen understanding of the link between education and a desire for justice. For a time, Douglass relates, he felt oppressed by the fact that he had become more educated than most other slaves and wished that he could be as ignorant as they. In time, however, his education helped him to escape slavery and to make substantial contributions to its abolition.

Douglass is keenly aware of his story's great irony: that the white masters who tried to prevent slaves from being educated on the grounds that it would make them unfit for slavery were absolutely correct. Education, Douglass insists, goes hand in hand with freedom, and the only way to keep people enslaved is to prevent them from learning and acquiring knowledge. The *Narrative of the Life of Frederick Douglass* is both a narrative of and a testimony to the emancipatory power of education.

Douglass relies heavily on emotional appeals as he narrates his early experiences with reading and literacy. These experiences were both positive and negative, and his emotional reflections are both joyful and disconcerting. They all, though, have the effect of pulling the reader in and creating sympathy for Douglass.

I LIVED IN MASTER HUGH's family about seven years. During this time, I succeeded in learning to read and write. In accomplishing this, I was compelled to resort
to various stratagems. I had no regular teacher. My mistress, who had kindly commenced to instruct me, had, in compliance with the advice and direction of her husband, not only ceased to instruct, but had set her face against my being instructed
by any one else. It is due, however, to my mistress to say of her, that she did not
adopt this course of treatment immediately. She at first lacked the depravity indispensable to shutting me up in mental darkness. It was at least necessary for her to
have some training in the exercise of irresponsible power, to make her equal to the
task of treating me as though I were a brute.

My mistress was, as I have said, a kind and tender-hearted woman; and in the
simplicity of her soul she commenced, when I first went to live with her, to treat
me as she supposed one human being ought to treat another. In entering upon the
duties of a slaveholder, she did not seem to perceive that I sustained to her the relation of a mere chattel, and that for her to treat me as a human being was not only
wrong, but dangerously so. Slavery proved as injurious to her as it did to me. When
I went there, she was a pious, warm, and tender-hearted woman. There was no sorrow or suffering for which she had not a tear. She had bread for the hungry, clothes
for the naked, and comfort for every mourner that came within her reach. Slavery
soon proved its ability to divest her of these heavenly qualities. Under its influence,
the tender heart became stone, and the lamblike disposition gave way to one of tiger-
like fierceness. The first step in her downward course was in her ceasing to instruct
me. She now commenced to practise her husband's precepts. She finally became
even more violent in her opposition than her husband himself. She was not satisfied with simply doing as well as he had commanded; she seemed anxious to do better. Nothing seemed to make her more angry than to see me with a newspaper. She
seemed to think that here lay the danger. I have had her rush at me with a face
made all up of fury, and snatch from me a newspaper, in a manner that fully revealed
her apprehension. She was an apt woman; and a little experience soon demonstrated,
to her satisfaction, that education and slavery were incompatible with each other.

From this time I was most narrowly watched. If I was in a separate room any considerable length of time, I was sure to be suspected of having a book, and was at once
called to give an account of myself. All this, however, was too late. The first step
had been taken. Mistress, in teaching me the alphabet, had given me the *inch*, and
no precaution could prevent me from taking the *ell*.[1]

The plan which I adopted, and the one by which I was most successful, was that
of making friends of all the little white boys whom I met in the street. As many of
these as I could, I converted into teachers. With their kindly aid, obtained at different times and in different places. I finally succeeded in learning to read. When I was

---

1. **Ell:** an archaic unit of measurement equal to
forty-five inches. The saying "give him and inch
and he will take an ell" is the forerunner of the
current proverb "give him an inch and he will
take a mile."

sent of errands, I always took my book with me, and by going one part of my errand quickly, I found time to get a lesson before my return. I used also to carry bread with me, enough of which was always in the house, and to which I was always welcome; for I was much better off in this regard than many of the poor white children in our neighborhood. This bread I used to bestow upon the hungry little urchins, who, in return, would give me that more valuable bread of knowledge. I am strongly tempted to give the names of two or three of those little boys, as a testimonial of the gratitude and affection I bear them; but prudence forbids;—not that it would injure me, but it might embarrass them; for it is almost an unpardonable offence to teach slaves to read in this Christian country. It is enough to say of the dear little fellows, that they lived on Philpot Street, very near Durgin and Bailey's ship-yard. I used to talk this matter of slavery over with them. I would sometimes say to them, I wished I could be as free as they would be when they got to be men. "You will be free as soon as you are twenty-one, *but I am a slave for life*! Have not I as good a right to be free as you have?" These words used to trouble them; they would express for me the liveliest sympathy, and console me with the hope that something would occur by which I might be free.

I was now about twelve years old, and the thought of being *a slave for life* began to bear heavily upon my heart. Just about this time, I got hold of a book entitled "The Columbian Orator." Every opportunity I got, I used to read this book. Among much of other interesting matter, I found in it a dialogue between a master and his slave. The slave was represented as having run away from his master three times. The dialogue represented the conversation which took place between them, when the slave was retaken the third time. In this dialogue, the whole argument in behalf of slavery was brought forward by the master, all of which was disposed of by the slave. The slave was made to say some very smart as well as impressive things in reply to his master—things which had the desired though unexpected effect; for the conversation resulted in the voluntary emancipation of the slave on the part of the master.

In the same book, I met with one of Sheridan's[2] mighty speeches on and in behalf of Catholic emancipation. These were choice documents to me. I read them over and over again with unabated interest. They gave tongue to interesting thoughts of my own soul, which had frequently flashed through my mind, and died away for want of utterance. The moral which I gained from the dialogue was the power of truth over the conscience of even a slaveholder. What I got from Sheridan was a bold denunciation of slavery, and a powerful vindication of human rights. The reading of these documents enabled me to utter my thoughts, and to meet the arguments brought forward to sustain slavery; but while they relieved me of one difficulty, they brought on another even more painful than the one of which I was relieved. The more I read, the more I was led to abhor and detest my enslavers. I could regard

5

2. **Sheridan's:** Richard Brinsley Sheridan (1751–1816) was a well-known Irish playwright and advocate for Catholic civil rights.

them in no other light than a band of successful robbers, who had left their homes, and gone to Africa, and stolen us from our homes, and in a strange land reduced us to slavery. I loathed them as being the meanest as well as the most wicked of men. As I read and contemplated the subject, behold! that very discontentment which Master Hugh had predicted would follow my learning to read had already come, to torment and sting my soul to unutterable anguish. As I writhed under it, I would at times feel that learning to read had been a curse rather than a blessing. It had given me a view of my wretched condition, without the remedy. It opened my eyes to the horrible pit, but to no ladder upon which to get out. In moments of agony, I envied my fellow-slaves for their stupidity. I have often wished myself a beast. I preferred the condition of the meanest reptile to my own. Any thing, no matter what, to get rid of thinking! It was this everlasting thinking of my condition that tormented me. There was no getting rid of it. It was pressed upon me by every object within sight or hearing, animate or inanimate. The silver trump of freedom had roused my soul to eternal wakefulness. Freedom now appeared, to disappear no more forever. It was heard in every sound, and seen in every thing. It was ever present to torment me with a sense of my wretched condition. I saw nothing without seeing it, I heard nothing without hearing it, and felt nothing without feeling it. It looked from every star, it smiled in every calm, breathed in every wind, and moved in every storm.

I often found myself regretting my own existence, and wishing myself dead; and but for the hope of being free, I have no doubt but that I should have killed myself, or done something for which I should have been killed. While in this state of mind, I was eager to hear any one speak of slavery. I was a ready listener. Every little while, I could hear something about the abolitionists. It was some time before I found what the word meant. It was always used in such connections as to make it an interesting word to me. If a slave ran away and succeeded in getting clear, or if a slave killed his master, set fire to a barn, or did any thing very wrong in the mind of a slaveholder, it was spoken of as the fruit of *abolition*. Hearing the word in this connection very often, I set about learning what it meant. The dictionary afforded me little or no help. I found it was "the act of abolishing"; but then I did not know what was to be abolished. Here I was perplexed. I did not dare to ask any one about its meaning, for I was satisfied that it was something they wanted me to know very little about. After a patient waiting, I got one of our city papers, containing an account of the number of petitions from the north, praying for the abolition of slavery in the District of Columbia, and of the slave trade between the States. From this time I understood the words *abolition* and *abolitionist*, and always drew near when that word was spoken, expecting to hear something of importance to myself and fellow-slaves. The light broke in upon me by degrees. I went one day down on the wharf of Mr. Waters; and seeing two Irishmen unloading a scow of stone, I went, unasked, and helped them. When we had finished, one of them came to me and asked me if I were a slave. I told him I was. He asked, "Are ye a slave for life?" I told him that I was. The good Irishman seemed to be deeply affected by the statement. He said to the other that it was a pity so fine a little fellow as myself should be a slave for life. He said it was a shame to hold me. They both advised me to run away to the north; that I should find friends there, and that I should be free. I pretended not to be interested in what they said, and treated them as if I did not understand them; for I feared they might be treacherous. White men have been known to encourage slaves to escape, and then, to get the reward, catch them and return them to their masters. I was afraid that these seemingly good men might use me so; but I nevertheless remembered their advice, and from that time I resolved to run away. I looked forward to a time at which it would be safe for me to escape. I was too young to think of doing so immediately; besides, I wished to learn how to write, as I might have occasion to write my own pass. I consoled myself with the hope that I should one day find a good chance. Meanwhile, I would learn to write.

The idea as to how I might learn to write was suggested to me by being in Durgin and Bailey's ship-yard, and frequently seeing the ship carpenters, after hewing, and getting a piece of timber ready for use, write on the timber the name of that part of the ship for which it was intended. When a piece of timber was intended for the larboard side, it would be marked thus—"L." When a piece was for the starboard side, it would be marked thus—"S." A piece for the larboard side forward, would be marked thus—"L. F." When a piece was for starboard side forward it would be marked thus—"S. F." For larboard aft, it would be marked thus— "L. A." For starboard aft, it would be marked thus— "S. A." I soon learned the names of these letters, and for what they were intended when placed upon a piece of timber in the shipyard. I immediately commenced copying them, and in a short time was able to make the four letters named. After that, when I met with any boy who I knew could write, I would tell him I could write as well as he. The next word would be, "I don't believe you. Let me see you try it." I would then make the letters which I had been so fortunate as to learn, and ask him to beat that. In this way I got a good many lessons in writing, which it is quite possible I should never have gotten in any other way. During this time, my copy-book was the board fence, brick wall, and pavement; my pen and ink was a lump of chalk. With these, I learned mainly how to write. I then commenced and continued copying the Italics in Webster's Spelling Book, until I could make them all without looking on the book. By this time, my little Master Thomas had gone to school, and learned how to write, and had written over a number of copy-books. These had been brought home, and shown to some of our near neighbors, and then laid aside. My mistress used to go to class meeting at the Wilk Street meetinghouse every Monday afternoon, and leave me to take care of the house. When left thus, I used to spend the time in writing in the spaces left in Master Thomas's copy-book, copying what he had written. I continued to do this until I could write a hand very similar to that of Master Thomas. Thus, after a long, tedious effort for years, I finally succeeded in learning how to write.

UNDERSTANDING THE TEXT

1. What effect does Douglass believe slavery has on slaveholders? How do the actions of his former mistress support his assertion?

2. Why does Douglass not name the white boys who helped him learn to read? What does this decision say about the society he was living in when he wrote his autobiography?

3. What kinds of ideas did Douglass encounter when he read *The Columbian Orator*? How did these ideas influence him?

4. Why did Douglass become depressed after reading *The Columbian Orator*? Why did he feel that he would have been better off not knowing how to read?

5. What role does Douglass suggest education has in ending oppression? Why do oppressors keep their victims in ignorance?

6. How well does Douglass's narrative support his argument? How would you phrase that argument as a single thesis (p. 579)?

MAKING CONNECTIONS

1. Compare "Learning to Read" with Martin Luther King Jr.'s "Letter from Birmingham City Jail" (p. 203). How does each writer draw on noncontroversial sources and ideas to support his then-controversial assertions?

2. Compare Douglass's experience of educating himself with John Henry Newman's understanding of "liberal education" (p. 53). How well does Douglass's learning correspond to the kind of education that Newman advocates? How "useful" to Douglass are the things he learns?

3. Compare Douglass's view of education's liberating effects with Paulo Friere's in "The Banking Concept of Education" (p. 62). How is Douglass an example of the principles that Friere articulates?

4. What role does rhetoric, as exemplified by the dialogue and speech in *The Columbian Orator*, play in Douglass's education? Consider the impact of this material on Douglass from the standpoint of Plato's (p. 478) and Aristotle's (p. 489) conflicting views on the usefulness of rhetoric.

5. Contrast Douglass's view of the importance of learning to read and write in Standard English with the views of Gloria Anzaldúa (p. 527) and Kisautaq Leona Okakok (p. 76) on the importance of cultural minorities' retaining their linguistic distinctiveness. Might the two positions be reconciled? Why or why not?

WRITING ABOUT THE TEXT

1. Write a personal essay about an early experience that significantly influenced your education. If appropriate, describe how something that you read had an impact on you and your course(s) of study.

2. Imagine that a person from another country arrived in your community able to speak English but not able to read and write. You are that person's tutor. How would you begin to teach? What reading materials would you use?

3. Other abolitionists criticized Douglass for accepting the tenets of the U.S. Constitution, because it did not repudiate slavery. Write an essay examining the Constitution as it stood in Douglass's day and arguing for or against Douglass's proposition that it is inherently antislavery. Perhaps also examine other founding American documents and judge how Douglass might have viewed them.

4. Explain the connections between education and liberty by using Seneca (p. 16) as a theoretical background and Douglass as a primary example.

John Henry Newman
from *Knowledge Its Own End*
(1852)

IN 1845, John Henry Newman (1801–1890) shocked his students, his colleagues, and much of England when he resigned his positions as Anglican minister and Oxford professor and converted to Roman Catholicism. At the time, Catholics held an extremely tenuous position in English society; they had received the right to vote only sixteen years earlier, in 1829, and the Catholic Church had no formal organization in England. Newman's conversion was a matter of deep, personal conviction, which he discussed in his famous 1864 autobiography, *Apologia Pro Vita Sua*. In 1879, Pope Leo XIII named Newman a cardinal, and in 1991, Pope John Paul II set in motion the process to proclaim him a saint. Newman was as committed to education as he was to Catholicism, and, from his conversion to his death, he was a prominent spokesperson for both.

Newman's conversion meant that he was forbidden to teach at Oxford or any other English university. However, the Catholic population of Ireland was large enough to support a major university. In 1852, Newman traveled to Dublin to deliver a series of lectures on the importance of Catholic education. Two years later, in 1854, he helped found the Catholic University of Ireland and was named its first rector. In this capacity, he revised his early lectures on education, which were published in 1873 as *The Idea of a University*.

The Idea of a University reflects on much more than the role of education in a religious life. Newman understood "Catholic" in its broadest sense, including the meaning "universal," and he believed that a "Catholic education" involved all branches of knowledge. *The Idea of a University* argues for a "liberal" education, meaning an education that crosses disciplinary boundaries and gives students a solid background in the arts, sciences, and humanities. Newman's concept of a liberal education had a tremendous impact on the subsequent development of universities in England and the United States. Even today, most colleges and universities have a general education component whose core values can be traced back to the ideas that Newman articulates in this book.

"Knowledge Its Own End" was the fifth of Newman's original lectures on education to Irish Catholics. In it, Newman argues that a true education need not, and in many cases cannot, be attached to practical purposes. Relying on quotations from Cicero, Aristotle, and Francis Bacon, Newman draws a sharp distinction between "useful knowledge" (knowledge that has a practical application) and "liberal knowledge" (knowledge that is pursued for its own sake). Newman acknowledges that useful knowledge is important—people need to be trained for careers, taught to accomplish tasks, and provided with ways to make their lives more fulfilling. However, Newman also sees tremendous value in education that exists solely for the sake of imparting knowledge and fostering inquiry. This kind of knowledge, for Newman, lies at the heart of a university. Newman relies heavily on quotations and examples from ancient authors such as Aristotle, Cicero, and Xenophon. His own essay on liberal education draws much of its authority from the words of thinkers that most educated people in Newman's day were familiar with. 🖎

2.

I AM ASKED what is the end of University Education, and of the Liberal or Philosophical Knowledge which I conceive it to impart: I answer, that what I have already said has been sufficient to show that it has a very tangible, real, and sufficient end, though the end cannot be divided from that knowledge itself. Knowledge is capable of being its own end. Such is the constitution of the human mind, that any kind of knowledge, if it be really such, is its own reward. And if this is true of all knowledge, it is true also of that special Philosophy, which I have made to consist in a comprehensive view of truth in all its branches, of the relations of science to science, of their mutual bearings, and their respective values. What the worth of such an acquirement is, compared with other objects which we seek,—wealth or power or honour or the conveniences and comforts of life, I do not profess here to discuss; but I would maintain, and mean to show, that it is an object, in its own nature so really and undeniably good, as to be the compensation of a great deal of thought in the compassing, and a great deal of trouble in the attaining.

Now, when I say that Knowledge is, not merely a means to something beyond it, or the preliminary of certain arts into which it naturally resolves, but an end sufficient to rest in and to pursue for its own sake, surely I am uttering no paradox, for I am stating what is both intelligible in itself, and has ever been the common judgment of philosophers and the ordinary feeling of mankind. I am saying what at least the public opinion of this day ought to be slow to deny, considering how much we have heard of late years, in opposition to Religion, of entertaining, curious, and various knowledge. I am but saying what whole volumes have been written to illustrate, viz.,[1] by a "selection from the records of Philosophy, Literature, and Art, in all ages and countries, of a body of examples, to show how the most unpropitious circumstances have been unable to conquer an ardent desire for the acquisition of knowledge."[2] That further advantages accrue to us and redound to others by its possession, over and above what it is in itself, I am very far indeed from denying; but, independent of these, we are satisfying a direct need of our nature in its very aquisition; and whereas our nature, unlike that of the inferior creation, does not at once reach its perfection, but depends, in order to it, on a number of external aids and appliances, Knowledge, as one of the principal of these, is valuable for what its very pres-

1. **Viz.:** namely.
2. The quotation is from *The Pursuit of Knowl-* *edge under Difficulties* (1866), by the American essayist Mary Abigail Dodge (1833–1896).

ence in us does for us after the manner of a habit, even though it be turned to no further account, nor subserve any direct end.

3.

Hence it is that Cicero,[3] in enumerating the various heads of mental excellence, lays down the pursuit of Knowledge for its own sake, as the first of them. "This pertains most of all to human nature," he says, "for we are all of us drawn to the pursuit of Knowledge; in which to excel we consider excellent, whereas to mistake, to err, to be ignorant, to be deceived, is both an evil and a disgrace." And he considers Knowledge the very first object to which we are attracted, after the supply of our physical wants. After the calls and duties of our animal existence, as they may be termed, as regards ourselves, our family, and our neighbours, follows, he tells us, "the search after truth. Accordingly, as soon as we escape from the pressure of necessary cares, forthwith we desire to see, to hear, and to learn; and consider the knowledge of what is hidden or is wonderful a condition of our happiness."

This passage, though it is but one of many similar passages in a multitude of authors, I take for the very reason that it is so familiarly known to us; and I wish you to observe, Gentlemen, how distinctly it separates the pursuit of Knowledge from those ulterior objects to which certainly it can be made to conduce, and which are, I suppose, solely contemplated by the persons who would ask of me the use of a University or Liberal Education. So far from dreaming of the cultivation of Knowledge directly and mainly in order to our physical comfort and enjoyment, for the sake of life and person, of health, of the conjugal and family union, of the social tie and civil security, the great Orator implies, that it is only after our physical and political needs are supplied, and when we are "free from necessary duties and cares," that we are in a condition for "desiring to see, to hear, and to learn." Nor does he contemplate in the least degree the reflex or subsequent action of Knowledge, when acquired, upon those material goods which we set out by securing before we seek it; on the contrary, he expressly denies its bearing upon social life altogether, strange as such a procedure is to those who live after the rise of the Baconian philosophy,[4] and he cautions us against such a cultivation of it as will interfere with our duties to our fellow-creatures. "All these methods," he says, "are engaged in the investigation of truth; by the pursuit of which to be carried off from public occupations is a transgression of duty. For the praise of virtue lies altogether in action; yet intermissions often occur, and then we recur to such pursuits; not to say that the incessant activity of the mind is vigorous enough to carry us on in the pursuit of knowledge, even without any exertion of our own." The idea of benefiting society by means of

---

3. **Cicero:** Marcus Tullius Cicero (106–43 BCE), Roman orator and statesman. The quotation below comes from his work *De Officiis*, or "On Duties" (44 BCE).

4. **Baconian philosophy:** the theory of knowledge derived from the writings of Francis Bacon (1561–1626), who emphasized the way that scientific inquiry could improve the human condition.

"the pursuit of science and knowledge" did not enter at all into the motives which he would assign for their cultivation. . . .

4.

Things, which can bear to be cut off from every thing else and yet persist in living, must have life in themselves; pursuits, which issue in nothing, and still maintain their ground for ages, which are regarded as admirable, though they have not as yet proved themselves to be useful, must have their sufficient end in themselves, whatever it turn out to be. And we are brought to the same conclusion by considering the force of the epithet, by which the knowledge under consideration is popularly designated. It is common to speak of "*liberal* knowledge," of the "*liberal* arts and studies," and of a "*liberal* education," as the especial characteristic or property of a University and of a gentleman; what is really meant by the word? Now, first, in its grammatical sense it is opposed to *servile*; and by "servile work" is understood, as our catechisms inform us, bodily labour, mechanical employment, and the like, in which the mind has little or no part. . . . As far as this contrast may be considered as a guide into the meaning of the word, liberal education and liberal pursuits are exercises of mind, of reason, of reflection.

But we want something more for its explanation, for there are bodily exercises which are liberal, and mental exercises which are not so. For instance, in ancient times the practitioners in medicine were commonly slaves; yet it was an art as intellectual in its nature, in spite of the pretence, fraud, and quackery with which it might then, as now, be debased, as it was heavenly in its aim. And so in like manner, we contrast a liberal education with a commercial education or a professional; yet no one can deny that commerce and the professions afford scope for the highest and most diversified powers of mind. There is then a great variety of intellectual exercises, which are not technically called "liberal;" on the other hand, I say, there are exercises of the body which do receive that appellation. Such, for instance, was the palæstra,[5] in ancient times; such the Olympic games, in which strength and dexterity of body as well as of mind gained the prize. In Xenophon[6] we read of the young Persian nobility being taught to ride on horseback and to speak the truth; both being among the accomplishments of a gentleman. War, too, however rough a profession, has ever been accounted liberal, unless in cases when it becomes heroic, which would introduce us to another subject.

Now comparing these instances together, we shall have no difficulty in determining the principle of this apparent variation in the application of the term which I am examining. Manly games, or games of skill, or military prowess, though bodily, are, it seems, accounted liberal; on the other hand, what is merely professional,

---

5. **The palæstra:** in ancient Greece, the site of boxing, wrestling, and other physical competitions.
6. **Xenophon:** a student (circa 431–circa 352 BCE) of Socrates and contemporary of Plato who wrote a series of works on the history of Athens during his own times. His best-known work, the *Anabasis*, tells of his travels through the Persian Empire.

though highly intellectual, nay, though liberal in comparison of trade and manual labour, is not simply called liberal, and mercantile occupations are not liberal at all. Why this distinction? because that alone is liberal knowledge, which stands on its own pretensions, which is independent of sequel, expects no complement, refuses to be *informed* (as it is called) by any end, or absorbed into any art, in order duly to present itself to our contemplation. The most ordinary pursuits have this specific character, if they are self-sufficient and complete; the highest lose it, when they minister to something beyond them. It is absurd to balance, in point of worth and importance, a treatise on reducing fractures with a game of cricket or a fox-chase; yet of the two the bodily exercise has that quality which we call "liberal," and the intellectual has it not. And so of the learned professions altogether, considered merely as professions; although one of them be the most popularly beneficial, and another the most politically important, and the third the most intimately divine of all human pursuits, yet the very greatness of their end, the health of the body, or of the commonwealth, or of the soul, diminishes, not increases, their claim to the appellation "liberal," and that still more, if they are cut down to the strict exigencies of that end. If, for instance, Theology, instead of being cultivated as a contemplation, be limited to the purposes of the pulpit or be represented by the catechism, it loses,—not its usefulness, not its divine character, not its meritoriousness (rather it gains a claim upon these titles by such charitable condescension),—but it does lose the particular attribute which I am illustrating; just as a face worn by tears and fasting loses its beauty, or a labourer's hand loses its delicateness;—for Theology thus exercised is not simple knowledge, but rather is an art or a business making use of Theology. And thus it appears that even what is supernatural need not be liberal, nor need a hero be a gentleman, for the plain reason that one idea is not another idea. And in like manner the Baconian Philosophy, by using its physical sciences in the service of man, does thereby transfer them from the order of Liberal Pursuits to, I do not say the inferior, but the distinct class of the Useful. And, to take a different instance, hence again, as is evident, whenever personal gain is the motive, still more distinctive an effect has it upon the character of a given pursuit; thus racing, which was a liberal exercise in Greece, forfeits its rank in times like these, so far as it is made the occasion of gambling.

All that I have been now saying is summed up in a few characteristic words of the great Philosopher. "Of possessions," he says, "those rather are useful, which bear fruit; those *liberal, which tend to enjoyment.* By fruitful, I mean, which yield revenue; by enjoyable, where *nothing accrues of consequence beyond the using.*"[7] . . .

9.

Useful Knowledge then, I grant, has done its work; and Liberal Knowledge as certainly has not done its work,—that is, supposing, as the objectors assume, its

---

7. This quotation comes from the fifth chapter of the first book of Aristotle's *Rhetoric.*

direct end, like Religious Knowledge, is to make men better; but this I will not for an instant allow, and, unless I allow it, those objectors have said nothing to the purpose. I admit, rather I maintain, what they have been urging, for I consider Knowledge to have its end in itself. For all its friends, or its enemies, may say, I insist upon it, that it is as real a mistake to burden it with virtue or religion as with the mechanical arts. Its direct business is not to steel the soul against temptation or to console it in affliction, any more than to set the loom in motion, or to direct the steam carriage; be it ever so much the means or the condition of both material and moral advancement, still, taken by and in itself, it as little mends our hearts as it improves our temporal circumstances. And if its eulogists claim for it such a power, they commit the very same kind of encroachment on a province not their own as the political economist who should maintain that his science educated him for casuistry or diplomacy. Knowledge is one thing, virtue is another; good sense is not conscience, refinement is not humility, nor is largeness and justness of view faith. Philosophy, however enlightened, however profound, gives no command over the passions, no influential motives, no vivifying principles. Liberal Education makes not the Christian, not the Catholic, but the gentleman. It is well to be a gentleman, it is well to have a cultivated intellect, a delicate taste, a candid, equitable, dispassionate mind, a noble and courteous bearing in the conduct of life;—these are the natural qualities of a large knowledge; they are the objects of a University; I am advocating, I shall illustrate and insist upon them; but still, I repeat, they are no guarantee for sanctity or even for conscientiousness, they may attach to the man of the world, to the profligate, to the heartless,—pleasant, alas, and attractive as he shows when decked out in them. Taken by themselves, they do but seem to be what they are not; they look like virtue at a distance, but they are detected by close observers, and on the long run; and hence it is that they are popularly accused of pretence and hypocrisy, not, I repeat, from their own fault, but because their professors and their admirers persist in taking them for what they are not, and are officious in arrogating for them a praise to which they have no claim. Quarry the granite rock with razors, or moor the vessel with a thread of silk; then may you hope with such keen and delicate instruments as human knowledge and human reason to control against those giants, the passion and the pride of man.

Surely we are not driven to theories of this kind, in order to vindicate the value 10 and dignity of Liberal Knowledge. Surely the real grounds on which its pretensions rest are not so very subtle or abstruse, so very strange or improbable. Surely it is very intelligible to say, and that is what I say here, that Liberal Education, viewed in itself, is simply the cultivation of the intellect, as such, and its object is nothing more or less than intellectual excellence. Every thing has its own perfection, be it higher or lower in the scale of things; and the perfection of one is not the perfection of another. Things animate, inanimate, visible, invisible, all are good in their kind, and have a *best* of themselves, which is an object of pursuit. Why do you take such pains with your garden or your park? You see to your walks and turf and shrubberies; to your trees and drives; not as if you meant to make an orchard of the one, or corn or pasture land of the other, but because there is a special beauty in all that is goodly in wood, water, plain, and slope, brought all together by art into one shape, and grouped into the whole. Your cities are beautiful, your palaces, your public buildings, your territorial mansions, your churches; and their beauty leads to nothing beyond itself. There is a physical beauty and a moral: there is a beauty of person, there is a beauty of our moral being, which is natural virtue; and in like manner there is a beauty, there is a perfection, of the intellect. There is an ideal perfection in these various subject-matters, towards which individual instances are seen to rise, and which are the standards for all instances whatever. The Greek divinities and demigods, as the statuary has moulded them, with their symmetry of figure, and their high forehead and their regular features, are the perfection of physical beauty. The heroes, of whom history tells, Alexander, or Cæsar, or Scipio, or Saladin, are the representatives of that magnanimity or self-mastery which is the greatness of human nature. Christianity too has its heroes, and in the supernatural order, and we call them Saints. The artist puts before him beauty of feature and form; the poet, beauty of mind; the preacher, the beauty of grace: then intellect too, I repeat, has its beauty, and it has those who aim at it. To open the mind, to correct it, to refine it, to enable it to know, and to digest, master, rule, and use its knowledge, to give it power over its own faculties, application, flexibility, method, critical exactness, sagacity, resource, address, eloquent expression, is an object as intelligible. . . . as the cultivation of virtue, while, at the same time, it is absolutely distinct from it.

10.

This indeed is but a temporal object, and a transitory possession: but so are other things in themselves which we make much of and pursue. The moralist will tell us that man, in all his functions, is but a flower which blossoms and fades, except so far as a higher principle breathes upon him, and makes him and what he is immortal. Body and mind are carried on into an eternal state of being by the gifts of Divine Munificence; but at first they do but fail in a failing world; and if the powers of intellect decay, the powers of the body have decayed before them, and, as an Hospital or an Almshouse, though its end be ephemeral, may be sanctified to the service of religion, so surely may a University, even were it nothing more than I have as yet described it. We attain to heaven by using this world well, though it is to pass away; we perfect our nature, not by undoing it, but by adding to it what is more than nature, and directing it towards aims higher than its own.

UNDERSTANDING THE TEXT

1. What are some of the practical applications of different kinds of knowledge? Is Newman correct in saying that knowledge need not serve any "useful" social purpose to be worth acquiring? Why or why not?

2. How does Newman define "liberal" as it applies to knowledge? Which subjects in a contemporary college or university would Newman consider "liberal knowledge"? Which would he consider "useful knowledge"? Is this distinction valuable? Why or why not?

3. What kinds of physical exercises does Newman consider "liberal"? What is the difference between useful physical exercise and "liberal exercise"? Is the distinction the same as it is for intellectual pursuits?

4. According to Newman, what is the consequence of requiring that education correspond to certain notions of "virtue"?

5. In Newman's opinion, what role does enjoyment play in the motivation to acquire knowledge? In your opinion, is learning most enjoyable for its own sake or for its use value?

6. Examine the ways that Newman incorporates (p. 632) quotations and references from ancient Greek and Roman authors. How well do these citations prove his points? How well do they illustrate his arguments?

7. Does Newman believe that liberal education is more valuable than career-oriented education? Which kinds of education would his ideal university accomplish?

MAKING CONNECTIONS

1. How does Newman's view of the value of education compare with that of Frederick Douglass (p. 46)? Do you think that Douglass would agree that acquiring knowledge is an end of its own? Why or why not?

2. Does Newman's religious approach to education resemble that of Hsün Tzu (p. 8), al-Ghazālī (p. 24), or the *New England Primer* (p. 32)? In what way can an education that does not specifically promote virtue be "religious"?

3. Compare Newman's understanding of the role of "useful education" with Richard Feynman's view that education must be practical and hands-on to be understood (p. 68). Do the two views contradict each other? Why or why not?

4. How might Newman respond to Gorgias (p. 478) or someone else who argues that rhetoric always has as its purpose the persuasion of others? Is it possible for rhetoric to be "liberal" in Newman's sense of the word?

WRITING ABOUT THE TEXT

1. Obtain a catalog from your own college or university and examine the general education curriculum. Write an essay discussing this curriculum in relation to Newman's "Knowledge Its Own End." Support or oppose these requirements for all students, regardless of their majors.

2. Compare Newman's view of liberal education with Seneca's (p. 16). In what ways does Seneca mirror Newman's contention that education does not need to be useful?

3. How "useful" or helpful do you find Newman's distinction between "useful" and "liberal" knowledge? Consider your education thus far. How much of your knowledge meets all the qualifications of "liberal knowledge"? How much is "useful" and practical? Where do the two kinds overlap?

4. Write an essay titled "The Idea of a University," explaining your view of what college should be and how it should function. Do not feel bound to Newman's ideas, but refer to them when appropriate.

Paulo Freire
The Banking Concept of Education
(1970)

THROUGHOUT HIS LIFE, the Brazilian educator and philosopher Paulo Freire (1921–1997) sought to create education theory that would meet the needs of the poor, the colonized, and the politically oppressed. From 1946 to 1964, he developed models for teaching basic literacy to poor farm workers in the Brazilian state of Pernambuco, and in the early 1960s, his models were adopted throughout Brazil. However, the military government that came to power in 1964 ended these programs and arrested Freire as a subversive influence. After spending more than two months in jail, Freire left Brazil to work in Chile and, later, in the United States. As a visiting professor at Harvard University, Freire wrote his most famous book, *The Pedagogy of the Oppressed*, which established his reputation as one of the most important education theorists of the twentieth century.

Freire's education theory begins with his belief that the relationship between teachers and students mirrors the relationship between political oppressors and the oppressed. In traditional classrooms, teachers have all of the institutional power. For students, therefore, "learning" means submitting to a teacher's absolute authority. Freire refers to this kind of education as "banking," in which teachers deposit knowledge into students' minds, which are empty until these deposits are made. Banking education emphasizes memorization, facts, formulas, and discipline.

In contrast to banking education, Freire proposes education practices modeled on progressive political relationships. Teachers must surrender their absolute authority, and students must take active responsibility for determining how and what they are taught. Such an education becomes a conversation among equals in which students and teachers learn from each other. Rather than forcing students to memorize facts, teachers pose problems whose answers are not certain, and the education process becomes a series of discussions about possible solutions. Education can be a tool for liberation only when educators refuse to reenact oppressive relationships in the classroom.

In the selection included here, from the second chapter of *Pedagogy of the Oppressed*, Freire outlines the ideological assumptions behind the banking concept of education. This model, he asserts, dehumanizes students and serves the interests of those who oppress them. The argument in this selection is based on an extended analogy between the process of depositing money in a bank and the vesion of education that Freire rejects. Through this analogy, he casts the prevailing model of education in his country as an automated, commercial transaction in which no real knowledge is created. 🍃

A CAREFUL ANALYSIS of the teacher-student relationship at any level, inside or outside the school, reveals its fundamentally *narrative* character. This relationship involves a narrating Subject (the teacher) and patient, listening objects (the students). The contents, whether values or empirical dimensions of reality, tend in the process of being narrated to become lifeless and petrified. Education is suffering from narration sickness.

The teacher talks about reality as if it were motionless, static, compartmentalized, and predictable. Or else he expounds on a topic completely alien to the existential experience of the students. His task is to "fill" the students with the contents of his narration—contents which are detached from reality, disconnected from the totality that engendered them and could give them significance. Words are emptied of their concreteness and become a hollow, alienated, and alienating verbosity.

The outstanding characteristic of this narrative education, then, is the sonority of words, not their transforming power. "Four times four is sixteen; the capital of Pará is Belém." The student records, memorizes, and repeats these phrases without perceiving what four times four really means, or realizing the true significance of "capital" in the affirmation "the capital of Pará is Belém," that is, what Belém means for Pará and what Pará means for Brazil.[1]

Narration (with the teacher as narrator) leads the students to memorize mechanically the narrated content. Worse yet, it turns them into "containers," into "receptacles" to be "filled" by the teacher. The more completely she fills the receptacles, the better a teacher she is. The more meekly the receptacles permit themselves to be filled, the better students they are.

Education thus becomes an act of depositing, in which the students are the depositories and the teacher is the depositor. Instead of communicating, the teacher issues communiqués and makes deposits which the students patiently receive, memorize, and repeat. This is the "banking" concept of education, in which the scope of action allowed to the students extends only as far as receiving, filing, and storing the deposits. They do, it is true, have the opportunity to become collectors or cataloguers of the things they store. But in the last analysis, it is the people themselves who are filed away through the lack of creativity, transformation, and knowledge in this (at best) misguided system. For apart from inquiry, apart from the praxis,[2] individuals cannot be truly human. Knowledge emerges only through invention and re-invention, through the restless, impatient, continuing, hopeful inquiry human beings pursue in the world, with the world, and with each other.

In the banking concept of education, knowledge is a gift bestowed by those who consider themselves knowledgeable upon those whom they consider to know noth-

1. **Pará . . . Belém:** The city of Belém is the capital of the northeastern Brazilian state of Pará.
2. **Praxis:** practical action that is grounded in a theory or set of ideals. Praxis is an important con-

cept in Marxism and other liberation philosophies, which teach that social and education theories cannot simply be appreciated intellectually; they must be translated into concrete action.

ing. Projecting an absolute ignorance onto others, a characteristic of the ideology of oppression, negates education and knowledge as processes of inquiry. The teacher presents himself to his students as their necessary opposite; by considering their ignorance absolute, he justifies his own existence. The students, alienated like the slave in the Hegelian dialectic,[3] accept their ignorance as justifying the teacher's existence—but, unlike the slave, they never discover that they educate the teacher.

The *raison d'être*[4] of libertarian education, on the other hand, lies in its drive towards reconciliation. Education must begin with the solution of the teacher-student contradiction, by reconciling the poles of the contradiction so that both are simultaneously teachers *and* students.

This solution is not (nor can it be) found in the banking concept. On the contrary, banking education maintains and even stimulates the contradiction through the following attitudes and practices, which mirror oppressive society as a whole:

(a) the teacher teaches and the students are taught;

(b) the teacher knows everything and the students know nothing;

(c) the teacher thinks and the students are thought about;

(d) the teacher talks and the students listen—meekly;

(e) the teacher disciplines and the students are disciplined;

(f) the teacher chooses and enforces his choice, and the students comply;

(g) the teacher acts and the students have the illusion of acting through the action of the teacher;

(h) the teacher chooses the program content, and the students (who were not consulted) adapt to it;

(i) the teacher confuses the authority of knowledge with his or her own professional authority, which she or he sets in opposition to the freedom of the students;

(j) the teacher is the Subject of the learning process, while the pupils are mere objects. . . .

The bank-clerk educator does not realize that there is no true security in his hypertrophied role, that one must seek to live *with* others in solidarity. One cannot impose oneself, nor even merely co-exist with one's students. Solidarity requires true communication, and the concept by which such an educator is guided fears and proscribes communication.

Yet only through communication can human life hold meaning. The teacher's *10* thinking is authenticated only by the authenticity of the students' thinking. The

3. **Hegelian dialectic:** a model developed by the German philosopher Georg Wilhelm Friedrich Hegel (1770–1831) by which two opposing ideas can be reconciled into a "synthesis." (See p. 624 for a fuller description of this model.)

4. **Raison d'être:** reason for being (French).

teacher cannot think for her students, nor can she impose her thought on them. Authentic thinking, thinking that is concerned about *reality*, does not take place in ivory tower isolation, but only in communication. If it is true that thought has meaning only when generated by action upon the world, the subordination of students to teachers becomes impossible. . . .

Unfortunately, those who espouse the cause of liberation are themselves surrounded and influenced by the climate which generates the banking concept, and often do not perceive its true significance or its dehumanizing power. Paradoxically, then, they utilize this same instrument of alienation in what they consider an effort to liberate. Indeed, some "revolutionaries" brand as "innocents," "dreamers," or even "reactionaries" those who would challenge this educational practice. But one does not liberate people by alienating them. Authentic liberation—the process of humanization—is not another deposit to be made in men. Liberation is a praxis: the action and reflection of men and women upon their world in order to transform it. Those truly committed to the cause of liberation can accept neither the mechanistic concept of consciousness as an empty vessel to be filled, nor the use of banking methods of domination (propaganda, slogans—deposits) in the name of liberation.

Those truly committed to liberation must reject the banking concept in its entirety, adopting instead a concept of women and men as conscious beings, and consciousness as consciousness intent upon the world. They must abandon the educational goal of deposit-making and replace it with the posing of the problems of human beings in their relations with the world. "Problem-posing" education, responding to the essence of consciousness—*intentionality*—rejects communiqués and embodies communication. It epitomizes the special characteristic of consciousness: being *conscious of*, not only as intent on objects but as turned in upon itself in a Jasperian "split"[5]— consciousness as consciousness *of* consciousness.

Liberating education consists in acts of cognition, not transferrals of information. It is a learning situation in which the cognizable object (far from being the end of the cognitive act) intermediates the cognitive actors—teacher on the one hand and students on the other. Accordingly, the practice of problem-posing education entails at the outset that the teacher-student contradiction be resolved. Dialogical relations—indispensable to the capacity of cognitive actors to cooperate in perceiving the same cognizable object—are otherwise impossible.

Indeed, problem-posing education, which breaks with the vertical patterns characteristic of banking education, can fulfill its function as the practice of freedom only if it can overcome the above contradiction. Through dialogue, the teacher-of-the-students and the students-of-the-teacher cease to exist and a new term emerges: teacher-student with students-teachers. The teacher is no longer merely the-one-

---

5. **Jasperian "split":** According to the German philosopher Karl Jaspers (1883–1969), human existence is split into "empirical existence," as physical beings occupying space—"consciousness-as-such," through which we process information rationally—and "spirit," through which we desire wholeness.

who-teaches, but one who is himself taught in dialogue with the students, who in turn while being taught also teach. They become jointly responsible for a process in which all grow. In this process, arguments based on "authority" are no longer valid; in order to function, authority must be *on the side of* freedom, not *against* it. Here, no one teachers another, nor is anyone self-taught. People teach each other, mediated by the world, by the cognizable objects which in banking education are "owned" by the teacher.

UNDERSTANDING THE TEXT

1. In what way does Freire see the problem with education as a "narration sickness"? What is the narrative upon which most education is based? What is the narration upon which he claims it should be based?

2. How well does Freire's list of the assumptions behind the banking concept (p. 64) mirror your own experience with education? Why aren't these assumptions limited to poor nations or politically oppressive regimes?

3. Why would those exercising political power want to use the banking model of education? According to Freire, how does this model allow the oppressive relationship to continue?

4. According to Freire, how do liberation movements become trapped in their own version of banking education?

5. Examine the analogy (p. 602), between education and banking, that forms the basis of this selection. Is the analogy valid? Or does it mislead by overstating the comparison?

MAKING CONNECTIONS

1. How does Freire's view of the potentially liberating nature of education compare with that espoused by Frederick Douglass in "Learning to Read" (p. 46)? Why were American slaveowners unwilling to allow their slaves to participate in even the kind of education that Freire labels "banking"?

2. What assumptions about human nature does Freire make in "The Banking Concept of Education"? Are they closer to those of Mencius (p. 94) or those of Hsün Tzu (p. 100)? Why do you say so?

3. Compare Freire's view of using education as a tool for the liberation of the poor with the economic views of Muhammad Yunus (p. 369), who has lifted thousands of people out of poverty through revolutionary banking practices. In what area do the two reformers rely on the same basic sets of assumptions?

4. How might the kind of education that Freire describes here account for the cultural differences that Kisautaq Leona Okalok describes in "Serving the Purpose of Education" (p. 76)?

WRITING ABOUT THE TEXT

1. Describe a classroom situation in which the teacher does not have any more authority than the students. Would such a classroom work at your college or university?

2. Compare Freire's theoretical approach to education with the practical observations of Richard Feynman in "O Americano Outra Vez" (p. 68).

3. Compare the banking model with the expectations that most students have for education. Do most college students expect teachers to be "bankers"? How many people would pay for an education in which no "banking" occurred? If you were Paulo Freire, how would you attempt to change students' expectations?

4. How does Freire's concept of education-as-praxis compare with John Henry Newman's view of "useless" liberal education (p. 53)? How would an educator in an underdeveloped country such as Brazil, working primarily with poor farm workers, view Newman's notion of "knowledge for its own sake"?

Richard Feynman
O Americano Outra Vez
(1985)

RICHARD P. FEYNMAN (1918–1988) was one of the most respected theoretical physicists of the twentieth century. As a young man, he worked on the Manhattan Project to develop a nuclear bomb during World War II. In the years that followed, he taught physics at both Cornell University and the California Institute of Technology and conducted research in quantum mechanics and particle physics. He received the Nobel Prize in Physics in 1965 for his contributions to the theory of quantum electrodynamics.

Unlike many of his colleagues in the highest levels of theoretical physics, Feynman had a reputation as a patient and talented classroom teacher. He frequently remarked that if a teacher could not explain a scientific concept clearly to a college freshman, the teacher didn't really understand it. His classroom lectures to undergraduate students at Caltech were compiled in the three-volume *Feynman Lectures on Physics* (1970), which has become a widely read introductory text to some of science's most difficult concepts.

In the later part of his life, Feynman became a public figure whose reputation as a quirky nonconformist was almost as well known as his reputation as a brilliant scientist. Much of this reputation derives from two bestselling books: *Surely You're Joking, Mr. Feynman* (1985) and *What Do You Care What Other People Think* (1988). Both are composed of short, oral reminiscences collected and edited by Feynman's friend, Ralph Leighton. In these stories, Feynman presents himself as someone who has little use for rules, authorities, and structures. A recurring theme is his unwillingness to observe the rules of polite behavior and pretend to be impressed with people just because they are wealthy, famous or in charge of resources. The Richard Feynman that emerges from these books is a man with an obsessive and insatiable curiosity—someone who grew up fixing radios and picking locks and never stopped trying to figure out how things worked.

"O Americano Outra Vez" ("The American Again") is taken from *Surely You're Joking, Mr. Feynman*. It tells the story of Feynman's trip to Brazil in the summer of 1950 to spend time at the Brazilian Center for Physical Research. While there, Feynman interacted with a number of Brazilian students who were preparing for teaching careers. He discovered that their educations had equipped them with surface facts about physics rather than a genuine understanding of physical processes. This experience became a platform for Feynman to discuss the difference between learning something and learning *about* something—one of the most important themes in all of his lectures and published works. "You can know the name of a bird in all the languages of world, but when you're finished, you'll know absolutely nothing whatever about the bird," Feynman once wrote. "So let's look at the bird and see what its doing—that's what counts."

Feynman organizes this selection as a single narrative from which he draws a simple conclusion. He goes on, though, to use inductive reasoning to generalize this conclusion to the whole country of Brazil and its educational system. ❧

In regard to education in Brazil, I had a very interesting experience. I was teaching a group of students who would ultimately become teachers, since at that time there were not many opportunities in Brazil for a highly trained person in science. These students had already had many courses, and this was to be their most advanced course in electricity and magnetism—Maxwell's equations,[1] and so on.

The university was located in various office buildings throughout the city, and the course I taught met in a building which overlooked the bay.

I discovered a very strange phenomenon: I could ask a question, which the students would answer immediately. But the next time I would ask the question—the same subject, and the same question, as far as I could tell—they couldn't answer it at all! For instance, one time I was talking about polarized light, and I gave them all some strips of polaroid.

Polaroid passes only light whose electric vector is in a certain direction, so I explained how you could tell which way the light is polarized from whether the polaroid is dark or light.

We first took two strips of polaroid and rotated them until they let the most light 5 through. From doing that we could tell that the two strips were now admitting light polarized in the same direction—what passed through one piece of polaroid could also pass through the other. But then I asked them how one could tell the *absolute* direction of polarization, from a *single* piece of polaroid.

They hadn't any idea.

I knew this took a certain amount of ingenuity, so I gave them a hint: "Look at the light reflected from the bay outside."

Nobody said anything.

Then I said, "Have you ever heard of Brewster's Angle?"

"Yes, sir! Brewster's Angle is the angle at which light reflected from a medium 10 with an index of refraction is completely polarized."

"And which way is the light polarized when it's reflected?"

"The light is polarized perpendicular to the plane of reflection, sir." Even now, I have to think about it; they knew it cold! They even knew the tangent of the angle equals the index!

I said, "Well?"

Still nothing. They had just told me that light reflected from a medium with an

---

1. **Maxwell's equations:** equations that describe the properties of electric and magnetic fields.

index, such as the bay outside, was polarized; they had even told me which *way* it was polarized.

I said, "Look at the bay outside, through the polaroid. Now turn the polaroid." 15

"Ooh, it's polarized!" they said.

After a lot of investigation, I finally figured out that the students had memorized everything, but they didn't know what anything meant. When they heard "light that is reflected from a medium with an index," they didn't know that it meant a material *such as water*. They didn't know that the "direction of the light" is the direction in which you *see* something when you're looking at it, and so on. Everything was entirely memorized, yet nothing had been translated into meaningful words. So if I asked, "What is Brewster's Angle?" I'm going into the computer with the right key-words. But if I say, "Look at the water," nothing happens—they don't have anything under "Look at the water!"

Later I attended a lecture at the engineering school. The lecture went like this, translated into English: "Two bodies . . . are considered equivalent . . . if equal torques . . . will produce . . . equal acceleration. Two bodies, are considered equivalent, if equal torques, will produce equal acceleration." The students were all sitting there taking dictation, and when the professor repeated the sentence, they checked it to make sure they wrote it down all right. Then they wrote down the next sentence, and on and on. I was the only one who knew the professor was talking about objects with the same moment of inertia, and it was hard to figure out.

I didn't see how they were going to learn anything from that. Here he was talking about moments of inertia, but there was no discussion about how hard it is to push a door open when you put heavy weights on the outside, compared to when you put them near the hinge—*nothing!*

After the lecture, I talked to a student: "You take all those notes—what do you 20 do with them?"

"Oh, we study them," he says. "We'll have an exam."

"What will the exam be like?"

"Very easy. I can tell you now one of the questions." He looks at his notebook and says, "'When are two bodies equivalent?' And the answer is, 'Two bodies are considered equivalent if equal torques will produce equal acceleration.'" So, you see, they could pass the examinations, and "learn" all this stuff, and not *know* anything at all, except what they had memorized.

Then I went to an entrance exam for students coming into the engineering school. It was an oral exam, and I was allowed to listen to it. One of the students was absolutely super: He answered everything nifty! The examiners asked him what diamagnetism was, and he answered it perfectly. Then they asked, "When light comes at an angle through a sheet of material with a certain thickness, and a certain index N, what happens to the light?"

"It comes out parallel to itself, sir—displaced." 25

"And how much is it displaced?"

"I don't know, sir, but I can figure it out." So he figured it out. He was very good. But I had, by this time, my suspicions.

After the exam I went up to this bright young man, and explained to him that I was from the United States, and that I wanted to ask him some questions that would not affect the result of his examination in any way. The first question I ask is, "Can you give me some example of a diamagnetic substance?"[2]

"No."

Then I asked, "If this book was made of glass, and I was looking at something on   30
the table through it, what would happen to the image if I tilted the glass?"

"It would be deflected sir, by twice the angle that you've turned the book."

I said, "You haven't got it mixed up with a mirror, have you?"

"No, sir!"

He had just told me in the examination that the light would be displaced, parallel to itself, and therefore the image would move over to one side, but would not be turned by any angle. He had even figured out how *much* it would be displaced, but he didn't realize that a piece of glass is a material with an index, and that his calculation had applied to my question.

I taught a course at the engineering school on mathematical methods in physics,   35
in which I tried to show how to solve problems by trial and error. It's something that people don't usually learn, so I began with some simple examples of arithmetic to illustrate the method. I was surprised that only about eight out of the eighty or so students turned in the first assignment. So I gave a strong lecture about having to actually *try* it, not just sit back and watch *me* do it.

After the lecture some students came up to me in a little delegation, and told me that I didn't understand the backgrounds that they have, that they can study without doing the problems, that they have already learned arithmetic, and that this stuff was beneath them.

So I kept going with the class, and no matter how complicated or obviously advanced the work was becoming, they were never handing a damn thing in. Of course I realized what it was: They couldn't *do* it!

One other thing I could never get them to do was to ask questions. Finally, a student explained it to me: "If I ask you a question during the lecture, afterwards everybody will be telling me, 'what are you wasting our time for in the class? We're trying to *learn* something. And you're stopping him by asking a question.'"

It was a kind of one-upmanship, where nobody knows what's going on, and they'd put the other one down as if they *did* know. They all fake that they know, and if one student admits for a moment that something is confusing by asking a question, the others take a high-handed attitude, acting as if it's not confusing at all, telling him that he's wasting their time.

2. **Diamagnetic substance:** a substance that creates a magnetic field when another magnetic field is applied externally.

I explained how useful it was to work together, to discuss the questions, to talk 40 it over, but they wouldn't do that either, because they would be losing face if they had to ask someone else. It was pitiful! All the work they did, intelligent people, but they got themselves into this funny state of mind, this strange kind of self-propagating "education" which is meaningless, utterly meaningless!

At the end of the academic year, the students asked me to give a talk about my experiences of teaching in Brazil. At the talk there would be not only students, but professors and government officials, so I made them promise that I could say whatever I wanted. They said, "Sure. Of course. It's a free country."

So I came in, carrying the elementary physics textbook that they used in the first year of college. They thought this book was especially good because it had different kinds of typeface—bold black for the most important things to remember, lighter for less important things, and so on.

Right away somebody said, "You're not going to say anything bad about the textbook, are you? The man who wrote it is here, and everybody thinks it's a good textbook."

"You promised I could say whatever I wanted."

The lecture hall was full. I started out by defining science as an understanding of 45 the behavior of nature. Then I asked, "What is a good reason for teaching science? Of course, no country can consider itself civilized unless . . . yak, yak, yak." They were all sitting there nodding, because I know that's the way they think.

Then I say, "That, of course, is absurd, because why should we feel we have to keep up with another country? We have to do it for a *good* reason, a *sensible* reason; not just because other countries do." Then I talked about the utility of science, and its contribution to the improvement of the human condition, and all that—I really teased them a little bit.

Then I say, "The main purpose of my talk is to demonstrate to you that *no* science is being taught in Brazil!"

I can see them stir, thinking, "What? No science? This is absolutely crazy! We have all these classes."

So I tell them that one of the first things to strike me when I came to Brazil was to see elementary school kids in bookstores, buying physics books. There are so many kids learning physics in Brazil, beginning much earlier than kids do in the United States, that it's amazing you don't find many physicists in Brazil—why is that? So many kids are working so hard, and nothing comes of it.

Then I gave the analogy of a Greek scholar who loves the Greek language, who 50 knows that in his own country there aren't many children studying Greek. But he comes to another country, where he is delighted to find everybody studying Greek— even the smaller kids in the elementary schools. He goes to the examination of a student who is coming to get his degree in Greek, and asks him, "What were Socrates' ideas on the relationship between Truth and Beauty?"—and the student can't answer.

Then he asks the student, "What did Socrates say to Plato in the Third Symposium?" the student lights up and goes, "*Brrrrrrrrr-up*"—he tells you everything, word for word, that Socrates said, in beautiful Greek.

But what Socrates was talking about in the Third Symposium was the relationship between Truth and Beauty!

What this Greek scholar discovers is, the students in another country learn Greek by first learning to pronounce the letters, then the words, and then sentences and paragraphs. They can recite, word for word, what Socrates said, without realizing that those Greek words actually *mean* something. To the student they are all artificial sounds. Nobody has ever translated them into words the students can understand.

I said, "That's how it looks to me, when I see you teaching the kids 'science' here in Brazil." (Big blast, right?)

Then I held up the elementary physics textbook they were using. "There are no experimental results mentioned anywhere in this book, except in one place where there is a ball, rolling down an inclined plane, in which it says how far the ball got after one second, two seconds, three seconds, and so on. The numbers have 'errors' in them—that is, if you look at them, you think you're looking at experimental results, because the numbers are a little above, or a little below, the theoretical values. The book even talks about having to correct the experimental errors—very fine. The trouble is, when you calculate the value of the acceleration constant from these values, you get the right answer. But a ball rolling down an inclined plane, *if it is actually done*, has an inertia to get it to turn, and will, *if you do the experiment*, produce five-sevenths of the right answer, because of the extra energy needed to go into the rotation of the ball. Therefore this single example of experimental 'results' is obtained from a *fake* experiment. Nobody had rolled such a ball, or they would never have gotten those results!

"I have discovered something else," I continued. "By flipping the pages at random, and putting my finger in and reading the sentences on that page, I can show you what's the matter—how it's not science, but memorizing, in *every* circumstance. Therefore I am brave enough to flip through the pages now, in front of this audience, to put my finger in, to read, and to show you."

So I did it. *Brrrrrrup*—I stuck my finger in, and I started to read: "Triboluminescence. Triboluminescence is the light emitted when crystals are crushed . . . "

I said, "And there, have you got science? No! You have only told what a word means in terms of other words. You haven't told anything about nature—*what* crystals produce light when you crush them, *why* they produce light. Did you see any student go home and *try* it? He can't.

"But if, instead, you were to write, 'When you take a lump of sugar and crush it with a pair of pliers in the dark, you can see a bluish flash. Some other crystals do that too. Nobody knows why. The phenomenon is called "triboluminescence."' Then someone will go home and try it. Then there's an experience of nature." I used that example to show them, but it didn't make any difference where I would have put my finger in the book; it was like that everywhere.

Finally, I said that I couldn't see how anyone could be educated by this self-propagating system in which people pass exams, and teach others to pass exams, but nobody knows anything. "However," I said, "I must be wrong. There were two students in my class who did very well, and one of the physicists I know was educated entirely in Brazil. Thus, it must be possible for some people to work their way through the system, bad as it is."

Well, after I gave the talk, the head of the science education department got up and said, "Mr. Feynman has told us some things that are very hard for us to hear, but it appears to be that he really loves science, and is sincere in his criticism. Therefore, I think we should listen to him. I came here knowing we have some sickness in our system of education; what I have learned is that we have a *cancer!*"—and he sat down.

That gave other people the freedom to speak out, and there was a big excitement. Everybody was getting up and making suggestions. The students got some committee together to mimeograph the lectures in advance, and they got other committees organized to do this and that.

Then something happened which was totally unexpected for me. One of the students got up and said, "I'm one of the two students whom Mr. Feynman referred to at the end of his talk. I was not educated in Brazil; I was educated in Germany, and I've just come to Brazil this year."

The other student who had done well in class had a similar thing to say. And the professor I had mentioned got up and said, "I was educated here in Brazil during the war, when, fortunately, all of the professors had left the university, so I learned everything by reading alone. Therefore I was not really educated under the Brazilian system."

I didn't expect that. I knew the system was bad, but 100 percent—it was terrible!

Since I had gone to Brazil under a program sponsored by the United States Government, I was asked by the State Department to write a report about my experiences in Brazil, so I wrote out the essentials of the speech I had just given. I found out later through the grapevine that the reaction of somebody in the State Department was, "That shows you how dangerous it is to send somebody to Brazil who is so naive. Foolish fellow; he can only cause trouble. He didn't understand the problems." Quite the contrary! I think this person in the State Department was naive to think that because he saw a university with a list of courses and descriptions, that's what it was.

UNDERSTANDING THE TEXT

1. How would you characterize the difference between the knowledge possessed by the students that Feynman encounters and the knowledge that Feynman believes that they should have?

2. What is the purpose of examinations in the educational system that Feynman describes?

3. How does Feynman characterize the role of social pressures in perpetuating Brazil's flawed educational system? What kinds of peer pressures do the students he meets describe?

4. How would Feynman recommend that science be taught in elementary schools? How does this compare with the way that science usually is taught? Compare your own educational experiences to those described in the text.

5. How does Feynman characterize his experience with the U.S. government when he wrote a report about his experience in Brazil? Why do you think he included this final reflection? What parallels can we draw between Brazilian science students and American government workers?

Making Connections

1. The students that Feynman describes in "O Americano Outra Vez" are products of the same Brazilian educational system that Paulo Freire describes (p. 62). Do Feynman's experiences confirm or contradict Freire's observations about the "banking concept of education"? Explain.

2. Are the methods of teaching physics that Feynman describes culturally specific phenomena, such as those described by Ruth Benedict (p. 132)? Is it unreasonable for Feynman to expect students in a different culture to understand and teach science the way that he does? Why or why not?

3. Compare Feynman's approach to teaching physics with David Suzuki's understanding of nature in "The Sacred Balance" (p. 427). How might Feynman characterize the "sense of wonder" that is central to Suzuki's work?

Writing about the Text

1. Describe your own experience learning science in school. Was your education one that Feynman would have approved of, or would he have made the same accusations of your instructors as he did of the Brazilian educational system?

2. Many educators would challenge Feynman's belief that knowing the names of things and being able to define them is "meaningless." Being able to define concepts, they argue, is an essential part of being able to understand them at any level. Write an essay in which you agree or disagree with this position.

3. Describe how Feynman's distinction between knowing the name of a thing and truly understanding how to do it applies to the writing process. Which do you believe is the more effective way to teach writing? Why?

Kisautaq Leona Okakok
Serving the Purpose of Education
(1989)

WHEN SHE WROTE her groundbreaking essay "Serving the Purpose of Education," Kisautaq Leona Okakok was the deputy director of the North Slope Borough School District in Alaska. The North Slope consists of nearly 100,000 square miles in the extreme north of Alaska. It is one of the northernmost populated regions in the world, though the population is extremely sparse—about 7,000 people live in an area the size of the state of Michigan.

The majority of inhabitants of the North Slope are the Inupiat, the predominant Alaskan Inuit (Eskimo) group. The native Inupiat population of Alaska lives a largely traditional lifestyle, with hunting, fishing, and whaling forming the core of the community's economic life. In recent years, oil revenues have also become important to the Inupiat. The largest city in the North Slope is Barrow, Alaska, with a population of about 4,000 people. Barrow is the northernmost settlement in North America. It is the home of a school district with a reputation for innovation and of Ilisagvik College, a public college that emphasizes and preserves Inupiat culture.

As an Inupiaq woman ("Inupiaq" is a variant of "Inupiat") working in the North Slope School District, Okakok faced challenges unknown to most American educators. The cold temperatures, irregular daylight hours, and extremely long distances between population centers make the mechanics of running a school district difficult to begin with. Even more importantly, Okakok faced the task of integrating a modern Western educational system with a strong native culture and language without distorting either one.

In additional to her work in educational theory, Okakok has also translated a number of Inupiat stories into English. Her translation and transcription of the 1978 North Shore Borough Elder's Conference is published in book form under the title *Puiguitkaat*, an Inupiat word that means "Things We Cannot Forget."

Okakok uses well-selected examples to support her claim. By pointing out that ideas presented to children as facts are, in certain cases, not facts at all, she provides strong support for her assertions about the need for education to take cultural perceptions into account. 🍃

The Role of Local Culture in the Learning Process

WE, THE INDIGENOUS PEOPLE of the United States, have had to overcome many obstacles in order to acquire basic education. One of the main obstacles was language. Not only were we required to learn to read, at the same time we also had to learn the language we were learning to read in. In the late 1930s and early 1940s, in order to help children learn English, teachers visited Inupiaq[1] parents and instructed them to speak only English to their children. Most parents knew very little, if any, English, so they were effectively being told to sever communication with their children. Parents were willing to comply with this instruction, except that their great love for their children and the necessity to interact with them sustained Inupiaq in the household, thus keeping alive the foundation of our culture. But severe retardation of our native language did take place in time. Besides ordering that English be spoken at home, teachers punished children for speaking their mother tongue in the classroom. I remember clearly catching myself many times speaking in Inupiaq during my first few years in school and feeling guilty for doing so. I was rarely caught and, therefore, rarely punished, but others were not so lucky. Many times we'd hear the whack of the ruler either on the head or the palm of the hand of any student caught being "naughty" and speaking in our language.

But we spoke in our own language in order to survive. Imagine learning to say a word in a language you did not know, and having no earthly idea what that word represented. As hard as learning a foreign language was, however, it was easier than absorbing the content of Western education. The world view of the West, the perspective from which our schoolbooks were written, was totally different from ours. Therefore, understanding what we were learning to read in the English language came very hard. For example, as I was learning to read, one of my earliest realizations was that, in the Western world, grandparents and other relatives are not people you see or visit every day, even when they live nearby in the same town or city. A visit from them is an occasion, a cause for special preparations. This behavior was so foreign to my experience that it took me a long time to understand what I was reading and to realize that extended families are not the norm in the Western world.

In our communities, visiting relatives is a frequent, everyday occurrence, learned in early childhood. Unplanned, spontaneous visits (as opposed to purposeful visits) bond our relationships with relatives and friends. When visiting is unplanned, it does not require a formal invitation; tea or a soft drink is usually served unless it is near mealtime, when visitors will be expected to join in the meal. Other cultural practices, such as the special relationships between grandparents and grandchildren, reinforce these visiting patterns. A high degree of social interaction is the norm in our communities.

During the years my husband and I attended the University of Alaska in Fairbanks, my father's first cousin, an elderly lady, lived right in town, an area where I frequently shopped. When I took my father there for a visit I was soundly scolded for visiting only when I had a purpose—in this instance, taking my father to see her. Although I was living in the same town, I had not nurtured my relationship with my aunt with intermittent, spontaneous visits.

---

1. **Inupiaq:** *Inupiaq* is a variant of *Inupiat.*

In the Western world privacy is considered such a basic right that I am afraid 5
many find it hard to understand the value of spontaneous visits. It is equally hard
for us to understand why anyone would want to have so much privacy that developing nurturing relationships becomes very difficult, if not impossible. This is an
example of one area where two very diverse cultures have different but equally valid
values; members of both cultures have to strive to acknowledge and to understand
each other's differences.

Another example of the proliferation of Western concepts and Western "realities" contained within textbooks is the "fact" that the sun rises in the East and sets
in the West. This is included in tests that evaluate the child's understanding of the
world around him or her. In the arctic, however, the sun behaves differently. Depending on the time of year, it can do almost anything, six examples of which are: 1) it
doesn't rise at all; 2) it peeks through the horizon for a few minutes; 3) it rises in
the South and sets in the South a few minutes later; 4) it rises in the East and sets
in the West; 5) it rises in the North and sets in the North almost twenty-four hours
later; *or* 6) it doesn't see at all. During the whole process of moving from the first
instance to the last, so gradual is the sun's movement along the continuum that it
is almost imperceptible. You will note that the Western world's "fact" about the sun
rising in the East and setting in the West is only one of various northern Alaskan
realities. Saying that the sun rises in the East and sets in the West up here would
be like saying that a yo-yo with a two-foot string reaches twelve inches. Certainly
it does, at some instant, reach the twelve-inch point, but there are infinite points
along the string that it also reaches, including being fully wound and fully extended.

Because the rising and setting of the sun rarely changes in the rest of the United
States, it does seem a useful gauge in determining a child's learning. But for children in the far North, there are too many variables for "the" fact of where the sun
rises and sets for it to be useful. For Western students, the direction of shadows or
looking in the direction of the rising or setting sun are obvious clues to the time of
day. But when these clues were presented in schoolbooks, I was always looking also
for clues as to the time of year, which, I later realized, even if they were given, would
not have helped at all. Although I am a puzzle fan, I was often understandably
stumped by what I later learned was no puzzle at all to Western students.

Those of us who experienced these problems during our schooling realized that
we had to find a better way to teach our children. We who work at the grassroots
level of education—the local PTAs, advisory committees, and school boards—are
in a unique position to observe schooling in action. We are often the first to know
when something works and when it doesn't.

Contrasting Definitions of Education

To me, educating a child means equipping him or her with the capability to succeed
in the world he or she will live in. In our Inupiat communities, this means learning
not only academics, but also to travel, camp, and harvest wildlife resources in the

surrounding land and sea environments. Students must learn about responsibilities to the extended family and elders, as well as about our community and regional governments, institutions, and corporations, and significant issues in the economic and social system.

"Education" and "schooling" have become quite interchangeable in everyday speech. When we talk of a person being educated we usually mean he or she has gone through a series of progressively higher formal systems of learning. Although a person may be an authority on a subject, we don't usually think of him or her as "educated" if he or she is self-taught. Since all of our traditional knowledge and expertise is of this latter type, the concept of "an educated person" has worked against us as a people, creating conflicting attitudes, and weakening older and proven instructional methods and objects of knowledge. Therefore, we, the North Slope Borough[2] School District School Board, have defined "education" as a lifelong process, and "schooling" as our specific responsibility. This is expressed in our Educational Philosophy statement:

> Education, a lifelong process, is the sum of learning acquired through interaction with one's environment, family, community members, schools and other institutions and agencies. Within the Home Rule Municipality of the North Slope Borough, "schooling" is the specific, mandated responsibility of the North Slope Borough School District Board of Education.
>
> The Board of Education is committed to providing academic excellence in the "schooling" environment. This commitment to academic excellence shall focus on the learner, recognizing that each student brings to the "schooling" environment his own interests, learning styles, cultural background and abilities.[3]

We decided that our role is to control the environment of the schooling process: the building, the equipment and materials, the quality of teaching and counselling services—everything about our schools—to ensure that education can take place in the classroom.

Remember that education is also the passing down of a society's values to children. Although I suppose there are people who would disagree, I think teachers pass down values by what they do in certain situations. Showing approval to a child for quickly attempting to answer a question—even wrongly—is valuing a quick answer to questions. At home, this same child may have been taught not to stay anything until he or she has observed and observed and *observed*, and feels certain that his or her answer is correct. At home, the parents value accuracy more highly than a quick

---

2. **North Slope Borough:** Alaska does not have counties but is divided into sixteen boroughs. The North Slope Borough covers almost 6,000 square miles of land in the northern portion of the state.

3. North Slope Borough School District Policy Manual, Policy AD (Educational Philosophy), Adopted 10/13/76, Revised 8/11/87. [Author's note]

10

answer. They know that accuracy may mean the difference between life and death in the Arctic. In grade school, however, many of us learned that the teacher would "reward" us when we spoke up, whether we were right or wrong. Only by hearing our responses could she determine whether or not learning was taking place. If the answer was correct, she would have the opportunity to praise us. If a wrong answer was given, this gave her the opportunity to correct us.

Education is more than book learning, it is also value-learning. To address this issue we, as a board, have incorporated a cultural component into our new-hire orientation. The bilingual department is an integral part of the orientation, highlighting differences in how our children learn. We hope that awareness lessens the frustration of teaching children who do not respond in ways teachers usually expect.

It is interesting that the root of the English word "educate" is very similar to our Inupiaq concept of education. According to Webster:

> It has often been said that *educate* means 'to draw out' a person's talent as opposed to putting in knowledge or instructions. This is an interesting idea, but it is not quite true in terms of the etymology of the word. 'Educate' comes from Latin *educare*, 'to educate', which is derived from a specialized use of Latin *educere* (from *e-*'out,' and *ducere*, 'to lead') meaning 'to assist at the birth of a child.'[4]

This old meaning of the English word "educate" is similar to our own Inupiat Eskimo word "iñuguq-"[5]—which literally means "to cause to become a person." It refers to someone who attends to the child in the formative years and helps him or her to become a person. In our Inupiat Eskimo society, the first few years of a child's life are a time when they are "becoming a person." Anyone who attends to the child during that time of his or her life is said to cause him or her to become a person, "iñuguġaa."

We Inupiat believe that a child starts becoming a person at a young age, even while he or she is still a baby. When a baby displays characteristics of individual behavior, such as a calm demeanor or a tendency to temper tantrums, we say "he or she is becoming a person." In our culture, such characteristics are recognized and accommodated from early childhood. As each child shows a proclivity toward a certain activity, it is quickly acknowledged and nurtured. As these children and adults in the community interact, bonds are established that help determine the teacher and the activities which will be made available to that particular child. As education progresses, excellence is pursued naturally.

4. *Webster's 11 New Riverside University Dictionary* (Boston: Houghton Mifflin, 1984), p. 418. [Author's note]
5. Inupiaq words followed by a hyphen are stems that need at least an ending to make sense. For those interested in more information about the structure of the language, please see the introduction to *Inupiallu Tangilla Uqalunisa Ilanich. Abridged Inupiaq and English Dictionary*, compiled by Adna Abgeak MacLean (University of Alaska, 1980). [Author's note]

Parents often stand back and let a child explore and experience things, observing the child's inclination. If a child shows an aptitude for skills that the parents don't possess, they might arrange for their child to spend time with an expert, or an adult may ask to participate in the education of the child. Thus, many adults in the community have a role in the education of our children.

When you hear the word "educate," you may think more often of the primary Webster definition, which is "to provide with training or knowledge, especially via formal education." In the Western tradition, educating children depends heavily on a system of formal schooling with required attendance until a certain age.

Our concept of education has much in common with the Western concept of "child-rearing." It is interesting to us that Eskimo practices of child-rearing are commonly regarded as "permissive," in contrast to Western methods. Our perception is that Western child-rearing practices are overly directive and controlling, essentially interfering and intruding in the development of the child. The development of individuality is constrained and childhood is prolonged in Western society.

Though most of the education in our traditional society was not formal, it was serious business. For us, education meant equipping the child with the wherewithal to survive in our world. Because social interaction is a part of survival in the Arctic, this included education in proper social behavior, as well as in equipping the child with the means with which to make a living. As Robert F. Spencer wrote in his description of traditional North Alaskan Eskimo society: "The educative process . . . succeeded in a remarkable way [to produce] an individual capable of living in the cooperative situation demanded by the social and natural environment."[6]

In the traditional Inupiat Eskimo culture, education was everybody's business. It was okay to admonish, scold, or otherwise correct the behavior of any child, whether or not one was a relative. The success of the child's education depended in large part on how well his or her parents accepted admonishment of their child by other members of their own community. We as a people valued this acceptance highly because we knew that every member of our village was involved in some way with equipping our child for success.

UNDERSTANDING THE TEXT

1. Why did Leona feel, as a child, that speaking her native language was "naughty"? Do you think that it is a good idea to encourage parents not to speak native languages in the homes of children learning English? Why or why not?

---

6. *The Northern Alaskan Eskimo*, p. 239. [Author's note]

2. How does Okakok characterize the differences in the ways that Western and Inupiaq people perceived extended family relationships? Do you believe that her characterization of Western culture is accurate?

3. What scientific "facts" does Okakok present as contingent on certain cultural assumptions? Can you think of other examples where this might be the case?

4. What are the fundamental principles of the Inupiaq concept of education? How does Okakok distinguish these concepts from those found in Western education? What does she see as the difference between "education" and "schooling"?

5. Do you agree with Okakok's statement that "education is . . . the passing down of a society's values to children"? Should this be the purpose of education in a public school? Why or why not?

MAKING CONNECTIONS

1. Compare Okakok's explanation of the cultural differences between Inupiaq and Western people with the views on cultural conditioning expressed by Ruth Benedict in "The Individual and the Pattern of Culture" (p. 132). Are Okakok's examples the sort of phenomena that Benedict describes? Why or why not?

2. How might Okakok's use of Inupiaq words and phrases to express cultural concepts compare with N. Scott Momaday's (p. 519) or Chinua Achebe's (p. 506) presentation of the functions of language in shaping our worldview?

3. Does Okakok's definition of "Western" educational ideas also fit the non-Western writings of Hsün Tzu (p. 8) and al-Ghazālī (p. 24)? Explain.

WRITING ABOUT THE TEXT

1. Argue for or against Okakok's characterization of privacy as a basic Western right. Use your own experience with family and friends to support or refute her argument that "many [Westerners] find it hard to understand the value of spontaneous visits."

2. Compare Okakok's experiences speaking her native language with those of Gloria Anzaldúa in "How to Tame a Wild Tongue" (p. 527). What do both pieces suggest about the languages of minority cultures?

3. Consider Okakok's characterization of certain natural "facts" that are untrue in the extreme North. Give an example of one or more similarly well-known principles that are only true in certain circumstances.

4. Compare Okakok's presentation of the Inupiaq view of education with that of either Seneca (p. 16) or John Henry Newman (p. 53). Focus especially on the question of "useful knowledge."

2

HUMAN NATURE

WHAT IS THE ESSENCE OF HUMANITY?

A man is a featherless biped with broad, flat nails.
—*philosophers at Plato's Academy*

ACCORDING TO A LEGEND of ancient Greek philosophy, the students at Plato's Academy once tried to unassailably define the phrase "human being." After months of wrangling over every fine point, the philosophical elite of Athens finally settled on a definition that would, they felt, stand throughout time: a human being is a "featherless biped." On the day that the Academy was set to announce this truth to the world, however, the famous philosopher Diogenes of Sinope—a member of the group called the Cynics (from whose name the modern word "cynic" derives)—brought a plucked chicken to the school. The philosophers, unwilling to see months of work shattered, amended their definition and announced that a human being "is a featherless biped with broad, flat nails."

For a very long time, humans have been obsessed with defining their own nature and yet have been unable to do so in any convincing fashion—even in an arena of pure speculation such as Plato's Academy. Not only has there never been a universally accepted definition of human nature, the definitions and ideas that have been proposed have historically led to very different ways of organizing and governing societies. If, for example, human beings are inherently selfish, aggressive, and antisocial, then strong laws and harsh punishments may be necessary to check their natural tendencies and ensure the cohesion of society. This was the argument of the Chinese school of thought known as Legalism, which, working from the premise that human beings were naturally evil, unified all of China under the tyrannical rule of the Ch'in Dynasty. If, on the other hand, human beings have an innate sense of morality and justice, then it follows that people should be trusted to organize their own governments and elect their own leaders. This idea led to both America's Declaration of Independence and the development of democratic governments throughout the world.

This chapter opens with one of the first known attempts to depict a human figure: the "Shaft of the Dead Man" cave painting in a cave of Lascaux, France. Found amidst more than two thousand representations of animals, footprints, and obscure symbols, this "Dead Man" is the only attempt by the cave artists to represent a human form. Two other representations of human forms are included in this chapter: Leonardo da Vinci's *Vitruvian Man*, from the Italian Renaissance, and a clay statue of a mother and child created by an anonymous artist of the Igbo people of southern Nigeria. These works of art all depict human figures very differently, but together they show that a powerful urge to visually represent the human condition cuts across time and culture.

The first written text in this chapter comes from Plato's *Symposium*, a series of speeches paying tribute to love. The speech included here attempts to explain the nature of love allegorically, by telling of a mythical time when human beings were physically connected to each other. Through this allegory, Plato presents humans as fragmented beings in dire need of others who can complete them. The readings continue with a vigorous debate about the moral nature of humanity between two of China's most esteemed Confucian scholars: Mencius, who saw humans as essentially good, and Hsün Tzu, who believed that humans were inherently evil. These writings are followed by a classical Buddhist text, "The Precious Garland," which emphasizes the illusory nature of the self.

During the European Enlightenment, philosophers attempted to define human nature by imagining what people would be like in a "state of nature," in which there were no social or cultural influences to constrain human behavior. Versions of this natural state ranged from wistful descriptions of "noble savages" living idyllic, uncontaminated lives to disturbing portrayals of lawless brutes, barely better than animals, robbing each other regularly and killing at the slightest provocation. Foremost among those who held the latter view of the state of nature was the English political theorist Thomas Hobbes, whose major work *Leviathan* is excerpted here. The next writer, John Locke, was a contemporary of Hobbes who believed that human beings were neither essentially good or essentially bad but were *tabula rasas*, "blank slates," to be formed by experience.

The final two selections in the chapter come from more modern writers, who have attempted to explain the forces that interact to create a human being. The first of these writers, Ruth Benedict, was one of the foremost anthropologists of the twentieth century. She argues that much of what others have labeled "human nature" actually arises out of a complicated interplay between human beings and the cultures in which they live. Benedict asserts that such things as values, morals, and defining "human" traits can be studied only when they are connected to a specific culture.

The final selection, Edward O. Wilson's "The Fitness of Human Nature," argues for an evolutionary view of human nature. Wilson believes that human psychology has been formed largely by natural selection that has, over millions of years, selected for traits that promote survival and reproduction.

Diogenes and the philosophers at Plato's Academy were just one part of the world's very long tradition of debating the nature of human beings. The earliest narratives that have been recorded in human cultures—the Epic of Gilgamesh, the Rig Veda, the Book of Genesis, the *Iliad*—contain not only intense descriptions of human nature but also full-scale internal debates about the subject that are never entirely resolved. Are human beings inherently good or inherently evil? Does civilization redeem or contaminate the natural human condition? Do we make choices freely, or do we simply follow a script that has been written by history, culture, or God? Perhaps the most convincing evidence for the existence of some kind of core human nature is the fact that we persist in asking questions such as these.

The Shaft of the Dead Man
(15,000–13,000 BCE)

ON SEPTEMBER 12, 1940, four French teenagers were exploring the woods just south of their village when a dog belonging to one of them fell into a hole. Their attempt to rescue the dog led to one of the most important archeological finds in history: the discovery of the Lascaux caves. These interlocking caves contain more than two thousand paintings dating back to the late Paleolithic period, between 15,000 and 13,000 BCE.

The paintings in the Lascaux caves are more extensive than any other cave paintings ever discovered. They have been divided into six "galleries," or series of paintings, with the deepest gallery lying some 250 feet from the entrance. The paintings depict a wide range of human and animal subjects, including horses, bison, reindeer, bears, birds, fish, and several animals now extinct. Some of the paintings are arranged in series that portray a narrative composed of four or five scenes, such as a stag crossing a river or a large animal being hunted and killed.

The exact purpose of cave art such as that found at Lascaux remains a mystery. It was probably not decorative, since no evidence indicates that these caves were used for regular human habitation. Some have suggested that the art served a religious purpose or composed a historical record of major events in the life of a particular tribe or community. What is clear is that prehistoric cultures devoted substantial resources to the creation of these paintings. At Lascaux alone, archeologists have found more than 150 mineral fragments used to mix colors, pestles and mortars used to mix the ingredients, and traces of early torches that were used to provide light for the artists who spent hours in cramped conditions creating these paintings. It is remarkable that a hunter-gatherer culture—one that almost certainly had to expend much of its available energy just to collect food—would devote these kinds of resources to creating art that does not appear to have provided any immediate advantage for survival.

Of all the paintings in the Lascaux caves, none is as mysterious as "The Shaft of the Dead Man," which, alone, constitutes one of the six major "galleries" of the caves. Its subject matter is unlike anything else in Lascaux. This scene portrays a human figure with a birdlike head, either before or after the attack of a charging bison. The figure probably represents a dead (or soon to be dead) person, hence the title "Shaft of the Dead Man." To the right of the figure, a rhinoceros appears to be fleeing the scene. Directly underneath his right hand, a staff or stick is capped by the image of a bird's head. This strange interplay among bison, bird, rhinoceros, and human being has puzzled generations of scholars and historians. No one who sees "The Shaft of the Dead Man" or the other cave paintings at Lascaux can doubt, however, that the urge to represent experience in art forms a very deep part of what it means to be human. 🍃

Rock painting, Lascaux caves, Dordogne, France, 15,000–13,000 BCE.
Bridgeman Art Library
See p. C-1 in the color insert for a full-color reproduction of this image.

UNDERSTANDING THE TEXT

1. Why does the human figure have a bird's head? What does this combination suggest about the culture that produced this scene?

2. Why is the human figure disproportionately large compared to the bison? What kind of relationship between humans and the natural world does the painting suggest?

3. Some have suggested that the figure in the drawing is a religious shaman who is in a dreamlike trance. Is this a plausible interpretation of the painting? If so, should the other animals be read literally or symbolically?

4. Based on the available evidence, what do you believe was the purpose of the cave art at Lascaux? What facts support your interpretation? How might this interpretation account for "The Shaft of the Dead Man"?

MAKING CONNECTIONS

1. What kinds of contemporary art draws, on creative processes similar to those that led to the cave paintings? Speculate about the time and resources expended on the primitive art and the contemporary art. What conclusions can you draw about the cultural importance of art in each period?

2. Compare "The Shaft of the Dead Man" with both the painting *Vitruvian Man* (p. 116), by a professional artist, and the Igbo mother and child statue (p. 129), by an ordinary community member. What aspects of the Lascaux painting suggest that its creator was a professional—a community member whose major function is to produce art—or, alternatively, a nonprofessional?

3. Compare "The Shaft of the Dead Man" with Picasso's *Guernica* (p. 272). What do the similarities in imagery tell you about the relationship between primitive art and modern art? Do they suggest any similarities of artistic methods?

4. Which of the theories of human nature presented in this chapter best accounts for art such as "The Shaft of the Dead Man"? Why?

WRITING ABOUT THE TEXT

1. Use this chapter's selection from Hobbes (p. 119), Benedict (p. 132), or Wilson (p. 144) as the basis for an interpretation of "The Shaft of the Dead Man." How does this philosophy of human nature account for the art found in the Lascaux caves?

2. Imagine you are an archeologist living fifteen thousand years in the future and that you have just discovered a preserved college dorm room from twenty-first-century America. Write a paper in which you draw conclusions about an "ancient" culture that are based solely on the room's posters and other wall decorations.

3. Speculate about the purpose of cave art. Determine whether paintings such as "The Shaft of the Dead Man" served within religious ritual or as forms of entertainment, historical recording, education, or something else. Use all the visual clues at your disposal and conduct extra research as appropriate.

4. Compare ancient and modern uses of nature imagery in visual arts. What do the different forms of art say about human responses and connections to nature?

Plato
The Speech of Aristophanes
(385 BCE)

THE GREEK PHILOSOPHER PLATO (circa 428–348 or 347 BCE) was one of the most influential thinkers of the ancient world. Chronologically, he was the second of three towering figures. His student, Aristotle (384–322 BCE) was the first to attempt to catalog and interpret the knowledge of his day in a structured, methodical way. Plato's mentor, Socrates (469–399 BCE), invented the term *philosophy* ("love of wisdom") and was an important public figure in Athens until his execution in 399 for the crimes of impiety and corrupting the youth. Socrates did not leave behind any written records of his own. We know him only through the descriptions of others—chiefly the descriptions of Plato, who made Socrates a character in many of his works.

Most of Plato's philosophical writings take the form of dialogues between Socrates and one or more companions. In these dialogues Socrates leads his interlocutors to the point that Plato wants to make. The *Symposium*, however, from which this selection is taken, reads more like a complete story than most of Plato's dialogues. It is the story of an evening of drinking and making speeches (*symposium* comes from a Greek word meaning "drinking party") in the home of the young poet Agathon, who has won first prize in the annual tragedy competition and is celebrating with his friends. As the party progresses, the participants each agree to make a speech in praise of love.

Among the participants are both Socrates and the comic poet Aristophanes, whose play *The Clouds* had viciously satirized Socrates as a manipulative, impractical teacher who taught students to circumvent the law. Given Plato's dislike and suspicion of Aristophanes—in *Apology* he calls *The Clouds* one of the primary reasons that the people of Athens mistrusted Socrates—we might expect the character of Aristophanes in *Symposium* to appear foolish or cruel. However, Plato assigns him the most memorable and beautiful speech in the entire volume. Aristophanes' speech takes the form of a creation myth—the story of an ancestral race of human beings who were neither male nor female but a combination of both, who grew so strong that they challenged the gods and were each split into two incomplete halves.

Plato does not cast Aristophanes' story as a serious attempt to explain human history. Rather, he is trying to create a metaphor for something that he sees as a crucial element of human nature: the deep and aching need that people have for another person who can complete what they find lacking in themselves. This need forms the basis of erotic love, which, for Plato, was not entirely sexual, as the term generally implies today. An erotic relationship in the Platonic sense is a total and all-consuming connection with another person that—whether or not it has a sexual component—is primarily a meeting of minds and a mingling of intellects.

The central rhetorical device that Plato uses in "The Speech of Aristophanes" is an extended analogy between the creatures that Aristophanes describes and real human beings who feel the same sense of loss and emptiness that these creatures feel because we have been designed to be fulfilled by other people.

FIRST YOU MUST LEARN what Human Nature was in the beginning and what has happened to it since, because long ago our nature was not what it is now, but very different. There were there kinds of human beings, that's my first point—not two as there are now, male and female. In addition to these, there was a third, a combination of those two; its name survives, though the kind itself has vanished. At that time, you see, the word "androgynous" really meant something: a form made up of male and female elements, though now there's nothing but the word, and that's used as an insult. My second point is that the shape of each human being was completely round, with back and sides in a circle; they had four hands each, as many legs as hands, and two faces, exactly alike, on a rounded neck. Between the two faces, which were on opposite sides, was one head with four ears. There were two sets of sexual organs, and everything else was the way you'd imagine it from what I've told you. They walked upright, as we do now, whatever direction they wanted. And whenever they set out to run fast, they thrust out all their eight limbs, the ones they had then, and spun rapidly, the way gymnasts do cartwheels, by bringing their legs around straight.

Now here is why there were three kinds, and why they were as I described them: The male kind was originally an offspring of the sun, the female of the earth, and the one that combined both genders was an offspring of the moon, because the moon shares in both. They were spherical, and so was their motion, because they were like their parents in the sky.

In strength and power, therefore, they were terrible, and they had great ambitions. They made an attempt on the gods, and Homer's story about Ephialtes and Otos[1] was originally about them: how they tried to make an ascent to heaven so as to attack the gods. Then Zeus and the other gods met in council to discuss what to do, and they were sore perplexed. They couldn't wipe out the human race with thunderbolts and kill them all off, as they had the giants, because that would wipe out the worship they receive, along with the sacrifices we humans give them. On the other hand, they couldn't let them run riot. At last, after great effort, Zeus had an idea.

"I think I have a plan," he said, "that would allow human beings to exist and stop their misbehaving: they will give up being wicked when they lose their strength. So I shall now cut each of them in two. At one stroke they will lose their strength and

---

1. **Ephialtes and Otos:** giants and sons of Poseidon who attacked Mt. Olympus and were tricked into killing each other.

also become more profitable to us, owing to the increase in their number. They shall walk upright on two legs. But if I find they still run riot and do not keep the peace," he said, "I will cut them in two again, and they'll have to make their way on one leg, hopping."

So saying, he cut those human beings in two, the way people cut sorb-apples[2] before they dry them or the way they cut eggs with hairs. As he cut each one, he commanded Apollo to turn its face and half its neck towards the wound, so that each person would see that he'd been cut and keep better order. Then Zeus commanded Apollo to heal the rest of the wound, and Apollo did turn the face around, and he drew skin from all sides over what is now called the stomach, and there he made one mouth, as in a pouch with a drawstring, and fastened it at the center of the stomach. This is now called the navel. Then he smoothed out the other wrinkles, of which there were many, and he shaped the breasts, using some such tool as shoemakers have for smoothing wrinkles out of leather on the form. But he left a few wrinkles around the stomach and the navel, to be a reminder of what happened long ago.

Now, since their natural form had been cut in two, each one longed for its own other half, and so they would throw their arms about each other, weaving themselves together, wanting to grow together. In that condition they would die from hunger and general idleness, because they would not do anything apart from each other. Whenever one of the halves died and one was left, the one that was left still sought another and wove itself together with that. Sometimes the half he met came from a woman, as we'd call her now, sometimes it came from a man; either way, they kept on dying.

Then, however, Zeus took pity on them, and came up with another plan: he moved their genitals around to the front! Before then, you see, they used to have their genitals outside, like their faces, and they cast seed and made children, not in one another, but in the ground, like cicadas. So Zeus brought about this relocation of genitals, and in doing so he invented interior reproduction, *by* the man *in* the woman. The purpose of this was so that, when a man embraced a woman, he would cast his seed and they would have children; but when male embraced male, they would at least have the satisfaction of intercourse, after which they could stop embracing, return to their jobs, and look after their other needs in life. This, then, is the source of our desire to love each other. Love is born into every human being; it calls back the halves of our original nature together; it tries to make one out of two and heal the wound of human nature.

2. **Sorb-apples:** small, berry-sized fruit.

Understanding the Text

1. How does knowing that Aristophanes' speech was one of a series of speeches devoted to the same topic in a friendly competition affect your understanding of his words? How might he have framed the argument differently if he were writing a philosophical essay on the topic?

2. Why do you think that Plato chose to put this speech in the mouth of somebody whom, on other occasions, he strongly disagreed with? Do you think that Plato intended for us to read Aristophanes' speech as his own words?

3. Why does Aristophanes choose to make his point with a purely fictional story? Is the story meant to be humorous? What element of human nature does he hope to dramatize with this story?

4. How does Aristophanes understand the term *androgynous*? What does he suggest about the nature of masculinity and femininity with his depiction of beings that combine both natures in their own?

5. What role does divine intervention play in Aristophanes' allegory? What might he intend to symbolize by depicting Zeus as the creator of fragmented beings?

6. What does the allegory ultimately suggest about human nature?

Making Connections

1. How do Plato's arguments about erotic love compare with the sociobiological arguments advanced by Edward O. Wilson in "The Fitness of Human Nature" (p. 144)? Does modern evolutionary science support or contradict the notion that we have a deep-seated longing to form attachments with other people? How so?

2. Compare the erotic love discussed in Aristophanes' speech with the maternal love seen in Igbo Mother and Child (p. 129) and *Migrant Mother* (p. 342). How might Plato describe or allegorize the love that parents have for their children?

3. Compare the use of a mythical "state of nature" in the "Speech of Aristophanes" with that found in Thomas Hobbes's *Leviathan* (p. 119). What do philosophers gain by presenting human beings in a mythical past and drawing conclusions from their fictional portraits?

WRITING ABOUT THE TEXT

1. Use the "Speech of Aristophanes" as the basis for an essay about the nature of masculinity and femininity. Discuss whether or not the assumptions at the basis of the allegory can be used to derive valid points about human gender.

2. Compare Aristophanes' creation myth with another creation narrative or origin myth. Analyze the power of a narrative from the past to explain things about the present.

3. Explain, in your own words, the underlying argument about human nature at the heart of the "Speech of Aristophanes."

Mencius
Man's Nature Is Good
(circa 300 BCE)

OF THE HUNDREDS OF GREAT Chinese philosophers, poets, novelists, and states-men whose works have been read in the West, only two have been given Latin names: Kung Fu Tzu (551–479 BCE), who is known in the West as Confucius, and Meng Tzu (circa 371–circa 289 BCE), who is known as Mencius. After Confucius himself, Mencius is the most important figure in the development of Confucianism, a system of rites, rituals, and social observances that was the official state religion of China for nearly two thousand years.

Mencius lived and wrote during one of the most spectacular eras of social upheaval that the world has ever known: the Period of Warring States (475–221 BCE). During this period, the area now known as China consisted of numerous smaller states— all remnants of the great Chou Empire—who were constantly at war against each other. Confucianism, Legalism, Moism, and Taoism all emerged during this time as different ways to answer the most important question of the day: What is the best way to ensure political stability? The general Confucian answer to this question is that good government requires good leaders, and good leaders must be good people—people who honor their ancestors, observe the ancient rites, and act toward others with a spirit of rectitude and benevolence.

During Mencius's lifetime, Confucians were split on the question of human nature. Confucius had been puzzlingly vague on this matter, insisting only that all people had a duty to observe the rites and rituals handed down by their ancestors. Some, such as Mencius, took this to mean that humans were inherently good and, with the proper training, could become perfect. Others, such as Hsün Tzu, believed that the Confucian rites were necessary because humans were inherently evil and required rites to keep them in check. Mencius's arguments ultimately prevailed and influenced future generations of Confucians.

The excerpt here is drawn from chapter 21 of Mencius's major work, called the *Mencius*, and consists of a series of conversations between Mencius and the philosopher Kao Tzu and his disciples. Kao Tzu believed that human nature was neither inherently good nor inherently evil but a "blank slate" that could be conditioned in both directions. In Kao's philosophy, the love that people feel toward their relatives stems from internal human nature, but the respect that people show for strangers— and for the rites and traditions that were so important to Confucianism—must be conditioned by external forces. Mencius and his disciple Kung-tu refuse to make this distinction and insist that both love and respect proceed from internal feelings that form part of human beings' nature.

Mencius's rhetorical style is somewhat confusing at first because, like Plato in the "Gorgias," he advances his own arguments in a dialogue with others. Mencius adds an additional layer of complexity to this dialogue form by filtering Kao's arguments through a student, Kung-tu, who listens to both Kao and Mencius and tries to determine which of them speaks the truth.

1

MASTER KAO SAID: "The nature of things is like willow wood, and Duty is like cups and bowls. Shaping human nature into Humanity and Duty is like shaping willow wood into cups and bowls."

"Do you follow the nature of willow wood to shape cups and bowls," replied Mencius, "or do you maul it? If you maul willow wood to make cups and bowls, then I guess you maul human nature to make Humanity and Duty. It's talk like yours that will lead people to ravage Humanity and Duty throughout all beneath Heaven."

2

Master Kao said: "The nature of things is like swirling water: channel it east and it flows east, channel it west and it flows west. And human nature too is like water: it doesn't choose between good and evil any more than water chooses between east and west."

"It's true that water doesn't choose between east and west," replied Mencius, "but doesn't it choose between high and low? Human nature is inherently good, just like water flows inherently downhill. There's no such thing as a person who isn't good, just as there's no water that doesn't flow downhill.

"Think about water: if you slap it, you can make it jump over your head; and if you push and shove, you can make it stay on a mountain. But what does this have to do with the nature of water? It's only responding to the forces around it. It's like that for people too: you can make them evil, but that says nothing about human nature." . . .

6

Adept Kung-tu[1] said: "Master Kao said: *Human nature isn't good, and it isn't evil.* There are others who say: *Human nature can be made good, and it can be made evil.*

---

1. **Kung-tu:** Mencius's disciple.

That's why the people loved goodness when Wen and Wu ruled, and they loved cruelty when Yu and Li ruled.[2] And there are still others who say: *Human nature is inborn: some people are good and some evil. That's why a Hsiang could have Yao as his ruler, a Shun could have Blind Purblind as his father, a Lord Ch'i of Wei and Prince Pi Kan could have the tyrant Chou as their nephew and sovereign.*[3]

"But you say: *Human nature is good.* Does that mean all the others are wrong?"

"We are, by constitution, capable of being good," replied Mencius. "That's what I mean by good. If someone's evil, it can't be blamed on inborn capacities. We all have a heart of compassion and a heart of conscience, a heart of reverence and a heart of right and wrong. In a heart of compassion is Humanity, and in a heart of conscience is Duty. In a heart of reverence is Ritual, and in a heart of right and wrong is wisdom. Humanity, Duty, Ritual, wisdom—these are not external things we meld into us. They're part of us from the beginning, though we may not realize it. Hence the saying: *What you seek you will find, and what you ignore you will lose.* Some make more of themselves than others, maybe two or five or countless times more. But that's only because some people fail to realize their inborn capacities.

"The *Songs* say:

Heaven gave birth to humankind,
and whatever is has its own laws:
cleaving to what makes us human,
people delight in stately Integrity.

Of this, Confucius said: *Whoever wrote this song knew the Way well.* So whatever is must have its own laws, and whenever they cleave to what makes us human, the people must delight in stately Integrity."

7

Mencius said: "In good years, young men are mostly fine. In bad years, they're mostly cruel and violent. It isn't that Heaven endows them with such different capacities, only that their hearts are mired in such different situations. Think about barley: if you plant

---

2. **Yu and Li:** kings singled out in the Confucian tradition for their arrogance and recklessness. **Wen and Wu:** ancient kings who were singled out by Confucius as eminent examples of virtuous rulers. In Mencius's time, philosophers commonly appealed to well-known ancient kings, good and bad, to support their arguments about statecraft.

3. **Yao** was an ancient emperor frequently cited by Confucius as the model of a righteous king, and **Shun** was Yao's handpicked, equally right-

eous successor. **Blind Pureblind,** also called Ku-Sau, was Shun's wicked father. **Lord Ch'I of Wei** was a wise man who refused to serve the wicked tyrant **Chou,** who killed his own uncle **Prince Pi Kan.** The point of all these examples is to refute Mencius's major claim—that human nature is essentially good and made bad by environment—by showing that the same environments that produced some of the most righteous people in history also produced some of the worst.

the seeds carefully at the same time and in the same place, they'll all sprout and grow ripe by summer solstice. If they don't grow the same—it's because of inequities in richness of soil, amounts of rainfall, or the care given them by farmers. And so, all members belonging to a given species of thing are the same. Why should humans be the lone exception? The sage and I—surely we belong to the same species of thing.

"That's why Master Lung said: *Even if a cobbler makes a pair of sandals for feet he's never seen, he certainly won't make a pair of baskets.* Sandals are all alike because feet are the same throughout all beneath Heaven. And all tongues savor the same flavors. Yi Ya[4] was just the first to discover what our tongues savor. If taste differed by nature from person to person, the way horses and dogs differ by species from me, then how is it people throughout all beneath Heaven savor the tastes Yi Ya savored? People throughout all beneath Heaven share Yi Ya's tastes, therefore people's tongues are alike throughout all beneath Heaven.

"It's true for the ear too: people throughout all beneath Heaven share Maestro K'uang's[5] sense of music, therefore people's ears are alike throughout all beneath Heaven. And it's no less true for the eye: no one throughout all beneath Heaven could fail to see the beauty of Lord Tu. If you can't see his beauty, you simply haven't eyes.

"Hence it is said: *All tongues savor the same flavors, all ears hear the same music, and all eyes see the same beauty.* Why should the heart alone not be alike in us all? But what is it about our hearts that is alike? Isn't it what we call reason and Duty? The sage is just the first to discover what is common to our hearts. Hence, reason and Duty please our hearts just like meat pleases our tongues."

8

Mencius said: "The forests were once lovely on Ox Mountain.[6] But as they were near a great city, axes cleared them little by little. Now there's nothing left of their beauty. They rest day and night, rain and dew falling in plenty, and there's no lack of fresh sprouts. But people graze oxen and sheep there, so the mountain's stripped bare. When people see how bare it is, they think that's all the potential it has. But does that mean this is the nature of Ox Mountain?

"Without the heart of Humanity and Duty alive in us, how can we be human? When we abandon this noble heart, it's like cutting those forests: a few axe blows each day, and pretty soon there's nothing left. Then you can rest day and night, take

---

4. **Yi Ya:** an ancient chef who was revered for his culinary talents; according to legend, he once cooked his own son for his master's table.

5. **Maestro K'uang:** the most revered musician in Chinese history. Mencius makes the point that if everyone likes the cooking of Yi Ya and everyone likes the music of K'uang, then certain preferences in human nature are not subject to individual taste.

6. **Ox Mountain:** a mountain on the Pearl River Delta, near present-day Hong Kong. Mencius argues that, though it was in the nature of the mountain to have trees and lush vegetation, the human and animal population of the large state made it appear barren. The larger point is that even people's failure to act benevolently does not mean that they lack a natural disposition toward benevolence.

in the clarity of morning's healing *ch'i*—but the values that make you human keep thinning away. All day long, you're tangled in your life. If these tangles keep up day after day, even the clarity of night's healing *ch'i* isn't enough to preserve you. And if the clarity of night's healing *ch'i* isn't enough to preserve you, you aren't much different from an animal. When people see you're like an animal, they think that's all the potential you have. But does that mean this is the human constitution?

"With proper sustenance, anything will grow; and without proper sustenance, anything will fade away. Confucius said: *Embrace it and it endures. Forsake it and it dies. It comes and goes without warning, and no one knows its route.* He was speaking of the heart."

UNDERSTANDING THE TEXT

1. What is the rhetorical purpose of the character Kao at the beginning of this selection? How does he set up Mencius's argument? What kinds of objections to his own theory does this device allow Mencius to anticipate?

2. How does Mencius present the difference between "benevolence" and "righteousness"? Why does Kao Tzu see the first as internal to human nature and the second as external to human nature?

3. What role does human nature, for Mencius, play in the love we show to our family members? What role does it play in the respect that we show to strangers?

4. A great deal of the debate between Mencius and Kao Tzu concerns the origin of propriety, or proper social behavior, which is synonymous in the text with "righteousness." For Kao Tzu, propriety is a matter of social convention that has nothing to do with human nature. For Mencius, the standards of propriety are based on qualities that are inherently part of human nature. Which of these views do you find more convincing? Why?

5. How might Mencius perceive the nature of evil? If human beings are naturally good, where might evil originate? Support your answer with evidence from the text.

6. Do you agree with Mencius's statement, "Men's mouths agree in having the same relishes; their ears agree in enjoying the same sounds; their eyes agree in recognising the same beauty"? How does this idea of conformity, and with it Mencius's argument, conflict with modern ideas of the individual?

MAKING CONNECTIONS

1. Mencius and Hsün Tzu (p. 100) disagree completely about human nature, yet both are dedicated Confucians. What elements of their respective philosophies justify their inclusion as members of the same school of thought?

2. Compare the thoughts of Mencius and Kao Tzu with those of Ruth Benedict (p. 132) or Edward O. Wilson (p. 144). Does the comparison between East and West, ancient and modern, bring you closer to either Chinese philosopher? Why?

3. What does Mencius imply about people who change the appearance of natural phenomena, such as trees or mountains? What similarities do you see to the arguments about nature made by Rachel Carson in "The Obligation to Endure" (p. 419)?

4. How would you extend Mencius's view of human nature to answer the question "What is good government?" If human beings are essentially good, then what kind of government serves them best? How does this compare to Lao Tzu's thoughts on government (p. 158)?

WRITING ABOUT THE TEXT

1. Take one of the metaphors that Kao Tzu and Mencius debate over—either the willow metaphor or the water metaphor—and use it to support your own view of human nature.

2. Compare Mencius's and Hsün Tzu's (p. 100) ideas about human nature. How are the two texts similar?

3. Examine the role of ritual in contemporary society. Where do social conventions such as manners, dating behavior, dressing and grooming practices, and so on, come from? Do they have as their basis anything natural to human beings?

4. What kinds of government best suit, respectively, Mencius's and Kao Tzu's assumptions about human nature? Write an essay exploring this question, being sure to explain how different perceptions about the nature of human beings lead to different assumptions about the role of government.

Hsün Tzu
Man's Nature Is Evil
(circa 300 BCE)

IN BOTH THE STYLE OF HIS WRITING and the nature of his philosophy, the Chinese scholar Hsün Tzu (circa 300–230 BCE) could not have differed more from his slightly older contemporary Mencius (circa 371–circa 289 BCE). The writings of Mencius consist largely of parables and of what appear to be transcripts of debates that he had with other philosophers. Hsün Tzu wrote sustained, well-developed philosophical arguments that, while they feel quite familiar to the modern reader, were something of an anomaly in his own time.

Both men were Confucians, but Hsün Tzu did not share Mencius's belief that human nature is inherently good, even divine. Whereas for Mencius the Confucian sense of propriety derived from inclinations that all people possessed, Hsün Tzu saw Confucian rites as valuable because they restrained and redirected humanity's inherent disposition toward evil. Hsün Tzu believed that strict discipline could make human beings good despite their natural inclinations. Most of his known writings deal with forces that, in his estimation, steered people toward righteousness: education, music, ritual, and law.

Hsün Tzu's philosophy had an enormous effect on the Chinese philosophy of Legalism. One of his pupils, Han Fei Tzu, the major theorist of that school, argued that human beings must be forced into rectitude by strict laws and harsh penalties for disobedience. When the state of Ch'in unified China into a single empire (221 BCE), another of Hsün Tzu's pupils, Li Ssu, became the prime minister and put the authoritarian principles of Legalism into practice. When the Ch'in Dynasty collapsed—a mere fifteen years after it was established—the backlash against Legalist rule led subsequent regimes to ban Hsün Tzu's teachings.

The reading included here, "Man's Nature Is Evil," is section 23 of the *Hsün Tzu*, the standard collection of Hsün Tzu's writings. This essay specifically addresses the arguments about human nature Mencius advanced one generation earlier. Like Mencius, Hsün Tzu argues frequently by analogy, but unlike his predecessor, he argues just as frequently with sustained, developed arguments. Like modern writers, he states his thesis early (in the very first sentence), repeats it throughout the essay, and focuses on proving this thesis. 🖋

Man's NATURE IS EVIL; goodness is the result of conscious activity. The nature of man is such that he is born with a fondness for profit. If he indulges this fondness, it will lead him into wrangling and strife, and all sense of courtesy and humility will

---

Some of the the the translator's footnotes have been omitted. Bracketed insertions are the translator's.

disappear. He is born with feelings of envy and hate, and if he indulges these, they will lead him into violence and crime, and all sense of loyalty and good faith will disappear. Man is born with the desires of the eyes and ears, with a fondness for beautiful sights and sounds. If he indulges these, they will lead him into license and wantonness, and all ritual principles and correct forms will be lost. Hence, any man who follows his nature and indulges his emotions will inevitably become involved in wrangling and strife, will violate the forms and rules of society, and will end as a criminal. Therefore, man must first be transformed by the instructions of a teacher and guided by ritual principles, and only then will he be able to observe the dictates of courtesy and humility, obey the forms and rules of society, and achieve order. It is obvious from this, then, that man's nature is evil, and that his goodness is the result of conscious activity.

A warped piece of wood must wait until it has been laid against the straightening board, steamed, and forced into shape before it can become straight; a piece of blunt metal must wait until it has been whetted on a grindstone before it can become sharp. Similarly, since man's nature is evil, it must wait for the instructions of a teacher before it can become upright, and for the guidance of ritual principles before it can become orderly. If men have no teachers to instruct them, they will be inclined towards evil and not upright; and if they have no ritual principles to guide them, they will be perverse and violent and lack order. In ancient times the sage kings realized that man's nature is evil, and that therefore he inclines toward evil and violence and is not upright or orderly. Accordingly they created ritual principles and laid down certain regulations in order to reform man's emotional nature and make it upright, in order to train and transform it and guide it in the proper channels. In this way they caused all men to become orderly and to conform to the Way.[1] Hence, today any man who takes to heart the instructions of his teacher, applies himself to his studies, and abides by ritual principles may become a gentleman, but anyone who gives free rein to his emotional nature, is content to indulge his passions, and disregards ritual principles becomes a petty man. It is obvious from this, therefore, that man's nature is evil, and that his goodness is the result of conscious activity.

Mencius states that man is capable of learning because his nature is good, but I say that this is wrong. It indicates that he has not really understood man's nature nor distinguished properly between the basic nature and conscious activity. The nature is that which is given by Heaven; you cannot learn it, you cannot acquire it by effort. Ritual principles, on the other hand, are created by sages; you can learn to apply them, you can work to bring them to completion. That part of man which cannot be learned or acquired by effort is called the nature; that part of him which can be acquired by learning and brought to completion by effort is

1. **The Way:** Chinese philosophers from every school speak about "the Way," or the *Tao*, though each school uses the term in a different sense. For Taoists, "the Way" means "the natu- ral order of things" and is beyond human influence. For Confucians, "the Way" means something like "the way things should be" and incorporates ideals of rectitude and propriety.

called conscious activity. This is the difference between nature and conscious activity.

It is a part of man's nature that his eyes can see and his ears can hear. But the faculty of clear sight can never exist separately from the eye, nor can the faculty of keen hearing exist separately from the ear. It is obvious, then, that you cannot acquire clear sight and keen hearing by study. Mencius states that man's nature is good, and that all evil arises because he loses his original nature. Such a view, I believe, is erroneous. It is the way with man's nature that as soon as he is born he begins to depart from his original naïveté and simplicity, and therefore he must inevitably lose what Mencius regards as his original nature. It is obvious from this, then, that the nature of man is evil.

Those who maintain that the nature is good praise and approve whatever has   5 not departed from the original simplicity and naïveté of the child. That is, they consider that beauty belongs to the original simplicity and naïveté and goodness to the original mind in the same way that clear sight is inseparable from the eye and keen hearing from the ear. Hence, they maintain that [the nature possesses goodness] in the same way that the eye possesses clear vision or the ear keenness of hearing. Now it is the nature of man that when he is hungry he will desire satisfaction, when he is cold he will desire warmth, and when he is weary he will desire rest. This is his emotional nature. And yet a man, although he is hungry, will not dare to be the first to eat if he is in the presence of his elders, because he knows that he should yield to them, and although he is weary, he will not dare to demand rest because he knows that he should relieve others of the burden of labor. For a son to yield to his father or a younger brother to yield to his elder brother, for a son to relieve his father of work or a younger brother to relieve his elder brother—acts such as these are all contrary to man's nature and run counter to his emotions. And yet they represent the way of filial piety and the proper forms enjoined by ritual principles. Hence, if men follow their emotional nature, there will be no courtesy or humility; courtesy and humility in fact run counter to man's emotional nature. From this it is obvious, then, that man's nature is evil, and that his goodness is the result of conscious activity.

Someone may ask: if man's nature is evil, then where do ritual principles come from? I would reply: all ritual principles are produced by the conscious activity of the sages; essentially they are not products of man's nature. A potter molds clay and makes a vessel, but the vessel is the product of the conscious activity of the potter, not essentially a product of his human nature. A carpenter carves a piece of wood and makes a utensil, but the utensil is the product of the conscious activity of the carpenter, not essentially a product of his human nature. The sage gathers together his thoughts and ideas, experiments with various forms of conscious activity, and so produces ritual principles and sets forth laws and regulations. Hence, these ritual principles and laws are the products of the conscious activity of the sage, not essentially products of his human nature.

Phenomena such as the eye's fondness for beautiful forms, the ear's fondness for beautiful sounds, the mouth's fondness for delicious flavors, the mind's fondness for profit, or the body's fondness for pleasure and ease—these are all products of the emotional nature of man. They are instinctive and spontaneous; man does not have to do anything to produce them. But that which does not come into being instinctively but must wait for some activity to bring it into being is called the product of conscious activity. These are the products of the nature and of conscious activity respectively, and the proof that they are not the same. Therefore, the sage transforms his nature and initiates conscious activity; from this conscious activity he produces ritual principles, and when they have been produced he sets up rules and regulations. Hence, ritual principles and rules are produced by the sage. In respect to human nature the sage is the same as all other men and does not surpass them; it is only in his conscious activity that he differs from and surpasses other men.

It is man's emotional nature to love profit and desire gain. Suppose now that a man has some wealth to be divided. If he indulges his emotional nature, loving profit and desiring gain, then he will quarrel and wrangle even with his own brothers over the division. But if he has been transformed by the proper forms of ritual principle, then he will be capable of yielding even to a complete stranger. Hence, to indulge the emotional nature leads to the quarreling of brothers, but to be transformed by ritual principles makes a man capable of yielding to strangers.

Every man who desires to do good does so precisely because his nature is evil. A man whose accomplishments are meager longs for greatness; an ugly man longs for beauty; a man in cramped quarters longs for spaciousness; a poor man longs for wealth; a humble man longs for eminence. Whatever a man lacks in himself he will seek outside. But if a man is already rich, he will not long for wealth, and if he is already eminent, he will not long for greater power. What a man already possesses in himself he will not bother to look for outside. From this we can see that men desire to do good precisely because their nature is evil. Ritual principles are certainly not a part of man's original nature. Therefore, he forces himself to study and to seek to possess them. An understanding of ritual principles is not a part of man's original nature, and therefore he ponders and plans and thereby seeks to understand them. Hence, man in the state in which he is born neither possesses nor understands ritual principles. If he does not possess ritual principles, his behavior will be chaotic, and if he does not understand them, he will be wild and irresponsible. In fact, therefore, man in the state in which he is born possesses this tendency towards chaos and irresponsibility. From this it is obvious, then, that man's nature is evil, and that his goodness is the result of conscious activity.

Mencius states that man's nature is good, but I say that this view is wrong. All men in the world, past and present, agree in defining goodness as that which is upright, reasonable, and orderly, and evil as that which is prejudiced, irresponsible, and chaotic. This is the distinction between good and evil. Now suppose that man's nature was in fact intrinsically upright, reasonable, and orderly—then what need would there be for sage kings and ritual principles? The existence of sage kings and ritual principles could certainly add nothing to the situation. But because man's nature is in fact evil, this is not so. Therefore, in ancient times the sages, realizing that man's nature is evil, that it is prejudiced and not upright, irresponsible and lacking in order, for this reason established the authority of the ruler to control it, elucidated ritual principles to transform it, set up laws and standards to correct it, and meted out strict punishments to restrain it. As a result, all the world achieved order and conformed to goodness. Such is the orderly government of the sage kings and the transforming power of ritual principles. Now let someone try doing away with the authority of the ruler, ignoring the transforming power of ritual principles, rejecting the order that comes from laws and standards, and dispensing with the restrictive power of punishments, and then watch and see how the people of the world treat each other. He will find that the powerful impose upon the weak and rob them, the many terrorize the few and extort from them, and in no time the whole world will be given up to chaos and mutual destruction. It is obvious from this, then, that man's nature is evil, and that his goodness is the result of conscious activity.

Those who are good at discussing antiquity must demonstrate the validity of what they say in terms of modern times; those who are good at discussing Heaven must show proofs from the human world. In discussions of all kinds, men value what is in accord with the facts and what can be proved to be valid. Hence if a man sits on his mat propounding some theory, he should be able to stand right up and put it into practice, and show that it can be extended over a wide area with equal validity. Now Mencius states that man's nature is good, but this is neither in accord with the facts, nor can it be proved to be valid. One may sit down and propound such a theory, but he cannot stand up and put it into practice, nor can he extend it over a wide area with any success at all. How, then, could it be anything but erroneous?

If the nature of man were good, we could dispense with sage kings and forget about ritual principles. But if it is evil, then we must go along with the sage kings and honor ritual principles. The straightening board is made because of the warped wood; the plumb line is employed because things are crooked; rulers are set up and ritual principles elucidated because the nature of man is evil. From this it is obvious, then, that man's nature is evil, and that his goodness is the result of conscious activity. A straight piece of wood does not have to wait for the straightening board to become straight; it is straight by nature. But a warped piece of wood must wait until it has been laid against the straightening board, steamed, and forced into shape before it can become straight, because by nature it is warped. Similarly, since man's nature is evil, he must wait for the ordering power of the sage kings and the transforming power of ritual principles; only then can he achieve order and conform to goodness. From this it is obvious, then, that man's nature is evil, and that his goodness is the result of conscious activity.

Someone may ask whether ritual principles and concerted conscious activity are not themselves a part of man's nature, so that for that reason the sage is capable of producing them. But I would answer that this is not so. A potter may mold clay and produce an earthen pot, but surely molding pots out of clay is not a part of the potter's human nature. A carpenter may carve wood and produce a utensil, but surely carving utensils out of wood is not a part of the carpenter's human nature. The sage stands in the same relation to ritual principles as the potter to the things he molds and produces. How, then, could ritual principles and concerted conscious activity be a part of man's basic human nature?

As far as human nature goes, the sages Yao and Shun possessed the same nature as the tyrant Chieh or Robber Chih, and the gentleman possesses the same nature as the petty man.[2] Would you still maintain, then, that ritual principles and concerted conscious activity are a part of man's nature? If you do so, then what reason is there to pay any particular honor to Yao, Shun, or the gentleman? The reason people honor Yao, Shun, and the gentleman is that they are able to transform their nature, apply themselves to conscious activity, and produce ritual principles. The sage, then, must stand in the same relation to ritual principles as the potter to the things he molds and produces. Looking at it this way, how could ritual principles and concerted conscious activity be a part of man's nature? The reason people despise Chieh, Robber Chih, or the petty man is that they give free rein to their nature, follow their emotions, and are content to indulge their passions, so that their conduct is marked by greed and contentiousness. Therefore, it is clear that man's nature is evil, and that his goodness is the result of conscious activity.

Heaven did not bestow any particular favor upon Tseng Tzu, Min Tzu-ch'ien, or Hsiao-i that it withheld from other men.[3] And yet these three men among all others proved most capable of carrying out their duties as sons and winning fame for their filial piety. Why? Because of their thorough attention to ritual principles. Heaven has not bestowed any particular favor upon the inhabitants of Ch'i and Lu which it has withheld from the people of Ch'in.[4] And yet when it comes to observing the duties of father and son and the separation of roles between husband and wife, the inhabitants of Ch'in cannot match the filial reverence and respect for proper form which marks the people of Ch'i and Lu. Why? Because the people of Ch'in give free rein to their emotional nature, are content to indulge their passions, and are careless of ritual principles. It is certainly not due to any difference in human nature between the two groups.

15

---

2. The category of **gentleman** (*chün tzu*) represents the ideal human being in the Confucian system of thought. The gentleman possesses rectitude, benevolence, integrity, honor, and a proper respect for the ancestors and the rites. The opposite of a gentleman is a "petty man" (*hsiao jen*). The terms do not have any class-based connotations. **Yao and Shun:** mythical ancient kings advanced by Confucians as ideals of righteous rulers. **Tyrant Chieh or Robber Chih:** According to tradition, Chieh was an evil ruler who brought down the great Hsia Dynasty. **Robber Chih** led a band of nine thousand criminals; legend has it that Confucius once tried in vain to reform him.

3. **Tseng Tzu, Min Tzu-ch'ien:** followers of Confucius who were considered especially righteous. Not much is known about **Hsiao-i**.

4. **Ch'in's** government was officially anti-Confucian (see p. 100). **Ch'i and Lu** were areas where Confucianism was very influential.

The man in the street can become a Yü.[5] What does this mean? What made the sage emperor Yü a Yü, I would reply, was the fact that he practiced benevolence and righteousness and abided by the proper rules and standards. If this is so, then benevolence, righteousness, and proper standards must be based upon principles which can be known and practiced. Any man in the street has the essential faculties needed to understand benevolence, righteousness, and proper standards, and the potential ability to put them into practice. Therefore it is clear that he can become a Yü.

Would you maintain that benevolence, righteousness, and proper standards are not based upon any principles that can be known and practiced? If so, then even a Yü could not have understood or practiced them. Or would you maintain that the man in the street does not have the essential faculties needed to understand them or the potential ability to put them into practice? If so, then you are saying that the man in the street in his family life cannot understand the duties required of a father or a son and in public life cannot comprehend the correct relationship between ruler and subject. But in fact this is not true. Any man in the street *can* understand the duties required of a father or a son and *can* comprehend the correct relationship between ruler and subject. Therefore, it is obvious that the essential faculties needed to understand such ethical principles and the potential ability to put them into practice must be a part of his make-up. Now if he takes these faculties and abilities and applies them to the principles of benevolence and righteousness, which we have already shown to be knowable and practicable, then it is obvious that he can become a Yü. If the man in the street applies himself to training and study, concentrates his mind and will, and considers and examines things carefully, continuing his efforts over a long period of time and accumulating good acts without stop, then he can achieve a godlike understanding and form a triad with Heaven and earth. The sage is a man who has arrived where he has through the accumulation of good acts.

You have said, someone may object, that the sage has arrived where he has through the accumulation of good acts. Why is it, then, that everyone is not able to accumulate good acts in the same way? I would reply: everyone is capable of doing so, but not everyone can be made to do so. The petty man is capable of becoming a gentleman, yet he is not willing to do so; the gentleman is capable of becoming a petty man but he is not willing to do so. The petty man and the gentleman are perfectly capable of changing places; the fact that they do not actually do so is what I mean when I say that they are capable of doing so but they cannot be made to do so. Hence, it is correct to say that the man in the street is *capable* of becoming a Yü but it is not necessarily correct to say that he will in fact find it possible to do so. But although he does not find it possible to do so does not prove that he is incapable of doing so.

5. **Yü:** the virtuous king and founder of the ancient Hsia Dynasty. "The man in the street can become a Yü" refers to the assertion, found in section 22 of the *Mencius*, that "all men may be Yaos and Shuns" (see note 2 above).

A person with two feet is theoretically capable of walking to every corner of the earth, although in fact no one has ever found it possible to do so. Similarly, the artisan, the carpenter, the farmer, and the merchant are theoretically capable of exchanging professions, although in actual practice they find it impossible to do so. From this we can see that, although someone may be theoretically capable of becoming something, he may not in practice find it possible to do so. But although he does not find it possible to do so, this does not prove that he is not capable of doing so. To find it practically possible or impossible to do something and to be capable or incapable of doing something are two entirely different things. It is perfectly clear, then, that a man is theoretically capable of becoming something else.

Yao asked Shun, "What are man's emotions like?" Shun replied, "Man's emotions are very unlovely things indeed! What need is there to ask any further? Once a man acquires a wife and children, he no longer treats his parents as a filial son should. Once he succeeds in satisfying his cravings and desires, he neglects his duty to his friends. Once he has won a high position and a good stipend, he ceases to serve his sovereign with a loyal heart. Man's emotions, man's emotions—they are very unlovely things indeed! What need is there to ask any further? Only the worthy man is different from this." 20

There is the understanding of the sage, the understanding of the gentleman and man of breeding, the understanding of the petty man, and the understanding of the menial. He speaks many words but they are graceful and well ordered; all day he discourses on his reasons, employing a thousand different and varied modes of expression, and yet all that he says is united around a single principle: such is the understanding of the sage. He speaks little but what he says is brief and to the point, logical and clearly presented, as though laid out with a plumb line: such is the understanding of the gentleman and man of breeding. His words are all flattery, his actions irresponsible; whatever he does is shot through with error: such is the understanding of the petty man. His words are rapid and shrill but never to the point; his talents are varied and many but of no practical use; he is full of subtle distinctions and elegant turns of phrase that serve no practical purpose; he ignores right or wrong, disdains to discuss crooked or straight, but seeks only to overpower the arguments of his opponent: such is the understanding of the menial.

There is superior valor, there is the middle type of valor, and there is inferior valor. When proper standards prevail in the world, to dare to bring your own conduct into accord with them; when the Way of the former kings prevails, to dare to follow its dictates; to refuse to bow before the ruler of a disordered age, to refuse to follow the customs of the people of a disordered age; to accept poverty and hardship if they are in the cause of benevolent action; to reject wealth and eminence if they are not consonant with benevolent action; if the world recognizes you, to share in the world's joys; if the world does not recognize you, to stand alone and without fear: this is superior valor. To be reverent in bearing and modest in intention; to value honor and make light of material goods; to dare to promote and honor the worthy, and reject and cast off the unworthy: such is the middle type of valor. To ignore your own safety in the quest for wealth; to make light of danger and try to talk your way out of every difficulty; to rely on lucky escapes; to ignore right and wrong, just and unjust, and seek only to overpower the arguments of your opponents: such is inferior valor. . . .

A man, no matter how fine his nature or how keen his mind, must seek a worthy teacher to study under and good companions to associate with. If he studies under a worthy teacher, he will be able to hear about the ways of Yao, Shun, Yü, and T'ang,[6] and if he associates with good companions, he will be able to observe conduct that is loyal and respectful. Then, although he is not aware of it, he will day by day progress in the practice of benevolence and righteousness, for the environment he is subjected to will cause him to progress. But if a man associates with men who are not good, then he will hear only deceit and lies and will see only conduct that is marked by wantonness, evil, and greed. Then, although he is not aware of it, he himself will soon be in danger of severe punishment, for the environment he is subjected to will cause him to be in danger. An old text says, "If you do not know a man, look at his friends; if you do not know a ruler, look at his attendants." Environment is the important thing! Environment is the important thing!

UNDERSTANDING THE TEXT

1. Why does Hsün Tzu repeat his thesis (p. 579) throughout this piece? Does this technique make his argument more effective? What other types of repetition does Hsün Tzu use? How does he use the repeating images or scenarios to illustrate different aspects of his argument?

2. What distinction does Hsün Tzu draw between "nature" and "conscious activity"? Are these categories mutually exclusive? What kinds of things does he place in each category?

3. What does Hsün Tzu see as the origin of ritual principles? How does this differ from Mencius's view (p. 94)?

4. Why does Hsün Tzu assert that "every man who desires to do good does so precisely because his nature is evil"? Do you agree? Are his comparisons to men who are unaccomplished, ugly, cramped, poor, and humble valid? Is it possible to desire to be something that *is* part of one's nature?

5. How does Hsün Tzu define "good" and "evil"? Do his definitions concur with contemporary definitions of the same words?

6. **T'ang:** a righteous king in mythical ancient China; should not be confused with the T'ang Dynasty, which ruled China from 618 to 907 CE, nearly a thousand years after Hsün Tzu's time.

6. How does Hsün Tzu differentiate between capability and possibility? How are they related, and does this inclusion weaken or strengthen the validity of Hsün Tzu's argument?

7. According to Hsün Tzu, what role does environment play in how humans deal with their nature? What kind of environmental factors determine a person's inclination or rejection of human nature?

MAKING CONNECTIONS

1. How does Hsün Tzu's writing style compare with that of Mencius (p. 94)? Are his rhetorical strategies more or less effective than those of his major philosophical opponent? Why?

2. What kind of political theory is suggested by Hsün Tzu's philosophy of human nature? How do perceptions of human nature affect political arguments? Which political theories covered in chapter 3, "Law and Government," best reflect the kind of government that Hsün Tzu would advocate?

3. Compare this essay by Hsün Tzu with the essay by him in chapter 1, "Education" (p. 8). How do his views on human nature affect his views on education?

4. Compare Hsün Tzu's use of the dialogue form with that of Plato in "Gorgias" (p. 478). Do the two philosophers use multiple voices for the same reasons? Explain.

WRITING ABOUT THE TEXT

1. Hsün Tzu states: "If a man is already rich, he will not long for wealth, and if he is already eminent, he will not long for greater power. What a man already possesses in himself he will not bother to look for outside. From this we can see that men desire to do good precisely because their nature is evil." Defend or refute this assertion, using historical examples to support your argument.

2. Compare Hsün Tzu's philosophy of human nature with that of Thomas Hobbes (p. 119). How does each philosopher feel that people should be governed?

3. Analyze the rhetoric of "Man's Nature Is Evil." What inductive and deductive arguments can you draw from the essay? (See pp. 597–604 for explanations and examples of inductive and deductive reasoning.) How logically sound are his arguments?

4. Compare Hsün Tzu's view of human nature with the one implicit in the argument of his contemporary Mo Tzu in "Against Music" (p. 308) and "Against Offensive Warfare" (p. 253). What elements do the texts share?

Nāgārjuna
The Precious Garland
(circa 200 BCE)

LITTLE IS KNOWN about the life of Acharya Nāgārjuna (circa 150–250 CE), the Indian philosopher who, many people believe, contributed more to the development of Buddhism than anyone other than the Buddha himself. According to tradition, Nāgārjuna was born to an upper-caste Brahmin family in southern India. A Hindu by birth, he later converted to Buddhism, but he continued to write in Sanskrit rather than in the Pali language favored by other Buddhist writers of his day. He is considered the founder of the school of Buddhism known as *Madhyamaka*, or "The Middle Path," which was eventually exported to China and became the foundation of many of the varieties of Buddhism practiced today.

Nāgārjuna's "Middle Path" was designed to offer an alternative to two competing perceptions of reality: "eternalism," the belief that all things have an external, unchanging reality, and "nihilism," the belief that nothing truly exists. *Madhyamaka* holds that human beings incorrectly attribute permanent and independent existence to things (both material objects and abstract concepts) instead of seeing them correctly as impermanent and dependent upon the shape and form of everything else. Things exist, but they do not exist in an unchangeable or absolute form. Rather, the form that a thing takes depends on its relationships to other things. People, place, things, and ideas all exist in Nāgārjuna's philosophy, but their existence is, in his words, "empty" until it is given significance through interaction with other people, places, things, and ideas.

"The Precious Garland" is Nāgārjuna's detailed explanation of the Buddhist philosophy of emptiness. The verses of "The Precious Garland" are addressed to an ancient Indian king named Sātavāhana. In the 500 quatrains that comprise the full poem, Nāgārjuna first explains the doctrine of emptiness and then goes onto explain the correct responses to this doctrine: We must recognize that the things we desire are impermanent and illusory, we must accept our deep connectedness to all other people and things, and we must act with the compassion that comes with feeling this connectedness. The twenty-two quatrains excerpted here contain Nāgārjuna's explanation of the nature of a human being.

Though originally written in India, the verses of "The Precious Garland" have become best known as part of the Buddhism of Tibet. The version of the text excerpted here is based on an oral Sanskrit and was translated into modern Tibetian by Tenzin Gyatso (b. 1935), the Fourteenth Dalai Lama of Tibet, whose extensive commentary on its content has been published in his 1984 book, *The Buddhism of Tibet*.

Rhetorically, "The Precious Garland" provides an excellent example of Hegelian synthesis. Nāgārjuna synthesizes the thesis of eternalism and the antithesis of nihilism to create a third doctrine that he presents as superior to the other two.

1

The doctrines of definite goodness are
Said by the Conquerors[1] to be deep,
Subtle and frightening to
Children who are not learned.

2

'I am not, I will not be.
I have not, I will not have',
That frightens all children
And kills fear in the wise.

3

By him who speaks only to help
Beings, it was said that they all
Have arisen from the conception of 'I'
And are enveloped with the conception of 'mine'.

4

'The "I" exists, the "mine" exists.'
These are wrong as ultimates,
For the two are not [established]
By a true and correct consciousness.

5

The mental and physical aggregates[2] arise
From the conception of 'I' which is false in fact.
How could what is grown
From a false seed be true?

---

1. **Conquerors:** In Buddhist writings, the term *conqueror* is often used to describe one who has conquered himself and achieved enlightenment.

2. **Aggregates:** the five sets of attributes that constitute a human being in Buddhist thought: form, feeling, perception, volition, and consciousness.

6

Having thus seen the aggregates as untrue,
The conception of 'I' is abandoned
And due to this abandonment
The aggregates arise no more.

7

Just as it is said
That an image of one's face is seen
Depending on a mirror
But does not in fact exist [as a face],

8

So the conception of 'I' exists
Dependent on the aggregates,
But like the image of one's face
In reality the 'I' does not exist.

9

Just as without depending on a mirror
The image of one's face is not seen,
So too the 'I' does not exist
Without depending on the aggregates.

10

When the superior Ānanda[3] had
Attained [insight into] what this means,
He won the eye of doctrine and taught it
Continually to the monks.

11

There is misconception of an 'I' as long
As the aggregates are misconceived,
When this conception of an 'I' exists,
There is action which results in birth.

---

3. **Ānanda:** the first cousin and disciple of Siddhartha Gautama, the founder of Buddhism.

12

With these three pathways mutually causing each
Other without a beginning, middle or an end,
This wheel of cyclic existence
Turns like the 'wheel' of a firebrand.[4]

13

Because this wheel is not obtained from self, other
Or from both, in the past, the present or the future,
The conception of an 'I' ceases
And thereby action and rebirth.

14

Thus one who sees how cause and effect
Are produced and destroyed
Does not regard the world
As really existent or non-existent.

15

Thus one who has heard but does not examine
The doctrine which destroys all suffering,
And fears the fearless state
Trembles due to ignorance.

16

That all these will not exist in nirvāna[5]
Does not frighten you [a Hīnayānist[6]],
Why does their non-existence
Explained here cause you fright?

---

4. **The 'wheel' of a firebrand:** the illusion of a wheel formed by swinging a stick with a burning end in a circular motion.
5. **Nirvāna:** Literally, "the extinguishing of a candle"; *nirvāna* refers to a state of mind free from attachment, craving, suffering, or illusion.
6. **Hīnayānist:** Buddhists who followed Nāgārjuna developed an expanded form of Buddhism that they called "Mahayana," or "the greater vehicle." Early Mahayana Buddhists coined the term *Hīnayāna*, or the "lesser vehicle," as a pejorative reference to those who favored a stricter interpretation of the Buddhist's writings. A modern equivalent would be the term *fundamentalist*.

17

'In liberation there is no self and are no aggregates.'
If liberation is asserted thus,
Why is the removal here of the self
And of the aggregates not liked by you?

18

If nirvāna is not a non-thing,
Just how could it have thingness?
The extinction of the misconception
Of things and non-things is called nirvāna.

19

In brief the view of nihilism[7] is
That actions bear no fruits; without
Merit and leading to a bad state,
It is regarded as the wrong view.

20

In brief the view of existence
Is that there are fruits of actions;
Meritorious and conducive to happy
Migrations, it is regarded as the right view.

21

Because 'is' and 'is not' are destroyed by wisdom,
There is a passage beyond merit and sin,
This, say the excellent, is liberation
From both bad and happy migrations.

7. **Nihilism:** the belief that nothing exists in an ultimate sense so that after the death of the physical body nothing about a person will remain. Nihilism and eternalism (the belief that every-thing will always exist in its current form) are the two extremes rejected by Nāgārjuna's "middle way."

UNDERSTANDING THE TEXT

1. What does the mirror represent in stanza 7? How might a reflection in a mirror represent something that both does and does not exist?

2. Why does Nāgārjuna compare the cycle of existence to the "'wheel' of a fire-brand"? Why are there quotation marks around the word "wheel"? What is the overall effect of the metaphor?

3. What constitutes liberation in Nāgārjuna's view of human nature? How is it possible to be liberated by "the removal of the self"?

4. What is the nature of the middle way that Nāgārjuna proposes between eternalism (the belief that everything, including the essence of a human being, exists in the same form forever) and nihilism (the belief that existence is an illusion)?

MAKING CONNECTIONS

1. Compare Nāgārjuna's view that a person's nature is dependent on relationships with Ruth Benedict's (p. 132) view that the meaning of an individual's characteristics or actions depends on the culture in which he or she is situated.

2. How does the view of external reality in "The Precious Garland" correspond to the Buddhist view that Matthieu Ricard offers in "The Universe in a Grain of Sand" (p. 435)?

3. How does the view of the ideal ruler in the *Tao te Ching* (p. 158) compare to the views of human nature that Nāgārjuna offers to King Śātavāhana? How do both philosophies use paradox and contradiction?

WRITING ABOUT THE TEXT

1. Summarize the view of human nature found in "The Precious Garland."

2. Compare or contrast Nāgārjuna's view of reality with that of Lao Tzu in the *Tao te Ching* (p. 158). Focus specifically on each author's view of perceptions as opposed to reality.

3. Explain the "middle way" position that Nāgārjuna stakes out in "The Precious Garland" by using the concept of the Hegelian synthesis found on pages 624–25. What positions constitute the "thesis" and the "antithesis"? How does the final position contain elements of each?

4. Using "The Precious Garland," compare the concepts of the self and human nature in Buddhism with those concepts in Islam or Christianity.

Leonardo da Vinci
Vitruvian Man
(1487)

VITRUVIAN MAN IS ONE OF the most recognizable images from the remarkable career of Leonardo da Vinci (1452–1519). Da Vinci was a major inspiration for the term *Renaissance Man*, which describes someone with a wide variety of talents. He was, among other things, a painter, writer, scientist, inventor, sculptor, and musician. In history and popular imagination, da Vinci is a symbol of the European Renaissance, or "rebirth," which lasted from the fourteenth through the seventeenth centuries and, like da Vinci himself, is known for its art, music, and literature as well as its explosive advances in science and technology. But the single word that best describes both da Vinci and the Renaissance is *humanism*, a passionate belief in the dignity and ingenuity of human beings and in the central position that humans occupy in creation.

The Renaissance was also known for a revival of interest in classical (Greek and Roman) art, literature, and philosophy. When Rome fell in the fifth century CE, many of the cultural achievements of the classical world were lost or ignored by the inhabitants of Europe. The Middle Ages did see renewed interest in classical arts, philosophy, science, and history, as cities were rebuilt and people rediscovered the works of Aristotle, Plato, and other ancient Greeks, but with the Renaissance that interest reached a fever pitch, and the era is named for its "rebirth" of classical culture.

Like many of his contemporaries, da Vinci was well versed in the works of the ancient Greeks and Romans, and it was one of these works—*De architectura*, by the Roman scholar Vitruvius—that provided the inspiration for *Vitruvian Man*. In *De architectura*, Vitruvius describes what he considers to be the perfect human body, characterized by exact geometrical proportions. The foot, for example, should be exactly one-sixth as long as the body is tall, and every other part of the body has its ideal size in proportion to the whole. By following these proportions, Vitruvius argued, the great artists and sculptors of the ancient world were able to create masterpieces whose perfections could be understood intuitively by those who viewed them.

In *Vitruvian Man*, da Vinci represents these proportions exactly. His ideal man is posed in two different positions inside of both a circle and a square. This arrangement also follows Vitruvius, who writes that "in the human body the central point is naturally the navel. For if a man be placed flat on his back, with his hands and feet extended, and a pair of compasses centered at his navel, the fingers and toes of his two hands and feet will touch the circumference of a circle described there from. And just as the human body yields a circular outline, so too a square figure may be found from it." The text accompanying *Vitruvian Man* is in Italian, but, like most of da Vinci's personal notes, it uses the convention of "mirror writing," text that can be read correctly only by viewing its reflection in a mirror. 🖊

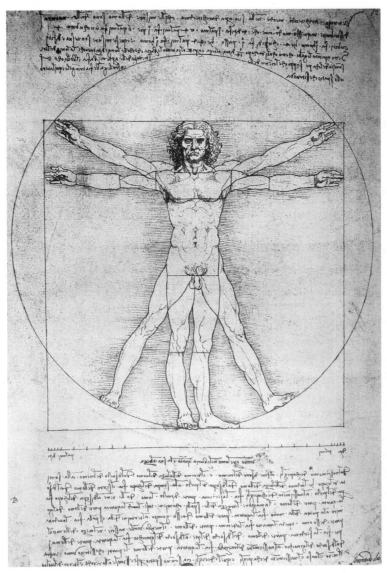

Vitruvian Man, 1487.
Photograph by Janaka Dharmasena/Dreamstime

UNDERSTANDING THE TEXT

1. Why does da Vinci draw the Vitruvian Man in two different positions? What is the effect of these images being combined into the same visual representation?

2. The numerical relationships between the different proportions in *Vitruvian Man* have been the source of numerous speculations in scholarly books and

articles and in popular works such as *The Da Vinci Code*. What do you believe attracted da Vinci to these proportions? Do you think that they reflect the actual proportions of an ideal human male? Why or why not?

3. Why is it important to the overall argument of the painting that the figure be a male? Would a "Vitruvian Woman" have the same proportions? What might da Vinci's choice of a male say about his views on gender?

4. Why do you think that da Vinci inserted his figure into two geometrical shapes, a circle and a square? Do these shapes have any symbolic meaning? What can circles and squares mean in your own culture? (Think of expressions such as a "circular argument" or a "square deal.")

5. What is the effect of the mirror text that da Vinci uses to describe *Vitruvian Man*? Why might it be important that the full meaning of the painting can be understood only by holding it to a mirror?

MAKING CONNECTIONS

1. Compare the ideal male image in *Vitruvian Man* with the ideal female image from Africa in *Igbo Mother and Child* (p. 129). What do you think accounts for the tremendous difference in these depictions?

2. Compare da Vinci's use of dual positions in *Vitruvian Man* with Pablo Picasso's use of several perspectives in *Guernica* (p. 271. Why do you think that the painters incorporate multiple viewpoints into one?

3. When most of us look at the picture of the Galaxy Cluster Abell 1689 (p. 452), we feel small in the hugeness of space. Da Vinci, on the other hand, placed humanity in the center of his drawing, with everything else orbiting it. How might you reconcile these views—that we are tiny and insignificant in the vastness of space, and that we are central to the universe?

WRITING ABOUT THE TEXT

1. Write a rebuttal to da Vinci's view of that a perfect body should be exactly proportioned. What definition of "perfection" does his view assume? What other definitions could you invoke to argue against da Vinci?

2. Examine modern views of "ideal beauty," either male or female. Where do such views usually come from? Select a photograph or other media representation of beauty and compare the assumptions behind that representation with those of da Vinci in *Vitruvian Man*.

3. Explain the idea of human nature that da Vinci advances in *Vitruvian Man*. Compare this with the idea of human nature behind another image, such as Dorothea Lange's *Migrant Mother* (p. 342) or the Aztec drawing from *Codex Mendoza* (p. 266).

Thomas Hobbes
from *Leviathan*
(1651)

LIKE THE PERIOD OF WARRING STATES in ancient China, the years between 1640 and 1714 in England saw great social upheaval. In 1642, a civil war broke out between King Charles I and the British Parliament under the leadership of Oliver Cromwell. The war ended in 1649 with the execution of King Charles, and for the next eleven years Cromwell ruled England as a commonwealth rather than a monarchy. Soon after Cromwell's death, Parliament invited Charles's son, Charles II, to return to the throne, but the hostilities among Anglicans, Catholics, and Dissenting Protestants continued for years and led to another revolution in 1689. Out of the chaos and uncertainty of the English revolutions emerged two of England's greatest political philosophers: Thomas Hobbes (1588–1679) and John Locke (1632–1704).

Both Locke's and Hobbes's theories of government imagine what people would be like in a "state of nature"—an environment without laws or social structures, one in which "human nature" existed without constraints. Locke and Hobbes posited that from a state of nature, humans established a "social contract" that required them to surrender some of their freedoms in exchange for the protections and opportunities of a civil society. The social contract arguments of Locke and Hobbes were extremely influential in their day. They were adopted by French philosophers such as the Baron de Montesquieu (1689–1755) and Jean-Jacques Rousseau (1712–1778) and by American revolutionaries such as Thomas Jefferson (1743–1826).

Each thinker's vision of the social contract depended on his understanding of human nature. Those who, like Locke, saw the natural state as reasonably safe and secure believed that people had the right to renegotiate, through violent revolution if necessary, their relationship with their government when that government ceased to protect them. For Hobbes, however, the state of nature was so horrible, and people in their natural state so degenerate, that any form of government was preferable to it. Hobbes therefore opposed revolution in any form, not because he thought that kings ruled by divine right but because he believed that authoritarian governments were necessary to keep human beings' worst impulses under control.

The reading that follows, "Of the Natural Condition of Mankind, As Concerning Their Felicity and Misery," is chapter 13 of Hobbes's most important political work, *Leviathan*. Though one of the shorter chapters in the book, it has become by far the most famous chapter. In it, Hobbes lays out his theory that the natural state of humanity is war, by which he means not necessarily armed conflict but a struggle in which each person's interests are inherently opposed to everyone else's. In such a state, human life is, in Hobbes's oft-quoted terms, "solitary, poor, nasty, brutish, and short."

This selection from *Leviathan* provides an example of reasoning by generalization. Hobbes begins by defining the nature of individual human beings and then generalizes this characterization to apply to entire societies. 🖉

Nature hath made men so equal in the faculties of body and mind as that, though there be found one man sometimes manifestly stronger in body or of quicker mind than another, yet when all is reckoned together the difference between man and man is not so considerable as that one man can thereupon claim to himself any benefit to which another may not pretend as well as he. For as to the strength of body, the weakest has strength enough to kill the strongest, either by secret machination, or by confederacy with others that are in the same danger with himself.[1]

And as to the faculties of the mind—setting aside the arts grounded upon words, and especially that skill of proceeding upon general and infallible rules called science (which very few have, and but in few things), as being not a native faculty (born with us), nor attained (as prudence) while we look after somewhat else—I find yet a greater equality amongst men than that of strength. For prudence is but experience, which equal time equally bestows on all men in those things they equally apply themselves unto. That which may perhaps make such equality incredible is but a vain conceit of one's own wisdom, which almost all men think they have in a greater degree than the vulgar, that is, than all men but themselves and a few others whom, by fame or for concurring with themselves, they approve. For such is the nature of men that howsoever they may acknowledge many others to be more witty, or more eloquent, or more learned, yet they will hardly believe there be many so wise as themselves. For they see their own wit at hand, and other men's at a distance. But this proveth rather that men are in that point equal, than unequal. For there is not ordinarily a greater sign of the equal distribution of anything than that every man is contented with his share.

From this equality of ability ariseth equality of hope in the attaining of our ends. And therefore, if any two men desire the same thing, which nevertheless they cannot both enjoy, they become enemies; and in the way to their end, which is principally their own conservation, and sometimes their delectation only, endeavour to destroy or subdue one another. And from hence it comes to pass that, where an invader hath no more to fear than another man's single power, if one plant, sow, build, or possess a convenient seat, others may probably be expected to come prepared with forces united, to dispossess and deprive him, not only of the fruit of his labour, but also of his life or liberty. And the invader again is in the like danger of another.

---

1. **By secret machination, or by confederacy:** Hobbes states that nobody is safe in a state of nature, since even the weakest people can kill the strongest, either by laying secret plans or by forming alliances with others.

And from this diffidence[2] of one another, there is no way for any man to secure himself so reasonable as anticipation, that is, by force or wiles to master the persons of all men he can, so long till he see no other power great enough to endanger him. And this is no more than his own conservation requireth, and is generally allowed. Also, because there be some that taking pleasure in contemplating their own power in the acts of conquest, which they pursue farther than their security requires, if others (that otherwise would be glad to be at ease within modest bounds) should not by invasion increase their power, they would not be able, long time, by standing only on their defence, to subsist. And by consequence, such augmentation of dominion over men being necessary to a man's conservation, it ought to be allowed him.

Again, men have no pleasure, but on the contrary a great deal of grief, in keep-   5
ing company where there is no power able to over-awe them all. For every man looketh that his companion should value him at the same rate he sets upon himself, and upon all signs of contempt, or undervaluing, naturally endeavours, as far as he dares (which amongst them that have no common power to keep them in quiet, is far enough to make them destroy each other), to extort a greater value from his contemners, by damage, and from others, by the example.

So that in the nature of man we find three principal causes of quarrel: first, competition; secondly, diffidence; thirdly, glory.

The first maketh men invade for gain; the second, for safety; and the third, for reputation. The first use violence to make themselves masters of other men's persons, wives, children, and cattle; the second, to defend them; the third, for trifles, as a word, a smile, a different opinion, and any other sign of undervalue, either direct in their persons, or by reflection in their kindred, their friends, their nation, their profession, or their name.

Hereby it is manifest that during the time men live without a common power to keep them all in awe, they are in that condition which is called war, and such a war as is of every man against every man. For WAR consisteth not in battle only, or the act of fighting, but in a tract of time wherein the will to contend by battle is sufficiently known. And therefore, the notion of *time* is to be considered in the nature of war, as it is in the nature of weather. For as the nature of foul weather lieth not in a shower or two of rain, but in an inclination thereto of many days together, so the nature of war consisteth not in actual fighting, but in the known disposition thereto during all the time there is no assurance to the contrary.[3] All other time is PEACE.

---

2. **Diffidence:** reservation. Hobbes means that people in a natural state can never trust or be genuinely close to other people because their interests might conflict and turn them into enemies.

3. Hobbes expands the common definition of "war" to include situations in which people do not have a reasonable assurance that they will not soon be at war. For Hobbes, then, "peace" means not only the absence of conflict but also the reasonable expectation that society has been structured to prevent conflict.

Whatsoever therefore is consequent to a time of war, where every man is enemy to every man, the same is consequent to the time wherein men live without other security than what their own strength and their own invention shall furnish them withal. In such condition there is no place for industry, because the fruit thereof is uncertain, and consequently, no culture of the earth, no navigation, nor use of the commodities that may be imported by sea, no commodious building, no instruments of moving and removing such things as require much force, no knowledge of the face of the earth, no account of time, no arts, no letters, no society, and which is worst of all, continual fear and danger of violent death, and the life of man, solitary, poor, nasty, brutish, and short.

It may seem strange, to some man that has not well weighed these things, that nature should thus dissociate, and render men apt to invade and destroy one another. And he may, therefore, not trusting to this inference made from the passions, desire perhaps to have the same confirmed by experience. Let him therefore consider with himself—when taking a journey, he arms himself, and seeks to go well accompanied; when going to sleep, he locks his doors; when even in his house, he locks his chests; and this when he knows there be laws, and public officers, armed, to revenge all injuries shall be done him—what opinion he has of his fellow subjects, when he rides armed; of his fellow citizens, when he locks his doors; and of his children and servants, when he locks his chests. Does he not there as much accuse mankind by his actions, as I do by my words? But neither of us accuse man's nature in it. The desires and other passions of man are in themselves no sin. No more are the actions that proceed from those passions, till they know a law that forbids them—which till laws be made they cannot know. Nor can any law be made, till they have agreed upon the person that shall make it.

It may peradventure[4] be thought, there was never such a time nor condition of war as this; and I believe it was never generally so, over all the world. But there are many places where they live so now. For the savage people in many places of *America* (except the government of small families, the concord whereof dependeth on natural lust)[5] have no government at all, and live at this day in that brutish manner as I said before. Howsoever, it may be perceived what manner of life there would be where there were no common power to fear, by the manner of life which men that have formerly lived under a peaceful government use to degenerate into, in a civil war.

But though there had never been any time wherein particular men were in a condition of war one against another, yet in all times kings and persons of sovereign authority, because of their independency, are in continual jealousies and in the state and posture of gladiators, having their weapons pointing and their eyes fixed on one

4. **Peradventure:** perhaps.
5. **The concord whereof dependeth on natural lust:** Hobbes relies on largely inaccurate portrayals of American Indians and other tribal people to assert that they have no form of civil government beyond that of the small family, which is kept together by sexual ties between partners and by affection for children.

another, that is, their forts, garrisons, and guns upon the frontiers of their kingdoms, and continual spies upon their neighbours, which is a posture of war. But because they uphold thereby the industry of their subjects, there does not follow from it that misery which accompanies the liberty of particular men.

To this war of every man against every man, this also is consequent: that nothing can be unjust. The notions of right and wrong, justice and injustice, have there no place. Where there is no common power, there is no law; where no law, no injustice. Force and fraud are in war the two cardinal virtues. Justice and injustice are none of the faculties neither of the body, nor mind. If they were, they might be in a man that were alone in the world, as well as his senses and passions. They are qualities that relate to men in society, not in solitude. It is consequent also to the same condition that there be no propriety, no dominion, no *mine* and *thine* distinct, but only that to be every man's that he can get, and for so long as he can keep it. And thus much for the ill condition which man by mere nature is actually placed in, though with a possibility to come out of it, consisting partly in the passions, partly in his reason.

The passions that incline men to peace are fear of death, desire of such things as are necessary to commodious living, and a hope by their industry to obtain them. And reason suggesteth convenient articles of peace, upon which men may be drawn to agreement. These articles are they which otherwise are called the Laws of Nature, whereof I shall speak more particularly in the two following chapters.

UNDERSTANDING THE TEXT

1. Why does Hobbes believe all humans are equal in the state of nature? In what ways can those who are physically weaker than others compensate for their weakness? According to Hobbes, is this equality good or bad? Why?

2. What makes people enemies in the state of nature? Is it possible to avoid this enmity? Why or why not?

3. What three principal causes of warfare and conflict does Hobbes name? Explain why Hobbes lists them in a particular order. How does one lead to the others? What do these causes imply about Hobbes's idea of human nature?

4. Under what conditions can peace occur? Considering the other tenets of human nature Hobbes puts forth, would these conditions ever be feasible?

5. According to Hobbes, how do people living in civilized states "degenerate into a civil war"? Why should people avoid doing this at all costs?

6. Why does Hobbes state that justice cannot exist in the state of nature? What conditions are necessary for it to exist?

7. What feelings propel human beings to seek "peace" and, therefore, civil government?

8. Which of Hobbes's passages appeal most to logic, or logos? Which appeal most to emotion, or pathos? Which of these two modes of persuasion (p. 597) are the most important to the presentation of his argument?

MAKING CONNECTIONS

1. Does Hobbes, like Hsün Tzu (p. 100), assert that human beings are evil? Does he advocate the same kinds of solutions to improve the natural condition of humankind? Explain.

2. According to Hobbes, any government should be tolerated because any state of peace is better than a state of war. How might Martin Luther King Jr. (p. 202) or Aung San Suu Kyi (p. 219) respond to this assertion?

3. How does Hobbes's take on the state of nature compare with Darwin's view of natural selection (p. 405)? How might Darwin evaluate the condition that Hobbes fears most: a social situation in which all humans compete with all other humans for survival?

5. How does Hobbes's idea of the state of nature compare to Plato's myth of human beings in their natural state in "The Speech of Aristophanes" (p. 89)?

WRITING ABOUT THE TEXT

1. Develop your own "state of nature" theory in which you describe how, in your opinion, human beings would behave in the absence of government or civil society.

2. Write a rebuttal to Hobbes using Martin Luther King Jr.'s distinction (p. 209) between "a negative peace which is the absence of tension" and "a positive peace which is the presence of justice" as the basis for your critique.

3. Compare Hobbes's assumptions about human nature to those of Hsün Tzu (p. 100). What kinds of assumptions might more likely lead to totalitarian governments, and what kinds might more likely lead to democratic governments?

John Locke
Of Ideas
(1690)

LIKE HIS CONTEMPORARY Thomas Hobbes, John Locke (1632–1704) lived during one of the most turbulent times in English history. A student at Oxford University in the 1650s, Locke came age during the brief period of republican rule that occurred in England after the execution of Charles I in 1649 and before the Restoration of Charles II in 1660. Unlike Hobbes, however, Locke did not see political unrest, or even revolution, as necessarily bad things, nor did he perceive human nature as inherently self-interested and aggressive.

In his *Second Treatise on Government* (1689), Locke argued that individuals enter into a two-way contract with the state, surrendering absolute liberty in exchange for the protection of life, liberty, and the right to own property. When the state fails to uphold its end of the bargain, he believed, the people have a right to renegotiate the terms of the contract. In his own day, Locke's ideas helped lay the groundwork for the Glorious Revolution of 1688–1689, when King James II was forced from the English throne without bloodshed. Nearly a hundred years later, Locke's ideas were incorporated almost verbatim into the American Declaration of Independence.

In addition to being one of the most important political theorists of the Enlightenment, Locke was also one of the founding figures of the school of philosophy known as "empiricism," the belief that all knowledge is gained through experience. In Locke's day, as in ours, empiricism contrasted directly with "nativism," the belief that all people share certain values and perceptions as part of their human inheritance—which can come from God, as many people in Locke's day believed, or from the mechanical operation of genes, as many scientists today affirm.

The selection below is drawn from Locke's influential *Essay Concerning Human Understanding* (1690), the work in which Locke gives the fullest expression to the principle of the *tabula rasa*. According to this principle, the human mind begins as a blank slate (in Latin, *tabula rasa*) and acquires knowledge through experience. For Locke, all such experience is either sensation (information acquired through the senses) or reflection (information that the mind derives through its own operations). Both sensation and reflection begin at birth, and together they entirely determine human understanding. Human nature, from this perspective, is simply the sum total of human experience.

At the heart of Locke's argument lies a simple but very powerful analogy: the human mind is like a blank slate. It has a certain shape and structure, but no innate content until it is "written on" by experience.

Of Ideas in general, and their Original

1. *Idea is the object of thinking.* Every man being conscious to himself that he thinks; and that which his mind is applied about whilst thinking being the ideas that are there, it is past doubt that men have in their minds several ideas, such as are those expressed by the words *whiteness, hardness, sweetness, thinking, motion, man, elephant, army, drunkenness,* and others: it is in the first place then to be inquired, How he come by them?

I know it is a received doctrine, that men have native ideas, and original characters, stamped upon their minds in their very first being.[1] This opinion I have at large examined already; and, I suppose what I have said in the foregoing Book[2] will be much more easily admitted, when I have shown whence the understanding may get all the ideas it has; and by what ways and degrees they may come into the mind; for which I shall appeal to every one's own observation and experience.

2. *All ideas come from sensation or reflection.* Let us then suppose the mind to be, as we say, white paper,[3] void of all characters, without any ideas: How comes it to be furnished? Whence comes it by that vast store which the busy and boundless fancy of man has painted on it with an almost endless variety? Whence has it all the materials of reason and knowledge? To this I answer, in one word, from EXPERIENCE. In that all our knowledge is founded; and from that it ultimately derives itself. Our observation employed either, about external sensible objects, or about the internal operations of our minds perceived and reflected on by ourselves, is that which supplies our understandings with all the materials of thinking. These two are the fountains of knowledge, from whence all the ideas we have, or can naturally have, do spring.

3. *The objects of sensation one source of ideas.* First, our Senses, conversant about particular sensible objects, do convey into the mind several distinct perceptions of things, according to those various ways wherein those objects do affect them. And thus we come by those ideas we have of yellow, white, heat, cold, soft, hard, bitter, sweet, and all those which we call sensible qualities; which when I say the senses convey into the mind, I mean, they from external objects convey into the mind what produces there those perceptions. This great source of most of the ideas we have, depending wholly upon our senses, and derived by them to the understanding, I call SENSATION.

---

1. The "received doctrine" of nativism, the belief that all people share certain ideas and values simply because they are all human, goes back to the philosophy of Plato; in Locke's day it was most associated with the philosophy of René Descartes (1596–1650). Some version of nativism is common in most of the world's major religious traditions.

2. **Foregoing book:** An *Essay Concerning Human*

Understanding is divided into four books. This selection is taken from the beginning of Book Two, "Of Ideas." The "foregoing book" refers to Book One, "Of Innate Notions."

3. **White paper:** Though *An Essay Concerning Human Understanding* is generally considered the source of the term *tabula rasa,* or "blank slate," Locke himself never uses either term. "White paper" is as close as he comes.

4. *The operations of our minds, the other source of them.* Secondly, the other fountain from which experience furnisheth the understanding with ideas is, the perception of the operations of our own mind within us, as it is employed about the ideas it has got; which operations, when the soul comes to reflect on and consider, do furnish the understanding with another set of ideas, which could not be had from things without. And such are perception, thinking, doubting, believing, reasoning, knowing, willing, and all the different actings of our own minds; which we being conscious of, and observing in ourselves, do from these receive into our understandings as distinct ideas as we do from bodies affecting our senses. This source of ideas every man has wholly in himself; and though it be not sense, as having nothing to do with external objects, yet it is very like it, and might properly enough be called internal sense. But as I call the other SENSATION, so I call this REFLECTION, the ideas it affords being such only as the mind gets by reflecting on its own operations within itself. By reflection then, in the following part of this discourse, I would be understood to mean, that notice which the mind takes of its own operations, and the manner of them, by reason whereof there come to be ideas of these operations in the understanding. These two, I say, viz. external material things, as the objects of SENSATION, and the operations of our own minds within, as the objects of REFLECTION, are to me the only originals from whence all our ideas take their beginnings. The term operations here I use in a large sense, as comprehending not barely the actions of the mind about its ideas, but some sort of passions arising sometimes from them, such as is the satisfaction or uneasiness arising from any thought.

5. *All our ideas are of the one or the other of these.* The understanding seems to me not to have the least glimmering of any ideas which it doth not receive from one of these two. External objects furnish the mind with the ideas of sensible qualities, which are all those different perceptions they produce in us; and the mind furnishes the understanding with ideas of its own operations.

These, when we have taken a full survey of them, and their several modes, combinations, and relations, we shall find to contain all our whole stock of ideas; and that we have nothing in our minds which did not come in one of these two ways. Let any one examine his own thoughts, and thoroughly search into his understanding; and then let him tell me, whether all the original ideas he has there, are any other than of the objects of his senses, or of the operations of his mind, considered as objects of his reflection. And how great a mass of knowledge soever he imagines to be lodged there, he will, upon taking a strict view, see that he has not any idea in his mind but what one of these two have imprinted; though perhaps, with infinite variety compounded and enlarged by the understanding. . . .

UNDERSTANDING THE TEXT

1. What examples of "ideas" does Locke use to begin this passage? Is his list representative of the kinds of ideas that a person might have? Can you think of kinds of ideas that might not fit easily into his theory (i.e., ideas that do not appear to be based on either sensation or reflection)?

2. What does Locke present as the two subcategories of experience? Do you agree that neither of these contain innate ideas? Explain.

3. What does Locke mean by the term "sensible qualities"? How are such qualities experienced as ideas? What examples of this kind of idea does he give?

4. What kinds of "operations of our own minds" does Locke include under the heading "reflection"? Do you agree with him that these mental operations constitute a "kind of internal sense"? Explain.

5. What appeal does Locke make to the reader to the end of this passage? How does he suggest that his ideas can be empirically tested and verified?

MAKING CONNECTIONS

1. Compare Locke's view of the reliability of sensory perception with that of Nāgārjuna in "The Precious Garland" (p. 110). According to Locke's theories, could a person understand a reality that exists beyond sensory perception, as Nāgārjuna argues that we should?

2. Locke and Hobbes (p. 119) are often contrasted with each other as polar opposites of Enlightenment political theory. Do the brief selections from Locke and Hobbes in this section support such a contrast? Why or why not?

3. Many modern scientists, including Edward O. Wilson (p. 144), reject Locke's idea of the human mind as a blank state. The mind, they argue, has been "written on" by the genes and contains innate perceptions that are common to all cultures. How do you think Locke might have responded to Wilson and others who argue for an innate, genetically determined human nature?

WRITING ABOUT THE TEXT

1. Write an essay comparing Locke's view of human nature with that of Mencius (p. 94) and Hsün Tzu (p. 100). How would Locke respond to the argument between these two ancient Confucians?

2. Refute Locke's theory that human beings are born "blank slates" with no innate ideas. Argue against it from a religious or a scientific perspective.

3. Write an essay in which you discuss the political implications of both Locke's and Hobbes's (p. 119) views of human nature. Conduct research into each author's actual political philosophies and discuss whether or not they flow logically from the brief passages in this chapter.

Igbo Mother and Child
(19th or 20th CENTURY)

FOR CENTURIES, the Igbo, or Ibo, people have inhabited the southern tip of what is now the nation of Nigeria. Their rich cultural and religious traditions were documented by Chinua Achebe in *Things Fall Apart* (1958), perhaps the most famous African novel of the twentieth century. Achebe, a native Igbo, considers his fiction an outgrowth of his people's art. In his essay "The Igbo World and Its Art," Achebe notes that each generation of Igbo destroys and then re-creates the art objects of the previous generation. In Igboland, art is a process rather than a product. "Process is motion while product is rest," Achebe writes. "When the product is preserved or venerated, the impulse to repeat is compromised. Therefore, the Igbo choose to eliminate the product and retain the process so that every occasion and every generation will receive its own impulses and kinesis of creation."

The statue shown here, which resides in New York City's Metropolitan Museum of Art, was originally crafted to adorn a religious shrine, probably associated with the compound of a large extended family. Such shrines are common in Igbo territory, and the figures that adorn them, called *ntpeke*, are seen as providing both decoration and protection. Older women are traditionally the artisans in the Igbo culture, as creation of life through art is seen as the responsibility of those who no longer have the power to create life through childbirth. The museum's caption for this piece describes it as follows:

> The work shown here, a tribute to motherhood, renders its classic subject in an especially sensitive and evocative manner. The female figure sits on a stool, which is fused with her lower back, legs extended before her. In her arms she cradles a child, who nurses at her breast. Her head is crowned by a coiffure composed of a series of five extensions that radiate outward and upward, conveying a sense of vitality.

The figure portrays a scene with universal relevance and appeal: a mother holding and nursing a child. In this sense, the artwork is similar to countless representations of Mary and Jesus in the Christian tradition. In Madonna and Child paintings, however, the mother enjoys a unique position among women, because her child is a divine being. The Igbo figures do not represent specific exceptional individuals. Rather, they represent the divine potential in all people—a potential that, in this case, is merged with the creative act of childbirth. 🍃

Igbo mother and child, 19th or 20th century (terracotta).
The Metropolitan Museum of Art, New York
Gift of Drs. Herbert F. and Teruko S. Neuwalder, 1982

UNDERSTANDING THE TEXT

1. How does the sculpture represent external nature? Why do the woman, her crown, the stool, and the child all seem to flow out of one another? What might this depiction suggest about the artist's culture?

2. Do you believe that the figure was intended to be realistic, allegorical, or both? If it is allegorical, what might it be seen as an allegory of?

3. Why do the woman's eyes appear to be closed? Where does she seem to be directing her attention? Why?

4. Does the sculpture betray signs that it was made by a woman? How might women in other cultures conceive of "motherhood" differently than men do? Why?

5. Why would a sculpture of a woman nursing a child have religious significance? Why would it be invested with the power to protect a shrine? Does this icon suggest a cultural view that equates maternity with physical power?

MAKING CONNECTIONS

1. Two of the works of art in this chapter—"The Shaft of the Dead Man" (p. 86) and the Igbo Mother and Child—appear to have had ritual or religious significance. What might the production process of each suggest about its respective culture's idea of community and human interaction with the holy or sacred?

2. What do the different works of art in this unit suggest about the human need to create art? Why is the urge to create artistic representations of human figures present in almost every culture ever discovered?

3. Compare the implicit ideal of human nature in Igbo Mother and Child with that of da Vinci's *Vitruvian Man* (p. 116). What do you think accounts for the widely different perceptions in these two works?

WRITING ABOUT THE TEXT

1. Explore the different ways that Igbo Mother and Child and *Vitruvian Man* (p. 116) render the human form. Then speculate about how each piece was produced. How might the specific creative process have affected the presentation of the human form?

2. Explore modern representations of motherhood or fatherhood in art, including music, movies, and television. What kind of "ideal parent" is constructed in those media? How does this representation of parenthood compare to the construction of the maternal in the Igbo statue?

3. Compare the function of art in Igbo culture with the function of art in contemporary American or European culture. How is the motivation for producing art different in different cultures? How is it universal?

Ruth Benedict
The Individual and the Pattern of Culture
(1934)

RUTH FULTON BENEDICT (1887–1948) was one of a key group of scholars who, in the early twentieth century, developed the discipline of cultural anthropology—a set of strategies and assumptions for studying different cultures. Benedict entered Columbia University in 1919 to study under the world-famous anthropologist Franz Boas (1858–1942). Four years later, she received a Ph.D. in anthropology and joined the faculty at Columbia, where one of her first doctoral students was Margaret Mead (1901–1978), who went on to become the best-known anthropologist of the century.

Benedict and her colleagues believed that cultures should be studied without the prejudices that most people experience when they encounter lifestyles and values different than their own. Unlike previous generations of anthropologists, who either made judgments about other cultures based on their own value systems or studied different peoples to discover "human universals" that could be applied across the spectrum of humanity, the cultural anthropologists observed other cultures impartially, evaluated them on the cultures' own terms, and described their findings without inserting their own values into the descriptions. Benedict called this approach "cultural relativism," referring to the belief that "right" and "wrong" were defined by individual cultures and could not be generalized in any fashion to all people or societies.

Benedict's first book, *Patterns of Culture*, became a national best seller and introduced millions of Americans to anthropology. In *Patterns of Culture*, Benedict examines the basic assumptions of three cultures: the gentle, austere Zuñi Pueblo Indians of New Mexico; the violent, brutal Dobu tribe of New Guinea; and the highly structured, hierarchical Kwakiutl Indians of the Pacific Northwest coast, near Vancouver. After considering the practices and values of these three cultures, Benedict proposes that human value structures are always situated within a cultural context and that a tremendous amount of what people call "human nature" must be attributed to the influence of culture.

In the selection here, the conclusion to *Patterns of Culture*, Benedict examines the relationship between the individual and his or her culture. She rejects the assumption that an inherent conflict exists between the needs of the individual and the needs of society and argues instead that individuals and society form an integrated whole, with individual personalities contributing to the fabric of a culture, and with that cultural fabric constraining the range of choices that any individual can make. Even those character traits that occur across the spectrum of human society are interpreted in very different ways by different cultures, leading to very different kinds of lives for those who possess them.

Like several other writers in this chapter, Benedict builds her argument on the form of inductive reasoning known as generalization. Specifically, she examines the conventions of several historical and contemporary societies and uses her conclusions as the basis for an argument about human nature in general. 🖎

THERE IS NO PROPER ANTAGONISM between the role of society and that of the individual. One of the most misleading misconceptions due to this nineteenth-century dualism[1] was the idea that what was subtracted from society was added to the individual and what was subtracted from the individual was added to society. Philosophies of freedom, political creeds of *laissez faire*,[2] revolutions that have unseated dynasties, have been built on this dualism. The quarrel in anthropological theory between the importance of the culture pattern and of the individual is only a small ripple from this fundamental conception of the nature of society.

In reality, society and the individual are not antagonists. His culture provides the raw material of which the individual makes his life. If it is meagre, the individual suffers; if it is rich, the individual has the chance to rise to his opportunity. Every private interest of every man and woman is served by the enrichment of the traditional stores of his civilization. The richest musical sensitivity can operate only within the equipment and standards of its tradition. It will add, perhaps importantly, to that tradition, but its achievement remains in proportion to the instruments and musical theory which the culture has provided. In the same fashion a talent for observation expends itself in some Melanesian[3] tribe upon the negligible borders of the magico-religious field. For a realization of its potentialities it is dependent upon the development of scientific methodology, and it has no fruition unless the culture has elaborated the necessary concepts and tools.

The man in the street still thinks in terms of a necessary antagonism between society and the individual. In large measure this is because in our civilization the regulative activities of society are singled out, and we tend to identify society with the restrictions the law imposes upon us. The law lays down the number of miles per hour that I may drive an automobile. If it takes this restriction away, I am by that much the freer. This basis for a fundamental antagonism between society and the individual is naïve indeed when it is extended as a basic philosophical and political

---

1. **Nineteenth-century dualism:** early anthropological theories that the rights of the individual fundamentally conflict with the needs of society.

2. *Laissez faire:* a French term meaning "let things alone." The economic doctrine of laissez-faire, often associated with Adam Smith, holds that government should not interfere with the running of the economy, but should allow economic forces to regulate themselves. In a larger political sense, a laissez-faire approach to government involves minimal laws, taxation, security procedures, and so on.

3. **Melanesian:** Melanesia refers to a group of Pacific islands north and northeast of Australia. The island of New Guinea, home to the Dobu tribe analyzed in *Patterns of Culture*, is by far the largest of these islands.

notion. Society is only incidentally and in certain situations regulative, and law is not equivalent to the social order. In the simpler homogeneous cultures collective habit or custom may quite supersede the necessity for any development of formal legal authority. American Indians sometimes say: 'In the old days, there were no fights about hunting grounds or fishing territories. There was no law then, so everybody did what was right.' The phrasing makes it clear that in their old life they did not think of themselves as submitting to a social control imposed upon them from without. Even in our civilization the law is never more than a crude implement of society, and one it is often enough necessary to check in its arrogant career. It is never to be read off as if it were the equivalent of the social order.

Society in its full sense . . . is never an entity separable from the individuals who compose it. No individual can arrive even at the threshold of his potentialities without a culture in which he participates. Conversely, no civilization has in it any element which in the last analysis is not the contribution of an individual. Where else could any trait come from except from the behaviour of a man or a woman or a child?

It is largely because of the traditional acceptance of a conflict between society and the individual, that emphasis upon cultural behaviour is so often interpreted as a denial of the autonomy of the individual. The reading of Sumner's *Folkways*[4] usually rouses a protest at the limitations such an interpretation places upon the scope and initiative of the individual. Anthropology is often believed to be a counsel of despair which makes untenable a beneficent human illusion. But no anthropologist with a background of experience of other cultures has ever believed that individuals were automatons, mechanically carrying out the decrees of their civilization. No culture yet observed has been able to eradicate the differences in the temperaments of the persons who compose it. It is always a give-and-take. The problem of the individual is not clarified by stressing the antagonism between culture and the individual, but by stressing their mutual reinforcement. This rapport is so close that it is not possible to discuss patterns of culture without considering specifically their relation to individual psychology.

We have seen that any society selects some segment of the arc of possible human behaviour, and in so far as it achieves integration its institutions tend to further the expression of its selected segment and to inhibit opposite expressions. But these opposite expressions are the congenial responses, nevertheless, of a certain proportion of the carriers of the culture. We have already discussed the reasons for believing that this selection is primarily cultural and not biological. We cannot, therefore, even on theoretical grounds imagine that all the congenial responses of all its people will be equally served by the institutions of any culture. To understand the behaviour of the

4. **Sumner's** *Folkways:* William Graham Sumner (1840–1910) was an American sociologist and Yale University professor. His 1907 book, *Folkways*, describes the way that cultures construct certain absolute values and beliefs, which are woven into the patterns of everyday life so that children internalize them from a very young age.

individual, it is not merely necessary to relate his personal life-history to his endowments, and to measure these against an arbitrarily selected normality. It is necessary
also to relate his congenial responses to the behaviour that is singled out in the institutions of his culture.

The vast proportion of all individuals who are born into any society always and
whatever the idiosyncrasies of its institutions, assume, as we have seen, the behaviour dictated by that society. This fact is always interpreted by the carriers of that
culture as being due to the fact that their particular institutions reflect an ultimate
and universal sanity. The actual reason is quite different. Most people are shaped
to the form of their culture because of the enormous malleability of their original
endowment. They are plastic to the moulding force of the society into which they
are born. It does not matter whether, with the Northwest Coast, it requires delu-
sions of self-reference, or with our own civilization the amassing of possessions. In
any case the great mass of individuals take quite readily the form that is presented
to them.

They do not all, however, find it equally congenial, and those are favoured and
fortunate whose potentialities most nearly coincide with the type of behaviour
selected by their society. Those who, in a situation in which they are frustrated, naturally seek ways of putting the occasion out of sight as expeditiously as possible are
well served in Pueblo culture. Southwest institutions, as we have seen, minimize the
situations in which serious frustration can arise, and when it cannot be avoided, as
in death, they provide means to put it behind them with all speed.

On the other hand, those who react to frustration as to an insult and whose
first thought is to get even are amply provided for on the Northwest Coast. They
may extend their native reaction to situations in which their paddle breaks or their
canoe overturns or to the loss of relatives by death. They rise from their first reaction of sulking to thrust back in return, to 'fight' with property or with weapons.
Those who can assuage despair by the act of bringing shame to others can register freely and without conflict in this society, because their proclivities are deeply
channelled in their culture. In Dobu those whose first impulse is to select a victim and project their misery upon him in procedures of punishment are equally
fortunate. . . .

The individuals we have so far discussed . . . illustrate the dilemma of the indi-   10
vidual whose congenial drives are not provided for in the institutions of his culture.
This dilemma becomes of psychiatric importance when the behaviour in question is
regarded as categorically abnormal in a society. Western civilization tends to regard
even a mild homosexual as an abnormal. The clinical picture of homosexuality
stresses the neuroses and psychoses to which it gives rise, and emphasizes almost
equally the inadequate functioning of the invert and his behaviour. We have only
to turn to other cultures, however, to realize that homosexuals have by no means
been uniformly inadequate to the social situation. They have not always failed to
function. In some societies they have even been especially acclaimed. Plato's *Repub-*

lic is, of course, the most convincing statement of the honourable estate of homosexuality. It is presented as a major means to the good life, and Plato's high ethical evaluation of this response was upheld in the customary behaviour of Greece at that period.

The American Indians do not make Plato's high moral claims for homosexuality, but homosexuals are often regarded as exceptionally able. In most of North America there exists the institution of the *berdache*, as the French called them. These men-women were men who at puberty or thereafter took the dress and the occupations of women. Sometimes they married other men and lived with them. Sometimes they were men with no inversion, persons of weak sexual endowment who chose this role to avoid the jeers of the women. The berdaches were never regarded as of first-rate supernatural power, as similar men-women were in Siberia, but rather as leaders in women's occupations, good healers in certain diseases, or, among certain tribes, as the genial organizers of social affairs. They were usually, in spite of the manner in which they were accepted, regarded with a certain embarrassment. It was thought slightly ridiculous to address as 'she' a person who was known to be a man and who, as in Zuñi, would be buried on the men's side of the cemetery. But they were socially placed. The emphasis in most tribes was upon the fact that men who took over women's occupations excelled by reason of their strength and initiative and were therefore leaders in women's techniques and in the accumulation of those forms of property made by women. One of the best known of all the Zuñis of a generation ago was the man-woman We-wha, who was, in the words of his friend, Mrs. Stevenson, 'certainly the strongest person in Zuñi, both mentally and physically.' His remarkable memory for ritual made him a chief personage on ceremonial occasions, and his strength and intelligence made him a leader in all kinds of crafts.

The men-women of Zuñi are not all strong, self-reliant personages. Some of them take this refuge to protect themselves against their inability to take part in men's activities. One is almost a simpleton, and one, hardly more than a little boy, has delicate features like a girl's. There are obviously several reasons why a person becomes a berdache in Zuñi, but whatever the reason, men who have chosen openly to assume women's dress have the same chance as any other persons to establish themselves as functioning members of the society. Their response is socially recognized. If they have native ability, they can give it scope; if they are weak creatures, they fail in terms of their weakness of character, not in terms of their inversion.

The Indian institution of the berdache was most strongly developed on the plains. The Dakota had a saying 'fine possessions like a berdache's,' and it was the epitome of praise for any woman's household possessions. A berdache had two strings to his bow, he was supreme in women's techniques, and he could also support his *ménage*[5] by the man's activity of hunting. Therefore no one was richer. When especially fine beadwork or dressed skins were desired for ceremonial occasions, the berdache's work was sought in preference to any other's. It was his social adequacy that was stressed above all else.

5. **Ménage:** household.

As in Zuñi, the attitude toward him is ambivalent and touched with malaise in the face of a recognized incongruity. Social scorn, however, was visited not upon the berdache but upon the man who lived with him. The latter was regarded as a weak man who had chosen an easy berth instead of the recognized goals of their culture; he did not contribute to the household, which was already a model for all households through the sole efforts of the berdache. His sexual adjustment was not singled out in the judgment that was passed upon him, but in terms of his economic adjustment he was an outcast.

When the homosexual response is regarded as a perversion, however, the invert is immediately exposed to all the conflicts to which aberrants are always exposed. His guilt, his sense of inadequacy, his failures, are consequences of the disrepute which social tradition visits upon him; and few people can achieve a satisfactory life unsupported by the standards of the society. The adjustments that society demands of them would strain any man's vitality, and the consequences of this conflict we identify with their homosexuality.

Trance is a similar abnormality in our society. Even a very mild mystic is aberrant in Western civilization. In order to study trance or catalepsy[6] within our own social groups, we have to go to the case histories of the abnormal. Therefore the correlation between trance experience and the neurotic and psychotic seems perfect. As in the case of the homosexual, however, it is a local correlation characteristic of our century. Even in our own cultural background other eras give different results. In the Middle Ages when Catholicism made the ecstatic experience the mark of sainthood, the trance experience was greatly valued, and those to whom the response was congenial, instead of being overwhelmed by a catastrophe as in our century, were given confidence in the pursuit of their careers. It was a validation of ambitions, not a stigma of insanity. Individuals who were susceptible to trance, therefore, succeeded or failed in terms of their native capacities, but since trance experience was highly valued, a great leader was very likely to be capable of it.

Among primitive peoples, trance and catalepsy have been honoured in the extreme. Some of the Indian tribes of California accorded prestige principally to those who passed through certain trance experiences. Not all of these tribes believed that it was exclusively women who were so blessed, but among the Shasta this was the convention. Their shamans were women, and they were accorded the greatest prestige in the community. They were chosen because of their constitutional liability to trance and allied manifestations. One day the woman who was so destined, while she was about her usual work, fell suddenly to the ground. She had heard a voice speaking to her in tones of the greatest intensity. Turning, she had seen a man with drawn bow and arrow. He commanded her to sing on pain of being shot through the heart by his arrow, but under the stress of the experience she fell senseless. Her family gathered. She was lying rigidly, hardly breathing. They knew that for some time she had

15

6. **Catalepsy:** a condition characterized by a lack of awareness of, or responsiveness to, one's surroundings.

had dreams of a special character which indicated a shamanistic calling, dreams of escaping grizzly bears, falling off cliffs or trees, or of being surrounded by swarms of yellow-jackets. The community knew therefore what to expect. After a few hours the woman began to moan gently and to roll about upon the ground, trembling violently. She was supposed to be repeating the song which she had been told to sing and which during the trance had been taught her by the spirit. As she revived, her moaning became more and more clearly the spirit's song until at last she called out the name of the spirit itself, and immediately blood oozed from her mouth.

When the woman had come to herself after the first encounter with her spirit, she danced that night her first initiatory shaman's dance. For three nights she danced, holding herself by a rope that was swung from the ceiling. On the third night she had to receive in her body her power from the spirit. She was dancing, and as she felt the approach of the moment she called out, 'He will shoot me, he will shoot me.' Her friends stood close, for when she reeled in a kind of cataleptic seizure, they had to seize her before she fell or she would die. From this time on she had in her body a visible materialization of her spirit's power, an icicle-like object which in her dances thereafter she would exhibit, producing it from one part of her body and returning it to another part. From this time on she continued to validate her supernatural power by further cataleptic demonstrations, and she was called upon in great emergencies of life and death, for curing and for divination and for counsel. She became, in other words, by this procedure a woman of great power and importance.

It is clear that, far from regarding cataleptic seizures as blots upon the family escutcheon[7] and as evidences of dreaded disease, cultural approval had seized upon them and made of them the pathway to authority over one's fellows. They were the outstanding characteristic of the most respected social type, the type which functioned with most honour and reward in the community. It was precisely the cataleptic individuals who in this culture were singled out for authority and leadership.

The possible usefulness of 'abnormal' types in a social structure, provided they are types that are culturally selected by that group, is illustrated from every part of the world. The shamans of Siberia dominate their communities. According to the ideas of these peoples, they are individuals who by submission to the will of the spirits have been cured of a grievous illness—the onset of the seizures—and have acquired by this means great supernatural power and incomparable vigour and health. Some, during the period of the call, are violently insane for several years; others irresponsible to the point where they have to be constantly watched lest they wander off in the snow and freeze to death; others ill and emaciated to the point of death, sometimes with bloody sweat. It is the shamanistic practice which constitutes their cure, and the extreme exertion of a Siberian séance leaves them, they claim, rested and able to enter immediately upon a similar performance. Cataleptic seizures are regarded as an essential part of any shamanistic performance. . . .

7. **Escutcheon:** coat of arms, here used to mean reputation.

It is clear that culture may value and make socially available even highly unsta- 20
ble human types. If it chooses to treat their peculiarities as the most valued variants
of human behaviour, the individuals in question will rise to the occasion and perform their social rôles without reference to our usual ideas of the types who can make
social adjustments and those who cannot. Those who function inadequately in any
society are not those with certain fixed 'abnormal' traits, but may well be those whose
responses have received no support in the institutions of their culture. The weakness of these aberrants is in great measure illusory. It springs, not from the fact that
they are lacking in necessary vigour, but that they are individuals whose native
responses are not reaffirmed by society. They are, as Sapir[8] phrases it, 'alienated from
an impossible world.'

The person unsupported by the standards of his time and place and left naked to
the winds of ridicule has been unforgettably drawn in European literature in the figure of Don Quixote. Cervantes turned upon a tradition still honoured in the abstract
the limelight of a changed set of practical standards, and his poor old man, the orthodox upholder of the romantic chivalry of another generation, became a simpleton.
The windmills with which he tilted were the serious antagonists of a hardly vanished world, but to tilt with them when the world no longer called them serious was
to rave. He loved his Dulcinea in the best traditional manner of chivalry, but another
version of love was fashionable for the moment, and his fervour was counted to him
for madness. . . .

We have been considering individuals from the point of view of their ability to
function adequately in their society. This adequate functioning is one of the ways
in which normality is clinically defined. It is also defined in terms of fixed symptoms, and the tendency is to identify normality with the statistically average. In practice this average is one arrived at in the laboratory, and deviations from it are defined
as abnormal.

From the point of view of a single culture this procedure is very useful. It shows
the clinical picture of the civilization and gives considerable information about its
socially approved behaviour. To generalize this as an absolute normal, however, is a
different matter. As we have seen, the range of normality in different cultures does
not coincide. Some, like Zuñi and the Kwakiutl, are so far removed from each other
that they overlap only slightly. The statistically determined normal on the Northwest Coast would be far outside the extreme boundaries of abnormality in the
Pueblos. The normal Kwakiutl rivalry contest would only be understood as madness
in Zuñi, and the traditional Zuñi indifference to dominance and the humiliation of
others would be the fatuousness of a simpleton in a man of noble family on the
Northwest Coast. Aberrant behaviour in either culture could never be determined

---

8. **Sapir:** Edward Sapir (1884–1939) was a lin-
guist and a close friend of Ruth Benedict. He is
best known for his contribution to the Sapir-

Whorf hypothesis, which claims that people's
ways of understanding the world are strongly
shaped by the structure of their language.

in relation to any least common denominator of behaviour. Any society, according to its major preoccupations, may increase and intensify even hysterical, epileptic, or paranoid symptoms, at the same time relying socially in a greater and greater degree upon the very individuals who display them.

This fact is important in psychiatry because it makes clear another group of abnormals which probably exists in every culture: the abnormals who represent the extreme development of the local cultural type. This group is socially in the opposite situation from the group we have discussed, those whose responses are at variance with their cultural standards. Society, instead of exposing the former group at every point, supports them in their furthest aberrations. They have a licence which they may almost endlessly exploit. For this reason these persons almost never fall within the scope of any contemporary psychiatry. They are unlikely to be described even in the most careful manuals of the generation that fosters them. Yet from the point of view of another generation or culture they are ordinarily the most bizarre of the psychopathic types of the period.

The Puritan divines of New England in the eighteenth century were the last persons whom contemporary opinion in the colonies regarded as psychopathic. Few prestige groups in any culture have been allowed such complete intellectual and emotional dictatorship as they were. They were the voice of God. Yet to a modern observer it is they, not the confused and tormented women they put to death as witches, who were the psychoneurotics of Puritan New England. A sense of guilt as extreme as they portrayed and demanded both in their own conversion experiences and in those of their converts is found in a slightly saner civilization only in institutions for mental diseases. They admitted no salvation without a conviction of sin that prostrated the victim, sometimes for years, with remorse and terrible anguish. It was the duty of the minister to put the fear of hell into the heart of even the youngest child, and to exact of every convert emotional acceptance of his damnation if God saw fit to damn him. It does not matter where we turn among the records of New England Puritan churches of this period, whether to those dealing with witches or with unsaved children not yet in their teens or with such themes as damnation and predestination, we are faced with the fact that the group of people who carried out to the greatest extreme and in the fullest honour the cultural doctrine of the moment are by the slightly altered standards of our generation the victims of intolerable aberrations. From the point of view of a comparative psychiatry they fall in the category of the abnormal.

In our own generation extreme forms of ego-gratification are culturally supported in a similar fashion. Arrogant and unbridled egoists as family men, as officers of the law and in business, have been again and again portrayed by novelists and dramatists, and they are familiar in every community. Like the behaviour of Puritan divines, their courses of action are often more asocial than those of the inmates of penitentiaries. In terms of the suffering and frustration that they spread about them there is probably no comparison. There is very possibly at least as great a degree of mental warping. Yet they are entrusted with positions of great influence and importance and are as a rule fathers of families. Their impress both upon their own children and upon the structure of our society is indelible. They are not described in our manuals of psychiatry because they are supported by every tenet of our civilization. They are sure of themselves in real life in a way that is possible only to those who are oriented to the points of the compass laid down in their own culture. Nevertheless a future psychiatry may well ransack our novels and letters and public records for illumination upon a type of abnormality to which it would not otherwise give credence. In every society it is among this very group of the culturally encouraged and fortified that some of the most extreme types of human behaviour are fostered.

Social thinking at the present time has no more important task before it than that of taking adequate account of cultural relativity. In the fields of both sociology and psychology the implications are fundamental, and modern thought about contacts of peoples and about our changing standards is greatly in need of sane and scientific direction. The sophisticated modern temper has made of social relativity, even in the small area which it has recognized, a doctrine of despair. It has pointed out its incongruity with the orthodox dreams of permanence and ideality and with the individual's illusions of autonomy. It has argued that if human experience must give up these, the nutshell of existence is empty. But to interpret our dilemma in these terms is to be guilty of an anachronism. It is only the inevitable cultural lag that makes us insist that the old must be discovered again in the new, that there is no solution but to find the old certainty and stability in the new plasticity. The recognition of cultural relativity carries with it its own values, which need not be those of the absolutist philosophies. It challenges customary opinions and causes those who have been bred to them acute discomfort. It rouses pessimism because it throws old formulae into confusion, not because it contains anything intrinsically difficult. As soon as the new opinion is embraced as customary belief, it will be another trusted bulwark of the good life. We shall arrive then at a more realistic social faith, accepting as grounds of hope and as new bases for tolerance the coexisting and equally valid patterns of life which mankind has created for itself from the raw materials of existence.

UNDERSTANDING THE TEXT

1. According to Benedict, what is the relationship between the individual and society? Should the concepts of "individual" and "society" be opposite or separate? How does the individual factor into the concept of society, and vice versa?

2. What relationship between the individual and culture does Benedict reject? Why does she believe individuals wrongly assume that their culture is against them? What does Benedict state concerning the average person's perception of laws and authority and other instruments of culture?

3. Does Benedict argue that people are locked into a fate dictated by the boundaries of their culture? Does her interpretation of culture allow room

for individuals to express themselves? Why, according to Benedict, do some people see anthropology as "a counsel of despair"? Does she agree?

4. What happens, in Benedict's analysis, to people within a culture whose natural inclinations are not valued by that culture? What kinds of people does your own culture perceive in this way?

5. How does Benedict argue by analogy throughout the selection? How does she employ examples and counterexamples to prove her thesis?

6. Why does Benedict bring up homosexuality? How have different cultures perceived homosexual relationships? How did Benedict's culture perceive such relationships?

7. What kind of people does Benedict identify as the "psychopathic types of the period"? What historical examples can you cite of people who were extremely successful in their own cultures but would be considered crazy today? Try to name someone who is extremely successful today but would probably be considered crazy by other cultures.

8. What does Benedict mean by "cultural relativity"? Why does she believe that it is important to view cultures through a relativistic lens?

Making Connections

1. How does Benedict's view of human nature compare with other views presented in this chapter? Would she agree, for example, that the various biological factors outlined by Wilson (p. 144) are universal to the human condition? How much of the behavior others have ascribed to "human nature" would Benedict describe as "culturally conditioned"?

2. How might Benedict respond to Hobbes's concept (p. 119) of a "state of nature" in which no cultural rules influenced human behavior? Is such a state possible, in Benedict's view?

3. Compare Benedict's view of culture with Margaret Mead's in "Warfare: An Invention—Not a Biological Necessity" (p. 274). What assumptions about human nature is each anthropologist working from?

4. In other chapters of *Patterns of Culture*, Benedict argues that the environment in which a culture develops strongly influences its values. She suggests, for example, that the Dobu are extremely competitive because they live in an area where food is scarce and that the Zuñi have no taboos against female adultery because their villages have traditionally had fewer women than men. How do such arguments show the influence of Darwin's principle of natural selection (p. 405)?

5. How does Benedict's analysis of traditional cultures from the outside compare with the analyses of N. Scott Momaday (p. 516) and Chinua Achebe (p. 506), who actually belong to the cultures that they write about? Is it possible for a writer to view another culture without any biases or preconceived notions? Why or why not?

WRITING ABOUT THE TEXT

1. Imagine you are an anthropologist from another planet examining the "primitive" culture of Americans. Write an essay describing American values and social institutions from the perspective of such an observer.

2. How has your culture shaped you? What are some things you do, say, or believe that have directly resulted from the society you were born into? What tenets of your society have you rejected? How does your personal nature work within the standards of your society? Write an essay reflecting on these questions.

3. Write a rebuttal to Benedict's assertion that other cultures should be observed without an imposition of the observer's values. Would it be possible, or even wise, for you to view such cultural practices as slavery, cannibalism, human sacrifice, or female genital mutilation from a value-neutral perspective?

4. Compare Benedict's view of human nature to Hobbes's (p. 119) or Wilson's (p. 144). Explain what elements of a human being would be considered "natural" by one of these writers and "cultural" by Benedict.

Edward O. Wilson
The Fitness of Human Nature
(1998)

IN HIS LONG CAREER as a teacher, writer, and researcher, Edward Osborn Wilson (b. 1929) has become one of America's most renowned, and controversial, scientists. Trained as an entomologist, Wilson's early work on ants and other social insects helped to explain why these creatures act in ways that humans consider altruistic. His 1971 book *The Insect Societies* remains a classic in the field of entomology. In 1990, Wilson teamed with German scientist Bert Hölldobler (b. 1936) to produce *The Ants*, an encyclopedic, 740-page analysis of ant behavior that won the 1991 Pulitzer Prize.

After years of scholarly work on the biological basis of insect society, Wilson began to explore ways that biology influences social behavior in other species, including human beings. In his 1976 book *Sociobiology*, he examined biologically based social interaction throughout the animal kingdom. The final chapter explores ways that natural selection might have influenced such human traits as love, loyalty, friendship, and faith. *Sociobiology* ignited a firestorm of controversy across the political spectrum. Conservatives denounced Wilson for assaulting the dignity of human beings by explaining our most cherished beliefs in biological terms. Progressives, on the other hand—led by Wilson's Harvard University colleagues Stephen Jay Gould and Richard Lewontin—felt that Wilson's ideas opened the door to racist and sexist beliefs about the nature of human beings, a charge that Wilson vehemently denied.

In 1979, Wilson received a second Pulitzer Prize for his book *Human Nature*, which advances the ideas about human evolution that he set forth in *Sociobiology*. Over the past thirty years, sociobiological ideas have become increasingly accepted by natural and social scientists alike. Current disciplines such as evolutionary psychology, evolutionary anthropology, population genetics, and even Darwinian literary criticism all trace their core ideas back to Wilson's initial work on sociobiology.

The selection here is taken from Wilson's 1998 book *Consilience: The Unity of Knowledge*. The word *consilience* means "jumping together," and Wilson uses this concept to frame his argument that a correct understanding of human biology—and of natural selection—can unify all branches of knowledge into a single, coherent area of study. By understanding the way that our minds evolved, Wilson believes, we can form better and more useful ideas about psychology, sociology, economics, politics, art, music, literature, religion, and any other area of study that involves human beings.

Wilson builds his argument in this chapter on a simple deductive proposition: if the process of natural selection has determined all complex biological functions, and the human brain contains complex biological function, then natural selection must have determined the operations of the human brain. 🖑

W HAT IS HUMAN NATURE? It is not the genes, which prescribe it, or culture, its ultimate product. Rather, human nature is something else for which we have only begun to find ready expression. It is the epigenetic rules,[1] the hereditary regularities of mental development that bias cultural evolution in one direction as opposed to another, and thus connect the genes to culture. . . .

By expressing gene-culture coevolution in such a simple manner, I have no wish either to overwork the metaphor of the selfish gene[2] or to minimize the creative powers of the mind. After all, the genes prescribing the epigenetic rules of brain and behavior are only segments of giant molecules. They feel nothing, care for nothing, intend nothing. Their role is simply to trigger the sequences of chemical reactions within the highly structured fertilized cell that orchestrate epigenesis. Their writ extends to the levels of molecule, cell, and organ. . . . The brain is a product of the very highest levels of biological order, which are constrained by epigenetic rules implicit in the organism's anatomy and physiology. Working in a chaotic flood of environmental stimuli, it sees and listens, learns, plans its own future. By that means the brain determines the fate of the genes that prescribed it. Across evolutionary time, the aggregate choices of many brains determine the Darwinian fate of everything human—the genes, the epigenetic rules, the communicating minds, and the culture.

Brains that choose wisely possess superior Darwinian fitness, meaning that statistically they survive longer and leave more offspring than brains that choose badly. That generalization by itself, commonly telescoped into the phrase "survival of the fittest," sounds like a tautology—the fit survive and those who survive are fit—yet it expresses a powerful generative process well documented in nature. During hundreds of millennia of Paleolithic history, the genes prescribing certain human epigenetic rules increased and spread at the expense of others through the species by means of natural selection. By that laborious process human nature assembled itself.

1. **Epigenetic rules:** In biology, "epigenetic" refers to a change in an organism that takes place without a change in the underlying DNA. Wilson uses the term "epigenetic rule" to refer to a set of instructions passed through the genes that triggers some kind of response when certain environmental conditions are met. The human ability to learn language, for example, is a consequence of an epigenetic rule. People do not inherit any knowledge of a specific language, but they are born with the ability to acquire language at a very young age if they are in a language-saturated environment.

2. **Selfish gene:** *The Selfish Gene* is a 1976 book by Richard Dawkins that argues for a gene-centered view of evolution. The "selfish gene" metaphor does not refer to a gene for selfish behavior, but to a view of natural selection that sees each gene in the body as a "replicator," whose primary function is to make copies of itself that survive into the next generation. Genes that contribute to an organism's ability to survive and reproduce achieve this end. The "selfish gene" theory of evolution is at odds with the organism-centered view of evolution, held by Stephen Jay Gould and others, which sees the whole organism, rather than individual genes, as the primary unit affected by natural selection.

What is truly unique about human evolution, as opposed say to chimpanzee or wolf evolution, is that a large part of the environment shaping it has been cultural. Therefore, construction of a special environment is what culture does to the behavioral genes. Members of past generations who used their culture to best advantage, like foragers gleaning food from a surrounding forest, enjoyed the greatest Darwinian advantage. During prehistory their genes multiplied, changing brain circuitry and behavior traits bit by bit to construct human nature as it exists today. Historical accident played a role in the assembly, and there were many particular expressions of the epigenetic rules that proved self-destructive. But by and large, natural selection, sustained and averaged over long periods of time, was the driving force of human evolution. Human nature is adaptive, or at least was at the time of its genetic origin. . . .

To take behavioral genes into account therefore seems a prudent step when assess-   5
ing human behavior. Sociobiology (or Darwinian anthropology, or evolutionary psychology, or whatever more politically acceptable term one chooses to call it) offers a key link in the attempt to explain the biological foundation of human nature. By asking questions framed in evolutionary theory, it has already steered research in anthropology and psychology in new directions. Its major research strategy in human studies has been to work from the first principles of population genetics and reproductive biology to predict the forms of social behavior that confer the greatest Darwinian fitness. The predictions are then tested with data taken from ethnographic archives and historical records, as well as from fresh field studies explicitly designed for the purpose. Some of the tests are conducted on preliterate and other traditional societies, whose conservative social practices are likely to resemble most closely those of Paleolithic ancestors. A very few societies in Australia, New Guinea, and South America in fact still have stone-age cultures, which is why anthropologists find them especially interesting. Other tests are conducted with data from modern societies, where fast-evolving cultural norms may no longer be optimally fit. In all these studies a full array of analytic techniques is brought to bear. They include multiple competing hypotheses, mathematical models, statistical analysis, and even the reconstruction of the histories of memes and cultural conventions by the same quantitative procedures used to trace the evolution of genes and species.

In the past quarter-century, human sociobiology has grown into a large and technically complex subject. Nevertheless, it is possible to reduce its primary evolutionary principles to some basic categories, which I will now briefly summarize.

Kin selection is the natural selection of genes based on their effects on individuals carrying them plus the effects the presence of the genes has on all the genetic relatives of the individuals, including parents, children, siblings, cousins, and others who still live and are capable either of reproducing or of affecting the reproduction of blood relatives. Kin selection is especially important in the origin of altruistic behavior. Consider two sisters, who share half their genes by virtue of having the same father and mother. One sacrifices her life, or at least remains childless, in order to help her sister. As a result the sister raises more than twice as many children as she would have otherwise. Since half of her genes are identical to those of her generous sister, the loss in genetic fitness is more than made up by the altruistic nature of the sacrifice. If such actions are predisposed by genes and occur commonly, the genes can spread through the population, even though they induce individuals to surrender personal advantage.

From this simple premise and elaborations of it have come a wealth of predictions about patterns of altruism, patriotism, ethnicity, inheritance rules, adoption practices, and infanticide. Many are novel, and most have held up well under testing.

Parental investment is behavior toward offspring that increases the fitness of the latter at the cost of the parent's ability to invest in other offspring. The different patterns of investment have consequences for the fitness of the genes that predispose individuals to select the patterns. Choose one, and you leave more offspring; choose another, and you leave fewer offspring. The idea has given rise to a biologically based "family theory," spinning off new insights on sex ratios, marriage contracts, parent-offspring conflict, grief at the loss of a child, child abuse, and infanticide. . . .

Mating strategy is influenced by the cardinal fact that women have more at stake in sexual activity than men, because of the limited age span in which they can reproduce and the heavy investment required of them with each child conceived. One egg, to put the matter in elemental terms, is hugely more valuable than a single sperm, which must compete with millions of other sperm for the egg. The achievement of pregnancy closes off further breeding opportunity of the mother for a substantial fraction of her remaining reproductive life, whereas the father has the physical capacity to inseminate another woman almost immediately. With considerable success, the nuances of this concept have been used by scientists to predict patterns of mate choice and courtship, relative degrees of sexual permissiveness, paternity anxiety, treatment of women as resources, and polygyny (multiple wives, which in the past at least has been an accepted arrangement in three-quarters of societies around the world). The optimum sexual instinct of men, to put the matter in the now familiar formula of popular literature, is to be assertive and ruttish, while that of women is to be coy and selective. Men are expected to be more drawn than women to pornography and prostitution. And in courtship, men are predicted to stress exclusive sexual access and guarantees of paternity, while women consistently emphasize commitment of resources and material security.

Status is central to all complex mammal societies, humanity included. To say that people generally seek status, whether by rank, class, or wealth, is to sum up a large part of the catalogue of human social behavior. In traditional societies genetic fitness of individuals is generally but not universally correlated with status. In chiefdoms and despotic states especially, dominant males have easy access to multiple women and produce more children, often in spectacular disproportion. Throughout history, despots (absolute rulers with arbitrary powers of life and death over their subjects) commanded access to hundreds or even thousands of women. Some states used explicit rules of distribution, as in Inca Peru, where by law petty chiefs were given seven women, governors of a hundred people eight, leaders of a thousand people fifteen, and lords and kings no fewer than seven hundred. Commoners took what was left over. The fathering of children was commensurately lopsided. In modern industrial states, the relationship between status and genetic fitness is more ambiguous. The data show that high male status is correlated with greater longevity and copulation with more women, but not necessarily the fathering of more children.

Territorial expansion and defense by tribes and their modern equivalents the nation states is a cultural universal. The contribution to survival and future reproductive potential, especially of tribal leaders, is overwhelming, and so is the warlike imperative of tribal defense. "Our country!" declared Commodore Stephen Decatur, hard-fighting hero of the War of 1812, "may she always be right; but our country, right or wrong." (Personal aggressiveness has its Darwinian limits, however; Decatur was killed in a duel in 1820.)

Biologists have determined that territoriality is not unavoidable during social evolution. It is apparently entirely absent in many animal species. The territorial instinct arises during evolution when some vital resource serves as a "density-dependent factor." That is, the growth of population density is slowed incrementally by an increasing shortage of food, water, nest sites, or the entire local terrain available to individuals searching for these resources. Death rates increase or birth rates decrease, or both, until the two rates come more or less into balance and population density levels off. Under such circumstances animal species tend to evolve territorial behavior. The theoretical explanation is that individuals hereditarily predisposed to defend private resources for themselves and their social group pass more genes on to the next generation.

In contrast, the growth of other species is not leveled off by limiting resources but by rising amounts of emigration, disease, or predation. When such alternative density-dependent factors are paramount, and resource control is therefore not required, territorial defense usually does not evolve as a hereditary response.

Humanity is decidedly a territorial species. Since the control of limiting resources has been a matter of life and death through millennia of evolutionary time, territorial aggression is widespread and reaction to it often murderous. It is comforting to say that war, being cultural in origin, can be avoided. Unfortunately, that bit of conventional wisdom is only a half truth. It is more nearly correct—and far more prudent—to say that war arises from both genes and culture and can best be avoided by a thorough understanding of the manner in which these two modes of heredity interact within different historical contexts.

Contractual agreement so thoroughly pervades human social behavior, virtually like the air we breathe, that it attracts no special notice—until it goes bad. Yet it deserves focused scientific research for the following reason. All mammals, including humans, form societies based on a conjunction of selfish interests. Unlike the worker castes of ants and other social insects, they resist committing their bodies and services to the common good. Rather, they devote their energies to their own welfare and that of close kin. For mammals, social life is a contrivance to enhance personal survival and reproductive success. As a consequence, societies of nonhuman mammalian species are far less organized than the insect societies. They depend on a combination of dominance hierarchies, rapidly shifting alliances, and blood ties. Human beings have loosened this constraint and improved social organization by extending kinshiplike ties to others through long-term contracts.

Contract formation is more than a cultural universal. It is a human trait as characteristic of our species as language and abstract thought, having been constructed from both instinct and high intelligence. Thanks to ground-breaking experiments by the psychologists Leda Cosmides and John Tooby at the University of California at Santa Barbara, we know that contract formation is not simply the product of a single rational faculty that operates equally across all agreements made among bargaining parties. Instead, one capacity, the detection of cheating, is developed to exceptional levels of sharpness and rapid calculation. Cheater detection stands out in acuity from mere error detection and the assessment of altruistic intent on the part of others. It is furthermore triggered as a computation procedure only when the cost and benefits of a social contract are specified. More than error, more than good deeds, and more even than the margin of profit, the possibility of cheating by others attracts attention. It excites emotion and serves as the principal source of hostile gossip and moralistic aggression by which the integrity of the political economy is maintained.

UNDERSTANDING THE TEXT

1. How does Wilson characterize the interaction between genes and culture— or, in the terms made familiar by earlier debates, between nature and nurture? How do "epigenetic rules" bridge the gap between these two sides?

2. According to Wilson, what role has natural selection played in the development of human psychology? Does he see any difference at all between the evolution of the mind and the evolution of the body?

3. How, according to Wilson, has human evolution been different from the evolution of any other species? What accounts for this key difference?

4. How have scientists such as Wilson gathered evidence for theories about human behavior in primitive conditions?

5. What does Wilson mean by the term "kin selection"? What evolutionary factors have led people to feel altruistic toward members of their own family?

6. What are the basic differences in mating strategies between males and females? How have these differences, according to Wilson, led to certain differences between male and female human nature?

7. Why, according to Wilson, are humans tribal and territorial? Are these traits that can be altered, or does Wilson present them as inherent parts of our psychological makeup? Explain.

8. What does Wilson say lies behind the human desire to cooperate and make agreements with other human beings? Why do we act altruistically toward people who are not closely related to us and do not therefore carry any of our genes?

MAKING CONNECTIONS

1. How does Wilson use the arguments of Charles Darwin in *Origin of Species* (p. 405)? Are his arguments about the evolution of human psychology consistent with Darwin's principles of evolution generally? Explain.

2. Do Wilson's theories tend to support Mencius's positive view of human nature (p. 94) or Hsün Tzu's more negative view (p. 100)? How might supporters of either of these theories appeal to biological or evolutionary evidence to support their claims?

3. How might biological evidence support or refute Thomas Hobbes's view of the state of nature as a state of perpetual war (p. 119)?

4. Would Wilson agree with Margaret Mead's view that warfare is a learned behavior rather than a biological imperative (p. 274)? What would Wilson single out as the basis of aggressive behavior in humans?

WRITING ABOUT THE TEXT

1. Compare or contrast Wilson's views on the interaction between nature and culture with those of Ruth Benedict in "The Individual and the Pattern of Culture" (p. 132).

2. Use Wilson's theories of human nature to suggest a reason that Stone Age people might have painted images in caves like "The Shaft of the Dead Man" (p. 86). What "epigenetic rules" might account for the desire to produce art?

3. Choose one of Wilson's categories of human behavior (kin selection, mating strategies, etc.) and use it as the basis for analyzing a book or a movie of your choice. You might, for example, examine the differences between male and female courtship strategies in a romantic comedy or the underlying reasons for violence in a war movie or historical epic.

4. Refute Wilson's argument that human behavior has a biological basis by arguing that humans don't behave as we would expect from the evolutionary factors that Wilson names. Include several examples in your response.

3

Law and Government

What Is the Role of Law and Government in Human Society?

... to bring about the rule of righteousness
in the land, to destroy the wicked and the evil-doers;
so that the strong should not harm the weak ...
                          —*Hammurabi's Code*

HAMMURABI'S CODE, the first known set of laws in history, was written in Babylon nearly thirty-eight hundred years ago, but its preface still sounds startlingly familiar. Before giving his list of laws, fines, and penalties, Hammurabi, the king of Mesopotamia and founder of the Babylonian Empire, states the purpose of his Code: "to bring about the rule of righteousness in the land, to destroy the wicked and the evil-doers; so that the strong should not harm the weak; so that I should rule over the black-headed people like Shamash, and enlighten the land, to further the well-being of mankind." We need make only a few surface changes in this and it sounds like the stated purpose of the Constitution of the United States, as set forth in its famous Preamble: to "establish justice, insure domestic tranquility, provide for the common defense, promote the general welfare, and secure the blessings of liberty to ourselves and our posterity." Many of the ideal functions of law and government have remained remarkably constant over the course of recorded history.

The fact that one of the oldest writings in history is a fully developed legal code testifies to the inseparability of law and civilization. According to social contract theorists (such as Thomas Hobbes, whose work *Leviathan* is excerpted in the previous chapter), society begins when people band together to protect themselves from conquest and their property from theft. Only societies with established laws, and with the governmental power necessary to enforce these laws, can provide the protection that people seek.

Two early readings in the chapter give very different views of the purpose of government from two of history's greatest civilizations. The first of these comes from Lao Tzu's *Tao te Ching*, a work of ancient Chinese philosophy. Written during a time of civil war and great upheaval, the *Tao te Ching* presents good government as the result of aggressive non-action. The forces of the universe act independently of human striving, Lao Tzu insists, and the role of government is to recognize and adapt to these forces rather than to alter or direct them. In "Perfect Associations and Perfect Rulers," the Muslim philosopher al-Farabi, writing during the golden age of Islamic society, argues that government requires virtuous rulers—a position very similar to that of the Chinese philosophy of Confucianism that the *Tao te Ching* positioned itself against.

Among the Western readings included in this chapter are complementary excerpts from Christine de Pizan's *The Treasure of the City of Ladies* and Niccolò Machiavelli's *The Prince*, both written toward the end of the Middle Ages in Europe. In these texts, Christine and Machiavelli focus on effective leadership, that is, on the practical nature of governing rather than on its moral aspects. This is especially true of Machiavelli, whose name, since the publication of *The Prince*, has been inextricably associated with cynical, opportunistic, amoral political maneuvering. Such maneuvering is often viewed in connection with *realpolitik* (from the German, meaning "realistic politics" or "the politics of reality"), politics based on practicality and not ideals or ethics.

One reading from early modern China highlights the difficulties that arise when governments and societies encounter each other on the international stage. In the early part of the nineteenth century, English merchants purchased highly desirable Chinese goods—such as tea, silk, and perfume—with the profits they made from opium produced in British India and sold illegally throughout China. Lin Tse-hsü, a Chinese official charged with stamping out the opium trade, wrote a letter to Queen Victoria asking her to force her subjects to obey the laws of the Chinese Empire. Though his pleas were unsuccessful, he raised many of the issues that would later become vital to the creation of international law.

Martin Luther King Jr.'s "Letter from Birmingham City Jail" describes the philosophy of "civil disobedience," or the belief that one is not obliged to submit to an unjust law. However, rather than proposing revolution—that is, a violent renegotiation of the social contract—King argues that even while refusing to obey an unjust law, one should respect legal authority by accepting the consequences of that disobedience. This argument, driven by King's passionate commitment to it, became the driving force of America's civil rights movement in the 1960s.

A commitment to peaceful reform also animates the final two readings of this chapter. The first of these comes from Burmese democracy advocate Aung San Suu Kyi, who was elected prime minister in an open election and then put under house arrest by a military dictatorship. She has remained under house arrest in Burma for most of the last twenty years but has refused to abandon her commitment to non-violence and peaceful reform. The second comes from Archbishop Desmond Tutu, a South African democracy advocate during the apartheid era who played a major role in his country's transition to democracy.

The two images in this chapter prompt questions about law and government. A portion of the Papyrus of Ani, itself drawn from the ancient Egyptian Book of the Dead, depicts the judgment of a soul in the afterworld. As a man is presented before the gods, his heart is weighed against a feather drawn from the wings of the goddess of truth and justice. How fair to the "accused," we must wonder, was this process? A frame from Leni Riefenstahl's movie *The Triumph of the Will*, which celebrates Adolf Hitler and the Nazi Party, forces us to ponder the transformation of law and government into the very mechanism by which the strong dominate, humiliate, and destroy the weakest members of a society. As Martin Luther King Jr. reminds us, "We can never forget that everything Hitler did in Germany was 'legal' and everything the Hungarian freedom fighters did in Hungary was 'illegal.'" The potential for serious abuse in any government structure makes it imperative for people to keep trying to answer the crucial questions about law and government, justice and citizenship, that are presented only briefly in this chapter.

The Papyrus of Ani
(circa 1240 BCE)

THE PAPYRUS OF ANI is one of the most spectacular examples ever uncovered of the ancient Egyptian Book of the Dead. This "book" consisted of a collection of texts that were copied onto long scrolls of papyrus, which were then buried with people to help them make their way into the afterlife. The spells, incantations, drawings, and declarations on the scrolls were designed to provide a guide for the ordeals that, the Egyptians believed, awaited a soul after death. This particular papyrus, which is more than seventy-eight feet long, was found in the ancient Egyptian capital city of Thebes (which should not be confused with the Greek city of the same name) and was purchased by the British Museum in 1888. E. A. Wallis Budge (1857–1934), a museum curator and legendary Egyptologist, translated the papyrus into English in 1895.

Very little is known about the subject of the papyrus, a scribe and nobleman named Ani. On the scroll, he bears three different titles: "Royal Scribe Veritable," "Scribe and Accountant of the Divine Offerings," and "The Governor of the Granary of the Lords of Abydos." Taken together, these titles suggest that Ani was in charge of revenues (probably in the form of grain) collected by the king on behalf of the gods. Though this would seem to be an important function, it is difficult to judge Ani's stature from the preserved papyrus, since we do not have other complete examples from the period to compare it to. But scholars have discovered enough references to other versions of the Book of the Dead to know that the Papyrus of Ani gives an accurate picture of Egyptian funerary and religious practices of the time.

The scene depicted here, the most famous portion of the papyrus, is the judgment of Ani. The drawing on the left shows Ani being led into the Hall of Judgment by his wife. In the Hall are a number of deities who have gathered to observe the ceremony. Anubis, the jackal-headed guide of the dead, is testing the balance of a scale. The scale weighs Ani's heart against an ostrich feather from the crown of Maat, the goddess of truth and justice. A heart heavy with sin will tip the balance of the scale, but a pure heart (a clear conscience) will balance perfectly with the demands of justice. Thoth, the judge of the dead, stands by to record the results. If Ani is judged worthy, Thoth will conduct him to the chamber of Osiris, the god of the underworld. If he is judged unworthy, he will be devoured by Amemet—part lion, part crocodile, and part hippopotamus—who stands behind Thoth.

The hieroglyphics surrounding the scene contain the "Negative Confession," a declaration of innocence consisting of forty-two statements that deny specific misdeeds. Though the actual denials differ in various versions of the Book of the Dead, there are always forty-two (though some denials are made more than once). This declaration gives us a clear picture of the kinds of laws and values that structured ancient Egyptian society.

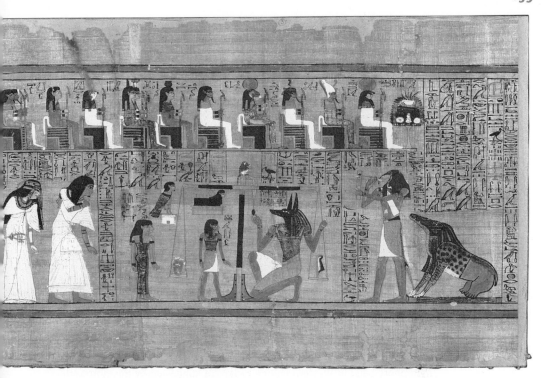

The Papyrus of Ani, circa 1240 BCE (painted papyrus).
British Museum, London, UK / Bridgeman Art Library
See p. C-2 in the color insert for a full-color reproduction of this image.

The Negative Confession

1. I have not done iniquity.
2. I have not robbed with violence.
3. I have not stolen.
4. I have done no murder; I have done no harm.
5. I have not defrauded offerings.
6. I have not minished oblations.[1]
7. I have not plundered the god.
8. I have spoken no lies.
9. I have not snatched away food.
10. I have not caused pain.
11. I have not committed fornication.
12. I have not caused shedding of tears.
13. I have not dealt deceitfully.
14. I have not transgressed.
15. I have not acted guilefully.
16. I have not laid waste the ploughed land.
17. I have not been an eavesdropper.
18. I have not set my lips in motion [against any man].
19. I have not been angry and wrathful except for a just cause.

---

1. **Minished oblations:** held back offerings to the gods.

20. I have not defiled the wife of any man.
21. I have not defiled the wife of any man.
22. I have not polluted myself.
23. I have not caused terror.
24. I have not transgressed.
25. I have not burned with rage.
26. I have not stopped my ears against the words of Right and Truth.
27. I have not worked grief.
28. I have not acted with insolence.
29. I have not stirred up strife.
30. I have not judged hastily.
31. I have not been an eavesdropper.
32. I have not multiplied words exceedingly.
33. I have done neither harm nor ill.
34. I have never cursed the king.
35. I have never fouled the water.
36. I have not spoken scornfully.
37. I have never cursed God.
38. I have not stolen.
39. I have not defrauded the offerings of the gods.
40. I have not plundered the offerings to the blessed dead.
41. I have not filched the food of the infant; neither have I sinned against the god of my native town.
42. I have not slaughtered with evil intent the cattle of the god.

Understanding the Text

1. Why is the judgment of Ani portrayed as the weighing of his heart? What metaphors used in Western culture today are suggested by this portrayal? Why does Ani's heart need only to balance, and not tip, the scale?

2. Why is the judgment scene so public? What about the nature of justice is suggested by a public, rather than a private, judicial accounting?

3. Why are all of the statements that Ani must make to justify himself *negative* statements, or statements of what he did *not* do? Why does he not state the good things that he has done? What might be implied here about the nature and limits of judicial proceedings?

4. What facts about ancient Egyptian culture can you infer from this view of justice, the gods, and the afterlife? How might you apply this same logic to another, perhaps contemporary culture?

Making Connections

1. Compare the "Negative Confession" with the declaration required by the South African Truth and Reconciliation Commission described by Desmond Tutu (p. 227). Why do both tribunals require a full disclosure of past events?

2. What conclusions can you draw about the ancient Egyptian religion from the drawing and the "Negative Confession"? How do the implied codes of conduct for this religion compare to those of other religious traditions?

3. Compare the treatment of death here with the morbid celebrations described by Octavio Paz in "The Day of the Dead" (p. 345). What does each culture's view of death suggest about the culture's values?

4. What might it say about ancient Egyptian culture that only the wealthy few were allowed to enter the afterworld with the benefits supposedly provided by the Book of the Dead?

WRITING ABOUT THE TEXT

1. Explore the importance of a culture's perception of death. Examine the beliefs about death, taboos surrounding death, and funerary customs of your own culture or a culture that you are familiar with and relate those ideas and practices to the culture's worldview.

2. Consider the understanding of the law's purpose behind the "Negative Confession." Why do laws generally attempt to discourage undesirable behavior rather than encourage desirable behavior?

3. Examine the scale as a metaphor for law. Why has this symbol persisted in cultures from the ancient Egyptians' to our own?

Lao Tzu
from the *Tao te Ching*
(600–400 BCE)

WHEN THE MIGHTY Chou Dynasty collapsed, in about 770 BCE, ancient China dissolved into seven small states. Between 475 and 221 BCE, these states fought furiously with each other, each attempting to reunify China under its banner. This "Period of Warring States" was also, not coincidentally, a golden age of Chinese political thought. Hundreds of philosophers, representing dozens of different schools of thought, emerged during this time to propose answers to the burning question of the day: what is the best system of government under which we can reunify China?

Of all of the proposed solutions, however, none was as simple—or as radical—as that offered by the Taoists: maybe, they suggested, China should not be unified. If nature or fate had divided the old empire into separate states, then why not let them remain separate? This political philosophy is consistent with the founding text of Taoism, the *Tao te Ching*.

Very little is known about the origin of this short collection. Some of the verses appear to have been engraved on stones as early as 300 BCE, but not until the Han Dynasty (206 BCE–220 CE) was the *Tao te Ching* referred to in other texts. However, authorship of the volume is traditionally attributed to an ancient sage, Lao Tzu ("the Old Master," or "the Old Boy"), around 600 BCE. According to the legend, Lao Tzu, disgusted with the Chinese and their inability to learn, planned to ride off forever on a yak. On his way out of town, he hastily wrote the *Tao te Ching* to give his disciples something to remember him by.

The overall argument of the *Tao te Ching* is that human beings constitute a small part of a much larger whole, referred to as "the Tao," or "the Way." Humans cannot change the Way; it goes on with or without our presence. We can, however, work to bring our lives in accordance with its principles. For the Taoist, the world is a great river, and we are all floating on rafts. We can spend our efforts trying to row upstream, making ourselves miserable in the process, or we can relax, make sure that our raft points downstream, and enjoy wherever the river takes us. As a political philosophy, Taoism translates into a minimal approach to governing. Rulers lead most successfully when they give up ambition; they should not make changes simply for the sake of making changes; and they should govern in a way that works with, rather than against, the natural order of the universe.

The *Tao te Ching*'s rhetorical style combines two major strategies: short, declarative statements and intentional contradictions. The first of these strategies creates memorable phrases, while the second, much like the Hegelian dialectic, forces us to create our own reconciliations of the supposed contradictions. 🍃

17

In ancient times
The people knew that they had rulers.
Then they loved and praised them,
Then they feared them,
Then they despised them.

The rulers did not trust the people,
The people did not trust the rulers.

The rulers were grave, their words were precious.
The people having finished their work,
    and brought it to a successful issue, said:—
        "We are sufficient in ourselves."[1] . . .

19

If the people renounce self-control and reject wisdom,
Let them gain simplicity and purity.

If the people renounce duty to man and reject right conduct,
Let them return to filial piety deep, deep in the heart.

If they renounce skill and leave off search for profit,
Let them rob and by violence take possession of spiritual life.

These three things do not help our progress.
Therefore now let us seek
To perceive simplicity,
To conserve beauty in the heart,
To curb selfishness and to have few desires. . . .

29

If you desire to gain the kingdom by action,
I see that you will not succeed.
The kingdom is a spiritual vessel,
It cannot be gained by action.
He who acts, destroys it. ✣
He who grasps, loses it. ✣

The translator's footnotes have been omitted. The original title of the translation, *Tao Teh King*, has been changed to the more familiar *Tao te Ching*. The Chinese word *tao* has generally been rendered as "the Way," and "Teh" has been rendered as "Te" throughout.

1. **"We are sufficient in ourselves":** that is, "We did not need the ruler." According to Lao Tzu, the actions of the most effective leaders are not even noticed by the people, who see them as simply the results of nature.

Therefore behold the animals:
>   Some go in front, others follow;
>   Some are warm, others are cold;
>   Some are strong, others are feeble;
>   Some keep moving, others are still.

That is why the self-controlled man
>   puts away excess,
>   he puts away egotism,
>   he puts away easy living.

30

He who would help a Ruler of men by the Way
Does not take soldiers to give strength to the kingdom.
His service is well rewarded.

Where troops dwell, there grow thorns and briers.
After great wars, there follow bad years.

He who loves, bears fruit unceasingly,
He does not dare to conquer by strength.
He bears fruit, but not with assertiveness,
He bears fruit, but not with boastfulness,
He bears fruit, but not with meanness,
He bears fruit, but not to obtain it for himself,
He bears fruit, but not to shew his strength.

Man is great and strong, then he is old,
In this he is not of the Way.
If he is not of the Way
He quickly will perish. . . .

33

He who knows men is wise,
He who knows himself can see clearly.

He who conquers men has strength,
He who conquers himself has power.

He who knows that he has enough is rich,
He who acts with energy has a strong will.

He who fails not to find the Self shall endure,
He who dies, but does not perish, shall endure for ever. . . .

35

Hold fast the idea of "The Great,"
Then all men will be drawn to you.
They will come to you and receive no hurt,
But rest, peace and great calm.

When you provide music and exquisite food
The traveller will stay with you gladly.
When the Way flows out from you to him
By his palate he does not detect its savour,
By his eyes he cannot perceive it,
By his ears he cannot hear it,
But in using it he finds it to be inexhaustible.

36

If you desire to breathe deeply,
     you must first empty the lungs.
If you desire to be strong,
     you must first learn to be weak.
If you desire to be in a lofty position,
     you must first learn to take a lowly position.
If you desire to be enriched by gifts,
     you must first give away all that you have.
This is called concealment and enlightenment.

The soft overcomes the hard.
The weak overcomes the strong.
Fish cannot swim safely in shallow waters.
The secrets of government of a kingdom
     should not be revealed to the people. . . .

38

To assume virtue without being really virtuous
     is to be virtuous from duty;
To be less virtuous, yet not to lose real virtue,
     is to be virtuous from Inner Life.

Supreme virtue comes through activity of Inner Life;
     then let us actively seek Inner Life.
To be less virtuous and to practise it,
     let us be active in the performance of duty.

To assume benevolence and practise it
    let us actively seek Inner Life.
To assume right conduct and practise it
    let us be active in the performance of duty.
To assume expediency and practise it is to find that no one honours it;
    then it bares the arm, and asserts itself by force.

Therefore, when the Way is lost, follow Virtue;
    when virtue is lost, follow benevolence;
    when benevolence is lost, follow right conduct;
    when right conduct is lost, follow expediency.

Those who are Masters of expediency
    have in the heart only the shadow of faith,
    and in the mind only confusion.

Those who are Leaders of politeness
    have only the husk of the Way,
    which is the source of ignorance.

That is why the greatest of the Masters
    abide in the real,
    they do not abide in the shadow.
They hold to the fruit,
    they do not hold to the husk.
Therefore they put away the latter
    and take hold of the former. . . .

46

When the Way was manifested to men,
Horses were used for cultivating the fields.

When the Way was hid within Itself,
War horses were reared on the frontiers.

There is no sin greater than desire,
There is no misfortune greater than discontent,
There is no calamity greater than the wish to acquire,
Therefore to be satisfied is an everlasting sufficiency. . . .

49

The Heart of the self-controlled man
    is always in the Inner Kingdom.
He draws the hearts of all men into his Heart.

If a man is good, he blesses him;
If a man is not good, still he blesses him with the Blessing of Te.[2]
If a man is faithful, he is faithful to him;
If a man is not faithful, still he is faithful to him with the Faithfulness of Te.

The self-controlled man dwells in the world.
Patiently and persistently
He brings the whole world into active community of Heart.

All men turn their ears and their eyes towards him.
They are all the children of the self-controlled man. . . .

57

To govern a kingdom, use righteousness.
To conduct a war, use strategy.
To be a true world-ruler, be occupied with Inner Life.

How do I know that this is so?
By this:—
  The more restrictive the laws,
    the poorer the people.
  The more machinery used,
    the more trouble in a kingdom.
  The more clever and skilful the people,
    the more do they make artificial things.
  The more the laws are in evidence,
    the more do thieves and robbers abound.

That is why the self-controlled man says:—
  If I act from Inner Life
    the people will become transformed in themselves.
  If I love stillness
    the people will become righteous in themselves.
  If I am occupied with Inner Life
    the people will become enriched in themselves.
  If I love the Inner Life
    the people will become pure in themselves.

---

2. **Te:** in the philosophy of the *Tao te Ching*, the counterpart of "Tao." Whereas "Tao" is the universal way of nature, "Te" is the ability of an individual to live according to the "Tao." "Te" is normally translated into English as either "virtue" or "power," and it contains elements of both concepts.

58

If the government is from the heart
    the people will be richer and richer.
If the government is full of restrictions
    the people will be poorer and poorer.

Miserable! you rely upon coming happiness.
Happy! you crouch under dread of coming misery.
You may know the end from the beginning.

If a ruler is in line with Inner Life
    his strategy will come right,
    his bad luck will become good,
    and the people will be astonished.
    Things have been so for a long time.

That is why the self-controlled man
    is just and hurts no one,
    is disinterested and does no wrong,
    is true and takes no licence;
    he shines, and offends not by his brightness. . . .

60

Govern a great State
As you would cook a small fish (do it gently).

When the Way is manifest in the world
Evil spirits have no power.

When evil spirits have no power
They cannot hurt men.

Evil spirits cannot hurt men.
The self-controlled man does not hurt men.
The Master also does not hurt men.
Therefore they unite in manifesting Te. . . .

61

A great kingdom, lowly like running water,
    is the Meeting-place of the world.
It is the feminine quality of the world.

The feminine quality always overcomes the
    masculine by stillness.

In order to be still, we must become lowly.

Therefore, if a great kingdom is lowly towards a little kingdom
    it will take possession of the little kingdom.
If a little kingdom is lowly towards a great kingdom
    it will take possession of the great kingdom.
So the one becomes lowly in order to conquer,
The other is lowly and yet it conquers.

If a great kingdom only desires to unify and nourish men,
If a small kingdom only desires to enter in and serve men,
Then the Master, in each case, shall obtain his desire.

He who is great ought to be lowly. . . .

62

He who has the Way is the refuge of all beings.
He is the treasure of the good man,
He is the support of the man who is not good.

Beautiful words through the Way gain power,
Man by following it gains steadfastness in action,
But, by the evil man, its possession is ignored.

The Son of Heaven sits enthroned,
His three Ministers are appointed.
One carries in his hand a tablet of jade;
Another is followed by a mounted retinue.
But the one who is most valued
    sits quietly, and offers as his gift the Way.

How was the Way prized by men of Old?
Daily they sought for it.
They found it, hid within the Self.
It gives a way of escape to the guilty.
Therefore it is prized by all men. . . .

65

Of Old, he who was active in the Way
    did not use it to make people enlightened,
    but to make them more kind.

If people are difficult to govern
    it is because they have too much knowledge.

Therefore if you govern a kingdom by knowledge,
    you will be an oppressor of the kingdom.

But if you govern a kingdom by wisdom,
    you will give happiness to the kingdom.

If you know and do these things
    you will be a pattern for men.
Knowledge of how to be always a pattern for men
    is called profound Te.

Profound Te is in the very source of life,
    it pervades the utmost limits of life,
    it returns and dwells in every being.

When fully manifested,
    it unites all beings in a great harmony.

66

The Rivers and the Seas (because they seek a lowly place)
    are Lords of a hundred valleys.
Let your love flow, seek a lowly place,
    you will be Lord of a hundred valleys.

That is why
    if the self-controlled man desires to exalt the people,
    in his speech he must take a lowly place;
    if he desires to put the people first,
    he must put himself after them.

Thus, though he dwells above them,
    the people are not burdened by him.
Though he is placed before them,
    the people are not obstructed by him,

Therefore men serve him gladly,
    they do not tire in serving him.
Because he does not strive,
    no one in the world can strive against him. . . .

74

If the people do not fear death,
How then can you frighten them by death?

But if you cause the people continually to fear death,
And if one of them becomes a great criminal,
Can you take hold of him and slay him?

Would you dare to do this?
There is always one, the Executioner, who kills men.

But, on the contrary, if you kill as if you were Executioner,
It would be as if you tried to do the work of a Master Carpenter.

In attempting to do the work of a Master Carpenter,
Few there be who do not wound their own hands.

75

The people are hungry.
Because they who are over the food tax it heavily
That is why the people are hungry.

The people are difficult to govern.
Because the rulers trust in possessions and activities,
That is why the people are difficult to govern.

The people make light of death.
Because they work hard in order to save their life,
That is why they make light of death.

A Master indeed is he whose life-activities are from within.
He excels all men in his appreciation of Life. . . .

79

To harmonise great enemies
We must possess that which far surpasses enmity.

We must be able to be at peace
In order to be active in Love.

That is why the self-controlled man
   holds the left-hand portion of the contract,
   but does not insist upon the other man producing his portion.

He who is virtuous may rule by a contract,
He whose virtue is within may rule by destroying it.

Akin to the Way is Inner Life.
A constant giver is the man who loves.

80

Take a small kingdom and few people,
Cause ten or a hundred of them to carry weapons,
But not to use them.

Cause the people to fear death,
Do not let them travel far,
Though they may have boats and carriages,
Let them use them only within the kingdom.
Though they may have soldiers in uniform,
Let them parade only within the kingdom.
Cause the people again to have knotted cords,
And to use them (instead of the written character).

Their food would be sweet,
Their clothing would be beautiful in their own eyes,
Their dwellings would be resting-places,
They would love simple ways.

If another kingdom were so near
That they could hear the sounds of dogs and fowls,
They would not come into mutual contact
Until they all grew old and died. . . .

UNDERSTANDING THE TEXT

1. How does paradox function in the *Tao te Ching*? What is the rhetorical effect of presenting concepts as integrally connected to their opposites? What overall philosophy does this support?

2. Why does Lao Tzu advocate a leader who shows no ambition and takes no action? Is it always necessary for a leader to act, or is it possible to be a good leader by simply allowing things to happen on their own?

3. What does Lao Tzu mean by "the Inner Life"? In what contexts does he generally employ this phrase? How is it related to "the Way"?

4. Why is having too many desires presented as a crime? How would having desires make following the *Tao te Ching*'s other suggestions difficult? According to the *Tao te Ching*, what makes desire the root of all unrest?

5. Which qualities does Lao Tzu label as "feminine"? Which does he label as "masculine"? How do these two sets of qualities interact?

6. What does it mean for a ruler to take the "lower position"? What metaphors does Lao Tzu use to get this point across?

Making Connections

1. How does Lao Tzu's view of government differ from Mach[iavelli's?] What are the major differences between the ideal Taoist r[uler and Mach]avellian "Prince"?

2. For many centuries, Taoism and Confucianism have repr[esented the two] poles of Chinese thought: while Confucians attempt to c[ontrol human] nature through rigid adherence to rites and rituals, Taoi[sts believe it] cannot be controlled or restrained. With these ideas in mind, compare the passages from the *Tao te Ching* with the selection by either Mencius (p. 94) or Hsün Tzu (p. 100).

3. In what ways might the *Tao te Ching* have influenced Sun Tzu's *The Art of War* (p. 256)?

4. Can you detect in the *Tao te Ching* an environmentalist ethic? Would a contemporary environmentalist, such as Rachel Carson (p. 419) or David Suzuki (p. 427), agree with Lao Tzu's opinion that the natural world should simply be left alone? Explain.

5. How do Lao Tzu's ideas about the role of the ruler contrast with those of al-Farabi in "Perfect Associations and Perfect Rulers" (p. 170)? Would Lao Tzu agree that a good ruler must be a virtuous person? Explain?

Writing about the Text

1. To explore the political philosophy of the *Tao te Ching*, choose a contemporary government and imagine the changes it would have to make in order to follow Taoist principles.

2. Analyze the paradox of "leading without doing anything." Explain how a leader could be effective simply by allowing a natural flow rather than by making changes or inventing programs.

3. The translation of the *Tao te Ching* included here is from 1922. Try modernizing one passage, using your own words. Is it possible to use contemporary language and examples and still preserve the meaning?

4. Refute or support the *Tao te Ching*'s assertion that desires are disastrous, using historical examples to back up your argument. How does desire relate to ambition? How would Lao Tzu view ambition within government?

Abu Nasr al-Farabi
Perfect Associations and Perfect Rulers
(circa 900 CE)

THE ARAB SCIENTIST and philosopher Abu Nasr al-Farabi (870–950 CE) was born
in Turkestan during what is called the "Golden Age of Islam," a time when the Muslim religion spread from Spain to India and when Islamic scholars, scientists, mathematicians, and jurists shone. He spent much of his life in Baghdad with other
scholars and intellectuals. Like da Vinci and the "Renaissance men" of fifteenth-
century Europe, al-Farabi was accomplished in nearly all of the important branches
of knowledge of his day. He wrote more than 100 treatises on subjects such as music,
logic, philosophy, physics, politics, and religion.

Like many other Islamic philosophers of his day, al-Farabi was an avid student of
both Plato and Aristotle. One of his most important influential works, in fact, was an
extensive analysis of the work of both philosophers. Al-Farabi was one of a group of
philosophers in Baghdad who worked on creating a synthesis between Aristotelian
thought and Muslim theology. This mode of thought dominated Islamic philosophy
for several hundred years until it was categorically denounced as un-Islamic in al-
Ghazālī's enormously influential work *The Incoherence of the Philosophers* (circa 1095).

Unlike most of the contemporaries, al-Farabi often veered away from theology and
metaphysics and wrote about more practical sociological and political issues. The
work in which this selection appears, *On the Perfect State*, is one of the Islamic world's
earliest and best-known works of political philosophy. Al-Farabi modeled this work
on Plato's *Republic*, which also purports to describe the perfect state. Unlike Plato's
republic, however, al-Farabi's perfect state was a theocracy whose rulers were not
only educated in philosophy, but were also exemplary Muslims.

In "Perfect Associations and Perfect Rulers," al-Farabi uses the common metaphor
of the political state as a single body, with every member playing a distinct role in
its healthy operation. The ruler, al-Farabi insists, is the heart of the state and must
meet a long list of ideal characteristics. The twelve characteristics he identifies are
drawn from both Greek philosophy and Islamic theology. But like Plato, al-Farabi is
describing an unobtainable ideal rather than a realistic personality for a ruler.

Al-Farabi advances his argument in two distinct ways. In the first half of the selection, he argues from an extended analogy, comparing a state to a human body. In the
second half, he simply lists the traits that a perfect leader should possess. 🍃

IN ORDER TO PRESERVE HIMSELF and to attain his highest perfections every human
being is by his very nature in need of many things which he cannot provide all by
himself. He is indeed in need of people who each supply him with some particular

need of his. Everybody finds himself in the same relation to everybody in this respect. Therefore man cannot attain the perfection, for the sake of which his inborn nature has been given to him, unless many societies of people who co-operate come together who each supply everybody else with some particular need of his, so that as result of the contribution of the whole community all the things are brought together which everybody needs in order to preserve himself and to attain perfection. Therefore human individuals have come to exist in great numbers, and have settled in the inhabitable region of the earth, so that human societies have come to exist in it, some of which are perfect, others imperfect. . . .

The excellent city resembles the perfect and healthy body, all of whose limbs co-operate to make the life of the animal perfect and to preserve it in this state. Now the limbs and organs of the body are different and their natural endowments and faculties are unequal in excellence, there being among them one ruling organ, namely the heart, and organs which are close in rank to that ruling organ, each having been given by nature a faculty by which it performs its proper function in conformity with the natural aim of that ruling organ. Other organs have by nature faculties by which they perform their functions according to the aims of those organs which have no intermediary between themselves and the ruling organ; they are in the second rank. Other organs, in turn, perform their functions according to the aim of those which are in the second rank, and so on until eventually organs are reached which only serve and do not rule at all.

The same holds good in the case of the city. Its parts are different by nature, and their natural dispositions are unequal in excellence: there is in it a man who is the ruler, and there are others whose ranks are close to the ruler, each of them with a disposition and a habit through which he performs an action in conformity with the intention of that ruler; these are the holders of the first ranks. Below them are people who perform their actions in accordance with the aims of those people; they are in the second rank. Below them in turn are people who perform their actions according to the aims of the people mentioned in the second instance, and the parts of the city continue to be arranged in this way, until eventually parts are reached which perform their actions according to the aims of others, while there do not exist any people who perform their actions according to their aims; these, then, are the people who serve without being served in turn, and who are hence in the lowest rank and at the bottom of the scale. . . .

The ruling organ in the body is by nature the most perfect and most complete of the organs in itself and in its specific qualification, and it also has the best of everything of which another organ has a share as well; beneath it, in turn, are other organs which rule over organs inferior to them, their rule being lower in rank than the rule of the first and indeed subordinate to the rule of the first; they rule and are ruled.

In the same way, the ruler of the city is the most perfect part of the city in his specific qualification and has the best of everything which anybody else shares with him; beneath him are people who are ruled by him and rule others.

The heart comes to be first and becomes then the cause of the existence of the other organs and limbs of the body, and the cause of the existence of their faculties in them and of their arrangement in the ranks proper to them, and when one of its organs is out of order, it is the heart which provides the means to remove that disorder. In the same way the ruler of this city must come to be in the first instance, and will subsequently be the cause of the rise of the city and its parts and the cause of the presence of the voluntary habits of its parts and of their arrangement in the ranks proper to them; and when one part is out of order he provides it with the means to remove its disorder.

The parts of the body close to the ruling organ perform of the natural functions, in agreement—by nature—with the aim of the ruler, the most noble ones; the organs beneath them perform those functions which are less noble, and eventually the organs are reached which perform the meanest functions. In the same way the parts of the city which are close in authority to the ruler of the city perform the most noble voluntary actions, and those below them less noble actions, until eventually the parts are reached which perform the most ignoble actions. The inferiority of such actions is sometimes due to the inferiority of their matter, although they may be extremely useful—like the action of the bladder and the action of the lower intestine in the body; sometimes it is due to their being of little use; at other times it is due to their being very easy to perform. This applies equally to the city and equally to every whole which is composed by nature of well-ordered coherent parts: they have a ruler whose relation to the other parts is like the one just described. . . .

The ruler of the excellent city cannot just be any man, because rulership requires two conditions: (a) he should be predisposed for it by his inborn nature, (b) he should have acquired the attitude and habit of will for rulership which will develop in a man whose inborn nature is predisposed for it. Nor is every art suitable for rulership; most of the arts, indeed, are rather suited for service within the city, just as most men are by their very nature born to serve. Some of the arts rule certain (other) arts while serving others at the same time, whereas there are other arts which, not ruling anything at all, only serve. Therefore the art of ruling the excellent city cannot just be any chance art, nor due to any chance habit whatever. For just as the first ruler in a genus cannot be ruled by anything in that genus—for instance the ruler of the limbs cannot be ruled by any other limb, and this holds good for any ruler of any composite whole—so the art of the ruler in the excellent city of necessity cannot be a serving art at all and cannot be ruled by any other art, but his art must be an art towards the aim of which all the other arts tend, and for which they strive in all the actions of the excellent city. . . .

But this state can only be reached by a man in whom twelve natural qualities are found together, with which he is endowed by birth. (1) One of them is that he should have limbs and organs which are free from deficiency and strong, and that they will make him fit for the actions which depend on them; when he intends to perform an action with one of them, he accomplishes it with ease. (2) He should by nature be good at understanding and perceiving everything said to him, and grasp it in his mind according to what the speaker intends and what the thing itself demands. (3) He should be good at retaining what he comes to know and see and hear and apprehend in general, and forget almost nothing. (4) He should be well provided with ready intelligence and very bright; when he sees the slightest indication of a thing, he should grasp it in the way indicated. (5) He should have a fine diction, his tongue enabling him to explain to perfection all that is in the recess of his mind. (6) He should be fond of learning and acquiring knowledge, be devoted to it and grasp things easily, without finding the effort painful, nor feeling discomfort about the toil which it entails. (7) He should by nature be fond of truth and truthful men and hate falsehood and liars. (8) He should by nature not crave for food and drink and sexual intercourse, and have a natural aversion to gambling and hatred of the pleasures which these pursuits provide. (9) He should be proud of spirit and fond of honour, his soul being by his nature above everything ugly and base, and rising naturally to the most lofty things. (10) Dirham and dinar[1] and the other worldly pursuits should be of little amount in his view. (11) He should by nature be fond of justice and of just people, and hate oppression and injustice and those who practice them, giving himself and others their due, and urging people to act justly and showing pity to those who are oppressed by injustice; he should lend his support to what he considers to be beautiful and noble and just; he should not be reluctant to give in nor should he be stubborn and obstinate if he is asked to do justice; but he should be reluctant to give in if he is asked to do injustice and evil altogether. (12) He should be strong in setting his mind firmly upon the thing which, in his view, ought to be done, and daringly and bravely carry it out without fear and weak-mindedness.

UNDERSTANDING THE TEXT

1. According to al-Farabi, how are people within a society connected to each other? What fact lies at the heart of this connection? How does al-Farabi use the body as a metaphor for the society?

2. Why does al-Farabi believe that a ruler must have "the best of everything"? Does this statement refer to the inborn qualities of a ruler or to his material possessions?

3. To what part of the body does al-Farabi compare the ruler of the state? Why?

4. Look at the twelve qualifications that al-Farabi prescribes for the ideal ruler. Are these qualifications that can be acquired, or must a person be born with them? Why do you say so? Do you agree that these qualifications are important for those who govern? Why or why not?

1. **Dirham and dinar:** currencies found in various Arab countries.

MAKING CONNECTIONS

1. How does al-Farabi's perfect ruler compare to Lao Tzu's sage (p. 158)? What is the primary difference between the two views of the ideal leader?

2. Compare al-Farabi's view of human beings in nature with that of Thomas Hobbes (p. 119). Would Hobbes agree with al-Farabi's assertion that human beings need each other to fulfill their needs? Why or why not? How might Buddhists such as Matthieu Ricard and Trinh Xuan Thuan (p. 435) view this connectedness?

3. Do you think al-Farabi's ideal ruler could survive in the political environment described by Machiavelli (p. 184)? What qualifications does the Machiavellian ideal ruler have that al-Farabi's does not? What difference would these qualifications make in a ruler's success?

4. Which of al-Farabi's qualities of the ideal ruler have to do with rhetorical or persuasive ability? How might Plato (p. 478) or Aristotle (p. 489) respond to his emphasis on these factors?

WRITING ABOUT THE TEXT

1. Divide al-Farabi's twelve qualities of the ideal ruler into three or four larger categories and explain which ones go into which categories, and why.

2. Choose one of al-Farabi's ideal qualities and a contemporary political figure. Does he or she display the ideal quality? How so? How might the presence or lack of this quality contribute to the figure's political successes or failures?

3. Refute al-Farabi's argument that a ruler must be superior to those that he rules. Consider contemporary government figures in your response.

4. Contrast the ideal ruler of an Islamic state in "Perfect Associations and Perfect Rulers" with the ideal ruler of a Buddhist state presented in Aung San Suu Kyi's "In Quest of Democracy" (p. 219).

Christine de Pizan
from *The Treasure of the City of Ladies*
(1405)

BORN IN VENICE, Christine de Pizan (circa 1365–circa 1430) spent much of her early life at the court of the French king Charles V, where her father was the court physician and an esteemed astrologer. She was married at a young age to a court official and had three children. When King Charles died, in 1380, her father and her husband lost their positions at court and much of their financial support. After the deaths of her father around 1387 and her husband around 1390, Christine found herself trying to raise her children without the advantage of position or money. She responded by writing poetry and dedicating it to the rich and powerful in hopes of attracting patronage—an occupation well established for men of her education and family background but almost unheard of for women. She succeeded nonetheless, becoming the first woman in the history of France to earn a living through her writing.

Within ten years, Christine had acquired a substantial following. Rather than continuing to write pleasant poems praising wealthy patrons, however, she turned to writing philosophy and social commentary. Her first book in this vein was *Letter to the God of Love* (1399), an attack on the immorality and misogyny of Guillaume de Lorris and Jean de Meun's *The Romance of the Rose*, one of the most popular French poems of the Middle Ages. In 1404, she wrote a utopian treatise, *The Book of the City of Ladies*, which was modeled partly on Augustine's *City of God*. *The Book of the City of Ladies* chronicled the historical oppression of women, defended the female sex against charges of inferiority, and imagined a city in which women were authors, inventors, rulers, and religious leaders and participated fully in the life of the community.

Whereas *The Book of the City of Ladies* addressed the world as it might have become, her follow-up, *The Treasure of the City of Ladies* (1405), sometimes called *The Book of the Three Virtues*, dealt with the world as it was. If the earlier book looked back to Augustine for its inspiration, the later book anticipated the work of Niccoló Machiavelli, whose advice to princes in 1513 lacked the soft edges, but not the essential pragmatism, of Christine's advice to queens, princesses, ladies of rank, and women of substantial fortunes. Christine argues that such women—and the way that they behave in public ceremonies and in private conversations with their husbands—are essential to the prosperity of the state.

Christine's rhetoric relies primarily on her ethos—both the ethos that she constructs in the text as a gentle, knowledgable participant in civic affairs and the ethos that she brings to the text as a poet and a noblewoman. 🖎

16. The Fifth Teaching of Prudence, which Is How the Wise Princess Will Try Her Best to be in Favour with, and Have the Good Wishes of, All Classes of Her Subjects.

As IT IS FITTING for the wise and prudent princess to wish to regulate her actions so that she seeks and follows all the paths that honour demands, she will want for this reason (which is the fifth teaching) to enjoy the favour of the clergy and to be on good terms with persons in religious orders, leaders of the Church, prelates and councillors, as well as the middle classes and even the common people. No one can be surprised that we say she should especially cultivate these people more than the barons and nobles. The reason for this is that we suppose that she already associates with barons and nobles, for it would be according to the common custom for her to be acquainted with them. She wishes to be in favour with the above-mentioned persons for two reasons.

The first is so that the good and devout will pray to God for her, and the second is that she may be praised by them in their sermons and homilies so that, if the need arises, their voices and words can be a shield and defence against the rumours and reports of her slanderous enemies and can negate them. By this strategy she will have more of her husband's love and also that of the common people, who will hear good things about their lady, and also she may be supported by the most powerful people in an emergency. She will find out which of the clerks and scholars, those in religious orders as well as others, will be the most useful and of the greatest authority and in whom and in whose word people place the most confidence. Those persons will inspire the others with confidence in her. She will speak to them all very amiably and want to have their advice and make use of it. She will sometimes ask them to dinner at her court, together with her confessor and the people of her chapel, who will all be honourable people. She will accord them great honour and will wish them to be honoured by her household, which is a very seemly thing, for truly those who are ennobled by learning ought to be honoured. She will do them all the good in her power and contribute to their colleges and monasteries.

Although almsgiving[1] should be done secretly (the reason for this is so that the person who gives them may not be puffed up with pride about it, for that is a mortal sin), if she did not feel any pride in her heart, it would be better to give publicly than in secret, because she would set a good example to others. Whoever does it in this frame of mind doubles her merit and does well. This wise lady who knows how

---

1. **Almsgiving:** making charitable contributions. According to Jesus's Sermon on the Mount, almsgiving should always be done in secret, so as to avoid public displays of charity that are designed to bring recognition to the giver. Matthew 6:2–3 states: "Therefore when thou doest thine alms, do not sound a trumpet before thee, as the hypocrites do in the synagogues and in the streets, that they may have glory of men. Verily I say unto you, They have their reward. But when thou doest alms, let not thy left hand know what thy right hand doeth."

to protect herself from this vice will indeed wish that the gifts and alms that she gives in this way will be known and recorded (if they are notable; such as for rebuilding churches and monasteries or some other necessary thing) in perpetual memory on tablets in their churches so that the people will pray to God for her. Or her name may appear on other lists of benefactors, or her gifts may be announced publicly. Others will follow her example and give similarly, and by their actions they will gain a good reputation. It may seem that she has a small streak of hypocrisy or that she is getting a name for it, yet it may be called a 'just hypocrisy', so to speak, for it strives towards good and the avoidance of evil. We do not mean that under cover of almsgiving they ought to commit evil deeds and sin, nor that great vanity ought to arise in their hearts. Certainly being 'hypocritical' in the cause of good will not offend any person who desires honour. We repeat that this kind of 'just hypocrisy' is almost necessary, especially to princes and princesses who must rule over others and to whom more reverence is due than to other people. As for that, it is written in the book of Valerius[2] that formerly princes claimed that they were descended from the gods so that their subjects would hold them in greater reverence and fear them more.

The wise lady will wish her husband's counsellors to think well of her, be they prelates, chancellors or others. She will command them to come to her. She will receive them honourably and speak to them intelligently. As best she can, she will try to be worthy of their great esteem. This approach will be valuable to her in several ways. They will praise her good sense and conduct, which they will regard as outstanding. If it happens that any envious person wishes to intrigue against her, they will not allow any decisions to be made to her prejudice. They will dissuade the prince if he has been misinformed by any other people. If she desired anything to be discussed in council they would be more friendly and favourable to her.

In addition, this lady will wish to have the good will of the clergy, who become   5
embroiled with the 'common causes' of the people, as we say in Paris, with advocates in Parliament and elsewhere. She will wish to see such defenders of causes on certain days, the leaders and principal men among them and the other most notable ones. She will confer with them amiably and want them to understand her honourable position. She will do this not so that she may speak to them from motives of vengeance, but so that they should perceive the effect of her conduct and great knowledge. To have such a custom can be valuable for the increase of her honour and praise. The reason for this is that she will wish all sorts and conditions of the legal fraternity, the leading citizens of towns and cities in her husband's jurisdiction, and also great merchants and even some of the most respectable artisans to come to her from time to time. She will welcome them warmly and try hard to be well regarded by them, so that if she were to have any difficulty and if she needed some ready money, these merchants, being well disposed towards her, would gladly help her. If

---

2. **Book of Valerius:** Valerius Antias was a Roman historian in the first century BCE.

she must borrow and if she wishes to honour her commitments, she ought to render payment without fail on the appointed day. If she always keeps her word sincerely and unswervingly, people will consequently believe in it.

While we have been telling in this chapter how the wise princess ought to be well regarded by her subjects, it could seem wrong to some readers to say such a pointless thing. They might think that it was not the princess's business to court her subjects, but rather she ought to command her pleasures boldly, and her subjects ought to obey and take pains to court *her* love and not the other way around, or otherwise they will not be subjects and she the mistress. But to this we will reply that, with no disrespect to the speakers, it is appropriate to do this, not only for princesses but for princes. There are many reasons, but we will discuss only two, for this matter could be enlarged upon much more. The first reason is that although the prince may be lord and master of his subjects, the subjects nevertheless make the lord and not the lord the subjects. They would very much more easily find someone who would take them on as subjects (if they wished to overthrow him) than he would find people who would receive him as lord! And for this reason, and also because he would not be able to overcome them by himself if they rebelled against him (and even if he then had the power to destroy them, he would forbear to do it), he must necessarily keep their affection, not by harshness but in such a way that from this love comes fear, or otherwise his authority is in peril. The common proverb is quite true that avers, 'There is no lord of a land who is hated by his men.' As for keeping their affection, truly one who sincerely wishes to be called 'lord' could do nothing more sensible, for he could have neither city nor fortress of such a great defensive strength and power as the love and benevolence of true subjects.

The other reason is that, supposing that the subjects feel good will towards the prince and princess, if they never have the courage to go freely to their rulers and if they have never been invited to do so, it would not be their place to begin. Therefore, the prince or princess ought to make the overture. It is perfectly natural for the subjects to celebrate this with great joy and consider themselves quite honoured by it. It ought to double their love and loyalty, and they will then find still more kindness from their rulers. Speaking on this subject, a wise man has said that there is nothing that wins over the hearts of a ruler's subjects more nor that draws them to their lord so much as when they find gentleness and kindness in him, such as is written of a good emperor who said that he wished to behave towards his subjects in such a manner that they themselves would desire him to be their emperor. Bearing this firmly in mind, the wise princess will sometimes invite the wives to visit her, and she will make them very welcome and speak to everyone so amiably that they will be very content and praise her wisdom. Her whole court will celebrate their lyings-in and the weddings of their children, and the princess will wish the women to be in the company of ladies and damsels. From all this she will acquire much love from all men and women. . . .

18. The Seventh Teaching Describes How the Wise Princess Will Keep a Careful Eye on Her Revenues and Finances and on the State of Her Court.

The seventh teaching of Prudence to the wise princess is that she will carefully look after her revenue and her expenditure, which not only princes and princesses ought to consider, but likewise all people who wish their lives to be regulated by wisdom. She herself will feel no shame in wishing to know the sum of her revenues or payments; on certain days she will have her collectors and the administrators of her finances do their accounts in her presence. She will want to know how the masters of her household govern their staffs, command their underlings and distribute food. In the same way the princess will want to be familiar with other departments of her court. She will want to know that all her officers, whether great or little, are prudent, lead a good life and are the true gentlemen that she takes them for. If she finds out the contrary, she will immediately dismiss them.

She will want to know what the household expenses are. She will want to know what has been bought for her out of her funds from merchants and from her subjects, and she will command that the bills be fully paid on a certain day, for she will certainly not want the curses or the ill will of creditors. She will wish to owe nothing; she will prefer to manage with less and to spend her money more moderately. She will not permit anyone to take anything from the people against their will or at an unfair price, and she will stipulate that her staff must pay promptly and not oblige the poor people of the villages and other places, at great expense and trouble, to come time and time again to deliver a memorandum of a debt to her private apartments or to her finance officers before they are paid. She will not want her treasurers or stewards to be liars, as is the common custom, nor to put the people off with hollow promises and one delay after another.

This wise lady will organize the management of her revenues in the following man- 10 ner. She will divide her income into five parts. The first will be the portion that she wants to devote to alms and give to the poor. The second part is her household expenses: she will know what the total amounts to—indeed, if need be, she should find out what it is and request her husband not to settle the accounts without involving her in the transaction. The third part is for payment to her officers and women servants. The fourth is for gifts to strangers or others who are particularly deserving of them. And the fifth part she will save and use when she decides to spend something on herself for jewels, gowns and other clothing. Each portion of the amount will be what she sees that she can afford according to her revenue. By means of this rule she will be able to keep her affairs orderly and without confusion, nor will she lack money to fulfill any of the above-mentioned items. For this reason she needs to have some ready money in reserve, and that would not be possible if she had indulged in lavish expenditure and waste.

In this manner the princess will be able to follow the above seven teachings of Prudence, with the other virtues. These things are not at all hard to do, but rather are agreeable and pleasant provided that she is sincere and that she had made something of a habit of them. The wise lady will be able to acquire glory, renown and great honour in this world and eventually in Paradise, which is promised to those who live virtuously.

19. How the Wise Princess Ought to Extend Largesse and Liberality.

As we have spoken at some length about the other virtues appropriate to princesses and we have touched only briefly on a suitable generosity in gifts outside her ordinary expenditure, and as it is out of the ordinary and is something about which a princess ought to be informed, we will now treat it at greater length.

The wise princess wishing to be without reproach will take special care that neither the vice of meanness and avarice may be seen in her, nor foolish generosity, which is no less a vice. Therefore, she will distribute these gifts with great discretion and prudence, for munificence is one of the things that most magnifies the reputation of great lords and ladies. John of Salisbury[3] proves this in *Polycraticus* (book three, chapter twenty-four) by demonstrating that the virtue of generosity is necessary for those who rule over public affairs. For example, Titus,[4] the noble emperor, acquired such renown through his generosity that he was known as the benefit, the relief and the help of all persons. He loved this virtue of largesse so much that the day he had not given any gift he could not be happy. In this way he acquired the general favour and love of everyone.

The wise lady will demonstrate her generosity like this: if she has the power to give, and she learns that some foreign gentlemen or other people have lost much of their wealth through long imprisonment or ransom or are suffering great penury, she will help them with her own resources very willingly and liberally as a matter of course, according to her ability. As largesse does not consist only in material gifts, as a wise man has said, but also in comforting words, she will comfort them with hopes for a better future. This comfort will perhaps do them as much good as, or even more good than, the money that she gives them, for it is very agreeable to any person when a prince or princess comforts him, even just in words.

If this lady sees any gentleman, be he knight or squire, of good courage who has a great desire to increase his honour but does not have much money to outfit himself properly, and if she sees that it is worth while to help him, the gentle lady will do so, for she has within her all good impulses for honour and gentility and for always encouraging noble and valiant actions. And thus in various situations that may arise 15

---

3. **John of Salisbury:** English philosopher and bishop of Chartres (1115 or 1120–1180). His *Polycraticus, or The Statesman's Book* was an important work of medieval political theory.

4. **Titus:** Roman emperor (39–81 CE) who gained fame by providing generous relief efforts after the city of Pompeii was destroyed by the eruption of Mount Vesuvius in 79 CE.

this lady will extend wise and well-considered largesse. And if any great lords give her presents or gifts she will reward the messengers so generously that they will have cause to rejoice. She will give more to foreigners than to other people so that in their country they may mention for generosity to their lords. She will want her stewards to deliver the gifts promptly. If great ladies give her presents, she will send them some of her jewels and fine things, but more generously. If a poor or simple person does her any service or kindly presents her with some curiosity, she will consider the abilities of the person and his or her social position and the importance of the service, or the value, beauty or novelty of the gift, according to the case. Whatever the remuneration is, she will give it so abundantly that the person will rejoice. Furthermore, she will receive the thing with such a delighted expression that it will be half the payment by itself.

She will certainly not do what we saw happen once, something that we thought was deplorable at a sophisticated court of a prince or princess. A person was summoned there who was considered wise, so that the court might hear and learn his knowledge. He attended the court several times and everyone felt greatly satisfied with his deeds and his counsel. As a result of his knowledge he did the ruler certain just, good and laudable services that were worthy of commendation and reward. At the same time another person frequented this same court who had the reputation of being a buffoon and was in the habit of entertaining the lords and ladies with jests and stories of what everyone was doing everywhere and with worthless chatter in the way of mockery and jokes. It was decided that they both be remunerated, and so gifts were given both to the person who was reputed to be wise and who had deserved them because of his knowledge and to the person reputed to be a fool who had done nothing but tell his jokes. A gift was given to this buffoon that was valued at forty *écus* and to the other a gift worth twelve *écus*. When we three sisters, Reason, Rectitude,[5] and Justice, saw this, we hid our faces with shame at seeing such improper valuation and such blind ignorance in a court that is supposed to be famous. We were ashamed not for the value of the gifts but for the relative esteem for the persons and their deeds. The wise princess will not behave in this way and will not have to do with foolish people or those who imitate the ways of this court. Neither will she have much time for worthless things, nor will she offer her gifts for them, but to the virtuous and to those who have done something worth while.

---

5. **Rectitude:** righteousness. Reason, Rectitude, and Justice are the three "goddess" figures at the heart of *The Book of the City of Ladies*.

UNDERSTANDING THE TEXT

1. What does Christine suggest a "wise and prudent" princess should do to establish and keep order in her kingdom? How do personal relations between royalty and subjects factor into government processes? How is amiability between the two classes important in maintaining order and peace?

2. Why does Christine advise princesses to give charitable contributions publicly if they can do so without pride? How does she use this formulation to get around the scriptural injunction to give alms in secret?

3. In what ways does Christine construct an ethos (pp. 608–11) that suggests both knowledge and trustworthiness? What other personal characteristics does her writing style suggest?

4. What role does Christine believe that a woman should play in her husband's government? Why is it important that "her husband's counsellors . . . think well of her"?

5. Are the aims of "the wise princess" completely selfish? Would her attempts to be "well regarded by her subjects" remain effective, even if they are motivated by self-interest? What are her reasons for "courting" her subjects? Is this reasoning sound?

6. Why is it important for a princess to understand household finances? What correlation does Christine suggest between a well-run household and a well-run state?

7. Why should a princess cultivate a reputation for generosity? What are the advantages of such a reputation, both to the state and to her personally?

MAKING CONNECTIONS

1. How does the advice that Christine gives to princesses compare with the advice that Niccoló Machiavelli gives to princes (p. 184)? Can *The Treasure of the City of Ladies* be considered realpolitik (p. 184)? Why or why not?

2. How does Christine believe that Christian principles should influence government? How do her views compare with those of another Christian thinker, Thomas Aquinas (p. 260)?

3. How does Christine's feminism compare with that of Mary Wollstonecraft (p. 35) and Gloria Anzaldúa (p. 527)? According to each thinker, what strategies can women in male-dominated societies use to make their voices heard?

WRITING ABOUT THE TEXT

1. Argue for or against Christine de Pizan's notion of "just hypocrisy." Is it possible to accomplish a noble end through evil means? Why or why not?

2. Compare the advice of Christine de Pizan and Niccolò Machiavelli (p. 184).

3. Write an essay arguing that Christine de Pizan should be considered a feminist, because she advocates an expanded role for women in public life, or an antifeminist, because she treats women as subordinate to their husbands.

4. Examine the role of appearance (versus reality) in *The Treasure of the City of Ladies*. Which, for Christine de Pizan, is more important: for a princess to be good or for a princess to be considered good?

Niccolò Machiavelli
from *The Prince*
(1513)

FOR NEARLY FIVE HUNDRED YEARS, Niccolò Machiavelli (1469–1527), his book *The Prince*, and the adjective "Machiavellian" have been associated with dishonesty, underhandedness, political maneuvering, and the philosophy that "the end justifies the means." These associations, while carrying an element of truth, have too often been used to dismiss one of the most perceptive works ever written about the way that power works in a political state.

Machiavelli was deeply concerned with the stability of governments, a natural result of the political climate of his native Italy. During his lifetime, Italy had no central government and was divided into city-states, which were constantly at war with each other. Machiavelli, a loyal Florentine, believed that Florence had the potential to unite the other Italian states under its banner.

His devotion to Florence led to a successful career in public service. At a young age, Machiavelli achieved distinction as a Florentine ambassador to the courts of Europe. He wrote a series of insightful reports on foreign governments and thus gained great influence with the government that he served; and he observed countless instances of the damaging effects of weak leaders, unstable governments, and revolutions, experiences that directly shaped the advice he gave to rulers in *The Prince*. Despite its modern reputation for advising ruthlessness, guile, and secrecy, *The Prince* was intended to help rulers work for good by staying in power longer—a stable government, Machiavelli argues, would be able to prevent the misery caused by warfare and civic unrest. Ironically, Machiavelli did not write *The Prince* until the Republic of Florence had fallen and been replaced by the powerful autocrat Lorenzo de' Medici (1449–1492). Machiavelli dedicated *The Prince* to the new ruler in an attempt to earn his favor, but he was unsuccessful and forced to retire.

The Prince begins with the premise that political power is exercised in the real world and must therefore take into account the unsavory characteristics of real human beings: ambition, cruelty, greed, gullibility, and incompetence. This approach to politics is now known as "realpolitik" and is more associated with Machiavelli than with any other figure in history.

Unlike almost every well-known political theorist who preceded him, Machiavelli does not attempt to instruct rulers how to be moral. He attempts, rather, to show them how to be effective—how to accumulate, exercise, and maintain power. For Machiavelli, this means that, at times, rulers must be cruel, dishonest, duplicitous, and manipulative. Those who loosen their holds on power and focus on enjoying the fruits of power or the luxury of position will not, in the long run, succeed—their principalities will experience misrule, even chaos.

Machiavelli's arguments are inductive in nature and generally proceed from historical examples. Throughout *The Prince*, Machiavelli studies the lives of successful leaders and from them generalizes the ideal qualities of princes. ✎

Chapter XV

CONCERNING THINGS FOR WHICH MEN, AND ESPECIALLY PRINCES, ARE PRAISED OR BLAMED

It REMAINS NOW to see what ought to be the rules of conduct for a prince towards subject and friends. And as I know that many have written on this point, I expect I shall be considered presumptuous in mentioning it again, especially as in discussing it I shall depart from the methods of other people. But, it being my intention to write a thing which shall be useful to him who apprehends it, it appears to me more appropriate to follow up the real truth of a matter than the imagination of it; for many have pictured republics and principalities which in fact have never been known or seen, because how one lives is so far distant from how one ought to live, that he who neglects what is done for what ought to be done, sooner effects his ruin than his preservation; for a man who wishes to act entirely up to his professions of virtue soon meets with what destroys him among so much that is evil.

Hence it is necessary for a prince wishing to hold his own to know how to do wrong, and to make use of it or not according to necessity. Therefore, putting on one side imaginary things concerning a prince, and discussing those which are real, I say that all men when they are spoken of, and chiefly princes for being more highly placed, are remarkable for some of those qualities which bring them either blame or praise; and thus it is that one is reputed liberal, another miserly, using a Tuscan[1] term (because an avaricious person in our language is still he who desires to possess by robbery, whilst we call one miserly who deprives himself too much of the use of his own); one is reputed generous, one rapacious; one cruel, one compassionate; one faithless, another faithful; one effeminate and cowardly, another bold and brave; one affable, another haughty; one lascivious, another chaste; one sincere, another cunning; one hard, another easy; one grave, another frivolous; one religious, another unbelieving, and the like. And I know that every one will confess that it would be most praiseworthy in a prince to exhibit all the above qualities that are considered good; but because they can neither be entirely possessed nor observed, for human conditions do not permit it, it is necessary for him to be sufficiently prudent that he may know how to avoid the reproach of those vices which would lose him his state; and also to keep himself, if it be possible, from those which would not lose him it; but this not being possible, he may with less hesita-

---

1. **Tuscan:** from Tuscany, the region in central Italy that includes Florence. **Liberal:** The term here means generous, rather than politically progressive.

tion abandon himself to them. And again, he need not make himself uneasy at incurring a reproach for those vices without which the state can only be saved with difficulty, for if everything is considered carefully, it will be found that something which looks like virtue, if followed, would be his ruin; whilst something else, which looks like vice, yet followed brings him security and prosperity.

Chapter XVI

CONCERNING LIBERALITY AND MEANNESS

Commencing then with the first of the above-named characteristics, I say that it would be well to be reputed liberal. Nevertheless, liberality exercised in a way that does not bring you the reputation for it, injures you; for if one exercises it honestly and as it should be exercised, it may not become known, and you will not avoid the reproach of its opposite. Therefore, any one wishing to maintain among men the name of liberal is obliged to avoid no attribute of magnificence; so that a prince thus inclined will consume in such acts all his property, and will be compelled in the end, if he wish to maintain the name of liberal, to unduly weigh down his people, and tax them, and do everything he can to get money. This will soon make him odious to his subjects, and becoming poor he will be little valued by anyone; thus, with his liberality, having offended many and rewarded few, he is affected by the very first trouble and imperilled by whatever may be the first danger; recognizing this himself, and wishing to draw back from it, he runs at once into the reproach of being miserly.

Therefore, a prince, not being able to exercise this virtue of liberality in such a way that it is recognized, except to his cost, if he is wise he ought not to fear the reputation of being mean, for in time he will come to be more considered than if liberal, seeing that with his economy his revenues are enough, that he can defend himself against all attacks, and is able to engage in enterprises without burdening his people; thus it comes to pass that he exercises liberality towards all from whom he does not take, who are numberless, and meanness towards those to whom he does not give, who are few.

We have not seen great things done in our time except by those who have been considered mean; the rest have failed. Pope Julius the Second was assisted in reaching the papacy by a reputation for liberality, yet he did not strive afterwards to keep it up, when he made war on the King of France; and he made many wars without imposing any extraordinary tax on his subjects, for he supplied his additional expenses out of his long thriftiness. The present King of Spain[2] would not have undertaken or conquered in so many enterprises if he had been reputed liberal. A prince, therefore, provided that he has not to rob his subjects, that he can

---

2. **Present King of Spain:** King Ferdinand II (1452–1516), who united the kingdoms of Castile and Aragon through his marriage to Isabella and defeated the last Islamic stronghold in Spain, the kingdom of Grenada. Ferdinand also commissioned Christopher Columbus's first expedition, thus paving the way for Spain's conquests of the New World.

defend himself, that he does not become poor and abject, that he is not forced to become rapacious, ought to hold of little account a reputation for being mean, for it is one of those vices which will enable him to govern.

And if any one should say: Caesar obtained empire by liberality, and many others have reached the highest positions by having been liberal, and by being considered so, I answer: Either you are a prince in fact, or in a way to become one. In the first case this liberality is dangerous, in the second it is very necessary to be considered liberal; and Caesar was one of those who wished to become pre-eminent in Rome; but if he had survived after becoming so, and had not moderated his expenses, he would have destroyed his government. And if anyone should reply: Many have been princes, and have done great things with armies, who have been considered very liberal, I reply: Either a prince spends that which is his own or his subjects' or else that of others. In the first case he ought to be sparing, in the second he ought not to neglect any opportunity for liberality. And to the prince who goes forth with his army, supporting it by pillage, sack, and extortion, handling that which belongs to others, this liberality is necessary, otherwise he would not be followed by soldiers. And of that which is neither yours nor your subjects' you can be a ready giver, as were Cyrus, Caesar, and Alexander; because it does not take away your reputation if you squander that of others, but adds to it; it is only squandering your own that injures you.

And there is nothing wastes so rapidly as liberality, for even whilst you exercise it you lose the power to do so, and so become either poor or despised, or else, in avoiding poverty, rapacious and hated. And a prince should guard himself, above all things, against being despised and hated; and liberality leads you to both. Therefore it is wiser to have a reputation for meanness which brings reproach without hatred, than to be compelled through seeking a reputation for liberality to incur a name for rapacity which begets reproach with hatred.

Chapter XVII

CONCERNING CRUELTY AND CLEMENCY, AND WHETHER IT IS BETTER TO BE LOVED THAN FEARED

Coming now to the other qualities mentioned above, I say that every prince ought to desire to be considered clement and not cruel. Nevertheless he ought to take care not to misuse this clemency. Cesare Borgia was considered cruel; notwithstanding, his cruelty reconciled the Romagna, unified it, and restored it to peace and loyalty.[3]

3. **Cesare Borgia:** The son of Rodrigo Borgia (1431–1503), who became Pope Alexander VI in 1492. Alexander was an intensely political pope, bent on increasing the power of the papacy and the extent of papal lands, and Cesare Borgia (1475 or 1476–1507) led a sustained attempt, with his father's help, to unify the central Italian states known as the **Romagna** into a single political entity. Machiavelli greatly admired Borgia, and some scholars have argued that he is the model "prince" that Machiavelli had in mind throughout the work.

And if this be rightly considered, he will be seen to have been much more merciful than the Florentine people, who, to avoid a reputation for cruelty, permitted Pistoia to be destroyed. Therefore a prince, so long as he keeps his subjects united and loyal, ought not to mind the reproach of cruelty; because with a few examples he will be more merciful than those who, through too much mercy, allow disorders to arise, from which follow murders or robberies; for these are wont to injure the whole people, whilst those executions which originate with a prince offend the individual only.

And of all princes, it is impossible for the new prince to avoid the imputation of cruelty, owing to new states being full of dangers. . . . Nevertheless he ought to be slow to believe and to act, nor should he himself show fear, but proceed in a temperate manner with prudence and humanity, so that too much confidence may not make him incautious and too much distrust render him intolerable.

Upon this a question arises: whether it be better to be loved than feared or feared than loved? It may be answered that one should wish to be both, but, because it is difficult to unite them in one person, it is much safer to be feared than loved, when, of the two, either must be dispensed with. Because this is to be asserted in general of men, that they are ungrateful, fickle, false, cowardly, covetous, and as long as you succeed they are yours entirely; they will offer you their blood, property, life, and children, as is said above, when the need is far distant; but when it approaches they turn against you. And that prince who, relying entirely on their promises, has neglected other precautions, is ruined; because friendships that are obtained by payments, and not by greatness or nobility of mind, may indeed be earned, but they are not secured, and in time of need cannot be relied upon; and men have less scruple in offending one who is beloved than one who is feared, for love is preserved by the link of obligation which, owing to the baseness of men, is broken at every opportunity for their advantage; but fear preserves you by a dread of punishment which never fails.

Nevertheless a prince ought to inspire fear in such a way that, if he does not win love, he avoids hatred; because he can endure very well being feared whilst he is not hated, which will always be as long as he abstains from the property of his citizens and subjects and from their women. But when it is necessary for him to proceed against the life of someone, he must do it on proper justification and for manifest cause, but above all things he must keep his hands off the property of others, because men more quickly forget the death of their father than the loss of their patrimony. Besides, pretexts for taking away the property are never wanting; for he who has once begun to live by robbery will always find pretexts for seizing what belongs to others; but reasons for taking life, on the contrary, are more difficult to find and sooner lapse. But when a prince is with his army, and has under control a multitude of soldiers, then it is quite necessary for him to disregard the reputation of cruelty, for without it he would never hold his army united or disposed to its duties.

Among the wonderful deeds of Hannibal[4] this one is enumerated: that having led an enormous army, composed of many various races of men, to fight in foreign lands, no dissensions arose either among them or against the prince, whether in his bad or in his good fortune. This arose from nothing else than his inhuman cruelty, which, with his boundless valour, made him revered and terrible in the sight of his soldiers, but without that cruelty, his other virtues were not sufficient to produce this effect. And shortsighted writers admire his deeds from one point of view and from another condemn the principal cause of them. That it is true his other virtues would not have been sufficient for him may be proved by the case of Scipio,[5] that most excellent man, not only of his own times but within the memory of man, against whom, nevertheless, his army rebelled in Spain; this arose from nothing but his too great forbearance, which gave his soldiers more licence than is consistent with military discipline. For this he was upbraided in the Senate by Fabius Maximus, and called the corrupter of the Roman soldiery. The Locrians were laid waste by a legate of Scipio, yet they were not avenged by him, nor was the insolence of the legate[6] punished, owing entirely to his easy nature. Insomuch that someone in the Senate, wishing to excuse him, said there were many men who knew much better how not to err than to correct the errors of others. This disposition, if he had been continued in the command, would have destroyed in time the fame and glory of Scipio; but, he being under the control of the Senate, this injurious characteristic not only concealed itself, but contributed to his glory.

Returning to the question of being feared or loved, I come to the conclusion that, men loving according to their own will and fearing according to that of the prince, a wise prince should establish himself on that which is in his own control and not in that of others; he must endeavour only to avoid hatred, as is noted.

Chapter XVIII

CONCERNING THE WAY IN WHICH PRINCES SHOULD KEEP FAITH

Everyone admits how praiseworthy it is in a prince to keep faith, and to live with integrity and not with craft. Nevertheless our experience has been that those princes who have done great things have held good faith of little account, and have known how to circumvent the intellect of men by craft, and in the end have overcome those who have relied on their word. You must know there are two ways of contesting, the one by the law, the other by force; the first method is proper to men, the second to

4. **Hannibal:** legendary Carthaginian general (247–183 BCE), who defeated the Romans in 218 BCE by leading an army of nearly forty thousand men across the Alps—a feat that no one believed possible—and catching the Romans completely off guard.
5. **Scipio:** the name of a Roman family that included two generals, father and son, who fought against Hannibal during the Second Punic War. Machiavelli refers here to the younger of the two, Scipio Africanus Major (236–184 or 183 BCE), the general who finally defeated Hannibal in 202 BCE.
6. **Legate:** assistant to a Roman general. **Locrians:** inhabitants of the ancient Greek region of Locris.

beasts; but because the first is frequently not sufficient, it is necessary to have recourse to the second. Therefore it is necessary for a prince to understand how to avail himself of the beast and the man. This has been figuratively taught to princes by ancient writers, who describe how Achilles and many other princes of old were given to the Centaur Chiron[7] to nurse, who brought them up in his discipline; which means solely that, as they had for a teacher one who was half beast and half man, so it is necessary for a prince to know how to make use of both natures, and that one without the other is not durable. A prince, therefore, being compelled knowingly to adopt the beast, ought to choose the fox and the lion; because the lion cannot defend himself against snares and the fox cannot defend himself against wolves. Therefore, it is necessary to be a fox to discover the snares and a lion to terrify the wolves. Those who rely simply on the lion do not understand what they are about. Therefore a wise lord cannot, nor ought he to, keep faith when such observance may be turned against him, and when the reasons that caused him to pledge it exist no longer. If men were entirely good this precept would not hold, but because they are bad, and will not keep faith with you, you too are not bound to observe it with them. Nor will there ever be wanting to a prince legitimate reasons to excuse this nonobservance. Of this endless modern examples could be given, showing how many treaties and engagements have been made void and of no effect through the faithlessness of princes; and he who has known best how to employ the fox has succeeded best.

But it is necessary to know well how to disguise this characteristic, and to be a great pretender and dissembler; and men are so simple, and so subject to present necessities, that he who seeks to deceive will always find someone who will allow himself to be deceived. One recent example I cannot pass over in silence. Alexander VI did nothing else but deceive men, nor ever thought of doing otherwise, and he always found victims; for there never was a man who had greater power in asserting, or who with greater oaths would affirm a thing, yet would observe it less; nevertheless his deceits always succeeded according to his wishes, because he well understood this side of mankind.

Therefore it is unnecessary for a prince to have all the good qualities I have enumerated, but it is very necessary to appear to have them. And I shall dare to say this also, that to have them and always to observe them is injurious, and that to appear to have them is useful; to appear merciful, faithful, humane, religious, upright, and to be so, but with a mind so framed that should you require not to be so, you may be able and know how to change to the opposite.

And you have to understand this, that a prince, especially a new one, cannot observe all those things for which men are esteemed, being often forced, in order to maintain the state, to act contrary to faith, friendship, humanity, and religion. Therefore it is

7. **Centaur Chiron:** In Greek mythology, Chiron the Centaur (half-horse, half-man) was a gifted tutor whose pupils included many heroes of ancient Greece, including Achilles, the great hero of the Trojan War.

necessary for him to have a mind ready to turn itself accordingly as th
ations of fortune force it, yet, as I have said above, not to diverge fr
can avoid doing so, but, if compelled, then to know how to set abo

For this reason a prince ought to take care that he never lets a
his lips that is not replete with the above-named five qualities, th
to him who sees and hears him altogether merciful, faithful, hun
religious. There is nothing more necessary to appear to have tha
inasmuch as men judge generally more by the eye than by the hand, because it
belongs to everybody to see you, to few to come in touch with you. Every one sees
what you appear to be, few really know what you are, and those few dare not oppose
themselves to the opinion of the many, who have the majesty of the state to defend
them; and in the actions of all men, and especially of princes, which it is not prudent to challenge, one judges by the result.

For that reason, let a prince have the credit of conquering and holding his state,
the means will always be considered honest, and he will be praised by everybody;
because the vulgar are always taken by what a thing seems to be and by what comes
of it; and in the world there are only the vulgar, for the few find a place there only
when the many have no ground to rest on.

One prince of the present time, whom it is not well to name, never preaches any-   20
thing else but peace and good faith, and to both he is most hostile, and either, if he
had kept it, would have deprived him of reputation and kingdom many a time.

Understanding the Text

1. Why must a prince "know how to do wrong"? What connection, if any, does
   Machiavelli see between ethics and politics?

2. How does Machiavelli justify being "miserly" as a leader? List the major reasons for this assertion: "And a prince should guard himself, above all things,
   against being despised and hated; and liberality leads you to both."

3. Why does Machiavelli reason that it is better for a prince to be feared than
   loved? How is cruelty a motivating force to keep order? What restraints does
   he put on inflicting fear? Why does he name these limits?

4. How does Machiavelli use the analogies of the fox and the lion as part of
   his argument? What qualities of a leader does each represent? How does
   the ideal leader combine these qualities?

5. Do you believe that Machiavelli is correct in his estimation that having a reputation for good character traits is actually better than having those character
   traits? What is the difference, in political terms, between reputation and reality?

6. Why are the historical references to past rulers important to Machiavelli's
   argument? What points of his argument concerning the essential duality of a
   leader do these stories illustrate?

Making Connections

1. How does Machiavelli employ the "just hypocrisy" argument that Christine de Pizan (p. 175) also proposes? Are the two operating from the same basic presumptions?

2. How does Machiavelli instruct princes to deal with the negative aspects of human nature, such as lust, greed, ambition, and dishonesty? How does he instruct princes to deal with the more positive aspects of human nature, such as trust, loyalty, and a willingness to believe in the good of others? Is it possible to deduce from *The Prince* a sense of Machiavelli's overall conception of human nature?

3. How does Machiavelli's pragmatism compare to that of Sun Tzu in *The Art of War* (p. 256)? The two types have often been grouped as examples of "win at any cost" thinking. Do you agree? Explain.

4. Does Machiavelli's approach to leadership suggest a kind of natural selection comparable to what Darwin saw in nature (p. 405)? Are political leaders subject to the same "survival of the fittest" rules that pervade the natural world? Why or why not?

Writing about the Text

1. Consider whether Machiavelli's idea that it is better for a ruler to be feared than loved applies to contemporary politics. Does the emergence of democracy in many parts of the world alter this equation? If so, how so? If not, why not?

2. Examine the underlying ethical structure of Machiavelli's argument that the goal of political stability justifies cruelty, deception, and hypocrisy. Do you believe that this is true? Do the peace and prosperity brought about by political stability justify the kind of leadership that Machiavelli proposes?

3. Compare the concepts of human nature in Hobbes's *Leviathan* (p. 119) with those in Machiavelli's *The Prince* (p. 184).

4. Rebut Machiavelli's argument that effective leadership requires duplicity. Cite examples of cases in which honesty and straightforwardness have produced strong and effective leaders.

5. Examine Machiavelli's use of historical examples. Is he ultimately writing a prescriptive argument (one that instructs rulers how they should exercise power most effectively) or a descriptive argument (one that simply describes how power has been exercised effectively in the past)?

Lin Tse-hsü
A Letter to Queen Victoria
(1839)

BETWEEN 1839 AND 1860, the British and Chinese Empires became involved in two trade disputes that are known collectively as the Opium Wars. As the name suggests, the root cause of both conflicts was opium—specifically, the Chinese desire to prevent British merchants from importing opium into China as payment for Chinese goods, like tea and silk, that were in great demand throughout the British Empire. Earlier in the seventeenth century, the British had purchased these products with either silver or British currency, but this activity had produced a huge trade deficit that threatened to cripple the British economy. The only way to reverse the deficit was to export British goods to China, but this enterprise was made difficult both by the low demand for British products and by the Chinese government's protectionist policies, which made it almost impossible for British merchants to penetrate Chinese markets.

The solution that the British came up with was opium, which could be produced in British India and smuggled into China, where its addictive properties ensured a stable market. The money from the opium trade was then used to buy tea, which the British sold throughout Europe, where demand for it was almost insatiable. Predictably, the sharp increase in opium use had disastrous effects in China. As early as 1729, the Chinese emperor outlawed the consumption of opium for non-medical reasons. In 1799, the importation of opium was outlawed. These decrees did very little to stop the flow of opium into the country, however. The combination of a determined supplier, a large population of addicts, and weak imperial control in southern China led to a full-fledged drug crisis throughout China.

In 1839, the emperor sent Lin Tse-hsü (1785–1850) to the Canton Province in southern China, which had become the center of opium imports to China. Lin was a strict Confucian public official who had become known as an opium opponent in previous positions. As soon as he arrived, Lin set out to crush the opium trade. He confiscated tens of thousands of opium pipes, arrested thousands of dealers, and confiscated and destroyed millions of pounds of the drug. As a public official, Lin was dismayed by the economic effects of opium addiction, but as a Confucian, his primary objections were moral. For both moral and pragmatic reasons, then, Lin decided to appeal directly to Queen Victoria by way of a direct letter. In this letter, Lin assumes that Victoria does not know what British traders are doing in her name and appeals to her sense of justice and morality to end the export of opium into China.

It is unlikely that Queen Victoria ever saw the letter or had any opportunity to respond. Lin's plea fell on deaf ears, and soon after he wrote the letter, hostilities between the two empires escalated into the first of two armed conflicts. The British won that conflict, resulting in the legalization of the opium trade and a series of concessions that would eventually facilitate the colonization of China in the nineteenth century.

Lin Tse-hsü's rhetoric relies strongly on pathos, the appeal to the reader's emotions. He also appeals to the queen's sense of fairness in arguing that the British should allow the Chinese the same freedom that they themselves enjoy in controlling harmful substances within their borders. 🖋

A COMMUNICATION: magnificently our great Emperor soothes and pacifies China and the foreign countries, regarding all with the same kindness. If there is profit, then he shares it with the peoples of the world; if there is harm, then he removes it on behalf of the world. This is because he takes the mind of heaven and earth as his mind.

The kings of your honorable country by a tradition handed down from generation to generation have always been noted for their politeness and submissiveness. We have read your successive tributary memorials saying, "In general our countrymen who go to trade in China have always received His Majesty the Emperor's gracious treatment and equal justice," and so on. Privately we are delighted with the way in which the honorable rulers of your country deeply understand the grand principles and are grateful for the Celestial grace. For this reason the Celestial Court[1] in soothing those from afar has redoubled its polite and kind treatment. The profit from trade has been enjoyed by them continuously for two hundred years. This is the source from which your country has become known for its wealth.

But after a long period of commercial intercourse, there appear among the crowd of barbarians[2] both good persons and bad, unevenly. Consequently there are those who smuggle opium to seduce the Chinese people and so cause the spread of the poison to all provinces. Such persons who only care to profit themselves, and disregard their harm to others, are not tolerated by the laws of heaven and are unanimously hated by human beings. His Majesty the Emperor, upon hearing of this, is in a towering rage. He has especially sent me, his commissioner, to come to Kwangtung,[3] and together with the governor-general and governor jointly to investigate and settle this matter.

All those people in China who sell opium or smoke opium should receive the death penalty. If we trace the crime of those barbarians who through the years have been selling opium, then the deep harm they have wrought and the great profit they

---

1. **Celestial Court:** formerly, the home of the gods in the Taoist pantheon; here used to refer to the Imperial headquarters of China.

2. **Barbarians:** used here simply to mean an outsider or a non-Chinese person.

3. **Kwangtung:** the major Chinese port for the opium trade; known in English as Canton.

have usurped should fundamentally justify their execution according to law. We take into consideration, however, the fact that the various barbarians have still known how to repent their crimes and return to their allegiance to us by taking the 20,183 chests of opium from their storeships and petitioning us, through their consular officer, Elliot,[4] to receive it. It has been entirely destroyed and this has been faithfully reported to the Throne in several memorials by this commissioner and his colleagues.

Fortunately we have received a specially extended favor from His Majesty the Emperor, who considers that for those who voluntarily surrender there are still some circumstances to palliate their crime, and so for the time being he has magnanimously excused them from punishment. But as for those who again violate the opium prohibition, it is difficult for the law to pardon them repeatedly. Having established new regulations, we presume that the ruler of your honorable country, who takes delight in our culture and whose disposition is inclined towards us, must be able to instruct the various barbarians to observe the law with care. It is only necessary to explain to them the advantages and disadvantages and then they will know that the legal code of the Celestial Court must be absolutely obeyed with awe.

We find that your country is sixty or seventy thousand *li* [three *li* make one mile, ordinarily] from China. Yet there are barbarian ships that strive to come here for trade for the purpose of making a great profit. The wealth of China is used to profit the barbarians. That is to say, the great profit made by barbarians is all taken from the rightful share of China. By what right do they then in return use the poisonous drug to injure the Chinese people? Even though the barbarians may not necessarily intend to do us harm, yet in coveting profit to an extreme, they have no regard for injuring others. Let us ask, where is your conscience? I have heard that the smoking of opium is very strictly forbidden by your country,[5] that is because the harm caused by opium is clearly understood. Since it is not permitted to do harm to your own country, then even less should you let it be passed on to the harm of other countries—how much less to China! Of all that China exports to foreign countries, there is not a single thing which is not beneficial to people: they are of benefit when eaten, or of benefit when used, or of benefit when resold: all are beneficial. Is there a single article from China which has done any harm to foreign countries? Take tea and rhubarb, for example; the foreign countries cannot get along for a single day without them. If China cuts off these benefits with no sympathy for those who are to suffer, then what can the barbarians rely upon to keep themselves alive? Moreover the woolens, camlets, and longells [i.e., textiles] of foreign countries cannot be woven unless they obtain Chinese silk. If China, again, cuts off this beneficial export, what profit can the barbarians expect to make? As for other food-stuffs, beginning

---

4. **Elliot:** Charles Elliot (1801–1875), British Chief Superintendent of Trade in China before the Opium Wars.

5. **Strictly forbidden by your own country:** Opium was actually not illegal in England until 1868, when it was restricted to medical uses by the 1868 Pharmacy Act.

with candy, ginger, cinnamon, and so forth, and articles for use, beginning with silk, satin, chinaware, and so on, all the things that must be had by foreign countries are innumerable. On the other hand, articles coming from the outside to China can only be used as toys. We can take them or get along without them. Since they are not needed by China, what difficulty would there be if we closed the frontier and stopped the trade? Nevertheless our Celestial Court lets tea, silk, and other goods be shipped without limit and circulated everywhere without begrudging it in the slightest. This is for no other reason but to share the benefit with the people of the whole world.

The goods from China carried away by your country not only supply your own consumption and use, but also can be divided up and sold to other countries, producing a triple profit. Even if you do not sell opium, you still have this threefold profit. How can you bear to go further, selling products injurious to others in order to fulfill your insatiable desire?

Suppose there were people from another country who carried opium for sale to England and seduced your people into buying and smoking it; certainly your honorable ruler would deeply hate it and be bitterly aroused. We have heard heretofore that your honorable ruler is kind and benevolent. Naturally you would not wish to give unto others what you yourself do not want. We have also heard that the ships coming to Canton have all had regulations promulgated and given to them in which it is stated that it is not permitted to carry contraband goods. This indicates that the administrative orders of your honorable rule have been originally strict and clear. Only because the trading ships are numerous, heretofore perhaps they have not been examined with care. Now after this communication has been dispatched and you have clearly understood the strictness of the prohibitory laws of the Celestial Court, certainly you will not let your subjects dare again to violate the law.

We have further learned that in London, the capital of your honorable rule, and in Scotland, Ireland, and other places, originally no opium has been produced. Only in several places of India under your control such as Bengal, Madras, Bombay, Patna, Benares, and Malwa has opium been planted from hill to hill, and ponds have been opened for its manufacture. For months and years work is continued in order to accumulate the poison. The obnoxious odor ascends, irritating heaven and frightening the spirits. Indeed you, O King, can eradicate the opium plant in these places, hoe over the fields entirely, and sow in its stead the five grains [i.e., millet, barley, wheat, etc.]. Anyone who dares again attempt to plant and manufacture opium should be severely punished. This will really be a great, benevolent government policy that will increase the common weal and get rid of evil. For this, Heaven must support you and the spirits must bring you good fortune, prolonging your old age and extending your descendants. All will depend on this act.

As for the barbarian merchants who come to China, their food and drink and habitation are all received by the gracious favor of our Celestial Court. Their accumulated wealth is all benefit given with pleasure by our Celestial Court. They spend rather few

10

days in their own country but more time in Canton. To digest clearly the legal penalties as an aid to instruction has been a valid principle in all ages. Suppose a man of another country comes to England to trade, he still has to obey the English laws; how much more should he obey in China the laws of the Celestial Dynasty?

Now we have set up regulations governing the Chinese people. He who sells opium shall receive the death penalty and he who smokes it also the death penalty. Now consider this: if the barbarians do not bring opium, then how can the Chinese people resell it, and how can they smoke it? The fact is that the wicked barbarians beguile the Chinese people into a death trap. How then can we grant life only to these barbarians? He who takes the life of even one person still has to atone for it with his own life; yet is the harm done by opium limited to the taking of one life only? Therefore in the new regulations, in regard to those barbarians who bring opium to China, the penalty is fixed at decapitation or strangulation. This is what is called getting rid of a harmful thing on behalf of mankind.

Moreover we have found that in the middle of the second month of this year [April 9] Consul Elliot of your nation, because the opium prohibition law was very stern and severe, petitioned for an extension of the time limit. He requested a limit of five months for India and its adjacent harbors and related territories, and ten months for England proper, after which they would act in conformity with the new regulations. Now we, the commissioner and others, have memorialized and have received the extraordinary Celestial grace of His Majesty the Emperor, who has redoubled his consideration and compassion. All those who within the period of the coming one year (from England) or six months (from India) bring opium to China by mistake, but who voluntarily confess and completely surrender their opium, shall be exempt from their punishment. After this limit of time, if there are still those who bring opium to China then they will plainly have committed a wilful violation and shall at once be executed according to law, with absolutely no clemency or pardon. This may be called the height of kindness and the perfection of justice.

Our Celestial Dynasty rules over and supervises the myriad states, and surely possesses unfathomable spiritual dignity. Yet the Emperor cannot bear to execute people without having first tried to reform them by instruction. Therefore he especially promulgates these fixed regulations. The barbarian merchants of your country, if they wish to do business for a prolonged period, are required to obey our statutes respectfully and to cut off permanently the source of opium. They must by no means try to test the effectiveness of the law with their lives. May you, O King, check your wicked and sift your vicious people before they come to China, in order to guarantee the peace of your nation, to show further the sincerity of your politeness and submissiveness, and to let the two countries enjoy together the blessing of peace. How fortunate, how fortunate indeed! After receiving this dispatch will you immediately give us a prompt reply regarding the details and circumstances of your cutting off the opium traffic. Be sure not to put this off.

UNDERSTANDING THE TEXT

1. Why does Lin begin with two paragraphs of praise for Queen Victoria and the British Empire? Do you believe that this praise is sincere? Why or why not?

2. Whom does Lin blame for the importation of opium into China? How does he feel about Chinese who sell opium to other Chinese? Who are the "barbarians" that he refers to?

3. How does Lin compare Chinese exports with British exports? Why do you think he suggests that foreign countries would have a hard time living without certain Chinese products?

4. Why does Lin believe that, once the queen finds out about the opium trade and the Chinese laws against it, she will put an end to it?

5. According to Lin, is one nation obligated to obey the laws of another nation? Explain. What reasons does he give in support of his position?

MAKING CONNECTIONS

1. Does the English policy of opium importation into China qualify as an unjust law under any of the definitions offered by Martin Luther King Jr. in "Letter from Birmingham City Jail" (p. 202)? Explain.

2. Compare the amnesty that Lin offers to those who acknowledge their participation in the opium trade with the amnesty offered by the Truth Reconciliation Commission in Desmond Tutu's "Nuremberg or National Amnesia: A Third Way" (p. 227). What is the social value of somebody acknowledging their participation in a crime?

3. Do the actions of the British, as described in Lin's letter, constitute a justifiable cause for war under the definitions of Thomas Aquinas (p. 260) or Jean Bethke Elshtain (p. 293)?

4. Evaluate the persuasiveness of Lin's argument using Aristotle's three forms of persuasion: pathos, ethos, and logos (p. 597–611). Which of these three forms does Lin use most effectively?

WRITING ABOUT THE TEXT

1. Explore the connections between the opium trade that Lin describes and contemporary drug trafficking. Whom might somebody write to today in an attempt to stop drug trafficking? Why?

2. Write an essay that analyzes Lin's Confucian beliefs about human nature in the context of the debate between the ancient Confucian scholars Mencius (p. 94) and Hsün Tzu (p. 100). Which of the two Confucian views of human nature does Lin's argument rely on?

3. Compare Lin's letter to Queen Victoria with Martin Luther King Jr.'s "Letter from Birmingham City Jail" (p. 202). Explore the way that both authors use their audiences' own moral values to argue against those audiences' actions.

Leni Riefenstahl
from *The Triumph of the Will*
(1935)

GERMANY'S DEFEAT IN WORLD WAR I left the country humiliated and economically battered. In 1919, a German government known as the Weimar Republic established Germany's first representative democracy. However, a radical fringe party known as the National Socialists, or Nazis, became increasingly successful at converting disaffected Germans to their platform of ultranationalism, militarism, and racial purity. Under the leadership of Adolf Hitler (1889–1945), the Nazis won major victories in Germany's legislative body, the Reichstag, particularly after the international Great Depression further crippled the German economy. By 1932, the Nazis were the largest political party in Germany, and in 1933, President Paul von Hindenburg, who had defeated Hitler for the presidency a year earlier, asked Hitler to become Germany's chancellor. In 1934, Hindenburg died, and Hitler proclaimed himself both president and chancellor—allowing the Nazi Party to take control of Germany and establish a totalitarian regime.

The Nazis keenly understood the power of political spectacle, and they organized massive rallies to display their might. The 1934 Nuremberg Rally was one of the first major propaganda events that Hitler staged after assuming control of the German state, and every detail was planned to create an impression of the power and virility of the Nazi Party. The rally was held outdoors, in a large arena decorated by huge, swastika-bearing banners designed by the famous Nazi architect, Albert Speer (1905–1981). To spread the message as widely as possible, Hitler commissioned Leni Riefenstahl (1902–2003), a young, highly innovative filmmaker, to create a movie of the event that could be distributed throughout Germany and the world. The film, which would become the most famous propaganda film in history, was called *The Triumph of the Will*.

The technical brilliance of *The Triumph of the Will* has never been in dispute. Using thirty-five cameras and a film crew of 120 people, Riefenstahl broke new ground in the use of camera angles, lighting, and film-editing techniques—and, as a result, she changed the way that films were made. But *The Triumph of the Will* has also endured because it helps people understand the appeal that Hitler's brand of fascism originally had for ordinary Germans. The Nuremberg Rally's elaborate pageantry, its projection of strength, and its overall hugeness were designed to make individual Germans feel that they were a part of something larger, something to which they should subordinate their individual wills and desires. In the still shown here, 160,000 German citizens look on as the three highest-ranking officials of the Nazi Party—Adolf Hitler, Heinrich Himmler (1900–1945), and Viktor Lutze (1890–1943)—walk reverently through the crowd toward a ceremonial wreath honoring German soldiers who have died in the line of duty. 🖉

Leni Riefenstahl
Still from *The Triumph of the Will*, 1935.

Understanding the Text

1. What is the effect of the crowd size on the composition of the picture? How does the camera angle maximize this effect? What is the visual relationship between the crowd and the three men in the center of the picture?

2. What is the effect of the huge banners on the composition of the picture? What emotional effect might they have had on the crowd?

3. What characteristics of the Nazi Party and of fascist ideology are suggested by this image? Why would people be attracted to these characteristics?

4. This was a peaceful rally of a newly elected government at a time of peace. Why is the military so conspicuous in the scene?

5. What do you see as the ultimate message that Hitler and the Nazis hoped to broadcast to the world with *The Triumph of the Will*?

MAKING CONNECTIONS

1. Compare the tone of this still with that of *Liberty Leading the People* (p. 268). Both are highly nationalistic images meant to provoke patriotic reactions. How differently do they present their messages? Why is one image now an unmistakable symbol of tyranny while the other one symbolizes freedom?

2. The site of this rally, Nuremberg, is also the site of the war crimes trials described in Desmond Tutu's "Nuremberg or National Amnesia: A Third Way" (p. 227). What about the 1936 Nazi Party rally might have suggested Nuremberg as the host of a tribunal designed to achieve some kind of reconciliation?

3. Compare the persuasive techniques of *The Triumph of the Will* with those found in Norman Rockwell's *Freedom of Speech* (p. 504). Does Rockwell tap into any of the same kinds of patriotic feelings that the Nazis tapped into? How do the treatments of the crowds differ?

WRITING ABOUT THE TEXT

1. View the film *The Triumph of the Will* and examine Riefenstahl's use of persuasive techniques. In what ways do elements such as lighting, camera angle, contrasts, and choice of specific subject matter contribute to the film's value as propaganda?

2. Using external sources, define "fascism" and its manifestations as forms of government. How does this image from *The Triumph of the Will* encapsulate that definition?

3. One of the key logical fallacies in the argument of this image is "bandwagoning" (p. 606), or equating an idea's worth with its popularity. Compare uses of this technique in *The Triumph of the Will* (either this picture or the entire film) with ones in modern commercial or political advertising.

Martin Luther King Jr.
Letter from Birmingham City Jail
(1963)

IN THE FIRST HALF OF THE TWENTIETH CENTURY, "Jim Crow" laws ensured that whites and blacks in America remained segregated in all areas of public life— on buses, on railroads, in schools, in restaurants, and elsewhere. However, in 1954, the Supreme Court ruled in the case of *Brown v. Board of Education of Topeka* that separating students of different races into different schools was unconstitutional. That decision signaled the beginning of the end of the segregation laws. In the following years, schools across the country would be integrated, followed by other public facilities and public transportation.

The Reverend Martin Luther King Jr. (1929–1968) gained wide exposure as a civil rights leader in 1955, when, while serving as a pastor in Montgomery, Alabama, he led a boycott against that city's bus lines that resulted in their desegregation the following year. In 1957, after the success of the bus boycott, King founded the Southern Christian Leadership Conference (SCLC) and began a series of nonviolent campaigns aimed at ending racial segregation across the South. In 1963, the SCLC led a series of highly publicized protests and demonstrations in Birmingham, Alabama, that proved to be one of the turning points in the struggle for civil rights.

King, who was well versed in the philosophy and practice of nonviolent civil disobedience, understood that one powerful application of this philosophy was to disobey unjust laws publicly and to accept the consequences of that disobedience. Consequently, when a local judge issued a blatantly unconstitutional injunction that forbade King and others from engaging in protest activities, he defied the order and went to jail. While in jail, he read, with dismay, an open letter from eight moderate, white clergymen in Birmingham condemning the demonstrations as "unwise and untimely . . . extreme measures [that were] led . . . by outsiders." In its conclusion, the letter states, "we . . . urge our own Negro community to withdraw support from these demonstrations, and to unite locally in working peacefully for a better Birmingham. When rights are consistently denied, a cause should be pressed in the courts and in negotiations among local leaders, and not in the streets. We appeal to both our white and Negro citizenry to observe the principles of law and order and common sense."

King was disheartened by this rebuke from the very Christian and Jewish leaders he had hoped would support his cause. He used their letter as the platform for what would become one of the most famous arguments for civil disobedience ever written: his "Letter from Birmingham City Jail." Because he wrote this response to fellow members of the clergy, and because he rooted his activism in Christianity, King based his argument firmly in the Judeo-Christian tradition. He invoked passages from both the Old and New Testaments to support two different propositions: that segregation was unjust in the eyes of God, and that the Judeo-Christian tradition allowed, and even at times required, disobedience to unjust laws.

The "Letter from Birmingham City Jail" is dated April 16, 1963. King could not send the letter directly to those it addressed; friends had to smuggle it out of the jail in pieces and reassemble it later. The letter was included in King's book *Why We Can't Wait*, which was published in 1964, the year that King became, at thirty-five, the youngest person ever to be awarded the Nobel Prize for Peace.

The "Letter from Birmingham City Jail" has long been considered a casebook of different rhetorical approaches. King takes great pains to establish an ethos of a trusted and knowledgeable member of the clergy, but he also makes powerful appeals to emotions involving justice and fairness, and his arguments about just and unjust laws give an excellent example of deductive reasoning in action. ✎

My dear Fellow Clergymen,

While confined here in the Birmingham city jail, I came across your recent statement calling our present activities "unwise and untimely." Seldom, if ever, do I pause to answer criticism of my work and ideas. If I sought to answer all of the criticisms that cross my desk, my secretaries would be engaged in little else in the course of the day, and I would have no time for constructive work. But since I feel that you are men of genuine good will and your criticisms are sincerely set forth, I would like to answer your statement in what I hope will be patient and reasonable terms.

I think I should give the reason for my being in Birmingham, since you have been influenced by the argument of "outsiders coming in." I have the honor of serving as president of the Southern Christian Leadership Conference, an organization operating in every southern state, with headquarters in Atlanta, Georgia. We have some eighty-five affiliate organizations all across the South—one being the Alabama Christian Movement for Human Rights. Whenever necessary and possible we share staff, educational and financial resources with our affiliates. Several months ago our local affiliate here in Birmingham invited us to be on call to engage in a nonviolent direct-action program if such were deemed necessary. We readily consented and when the hour came we lived up to our promises. So I am here, along with several members of my staff, because we were invited here. I am here because I have basic organizational ties here.

Beyond this, I am in Birmingham because injustice is here. Just as the eighth century prophets[1] left their little villages and carried their "thus saith the Lord" far beyond the boundaries of their hometowns; and just as the Apostle Paul left his lit-

---

1. **Eighth century prophets:** a group of Hebrew prophets—including Isaiah, Amos, Hosea, Jonah, and Elijah—who preached against idolatry. Like King and the Southern Christian Lead-ership Conference, these prophets were often seen as "outside agitators" by the people they preached to.

tle village of Tarsus and carried the gospel of Jesus Christ to practically every ham-
let and city of the Graeco-Roman world, I too am compelled to carry the gospel of
freedom beyond my particular hometown. Like Paul, I must constantly respond to
the Macedonian call for aid.[2]

Moreover, I am cognizant of the interrelatedness of all communities and states. I
cannot sit idly by in Atlanta and not be concerned about what happens in Birmingham. Injustice anywhere is a threat to justice everywhere. We are caught in an
inescapable network of mutuality, tied in a single garment of destiny. Whatever
affects one directly affects all indirectly. Never again can we afford to live with the
narrow, provincial "outside agitator" idea. Anyone who lives in the United States
can never be considered an outsider anywhere in this country.

You deplore the demonstrations that are presently taking place in Birming-   5
ham. But I am sorry that your statement did not express a similar concern for the
conditions that brought the demonstrations into being. I am sure that each of you
would want to go beyond the superficial social analyst who looks merely at effects,
and does not grapple with underlying causes. I would not hesitate to say that it
is unfortunate that so-called demonstrations are taking place in Birmingham at
this time, but I would say in more emphatic terms that it is even more unfortunate that the white power structure of this city left the Negro community with
no other alternative.

In any nonviolent campaign there are four basic steps: (1) collection of the facts
to determine whether injustices are alive, (2) negotiation, (3) self-purification, and
(4) direct action. We have gone through all of these steps in Birmingham. There
can be no gainsaying of the fact that racial injustice engulfs this community.

Birmingham is probably the most thoroughly segregated city in the United States.
Its ugly record of police brutality is known in every section of this country. Its injust
treatment of Negroes in the courts is a notorious reality. There have been more
unsolved bombings of Negro homes and churches in Birmingham than any city in
this nation. These are the hard, brutal and unbelievable facts. On the basis of these
conditions Negro leaders sought to negotiate with the city fathers. But the political
leaders consistently refused to engage in good faith negotiation.

Then came the opportunity last September to talk with some of the leaders of
the economic community. In these negotiating sessions certain promises were made

---

2. **Macedonian call for aid:** Paul was an early
Christian missionary who established Christian
congregations in many of the major cities of
the Roman Empire, such as Corinth, Galatia,
Philippi, Thessalonica, and Rome itself. Much
of the latter part of the New Testament consists
of Paul's letters to these various congregations.
Macedonia was a region of the Roman Empire
north of Greece, in which several of these congregations were located. The **Macedonian call**
refers to a vision that Paul had, which is
described in Acts 16:9–10: "And a vision
appeared to Paul in the night; There stood a man
of Macedonia, and prayed him, saying, Come
over into Macedonia, and help us. And after he
had seen the vision, immediately we endeav-
oured to go into Macedonia, assuredly gathering
that the Lord had called us for to preach the
gospel unto them."

by the merchants—such as the promise to remove the humiliating racial signs from the stores. On the basis of these promises Rev. Shuttlesworth[3] and the leaders of the Alabama Christian Movement for Human Rights agreed to call a moratorium on any type of demonstrations. As the weeks and months unfolded we realized that we were the victims of a broken promise. The signs remained. Like so many experiences of the past we were confronted with blasted hopes, and the dark shadow of a deep disappointment settled upon us. So we had no alternative except that of preparing for direct action, whereby we would present our very bodies as a means of laying our case before the conscience of the local and national community. We were not unmindful of the difficulties involved. So we decided to go through a process of self-purification. We started having workshops on nonviolence and repeatedly asked ourselves the questions, "Are you able to accept blows without retaliating?" "Are you able to endure the ordeals of jail?" We decided to set our direct-action program around the Easter season, realizing that with the exception of Christmas, this was the largest shopping period of the year. Knowing that a strong economic withdrawal program would be the by-product of direct action, we felt that this was the best time to bring pressure on the merchants for the needed changes. Then it occurred to us that the March election was ahead and so we speedily decided to postpone action until after election day. When we discovered that Mr. Connor[4] was in the run-off, we decided again to postpone action so that the demonstrations could not be used to cloud the issues. At this time we agreed to begin our nonviolent witness the day after the run-off.

This reveals that we did not move irresponsibly into direct action. We too wanted to see Mr. Connor defeated; so we went through postponement after postponement to aid in this community need. After this we felt that direct action could be delayed no longer.

You may well ask, "Why direct action? Why sit-ins, marches, etc.? Isn't negotiation a better path?" You are exactly right in your call for negotiation. Indeed, this is the purpose of direct action. Nonviolent direct actions seeks to create such a crisis and establish such creative tension that a community that has constantly refused to negotiate is forced to confront the issue. It seeks so to dramatize the issue that it can no longer be ignored. I just referred to the creation of tension as a part of the work of the nonviolent resister. This may sound rather shocking. But I must confess that I am not afraid of the word tension. I have earnestly worked and preached against violent tension, but there is a type of constructive nonviolent tension that is necessary for growth. Just as Socrates felt that it was necessary to create a tension

10

---

3. **Rev. Shuttlesworth:** The Reverend Fred Shuttlesworth (b. 1922) was one of the cofounders, with King, of the SCLC.

4. **Mr. Connor:** Theophilus Eugene "Bull" Connor (1897–1973), a police commissioner in Birmingham, was noted for using vicious methods—including fire hoses and police dogs—to suppress civil rights demonstrations. Images of Connor using these tactics on peaceful demonstrators in Birmingham were broadcast all over the world, generating an outrage that helped pass the 1963 and 1964 Civil Rights Acts.

in the mind so that individuals could rise from the bondage of myths and half-truths to the unfettered realm of creative analysis and objective appraisal, we must see the need of having nonviolent gadflies to create the kind of tension in society that will help men to rise from the dark depths of prejudice and racism to the majestic heights of understanding and brotherhood. So the purpose of the direct action is to create a situation so crisis-packed that it will inevitably open the door to negotiation. We, therefore, concur with you in your call for negotiation. Too long has our beloved Southland been bogged down in the tragic attempt to live in monologue rather than dialogue.

One of the basic points in your statement is that our acts are untimely. Some have asked, "Why didn't you give the new administration time to act?" The only answer that I can give to this inquiry is that the new administration must be prodded about as much as the outgoing one before it acts. We will be sadly mistaken if we feel that the election of Mr. Boutwell[5] will bring the millennium to Birmingham. While Mr. Boutwell is much more articulate and gentle than Mr. Connor, they are both segregationists, dedicated to the task of maintaining the status quo. The hope I see in Mr. Boutwell is that he will be reasonable enough to see the futility of massive resistance to desegregation. But he will not see this without pressure from the devotees of civil rights. My friends, I must say to you that we have made a single gain in civil rights without determined legal and nonviolent pressure. History is the long and tragic story of the fact that privileged groups seldom give up their privileges voluntarily. Individuals may see the moral light and voluntarily give up their unjust posture; but as Reinhold Niebuhr has reminded us, groups are more immoral than individuals.[6]

We know through painful experience that freedom is never voluntarily given by the oppressor; it must be demanded by the oppressed. Frankly, I have never yet engaged in a direct action movement that was "well-timed," according to the timetable of those who have not suffered unduly from the disease of segregation. For years now I have heard the word "Wait!" It rings in the ear of every Negro with a piercing familiarity. This "Wait" has almost always meant "Never." It has been a tranquilizing thalidomide,[7] relieving the emotional stress for a moment, only to give birth to an ill-formed infant of frustration. We must come to see with the distinguished jurist of yesterday that "justice too long delayed is justice denied." We have waited for more than 340 years for our constitutional and God-given rights. The nations of Asia and Africa are moving with jetlike speed toward the goal of political independence, and we still creep at horse and buggy pace toward the gain-

5. **Mr. Boutwell:** Albert Boutwell (1904–1978) defeated Bull Connor in the 1963 race for mayor of Birmingham.
6. **Reinhold Niebuhr:** American Protestant theologian (1892–1971) and professor at New York's Union Theological Seminary. The asser-

tion that King references here is the subject of Niebuhr's 1932 book *Moral Man and Immoral Society.*
7. **Thalidomide:** a sedative drug that was discovered to cause birth defects.

ing of a cup of coffee at a lunch counter. I guess it is easy for those who have never felt the stinging darts of segregation to say, "Wait." But when you have seen vicious mobs lynch your mothers and fathers at will and drown your sisters and brothers at whim; when you have seen hate-filled policemen curse, kick, brutalize and even kill your black brothers and sisters with impunity; when you see the vast majority of your twenty million Negro brothers smothering in an airtight cage of poverty in the midst of an affluent society; when you suddenly find your tongue twisted and your speech stammering as you seek to explain to your six-year-old daughter why she can't go to the public amusement park that has just been advertised on television, and see tears welling up in her little eyes when she is told that Funtown is closed to colored children, and see the depressing clouds of inferiority begin to form in her little mental sky, and see her begin to distort her little personality by unconsciously developing a bitterness toward white people; when you have to concoct an answer for a five-year-old son asking in agonizing pathos: "Daddy, why do white people treat colored people so mean?"; when you take a cross-country drive and find it necessary to sleep night after night in the uncomfortable corners of your automobile because no motel will accept you; when you are humiliated day in and day out by nagging signs reading "white" and "colored"; when your first name becomes "nigger" and your middle name becomes "boy" (however old you are) and your last name becomes "John," and when your wife and mother are never given the respected title "Mrs."; when you are harried by day and haunted by night by the fact that you are a Negro, living constantly at tiptoe stance never quite knowing what to expect next, and plagued with inner fears and outer resentments; when you are forever fighting a degenerating sense of "nobodiness"; then you will understand why we find it difficult to wait. There comes a time when the cup of endurance runs over, and men are no longer willing to be plunged into an abyss of injustice where they experience the blackness of corroding despair. I hope, sirs, you can understand our legitimate and unavoidable impatience.

You express a great deal of anxiety over our willingness to break laws. This is certainly a legitimate concern. Since we so diligently urge people to obey the Supreme Court's decision of 1954 outlawing segregation in the public schools, it is rather strange and paradoxical to find us consciously breaking laws. One may well ask, "How can you advocate breaking some laws and obeying others?" The answer is found in the fact that there are two types of laws: there are *just* and there are *unjust* laws. I would agree with Saint Augustine[8] that "An unjust law is no law at all."

Now what is the difference between the two? How does one determine when a law is just or unjust? A just law is a man-made code that squares with the moral law or the law of God. An unjust law is a code that is out of harmony with the moral law. To put it in the terms of Saint Thomas Aquinas,[9] an unjust law is a

---

8. **Saint Augustine:** early Christian writer (354–430 CE) and bishop of the North African town of Hippo (in present-day Algeria).

9. **Saint Thomas Aquinas:** Italian theologian (1224 or 1225–1274) whose *Summa Theologica* (1265–74) is a classic of Christian thought.

human law that is not rooted in eternal and natural law. Any law that uplifts human personality is just. Any law that degrades human personality is unjust. All segregation statutes are unjust because segregation distorts the soul and damages the personality. It gives the segregator a false sense of superiority, and the segregated a false sense of inferiority. To use the words of Martin Buber,[10] the great Jewish philosopher, segregation substitutes an "I-it" relationship for the "I-thou" relationship, and ends up relegating persons to the status of things. So segregation is not only politically, economically and sociologically unsound, but it is morally wrong and sinful. Paul Tillich[11] has said that sin is separation. Isn't segregation an existential expression of man's tragic separation, an expression of his awful estrangement, his terrible sinfulness? So I can urge men to disobey segregation ordinances because they are morally wrong.

Let us turn to a more concrete example of just and unjust laws. An unjust law is a code that a majority inflicts on a minority that is not binding on itself. This is difference made legal. On the other hand a just law is a code that a majority compels a minority to follow that it is willing to follow itself. This is sameness made legal.

Let me give another explanation. An unjust law is a code inflicted upon a minority which that minority had no part in enacting or creating because they did not have the unhampered right to vote. Who can say that the legislature of Alabama which set up the segregation laws was democratically elected? Throughout the state of Alabama all types of conniving methods are used to prevent Negroes from becoming registered voters and there are some counties without a single Negro registered to vote despite the fact that the Negro constitutes a majority of the population. Can any law set up in such a state be considered democratically structured?

These are just a few examples of unjust and just laws. There are some instances when a law is just on its face and unjust in its application. For instance, I was arrested Friday on a change of parading without a permit. Now there is nothing wrong with an ordinance which requires a permit for a parade, but when the ordinance is used to preserve segregation and to deny citizens the First Amendment privilege of peaceful assembly and peaceful protest, then it becomes unjust.

I hope you can see the distinction I am trying to point out. In no sense do I advocate evading or defying the law as the rabid segregationist would do. This would lead to anarchy. One who breaks an unjust law must do it *openly*, *lovingly* (not hatefully as the white mothers did in New Orleans when they were seen on television screaming, "nigger, nigger, nigger"), and with a willingness to accept the penalty. I submit that an individual who breaks a law that conscience tells him is unjust, and willingly accepts the penalty by staying in jail to arouse the conscience

10. **Martin Buber:** Israeli (Austrian-born) Jewish philosopher (1878–1965) and theologian who wrote the well-known ethical treatise *I and Thou* in 1923.

11. **Paul Tillich:** American (German-born) Protestant theologian (1886–1965).

of the community over its injustice, is in reality expressing the very highest respect for law.

Of course, there is nothing new about this kind of civil disobedience. It was seen sublimely in the refusal of Shadrach, Meshach and Abednego to obey the laws of Nebuchadnezzar because a higher moral law was involved.[12] It was practiced superbly by the early Christians who were willing to face hungry lions and the excruciating pain of chopping blocks, before submitting to certain unjust laws of the Roman Empire. To a degree academic freedom is a reality today because Socrates practiced civil disobedience.

We can never forget that everything Hitler did in Germany was "legal" and every-thing the Hungarian freedom fighters did in Hungary was "illegal." It was "illegal" to aid and comfort a Jew in Hitler's Germany. But I am sure that if I had lived in Germany during that time I would have aided and comforted my Jewish brothers even though it was illegal. If I lived in a Communist country today where certain principles dear to the Christian faith are suppressed, I believe I would openly advo-cate disobeying these anti-religious laws. I must make two honest confessions to you, my Christian and Jewish brothers. First, I must confess that over the last few years I have been gravely disappointed with the white moderate. I have almost reached the regrettable conclusion that the Negro's great stumbling block in the stride toward freedom is not the White Citizen's Counciler[13] or the Ku Klux Klanner, but the white moderate who is more devoted to "order" than to justice; who prefers a neg-ative peace which is the absence of tension to a positive peace which is the pres-ence of justice; who constantly says, "I agree with you in the goal you seek, but I can't agree with your methods of direct action"; who paternalistically feels that he can set the timetable for another man's freedom; who lives by the myth of time and who constantly advised the Negro to wait until a "more convenient season." Shal-low understanding from people of good will is more frustrating than absolute mis-understanding from people of ill will. Lukewarm acceptance is much more bewildering than outright rejection.

I had hoped that the white moderate would understand that law and order exist for the purpose of establishing justice, and that when they fail to do this they become dangerously structured dams that block the flow of social progress. I had hoped that the white moderate would understand that the present tension of the South is merely a necessary phase of the transition from an obnoxious negative peace, where the

20

---

12. **Shadrach, Meshach and Abednego:** In the third chapter of the Book of Daniel, these three young Hebrew men are condemned to die by fire because they refuse to worship a golden image. God saves them from harm, and they end up being promoted to high positions in the Baby-lonian empire. King invokes them to provide a biblical example of civil disobedience.

13. **White Citizen's Counciler:** After the Supreme Court ordered the desegregation of public schools in 1954, groups known as White Citizen's Councils rose in the South to support continued segregation. Unlike the Ku Klux Klan, the Councils were not secretive or openly violent; however, many committed segregation-ists were members of both organizations.

Negro passively accepted his unjust plight, to a substance-filled positive peace, where all men will respect the dignity and worth of human personality. Actually, we who engage in nonviolent direct action are not the creators of tension. We merely bring to the surface the hidden tension that is already alive. We bring it out in the open where it can be seen and dealt with. Like a boil that can never be cured as long as it is covered up but must be opened with all its pus-flowing ugliness to the natural medicines of air and light, injustice must likewise be exposed, with all of the tension its exposing creates, to the light of human conscience and the air of national opinion before it can be cured.

In your statement you asserted that our actions, even though peaceful, must be condemned because they precipitate violence. But can this assertion be logically made? Isn't this like condemning the robbed man because his possession of money precipitated the evil act of robbery? Isn't this like condemning Socrates because his unswerving commitment to truth and his philosophical delvings precipitated the misguided popular mind to make him drink the hemlock? Isn't this like condemning Jesus because His unique God-consciousness and never-ceasing devotion to his will precipitated the evil act of crucifixion? We must come to see, as federal courts have consistently affirmed, that it is immoral to urge an individual to withdraw his efforts to gain his basic constitutional rights because the quest precipitates violence. Society must protect the robbed and punish the robber.

I had also hoped that the white moderate would reject the myth of time. I received a letter this morning from a white brother in Texas which said: "All Christians know that the colored people will receive equal rights eventually, but it is possible that you are in too great of a religious hurry. It has taken Christianity almost two thousand years to accomplish what it has. The teachings of Christ take time to come to earth." All that is said here grows out of a tragic misconception of time. It is the strangely irrational notion that there is something in the very flow of time that will inevitably cure all ills. Actually time is neutral. It can be used either destructively or constructively. I am coming to feel that the people of ill will have used time much more effectively than the people of good will. We will have to repent in this generation not merely for the vitriolic words and actions of the bad people, but for the appalling silence of the good people. We must come to see that human progress never rolls in on wheels of inevitability. It comes through the tireless efforts and persistent work of men willing to be co-workers with God, and without this hard work time itself becomes an ally of the forces of social stagnation. We must use time creatively, and forever realize that the time is always ripe to do right. Now is the time to make real the promise of democracy, and transform our pending national elegy into a creative psalm of brotherhood. Now is the time to lift our national policy from the quicksand of racial injustice to the solid rock of human dignity.

You spoke of our activity in Birmingham as extreme. At first I was rather disappointed that fellow clergymen would see my nonviolent efforts as those of the extremist. I started thinking about the fact that I stand in the middle of two opposing forces in the Negro community. One is a force of complacency made up of Negroes who, as a result of long years of oppression, have been so completely drained of self-respect and a sense of "somebodiness" that they have adjusted to segregation, and, of a few Negroes in the middle class who, because of a degree of academic and economic security, and because at points they profit by segregation, have unconsciously become insensitive to the problems of the masses. The other force is one of bitterness and hatred, and comes perilously close to advocating violence. It is expressed in the various black nationalist groups that are springing up over the nation, the largest and best known being Elijah Muhammad's Muslim movement.[14] This movement is nourished by the contemporary frustration over the continued existence of racial discrimination. It is made up of people who have lost faith in America, who have absolutely repudiated Christianity, and who have concluded that the white man is an incurable "devil." I have tried to stand between these two forces, saying that we need not follow the "do-nothingism" of the complacent or the hatred and despair of the black nationalist. There is the more excellent way of love and nonviolent protest. I'm grateful to God that, through the Negro church, the dimension of nonviolence entered our struggle. If this philosophy had not emerged, I am convinced that by now many streets of the South would be flowing with floods of blood. And I am further convinced that if our white brothers dismiss us as "rabble-rousers" and "outside agitators" those of us who are working through the channels of nonviolent direct action and refuse to support our nonviolent efforts, millions of Negroes, out of frustration and despair, will seek solace and security in black nationalist ideologies, a development that will lead inevitably to a frightening racial nightmare.

Oppressed people cannot remain oppressed forever. The urge for freedom will   25
eventually come. This is what happened to the American Negro. Something within has reminded him of his birthright of freedom; something without has reminded him that he can gain it. Consciously and unconsciously, he has been swept in by what the Germans call the Zeitgeist,[15] and with his black brothers of Africa, and his brown and yellow brothers of Asia, South America and the Caribbean, he is moving with a sense of cosmic urgency toward the promised land of racial justice. Recognizing this vital urge that has engulfed the Negro community, one should readily understand public demonstrations. The Negro has many pent-up resentments and latent frustrations. He has to get them out. So let him march sometime; let him have his prayer pilgrimages to the city hall; understand why he must

---

14. **Elijah Muhammad's Muslim movement:** Elijah Muhammad (1897–1975) led the Nation of Islam, a group that preached black supremacy and advocated the creation of a separate African-American nation within the United States. Muhammad's most famous disciple was Malcolm X (1925–1965), who broke with the movement after making a pilgrimage to Mecca and fully converting to Islam; the latter process required him to renounce the belief that any one race was superior to any other.

15. **Zeitgeist:** German word meaning "spirit of the time."

have sit-ins and freedom rides. If his repressed emotions do not come out in these nonviolent ways, they will come out in ominous expressions of violence. This is not a threat; it is a fact of history. So I have not said to my people "get rid of your discontent." But I have tried to say that this normal and healthy discontent can be channelized through the creative outlet of nonviolent direct action. Now this approach is being dismissed as extremist. I must admit that I was initially disappointed in being so categorized.

But as I continued to think about the matter I gradually gained a bit of satisfaction from being considered an extremist. Was not Jesus an extremist in love—"Love your enemies, bless them that curse you, pray for them that despitefully use you." Was not Amos an extremist for justice—"Let justice roll down like waters and righteousness like a mighty stream." Was not Paul an extremist for the gospel of Jesus Christ—"I bear in my body the marks of the Lord Jesus." Was not Martin Luther an extremist— "Here I stand; I can do none other so help me God." Was not John Bunyan[16] an extremist—"I will stay in jail to the end of my days before I make a butchery of my conscience." Was not Abraham Lincoln an extremist—"This nation cannot survive half slave and half free." Was not Thomas Jefferson an extremist—"We hold these truths to be self-evident, that all men are created equal." So the question is not whether we will be extremist but what kind of extremist will we be. Will we be extremists for hate or will we be extremists for love? Will we be extremists for the preservation of injustice—or will we be extremists for the cause of justice? In that dramatic scene on Calvary's hill, three men were crucified. We must not forget that all three were crucified for the same crime—the crime of extremism. Two were extremists for immorality, and thusly fell below their environment. The other, Jesus Christ, was an extremist for love, truth and goodness, and thereby rose above his environment. So, after all, maybe the South, the nation and the world are in dire need of creative extremists.

I had hoped that the white moderate would see this. Maybe I was too optimistic. Maybe I expected too much. I guess I should have realized that few members of a race that has oppressed another race can understand or appreciate the deep groans and passionate yearnings of those that have been oppressed and still fewer have the vision to see that injustice must be rooted out by strong, persistent and determined action. I am thankful, however, that some of our white brothers have grasped the meaning of this social revolution and committed themselves to it. They are still all too small in quantity, but they are big in quality. Some like Ralph McGill, Lillian Smith, Harry Golden and James Dabbs have written about our struggle in eloquent, prophetic and understanding terms. Others have marched with us down nameless streets of the South. They have languished in filthy roach-infested jails, suffering the abuse and brutality of angry policemen who see them as "dirty nigger-lovers." They, unlike so many of their moderate brothers and sisters, have recognized the urgency

16. **Bunyan:** English preacher (1628–1688), author of *Pilgrim's Progress.* **Luther:** German reformer (1483–1546) who launched the Protestant Reformation by protesting policies of the Catholic Church.

of the moment and sensed the need for powerful "action" antidotes to combat the disease of segregation.

Let me rush on to mention my other disappointment. I have been so greatly disappointed with the white church and its leadership. Of course, there are some notable exceptions. I am not unmindful of the fact that each of you has taken some significant stands on this issue. I commend you, Rev. Stallings,[17] for your Christian stance on this past Sunday, in welcoming Negroes to your worship service on a nonsegregated basis. I commend the Catholic leaders of this state for integrating Springhill College several years ago.

But despite these notable exceptions I must honestly reiterate that I have been disappointed with the church. I do not say that as one of the negative critics who can always find something wrong with the church. I say it as a minister of the gospel, who loves the church; who was nurtured in its bosom; who has been sustained by its spiritual blessings and who will remain true to it as long as the cord of life shall lengthen.

I had the strange feeling when I was suddenly catapulted into the leadership of the bus protest in Montgomery several years ago that we would have the support of the white church. I felt that the white ministers, priests and rabbis of the South would be some of our strongest allies. Instead, some have been outright opponents, refusing to understand the freedom movement and misrepresenting its leaders; all too many others have been more cautious than courageous and have remained silent behind the anesthetizing security of the stained-glass windows. 30

In spite of my shattered dreams of the past, I came to Birmingham with the hope that the white religious leadership of this community would see the justice of our cause, and with deep moral concern, serve as the channel through which our just grievances would get to the power structure. I had hoped that each of you would understand. But again I have been disappointed. I have heard numerous religious leaders of the South call upon their worshippers to comply with a desegregation decision because it is the *law,* but I have longed to hear white ministers say, "Follow this decree because integration is morally *right* and the Negro is your brother." In the midst of blatant injustices inflicted upon the Negro, I have watched white churches stand on the sideline and merely mouth pious irrelevancies and sanctimonious trivialities. In the midst of a mighty struggle to rid our nation of racial and economic injustice, I have heard so many ministers say, "Those are social issues with which the gospel has no real concern," and I have watched so many churches commit themselves to a completely otherworldly religion which made a strange distinction between body and soul, the sacred and the secular.

So here we are moving toward the exit of the twentieth century with a religious community largely adjusted to the status quo, standing as a taillight behind other community agencies rather than a headlight leading men to higher levels of justice.

---

17. **Rev. Stallings:** The Reverend Earl Stallings, pastor of the First Baptist Church in Birmingham, was one of the eight clergymen who had signed the letter that King was responding to.

I have traveled the length and breadth of Alabama, Mississippi and all the other southern states. On sweltering summer days and crisp autumn mornings I have looked at her beautiful churches with their lofty spires pointing heavenward. I have beheld the impressive outlay of her massive religious education buildings. Over and over again I have found myself asking: "What kind of people worship here? Who is their God? Where were their voices when the lips of Governor Barnett dripped with words of interposition and nullification?[18] Where were they when Governor Wallace gave the clarion call for defiance and hatred?[19] Where were their voices of support when tired, bruised and weary Negro men and women decided to rise from the dark dungeons of complacency to the bright hills of creative protest?"

Yes, these questions are still in my mind. In deep disappointment, I have wept over the laxity of the church. But be assured that my tears have been tears of love. There can be no deep disappointment where there is not deep love. Yes, I love the church; I love her sacred walls. How could I do otherwise? I am in the rather unique position of being the son, the grandson and the great-grandson of preachers. Yes, I see the church as the body of Christ. But, oh! How we have blemished and scarred that body through social neglect and fear of being nonconformists.

There was a time when the church was very powerful. It was during that period when the early Christians rejoiced when they were deemed worthy to suffer for what they believed. In those days the church was not merely a thermometer that recorded the ideas and principles of popular opinion; it was a thermostat that transformed the mores of society. Wherever the early Christians entered a town the power structure got disturbed and immediately sought to convict them for being "disturbers of the peace" and "outside agitators." But they went on with the conviction that they were "a colony of heaven," and had to obey God rather than man. They were small in number but big in commitment. They were too God-intoxicated to be "astronomically intimidated." They brought an end to such ancient evils as infanticide and gladiatorial contest.

Things are different now. The contemporary church is often a weak, ineffectual voice with an uncertain sound.[20] It is so often the arch-supporter of the status quo.

35

---

18. **Governor Barnett:** Ross Barnett (1898–1987) was the governor of Mississippi in 1962, when the Supreme Court ordered that James Meredith (b. 1933), an African-American, be admitted to the University of Mississippi. Barnett attempted to nullify the order, swearing that he would go to jail before he would allow a Mississippi school to be integrated.

19. **Governor Wallace:** George Wallace (1919–1998) was elected governor of Alabama in 1962.

In his inaugural address, Wallace declared "segregation now, segregation tomorrow, and segregation forever." In 1963, he stood outside the University of Alabama and tried to prevent two black students from enrolling.

20. **Uncertain sound:** King alludes here to Paul's criticisms of the Corinthian church in 1 Corinthians 14:8: "For if the trumpet give an uncertain sound, who shall prepare himself to the battle?"

Far from being disturbed by the presence of the church, the power structure of the average community is consoled by the church's silent and often vocal sanction of things as they are.

But the judgment of God is upon the church as never before. If the church of today does not recapture the sacrificial spirit of the early church, it will lose its authentic ring, forfeit the loyalty of millions, and be dismissed as an irrelevant social club with no meaning for the twentieth century. I am meeting young people every day whose disappointment with the church has risen to outright disgust.

Maybe again, I have been too optimistic. Is organized religion too inextricably bound to the status quo to save our nation and the world? Maybe I must turn my faith to the inner spiritual church, the church within the church, as the true ecclesia[21] and the hope of the world. But again I am thankful to God that some noble souls from the ranks of organized religion have broken loose from the paralyzing chains of conformity and joined us as active partners in the struggle for freedom. They have left their secure congregations and walked the streets of Albany, Georgia, with us. They have gone through the highways of the South on tortuous rides for freedom.[22] Yes, they have gone to jail with us. Some have been kicked out of their churches, and lost support of their bishops and fellow ministers. But they have gone with the faith that right defeated is stronger than evil triumphant. These men have been the leaven in the lump of the race. Their witness has been the spiritual salt that has preserved the true meaning of the gospel in these troubled times. They have carved a tunnel of hope through the dark mountain of disappointment.

I hope the church as a whole will meet the challenge of this decisive hour. But even if the church does not come to the aid of justice, I have no despair about the future. I have no fear about the outcome of our struggle in Birmingham, even if our motives are presently misunderstood. We will reach the goal of freedom in Birmingham and all over the nation, because the goal of America is freedom. Abused and scorned though we may be, our destiny is tied up with the destiny of America. Before the Pilgrims landed at Plymouth we were here. Before the pen of Jefferson etched across the pages of history the majestic words of the Declaration of Independence, we were here. For more than two centuries our foreparents labored in this country without wages; they made cotton king; and they built the homes of their masters in the midst of brutal injustice and shameful humiliation—and yet out of a bottomless vitality they continued to thrive and develop. If the inexpressible cruelties of slav-

---

21. **Ecclesia:** Latin form of *ekklesia*, the Greek root of English words such as "ecclesiastical." In the early days of the Church, *ekklesia* was used to refer to a Christian community. Later, it came to mean the collective body of the Church or of all Christian believers.

22. **Rides for freedom:** In 1961, a year after the Supreme Court outlawed racial segregation in interstate public facilities, integrated groups of student volunteers rode together on buses throughout the South. The "Freedom Rides" were organized by the Congress on Racial Equality (CORE) and the Student Nonviolent Coordinating Committee (SNCC).

ery could not stop us, the opposition we now face will surely fail. We will win our freedom because the sacred heritage of our nation and the eternal will of God are embodied in our echoing demands.

I must close now. But before closing I am impelled to mention one other point in your statement that troubled me profoundly. You warmly commended the Birmingham police force for keeping "order" and "preventing violence." I don't believe you would have so warmly commended the police force if you had seen its angry violent dogs literally biting six unarmed, nonviolent Negroes. I don't believe you would so quickly commend the policemen if you would observe their ugly and inhuman treatment of Negroes here in the city jail; if you would watch them push and curse old Negro women and young Negro girls; if you would see them slap and kick old Negro men and young boys; if you will observe them, as they did on two occasions, refuse to give us food because we wanted to sing our grace together. I'm sorry that I can't join you in your praise for the police department. 40

It is true that they have been rather disciplined in their public handling of the demonstrators. In this sense they have been rather publicly "nonviolent." But for what purpose? To preserve the evil system of segregation. Over the last few years I have consistently preached that nonviolence demands that the means we use must be as pure as the ends we seek. So I have tried to make it clear that it is wrong to use immoral means to attain moral ends. But now I must affirm that it is just as wrong, or even more so, to use moral means to preserve immoral ends. May be Mr. Connor and his policemen have been rather publicly nonviolent, as Chief Pritchett was in Albany, Georgia, but they have used the moral means of nonviolence to maintain the immoral end of flagrant racial injustice. T. S. Eliot has said that there is no greater treason than to do the right deed for the wrong reason.[23]

I wish you had commended the Negro sit-inners and demonstrators of Birmingham for their sublime courage, their willingness to suffer and their amazing discipline in the midst of the most inhuman provocation. One day the South will recognize its real heroes. They will be the James Merediths,[24] courageously and with a majestic sense of purpose facing jeering and hostile mobs and the agonizing loneliness that characterizes the life of the pioneer. They will be old, oppressed, battered Negro women, symbolized in a seventy-two-year-old woman of Montgomery, Alabama, who rose up with a sense of dignity and with her people decided not to ride the segregated buses, and responded to one who inquired about her tiredness with ungrammatical profundity: "My feet is tired, but my soul is rested." They will be the young high school and college students, young ministers of the gospel and a host of their elders courageously and nonviolently sitting-in at lunch counters and willingly going to jail for conscience's sake. One day the South will know that when these

23. **T. S. Eliot:** British (American-born) poet (1888–1965); the text is from his play *Murder in the Cathedral.*   24. **The James Merediths:** See note 18.

disinherited children of God sat down at lunch counters they were in reality standing up for the best in the American dream and the most sacred values in our Judeo-Christian heritage, and thusly, carrying our whole nation back to those great wells of democracy which were dug deep by the Founding Fathers in the formulation of the Constitution and the Declaration of Independence.

Never before have I written a letter this long (or should I say a book?). I'm afraid that it is much too long to take your precious time. I can assure you that it would have been much shorter if I had been writing from a comfortable desk, but what else is there to do when you are alone for days in the dull monotony of a narrow jail cell other than write long letters, think strange thoughts, and pray long prayers?

If I have said anything in this letter that is an overstatement of the truth and is indicative of an unreasonable impatience, I beg you to forgive me. If I have said anything in this letter that is an understatement of the truth and is indicative of my having a patience that makes me patient with anything less than brotherhood, I beg God to forgive me.

I hope this letter finds you strong in the faith. I also hope that circumstances will   45
soon make it possible for me to meet each of you, not as an integrationist or a civil rights leader, but as a fellow clergyman and a Christian brother. Let us all hope that the dark clouds of racial prejudice will soon pass away and the deep fog of misunderstanding will be lifted from our fear-drenched communities and in some not too distant tomorrow the radiant stars of love and brotherhood will shine over our great nation with all of their scintillating beauty.

Yours for the cause of Peace and Brotherhood,
Martin Luther King, Jr.

UNDERSTANDING THE TEXT

1. How does King answer the major criticisms raised in the letter: that the Birmingham demonstrations are being directed by outsiders, that they are making tensions worse, and that they are encouraging disrespect for the law?

2. What portions of the letter speak to people other than (or in addition to) the clergymen to whom it is addressed? Through what elements does King appeal to the letter's potential nonclerical audience?

3. What does King mean by "we would present our very bodies as a means of laying our case before the conscience of the local and national community"?

4. What criteria does King give for determining whether or not a law is unjust? What different definitions of "unjust law" does he propose?

5. Why does King consider white moderates to be more of an obstacle than overt racists to the progress of civil rights? Why does he seem more concerned about the lack of support from those who agree with his ends than about those who want to defeat everything that he stands for?

6. How does King contrast Elijah Muhammad's Black Muslim movement with his own activism? What is the rhetorical effect of this comparison?

7. How does King respond to the charge that he is an "extremist"? In what way does he redefine the traditional definition of "extremism"?

MAKING CONNECTIONS

1. Does King's implicit assertion that the ends of segregation justify the means of breaking the law constitute a Machiavellian argument (p. 184)? How so? Does King say that any means are acceptable to this end? Or does he argue that certain means (such as violence) are inherently unacceptable?

2. Compare King's views of democracy, civil disobedience, and nonviolence with those of Aung San Suu Kyi (p. 219). How might the two figures be seen as parts of the same philosophical tradition, despite their differences in religion and culture?

3. Thomas Aquinas (p. 260), whom King quotes in this essay for his opposition to unjust laws, is an important thinker in the "just war" tradition. What basic conception of natural law underlies the ideas of "just law" and "just war"?

4. How do King's experiences with segregation compare with the experience of apartheid described in Desmond Tutu's "Nuremberg or National Amnesia: A Third Way" (p. 227)?

WRITING ABOUT THE TEXT

1. Use King's definitions of "just" and "unjust" laws to make the argument that a certain current law (national or local) or policy of your school is "unjust."

2. Think of conditions that would cause you to disobey a law. Write a "Letter from _____" to explain your disobedience.

3. Evaluate the potential effectiveness of nonviolent direct action in different kinds of political systems. Would the kinds of demonstrations that Martin Luther King Jr. staged in Birmingham work in other, more repressive political situations? (Consider, for example, Nazi Germany, where "civil disobedients" were routinely rounded up and shot.) At what point, if any, should a belief in nonviolence give way to advocacy of a "just war"?

4. Examine the rhetorical effectiveness of the "Letter from Birmingham City Jail." What aspects of the work made it such an effective argument in its own day?

5. Choose a biblical theme or pattern of biblical allusions that King uses in the "Letter from Birmingham City Jail" (such as the writings of Paul, the wanderings of the prophets, the laws of Babylon, etc.). Trace this concept through the letter and show how it supports King's overall argument.

Aung San Suu Kyi
from *In Quest of Democracy*
(1990)

IN 1886, the British invaded the Kingdom of Burma and made it part of the massive colonial enterprise known as British India (encompassing present-day India, Pakistan, Burma, Bangladesh, and Sri Lanka). During World War II, Aung San Suu Kyi's father and partial namesake, the nationalist leader Aung San (1915–1947), enlisted the aid of the Japanese to expel the British and proclaim independence. However, Aung San soon became disillusioned by Japanese militarism and fascism, and he turned his forces against the Japanese. As the war ended, Aung San negotiated with the British for Burma's permanent independence, and he would almost certainly have been its first prime minister had he not been assassinated by a rival politician six months before the official transfer of power occurred.

Though she was the daughter of Burma's most revered hero, Aung San Suu Kyi (b. 1945) spent most of her life outside her native country. She attended high school in New Delhi, where her mother was the Burmese ambassador to India. Upon graduating, she studied at England's Oxford University, where she met and married Michael Aris, a leading scholar of Tibetan culture. During this time, events in Burma were quickly deteriorating. The country's democratically elected government was overthrown in 1962 by the Marxist dictator Ne Win (1910 or 1911–2002), whose authoritarian regime plunged Burma deeper and deeper into poverty and international isolation. In 1988, Aung San Suu Kyi was doing advanced graduate work at London's prestigious School of Oriental and African Studies when her mother suffered a severe stroke. She returned to Burma in April 1988, five months before massive popular uprisings ended Ne Win's twenty-six-year rule.

In the chaos that followed the revolts, Aung San Suu Kyi emerged as a strong political leader and democracy advocate, but a military junta seized power (and officially, though controversially, changed the English version of the country's name from Burma to Myanmar). Despite promising free elections, the junta had no intention of handing control to an elected government; they scheduled immediate elections in 1990 under the assumption that no opposition to their rule could organize in such a short amount of time. To ensure their victory, Aung San Suu Kyi was declared ineligible to run for office and placed under house arrest, and the political party that she formed, the National League for Democracy (NLD), was barred from taking part in the elections in any way. Nonetheless, the NLD won 82 percent of the popular vote, forcing the junta to void the election and rule as an unelected dictatorship. Instead of taking her rightful place as the elected prime minister, Aung San Suu Kyi remained under house arrest. When she was awarded the Nobel Peace Prize in 1991, her oldest son accepted the award in her stead. She was released in

1995 but was placed under house arrest again from 2000 to 2002 and yet again in 2003. Despite the military's attempts to silence her, Aung San Suu Kyi has become an important voice for freedom and democracy in her native country and throughout the world.

In the essay "In Quest of Democracy," a selection from which appears here, Aung San Suu Kyi attempts to answer one of the standard charges made by non-democratic governments throughout the world: that democracy is a Western form of government and a remnant of imperialism that represents values alien to the non-Western world. To answer this charge, Aung San Suu Kyi argues deductively. First she examines the role of government in Buddhist scripture (nearly 90 percent of the population of Burma/Myanmar is Buddhist). She narrates the story of the original social contract in Buddhist scripture and briefly explains the ten duties of kingship in the Buddhist tradition. She then applies these principles to the present definition of "democracy." The essential elements of democracy, fairness, and respect for human rights, she asserts, have always been present in the Buddhist traditions of her people. 🖋

1

OPPONENTS OF THE MOVEMENT for democracy in Burma[1] have sought to undermine it by on the one hand casting aspersions on the competence of the people to judge what was best for the nation and on the other condemning the basic tenets of democracy as un-Burmese. There is nothing new in Third World governments seeking to justify and perpetuate authoritarian rule by denouncing liberal democratic principles as alien. By implication they claim for themselves the official and sole right to decide what does or does not conform to indigenous cultural norms. Such conventional propaganda aimed at consolidating the powers of the establishment has been studied, analysed and disproved by political scientists, jurists and sociologists. But in Burma, distanced by several decades of isolationism from political and intellectual developments in the outside world, the people have had to draw on their own resources to explode the twin myths of their unfitness for political responsibility and the unsuitability of democracy for their society. As soon as the movement for democracy spread out across Burma there was a surge of intense interest in the meaning of the word 'democracy', in its history and its practical implications. More than a quarter-century of narrow authoritarianism under which

---

1. **Burma:** The Union of Burma was established in 1948, having previously been part of British India. In 1989, the ruling military junta declared that the country would be known as the Union of Myanmar, with the designated short form Myanmar. This change has been adopted by the United Nations and by some other international organizations, but is rejected by prodemocracy forces within Burma because it was not ratified by any elected body. The governments of the United States, Great Britain, and Canada continue to call the country Burma, as does Aung San Suu Kyi.

they had been fed a pabulum[2] of shallow, negative dogma had not blunted the perceptiveness or political alertness of the Burmese. On the contrary, perhaps not all that surprisingly, their appetite for discussion and debate, for uncensored information and objective analysis, seemed to have been sharpened. Not only was there an eagerness to study and to absorb standard theories on modern politics and political institutions, there was also widespread and intelligent speculation on the nature of democracy as a social system of which they had had little experience but which appealed to their common-sense notions of what was due to a civilized society. There was a spontaneous interpretative response to such basic ideas as representative government, human rights and the rule of law. The privileges and freedoms which would be guaranteed by democratic institutions were contemplated with understandable enthusiasm. But the duties of those who would bear responsibility for the maintenance of a stable democracy also provoked much thoughtful consideration. It was natural that a people who have suffered much from the consequences of bad government should be preoccupied with theories of good government.

Members of the Buddhist *sangha*[3] in their customary role as mentors have led the way in articulating popular expectations by drawing on classical learning to illuminate timeless values. But the conscious effort to make traditional knowledge relevant to contemporary needs was not confined to any particular circle—it went right through Burmese society from urban intellectuals and small shopkeepers to doughty village grandmothers.

Why has Burma with its abundant natural and human resources failed to live up to its early promise as one of the most energetic and fastest-developing nations in South-east Asia? International scholars have provided detailed answers supported by careful analyses of historical, cultural, political and economic factors. The Burmese people, who have had no access to sophisticated academic material, got to the heart of the matter by turning to the words of the Buddha on the four causes of decline and decay: failure to recover that which had been lost, omission to repair that which had been damaged, disregard of the need for reasonable economy, and the elevation to leadership of men without morality or learning. Translated into contemporary terms, when democratic rights had been lost to military dictatorship sufficient efforts had not been made to regain them, moral and political values had been allowed to deteriorate without concerted attempts to save the situation, the economy had been badly managed, and the country had been ruled by men without integrity or wisdom. A thorough study by the cleverest scholar using the best and latest methods of research could hardly have identified more correctly or succinctly the chief causes of Burma's decline since 1962.

---

2. **Pabulum:** food, or a diet. Because of historical confusion with the word "pablum," or food for infants, the word has come to connote shallow or trite thought.

3. **Sangha:** a collective word for the ordained monks and nuns in the Buddhist religion, similar, in some respects, to the English word "clergy."

Under totalitarian socialism, official policies with little relevance to actual needs had placed Burma in an economic and administrative limbo where government bribery and evasion of regulations were the indispensable lubricant to keep the wheels of everyday life turning. But through the years of moral decay and material decline there has survived a vision of a society in which the people and the leadership could unite in principled efforts to achieve prosperity and security. In 1988 the movement for democracy gave rise to the hope that the vision might become reality. At its most basic and immediate level, liberal democracy would mean in institutional terms a representative government appointed for a constitutionally limited term through free and fair elections. By exercising responsibly their right to choose their own leaders the Burmese hope to make an effective start at reversing the process of decline. They have countered the propagandist doctrine that democracy is unsuited to their cultural norms by examining traditional theories of government.

The Buddhist view of world history tells that when society fell from its original state of purity into moral and social chaos a king was elected to restore peace and justice. The ruler was known by three titles: *Mahasammata*, 'because he is named ruler by the unanimous consent of the people'; *Khattiya*, 'because he has dominion over agricultural land'; and *Raja*, 'because he wins the people to affection through observance of the *dhamma* (virtue, justice, the law)'. The agreement by which their first monarch undertakes to rule righteously in return for a portion of the rice crop represents the Buddhist version of government by social contract. The *Mahasammata* follows the general pattern of Indic kingship in South-east Asia. This has been criticized as antithetical to the idea of the modern state because it promotes a personalized form of monarchy lacking the continuity inherent in the western abstraction of the king as possessed of both a body politic and a body natural. However, because the *Mahasammata* was chosen by popular consent and required to govern in accordance with just laws, the concept of government elective and *sub lege*[4] is not alien to traditional Burmese thought.

The Buddhist view of kingship does not invest the ruler with the divine right to govern the realm as he pleases. He is expected to observe the Ten Duties of Kings, the Seven Safeguards against Decline, the Four Assistances to the People, and to be guided by numerous other codes of conduct such as the Twelve Practices of Rulers, the Six Attributes of Leaders, the Eight Virtues of Kings and the Four Ways to Overcome Peril. There is logic to a tradition which includes the king among the five enemies or perils and which subscribes to many sets of moral instructions for the edification of those in positions of authority. The people of Burma have had much experience of despotic rule and possess a great awareness of the unhappy gap that can exist between the theory and practice of government.

4. **Sub lege:** "Under the law"; the phrase here refers to a government that is bound by, and accountable to, legal authorities.

The Ten Duties of Kings are widely known and generally accepted as a yardstick which could be applied just as well to modern government as to the first monarch of the world. The duties are: liberality, morality, self-sacrifice, integrity, kindness, austerity, non-anger, non-violence, forbearance and non-opposition (to the will of the people).

The first duty of liberality (*dana*) which demands that a ruler should contribute generously towards the welfare of the people makes the tacit assumption that a government should have the competence to provide adequately for its citizens. In the context of modern politics, one of the prime duties of a responsible administration would be to ensure the economic security of the state.

Morality (*sila*) in traditional Buddhist terms is based on the observance of the five precepts, which entails refraining from destruction of life, theft, adultery, falsehood and indulgence in intoxicants. The ruler must bear a high moral character to win the respect and trust of the people, to ensure their happiness and prosperity and to provide a proper example. When the king does not observe the *dhamma*, state functionaries become corrupt, and when state functionaries are corrupt the people are caused much suffering. It is further believed that an unrighteous king brings down calamity on the land. The root of a nation's misfortunes has to be sought in the moral failings of the government.

The third duty, *paricagga*, is sometimes translated as generosity and sometimes as self-sacrifice. The former would constitute a duplication of the first duty, *dana*, so self-sacrifice as the ultimate generosity which gives up all for the sake of the people would appear the more satisfactory interpretation. The concept of selfless public service is sometimes illustrated by the story of the hermit Sumedha who took the vow of Buddhahood.[5] In so doing he who could have realized the supreme liberation of *nirvana* in a single lifetime committed himself to countless incarnations that he might help other beings free themselves from suffering. Equally popular is the story of the monkey king who sacrificed his life to save his subjects, including one who had always wished him harm and who was the eventual cause of his death. The good ruler sublimates his needs as an individual to the service of the nation.

Integrity (*ajjava*) implies incorruptibility in the discharge of public duties as well as honesty and sincerity in personal relations. There is a Burmese saying: 'With rulers, truth, with (ordinary) men, vows'. While a private individual may be bound only by the formal vows that he makes, those who govern should be wholly bound by the truth in thought, word and deed. Truth is the very essence of the teachings of the Buddha, who referred to himself as the *Tathagata* or 'one who has come to the truth'. The Buddhist king must therefore live and rule by truth, which is the perfect uniformity between

10

---

5. **Sumedha:** In Buddhist tradition, Sumedha was a man who inherited great wealth from his parents but, instead of accepting it, opened his treasury to the people of the village and declared that anyone could take whatever they wanted. Upon renouncing his wealth, Sumedha became a hermit and attained the status of a Buddha.

nomenclature and nature.[6] To deceive or to mislead the people in any way would be an occupational failing as well as a moral offence. 'As an arrow, intrinsically straight, without warp or distortion, when one word is spoken, it does not err into two.'

Kindness (*maddava*) in a ruler is in a sense the courage to feel concern for the people. It is undeniably easier to ignore the hardships of those who are too weak to demand their rights than to respond sensitively to their needs. To care is to accept responsibility, to dare to act in accordance with the dictum that the ruler is the strength of the helpless. In *Wizaya*, a well-known nineteenth-century drama based on the *Mahavamsa* story of Prince Vijaya, a king sends away into exile his own son whose wild ways have caused the people much distress: 'In the matter of love, to make no distinction between citizen and son, to give equally of loving kindness, that is the righteousness of kings.'

The duty of austerity (*tapa*) enjoins the king to adopt simple habits, to develop self-control and to practise spiritual discipline. The self-indulgent ruler who enjoys an extravagant lifestyle and ignores the spiritual need for austerity was no more acceptable at the time of the *Mahasammata* then he would be in Burma today.

The seventh, eighth and ninth duties—non-anger (*akkodha*), non-violence (*avi-hamsa*) and forbearance (*khanti*)—could be said to be related. Because the displeasure of the powerful could have unhappy and far-reaching consequences, kings must not allow personal feelings of enmity and ill will to erupt into destructive anger and violence. It is incumbent on a ruler to develop the true forbearance which moves him to deal wisely and generously with the shortcomings and provocations of even those whom he could crush with impunity. Violence is totally contrary to the teachings of Buddhism. The good ruler vanquishes ill will with loving kindness, wickedness with virtue, parsimony with liberality, and falsehood with truth. The Emperor Ashoka[7] who ruled his realm in accordance with the principles of non-violence and compassion is always held up as an ideal Buddhist king. A government should not attempt to enjoin submission through harshness and immoral force but should aim at *dhamma-vijaya*, a conquest by righteousness.

The tenth duty of kings, non-opposition to the will of the people (*avirodha*), tends to be singled out as a Buddhist endorsement of democracy, supported by well-known stories from the *Jakatas*.[8] Pawridasa, a monarch who acquired an unfortunate taste for human flesh, was forced to leave his kingdom because he would not heed the people's demand that he should abandon his cannibalistic habits. A very different

15

---

6. **Nomenclature:** a system of naming. **Uniformity between nomenclature and nature** means that what is said to be true corresponds to what is true.

7. **Emperor Ashoka:** ruler (d. 232 BCE) of the Mauryan Empire, the first political entity that united nearly all of the Indian subcontinent. In the early part of his reign, Ashoka was violent and ruthless, but after converting to Buddhism, he became renowned for his compassionate government and commitment to peace.

8. *Jakatas:* a collection of stories about the Buddha's lives in previous incarnations. Traditionally, the 550 *Jakatas* represent the Buddha's 550 previous lives.

kind of ruler was the Buddha's penultimate incarnation on earth, the pious King Vessantara.[9] But he too was sent into exile when in the course of his strivings for the perfection of liberality he gave away the white elephant of the state without the consent of the people. The real duty of non-opposition is a reminder that the legitimacy of government is founded on the consent of the people, who may withdraw their mandate at any time if they lose confidence in the ability of the ruler to serve their best interests.

By invoking the Ten Duties of Kings the Burmese are not so much indulging in wishful thinking as drawing on time-honoured values to reinforce the validity of the political reforms they consider necessary. It is a strong argument for democracy that governments regulated by principles of accountability, respect for public opinion and the supremacy of just laws are more likely than an all-powerful ruler or ruling class, uninhibited by the need to honour the will of the people, to observe the traditional duties of Buddhist kingship. Traditional values serve both to justify and to decipher popular expectations of democratic government.

UNDERSTANDING THE TEXT

1. What two kinds of arguments have opponents of democracy in Burma used to discredit their opponents? How does Aung San Suu Kyi refute these charges?

2. Why is democracy a relatively new concept to the Burmese people? In the words of the Buddha, what four causes of decline and decay have prevented Burma from fully prospering? How are these causes relatable to other troubled countries and governments in today's world?

3. By what three names is the legitimate ruler known in Buddhist tradition? What does each name signify? How does Aung San Suu Kyi translate these concepts into a more contemporary setting?

4. How does Aung San Suu Kyi combine the idea of a democratic government with Buddhist principles? How does one support the other? How are the Ten Duties of Kings similar to tenets of a democratic government? How do these duties protect the citizens from the government?

5. To what purpose does Aung San Suu Kyi use the traditional Buddhist stories of Sumedha, Pawridasa, and Vessantara? How does each story support the point that political power ultimately rests in the people's hands?

9. **Vessantara:** one of the most recent incarnations of the Buddha, in the best-known *Jakata* tale. As a prince, Vessantara was known for his generosity. As a young king, he gave away a great white elephant that had become a symbol of his country. The people were so disheartened by the loss of the elephant that they lost their confidence in his leadership, leading him to relinquish the throne to his father and become an ascetic.

MAKING CONNECTIONS

1. Compare Martin Luther King Jr. (p. 202), Mohandas K. Gandhi (p. 332), and Aung San Suu Kyi as religious social reformers. In what way does each of them bring religious belief directly to bear on social problems?

2. How does the Buddhist narrative that Aung San Suu Kyi retells here compare with the Buddhist poem "The Precious Garland" (p. 110)? What themes, if any, do the two works have in common?

3. Compare the ways that the religious views of Aung San Suu Kyi, al-Farabi (p. 170), and Desmond Tutu (p. 227) influence their understanding of government's role.

WRITING ABOUT THE TEXT

1. Explore democratic governments' ability to incorporate traditional belief systems into policy. What gives democracy this flexibility? What are the pros and cons of, for instance, religious influences on contemporary American lawmaking?

2. Compare Martin Luther King Jr.'s use of Christianity in the "Letter from Birmingham City Jail" (p. 202) with Aung San Suu Kyi's use of Buddhism in "In Quest of Democracy."

3. Compare different notions of the "social contract" across various cultures. How does Aung San Suu Kyi's understanding of this contract differ from Hobbes's (p. 119)?

Desmond Tutu
Nuremberg or National Amnesia: A Third Way
(1997)

In 1984, the year that Desmond Tutu (b. 1931) won the Nobel Peace Prize, his country of South Africa was at the center of an international firestorm over its practice of apartheid. Apartheid, or "apartness," was a system of racial segregation that disenfranchised the black South African majority and subjected them to officially mandated inequalities in education, employment, legal status, and police protection. When it began in 1948, apartheid was comparable to the official segregation that existed in the American South and other regions of the world—except that, in South Africa, whites accounted for less than 10 percent of the total population.

By the 1980s, however, the civil rights movement in America and the decolonization of Asia and Africa had eliminated official segregation in nearly every other industrialized nation. South Africa became a pariah nation, subject to boycotts and diplomatic pressures from other countries and increasing protests at home. During this time, Tutu, an Anglican bishop and democracy advocate, became an international symbol of the struggle against apartheid. After winning the Nobel Prize in 1984, he became the Bishop of Johannesburg in 1985 and the Archbishop of Cape Town—as well as the first black cleric to lead the Anglican Church in South Africa—in 1986. All the while, he continued his resistance to apartheid and his advocacy of nonviolent resistance in the tradition of Mahatma Gandhi and Martin Luther King Jr.

Racial tensions nearly plunged South Africa into a civil war. Chaos was averted, however, when F. W. de Klerk (b. 1936) became prime minister in 1989 and, less than a year later, began dismantling the apartheid system. He rescinded the long-standing ban on the African National Congress and released its leader, Nelson Mandela (b. 1918), from jail after twenty-seven years of incarceration. In 1994, Mandela became the president of the newly democratic Republic of South Africa, with F. W. de Klerk as deputy president.

With the transition to democracy, South Africa's new government had to find a way to address the atrocities that had occurred during the apartheid regime without destroying the fragile truce that existed between the old and the new governments. It was Desmond Tutu who provided the solution to this problem. In 1996, Tutu retired as the Archbishop of Cape Town to become the chair of the Truth and Reconciliation Commission, which was set up in an attempt provide healing, rather than retributive, justice. The commission was empowered to grant amnesty for criminal acts committed by both white officials and black protesters, on the condition that they fully disclosed the crimes for which they were seeking amnesty. Under Tutu's leadership, the Truth and Reconciliation Commission, whose purpose he explains here, became an important element in the creation of a stable democracy in South Africa.

"Nuremberg or National Amnesia: A Third Way" is the second chapter of Tutu's 1999 book *No Future without Forgiveness*.

This selection from Tutu's book presents a clear example of an argument based on a Hegelian synthesis. Tutu considers two antithetical solutions to the problem of dealing with South Africa's past. By placing these propositions in opposition to each other, he succeeds in rejecting them both and constructing a third alternative to take their place. ◩

THE DEBILITATING LEGACY of apartheid is going to be with us for many a long day yet. No one possesses a magic wand which the architects of the new dispensation could wave and, "Hey presto!" things will be transformed overnight into a promised land flowing with milk and honey. Apartheid, firmly entrenched for a long half century and carried out with a ruthless efficiency, was too strong for that. It is going to take a long time for the pernicious effects of apartheid's egregiousness to be eradicated.

Apart from the systematic and devastating violation of all sorts of human rights by the nature of apartheid itself—described by five senior judges in a deposition to the commission as "in itself and in the way it was implemented . . . a gross abuse of human rights"—many South Africans remembered that awful deeds had been perpetrated in the past. They remembered the Sharpeville massacre when, on March 21, 1960, a peaceful crowd demonstrated against the pass laws and sixty-nine people were mown down when the police panicked and opened fire on the demonstrators, most of whom were shot in the back while fleeing.

People recalled the Soweto uprising of June 16, 1976, when unarmed schoolchildren were shot and killed as they demonstrated against the use of the Afrikaans language as a medium of instruction. Afrikaans was regarded as the language of the enforcers of the apartheid policy that an overwhelmingly Afrikaans-speaking political party, the Nationalist Party, had inflicted on the nation from 1948.

South Africa remembered that several people had died mysteriously while they were in police detention. It was alleged by the authorities who might perhaps have been believed by most of the white community—they were certainly not believed by most of the black community—that they had committed suicide by hanging themselves with their belts, or they had slipped on soap while showering, or they tended to have a penchant for jumping out of the windows of the buildings where they were being detained and questioned. Others died, so we were told, from self-inflicted injuries. One such was Steve Biko, the young student founder of the Black Consciousness Movement. It was said he had banged his head against the wall in an inexplicable and quite unreasonable altercation with his interrogators in September 1977. People recalled that when the then Minister of Police was told of Steve's death he had callously and memorably declared that his death "leaves me cold." People recalled that Steve had been driven naked on the back of a police truck over 1500 kilometers to Pretoria, where it was reported he would have received medical treatment, except that he died soon after he arrived there. No one ever explained why he could not have got the emergency treatment in Port Elizabeth where he had been detained, nor why if he had had to be taken to Pretoria he had had to be humiliated, comatose as he was, by being transported without any clothes on.

People remembered the bombing in Amanzimtoti, KwaZulu/Natal, in 1985 when a limpet mine placed in a refuse bin outside a shopping center exploded among holidaymakers doing last-minute Christmas shopping, killing five persons and injuring over sixty.

South Africa recalled the Magoo's Bar bombing of June 1986, when three people were killed and about sixty-nine injured by a car bomb planted by Robert McBride and his two accomplices, allegedly on the orders of a commander of the ANC's armed wing, Umkhonto weSizwe,[1] based in neighboring Botswana.

People had been filled with revulsion when they saw how people were killed so 5 gruesomely through the so-called "necklace," a tire placed around the victim's neck and filled with petrol and then set alight. This horrible way of execution was used by township ANC-supporting "comrades" especially against "sellouts," those who were suspected of being collaborators with the state. It was also used in the internecine strife between warring liberation movements, such as the United Democratic Front (UDF), which largely comprised ANC sympathizers while that party was banned, and the Azanian People's Organization (Azapo), the party espousing the principles of black consciousness developed by Steve Biko and his colleagues. You were appalled that human beings, children even, could actually dance around the body of someone dying in such an excruciating fashion. Apartheid had succeeded only too well in dehumanizing its victims and those who implemented it. People remembered that all this was very much a part of our past, a part of our history.

People were appalled at the carnage in Church Street, Pretoria, in May 1983 when a massive bomb exploded outside the administrative headquarters of the South African Air Force. Twenty-one people died and over two hundred were injured. The ANC claimed responsibility for this outrage.

More recently people recalled the St. James' Church massacre in Cape Town in July 1993. In that attack, two members of the armed wing of the Pan Africanist Congress (PAC)—the liberation movement which had broken away from the ANC in 1959—burst into a Sunday church service and fired machine guns, killing eleven worshipers and injuring fifty-six. Nothing, it seemed, was sacrosanct anymore in this urban guerrilla warfare.

These and similar atrocities pockmarked our history and on all sides it was agreed 10 that we had to take this past seriously into account. We could not pretend that it had not happened. Much of it was too fresh in the memories of many communities.

There was in fact hardly any controversy about whether we should deal effectively with our past if we were going to be making the transition to a new dispen-

---

1. **Umkhonto weSizwe:** translates as "Spear of the Nation." [Author's note]

sation. No, the debate was not on *whether* but on *how* we might deal with this only too real past.

There were those who wanted to follow the Nuremberg[2] trial paradigm, by bringing to trial all perpetrators of gross violations of human rights and letting them run the gauntlet of the normal judicial process. This, it turned out, was really not a viable option at all, perhaps mercifully for us in South Africa. In World War II the Allies defeated the Nazis and their allies comprehensively and were thus able to impose what has been described as "victor's justice." The accused had no say whatsoever in the matter, and because some of those who sat in judgment on the accused, such as the Russians, were themselves guilty of similar gross violations in the excesses perpetrated under Stalin, the whole process left a simmering resentment in many Germans as I found out when I participated in a BBC-TV panel discussion in the very room in Nuremberg where the trial had taken place fifty years previously. The Germans had accepted it because they were down and out and the victors, as it were, could kick the vanquished even as they lay on the ground. Thus the Nuremberg option was rejected by those who were negotiating the delicate process of transition to democracy, the rule of law, and respect for human rights. Neither side could impose victor's justice because neither side won the decisive victory that would have enabled it to do so, since we had a military stalemate.

It is as certain as anything that the security forces of the apartheid regime would not have supported the negotiated settlement which made possible the "miracle" of our relatively peaceful transition from repression to democracy—when most people had been making dire predictions of a blood bath, of a comprehensive disaster that would overwhelm us—had they known that at the end of the negotiations they would be for the high jump, when they would face the full wrath of the law as alleged perpetrators. They still controlled the guns and had the capacity to sabotage the whole process.

As the beneficiaries of a peaceful transition, citizens in a remarkable democratic dispensation, some South Africans—and others in the international community—enjoy the luxury of being able to complain that all the perpetrators ought to have been brought to justice. The fact of the matter is that we do unfortunately have remarkably short memories. We have in our amnesia forgotten that we were on tenterhooks until 1994, within a trice of the most comprehensive disaster, but that, in God's mercy, we were spared all of this. Those who now enjoy the new dispensation have forgotten too soon just how vulnerable and indeed how unlikely it was and why it is that the world can still look on in amazement that this miracle did in fact unfold. The miracle was the result of the negotiated settlement. There would have been no negotiated settlement and so no new democratic South Africa had the negotiators on one side insisted that all perpetrators be brought to trial. While the Allies could pack up and go home after Nuremberg, we in South Africa had to live with one another. . . .

2. **Nuremberg:** German city where Nazi officials were tried for war crimes after World War II.

There were other very cogent and important reasons that the Nuremberg trial option   15
found little favor with the negotiators. Even if we had been able to choose it, it would
have placed an intolerable burden on an already strained judicial system. We had some
experience of cases of this nature because the state had in two major trials prosecuted
Colonel Eugene de Kock, former head of a police death squad, in 1995 and 1996, and
General Magnus Malan, former Minister of Defense, and a number of generals
and other military officers in 1996. It had taken a whole bevy of Department of Justice and Safety and Security (police) personnel eighteen months to make a case successfully against de Kock, and since he had been a former state employee, the state
was obliged to foot his legal bill, which came to R5 million (nearly U.S. $1 million)—
an amount that did not include the cost of the prosecution and its bureaucracy, or an
expensive witness protection program. In the case of General Malan and his co-accused,
the prosecution failed to nail their men and the costs were astronomical, running into
nearly R12 million (U.S. $2 million) just for the defense, which again had to be borne
by the state. In a country strapped for cash and with a whole range of pressing prior-
ities in education, health, housing, and other fields, tough decisions had to be made
about what the country could be expected to afford.

We also could not have afforded to canvass day in and day out for an uncon-
scionably long time details which from the nature of the case would be distressing
to many and also too disruptive of a fragile peace and stability. We certainly would
not have been able to have the tenacity of Nazi hunters who more than fifty years
later are still at it. We have had to balance the requirements of justice, accountability, stability, peace, and reconciliation. We could very well have had justice, retributive justice, and had a South Africa lying in ashes—a truly Pyrrhic victory[3] if
ever there was one. Our country had to decide very carefully where it would spend
its limited resources to the best possible advantage.

Other important reasons why the trial option was not a viable one could still be
adduced. A criminal court requires the evidence produced in a case to pass the most
rigorous scrutiny and satisfy the criterion of proving the case beyond reasonable
doubt. In many of the cases which came before the commission, the only witnesses
to events who were still alive were the perpetrators and they had used the considerable resources of the state to destroy evidence and cover up their heinous deeds.
The commission proved to be a better way of getting at the truth than court cases:
amnesty applicants had to demonstrate that they had made a full disclosure to qualify for amnesty, so the normal legal process was reversed as applicants sought to discharge the onus on them to reveal all.

Most distressingly, we discovered in the course of the TRC investigations and
work that the supporters of apartheid were ready to lie at the drop of a hat. This

---

3. **Pyrrhic victory:** a victory that inflicts great
damage on the victor, named after the Greek
king Pyrrhus, whose army defeated the Romans
in 280 BCE but, in doing so, took devastating
casualties that limited his ability to fight future
wars.

applied to cabinet ministers, commissioners of police, and of course those in the lower echelons as well. They lied as if it were going out of fashion, brazenly and with very considerable apparent conviction. In the courts it was the word of one bewildered victim against that of several perpetrators, other officers in the police or armed forces who perjured themselves as they have now admitted in their applications for amnesty. It would have had to be a very brave judge or magistrate who would find in favor of the solitary witness who would in addition have the further disadvantage of being black facing a phalanx of white police officers who really could never do such a dastardly thing as to lie in court.

No wonder the judicial system gained such a notorious reputation in the black community. It was taken for granted that the judges and magistrates colluded with the police to produce miscarriages of justice. Until fairly recently the magistrates and judges were all white, sharing the apprehensions and prejudices of their white compatriots, secure in enjoying the privileges that the injustices of apartheid provided them so lavishly and therefore inclined to believe that all opposition to that status quo was Communist-inspired and generally supporting the executive and the legislative branches of government against the black person who was excluded by the law from a share in the governance of his motherland. Many judges in the old dispensation were blatantly political appointees and they did nothing to redeem the reputation of the judiciary as a willing collaborator with an unjust dispensation. Of course there were some exceptions, but by and large the dice were heavily loaded against the black litigant or accused or complainant. It will take some time for our black people to have confidence in the police and the judicial system, which was so badly discredited in the bad old days. . . .

When it came to hearing evidence from victims, because we were not a criminal court, we established facts on the basis of a balance of probability. Since we were exhorted by our enabling legislation to rehabilitate the human and civil dignity of victims, we allowed those who came to testify mainly to tell *their* stories in their own words. We did do all we could to corroborate these stories and we soon discovered that, as Judge Albie Sachs, a member of our Constitutional Court, has pointed out, there were in fact different orders of truth which did not necessarily mutually exclude one another. There was what could be termed forensic factual truth—verifiable and documentable—and there was "social truth, the truth of experience that is established through interaction, discussion and debate."[4] The personal truth—Judge Mahomed's "truth of wounded memories"—was a healing truth and a court of law would have left many of those who came to testify, who were frequently uneducated and unsophisticated, bewildered and even more traumatized than before, whereas many bore witness to the fact that coming to talk to the commission had had a marked therapeutic effect on them. We learned this from unsolicited comment by

20

4. In *The Healing of a Nation?* Alex Boraine, Janet Levy, eds., Justice in Transition, 1995. [Author's note]

the brother of one of the Cradock Four, ANC-supporting activists who left their homes in Cradock to attend a political rally in Port Elizabeth and never made it back home, having been gruesomely murdered by the police. The brother said to me after one of his relatives had testified at the TRC's first hearing, and before the policemen responsible had confessed and applied for amnesty: "Archbishop, we have told our story to many on several occasions, to newspapers and to the TV. This is the first time though that after telling it we feel as if a heavy load has been removed from our shoulders."

Thus the option of trials, which represented one extreme of the possible ways of dealing with our past, was rejected.

Then there were those others who opposed the trial option and suggested rather glibly that we let bygones be bygones. This was much sought after by the members of the previous government and those who had carried out their behest in their security forces. They clamored for a blanket or general amnesty as had happened in, for instance, Chile, where General Augusto Pinochet[5] and his cohorts gave themselves amnesty as a precondition to handing over from their military junta to a civilian government. Even though they agreed to the appointment of a Truth Commission, such a commission would deliberate only behind closed doors and the record of General Pinochet and his government and the security forces would not be scrutinized by the commission, certainly not for the purpose of apportioning blame. It has been important in the whole debate over impunity to point out that General Pinochet and his officers and government forgave themselves, they alone knew what precisely they had done; they were the accused, the prosecution, and the judges in their own case. In the absence of amnesty designed, as it was in South Africa, to establish accountability, I am a strong supporter of the recent extradition proceedings against General Pinochet. It would be quite intolerable that the perpetrator should decide not only whether he should get amnesty but that no one else should have the right to question the grounds on which he had so granted himself amnesty and for what offense.

In the South African case there was to be no general amnesty. This amnesty was not automatic and the applicant had to make an individual application, then appear before an independent panel which decided whether the applicant satisfied the stringent conditions for granting amnesty. So the other extreme, of blanket amnesty, was also rejected. Apart from the reasons given above, it was felt very strongly that general amnesty was really amnesia. It was pointed out that we none of us possess a kind of fiat by which we can say, "Let bygones be bygones" and, hey presto, they then become bygones. Our common experience in fact is the opposite—that the past, far

---

5. **Augusto Pinochet:** a Chilean military dictator (1915–2006) who was ousted in 1988 and, ten years later, arrested in Britain under a Spanish warrant for crimes committed against Spanish citizens during his dictatorship. In 2000, a British court allowed Pinochet to return to Chile rather than extraditing him to Spain to face trial for crimes against humanity.

from disappearing or lying down and being quiet, has an embarrassing and persistent way of returning and haunting us unless it has in fact been dealt with adequately. Unless we look the beast in the eye we find it has an uncanny habit of returning to hold us hostage.

The English and Afrikaners in South Africa are a perfect case study in point. During the Anglo-Boer War[6] at the turn of the century, the British incarcerated more than 200,000 people, including Boer women and children and black workers on Boer farms, in what was a new British invention at the time—concentration camps, which were to gain, appropriately, a foul reputation as a special feature of the Jewish Holocaust in Hitler's made obsession with Aryan purity. Nearly 50,000 of the inmates are estimated to have died in unacceptable conditions. At the end of the war neither side ever sat down with the other to talk about this aspect of their war. It seemed that in time the wounds inflicted then had healed and English and Afrikaner seemed to live happily together. Alas, however, the amicable relationship was only superficial and really quite unstable and uneasy. In 1998 I traveled by road from Zurich to attend the World Economic Forum in Davos. I was accompanied by a young Afrikaner who said he remembered so clearly his grandmother telling him of the awful things that had happened to his people in the concentration camps and he said with some feeling that he was ready to fight the Anglo-Boer War over again whenever he remembered his grandmother's stories.

At Dachau, the former concentration camp near Nuremberg, there is a museum   25
to commemorate what happened there—you can see the gas chambers and the ovens where the bodies of the Jews were incinerated. The gas chambers look so innocuous, like normal shower rooms, until you see the vents through which the lethal gas could be pumped into the chamber. In the museum are pictures of prisoners marching behind brass bands while they are carrying some inmate to his execution—macabre humor indeed. The Germans were so methodical and systematic. They recorded everything, including the experiments they carried out to see what depths and altitudes human beings could tolerate, and of course the guinea pigs were the subhuman, non-Aryan, Jewish inmates and it is all there to see in those photographs, showing faces grimacing like hideous gargoyles.

Over the entrance to this museum are philosopher George Santayana's[7] haunting words, "Those who forget the past are doomed to repeat it." Those who were negotiating our future were aware that, unless the past was acknowledged and dealt with adequately, it could put paid to that future as a baneful blight on it.

To accept national amnesia would be bad for another telling reason. It would in effect be to victimize the victims of apartheid a second time around. We would have

---

6. **Anglo-Boer War:** one of two conflicts fought in the late nineteenth century between Great Britain and Dutch settlers, known as Boers, for control of South Africa.

7. **George Santayana:** Spanish philosopher, novelist, and poet (1863–1952).

denied something that contributed to the identity of who they were. Ariel Dorfman, the Chilean playwright, wrote a play entitled *Death and the Maiden*. The maiden's husband has just been appointed to his country's Truth Commission. While she is busy in the kitchen someone whose car has broken down and who has been helped by her husband enters the house. The woman does not see him but hears him speak and she recognizes his voice as that of the man who tortured and raped her when she was in detention. She is then shown with the man completely at her mercy, tied up and helpless. She holds a gun to him and is ready to kill him because he denies strenuously that he could have done this and tries to produce an elaborate alibi. Much later, he eventually admits that he was the culprit and, very strangely, she lets him go. His denial hit at the core of her being, at her integrity, at her identity, and these were all tied up intimately with her experiences, with her memory. Denial subverted her personhood. She was in a real sense her memory, as someone who has Alzheimer's disease is no longer quite the same person we knew when she or he possessed all her or his faculties.

Our nation sought to rehabilitate and affirm the dignity and personhood of those who for so long had been silenced, had been turned into anonymous, marginalized ones. Now they would be able to tell their stories, they would remember, and in remembering would be acknowledged to be persons with an inalienable personhood.

Our country's negotiators rejected the two extremes and opted for a "third way," a compromise between the extreme of Nuremberg trials and blanket amnesty or national amnesia. And that third way was granting amnesty to individuals in exchange for a full disclosure relating to the crime for which amnesty was being sought. It was the carrot of possible freedom in exchange for truth and the stick was, for those already in jail, the prospect of lengthy prison sentences and, for those still free, the probability of arrest and prosecution and imprisonment. . . .

Let us conclude . . . by pointing out that ultimately this third way of amnesty was   30 consistent with a central feature of the African *Weltanschauung*[8]—what we know in our languages as *ubuntu*, in the Nguni group of languages, or *botho*, in the Sotho languages. What is it that constrained so many to choose to forgive rather than to demand retribution, to be so magnanimous and ready to forgive rather than wreak revenge?

Unbuntu is very difficult to render into a Western language. It speaks of the very essence of being human. When we want to give high praise to someone we say, "*Yu, u nobuntu*"; "Hey, so-and-so has *ubuntu*." Then you are generous, you are hospitable, you are friendly and caring and compassionate. You share what you have. It is to say, "My humanity is caught up, is inextricably bound up, in yours." We belong in a bundle of life. We say, "A person is a person through other persons." It is not, "I think therefore I am." It says rather: "I am human because I belong. I participate, I share." A person with *ubuntu* is open and available to others, affirming to others,

8. **Weltanschauung:** a German word meaning "worldview."

does not feel threatened that others are able and good, for he or she has a proper self-assurance that comes from knowing that he or she belongs in a greater whole and is diminished when others are humiliated or diminished, when others are tortured or oppressed, or treated as if they were less than who they are.

Harmony, friendliness, community are great goods. Social harmony is for us the *summum bonum*—the greatest good. Anything that subverts, that undermines this sought-after good, is to be avoided like the plague. Anger, resentment, lust for revenge, even success through aggressive competitiveness, are corrosive of this good. To forgive is not just to be altruistic. It is the best form of self-interest. What dehumanizes you inexorably dehumanizes me. It gives people resilience, enabling them to survive and emerge still human despite all efforts to dehumanize them.

UNDERSTANDING THE TEXT

1. Why does Tutu believe that the legacy of apartheid will extend far beyond its practice?

2. What kinds of events does Tutu describe to illustrate the crimes of the apartheid regime? Whom does he say is responsible for the violence that he cites?

3. What does Tutu see as the flaw in the Nuremberg trials that the Allies conducted after World War II? Why does he say the Nuremberg model would not have worked in South Africa?

4. Why did Tutu feel that it was important to reject the "let bygones be bygones" approach that would have extended blanket amnesty to anybody, on either side, involved in atrocities during the prior regime?

5. What is the point of the play *Death and the Maiden*, by Ariel Dorfman, as Tutu sees it? Why do you think that the woman in the play lets her former torturer go free?

6. How does Tutu translate the African term *ubantu*? Why is this concept important to his argument?

MAKING CONNECTIONS

1. How does Tutu's understanding of democracy compare to that of Aung San Suu Kyi (p. 219)? How are their views shaped by their religious beliefs?

2. Compare the system of apartheid described by Desmond Tutu with the American system of segregation described by Martin Luther King Jr. in "Letter from Birmingham City Jail" (p. 202). How does each writer respond to the political aspect of oppression?

3. Compare the declaration of responsibility required by the Truth and Reconciliation Committee with the "Negative Confession" shown in the Papyrus of Ani (p. 154) that, according to ancient Egyptian beliefs, will be required of all human beings after death. Why do both tribunals require one to account fully for one's deeds?

4. Compare the way that Tutu uses the native African concept of *ubantu* with the way that Chinua Achebe invokes African views of rhetoric and storytelling in "Language and the Destiny of Man" (p. 506).

WRITING ABOUT THE TEXT

1. Write an essay that applies the concept of synthesis, as described by Hegel (p. 624), to Tutu's rejection of both the Nuremberg model of justice and "national amnesia." How might Tutu's solution be considered a synthesis of the other two ways that society has used to address horrible crimes committed by the state?

2. Write an essay in which you argue that the amnesty offered by the Truth and Reconciliation Committee in South Africa is incompatible with a belief in justice. Conduct additional research into the process that Tutu describes.

3. Read or watch the play *Death and the Maiden* by Ariel Dorfman (a film version starring Sigourney Weaver and Ben Kingsley is widely available). Use this play as the basis for an argument about either the value of a tribunal such as the Truth and Recognition Commission or the problems that prevent such a tribunal from operating effectively.

Barack Obama
A More Perfect Union
(2008)

BARACK OBAMA was born in Hawaii in 1961. His parents—whom he would later describe as "a black man from Kenya and a white woman from Kansas"—were both students at the University of Hawaii in Manoa. As a child, Obama lived in Hawaii, Washington State, and Jakarta, Indonesia, the home country of his stepfather. After graduating from high school in Hawaii, Obama studied at Occidental College, Columbia University, and Harvard University before moving to Chicago, Illinois, where he became a professor of constitutional law at the University of Chicago and later a state legislator. In 2004, Obama was elected to the U.S. Senate, and in 2008, he was elected president of the United States, the first African American ever to hold that office.

Obama's campaign for the presidency began in February of 2007, just three years after his election to the U.S. Senate. His closest rival for the nomination of the Democratic Party was Senator Hillary Clinton; in the end, Obama won the nomination in one of the closest primary races in recent history and went on to defeat Senator John McCain, the Republican nominee, in November 2008. The most serious threat to Obama's campaign for the Democratic nomination came in March of 2008, when videos surfaced of Reverend Jeremiah Wright (b. 1941), Obama's long-time pastor at the Trinity United Church of Christ in Chicago, making inflammatory statements about the U.S. government and race relations in America. The videos, which showed Wright saying, among other things, that the government invented HIV "as a means of genocide against people of color," received heavy news coverage and associated Obama with divisive racial politics at a crucial point in a hotly contested Democratic primary.

On March 18, 2008, after several weeks of headlines about the Wright issue, Obama delivered the speech "A More Perfect Union" at the National Constitution Center in Philadelphia, Pennsylvania. In this speech, he responded to those who criticized his relationship with Wright, explaining why he disagreed with Wright and why he refused to denounce him altogether. In addition to addressing his relationship with Wright, Obama used "A More Perfect Union," whose title is taken from the Preamble to the Constitution, to address the broader issue of race in the United States.

Obama uses several rhetorical strategies in his speech. He supports his argument with anecdotes, historical facts, and logical reasoning. Underlying all of these strategies, however, is the creation of an ethos that is sympathetic to the diverse perspectives on race held by different members of his audience. At a number of places in his remarks, Obama refers to personal experiences as a multiracial American in order to establish his authority to speak knowledgeably from several perspectives.

"WE THE PEOPLE, in order to form a more perfect union."

Two hundred and twenty-one years ago, in a hall that still stands across the street, a group of men gathered and, with these simple words, launched America's improbable experiment in democracy. Farmers and scholars, statesmen and patriots who had traveled across an ocean to escape tyranny and persecution finally made real their declaration of independence at a Philadelphia convention that lasted through the spring of 1787.

The document they produced was eventually signed but ultimately unfinished. It was stained by this nation's original sin of slavery, a question that divided the colonies and brought the convention to a stalemate until the founders chose to allow the slave trade to continue for at least twenty more years, and to leave any final resolution to future generations.

Of course, the answer to the slavery question was already embedded within our Constitution—a Constitution that had at its very core the ideal of equal citizenship under the law; a Constitution that promised its people liberty, and justice, and a union that could be and should be perfected over time.

And yet words on a parchment would not be enough to deliver slaves from bondage, 5
or provide men and women of every color and creed their full rights and obligations as citizens of the United States. What would be needed were Americans in successive generations who were willing to do their part—through protests and struggle, on the streets and in the courts, through a civil war and civil disobedience, and always at great risk—to narrow the gap between the promise of our ideals and the reality of their time.

This was one of the tasks we set forth at the beginning of this campaign—to continue the long march of those who came before us, a march for a more just, more equal, more free, more caring, and more prosperous America. I chose to run for the presidency at this moment in history because I believe deeply that we cannot solve the challenges of our time unless we solve them together—unless we perfect our union by understanding that we may have different stories, but we hold common hopes; that we may not look the same and we may not have come from the same place, but we all want to move in the same direction—towards a better future for our children and our grandchildren.

This belief comes from my unyielding faith in the decency and generosity of the American people. But it also comes from my own American story.

I am the son of a black man from Kenya and a white woman from Kansas. I was raised with the help of a white grandfather who survived a Depression to serve in Patton's army during World War II and a white grandmother who worked on a bomber assembly line at Fort Leavenworth while he was overseas. I've gone to some of the best schools in America and lived in one of the world's poorest nations.[1]

1. **One of the world's poorest nations:** From 1967 through 1971, Obama lived in Indonesia with his mother and his stepfather, Lolo Soetoro, an Indonesian citizen.

I am married to a black American who carries within her the blood of slaves and slaveowners—an inheritance we pass on to our two precious daughters. I have brothers, sisters, nieces, nephews, uncles, and cousins, of every race and every hue, scattered across three continents, and for as long as I live, I will never forget that in no other country on Earth is my story even possible.

It's a story that hasn't made me the most conventional candidate. But it is a story that has seared into my genetic makeup the idea that this nation is more than the sum of its parts—that out of many, we are truly one.

Throughout the first year of this campaign, against all predictions to the contrary, we saw how hungry the American people were for this message of unity. Despite the temptation to view my candidacy through a purely racial lens, we won commanding victories in states with some of the whitest populations in the country. In South Carolina, where the Confederate flag still flies, we built a powerful coalition of African Americans and white Americans. 10

This is not to say that race has not been an issue in the campaign. At various stages in the campaign, some commentators have deemed me either "too black" or "not black enough." We saw racial tensions bubble to the surface during the week before the South Carolina primary. The press has scoured every exit poll for the latest evidence of racial polarization, not just in terms of white and black, but black and brown as well.

And yet, it has only been in the last couple of weeks that the discussion of race in this campaign has taken a particularly divisive turn.

On one end of the spectrum, we've heard the implication that my candidacy is somehow an exercise in affirmative action; that it's based solely on the desire of wide-eyed liberals to purchase racial reconciliation on the cheap. On the other end, we've heard my former pastor, Reverend Jeremiah Wright, use incendiary language to express views that have the potential not only to widen the racial divide, but views that denigrate both the greatness and the goodness of our nation; that rightly offend white and black alike.

I have already condemned, in unequivocal terms, the statements of Reverend Wright that have caused such controversy. For some, nagging questions remain. Did I know him to be an occasionally fierce critic of American domestic and foreign policy? Of course. Did I ever hear him make remarks that could be considered controversial while I sat in church? Yes. Did I strongly disagree with many of his political views? Absolutely—just as I'm sure many of you have heard remarks from your pastors, priests, or rabbis with which you strongly disagreed.

But the remarks that have caused this recent firestorm weren't simply controversial. They weren't simply a religious leader's effort to speak out against perceived injustice. Instead, they expressed a profoundly distorted view of this country—a view that sees white racism as endemic and that elevates what is wrong with America above all that we know is right with America; a view that sees the conflicts in the Middle East as rooted primarily in the actions of stalwart allies like Israel, instead of emanating from the perverse and hateful ideologies of radical Islam. 15

As such, Reverend Wright's comments were not only wrong but divisive, divisive at a time when we need unity; racially charged at a time when we need to come together to solve a set of monumental problems—two wars, a terrorist threat, a falling economy, a chronic health care crisis and potentially devastating climate change; problems that are neither black or white or Latino or Asian, but rather problems that confront us all.

Given my background, my politics, and my professed values and ideals, there will no doubt be those for whom my statements of condemnation are not enough. Why associate myself with Reverend Wright in the first place, they may ask? Why not join another church? And I confess that if all that I knew of Reverend Wright were the snippets of those sermons that have run in an endless loop on the television and YouTube, or if Trinity United Church of Christ conformed to the caricatures being peddled by some commentators, there is no doubt that I would react in much the same way.

But the truth is, that isn't all that I know of the man. The man I met more than twenty years ago is a man who helped introduce me to my Christian faith, a man who spoke to me about our obligations to love one another, to care for the sick and lift up the poor. He is a man who served his country as a U.S. Marine; who has studied and lectured at some of the finest universities and seminaries in the country, and who for over thirty years led a church that serves the community by doing God's work here on Earth—by housing the homeless, ministering to the needy, providing daycare services and scholarships and prison ministries, and reaching out to those suffering from HIV/AIDS.

In my first book, *Dreams From My Father*, I described the experience of my first service at Trinity:

> People began to shout, to rise from their seats and clap and cry out, a forceful wind carrying the reverend's voice up into the rafters. . . . And in that single note—hope!—I heard something else; at the foot of that cross, inside the thousands of churches across the city, I imagined the stories of ordinary black people merging with the stories of David and Goliath, Moses and Pharaoh, the Christians in the lion's den, Ezekiel's field of dry bones.[2] Those stories—of survival, and freedom, and hope—became our story, my story; the blood that had spilled was our blood, the tears our tears, until this black church, on this bright day, seemed once more a vessel carrying the story of a people into

---

2. **David and Goliath, Moses and Pharaoh, the Christians in the lion's den, Ezekiel's field of dry bones:** All of these references are to biblical stories that speak to persecution and to the eventual triumph of the persecuted. David was a shepherd who killed the giant Goliath. Moses led the Children of Israel out of Egypt in defiance of the pharaoh, who had forced them into slavery. The reference to "Christians in the lion's den" combines the biblical story of Daniel with the story of early Christians being fed to lions in Rome; Daniel was thrown into a den of lions when he refused to stop praying to his god but was ultimately saved by the Lord. The prophet Ezekiel saw a great vision of a field of bones that he brought to life through the power of God.

future generations and into a larger world. Our trials and triumphs became at once unique and universal, black and more than black; in chronicling our journey, the stories and songs gave us a means to reclaim memories that we didn't need to feel shame about . . . memories that all people might study and cherish—and with which we could start to rebuild.

That has been my experience at Trinity. Like other predominantly black churches across the country, Trinity embodies the black community in its entirety—the doctor and the welfare mom, the model student and the former gang-banger. Like other black churches, Trinity's services are full of raucous laughter and sometimes bawdy humor. They are full of dancing, clapping, screaming, and shouting that may seem jarring to the untrained ear. The church contains in full the kindness and cruelty, the fierce intelligence and the shocking ignorance, the struggles and successes, the love and, yes, the bitterness and bias that make up the black experience in America.

And this helps explain, perhaps, my relationship with Reverend Wright. As imperfect as he may be, he has been like family to me. He strengthened my faith, officiated my wedding, and baptized my children. Not once in my conversations with him have I heard him talk about any ethnic group in derogatory terms, or treat whites with whom he interacted with anything but courtesy and respect. He contains within him the contradictions—the good and the bad—of the community that he has served diligently for so many years.

I can no more disown him than I can disown the black community. I can no more disown him than I can my white grandmother—a woman who helped raise me, a woman who sacrificed again and again for me, a woman who loves me as much as she loves anything in this world, but a woman who once confessed her fear of black men who passed by her on the street, and who on more than one occasion has uttered racial or ethnic stereotypes that made me cringe.

These people are a part of me. And they are a part of America, this country that I love.

Some will see this as an attempt to justify or excuse comments that are simply inexcusable. I can assure you it is not. I suppose the politically safe thing would be to move on from this episode and just hope that it fades into the woodwork. We can dismiss Reverend Wright as a crank or a demagogue, just as some have dismissed Geraldine Ferraro,[3] in the aftermath of her recent statements, as harboring some deep-seated racial bias.

But race is an issue that I believe this nation cannot afford to ignore right now. We would be making the same mistake that Reverend Wright made in his offend-

---

3. **Geraldine Ferraro:** former member of Congress and 1984 Democratic vice-presidential candidate (b. 1935). Ferraro, who supported Hillary Clinton during the 2008 primary, caused a minor controversy when she told a California newspaper that "if Obama was a white man, he would not be in this position."

ing sermons about America—to simplify and stereotype and amplify the negative to the point that it distorts reality.

The fact is that the comments that have been made and the issues that have surfaced over the last few weeks reflect the complexities of race in this country that we've never really worked through—a part of our union that we have yet to perfect. And if we walk away now, if we simply retreat into our respective corners, we will never be able to come together and solve challenges like health care, or education, or the need to find good jobs for every American.

Understanding this reality requires a reminder of how we arrived at this point. As William Faulkner once wrote, "The past isn't dead and buried. In fact, it isn't even past."[4] We do not need to recite here the history of racial injustice in this country. But we do need to remind ourselves that so many of the disparities that exist in the African American community today can be directly traced to inequalities passed on from an earlier generation that suffered under the brutal legacy of slavery and Jim Crow.

Segregated schools were, and are, inferior schools; we still haven't fixed them, fifty years after *Brown v. Board of Education*,[5] and the inferior education they provided, then and now, helps explain the pervasive achievement gap between today's black and white students.

Legalized discrimination—where blacks were prevented, often through violence, from owning property, or loans were not granted to African American business owners, or black homeowners could not access FHA mortgages,[6] or blacks were excluded from unions, or the police force, or fire departments—meant that black families could not amass any meaningful wealth to bequeath to future generations. That history helps explain the wealth and income gap between black and white, and the concentrated pockets of poverty that persists in so many of today's urban and rural communities.

A lack of economic opportunity among black men, and the shame and frustration that came from not being able to provide for one's family, contributed to the erosion of black families—a problem that welfare policies for many years may have worsened. And the lack of basic services in so many urban black neighborhoods—parks for kids to play in, police walking the beat, regular garbage pick-up and building code enforcement—all helped create a cycle of violence, blight, and neglect that continue to haunt us. 30

This is the reality in which Reverend Wright and other African Americans of his generation grew up. They came of age in the late fifties and early sixties, a time

4. **William Faulkner:** American novelist (1897–1962) and winner of the 1949 Nobel Prize for Literature. Here, Obama paraphrases a passage from Faulkner's 1951 novel *Requiem for a Nun*.
5. *Brown v. Board of Education:* the 1954 Supreme Court decision that outlawed segregation in public schools.

6. **FHA mortgages:** loans insured by the Federal Housing Administration that help people secure mortgages for which they might otherwise not qualify.

when segregation was still the law of the land and opportunity was systematically constricted. What's remarkable is not how many failed in the face of discrimination, but rather how many men and women overcame the odds; how many were able to make a way out of no way for those like me who would come after them.

But for all those who scratched and clawed their way to get a piece of the American Dream, there were many who didn't make it—those who were ultimately defeated, in one way or another, by discrimination. That legacy of defeat was passed on to future generations—those young men and increasingly young women who we see standing on street corners or languishing in our prisons, without hope or prospects for the future. Even for those blacks who did make it, questions of race, and racism, continue to define their worldview in fundamental ways. For the men and women of Reverend Wright's generation, the memories of humiliation and doubt and fear have not gone away; nor has the anger and the bitterness of those years. That anger may not get expressed in public, in front of white co-workers or white friends. But it does find voice in the barbershop or around the kitchen table. At times, that anger is exploited by politicians, to gin up votes along racial lines, or to make up for a politician's own failings.

And occasionally it finds voice in the church on Sunday morning, in the pulpit and in the pews. The fact that so many people are surprised to hear that anger in some of Reverend Wright's sermons simply reminds us of the old truism that the most segregated hour in American life occurs on Sunday morning. That anger is not always productive; indeed, all too often it distracts attention from solving real problems; it keeps us from squarely facing our own complicity in our condition, and prevents the African American community from forging the alliances it needs to bring about real change. But the anger is real; it is powerful; and to simply wish it away, to condemn it without understanding its roots, only serves to widen the chasm of misunderstanding that exists between the races.

In fact, a similar anger exists within segments of the white community. Most working- and middle-class white Americans don't feel that they have been particularly privileged by their race. Their experience is the immigrant experience—as far as they're concerned, no one's handed them anything, they've built it from scratch. They've worked hard all their lives, many times only to see their jobs shipped overseas or their pension dumped after a lifetime of labor. They are anxious about their futures, and feel their dreams slipping away; in an era of stagnant wages and global competition, opportunity comes to be seen as a zero sum game, in which your dreams come at my expense. So when they are told to bus their children to a school across town; when they hear that an African American is getting an advantage in landing a good job or a spot in a good college because of an injustice that they themselves never committed; when they're told that their fears about crime in urban neighborhoods are somehow prejudiced, resentment builds over time.

Like the anger within the black community, these resentments aren't always expressed in polite company. But they have helped shape the political landscape for 35 at least a generation. Anger over welfare and affirmative action helped forge the Reagan Coalition.[7] Politicians routinely exploited fears of crime for their own electoral ends. Talk show hosts and conservative commentators built entire careers unmasking bogus claims of racism while dismissing legitimate discussions of racial injustice and inequality as mere political correctness or reverse racism.

Just as black anger often proved counterproductive, so have these white resentments distracted attention from the real culprits of the middle-class squeeze—a corporate culture rife with inside dealing,[8] questionable accounting practices, and short-term greed; a Washington dominated by lobbyists and special interests; economic policies that favor the few over the many. And yet, to wish away the resentments of white Americans, to label them as misguided or even racist, without recognizing they are grounded in legitimate concerns—this too widens the racial divide, and blocks the path to understanding.

This is where we are right now. It's a racial stalemate we've been stuck in for years. Contrary to the claims of some of my critics, black and white, I have never been so naïve as to believe that we can get beyond our racial divisions in a single election cycle, or with a single candidacy—particularly a candidacy as imperfect as my own.

But I have asserted a firm conviction—a conviction rooted in my faith in God and my faith in the American people—that working together we can move beyond some of our old racial wounds, and that in fact we have no choice if we are to continue on the path of a more perfect union.

For the African American community, that path means embracing the burdens of our past without becoming victims of our past. It means continuing to insist on a full measure of justice in every aspect of American life. But it also means binding our particular grievances—for better health care, and better schools, and better jobs—to the larger aspirations of all Americans—the white woman struggling to break the glass ceiling, the white man whose been laid off, the immigrant trying to feed his family. And it means taking full responsibility for own lives—by demanding more from our fathers, and spending more time with our children, and reading to them, and teaching them that while they may face challenges and discrimination in their own lives, they must never succumb to despair or cynicism; they must always believe that they can write their own destiny.

Ironically, this quintessentially American—and yes, conservative—notion of self-help found frequent expression in Reverend Wright's sermons. But what my former pastor too often failed to understand is that embarking on a program of self-help also requires a belief that society can change.

The profound mistake of Reverend Wright's sermons is not that he spoke about racism in our society. It's that he spoke as if our society was static; as if no progress

40

---

7. **Reagan Coalition:** Republicans and white, socially conservative Democrats who gave victories to Ronald Reagan in the 1980 and 1984 presidential elections.

8. **Inside dealing:** profiting, usually on the stock market, from information not available to the general public.

has been made; as if this country—a country that has made it possible for one of his own members to run for the highest office in the land and build a coalition of white and black; Latino and Asian, rich and poor, young and old—is still irrevocably bound to a tragic past. But what we know—what we have seen—is that America can change. That is the true genius of this nation. What we have already achieved gives us hope—the audacity to hope—for what we can and must achieve tomorrow.

In the white community, the path to a more perfect union means acknowledging that what ails the African American community does not just exist in the minds of black people; that the legacy of discrimination—and current incidents of discrimination, while less overt than in the past—are real and must be addressed. Not just with words, but with deeds—by investing in our schools and our communities; by enforcing our civil rights laws and ensuring fairness in our criminal justice system; by providing this generation with ladders of opportunity that were unavailable for previous generations. It requires all Americans to realize that your dreams do not have to come at the expense of my dreams; that investing in the health, welfare, and education of black and brown and white children will ultimately help all of America prosper.

In the end, then, what is called for is nothing more, and nothing less, than what all the world's great religions demand—that we do unto others as we would have them do unto us. Let us be our brother's keeper, Scripture tells us. Let us be our sister's keeper. Let us find that common stake we all have in one another, and let our politics reflect that spirit as well.

For we have a choice in this country. We can accept a politics that breeds division, and conflict, and cynicism. We can tackle race only as spectacle, as we did in the OJ trial, or in the wake of tragedy, as we did in the aftermath of Katrina,[9] or as fodder for the nightly news. We can play Reverend Wright's sermons on every channel, every day and talk about them from now until the election, and make the only question in this campaign whether or not the American people think that I somehow believe or sympathize with his most offensive words. We can pounce on some gaffe by a Hillary supporter as evidence that she's playing the race card, or we can speculate on whether white men will all flock to John McCain in the general election regardless of his policies.

We can do that.   45

But if we do, I can tell you that in the next election, we'll be talking about some other distraction. And then another one. And then another one. And nothing will change.

9. **Katrina:** In 2005, Hurricane Katrina devastated the city of New Orleans, especially its minority communities; many criticized the government for its slow response. **OJ trial:** In 1994, African American actor and former football player OJ Simpson was tried and acquitted for killing his ex-wife, Nicole Brown Simpson, and her friend Ronald Goldman, both of whom were white. Both incidents caused widespread discussion of the role of race in American society.

That is one option. Or, at this moment, in this election, we can come together and say, "Not this time." This time we want to talk about the crumbling schools that are stealing the future of black children and white children and Asian children and Hispanic children and Native American children. This time we want to reject the cynicism that tells us that these kids can't learn; that those kids who don't look like us are somebody else's problem. The children of America are not those kids, they are our kids, and we will not let them fall behind in a twenty-first-century economy. Not this time.

This time we want to talk about how the lines in the Emergency Room are filled with whites and blacks and Hispanics who do not have health care; who don't have the power on their own to overcome the special interests in Washington, but who can take them on if we do it together.

This time we want to talk about the shuttered mills that once provided a decent life for men and women of every race, and the homes for sale that once belonged to Americans from every religion, every region, every walk of life. This time we want to talk about the fact that the real problem is not that someone who doesn't look like you might take your job; it's that the corporation you work for will ship it overseas for nothing more than a profit.

This time we want to talk about the men and women of every color and creed 50 who serve together, and fight together, and bleed together under the same proud flag. We want to talk about how to bring them home from a war that never should've been authorized and never should've been waged, and we want to talk about how we'll show our patriotism by caring for them, and their families, and giving them the benefits they have earned.

I would not be running for president if I didn't believe with all my heart that this is what the vast majority of Americans want for this country. This union may never be perfect, but generation after generation has shown that it can always be perfected. And today, whenever I find myself feeling doubtful or cynical about this possibility, what gives me the most hope is the next generation—the young people whose attitudes and beliefs and openness to change have already made history in this election.

There is one story in particularly that I'd like to leave you with today—a story I told when I had the great honor of speaking on Dr. King's birthday at his home church, Ebenezer Baptist, in Atlanta.

There is a young, twenty-three-year-old white woman named Ashley Baia who organized for our campaign in Florence, South Carolina. She had been working to organize a mostly African American community since the beginning of this campaign, and one day she was at a roundtable discussion where everyone went around telling their story and why they were there.

And Ashley said that when she was nine years old, her mother got cancer. And because she had to miss days of work, she was let go and lost her health care. They had to file for bankruptcy, and that's when Ashley decided that she had to do something to help her mom.

She knew that food was one of their most expensive costs, and so Ashley convinced   55
her mother that what she really liked and really wanted to eat more than anything else
was mustard and relish sandwiches. Because that was the cheapest way to eat.

She did this for a year until her mom got better, and she told everyone at the
roundtable that the reason she joined our campaign was so that she could help the
millions of other children in the country who want and need to help their parents
too.

Now Ashley might have made a different choice. Perhaps somebody told her along
the way that the source of her mother's problems were blacks who were on welfare
and too lazy to work, or Hispanics who were coming into the country illegally. But
she didn't. She sought out allies in her fight against injustice.

Anyway, Ashley finished her story and then goes around the room and asks everyone else why they're supporting the campaign. They all have different stories and
reasons. Many bring up a specific issue. And finally they come to this elderly black
man who's been sitting there quietly the entire time. And Ashley asks him why he's
there. And he does not bring up a specific issue. He does not say health care or the
economy. He does not say education or the war. He does not say that he was there
because of Barack Obama. He simply says to everyone in the room, "I am here because
of Ashley."

"I'm here because of Ashley." By itself, that single moment of recognition between   60
that young white girl and that old black man is not enough. It is not enough to give
health care to the sick, or jobs to the jobless, or education to our children.

But it is where we start. It is where our union grows stronger. And as so many
generations have come to realize over the course of the two-hundred and twenty one
years since a band of patriots signed that document in Philadelphia, that is where
the perfection begins.

UNDERSTANDING THE TEXT

1. How does Obama use the phrase "a more perfect union" in the first part of
   his speech? How does his use of this phrase contrast with its use in the Preamble to the Constitution? (The Preamble is widely available online.) What
   about the early American republic does Obama present as imperfect?

2. How does Obama's invocation of "my own American story" help shape his
   ethos? In what way does he suggest his experiences are representative of the
   larger American experience?

3. What reason does Obama give for his refusal to disown Reverend Wright?
   What similarities does he find between Wright and his own grandmother? Is
   the comparison effective? Why or why not?

4. What issues does Obama feel can unite people of all races? Why does he
   use "This time we want to talk about . . ." to introduce each of these issues?

5. What is the point of the story about Ashley that Obama ends with? How does he invoke Martin Luther King Jr. in this story? Do you believe that this story provides a good conclusion to his remarks? Explain.

MAKING CONNECTIONS

1. Compare Obama's discussion of the role of churches in addressing racial issues with that of Martin Luther King Jr. in "Letter from Birmingham City Jail" (p. 202). Consider how the changes in American culture between 1963 and 2008 may affect their views.

2. Compare Obama's experience growing up on the edge of several cultures with those of Gloria Anzaldúa (p. 527) and Kisautaq Leona Okakok (p. 76). What common threads do you see in these three readings about the spaces between cultures?

3. How do Obama's views of the origins of poverty and inequality compare to Gandhi's (p. 332)? How do both men deal with historical causes for contemporary inequality?

4. Compare Obama's views of reconciliation with those of Desmond Tutu in "Nuremberg or National Amnesia: A Third Way" (p. 227). Though the historical contexts of the two works are very different, they both address the need for different cultures to learn to trust and forgive each other. Do the two selections appear to be motivated by the same overall philosophy of human nature? Explain.

WRITING ABOUT THE TEXT

1. Write an essay in which you compare "A More Perfect Union" to another major speech on race from a different time, such as Martin Luther King Jr.'s "I Have a Dream." (It is widely reprinted and available online.) Explore the ways that the speeches reflect changes in race relations in America.

2. Write an essay in which you analyze how "A More Perfect Union" is designed to appeal to different audiences at the same time. Consider how and how effectively Obama appeals to black and white Americans, to supporters and detractors, to religious voters, and to observers outside of the United States.

3. Watch the video of "A More Perfect Union" (it is available on YouTube and other Web sites) and write an essay in which you compare the effects of reading and viewing the speech. How is the experience of watching Obama deliver the speech different from the experience of reading it?

4. Write an essay in which you analyze the role of religious rhetoric in "A More Perfect Union." How does Obama connect religion and race in the United States? How does this affect his view on race relations? How might the speech's religious language and references affect the reactions and perceptions of his audience?

4

WAR AND PEACE

IS WAR EVER JUSTIFIED?

War is . . . inevitable unless we change our social system
and outlaw classes, the struggle for power, and possessions;
and in the event of our success warfare would disappear,
as a symptom vanishes when the disease is cured.
—Margaret Mead, "Warfare:
An Invention—Not a Biological Necessity"

THE DEDICATION PAGE of Kenneth Burke's highly influential 1945 treatise on rhetoric, *A Grammar of Motives*, reads simply "*Ad bellum purificandum*," a Latin phrase meaning "toward the purification of war." Argument, Burke believed, could be a socially beneficial outlet for the inherent human tendency toward conflict, a tendency that, if not carefully redirected, leads to violence. Rather than trying to eliminate the tendency, Burke held, we should encourage conflict while taking steps to ensure that it involves words and ideas, not guns and bombs. In this way, war can be "purified" into something useful.

History offers a great deal of evidence to support the premise of Burke's argument, that human beings are, by nature, quarrelsome and disposed to war. Early epic poems such as the *Iliad* and the *Mahābhārata* celebrate the prowess of great warriors in glorious combat; the world's major religious texts—such as the Hebrew Bible, the Quran, the *Tao te Ching*, and the *Bhagavad Gītā*—are replete with references to, and instructions for, warfare; and abundant historical evidence suggests that warfare has been carried out among the peoples of every continent in every historical period.

The reality of war, however, has always been accompanied by the ideal of peace. Few societies—not even militaristic and violent ones—have considered warfare desirable. Indeed, some of the most compelling art, literature, and philosophy has been produced in cultures so saturated by armed conflict that their greatest minds were enlisted to find ways to bring about peace. China's Period of Warring States, for example, lasted 250 years (475–221 BCE), during which seven separate states fought to unify China under one imperial banner. So many philosophers emerged that this time also became known as the Period of the Hundred Schools. Thinkers as diverse as Confucius, Lao Tzu, Mo Tzu, Mencius, Hsün Tzu, and Sun Tzu offered solutions to ending the wars and bringing about peace and stability. A similar burst of creative output is associated with the Peloponnesian Wars, between Athens and Sparta in ancient Greece; with the political instability and civil warfare of the Italian states during the Renaissance; with the Napoleonic Wars, in nineteenth-century Western Europe; and with the almost continuous state of war (either overt or, as in the Cold War indirect) between various superpowers, for most of the twentieth century.

This chapter begins with two readings from a period that saw some of the most sustained, continuous warfare in the history of the world: China's Period of Warring States. The first of these readings, Mo Tzu's "Against Offensive Warfare," takes to task all parties in the wars for ignoring the basic rules of human behavior in their large-scale interactions with other states. A very different view is offered by Mo Tzu's contemporary, Sun Tzu, a general who makes no attempt to evaluate the morality of war but simply insists that once the decision is made to engage in an armed conflict, the only rational aim is to win as quickly as possible.

These two Chinese readings are followed by a logical proof by the medieval Christian writer Thomas Aquinas, who lays out the theological requirements for considering a war "just." "The Progress of an Aztec Warrior," from the sixteenth-century Aztec *Codex Mendoza*, also looks at the connection between religion and warfare, here by depicting the ascension of an Aztec warrior-priest. A painting by Eugène Delacroix, *Liberty Leading the People*, presents another way to consider whether a war is just. It depicts a battle scene from the French Revolution in which Liberty, an allegory of the deep human need for freedom and the willingness to fight for it when necessary, leads the people of France to victory. The viewer is invited to consider the ideals behind a war and what things might be worth fighting for, killing for, dying for.

World-famous anthropologist Margaret Mead provides a rebuttal to those who consider war to be inevitable in her essay "Warfare: An Invention—Not a Biological Necessity." Mead marshals evidence from cultures throughout the world to argue that warfare is not an inherent part of the human condition but rather an invention that emerged to fulfill a certain function, an invention that can be replaced when another one emerges to fulfill that function more efficiently.

During the Spanish Civil War, Pablo Picasso addressed the toll of war in his famous 1937 painting *Guernica*. Painted soon after German planes, acting on behalf of Spanish dictator Francisco Franco, bombed thousands of innocent civilians in the Basque village of Guernica, its tortured, fragmented images portray the human cost of war, considered apart from the abstract ideals of war's justness or effectiveness. Writing soon after, at the height of World War II, George Orwell moves the discussion of warfare from the abstract ("What should human beings do about war?") to the very specific ("What should people in England and America do about Hitler?"). In his essay "Pacifism and the War," Orwell confronts head-on the question of what people who love peace and hate violence should do about a brutal dictator intent on destroying peace and perpetuating violence. Lofty ideals about peace and nonviolence, Orwell insists, have little value when one confronts a force that does not share those ideals and insists on making war.

The chapter closes with two essays written in response to two catastrophic acts of war that, together, frame the last half of the twentieth century. The first of these essays, Kenzaburo Oe's "The Unsurrendered People," addresses the bombing of Hiroshima at the end of World War II. After interviewing dozens of survivors of the bombing, Oe uses their experiences as the basis for his belief in the redemptive power of survival. In the second, American philosopher Jean Bethke Elshtain applies multiple just-war theories to the American response to the September 11, 2001, attacks on the World Trade Center and the Pentagon.

In very different and sometimes surprising ways, the texts in this chapter attempt to answer a series of fundamental questions: Is war inevitable? Is peace always desirable? Are ideals worth fighting for, killing for, dying for? Can deep conflict and division be managed without resorting to war? Perhaps no questions have been as important to the shape of societies in the past, and perhaps no answers are more important to the shape of humanity in the future.

Mo Tzu
Against Offensive Warfare
(circa 425 BCE)

CONTEMPORARY READERS often find the writings of the ancient Chinese philosopher Mo Tzu (circa 475 BCE) surprisingly accessible. Unlike many of his contemporaries, Mo Tzu did not write in riddles, paradoxes, and short aphorisms. Rather, he wrote in a format very similar to the modern philosophical essay, with a clear thesis statement at the beginning followed by evidence to support it. The content of Mo Tzu's writings also resonates with modern readers, who appreciate many of the arguments that he levied against the Confucians and the Taoists, the principal philosophical opponents of the philosophy, Mohism, that he founded.

Like Mencius and Hsün Tzu, Mo Tzu wrote during the Period of Warring States (475–221 BCE)—two and a half centuries of civil war among seven Chinese kingdoms who were struggling for control of the empire. During this time of war, Mo Tzu spoke chiefly of love—universal love, or the love of all human beings, which formed the cornerstone of Mohism. As innocent as this precept seems now, it caused tremendous controversy at the time. Confucians felt that the idea that people should love and respect each other equally undermined the traditional social structure, which called for people to love and respect some (ancestors, parents, elder brothers) more than others. Taoists objected to the Mohist belief that human beings are more deserving of love and respect than any other part of the cosmos, such as insects or rocks.

Along with universal love, Mo Tzu preached the pragmatic philosophy that people should only do that which produces tangible benefit for themselves and others. On these grounds, he opposed much of what was revered in Chinese culture, such as the observance of religious rituals, the staging of elaborate funerals, and the playing of music. These views further alienated him from devout Confucians, whose lives were structured around the rituals that, for Confucius, were essential to a moral life.

The idea of war was a frequent target for Mo Tzu and his followers. The slaughter of other human beings—so common during the Period of Warring States—clearly violated the principle of universal love. But Mo Tzu also believed that war was a foolish waste of resources. The selection presented here is the first, and shortest, of three treatises that Mo Tzu wrote in opposition to war.

Mo Tzu's rhetoric in this passage consists primarily of a series of analogies between war and individual acts of violence or theft. These analogies increase in persuasive power as Mo Tzu presents them and then asks how people can condemn all of the small atrocities and yet support the same actions when they are conducted on a large scale by states and armies. ✎

IF A MAN ENTERS AN ORCHARD and steals the peaches and plums, everyone who hears about it will condemn him, and if those above who administer the government catch him they will punish him. Why? Because he injures others to benefit himself. When it comes to carrying off dogs, swine, chickens, and piglings, the deed is even more unrighteous than entering an orchard to steal peaches and plums. Why? Because the loss to others is greater. It shows a greater lack of benevolence and is a more serious crime. When it comes to breaking into another man's stable and seizing his horses and cows, the deed is even more unrighteous than carrying off dogs, swine, chickens, and piglings. Why? Because the loss to others is greater, and if the loss is greater, it shows a greater lack of benevolence and is a more serious crime. And when it comes to murdering an innocent man, stripping him of his clothing, and appropriating his spear and sword, the deed is even more unrighteous than breaking into a stable and seizing someone's horses and cows. Why? Because the injury to others is even greater, and if the injury is greater, it shows a greater lack of benevolence and is a more serious crime.

Now all the gentlemen in the world know enough to condemn such acts and brand them as unrighteous. And yet when it comes to the even greater unrighteousness of offensive warfare against other states, they do not know enough to condemn it. On the contrary, they praise it and call it righteous. Is this what it means to know the difference between righteousness and unrighteousness?

If someone kills one man, he is condemned as unrighteous and must pay for his crime with is own life. According to this reasoning, if someone kills ten men, then he is ten times as unrighteous and should pay for his crime with ten lives, or if he kills a hundred men he is a hundred times as unrighteous and should pay for his crime with a hundred lives.

Now all the gentlemen in the world know enough to condemn such crimes and brand them as unrighteous. And yet when it comes to the even greater unrighteousness of offensive warfare against other states, they do not know enough to condemn it. On the contrary, they praise it and call it righteous. Truly they do not know what unrighteousness is. So they make a record of their wars to be handed down to posterity. If they knew that such wars were unrighteous, then what reason would they have for making a record of their unrighteous deeds to be handed down to posterity?

Now if there were a man who, on seeing a little bit of black, called it black but, on seeing a lot of black, called it white, we would conclude that he could not tell the difference between black and white. Or if there were a man who, on tasting a little bit of bitterness, called it bitter but, on tasting a lot, called it sweet, we would conclude that he could not distinguish between bitter and sweet. Now when a great wrong is committed and a state is attacked, men do not know enough to condemn it, but on the contrary praise it and call it righteous. Is this what it means to be able to distinguish between righteousness and unrighteousness? So we know that the gentlemen of the world are confused about the distinction between righteousness and unrighteousness.

UNDERSTANDING THE TEXT

1. What comparisons does Mo Tzu use to illustrate the immorality of war? Are these comparisons valid? Are they effective in presenting his argument?

2. What is the moral imperative at the heart of all of the actions, including war, that Mo Tzu considers evil? Can his position be reduced to a "golden rule" of appropriate behavior?

3. What is the point of Mo Tzu's discussion of black and white? What is he saying about human perceptions of scale?

4. What does Mo Tzu mean by "offensive warfare"? What do you think he would say about defensive warfare? What conditions does he suggest have to be present to make war immoral?

MAKING CONNECTIONS

1. Compare Mo Tzu's argument in "Against Offensive Warfare" with the argument that he makes in "Against Music" (p. 308). What features do offensive warfare and music have in common?

2. Which of Thomas Aquinas's principles of a just war would Mo Tzu agree with? Which might he disagree with? Why? What might he say about an offensive war conducted to try to achieve a moral or utilitarian purpose?

3. Why is Mo Tzu's utilitarian position so different from Garrett Hardin's argument in "Lifeboat Ethics: The Case against Helping the Poor" (p. 357), which is also based on utilitarian principles?

WRITING ABOUT THE TEXT

1. Analyze the movement that Mo Tzu makes from small-scale to large-scale moral arguments. Evaluate the effectiveness of this movement in terms of inductive reasoning (pp. 600–604).

2. Write a rebuttal to Mo Tzu's argument by invoking Thomas Aquinas, George Orwell, or Jean Bethke Elshtain to argue that there are some situations that justify even offensive warfare.

3. Compare Mo Tzu's view of the large-scale suffering caused by warfare with Kenzaburo Oe's recollections of the suffering caused by the bombing of Hiroshima (p. 288). Consider how Oe's personal observations might or might not confirm Mo Tzu's arguments.

Sun Tzu
from *The Art of War*
(400–320 BCE)

VERY LITTLE IS KNOWN about Sun Tzu, the Chinese general reputed to be the author of *The Art of War*, one of the most influential military treatises of all time. Scholars generally date the composition of the text to between 400 and 320 BCE, in the turbulent epoch of Chinese history known as the Period of Warring States (475–221 BCE), which occurred after the Chou Dynasty collapsed and before the Chinese mainland was unified under the Ch'in Dynasty. During this period of turmoil and constant warfare, the philosophies of Confucianism, Taoism, Moism, and Legalism emerged and competed for followers among the warring factions, and organized warfare became the subject of sustained and serious examination.

Though the existence of a historical figure named Sun Tzu cannot be conclusively demonstrated, the influence of *The Art of War* on Chinese military and political thought cannot be underestimated. Chinese texts from the classical period (about 500–200 BCE) refer to it continuously, and it shaped the military strategies of China, Japan, Korea, and Vietnam for nearly 2,500 years. One of Sun Tzu's most recent devotees, the communist leader Mao Tse Tung, used many of the work's principles to seize power in China in 1949.

Like many philosophical texts of ancient China, *The Art of War* is a series of epigrams rather than a consistent or systematic explanation of the author's point of view. Each sentence of Sun Tzu's work is designed to be read and pondered as an individual unit of thought; however, these maxims all work together to produce a pragmatic and surprisingly modern view of the process of warfare. Sun Tzu persuades his readers not through argument, but through a powerfully constructed ethos and through the startling resonance that these maxims have with many people's experiences.

The maxims of *The Art of War* go well beyond giving prescriptions for armed warfare. They touch, often in very deep ways, on the essential structure of human conflict. Perhaps this is why *The Art of War* was reborn in the late twentieth century as a handbook for corporate managers looking for ways to defeat their competition and advance their own product lines. The following maxims from *The Art of War* constitute the whole of chapter 3, "Attack by Stratagem."

1. GENERALLY IN WAR the best policy is to take a state intact; to ruin it is inferior to this.

2. To capture the enemy's army is better than to destroy it; to take intact a battalion, a company or a five-man squad is better than to destroy them.

3. For to win one hundred victories in one hundred battles is not the acme of skill. To subdue the enemy without fighting is the acme of skill.

4. Thus, what is of extreme importance in war is to attack the enemy's strategy.

5. Next best is to disrupt his alliances.

6. The next best is to attack his army.

7. The worst policy is to attack cities. Attack cities only when there is no alternative.

8. To prepare the shielded wagons and make ready the necessary arms and equipment requires at least three months; to pile up earthen ramps against the walls an additional three months will be needed.

9. If the general is unable to control his impatience and orders his troops to swarm up the wall like ants, one-third of them will be killed without taking the city. Such is the calamity of these attacks.

10. Thus, those skilled in war subdue the enemy's army without battle. They capture his cities without assaulting them and overthrow his state without protracted operations.

11. Your aim must be to take All-under-Heaven intact. Thus your troops are not worn out and your gains will be complete. This is the art of offensive strategy.

12. Consequently, the art of using troops is this: When ten to the enemy's one, surround him.

13. When five times his strength, attack him.

14. If double his strength, divide him.

15. If equally matched you may engage him.

16. If weaker numerically, be capable of withdrawing.

17. And if in all respects unequal, be capable of eluding him, for a small force is but booty for one more powerful.

18. Now the general is the protector of the state. If this protection is all-embracing, the state will surely be strong; if defective, the state will certainly be weak.

19. Now there are three ways in which a ruler can bring misfortune upon his army:

20. When ignorant that the army should not advance, to order an advance or ignorant that it should not retire, to order a retirement. This is described as "hobbling the army."

21. When ignorant of military affairs, to participate in their administration. This causes the officers to be perplexed.

22. When ignorant of command problems to share in the exercise of responsibilities. This engenders doubts in the minds of the officers.

23. If the army is confused and suspicious, neighbouring rulers will cause trouble. This is what is meant by the saying: "A confused army leads to victory."

24. Now there are five circumstances in which victory may be predicted:

25. He who knows when he can fight and when he cannot will be victorious.

26. He who understands how to use both large and small forces will be victorious.

27. He whose ranks are united in purpose will be victorious.

28. He who is prudent and lies in wait for an enemy who is not will be victorious.

29. He whose generals are able and not interfered with by the sovereign will be victorious.

30. It is in these five matters that the way to victory is known.

31. Therefore I say: "Know the enemy and know yourself; in a hundred battles you will never be in peril.

32. When you are ignorant of the enemy but know yourself, your chances of winning or losing are equal.

33. If ignorant of both your enemy and of yourself, you are certain in every battle to be in peril."

UNDERSTANDING THE TEXT

1. Why does Sun Tzu structure his advice on war as a series of short epigrams with no expansion or development? What is the rhetorical effect of this structure? Is it more or less effective than a traditional essay format?

2. What does "subdue the enemy without fighting" mean? How is it possible to achieve victory without conflict? Why would a peaceful victory be considered superior to winning an armed conflict?

3. Why did Sun Tzu hold that "the worst policy is to attack cities"?

4. Why does Sun Tzu place such great importance on a commander's self-knowledge? How is self-knowledge important beyond the scope of military conflict? What kinds of mistakes can be made by people who do not really understand themselves?

5. Can Sun Tzu's philosophy of war be applied beyond the scope of military affairs? Do any of his aphorisms seem relevant to other kinds of human conflict? Why has *The Art of War* become a best seller among American business professionals?

MAKING CONNECTIONS

1. Compare Sun Tzu's view of war with that of his contemporary Mo Tzu. Why do you think Mo Tzu writes exclusively about the morality of war while Sun Tzu refuses even to address the question?

2. How might Sun Tzu's advice on warfare be interpreted by George Orwell (p. 282), a former pacifist who believed that the Nazi threat made defensive warfare a moral requirement?

3. Sun Tzu was likely familiar with the teachings of Confucius and Lao Tzu. How does this chapter of *The Art of War* appear to have been influenced by Taoism as found in the *Tao te Ching* (p. 104) and Confucianism as found in the works of Mencius (p. 94) and Hsün Tzu (p. 100)?

4. What view of human nature do you detect in Sun Tzu's writings? What does he assert as the underlying motivations of most people? How do his views compare with other Chinese writers of the same period, such as Mencius (p. 94) and Hsün Tzu (p. 100)?

WRITING ABOUT THE TEXT

1. Write a chapter of *The Art of War for College Students*, *The Art of War for Corporate America*, or some other version of this classic text for a contemporary audience you know well. What simple, direct aphorisms could be relevant to contemporary situations involving conflict?

2. Analyze one or two underlying assumptions of *The Art of War*. What principle or principles are the aphorisms based on? Are these overall principles stated anywhere in the text, or are they left unstated, and why is this so?

3. Compare *The Art of War* with *The Prince* (p. 184). How do Sun Tzu and Machiavelli agree about the nature of effective leadership? How do they disagree?

St. Thomas Aquinas
from *Summa Theologica*
(1265–1274)

THOMAS AQUINAS (1224 or 1225–1274) was born Tommaso d'Aquino to an aristocratic family in Italy and received a classical education, first at the Benedictine monastery
of Montecassino, and later at the University of Naples. In 1243, against the strong
objections of his family, he joined the recently founded Dominican Order and began
to study theology at the University of Paris, where he was eventually awarded a doc-
torate in theology. He spent his life teaching in universities and writing several massive theological works, which have since become cornerstones of Catholic doctrine.

When Aquinas began his studies, Aristotle's works were becoming increasingly important in Christian Europe, and conflicts between faith and reason were occurring with
increasing frequency among European intellectuals. As a devoted student of classical
philosophy, Aquinas set out to reconcile Aristotle's rigorous methods of logical analysis
with what he believed to be the revealed truths of the Bible and Christianity. He wanted
not merely to synthesize Aristotle and the Bible but to reconcile faith and reason as they
were understood in his society. By far, his most ambitious work is the *Summa Theologica* ("a summary of theology"), a three-volume work that covers nearly every imaginable topic of Christian ethical and metaphysical belief.

The *Summa Theologica* is a series of thousands of deductive proofs on more than
six hundred major subjects. In a typical proof, Aquinas introduces a proposition and
lists possible objections to it; he then restates his position clearly and succinctly, citing both the Bible and the writings of the Church fathers, such as St. Augustine, and
proceeds to answer the objections in order. Once the proposition is thus "proved"—
all possible objections to it answered—it can serve as evidence in a later proof.

The following selection, from book 2 of the *Summa Theologica*, is the first of four
proofs that Aquinas offers on the subject of war. In this proof, Aquinas lays down
the conditions that must be met for an armed conflict to be considered a "just war."
As the Middle Ages progressed and Christian nations struggled to reconcile warfare
with a religion that emphasizes peace, Aquinas's conditions became the foundation
for the just war theory in Christian doctrine, a theory that the Catholic Church still
applies to wars. 🖋

"Whether It Is Always Sinful to Wage War?"

Objection 1: It would seem that it is always sinful to wage war. Because punishment
is not inflicted except for sin. Now those who wage war are threatened by Our Lord
with punishment, according to Mt. 26:52: "All that take the sword shall perish with
the sword." Therefore all wars are unlawful.

Objection 2: Further, whatever is contrary to a Divine precept is a sin. But war is contrary to a Divine precept, for it is written (Mt. 5:39): "But I say to you not to resist evil"; and (Rm. 12:19): "Not revenging yourselves, my dearly beloved, but give place unto wrath." Therefore war is always sinful.

Objection 3: Further, nothing, except sin, is contrary to an act of virtue. But war is contrary to peace. Therefore war is always a sin.

Objection 4: Further, the exercise of a lawful thing is itself lawful, as is evident in scientific exercises. But warlike exercises which take place in tournaments are forbidden by the Church, since those who are slain in these trials are deprived of ecclesiastical burial. Therefore it seems that war is a sin in itself.

On the contrary, Augustine[1] says in a sermon on the son of the centurion: "If the Christian Religion forbade war altogether, those who sought salutary advice in the Gospel would rather have been counselled to cast aside their arms, and to give up soldiering altogether. On the contrary, they were told: 'Do violence to no man . . . and be content with your pay'. If he commanded them to be content with their pay, he did not forbid soldiering."

I answer that, In order for a war to be just, three things are necessary. First, the authority of the sovereign by whose command the war is to be waged. For it is not the business of a private individual to declare war, because he can seek for redress of his rights from the tribunal of his superior. Moreover it is not the business of a private individual to summon together the people, which has to be done in wartime. And as the care of the common weal[2] is committed to those who are in authority, it is their business to watch over the common weal of the city, kingdom or province subject to them. And just as it is lawful for them to have recourse to the sword in defending that common weal against internal disturbances, when they punish evildoers, according to the words of the Apostle (Rm. 13:4): "He beareth not the sword in vain: for he is God's minister, an avenger to execute wrath upon him that doth evil"; so too, it is their business to have recourse to the sword of war in defending the common weal against external enemies. Hence it is said to those who are in authority (Ps. 81:4): "Rescue the poor: and deliver the needy out of the hand of the sinner"; and for this reason Augustine says (Contra Faust. xxii, 75): "The natural order conducive to peace among mortals demands that the power to declare and counsel war should be in the hands of those who hold the supreme authority."

Secondly, a just cause is required, namely that those who are attacked, should be attacked because they deserve it on account of some fault. Wherefore Augustine says

1. **Augustine:** early Christian writer (354–430 CE) and bishop of the North African town of Hippo (in present-day Algeria). Augustine's writings in *The City of God* and elsewhere are generally considered the starting point of the Christian just war tradition.

2. The **common weal,** or "commonweal," refers to the common interest of the general public.

(Questions. in Hept., qu. x, super Jos.): "A just war is wont to be described as one that avenges wrongs, when a nation or state has to be punished, for refusing to make amends for the wrongs inflicted by its subjects, or to restore what it has seized unjustly."

Thirdly, it is necessary that the belligerents should have a rightful intention, so that they intend the advancement of good, or the avoidance of evil. Hence Augustine says (De Verb. Dom.): "True religion looks upon as peaceful those wars that are waged not for motives of aggrandizement, or cruelty, but with the object of securing peace, of punishing evil-doers, and of uplifting the good." For it may happen that the war is declared by the legitimate authority, and for a just cause, and yet be rendered unlawful through a wicked intention. Hence Augustine says (Contra Faust. xxii, 74): "The passion for inflicting harm, the cruel thirst for vengeance, an unpacific and relentless spirit, the fever of revolt, the lust of power, and such like things, all these are rightly condemned in war."

Reply to Objection 1: As Augustine says (Contra Faust, xxii, 70): "To take the sword is to arm oneself in order to take the life of anyone, without the command or permission of superior or lawful authority." On the other hand, to have recourse to the sword (as a private person) by the authority of the sovereign or judge, or (as a public person) through zeal for justice, and by the authority, so to speak, of God, is not to "take the sword," but to use it as commissioned by another, wherefore it does not deserve punishment. And yet even those who make sinful use of the sword are not always slain with the sword, yet they always perish with their own sword, because, unless they repent, they are punished eternally for their sinful use of the sword.

Reply to Objection 2: Such like precepts, as Augustine observes (De Serm. Dom. in Monte i, 19), should always be borne in readiness of mind, so that we be ready to obey them, and, if necessary, to refrain from resistance or self-defense. Nevertheless it is necessary sometimes for a man to act otherwise for the common good, or for the good of those with whom he is fighting. Hence Augustine says (Ep. ad Marcellin. cxxxviii): "Those whom we have to punish with a kindly severity, it is necessary to handle in many ways against their will. For when we are stripping a man of the lawlessness of sin, it is good for him to be vanquished, since nothing is more hopeless than the happiness of sinners, whence arises a guilty impunity, and an evil will, like an internal enemy." 10

Reply to Objection 3: Those who wage war justly aim at peace, and so they are not opposed to peace, except to the evil peace, which Our Lord "came not to send upon earth" (Mt. 10:34). Hence Augustine says (Ep. ad Bonif. clxxxix): "We do not seek peace in order to be at war, but we go to war that we may have peace. Be peaceful, therefore, in warring, so that you may vanquish those whom you war against, and bring them to the prosperity of peace."

Reply to Objection 4: Manly exercises in warlike feats of arms are not all forbidden, but those which are inordinate and perilous, and end in slaying or plundering. In olden times warlike exercises presented no such danger, and hence they were called "exercises of arms" or "bloodless wars," as Jerome[3] states in an epistle.

UNDERSTANDING THE TEXT

1. What four moral objections to war does Aquinas raise at the beginning of this proof? How does he respond to each one? Are his replies effective? What is the rhetorical effect of Aquinas's raising the objections and then responding to them? What other objections might Aquinas have raised?

2. Choose one of the objections that Aquinas answers and write it as a deductive syllogism (pp. 597–600) with a major premise, a minor premise, and a conclusion.

3. Why does Aquinas consider it necessary for an appropriate "sovereign" to command the waging of war? What would constitute such an authority?

4. What kinds of causes does Aquinas consider sufficient rationale for the waging of war? What kinds of causes does he consider insufficient?

5. Aquinas's third necessary condition for waging war is a pure motive for doing so. Would it be possible, under the terms of Aquinas's argument, for a conflict to meet the first two conditions but be unjust because at least one nation has an impure motive?

6. Does Aquinas sufficiently prove the proposition that participating in a war is not always sinful? How would you argue against him? Try to formulate a logical proof to rebut his arguments.

MAKING CONNECTIONS

1. Compare Aquinas's requirements for a just war with Orwell's view of a necessary war. Does the conflict with fascism, as Orwell describes it, meet Aquinas's standards for a just war? Explain.

2. One of Aquinas's major purposes in the *Summa Theologica* was to harmonize Christian theology with Aristotle's logical methodology. Is the proof he offers here consistent with the philosophy of logic that Aristotle outlines in the *Rhetoric* (p. 489)? Explain.

3. How would Aquinas advise a soldier who was asked to fight in an unjust war? Would he say that it is more important to follow the will of the sovereign or to disobey that will in the way advocated by Martin Luther King Jr. in "Letter from Birmingham City Jail" (p. 202)?

3. **Jerome:** early Christian writer and scholar (circa 347–419 or 420 CE) best known as the translator of the Latin, or "Vulgate," version of the Bible, the standard version in Christian nations throughout the Middle Ages.

WRITING ABOUT THE TEXT

1. Analyze any modern armed conflict using Aquinas's three criteria for a "just war." Consider whether or not these seven-hundred-year-old principles still provide a useful lens through which to view events.

2. Evaluate Aquinas's use of deductive reasoning in this passage. (See pp. 597–600 for an introduction to deductive reasoning.) Does he construct valid syllogisms, in which the conclusions flow automatically from the premises?

3. Using Elshtain's "What Is a Just War?" (p. 293) as a framework for your comparison, contrast Aquinas's "just war" argument with Mo Tzu's argument in "Against Offensive Warfare" (p. 253).

4. Choose an important contemporary issue and construct a "proof" of your position on it, using this selection from *Summa Theologica* as a model. Follow Aquinas's organization: state a proposition, outline the potential objections to your case, summarize your basic argument, and respond to each objection.

The Progress of an Aztec Warrior
(1541)

IN 1521, Spanish conquistadores led by Hernán Cortés (1485–1547) conquered the Aztec empire, which had ruled much of what is now Mexico for nearly two hundred and fifty years. Soon afterwards, Spanish authorities, who wanted to document the culture of the Aztec people, commissioned a series of books known as codices. Each codex employed the talents of native artists and storytellers who could give first-hand accounts of Aztec life and culture before the conquest. Nearly five hundred Aztec codices from the period have been preserved.

The *Codex Mendoza*, where "The Progress of an Aztec Warrior" appears, was completed in 1541. It was commissioned by, and named for, Antonio de Mendoza (1495–1552), the Spanish viceroy of New Spain (what is now Central America and the southwestern United States) from 1535 to 1550. Unlike many of the codices from this period, which contained black and white drawings only, the *Codex Mendoza* featured lavish color paintings annotated with text in both Spanish and the Aztec language called *Nahuatl*. The codex was prepared for Emperor Charles V of the Holy Roman Empire (who was also King Charles I of Spain). The ship transporting it to Spain, however, was captured by pirates, and the codex ended up in England, where it languished in several private collections before finding its way to Oxford University's Bodleian Library in 1559.

The image presented here comes from the third and final section of the *Codex Mendoza*, which is devoted to visual representations of pre-conquest Aztec life. Several groups of paintings inhabit this illustration. First, two young novice priests are shown in different activities: taking care of a temple and then going off to war with a senior priest. A second group of paintings shows an important official (a *teculti*) and an assistant involved in public works projects. The final series—which begins in the second row of images and continues to the end of the page—shows the progression of an Aztec warrior through the various ranks of the Aztec military.

As the illustrations show, the main vehicle for military advancement in this culture was the capture of enemy combatant. Taking captives alive was an important part of Aztec warfare, as the elaborate human sacrifice rituals that the Aztecs practiced required a constant stream of offerings to the gods. As the warrior takes more and more captives, he is promoted through the ranks and receives increasingly elaborate battle gear, culminating in his elevation to the rank of *tlacatecatl*, or commanding general. 🖋

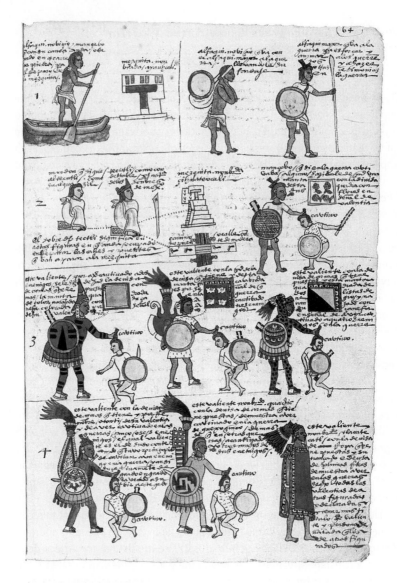

Progress of an Aztec Warrior, 1541.

See p. C-3 in the color insert for a full-color reproduction of this image.

UNDERSTANDING THE TEXT

1. Why do you think Aztec priests are depicted with both religious and military duties in the first two drawings? What might it say about the Aztec culture that these duties are combined in a single institution?

2. What function might the elaborate battle gear have played in Aztec society? Do the ornaments appear to have been useful in warfare, or do they appear to have had an entirely symbolic function? Explain.

3. Why did the Aztecs place such an emphasis on capturing opponents? What might this say about the way that they viewed warfare?

4. Why do you think that the artist provides close-up pictures of the uniform design for the first four ranks but not for the final three? Is there something about the final three uniforms that requires less explanation? Explain.

5. Can you detect a common thread running through the different sets of images in this illustration? Why do you think that they were all combined together on a single page?

MAKING CONNECTIONS

1. Compare the use of pictograms to explain important cultural practices in "The Progress of an Aztec Warrior" and the Papyrus of Ani (p. 154). Are there similarities in the way that these texts use their visual elements? What might account for those similarities, or for the lack thereof?

2. Both "The Progress of an Aztec Warrior" and *Liberty Leading the People* (p. 268) celebrate war. How are their depictions of war similar, and how are they different? What justifications do they each offer for warfare?

3. How might Margaret Mead (p. 274) interpret the celebration of warfare in Aztec culture? Do the Aztecs in "The Progress of an Aztec Warrior" appear to be using war in any of the ways that she describes in her essay?

4. Compare the religious nature of warfare in "The Progress of an Aztec Warrior" with the religious views of war found in the work of Thomas Aquinas (p. 260). Can you see any commonalities with the way that your culture views war and religion? Explain.

WRITING ABOUT THE TEXT

1. Compare the artwork in "The Progress of an Aztec Warrior" with that in the Papyrus of Ani (p. 154), "Greek Schoolchildren on a Kylix" (p. 5), or "The Shaft of the Dead Man" (p. 86). Then, using two or more of these texts as examples, explore the different ways that art can function in a culture.

2. Analyze the role of warfare in "The Progress of an Aztec Warrior." Focus especially on its relation to religion in the series of illustrations.

3. Conduct research into the culture of the Aztecs and write an informative essay about warfare in pre-Columbian Mesoamerica. Use images from "The Progress of an Aztec Warrior" as examples of ideas or concepts in your essay.

Eugène Delacroix
Liberty Leading the People
(1830)

THE FRENCH ARTIST Eugène Delacroix (1798–1863) was the most famous and influential of the Romantic painters, who rejected the balanced, moderate images of the preceding, Neoclassical period and emphasized passion and imagination in the creation of beauty. The Romantic movement swept across Europe during the first part of the nineteenth century and included, along with artists such as Delacroix, great writers, composers, architects, and philosophers. Important figures such as William Wordsworth, Samuel Taylor Coleridge, Lord Byron, Johann Wolfgang von Goethe, Ludwig von Beethoven, Richard Wagner, Jean-Jacques Rousseau, and Georg Wilhelm Friedrich Hegel are all associated with European Romanticism.

While Delacroix's paintings depicted contemporary or historical events, they also drew on literature and myth. Stylistically, Delacroix was a transitional figure in European art. He was heavily influenced by Renaissance art, which he studied passionately, but he also drew on impressionism, the painting style of, for example, Monet and Renoir, which dominated the last part of the nineteenth century. The French poet Charles Baudelaire famously referred to Delacroix as "the last of the great artists of the Renaissance and the first of the moderns."

Delacroix's best-known painting, *Liberty Leading the People, 28 July 1830*, was created to celebrate the July 1830 Revolution, which forced France's King Charles X to abdicate in favor of the much more popular and democratic King Louis-Phillippe. However, the painting has become indelibly associated with the French Revolution of 1789, which overthrew the old aristocracy of France and became one of the chief inspirations of European Romanticism. Liberty is allegorically portrayed in Delacroix's painting as a partially nude woman who is striding through a battlefield wearing a Phrygian cap (a hat traditionally associated with liberty in both classical times and during the French Revolution), carrying a musket in one hand and a French flag in the other.

Initial reactions to the painting were mixed. Some people, such as author Alexandre Dumas, thought that Delacroix had portrayed the crowd accompanying liberty as too rough and unruly. Others thought that his personification of liberty as a fighting woman was commonplace and vulgar. Having gained in popularity throughout the nineteenth century, the painting is now a recognizable symbol of the idealism behind the French Revolution and of the proposition that freedom must sometimes be won through armed conflict. From 1979 through 1994, the image was featured on the back of France's hundred-franc note.

EUGÈNE DELACROIX
Liberty Leading the People, 28 July 1830, 1830 (oil on canvas).
Louvre, Paris, France / Bridgeman Art Library
See p. C-4 in the color insert for a full-color reproduction of this image.

UNDERSTANDING THE TEXT

1. How would you describe the relationship between the actual scene that the painting depicts and the allegory that it represents?

2. What is the significance of Delacroix's representing liberty as a woman? Why might Delacroix have chosen to portray Liberty with her breasts exposed?

3. What argument about war does the juxtaposition of the items in Liberty's hands make?

4. What kind of social argument might be contained in the depictions of the people accompanying Liberty? (What does their dress indicate about their class status? Do all the people in the picture appear to be from the same social class?) How would you make this argument in words rather than a picture?

5. What do the lifeless bodies in the foreground of the painting symbolize? Why are they given such a prominent position in the painting?

MAKING CONNECTIONS

1. How do the living figures in *Liberty Leading the People* compare with the living figures in Picasso's *Guernica* (p. 271)? How does each painting's style affect its content? Its message?

2. How do the dead bodies in the foreground of *Liberty Leading the People* compare with the tortured human figures in *Guernica* (p. 271)? How do Delacroix and Picasso view the human costs of war?

3. How does *Liberty Leading the People* make the same point as Orwell's "Pacifism and the War" (p. 282)—that freedom sometimes must be won through violence? Does the painting or the essay argue more effectively? How so? What does this effectiveness suggest about rhetoric?

4. Which writers in this chapter might disagree with Delacroix's and Orwell's point (see #3)? Why?

WRITING ABOUT THE TEXT

1. Interpret *Liberty Leading the People*, focusing on Delacroix's attitude toward war.

2. Write an essay examining the representation of liberty as a woman. What qualities of liberty could plausibly be described as feminine?

3. Research the overall characteristics of European Romanticism and discuss *Liberty Leading the People* as a Romantic painting.

Pablo Picasso
Guernica
(1937)

IN A CAREER SPANNING more than seventy-five years, the Spanish painter and sculptor Pablo Picasso (1881–1973) produced thousands of paintings and was affiliated with dozens of artistic movements and media. His reputation, already highly esteemed during his life, continued to grow after his death, and he is now seen as one of the most influential artists who ever lived. In May of 2004, one of Picasso's early works, *Boy with a Pipe*, sold at auction for $104.1 million, then the highest price ever paid for a single painting.

In 1907, after more than ten years of painting realistic works, Picasso began working with the French artist Georges Braque (1882–1963) to develop a new artistic style that would eventually be called "cubism." The artistic theory behind cubism holds that an object must be seen from multiple perspectives to be truly understood. Thus, a cubist painting presents its subject from multiple perspectives—front view, side view, back view—all shown at once as part of the same image. Though cubism is only one of the many styles that Picasso used in his paintings, it is the one with which he is most often associated. And it is a style clearly evident in his 1937 masterpiece *Guernica*, which many critics consider his finest painting.

Though Picasso generally did not approve of overtly political art, *Guernica* is perhaps the most famous political statement by any artist in any age. An $11^1/_2 \times 25^1/_2$ foot mural commissioned by the Spanish Republican government for the 1937 Paris World's Fair, the painting depicts the bombing of Guernica, a Basque town in northern Spain, by German and Italian forces allied with General Francisco Franco during the Spanish Civil War. The German leader, Adolf Hitler, saw the unprovoked bombing raid against an unarmed civilian population as a way to test the destructive capability of his air force. As a result, an entire town was destroyed, and more than sixteen hundred people were killed. Devastated by the senseless destruction, Picasso created *Guernica* as a response to the brutality of the bombing and the senselessness of war. ✎

Pablo Picasso
Guernica, 1937 (oil on canvas).
Museo Nacional Centro de Arte Reina Sofia, Madrid, Spain / Bridgeman Art Library

Understanding the Text

1. What is the immediate visual effect of *Guernica*? What is the overall emotional effect? What elements of the painting elicit these reactions?

2. Notice the similarity between the woman holding the baby on the left side of the picture and the woman screaming on the right side. What is the significance of their likeness? Why are both of their heads facing upward at ninety-degree angles from their bodies?

3. Why do animals appear together with the people? What is the significance of the injured horse at the center of the painting and the tortured bull in the top left? Do these figures symbolize human elements of the conflict, or do they simply represent suffering caused by war?

4. What elements of cubism do you see in the painting? How do those elements contribute to Picasso's message?

5. What is the symbolic import of the broken dagger/sword in the bottom-center of the painting?

6. What do you think Picasso wanted to communicate through this painting? Why are glory and dignity absent from the work?

7. What symbolic roles do light sources, such as candles and lightbulbs, play in the painting? Is the painting itself a sort of "light source" designed to illuminate something? If so, what?

MAKING CONNECTIONS

1. Compare the portrayals of war in *Guernica* and *Liberty Leading the People* (p. 268). How are the political messages of both paintings connected to their artistic forms?

2. Compare *Guernica* to the paintings contained in chapter 7, "Language and Rhetoric": Norman Rockwell's *Freedom of Speech* (p. 503), which was used to sell war bonds, and the ad for China's One-Child Policy (p. 516). Should *Guernica* be included in the company of such propagandistic works of art? Why or why not?

3. Compare Picasso's response to fascist brutality to those of Aung San Suu Kyi (p. 219) and George Orwell (p. 282). What similarities and differences do you find?

4. What conception of human nature underlies *Guernica*? How are the animals portrayed in the painting related to that conception? How does Picasso's view of human nature compare with Hobbes's (p. 119) or Wilson's (p. 144)?

WRITING ABOUT THE TEXT

1. Think of a tragedy—personal, national, or global. Write an essay proposing an artwork that would communicate a strong emotional reaction and perhaps create one in the viewer. Would you render the scene visually realistic? What kinds of lines or colors would you use? What would the figures or components of the painting be doing? How would they interact to achieve your vision?

2. Try to translate Picasso's visual rhetoric (pp. 558–61) into words. Does the painting have an overall argument? How does it support that argument? What is lost when visual images are translated into written arguments?

3. Choose a single component of *Guernica*, such as the bull or the mother and child—and interpret its significance within the larger context of the painting. Pay special attention to the possible symbolism of the component.

4. Read two or three interpretations of *Guernica* (hundreds are readily available in any library or on the Internet) and write a paper identifying some of the problems of interpretation, or key areas of disagreement among scholars, that you uncover.

Symbolism
intertextuality

Margaret Mead
Warfare: An Invention—Not a Biological Necessity
(1940)

IN 1969, *TIME* MAGAZINE named anthropologist Margaret Mead (1901–1978) the "Mother of the World." This title stemmed in part from Mead's work with young girls in various cultures around the world, but it also recognized the moral and intellectual status that she earned during her fifty-year career as the world's most famous and respected anthropologist.

Mead was born in Philadelphia in 1901. She earned a doctoral degree in anthropology from Columbia University, where she studied under the legendary anthropologist Ruth Benedict. In 1925, Mead traveled to American Samoa for an extensive fieldwork project studying adolescent girls. She used this research as the basis for her first book, *Coming of Age in Samoa* (1928), which became a best seller and introduced a generation of nonspecialists to the field of anthropology. In 1929, Mead traveled to New Guinea for a similar study, which resulted in her second major book, *Growing Up in New Guinea* (1930). She continued doing fieldwork throughout the world, but maintained strong ties to New York, where for most of her career she worked at the American Museum of Natural History.

In the course of her career, Mead became known as an expert on both a diverse group of cultures and on human culture generally—on the ways that human beings form, maintain, and modify social relations. She refused to accept the common division of the world into "civilized" and "primitive" cultures, insisting instead that all cultures had things to learn from each other. The accessibility of her scholarly work, combined with her willingness to write articles for the popular press (she wrote a monthly column for *Redbook* magazine for seventeen years), put a human face on the often-obscure discipline of anthropology and gave Mead enormous influence with the American public.

The following essay, "Warfare: An Invention—Not a Biological Necessity," was originally published in *Asia* magazine in 1940. It is based on one of Mead's most cherished beliefs: that people can change by learning from other cultures. In this essay, Mead draws on her vast experience with other cultures to refute the popular argument that the inherent aggressiveness of human beings makes warfare inevitable.

Mead illustrates every major point that she makes with examples drawn from the cultures that she has studied. Each example argues, in effect, that a trait cannot be considered "universal" if there are people anywhere who do not possess it.

IS WAR A BIOLOGICAL NECESSITY, a sociological inevitability, or just a bad invention? Those who argue for the first view endow man with such pugnacious instincts that some outlet in aggressive behavior is necessary if man is to reach full human stature. It was this point of view which lay back of William James's famous essay, "The Moral Equivalent of War," in which he tried to retain the warlike virtues and channel them in new directions.[1] A similar point of view has lain back of the Soviet Union's attempt to make competition between groups rather than between individuals. A basic, competitive, aggressive, warring human nature is assumed, and those who wish to outlaw war or outlaw competitiveness merely try to find new and less socially destructive ways in which these biologically given aspects of man's nature can find expression. Then there are those who take the second view: warfare is the inevitable concomitant of the development of the state, the struggle for land and natural resources of class societies springing, not from the nature of man, but from the nature of history. War is nevertheless inevitable unless we change our social system and outlaw classes, the struggle for power, and possessions; and in the event of our success warfare would disappear, as a symptom vanishes when the disease is cured.

One may hold a compromise position between these two extremes; one may claim that all aggression springs from the frustration of man's biologically determined drives and that, since all forms of culture are frustrating, it is certain each new generation will be aggressive and the aggression will find its natural and inevitable expression in race war, class war, nationalistic war, and so on.

All three positions are very popular today among those who think seriously about the problems of war and its possible prevention, but I wish to urge another point of view, less defeatist perhaps than the first and third, and more accurate than the second: that is, that warfare, by which I mean organized conflict between two groups as *groups*, in which each group puts an army (even if the army is only fifteen Pygmies) into the field to fight and kill, if possible, some of the members of the army of the other group—that warfare of this sort is an invention like any other of the inventions in terms of which we order our lives, such as writing, marriage, cooking our food instead of eating it raw, trial by jury, or burial of the dead, and so on. Some of this list any one will grant are inventions: trial by jury is confined to very limited portions of the globe; we know that there are tribes that do not bury their dead but instead expose or cremate them; and we know that only part of the human race has had a knowledge of writing as its cultural inheritance. But, whenever a way of doing things is found universally, such as the use of fire or the practice of some form of marriage, we tend to think at once that it is not an invention at all but an attribute of humanity itself. And yet even such universals as marriage and the use of fire are inventions like the rest, very basic ones,

---

1. **William James's famous essay:** In the 1906 essay mentioned here, the American philosopher and psychologist William James (1842–1910) argues that the natural instincts of human beings toward competition, patriotism, and militarism can be channeled positively into public works projects and the fights against poverty and disease.

inventions which were perhaps necessary if human history was to take the turn it has taken, but nevertheless inventions. At some point in his social development man was undoubtedly without the institution of marriage or the knowledge of the use of fire.

The case for warfare is much clearer because there are peoples even today who have no warfare. Of these the Eskimo are perhaps the most conspicuous example, but the Lepchas of Sikkim[2] are an equally good one. Neither of these peoples understands war, not even the defensive warfare. The idea of warfare is lacking, and this lack is as essential to carrying on war as an alphabet or a syllabary[3] is to writing. But whereas the Lepchas are a gentle, unquarrelsome people, and the advocates of other points of view might argue that they are not full human beings or that they had never been frustrated and so had no aggression to expend in war-fare, the Eskimo case gives no such possibility of interpretation. The Eskimo are not a mild and meek people; many of them are turbulent and troublesome. Fights, theft of wives, murder, cannibalism occur among them—all outbursts of passion-ate men goaded by desire or intolerable circumstance. Here are men faced with hunger, men faced with loss of their wives, men faced with the threat of exter-mination by other men, and here are orphan children, growing up miserably with no one to care for them, mocked and neglected by those about them. The per-sonality necessary for war, the circumstances necessary to goad men to despera-tion are present, but there is no war. When a traveling Eskimo entered a settlement he might have to fight the strongest man in the settlement to establish his posi-tion among them, but this was a test of strength and bravery, not war. The idea of warfare, of one *group* organizing against another *group* to maim and wound and kill them, was absent. And without that idea passions might rage but there was no war.

But, it may be argued, isn't this because the Eskimo have such a low and unde- 5 veloped form of social organization? They own no land, they move from place to place, camping, it is true, season after season on the same site, but this is not some-thing to fight for as the modern nations of the world fight for land and raw materi-als. They have no permanent possessions that can be looted, no towns that can be burned. They have no social classes to produce stress and strains within the society which might force it to go to war outside. Doesn't the absence of war among the Eskimo, while disproving the biological necessity of war, just go to confirm the point that it is the state of development of the society which accounts for war, and noth-ing else?

2. **Lepchas of Sikkim:** Sikkim is a small state in the Himalayan mountains of northeastern India. Its original inhabitants, the Lepchas, are noted for their peaceful traditions. About fifty thousand Lepchas still live in India and eastern Nepal.

3. **Syllabary:** a writing system in which a char-acter represents a syllable rather than a single sound (as a character in an alphabet does).

We find the answer among the Pygmy peoples of the Andaman Islands in the Bay of Bengal.[4] The Andamans also represent an exceedingly low level of society: they are a hunting and food-gathering people; they live in tiny hordes without any class stratification; their houses are simpler than the snow houses of the Eskimo. But they knew about warfare. The army might contain only fifteen determined Pygmies marching in a straight line, but it was the real thing none the less. Tiny army met tiny army in open battle, blows were exchanged, casualties suffered, and the state of warfare could only be concluded by a peacemaking ceremony.

Similarly, among the Australian aborigines, who built no permanent dwellings but wandered from water hole to water hole over their almost desert country, warfare— and rules of "international law"—were highly developed. The student of social evolution will seek in vain for his obvious causes of war, struggle for lands, struggle for power of one group over another, expansion of population, need to divert the minds of a populace restive under tyranny, or even the ambition of a successful leader to enhance his own prestige. All are absent, but warfare as a practice remained, and men engaged in it and killed one another in the course of a war because killing is what is done in wars.

From instances like these it becomes apparent that an inquiry into the causes of war misses the fundamental point as completely as does an insistence upon the biological necessity of war. If a people have an idea of going to war and the idea that war is the way in which certain situations, defined within their society, are to be handled, they will sometimes go to war. If they are a mild and unaggressive people, like the Pueblo Indians, they may limit themselves to defensive warfare; but they will be forced to think in terms of war because there are peoples near them who have warfare as a pattern, and offensive, raiding, pillaging warfare at that. When the pattern of warfare is known, people like the Pueblo Indians will defend themselves, taking advantage of their natural defenses, the *mesa* village site, and people like the Lepchas, having no natural defenses and no idea of warfare, will merely submit to the invader. But the essential point remains the same. There is a way of behaving which is known to a given people and labeled as an appropriate form of behavior. A bold and warlike people like the Sioux or the Maori[5] may label warfare as desirable as well as possible; a mild people like the Pueblo Indians may label warfare as undesirable; but to the minds of both peoples the possibility of warfare is present. Their thoughts, their hopes, their plans are oriented about this idea, that warfare may be selected as the way to meet some situation.

4. **Pygmy peoples of the Andaman Islands in the Bay of Bengal:** Until the twentieth century, the inhabitants of the Andaman Islands, which lie off the eastern coast of India, were hunter-gatherers who had virtually no contact with modern civilization. In 1901, the estimated two thousand Andamanese had twelve distinct, constantly warring tribes.

5. **The Sioux or the Maori:** The Sioux, or Lakota, are a Native American tribe that originally inhabited the northern Great Plains; the Maori are the indigenous people of New Zealand. The **Pueblo Indians** inhabited the American Southwest.

So simple peoples and civilized peoples, mild peoples and violent, assertive peoples, will all go to war if they have the invention, just as those peoples who have the custom of dueling with have duels and peoples who have the pattern of vendetta will indulge in vendetta. And, conversely, peoples who do not know of dueling will not fight duels, even though their wives are seduced and their daughters ravished; they may on occasion commit murder but they will not fight duels. Cultures which lack the idea of the vendetta will not meet every quarrel in this way. A people can use only the forms it has. So the Balinese[6] have their special way of dealing with a quarrel between two individuals; if the two feel that the causes of quarrel are heavy, they may go and register their quarrel in the temple before the gods, and, making offerings, they may swear never to have anything to do with each other again. Under the Dutch government they registered such mutual "not-speaking" with the Dutch government officials. But in other societies, although individuals might feel as full of animosity and as unwilling to have any further contact as do the Balinese, they cannot register their quarrel with the gods and go on quietly about their business because registering quarrels with the gods is not an invention of which they know.

Yet, if it be granted that warfare is after all an invention, it may nevertheless be an   10
invention that lends itself to certain types of personality, to the exigent needs of autocrats, to the expansionist desires of crowded peoples, to the desire for plunder and rape and loot which is engendered by a dull and frustrating life. What, then, can we say of this congruence between warfare and its uses? If it is a form which fits so well, is not this congruence the essential point? But even here the primitive material causes us to wonder, because there are tribes who go to war merely for glory, having no quarrel with the enemy, suffering from no tyrant within their boundaries, anxious neither for land nor loot nor women, but merely anxious to win prestige which within that tribe has been declared obtainable only by war and without which no young man can hope to win his sweetheart's smile of approval. But if, as was the case with the Bush Negroes of Dutch Guiana,[7] it is artistic ability which is necessary to win a girl's approval, the same young man would have to be carving rather than going out on a war party.

In many parts of the world, war is a game in which the individual can win counters—counters which bring him prestige in the eyes of his own sex or of the opposite sex; he plays for these counters as he might, in our society, strive for a tennis championship. Warfare is a frame for such prestige-seeking merely because it calls for the display of certain skills and certain virtues; all of these skills—riding straight, shooting straight, dodging the missiles of the enemy, and sending one's own straight to the mark—can be equally well exercised in some other framework and, equally, the virtues—endurance, bravery, loyalty, steadfastness—can be displayed in other contexts. The tie-up between proving oneself a man and proving this by a success

---

6. **Balinese:** the people of the island of Bali, in present-day Indonesia.
7. **Dutch Guiana:** the country presently known as Suriname, located on the northeast coast of South America between Guyana and French Guiana.

in organized killing is due to a definition which many societies have made of man-
liness. And often, even in those societies which counted success in warfare a proof
of human worth, strange turns were given to the idea, as when the Plains Indians
gave their highest awards to the man who touched a live enemy rather than to the
man who brought in a scalp—from a dead enemy—because killing a man was less
risky. Warfare is just an invention known to the majority of human societies by
which they permit their young men either to accumulate prestige or avenge their
honor or acquire loot or wives or slaves or sago lands or cattle or appease the blood
lust of their gods or the restless souls of the recently dead. It is just an invention,
older and more widespread than the jury system, but none the less an invention.

But, once we have said this, have we said anything at all? Despite a few instances,
dear to the hearts of controversialists, of the loss of the useful arts, once an invention is made which proves congruent with human needs or social forms, it tends to
persist. Grant that war is an invention, that it is not a biological necessity nor the
outcome of certain special types of social forms, still, once the invention is made,
what are we to do about it? The Indian who had been subsisting on the buffalo for
generations because with his primitive weapons he could slaughter only a limited
number of buffalo did not return to his primitive weapons when he saw that the
white man's more efficient weapons were exterminating the buffalo. A desire for the
white man's cloth may mortgage the South Sea Islander to the white man's planta-
tion, but he does not return to making bark cloth, which would have left him free.
Once an invention is known and accepted, men do not easily relinquish it. The
skilled workers may smash the first steam looms which they feel are to be their undoing, but they accept them in the end, and no movement which has insisted upon
the mere abandonment of usable inventions has ever had much success. Warfare is
here, as part of our thought; the deeds of warriors are immortalized in the words of
our poets; the toys of our children are modeled upon the weapons of the soldier; the
frame of reference within which our statesmen and our diplomats work always contains war. If we know that it is not inevitable, that it is due to historical accident
that warfare is one of the ways in which we think of behaving, are we given any
hope by that? What hope is there of persuading nations to abandon war, nations so
thoroughly imbued with the idea that resort to war is, if not actually desirable and
noble, at least inevitable whenever certain defined circumstances arise?

In answer to this question I think we might turn to the history of other social
inventions, inventions which must once have seemed as firmly entrenched as warfare. Take the methods of trial which preceded the jury system: ordeal and trial by
combat.[8] Unfair, capricious, alien as they are to our feeling today, they were once

8. **Ordeal and trial by combat:** medieval methods of "trying cases." Trial by ordeal subjected
the accused to burning or drowning as a way of
allowing God to signal guilt or innocence. Trial
by combat allowed the accuser to challenge the
accused to a duel, which would "prove" the
alleged offender's guilt or innocence.

the only methods open to individuals accused of some offense. The invention of trial by jury gradually replaced these methods until only witches, and finally not even witches, had to resort to the ordeal. And for a long time the jury system seemed the one best and finest method of settling legal disputes, but today new inventions, trial before judges only or before commissions, are replacing the jury system. In each case the old method was replaced by a new social invention; the ordeal did not go out because people thought it unjust or wrong, it went out because a method more congruent with the institutions and feelings of the period was invented. And, if we despair over the way in which war seems such an ingrained habit of most of the human race, we can take comfort from the fact that a poor invention will usually give place to a better invention.

For this, two conditions at least are necessary. The people must recognize the defects of the old invention, and some one must make a new one. Propaganda against warfare, documentation of its terrible cost in human suffering and social waste, these prepare the ground by teaching people to feel that warfare is a defective social institution. There is further needed a belief that social invention is possible and the invention of new methods which will render warfare as out-of-date as the tractor is making the plow, or the motor car the horse and buggy. A form of behavior becomes out-of-date only when something else takes its place, and in order to invent forms of behavior which will make war obsolete, it is a first requirement to believe that an invention is possible.

UNDERSTANDING THE TEXT

1. What underlying assumption about human nature does Mead reject in this essay? What evidence does she supply for rejecting this assumption?

2. What arguments does Mead support through the examples of the Eskimos and the Lepchas? How do these two tribes differ? In what way are they similar? Which are most important for her argument, their differences or their similarities? How do the examples of the warlike Andaman Pygmies and Australian aborigines complement her arguments?

3. What factors does Mead see as determining whether a civilization will wage war? What kinds of changes would be required to eliminate this tendency?

4. What exactly does Mead mean by categorizing warfare as an "invention"? How does this idea change the traditional view of war? How does it give humanity hope of eliminating war?

MAKING CONNECTIONS

1. Compare Mead's view of human nature with that of Edward O. Wilson in "The Fitness of Human Nature" (p. 144). Would Wilson agree that war is not a biological imperative? Explain.

2. How does Mead's view of human nature compare with those of Mencius (p. 94), Hsün Tzu (p. 100), Hobbes (p. 119), or Machiavelli (p. 184)?

3. Mead studied with Ruth Benedict (p. 132). How might Benedict's theories about the cultural formation of human nature have influenced Mead's assertions about the nature of warfare?

WRITING ABOUT THE TEXT

1. Evaluate the effectiveness of Mead's argument. Does the evidence that Mead presents justify her article's claims? Could other factors account for that same evidence?

2. Define the terms "war," "violence," and "aggression" from Mead's perspective. How does her use of these terms account for some of her differences with one or two other thinkers in this chapter?

3. Consider Mead's contention that social inventions are often replaced with better inventions that solve the same problems. Write an essay speculating about the kind of invention that could achieve the same ends as armed conflict.

4. Examine the fundamental assumptions that Mead makes about human nature. Choose one reading in the chapter "Human Nature" as the basis for a comparison.

George Orwell
Pacifism and the War
(1942)

"GEORGE ORWELL" is the pen name of Eric Blair (1903–1950), one of the most important and controversial English writers of the twentieth century. Though he published nine novels and several collections of essays and occasional pieces, his reputation as a major author rests almost entirely on two of his last works: *Animal Farm* (1945), a satirical allegory that presents the events of the Russian Revolution as an uprising of the animals on a farm, and *Nineteen Eighty-Four* (1949), a dystopian novel about a futuristic totalitarian society based on surveillance, punishment, and disinformation.

Though Orwell considered himself a socialist and a political liberal, he greatly disdained rigid ideologies—even liberal ones—which, he believed, caused people to be intolerant, irrational, and susceptible to manipulation by cynical, power-hungry politicians. Orwell constantly angered other liberals by attacking their sacred cows and their cherished notions about the world. He especially scorned Soviet Communism, the totalitarianism of which he recognized and attacked at a time when many left-leaning intellectuals in Europe and America were still defending that system, and Spanish, Italian, and German fascism, which he saw as the greatest threat to freedom in history.

Orwell's passionate antifascism during the early stages of World War II led him into a conflict with the liberal pacifist movement in England and America. Though he had once considered himself a pacifist, the aggression of Spain's Francisco Franco, Italy's Benito Mussolini, and, most of all, Germany's Adolf Hitler had convinced him that failure to fight enemies of this kind would eventually cause more suffering and misery than even the bloodiest war. In 1942, he began attacking pacifists in his monthly "London Letter" column in the American magazine *Partisan Review*. His attacks generated numerous responses from pacifists, including letters from the prominent British intellectuals D. S. Savage, George Woodcock, and Alex Comfort. Orwell wrote the following commentary for *Partisan Review* as a collective response to these three letters.

In this response, Orwell identifies one of the most difficult philosophical questions for any pacifist philosophy to answer: how can one respond nonviolently to genuinely evil people, such as Hitler, who will use violence to further their own agendas and who will never respond to nonviolent persuasion? For Orwell, pacifism in the face of unwarranted aggression was morally untenable.

Orwell begins his argument with a single, declarative thesis that he supports through a series of deductive arguments. In the process, he refers to and refutes arguments made earlier by the writers that he is responding to. ✿

PACIFISM. PACIFISM IS objectively pro-Fascist. This is elementary common sense. If you hamper the war effort of one side you automatically help that of the other. Nor is there any real way of remaining outside such a war as the present one. In practice, "he that is not with me is against me". The idea that you can somehow remain aloof from and superior to the struggle, while living on food which British sailors have to risk their lives to bring you, is a bourgeois illusion bred of money and security. Mr Savage remarks that "according to this type of reasoning, a German or Japanese pacifist would be 'objectively pro-British'." But of course he would be! That is why pacifist activities are not permitted in those countries (in both of them the penalty is, or can be, beheading) while both the Germans and the Japanese do all they can to encourage the spread of pacifism in British and American territories. The Germans even run a spurious "freedom" station which serves out pacifist propaganda indistinguishable from that of the PPU.[1] They would stimulate pacifism in Russia as well if they could, but in that case they have tougher babies to deal with. In so far as it takes effect at all, pacifist propaganda can only be effective *against* those countries where a certain amount of freedom of speech is still permitted; in other words it is helpful to totalitarianism.

I am not interested in pacifism as a "moral phenomenon". If Mr Savage and others imagine that one can somehow "overcome" the German army by lying on one's back, let them go on imagining it, but let them also wonder occasionally whether this is not an illusion due to security, too much money and a simple ignorance of the way in which things actually happen. As an ex-Indian civil servant, it always makes me shout with laughter to hear, for instance, Gandhi[2] named as an example of the success of non-violence. As long as twenty years ago it was cynically admitted in Anglo-Indian circles that Gandhi was very useful to the British Government. So he will be to the Japanese if they get there. Despotic governments can stand "moral force" till the cows come home; what they fear is physical force. But though not much interested in the "theory" of pacifism, I *am* interested in the psychological processes by which pacifists who have started out with an alleged horror of violence end up with a marked tendency to be fascinated by the success and power of Nazism. Even pacifists who wouldn't own to any such fascination are beginning to claim that a Nazi victory is desirable in itself. In the letter you sent on to me, Mr Comfort considers that an artist in occupied territory ought to "protest against such evils as he sees", but considers

---

1. **PPU:** The Peace Pledge Union, a pacifist organization founded in 1934 by Richard Sheppard, an Anglican clergyman and radio broadcaster with a large following in England before World War II. Members of the PPU advocated conscientious objection during World War II and often faced persecution and even arrest for their beliefs.

2. **Gandhi:** Mohandas K. Gandhi (1896–1948), Indian political and spiritual leader who lead nonviolent protests against the British rule of India.

that this is best done by "temporarily accepting the *status quo*" (like Déat or Bergery,[3] for instance?). A few weeks back he was hoping for a Nazi victory because of the stimulating effect it would have upon the arts:

> As far as I can see, no therapy short of complete military defeat has any chance of re-establishing the common stability of literature and of the man in the street. One can imagine the greater the adversity the greater the sudden real-isation of a stream of imaginative work, and the greater the sudden katharsis of poetry, from the isolated interpretation of war as calamity to the realisation of the imaginative and actual tragedy of Man. When we have access again to the literature of the war years in France, Poland and Czechoslovakia, I am confident that that is what we shall find. . . .

I pass over the money-sheltered ignorance capable of believing that literary life is still going on in, for instance, Poland, and remark merely that statements like this justify me in saying that our English pacifists are tending towards active pro-Fascism. But I don't particularly object to that. What I object to is the intellectual cowardice of people who are objectively and to some extent emotionally pro-Fascist, but who don't care to say so and take refuge behind the formula "I am just as anti-Fascist as anyone, but—". The result of this is that so-called peace propaganda is just as dis-honest and intellectually disgusting as war propaganda. Like war propaganda, it con-centrates on putting forward a "case", obscuring the opponent's point of view and avoiding awkward questions. The line normally followed is "Those who fight against Fascism go Fascist themselves". In order to evade the quite obvious objections that can be raised to this, the following propaganda-tricks are used:

1. The Fascising processes occurring in Britain as a result of war are systemati-cally exaggerated.

2. The actual record of Fascism, especially its pre-war history, is ignored or pooh-poohed as "propaganda". Discussion of what the world would actually be like if the Axis[4] dominated it is evaded.

3. Those who want to struggle against Fascism are accused of being wholehearted defenders of capitalist "democracy". The fact that the rich everywhere tend to be pro-Fascist and the working class are nearly always anti-Fascist is hushed up.

4. It is tacitly pretended that the war is only between Britain and Germany. Men-tion of Russia and China,[5] and their fate if Fascism is permitted to win, is avoided. (You won't find one word about Russia or China in the three letters you sent to me.)

---

3. **Déat or Bergery:** Marcel Déat and Gaston Bergery were French politicians who collabo-rated with the Nazi forces occupying France dur-ing World War II. Bergery appealed to pacifism in arguing to cooperate with Adolf Hitler.

4. **The Axis:** Germany, Italy, Japan, and their allies during World War II.

5. **Russia and China:** A war between Britain and Germany could be viewed by Marxists as simply a clash between two corrupt bastions of industrial capitalism. This could not be said if Russia, the stronghold of world communism, and China, whose communist forces were on the verge of a successful revolution, were counted among Britain's allies in the fight against fascism.

Now as to one or two points of fact which I must deal with if your correspondents' letters are to be printed in full.

My past and present. Mr Woodcock tries to discredit me by saying that (a) I once served in the Indian Imperial Police, (b) I have written articles for the *Adelphi* and was mixed up with the Trotskyists[6] in Spain, and (c) that I am at the BBC "conducting British propaganda to fox the Indian masses". With regard to (a), it is quite true that I served five years in the Indian Police. It is also true that I gave up that job, partly because it didn't suit me but mainly because I would not any longer be a servant of imperialism. I am against imperialism because I know something about it from the inside. The whole history of this is to be found in my writings, including a novel[7] which I think I can claim was a kind of prophecy of what happened this year in Burma. (b) Of course I have written for the *Adelphi*. Why not? I once wrote an article for a vegetarian paper. Does that make me a vegetarian? I was associated with the Trotskyists in Spain. It was chance that I was serving in the POUM[8] militia and not another, and I largely disagreed with the POUM "line" and told its leaders so freely, but when they were afterwards accused of pro-Fascist activities I defended them as best I could. How does this contradict my present anti-Hitler attitude? It is news to me that Trotskyists are either pacifists or pro-Fascists. (c) Does Mr Woodcock really know what kind of stuff I put out in the Indian broadcasts? He does not—though I would be quite glad to tell him about it. He is careful not to mention what other people are associated with these Indian broadcasts. . . . Most of our broadcasters are Indian left-wing intellectuals, from Liberals to Trotskyists, some of them bitterly anti-British. They don't do it to "fox the Indian masses" but because they know what a Fascist victory would mean to the chances of India's independence. Why not try to find out what I am doing before accusing my good faith?

"Mr Orwell is intellectual-hunting again" (Mr Comfort). I have never attacked "the intellectuals" or "the intelligentsia" *en bloc.*[9] I have used a lot of ink and done myself a lot of harm by attacking the successive literary cliques which have infested this country, not because they were intellectuals but precisely because they were *not* what I mean by true intellectuals. The life of a clique is about five years and I have been writing long enough to see three of them come and two go—the Catholic gang, the Stalinist gang, and the present pacifist or, as they are sometimes nicknamed, Fascifist gang. My case against all of them is that they write mentally dis-

---

6. **Trotskyists:** followers of Leon Trotsky (see note 8).

7. *Burmese Days* (1934).

8. **POUM:** *Partido Obrero de Unificación Marxista* (Workers Party of Marxist Unification). In the Spanish Civil War, the POUM was a small, radical faction that opposed both the fascists and the Stalinists, or followers of the Soviet

leader, Joseph Stalin. The POUM followed Leon Trotsky, whom Stalin had exiled after a bitter power struggle. Orwell describes his association with the POUM in his memoir *Homage to Catalonia.* The power struggle between Stalin and Trotsky is the basis for his allegorical novel, *Animal Farm.*

9. **En bloc:** as a group.

honest propaganda and degrade literary criticism to mutual arse-licking. But even with these various schools I would differentiate between individuals. I would never think of coupling Christopher Dawson with Arnold Lunn, or Malraux with Palme Dutt, or Max Plowman with the Duke of Bedford.[10] And even the work of one individual can exist at very different levels. For instance Mr Comfort himself wrote one poem I value greatly ("The Atoll in the Mind"), and I wish he would write more of them instead of lifeless propaganda tracts dressed up as novels. But this letter he has chosen to send you is a different matter. Instead of answering what I have said he tries to prejudice an audience to whom I am little known by a misrepresentation of my general line and sneers about my "status" in England. (A writer isn't judged by his "status", he is judged by his work.) That is on a par with "peace" propaganda which has to avoid mention of Hitler's invasion of Russia, and it is not what I mean by intellectual honesty. It is just because I do take the function of the intelligentsia seriously that I don't like the sneers, libels, parrot phrases and financially profitable back-scratching which flourish in our English literary world, and perhaps in yours also.

12 July 1942
London, England

Understanding the Text

1. What kind of case is Orwell making? Does he perceive his audience as supportive, hostile, lacking in information, partially supportive, or unconvinced about the importance of the issue? Support your answer by drawing from the text.

2. What does Orwell mean when he says that during World War II pacifism was "objectively pro-Fascist"? From what you know about this conflict, judge whether it would have been possible to oppose the use of force by one side (the Allies) without supporting the ideology of the other side (the Axis).

3. Why, according to Orwell, was pacifism not permitted in Germany and Japan during World War II?

4. What is the basis of Orwell's distinction between "'moral force'" and "physical force"? Which does he see as more desirable in World War II?

10. Taken together, these six men represent the Catholic gang, the Stalinist gang, and the present pacifist . . . gang. Christopher Dawson was an esteemed Catholic historian whose 1937 essay "The Catholic Attitude to War" argues that true peace is impossible in a flawed world. Arnold Lunn was a Catholic aristocrat and adventurer whose attacks on the Trotskyists in the Spanish Civil War earned a rebuttal from Orwell in his 1944 essay "As I Please." André Malraux was a major French novelist with communist ties who eventually broke with Stalin and served in the French Resistance. Rajani Palme Dutt was the head of the British Communist Party and opposed Britain's entry into World War II. Max Plowman was a minor poet and a member of the Peace Pledge Union (PPU). The Duke of Bedford refers to Bertrand Russell, the great philosopher and mathematician, who was also a member of the PPU.

5. What arguments does Orwell characterize as "peace propaganda"? How is this related to "war propaganda"? What kinds of arguments might he see as the cornerstone of all kinds of propaganda?

6. What mistaken notions about fascism does Orwell attribute to the peace movement?

7. Against what personal attacks does Orwell defend himself? Are his defenses necessary? Are they effective?

MAKING CONNECTIONS

1. Compare Orwell's insistence that pacifism is pro-facist with Mo Tzu's argument that civilized people should never engage in offensive warfare (p. 253). Does Orwell's argument support only defensive warfare? Or would it justify an offensive first strike? Why or why not?

2. How does Orwell's argument about pacifism compare with the just war theories advocated by Thomas Aquinas (p. 260) and Jean Bethke Elshtain (p. 293)? Does his argument have religious overtones, or is it completely secular? Explain.

3. What beliefs about human nature are embedded in Orwell's argument? Would he agree with Hobbes (p. 119)? Do you believe that Orwell sees fascism as an extension of or as an aberration from human nature? Why?

4. How might Orwell's dismissal of "'moral force'" in this essay be reconciled with Martin Luther King Jr.'s very successful use of moral persuasion during the civil rights movement (p. 202)? What differences between the two situations allowed moral force to work in one and not the other?

WRITING ABOUT THE TEXT

1. Write a pacifist response to Orwell. Construct an argument for pacifism's morality, even in the face of unwarranted aggression.

2. Examine how Orwell's arguments about pacifism during World War II would apply to other military conflicts. Discuss whether Orwell's arguments are specific to the kind of ultimate evil represented by Hitler or whether they can be generalized to other armed conflicts.

3. Situate Orwell's argument in the just war tradition. Discuss what Orwell added to that tradition that is not found in the other readings in this chapter.

4. Evaluate the morality of pacifism in "the war on terror," "the war on drugs," or some other contemporary "conflict." Do Orwell's arguments apply?

Kenzaburo Oe
The Unsurrendered People
(1965)

KENZABURO OE (b. 1935) is well known in his native Japan as a writer of fiction, essays, memoirs, literary criticism, and cultural commentary—and as an important chronicler of postwar Japan's struggle to come to grips with its imperial past while joining the ranks of modern industrial democracies. In 1994, Oe became only the second Japanese citizen to receive the Nobel Prize for Literature, for creating a literary world "where life and myth condense to form a disconcerting picture of the human predicament today."

Oe began his career as a writer by studying French literature at Tokyo University, where he enrolled in 1953. He absorbed the works of Jean-Paul Sartre and other French existentialists and, while still a student, began publishing short fiction in well-regarded Japanese magazines. In 1958, at the age of 23, he was awarded the Akutagawa Prize, Japan's most prestigious literary award. That same year, he published his first novel, *Nip the Buds, Shoot the Kids*, and he began his celebrated career as a professional writer immediately upon graduation from college.

Oe was ten years old when American forces dropped atomic bombs on Hiroshima and Nagasaki in 1945, forcing the surrender of the Japanese empire and ending six years of war. This event, and the American occupation that followed, plays a central role in most of Oe's writings. Like many of his fellow citizens, Oe was caught up in the contradictions of trying to emulate American political and economic values, which he admired, without accepting the role of a conquered people or a vanquished culture. This ambiguity toward America was made worse by the fact that the American bombings of Hiroshima and Nagasaki unleashed on the people of Japan the greatest destructive force the world had ever known.

Oe's classic 1965 book, *Hiroshima Notes*, from which this reading is drawn, attempts to come to grips with the effects of the world's first atomic bombing. The bombing of Hiroshima on August 6, 1945, killed up to 140,000 people and caused injuries, trauma, and birth defects that affected residents for generations. Oe visited Hiroshima numerous times between 1963 and 1965 to interview survivors of the bombing. *Hiroshima Notes* confronts the destruction of Hiroshima head-on, without turning away from the horror that it produced. But Oe's tone is ultimately both positive and humanistic, as he chronicles the efforts of the people to rebuild their lives and their city despite the tragedy they have endured. For Oe, the survivors of Hiroshima are both an example of and a metaphor for the human spirit and its indomitable will to survive.

In presenting his argument, Oe emphasizes the sheer, almost unimaginable horror experienced by the people of Hiroshima. In this way, he makes a powerful emotional appeal to his readers, most of whom already have strong emotions about his subject matter. 🖎

Few people today view the world in terms of a dualism of good and evil. Certainly it is no longer fashionable to do so. But, all of a sudden one summer, an absolute evil intruded into the lives and consciousness of the A-bomb victims. To counter that absolute evil, it became necessary to have an absolute good in order to recover a human balance in the world and to persevere in resisting that evil. From that instant the atomic bomb exploded, it became the symbol of all human evil; it was a savagely primitive demon and a most modern curse. The attempt to accord it positive value as a means of ending the war quickly did not, however, bring peace even to the minds of all the airmen who carried out the atomic attack. The atomic bomb embodied the absolute evil of war, transcending lesser distinctions such as Japanese or Allies, attacker or attacked.

Even while the smoke still rose from the wasteland of total destruction, human goodwill began to go into action as people made their first moves toward recovery and restoration. This action was seen both in the injured victims' will to live and in the efforts of doctors who worked, in a virtual vacuum of supplies and support systems, to treat the victims. Initiated soon that summer morning by the people in Hiroshima, the acts of goodwill were essential to resisting that ultimate thrust of accumulated science which produced the atomic bomb. If one believes that there is some kind of human harmony or order in this world, then he must also believe that the efforts of the Hiroshima doctors were somehow sufficient to cope with the demonic aftermath of the atomic disaster.

For my part, I have a kind of nightmare about trusting in human strength, or in humanism; it is a nightmare about a particular kind of trust in human capability. Toward this kind of humanism (and it is nothing more than a kind of humanism), I have a strong antipathy; so much so that I cannot help thinking about it from time to time. My nightmare stems from a suspicion that a certain 'trust in human strength', or 'humanism', flashed across the minds of the American intellectuals who decided upon the project that concluded with the dropping of the atomic bomb on Hiroshima. That 'humanism' ran as follows: If this absolutely lethal bomb is dropped on Hiroshima, a scientifically predictable hell will result. But the hell will not be so thoroughly disastrous as to wipe out, once and for all, all that is good in human society. That hell will not be so completely beyond the possibility of human recovery that all mankind will despise their humanity merely at the thought of it. It will not be an unrelieved hell with no exit, or so devastatingly evil that President Truman will, throughout his life, be unable to sleep for thinking of it. There are, after all, people in Hiroshima who will make the hell as humane as they possibly can. . . . I suspect that the A-bomb planners thought in such a way; that in making the final decision, they trusted too much in the enemy's own human strength to cope with the hell that would follow the dropping of the atomic bomb. If so, theirs was a most paradoxical humanism.

Suppose that the atomic bomb had been dropped, say, on Leopoldville[1] in the Congo, instead of on Hiroshima. Initially, a huge number of people would have died instantly; then wounded survivors, forced to accept total surrender, would have continued to die for many months to come. Epidemics would have spread, and pests would have proliferated in the desolate ruins. The city would have become a wasteland where human beings perished without cease or succor. There would have been no one to dispose of the dead. And when the victor would come in to investigate the damage—after the threat of residual radiation had passed—they would have experienced the worst nausea ever. Some of them would never be sane, normal persons again. One whole city would have been rendered as deadly as a huge death chamber in a Nazi concentration camp. All the people would have been doomed to death, with no sign of hope to be found. . . . Such a scenario is shocking to even the toughest mind. Unless some slave driver's descendant had been available to make the decision, the dropping of an atomic bomb on Leopoldville would have been postponed without setting a future date.

What actually happened in Hiroshima when the atomic bomb was in fact dropped was not quite as horrible as the preceding scenario. For one thing, the people who survived in Hiroshima made no particular effort to impress on those who dropped the bomb what a dreadful thing they had done. Even though the city was utterly devastated and had become a vast, ugly death chamber, the Hiroshima survivors first began struggling to recover and rebuild. They did so, of course, for their own sakes; but doing so served also to lessen the burden on the consciences of those who had dropped the atomic bomb.

The recovery effort has continued for two decades, and continues even now. The fact that a girl with leukemia goes on suffering all her life, not committing suicide, surely lessens—by just one person's portion—the A-bomb droppers' burden of conscience.

It is quite abnormal that people in one city should decide to drop an atomic bomb on people in another city. The scientists involved cannot possibly have lacked the ability to imagine the hell that would issue from the explosion. The decision, nevertheless, was made. I presume that it was done on the basis of some calculation of a built-in harmony by virtue of which, if the incredibly destructive bomb were dropped, the greatest effort in history would be made to counterbalance the totality of the enormous evil to follow. The inhuman damage caused by this demonic weapon would be mitigated by the humane efforts of those struggling to find what hope they could in the desperate situation.

5

---

1. **Leopoldville:** the capital and largest city in the Democratic Republic of the Congo, with nearly ten million inhabitants. In 1966, the name of the city was changed to Kinshasa.

The notion of 'balancing' also reflects a 'confidence in human strength', itself a reflection of confidence in the strength of humanism. But it is the attacking wolf's confidence in the scapegoat's ability to set things straight after the pitiless damage is done. This is the gruesome nightmare I have about humanism. Perhaps it is no more than an overanxious delusion of mine.

I think of the patience of the A-bomb victims quietly awaiting their turns in the waiting room of the Atomic Bomb Casualty Commission[2] on the top of Hijiyama hill. At least it is true that their stoicism greatly reduces the emotional burden of the American doctors working there.

I have little knowledge of the Bible. It seems to me, though, that when God made   10
the rain fall for forty days and nights, he fully trusted that Noah would rebuild human society after the Great Flood ended. If Noah had been a lazy man, or a hysterical man given to despair, then there would have been great consternation in God's heaven. Fortunately, Noah had the needed will and ability, so the deluge played its part within God's plan for man, without playing the tyrant beyond God's expectations. Did God, too, count on a built-in harmony of 'balancing out'? (And if so, does God not seem rather vicious?)

The atomic destruction of Hiroshima was the worst 'deluge' of the twentieth century. The people of Hiroshima went to work at once to restore human society in the aftermath of this great atomic 'flood'. They were concerned to salvage their own lives, but in the process they also salvaged the souls of the people who had brought the atomic bomb. This Great Flood of the present age is a kind of Universal Deluge which, instead of receding, has become frozen; and we cannot foretell when it will thaw and flow away. To change the metaphor, the twentieth century has become afflicted with a cancer—the possession of nuclear weapons by various nations—for which there is no known cure. And the souls salvaged by the people of Hiroshima are the souls of all human beings alive today.

UNDERSTANDING THE TEXT

1. Why does Oe refer to the atomic bomb as an "absolute evil"? What might he say makes it more of an evil than a series of conventional explosions resulting in the same loss as life?

2. Why does Oe have a "nightmare" about a certain kind of humanism? What view of life does he refer to? What does he say that American intellectuals might have been thinking when they dropped the atomic bomb on Hiroshima?

2. **Atomic Bomb Casualty Commission:** a committee established by President Harry Truman after World War II to investigate the effects of radiation on the survivors of the Hiroshima and Nagasaki bombings. The commission's main facility was on the top of Hijiyama Hill in Hiroshima.

3. Do you agree with Oe's conclusion that, had the bomb been dropped some-where else, the resulting devastation would have been worse? Why does he make this argument?

4. What similarities does Oe see between those who suffered the effects of the atomic bomb and those who suffer "the burden of conscience" of having dropped it? What underlying assumption about human nature does Oe make here?

5. Why does Oe choose the title "The Unsurrendered People"? Does this selec-tion end with a note of optimism or a note of pessimism? What central insight of the author can be found in the final paragraph?

MAKING CONNECTIONS

1. Compare Oe's view of the suffering of the people of Hiroshima with the visual depictions of suffering that form the basis of Picasso's *Guernica* (p. 271). What are some of the similarities in Picasso's and Oe's depictions of the suffering of war?

2. Oe lists several justifications that the Allies gave for the bombing of Hiroshima—for instance, it brought a swift end to the war. Compare Oe's view of these justifications with Thomas Aquinas's assertion that some wars are just (p. 260). Would any of the proposed justifications meet Aquinas's criteria of a just war?

3. Compare Oe's discussion of the atomic bomb with Rachel Carson's discus-sion of DDT (p. 419) or Al Gore's discussion of global climate change (p. 454). What common themes run through these works? Can you detect a common set of attitudes and values behind those responsible for the destructive acts described by these works? Explain.

WRITING ABOUT THE TEXT

1. Use the personal, first-hand observations that Oe makes in this selection as the basis for challenging the just war theories of Thomas Aquinas and Jean Bethke Elshtain. Explain the difference between the abstract justness of a cause and the real suffering caused by a violent response.

2. Research the controversy surrounding the dropping of the atomic bombs on Hiroshima and Nagasaki to find out what arguments have been made for and against the bombings. Then write an essay in which you present both sides of the argument and then agree or disagree with Oe's arguments about the bombing. Remember to document your sources (pp. 637–43).

3. Write an essay analyzing Oe's view that the survivors of Hiroshima have, in some way, redeemed "the souls of all human beings alive today." What do you think he means by this statement? From what do human beings need to be redeemed? Do you agree?

Jean Bethke Elshtain
What Is a Just War?
(2003)

JEAN BETHKE ELSHTAIN (b. 1941) is the Laura Spelman Rockefeller Professor of Social and Political Ethics at the University of Chicago Divinity School and the author or editor of about two dozen books and more than five hundred articles on a wide variety of political topics. She chairs the board of directors of the Institute for American Values, a scholarly organization that defines its role as "contributing intellectually to the renewal of marriage and family life and the sources of competence, character, and citizenship."

In the aftermath of the September 11 terrorist attacks on the World Trade Center and the Pentagon, Elshtain joined more than sixty other academics and intellectuals in signing "What We're Fighting For: A Letter from America"—a written justification for an American military response to terrorist attacks that was widely published and vigorously debated throughout Europe and the Islamic world. In 2003, drawing largely on ideas contained in this letter, she wrote *Just War against Terror: The Burden of American Power in a Violent World*, the book from which the following selection is drawn.

In *Just War against Terror*, Elshtain argues that the September 11 attacks were perpetuated by a radical element whose stated objective was to destroy civic peace in the United States. Since one of the central purposes of any government is to maintain civic peace—to "insure domestic Tranquility," as stated in the Preamble to the Constitution—the U.S. government has a moral duty to respond to the attacks in a way that preserves civic peace and punishes the attackers. Elshtain traces the history of the "just war" tradition in Christian theology and offers this concept as a framework for guiding American responses to terrorist attacks and activities.

In the selection that follows, Elshtain draws heavily upon the just war tradition to discuss the appropriate responses to terrorism. She not only attempts to define the conditions that make a war just and therefore morally permissible; she also examines the conditions under which, because only military force can bring about justice, military force is morally necessary. In making her argument, she positions just war thinking between pacifism, the theory that violence is unacceptable in any situation, and realism, the belief that decisions about the use of force on political grounds are divorced from moral values. Just war thinking, she argues, provides a moral context in which the use of force can be justified when it prevents greater violence.

Elshtain's rhetoric frequently uses appeals to religious and philosophical authority. Ultimately, however, her argument is her own. She uses deductive reasoning to apply the general principles of "just war" theory to the comtemporary world events that she discusses. 🖋

IN THE IMMEDIATE AFTERMATH of September 11, I said to a friend, "Now we are reminded of what governments are for." The primary responsibility of government is to provide basic security—ordinary civic peace. St. Augustine[1] calls this form of earthly peace *tranquillitas ordinis*. This is not the perfect peace promised to believers in the Kingdom of God, the one in which the lion lies down with the lamb. On this earth, if the lion lies down with the lamb, the lamb must be replaced frequently, as Martin Luther[2] opined with his characteristic mordant wit. Portions of the U.S. Constitution refer specifically to security and public safety. "To ensure domestic tranquillity" was central to what the new order being created after the American Revolution was all about. None of the goods that human beings cherish, including the free exercise of religion, can flourish without a measure of civic peace and security.

What good or goods do I have in mind? Mothers and fathers raising their children; men and women going to work; citizens of a great city making their way on streets and subways; ordinary people flying to California to visit the grandchildren or to transact business with colleagues—all of these actions are simple but profound goods made possible by civic peace. They include the faithful attending their churches, synagogues, and mosques without fear, and citizens—men and women, young and old, black, brown, and white—lining up to vote on Election Day.

This civic peace is not the kingdom promised by scripture that awaits the end time. The vision of beating swords into plowshares and spears into pruning hooks, of creating a world in which "nation shall not lift up sword against nation, neither shall they learn war anymore," is connected with certain conditions that will always elude us. That vision presupposes that all persons are under one law. But our condition of pluralism and religious diversity alone precludes the rule of one law. Moreover, our condition of fallibility and imperfection precludes a world in which discontents never erupt.

That said, the civic peace that violence disrupts does offer intimations of the peaceable kingdom. If we live from day to day in fear of deadly attack, the goods we cherish become elusive. Human beings are fragile creatures. We cannot reveal the fullness of our being, including our deep sociality, if airplanes are flying into buildings or snipers are shooting at us randomly or deadly spores are being sent through the mail. As we have learned so shockingly, we can neither take this civic peace for granted nor shake off our responsibility to respect and promote the norms and rules that sustain civic peace.

We know what happens to people who live in pervasive fear. The condition of 5 fearfulness leads to severe isolation as the desire to protect oneself and one's family becomes overwhelming. It encourages harsh measures because, as the political the-

---

The author's footnotes have been omitted.
1. **St. Augustine:** early Christian writer (354–430 CE) and bishop of the North African town of Hippo (in present-day Algeria). Augustine's writings are generally considered the starting point of the Christian just war tradition.
2. **Martin Luther:** Protestant reformer and theologian (1483–1546). **Lion lies down with the lamb:** a paraphrase of a prophecy about the harmony of the Messianic reign: "The wolf also shall dwell with the lamb, and the leopard shall lie down with the kid; and the calf and the young lion and the fatling together; and a little child shall lead them" (Isaiah 11:6).

orist Thomas Hobbes wrote in his 1651 work *Leviathan*, if we live in constant fear of violent death we are likely to seek guarantees to prevent such. Chapter 13 of Hobbes's great work is justly renowned for its vivid depiction of the horrors of a "state of nature," Hobbes's description of a world in which there is no ordered civic peace of any kind. In that horrible circumstance, all persons have the strength to kill each other, "either by secret machination, or by confederacy with others." The overriding emotion in this nightmarish world is overwhelming, paralyzing *fear*, for every man has become an enemy to every other and

> men live without other security, than what their own strength, and their own invention shall furnish them withal. In such condition, there is no place for Industry; because the fruit thereof is uncertain, and consequently no Culture of the Earth; no Navigation, nor use of the commodities that may be imported by Sea; no commodious Building; no Instruments of moving, and removing such things as require much force; no Knowledge of the face of the Earth; no account of Time; no Arts; no Letters; no Society; and which is worst of all, continuall feare, and danger of violent death; And the life of man, solitary, poore, nasty, brutish, and short.

This is Hobbes's famous, or infamous, war of all against all.

To Prevent the Worst from Happening

Many, myself included, believe that Hobbes overstated his case. But there is a powerful element of truth in his depiction of the state of nature. Without civic peace—a basic framework of settled law and simple, everyday order—human life descends to its most primitive level. By primitive I mean rudimentary, the bare minimum—we struggle just to stay alive. The face of such worlds is known to us. We saw it in Somalia under the warlords. We saw it under the Taliban in Afghanistan, where horrible disorder prevailed in the name of order. When government becomes destructive of the most basic end for which it is instituted, *tranquillitas ordinis*, it abandons its minimal raison d'être and can no longer be said to be legitimate. This assumption is essential to political theory. All political theories begin with a notion of how to establish and sustain order among human beings. Some go beyond this minimal requirement to ask how human beings can work to attain justice, or serve the common good, or preserve and protect political liberty. But none of these other ends can be served without basic order. George Weigel defines *tranquillitas ordinis* as "the peace of public order in dynamic political community," insisting that there is nothing static about "the concept of *tranquillitas ordinis* as it evolved after Augustine."[3]

3. **George Weigel:** American scholar and Catholic theologian (b. 1951). The quotation comes from his book *Tranquillitas Ordinis: The Present Failure and Future Promise of American Catholic Thought on War and Peace* (1987).

The primary reason for the state's existence is to create those minimal conditions that prevent the worst from happening—meaning, the worst that human beings can do to one another. How do we prevent people from devouring one another like fishes, as Augustine put it? This task is in the first instance one of interdiction: preempting horrible things before they occur. Not all misfortune, catastrophe, or crime can be prevented. What Augustine calls "carking anxieties" are part of the human condition. But we can try to eliminate as many of the conditions that give rise to catastrophe as possible. We can refuse to tolerate violent crime and arbitrary, chaotic disorder. It is horrific to stand in the ruins of a once flourishing city or a section of a city and to know that a government could not prevent what happened there—or was, even worse, the agent of destruction. Imagine such horror as a daily occurrence. If this were our circumstance, we would rightly seek the restoration of basic, minimally decent civic peace and order. And we would rightly ask: Could none of this have been prevented? Is the government somehow responsible for the chaos and destruction? If our answer to the former question is yes, we are likely to call for a new government.

It is difficult for us to imagine anarchy and dread unless we have been victims of random violence of some kind. Otherwise, it is easy for us to lose a sense of urgency. But government cannot and must not lose that sense of urgency. Any government that fails to do what is within its rightful power and purview in these matters is guilty of dereliction of duty. Order is "the condition for the possibility of virtue in public life," Augustine believed, and "such a peace was not to be deprecated: It allowed fallen human beings to 'live and work together and attain the objects that are necessary for their earthly existence.'"

This does *not* mean that our absolute, unquestioned obedience to duly constituted authority is required. Given the temptations attendant upon the exercise of power, authority may overstep its rightful bounds, itself become lawless, and thereby lose its legitimacy.

Augustine appreciated that power is a basic reality of political life. How is power used? To what end? Augustine knew that questions concerning the ethics of power and its use or abuse are most exigent when it comes time to debate war and peace. Augustine launched a great tradition of reasoning on the ethics of the use of force called the *just war tradition*. It is this tradition that provides a conceptual framework for interpreting and analyzing America's war against terrorism.

Making a Case for the Just Use of Force

It is unsurprising that the events of September 11 inspired Americans, from President Bush to the average man and woman on the street, to speak of justice as a way to characterize our response to the intentional slaughter of almost three thousand innocent men, women, and children. When citizens evoke justice, they tap into the complex Western tradition called "just war." The origins of this tradition are usually traced from

St. Augustine's fourth-century masterwork, *The City of God.* In that massive text, Augustine grapples with how best to think about force and coercion in light of the fact that the Christian Savior was heralded as the Prince of Peace by angels proclaiming "peace on earth and goodwill" to all peoples. Jesus resisted taking up arms in his own behalf or asking others to do so. How, then, can a Christian take up arms? That is the question that animated the just war tradition, which had several aims: to articulate occasions for the legitimate resort to force; to ensure that war derives from the use of right authority by those responsible for public order; to limit the means to be deployed even in a just cause; and to hold warfare, one outgrowth of political rule, up to ethical scrutiny.

Consider the terms: *justice* and *war.* The presupposition of just war thinking is that war can sometimes be an instrument of justice; that, indeed, war can help to put right a massive injustice or restore a right order where there is a disorder, including those disorders that sometimes call themselves "peace." This latter concern was part of St. Augustine's brilliant deconstruction of the official rhetoric of the Roman Empire. The Romans, Augustine argues, created a desert and called it peace. "Peace and war had a contest in cruelty, and peace won the prize," he notes, lacing his commentary with characteristically heavy irony. So peace should not be universally lauded even as war is universally condemned. Each must be evaluated critically. Many horrors and injustices can traffic under the cover of "peace." Indeed, there are worse things than war. The twentieth century showed us many of those worse things, including gulags and genocides. The world would have been much better off if the violence of particular regimes had been confronted on the battlefield earlier; fewer lives would have been lost over the long run.

Many Christians claim for early Christianity a uniform peace tradition and peace politics. They insist that for its first three centuries Christianity was pacifist and then fell away from a tradition of nonviolence, its only authentic tradition. They believe that the teachings of Jesus rule out any use of force, even force deployed at the behest and under the limits of legitimate authority and ethical restraint. But this characterization of early Christianity does not bear up under close scrutiny. For one thing, the strongest pacifist arguments in the early church are associated with theologians who fell outside the Christian mainstream, such as Origen and Tertullian.[4] More powerful and more mainstream to the Christian tradition are the arguments of St. Augustine, St. Ambrose, and, later, St. Thomas Aquinas,[5] all associated with the just war tradition. These latter regarded their arguments as a consistent evolution from early Christian teaching, not a deviation from it. They knew that in a fallen

---

4. **Origen and Tertullian:** Origen of Alexandria (circa 185–circa 254 CE) was one of the first early Christian theologians to apply the ideas of Plato *and* Aristotle to Christianity. Tertullian (circa 150–after 220 CE) was an early Christian writer who left mainstream Christianity and joined a radical millenarian sect known as the Montanists.

5. **St. Augustine, St. Ambrose, and . . . St. Thomas Aquinas:** Christian writers and scholars who were elevated to sainthood, giving their work a stamp of official approval denied to Origen and Tertullian. Ambrose (339–397 CE) was bishop of Milan; for Aquinas, see p. 260.

world, filled with imperfect human beings, we cannot achieve perfection in earthly dominion, in religious life, or in anything else, and that—even more important— we all have a responsibility to and for one another to serve and to love our neighbors. If our neighbor is being slaughtered, do we stand by and do nothing?

Martial metaphors abounded in the early Church. One could be a nonviolent soldier who suffered violence bravely for Christ rather than assault others: These Christians were the *milites Christi*.[6] And indeed, being a soldier for Christ, with all the explicit imagery of stalwart fortitude, fit with the lore of the early Church. Sacralizing[7] suicide, or homicide, or other evils would certainly be inconsistent with Christian doctrine, but soldiering is another matter.

Christian involvement with force goes beyond metaphor, however. When Jesus made the distinction between serving God and serving Caesar, Christians were obliged to take the measure of earthly rule and dominion rather than condemn it or its necessities outright. The most famous—and to Christian pacifists nigh-infamous— passage in this regard is in St. Paul's Letter to the Romans, in which he calls upon believers to obey the governing authorities: "Let every person be subject to the governing authorities. For there is no authority except from God, and those that exist have been instituted by God" (Romans 13:1).

Most important for our purposes, St. Paul claims that earthly dominion has been established to serve God and to benefit all human beings. It is the *rightful authority* of earthly kings and kingdoms to punish wrongdoers. Matters of temporal justice must not be left to self-help. The prospect of leaving questions of righting injustice and imposing penalties in the hands of each and every person conjures up a nightmare of private warfare, vengeance, and vendettas. And that is precisely what the historic record displays in abundance when no entity has been assigned the legitimate use of force to forestall the chaos of private warfare. Because the Church is to serve all, and because Christians believe evil is real, both justice and charity may compel us to serve our neighbor and the common good by using force to stop wrongdoing and to punish wrongdoers.

Of course, earthly rule can become a greater disorder. In such a dire circumstance, the Christian may choose to suffer the evil of others, for protecting one's own life is not the highest value. But those in positions of authority and those who can help to spare others from suffering have an obligation to do so. Earthly peace, as imperfect as it is, is better than the nightmare of Thomas Hobbes's war of all against all. The early Christian community drew the line of obedience to the state at emperor worship, for "Thou shalt have no other gods before me." Because they refused to pay homage to the emperor, many early Christians were martyred. But in these first generations of Christian life after the crucifixion of Jesus, there is lit-

---

6. **Milites Christi:** Latin for "soldiers of Christ."
7. **Sacralizing:** making sacred or giving a holy purpose to. To sacralize suicide or homicide would be to supply a religious framework in which such acts could be considered righteous.

tle evidence that the faithful were enjoined from serving in either the Roman army or police forces.

Augustine also tells us that Christians, if called upon, should take up the worldly political vocation of judge. This is a tragic vocation, since a judge can rarely be absolutely certain about the guilt or innocence of defendants. Truth is often hidden, or the full truth is. Inevitably, a judge winds up punishing some who are innocent and releasing some who are guilty. But Christians, if called, are obliged to do this work.

The dilemmas of judging speak to the nature of earthly rule more generally. It   20
rarely admits of absolutes, and there are usually no bright lines separating alternatives. Carl von Clausewitz, the great German theorist of war, spoke famously of "the fog of war." Augustine would find that phrase apt as a characterization of governing overall. Responsible public authorities are always compelled to act in a kind of fog. As with waging war, the most certain thing about governing is its uncertainty. It is the armchair critics commenting from the sidelines who think the choices are absolutely clear. To be sure, a cause may be clear—opposing the indiscriminate horrors of terrorism, for example—but the means used to promote it may not admit of the same crystalline clarity. The just, or justified, war tradition recognizes this difference by giving us an account of comparative, not absolute, justice.

Although the just war tradition originated in early Christian history and was refined over the centuries by Christian theologians, it would become secularized, though not stripped of ethical content, when it was absorbed into the thinking of international law and many of its ethical restraints were encoded in both the Geneva and Hague Conventions. By the beginning of the twenty-first century, the just war tradition had become part of the way in which much of the world spoke of war and peace questions, especially such matters as noncombatant immunity, proportionality, and the treatment of prisoners. International law states that intentional attacks on noncombatants violate not only recognized rules of warfare but universal humanitarian standards.

How to Decide Whether a War Is Just

What occasions or events justify the use of violence? Augustine begins by specifying what is not permitted: Wars of aggression and aggrandizement are unacceptable because they violate not only the civic peace but the framework of justice. Once again we see that, in deciding whether a war is just, we must get the critical distinctions right, beginning with a distinction between peace and justice. Some versions of "peace" violate norms of justice and do so egregiously. For the sake of keeping the peace, statesmen often acquiesce in terrible injustices.

Peace is a good, and so is justice, but neither is an absolute good. Neither automatically trumps the other, save for those pacifists who claim that "violence is never the solution," "fighting never settled anything," and "violence only begets more vio-

lence." Does it? Not always, not necessarily. One can point to one historical example after another of force being deployed in the name of justice and leading to not
only a less violent world but a more just one.

Consider the force used to combat Japanese militarism in World War II. Defeating Japan in the war, occupying Japan in its aftermath and imposing a constitutional order did not incite further Japanese aggression of the sort witnessed
in its full horror in what came to be known as "the rape of Manchuria." What
emerged instead was a democratic Japan. Are there living Japanese who believe it
is time to return to a violent world of militarist dominance or the world of violent self-help associated with the samurai tradition? When the great Japanese writer
Yukio Mishima called for a mass uprising and restoration of the old militarism in
1970, only a couple of pathetic disciples responded. Mishima's bizarre fantasy of
the return of a more violent world was regarded by the Japanese as daft and nigh-
unintelligible.

All violence, including the rule-governed violence of warfare, is tragic. But even   25
more tragic is permitting gross injustices and massive crimes to go unpunished. Just
war stipulates that the goods of settled social life cannot be achieved in the face of
pervasive and unrelenting violence. The horror of today's so-called failed states is
testament to that basic requirement of the "tranquillity of order." In Somalia, as warlords have jostled for power for more than a decade, people have been abused cynically and routinely. Anyone at anytime may be a target. The tragedy of American
involvement in Somalia is not that U.S. soldiers were sent there, but that the American commitment was not sufficient to restore minimal civic peace and to permit
the Somalian people to begin to rebuild their shattered social framework. Can anyone doubt that a sufficient use of force to stop predators from killing and starving
people outright would have been the more just course in Somalia and, in the long
run, the one most conducive to civic peace?

Organized force, fighting under rules of engagement in order to minimize civilian casualties, can help to create the safe surround that permits civic peace—
tranquillitas ordinis—to flourish. Force used as an instrument of justice is not random,
uncontrolled violence. It is not violence as an instrument of terror for terror's sake.
It is not private violence. It is the use of force at the behest of *right authority*.

Some American films have done a better job of grappling with the question of
force than many contemporary analysts and commentators. One of the greatest, *The
Man Who Shot Liberty Valence*, directed by the incomparable John Ford, offers up a
reflection on violence in the service of politics and settled law in the absence of
viable right authority. Liberty Valence is a vicious outlaw who preys on innocents,
high and low. Everyone is terrified of him, including the local "right authority," the
sheriff in the small town of Shinbone. Lawyer Ransom Stoddard (played by James
Stewart) journeys west, but before arriving in town to set up a law office Stoddard
is introduced to lawless Shinbone when his stagecoach is robbed by Valence and his
gang. Stoddard is beaten to within an inch of his life.

Enter John Wayne as the tragic character, Tom Doniphon. The only way to deal with Valence, says Doniphon, is to run him out of the territory or disarm him, Doniphon tells the resistant Stoddard. Disarming Valence means killing him, for he will never disarm voluntarily and Shinbone's sheriff (played by Andy Devine) is too terrified to arrest him. Right authority has abandoned its post when confronted with untrammeled viciousness.

Doniphon's argument might be called an ethic of controlled violence. Law exists. Who will enforce it? The film tells us that settled law and its routine enforcement are possible only when random violence and the fear it instills have been pushed back. Doniphon proves to be right, although at the cost of personal tragedy to himself. *The Man Who Shot Liberty Valence* is a parable on the use of force at the service of civic peace in the fog of an undeclared war in which the forces of violence are pitted against all those who want to settle, raise their families, and educate their children. The film does not glorify the antiviolent use of force but shows it instead to be a tragic necessity.

Parables like *The Man Who Shot Liberty Valence* illustrate the just war tradition's 30 nuanced recognition that justice and force are not mutually incompatible. Although Augustine never wrote a systematic treatise on war, he put into play the characteristic form of moral reasoning that enters into the just war tradition. This way of thinking carves out a stance that is neither pacifist nor what is usually called "realist" or *realpolitik*.

Absolute pacifists hold that the use of force is never justifiable under any circumstances. This form of pacifism is associated with the practices of early Christians who tied their pacifism to certain ascetical norms and withdrawal from the world. Leaders charged with right authority within organized political bodies cannot withdraw from the world, of course, and thus are never pacifists. Anyone who accepts political leadership understands that he or she may be compelled to sanction the resort to force in certain circumstances. The just war tradition limits those circumstances in part because it shares with pacifism a strong presumption against violence and force, all other things being equal. The just war tradition does not discourage acts of forgiveness and reconciliation in political life but does recognize their limits in a world of conflicting human wills, one in which the ruthless would prevail if they faced neither restraint nor the prospect of punishment.

The other alternative to the just war tradition, *realpolitik*, is a tradition even older than Christianity. *Realpolitik* serves politics from ethics. There is no room in *realpolitik* for traditional ethical concerns about how and when to resort to force; for Machiavelli, the sixteenth-century Florentine diplomat and theorist after whom this way of thinking is named, this tradition of ethical restraint was synonymous with Christianity. By contrast, Machiavelli claimed that nothing should constrain the prince, the ruler of a principality, who can deploy even brutal techniques (some of which Machiavelli vividly describes) in order to seize and keep the reins of power. Justice is not the main concern for *realpolitikers*. Power is.

The just war thinker cannot accept the *realpolitikers'* "anything goes" approach to political violence. In a landmark study that helped to revive the just war tradition in contemporary debate, Michael Walzer[8] argues: "Our arguments and judgments shape what I want to call *the moral reality of war*—that is, all those experiences of which moral language is descriptive or within which it is necessarily employed."

To sum up, at least provisionally: For pacifists, the reigning word is *peace*. For realists, the reigning word is *power*. For just war thinkers, the reigning word is *justice*. Peace may sometimes be served by the just use of force, even as power is most certainly involved. (Power is also involved in peace politics in ways that many pacifists ignore.)

If we try to avoid the complexity of what is at issue when we debate the use of force, simplistic solutions are likely to win the day, whether of a pacifist or militarist bent. The just war tradition requires that the philosopher, the moralist, the politician, and the ordinary citizen consider a number of complex criteria when thinking about war. These criteria shape a continuous scrutiny of war that judges whether the resort to force is justified, and whether, once force is resorted to, its use has been kept within necessary limits. Although never regarding war as desirable, or as any kind of social "good," the just war tradition acknowledges that it may be better than the alternative.

Force as the Servant of Justice

How is justice served by the use of force? For Augustine, a resort to force may be an obligation of loving one's neighbor, a central feature of Christian ethics. An offense that triggers a forceful response may be suffered by a third party. Suppose one country has certain knowledge that genocide will commence on a particular date and time against a group of people in another country. The group to be slaughtered has no means to defend itself. Within the just war tradition, the first country may be justified in coming to the aid of the targeted group and using force to interdict and punish their would-be attackers.

For Augustine, using force under such circumstances protects the innocent from certain harm. The historic just war tradition grappled with Augustine's statement that war may be resorted to in order to preserve or to achieve peace—and not just any peace, but a just peace that leaves the world better off than it was prior to the resort to force. For early Christians like Augustine, killing to defend oneself alone was not enjoined: It is better to suffer harm than to inflict it. But the obligation of charity obliges one to move in another direction: To save the lives of others, it may be necessary to imperil and even take the lives of their tormenters. The latter response is the appropriate way, suggests the just war tradition, to meet the challenge of systematic violence. As the theologian Joseph E. Capizzi writes: "According to Augustine, nonviolence is required at the individual level and just-war is mandated at the societal level."

---

8. **Michael Walzer:** American philosopher and social critic. The quotation comes from his book *Just and Unjust Wars* (1977).

In addition to preventing harm to the innocent, what are the other criteria that morally justify an armed response, the so-called *jus ad bellum*?[9] First, a war must be openly declared or otherwise authorized by a legitimate authority, so as to forestall random, private, and unlimited violence. Second, a war must be a response to a specific instance of unjust aggression perpetrated against one's own people or an innocent third party, or fought for a just cause. Third, a war must begin with the right intentions. Fourth, a war must be a last resort after other possibilities for redress and defense of the values at stake have been explored. Another *ad bellum* criterion usually noted is the prudential one: Do not enter a conflict without reflecting on whether the cause has a reasonable chance of success. One should not resort to violence lightly or experimentally.

The just war tradition has been called upon repeatedly in criticisms of holy wars, crusades, and wars of imperial aggrandizement. Just war thinking could not be put to that use if it were just another way we have of talking about a crusade. But some critics have failed to see the deep and critical distinction between just war thinking—derived as it is from a religious tradition—and any other religiously based call to arms. Consider the vast gulf that separates just war restraint from Osama bin Laden's call for an unlimited attack by all Muslims everywhere against all infidels everywhere. This is the mentality of holy war, which aspires to limitlessness: One can never kill enough infidels. For holy warriors or crusaders, the occasion for war is the simple intention to spread their gospel, whether political or religious, through violence, whenever or wherever possible, against the infidels. For just warriors, both aims and means are limited, even if one has been grievously harmed.

UNDERSTANDING THE TEXT

1. How does Elshtain synthesize information from multiple sources (p. 614)? How does she incorporate the writings of historical figures such as Augustine and Hobbes—as well as those of contemporary philosophers—into her argument?

2. What does Elshtain see as the primary responsibility of a government?

3. What is the difference between "earthly peace" and the peace that Christians believe will be achieved in the Kingdom of God? How is this difference important to Elshtain's argument?

4. What does Elshtain see as "the worst" that can happen in a country or a community? What role should government play in preventing this from happening?

---

9. ***Jus ad bellum:*** Latin for "just war."

5. What did Augustine mean when he wrote that the Romans "created a desert and called it peace"? In what respect does an unjustified military conquest bring "peace"? Does peace mean more than simply the absence of war?

6. What kinds of things does Elshtain see as "worse . . . than war"? Do you agree with her assessment?

7. How, according to Elshtain, can war be an "instrument of justice"? Is there a difference between saying that a war is "just" and saying that a war is necessary to bring about justice? Do you agree that sometimes war is an essential part of justice? Why or why not?

8. What, for Elshtain, is the difference between a "just war" and a "holy war"? Are holy wars necessarily just? In what ways might wars fought in the name of religious values be unjust?

MAKING CONNECTIONS

1. How does Elshtain's understanding of the "just war" compare with Aquinas's (p. 260)? By what criteria do these thinkers determine whether a war is just? How do they perceive justice?

2. Why does Elshtain quote chapter 13 of Hobbes's *Leviathan* (p. 119)? What belief do she and Hobbes share about government's importance?

3. Compare Elshtain's view of pacifism to Orwell's view in "Pacifism and the War" (p. 282). Would Elshtain make the argument that, to paraphrase Orwell, "pacifism is objectively pro-terrorist"? Why or why not?

4. Compare Elshtain's position on war to the realpolitik advocated by Machiavelli (p. 184). In what areas would she and Machiavelli agree? Where would they disagree?

5. How does the peace of conquest that Elshtain refers to resemble the "negative peace" that Martin Luther King Jr. mentions in the "Letter from Birmingham City Jail" (p. 202)? Beyond the absence of conflict, what elements would have to appear in a meaningful definition of "peace"?

WRITING ABOUT THE TEXT

1. Apply the just war theory to recent American military actions in Afghanistan or Iraq. Argue for or against these actions by invoking the tradition that Elshtain describes.

2. Define "justice" and "peace." Assuming that both concepts are desirable, describe a society in which there is justice without peace or peace without justice. Ultimately, do you see justice or peace as more important to human happiness?

3. Watch *The Man Who Shot Liberty Valence* and write an essay analyzing its moral or political points. Compare your reading of the movie to Elshtain's.

5

WEALTH, POVERTY, AND SOCIAL CLASS

WHAT ARE THE ETHICAL IMPLICATIONS OF SOCIOECONOMIC INEQUALITY?

Ye cannot serve God and mammon.
—*Matthew 6:24, Luke 16:13*

THE FREQUENT CONDEMNATIONS of wealth in the New Testament (one of which is quoted above) are reinforced in nearly all of the world's great religious texts. The major religious figures—Confucius, the Buddha, Jesus, and Mohammed, to name only a few—have consistently taught their followers that focusing on material things is spiritually destructive and that allowing fellow human beings to live in poverty is evil. For thousands of years, poverty has been officially condemned by the belief systems that most people in the world subscribe to—yet it persists, and, in many areas of the world, seems worse than ever.

It is difficult to see why the problem of poverty has never been solved, even by societies that clearly have the resources to do so. Understanding this phenomenon means considering how the social mechanisms for distributing wealth are built into a society at a very basic level. The uneven distribution of wealth and the social stratification that accompanies it seem "normal" to most people because they flow directly from cultural assumptions that can be very difficult to question. The Hindu notion of karma, for example, functions as part of an elaborate caste system in which social stratification plays a crucial role in religious duty. Until very recent times, the Christian nations of Europe have viewed members of the aristocratic classes as naturally superior human beings whose right to control vast resources was ordained by God. And in China and other Asian nations, the cardinal Confucian virtue of *li*, which roughly translates as "respect," is manifest when one consistently acts in a way that is appropriate to one's economic and social station in life. The same religions and philosophies that discourage materialism and encourage charity, therefore, can also contribute to social forces that support the unequal distribution of wealth.

Moreover, religious and philosophical teachings tend to focus much more on poverty as it affects individuals than on the large-scale implications of economic policy. Political economics, which emerged in Western Europe in the eighteenth century, was one of the first great intellectual movements in the world to attempt to deal with issues of wealth and poverty on a large scale. Using all of the tools of modern philosophy, science, and mathematics, the great political economists—figures such as John Locke, Adam Smith, Thomas Malthus, Karl Marx, Jeremy Bentham, and John Stuart Mill—studied the same set of problems and came to completely different, mutually exclusive conclusions about the causes of, characteristics of, and cures for poverty. In the end, a macro-level, scientific approach has had as little success in eliminating poverty as a micro-level, religious approach has had.

The readings in this chapter, following the historical arc of the approach to wealth and poverty, move from mainly religious texts to works of specialized political economics. The readings begin with an essay by Mo Tzu, an ancient Chinese sage whose influence once rivaled that of Confucius. Though Mo Tzu's essay is titled "Against Music," its real concern is the diversion of resources to support luxurious lifestyles for the wealthy when the majority of people do not have enough food to eat. Mo Tzu is followed by a selection from the New Testament's Gospel of Luke, in which Jesus tells two parables that deal directly with wealth and poverty. These parables share many of Mo Tzu's concerns and point to a religious perspective on poverty that crosses cultural barriers.

An engraving by the eighteenth-century painter William Hogarth gives a more modern view of poverty. This engraving, entitled *Gin Lane*, shows a dilapidated London neighborhood whose inhabitants have allowed gin and despair to govern every aspect of their lives. The chapter's other image, Dorothea Lange's "Migrant Mother," tells a very different story of poverty. This iconic photograph, taken during the Great Depression, depicts a migrant farm worker in Nipomo, California, surrounded by three of her seven children.

The first major economist surveyed in this chapter is Thomas Malthus, who introduced the concept of "overpopulation." Malthus theorized that in any society, population will increase faster than the available food supply, unless it is kept in check by natural catastrophes or by civic regulations. Thus, unchecked population growth will always condemn large segments of a population to live at or below the level of bare subsistence. Malthus's ideas form the basis of Garrett Hardin's twentieth-century critique of food assistance to underdeveloped nations. Such assistance, he argues, is ultimately immoral because it allows a population to grow at an artificially high rate, thus increasing human misery in a severely overpopulated region and guaranteeing the population's collapse. For Hardin, as for Malthus, the most moral institutional response to poverty is to allow nature to take its course when populations exceed the resources of the lands that they inhabit.

A direct contrast to Malthus is given in a speech by Mohandas K. ("Mahatma") Gandhi to a group of British-trained economists in India in 1916. Rather than using his invitation to speak on his plans for "economic progress," as expected, Gandhi questions the very concept of economic progress. He argues that economic progress is inimical to "real" progress, which he defines as moral or spiritual progress. Nearly two thousand years after Jesus first uttered them, Gandhi once again invokes the words quoted at the beginning of this chapter: "Ye cannot serve God and mammon."

Three other selections from the twentieth century portray responses to poverty in developing nations. The first, Octavio Paz's "The Day of the Dead," argues that the Mexican custom of the fiesta—with all of the drunkenness, violence, and transgressive excess associated with it—serves as a crucial counterpoint to the solitary, poor lives that most Mexicans live. The second, Lucy Lameck's "Africans Are Not Poor," is from a speech Lameck gave to the parliament of the newly formed nation of Tanzania. She argues that it is wrong to speak of Africans as "poor" or as victims of European colonialism. Such language, Lameck insists, perpetuates a negative stereotype and conditions Africans to see themselves as helpless. The final selection of the chapter, Muhammad Yunus's "The Stool Makers of Jobra Village," tells the story of how a young economics professor found a remarkably effective way to combat poverty in one of the poorest countries in the world.

Mo Tzu
Against Music
(circa 425 BCE)

MO TZU HOLDS A UNIQUE POSITION in the canon of classical Chinese philosophers known as the hundred schools, which flourished from the sixth to the
third century BCE. He opposed and ridiculed both the Confucians, who he believed
were overly concerned with ritual, and the Legalists, whom he saw as totalitarian and immoral. Though he had many followers during his lifetime and in
the three centuries after his death, his influence steadily declined as Confucianism, rather than Moism, became the principal ethical philosophy of the Chinese
state.

Mo Tzu is best known for his philosophy of "universal love," which advocated a
general, impartial concern for all of humanity, with no person held in higher regard
than any other. This idea rankled the Confucians of his day because it implied that
the most honored relationships in Chinese culture—those between sons and their
fathers and between younger and older brothers—were no more important than relationships between strangers. Mo Tzu taught that the chief value of love lay in its uni-
versality and that family ties, which he saw as mere accidents of birth, did not make
people more worthy of this love.

Only slightly less disconcerting to Confucians were Mo Tzu's writings against
music. Confucian orthodoxy saw ritual music as a force for good; they believed it
helped to organize thoughts and regulate behavior. Mo Tzu, however, disapproved
of the fact that, in ancient China, music and its benefits were limited to an extremely
small number of people, namely the very wealthy. Musical instruments were expensive to manufacture, trained musicians were rare, and musical celebrations were usually accompanied by elaborate dancing and expensive feasts, all of which made
"music" virtually synonymous with "luxury."

At the center of "Against Music," part 1 of which follows, are two assertions: that
artistic pursuits such as music are not useful to society, and that people should not
be forced to pay—with their tax dollars—for artistic programs that do not benefit
them directly. Today, the first assertion often comes up in discussions about core
curricula (for example, should art and music classes be required for elementary school
students?). The second surfaces just as frequently in discussions about government
funding for the arts through programs such as the National Endowment for the Arts
and the National Endowment for the Humanities.

Mo Tzu employs several rhetorical strategies in this selection. He argues through
examples, close analysis, and appeals to authority. His most direct argument, how-

ever, is a simple deductive syllogism given in the first paragraph: benevolent men should promote what is beneficial; music is not beneficial; therefore, benevolent men should not promote music.

It is the business of the benevolent man to seek to promote what is beneficial to the world, to eliminate what is harmful, and to provide a model for the world. What benefits men he will carry out; what does not benefit men he will leave alone. Moreover, when the benevolent man plans for the benefit of the world, he does not consider merely what will please the eye, delight the ear, gratify the mouth, and give ease to the body. If in order to gratify the senses he has to deprive the people of the wealth needed for their food and clothing, then the benevolent man will not do so. Therefore Mo Tzu condemns music,[1] not because the sound of the great bells and rolling drums, the zithers and pipes, is not delightful; not because the sight of the carvings and ornaments is not beautiful, not because the taste of the fried and broiled meats is not delicious; and not because lofty towers, broad pavilions, and secluded halls are not comfortable to live in. But though the body finds comfort, the mouth gratification, the eye pleasure, and the ear delight, yet if we examine the matter, we will find that such things are not in accordance with the ways of the sage kings, and if we consider the welfare of the world we will find that they bring no benefit to the common people. Therefore Mo Tzu said: Making music is wrong!

Now if the rulers and ministers want musical instruments to use in their government activities, they cannot extract them from the sea water, like salt, or dig them out of the ground, like ore. Inevitably, therefore, they must lay heavy taxes upon the common people before they can enjoy the sound of great bells, rolling drums, zithers, and pipes. In ancient times the sage kings likewise laid heavy taxes on the people, but this was for the purpose of making boats and carts, and when they were completed and people asked, "What are these for?" the sage kings replied, "The boats are for use on water, and the carts for use on land, so that gentlemen may rest their feet and laborers spare their shoulders." So the common people paid their taxes and levies and did not dare to grumble. Why? Because they knew that the taxes would be used for the benefit of the people. Now if musical instruments were also used for the benefit of the people, I would not venture to condemn them. Indeed, if they were as useful as the boats and carts of the sage kings, I would certainly not venture to condemn them.

The translator's footnotes have been omitted. Bracketed insertions are the translator's.

1. **Music:** Mo Tzu means not only singing and playing instruments but also the dancing, banquets, and other expensive entertainments that went along with the enjoyment of music by wealthy people in ancient China.

There are three things the people worry about: that when they are hungry they will have no food, when they are cold they will have no clothing, and when they are weary they will have no rest. These are the three great worries of the people. Now let us try sounding the great bells, striking the rolling drums, strumming the zithers, blowing the pipes, and waving the shields and axes in the war dance. Does this do anything to provide food and clothing for the people? I hardly think so. But let us leave that point for the moment.

Now there are great states that attack small ones, and great families that molest small ones. The strong oppress the weak, the many tyrannize the few, the cunning deceive the stupid, the eminent lord it over the humble, and bandits and thieves rise up on all sides and cannot be suppressed. Now let us try sounding the great bells, striking the rolling drums, strumming the zithers, blowing the pipes, and waving the shields and axes in the war dance. Does this do anything to rescue the world from chaos and restore it to order? I hardly think so. Therefore Mo Tzu said: If you try to promote what is beneficial to the world and eliminate what is harmful by laying heavy taxes on the people for the purpose of making bells, drums, zithers, and pipes, you will get nowhere. So Mo Tzu said: Making music is wrong!

Now the rulers and ministers, seated in their lofty towers and broad pavilions, 5 look about them, and there are the bells, hanging like huge cauldrons. But unless the bells are struck, how can the rulers get any delight out of them? Therefore it is obvious that the rulers must have someone to strike the bells. But they cannot employ old men or young boys, since their eyes and ears are not keen enough and their arms are not strong, and they cannot make the sounds harmonious or see to strike the bells front and back. Therefore the rulers must have young people in their prime, whose eyes and ears are keen and whose arms are so strong that they can make the sounds harmonious and see to strike the bells front and back. If they employ young men, then they will be taking them away from their plowing and planting, and if they employ young women, they will be taking them away from their weaving and spinning. Yet the rulers and ministers will have their music, though their music-making interferes to such an extent with the people's efforts to produce food and clothing! Therefore Mo Tzu said: Making music is wrong!

Now let us suppose that the great bells, rolling drums, zithers, and pipes have all been provided. Still if the rulers and ministers sit quietly all alone and listen to the performance, how can they get any delight out of it? Therefore it is obvious that they must listen in the company of others, either humble men or gentlemen. If they listen in the company of gentlemen, then they will be keeping the gentlemen from attending to affairs of state, while if they listen in the company of humble men, they will be keeping the humble men from pursuing their tasks. Yet the rulers and ministers will have their music, though their music-making interferes to such an extent with the people's efforts to produce food and clothing! Therefore Mo Tzu said: Making music is wrong!

In former times Duke K'ang of Ch'i [404–379 BCE] loved the music of the Wan dance. The Wan dancers cannot wear robes of cheap cloth or eat coarse food, for it is said that unless they have the finest food and drink, their faces and complexions will not be fit to look at, and unless they have beautiful clothing, their figures and movements will not be worth watching. Therefore the Wan dancers ate only millet and meat,[2] and wore only robes of patterned and embroidered silk. They did nothing to help produce food or clothing, but lived entirely off the efforts of others. Yet the rulers and ministers will have their music, though their music-making interferes to such an extent with the people's efforts to produce food and clothing! Therefore Mo Tzu said: Making music is wrong!

Now man is basically different from the beasts, birds, and insects. The beasts, birds, and insects have feathers and fur for their robes and coats, hoofs and claws for their leggings and shoes, and grass and water for their food and drink. Therefore the male need not plow or plant, the female need not weave or spin, and still they have plenty of food and clothing. But man is different from such creatures. If a man exerts his strength, he may live, but if he does not, he cannot live. If the gentlemen do not diligently attend to affairs of state, the government will fall into disorder, and if humble men do not diligently pursue their tasks, there will not be enough wealth and goods.

If the gentlemen of the world do not believe what I say, then let us try enumerating the various duties of the people of the world and see how music interferes with them. The rulers and ministers must appear at court early and retire late, hearing lawsuits and attending to affairs of government—this is their duty. The gentlemen must exhaust the strength of their limbs and employ to the fullest the wisdom of their minds, directing bureaus within the government and abroad, collecting taxes on the barriers and markets and on the resources of the hills, forests, lakes, and fish weirs,[3] so that the granaries and treasuries will be full—this is their duty. The farmers must leave home early and return late, sowing seed, planting trees, and gathering large crops of vegetables and grain—this is their duty. Women must rise early and go to bed late, spinning, weaving, producing large quantities of hemp, silk, and other fibers, and preparing cloth—this is their duty. Now if those who occupy the position of rulers and ministers are fond of music and spend their time listening to it, then they will not be able to appear

2. **Millet and meat:** Meals composed solely of millet, a cereal grain, and meat would have been considered extremely luxurious by most Chinese in Mo Tzu's time.

3. **Fish weirs:** fenced-in areas in bodies of water, used to trap large quantities of migrating fish.

at court early and retire late, or hear lawsuits and attend to affairs of government, and as a result the state will fall into disorder and its altars of the soil and grain will be in danger. If those who occupy the position of gentlemen are fond of music and spend their time listening to it, then they will be unable to exhaust the strength of their limbs and employ to the fullest the wisdom of their minds in directing bureaus within the government and abroad, collecting taxes on the barriers and markets and on the resources of the hills, forests, lakes, and fish weirs, in order to fill the granaries and treasuries, and as a result the granaries and treasuries will not be filled. If those who occupy the position of farmers are fond of music and spend their time listening to it, then they will be unable to leave home early and return late, sowing seed, planting trees, and gathering large crops of vegetables and grain, and as a result there will be a lack of vegetables and grain. If women are fond of music and spend their time listening to it, then they will be unable to rise early and go to bed late, spinning, weaving, producing large quantities of hemp, silk, and other fibers, and preparing cloth, and as a result there will not be enough cloth. If you ask what it is that has caused the ruler to neglect the affairs of government and the humble man to neglect his tasks, the answer is music. Therefore Mo Tzu said: Making music is wrong!

How do we know that this is so? The proof is found among the books of the former kings, in T'ang's "Code of Punishment," where it says: "Constant dancing in the palace—this is the way of shamans! As a punishment, gentlemen shall be fined two measures of silk, but for common men the line shall be two hundred pieces of yellow silk." It also says: "Alas, all this dancing! The sound of the pipes is loud and clear. The Lord on High does not aid him, and the nine districts[4] are lost to him. The Lord on High does not approve him, but sends down a hundred misfortunes. His house will be destroyed." If we examine the reason why he lost the nine districts, we will find that it was because he idly spent his time arranging elaborate musical performances.

The "Wu kuan"[5] says: "Ch'i gave himself up to pleasure and music, eating and drinking in the fields. *Ch'iang-ch'iang*, the flutes and chimes sounded in unison! He drowned himself in wine and behaved indecently by eating in the fields. Splendid was the Wan dance, but Heaven clearly heard the sound and Heaven did not approve." So it was not approved by Heaven and the spirits above, and brought no benefit to the people below.

Therefore Mo Tzu said: If the rulers, ministers, and gentlemen of the world truly desire to promote what is beneficial to the world and eliminate what is harmful, they must prohibit and put a stop to this thing called music!

---

4. **Nine districts:** according to legend, the nine provinces of China in the distant past, which Mo Tzu would have considered "ancient."

5. **"Wu kuan":** an ancient Chinese text known to Mo Tzu but now lost.

UNDERSTANDING THE TEXT

1. What does Mo Tzu mean by "music"? What aspects of contemporary Western culture might fit into Mo Tzu's overall category of "music"?

2. Why does Mo Tzu begin the essay by acknowledging the delight and pleasure that music brings? What effect does this acknowledgment have on his ethos (pp. 608–10)?

3. According to Mo Tzu, what are the people's three primary concerns? How does he believe music will prevent people from performing their duties and therefore hurt the well-being of the entire community? Are his arguments reasonable? How so?

4. How might music affect government? What might then happen to the state?

5. What difference between humans and animals does Mo Tzu use to support his argument?

6. What kinds of activities does Mo Tzu claim are useful to society? Do you agree with his assessment? Why or why not?

MAKING CONNECTIONS

1. One of Mo Tzu's principal philosophical opponents, Hsün Tzu, wrote a direct rebuttal to "Against Music" that supported the value of music. Compare the way that Mo Tzu's assumptions about human nature differ from those of Hsün Tzu in "Man's Nature Is Evil" (p. 100).

2. In "Against Music," Mo Tzu asserts that rulers must make sure that all of their people are fed. How does his notion of that responsibility compare with the qualities of a good ruler in al-Farabi's "Perfect Associations and Perfect Rulers" (p. 170)?

3. How might Mo Tzu view the sometimes elaborate works of art produced in Egyptian funeral customs (The Papyrus of Ani, p. 154) or displayed in African communal shrines (Igbo Mother and Child, p. 129)? How do works of art (and literature) compare with music in terms of their social value?

4. How might advocates of a broad liberal education, such as Seneca (p. 16) and John Henry Newman (p. 53), defend music against Mo Tzu's charges?

WRITING ABOUT THE TEXT

1. Defend music against Mo Tzu's attacks. Construct an argument about the value of music to either the individual or society.

2. Choose a symbol of unfettered luxury from your own culture and write an essay attacking it in the style of Mo Tzu.

3. Drawing on Mo Tzu's arguments, refute or defend the proposition that colleges and universities should require students to study certain kinds of music (such as classical music) that have been judged superior to other kinds.

4. Compare Mo Tzu's utilitarian view in "Against Music" with John Henry Newman's argument in "Knowledge Its Own End" (p. 53) that the pursuit of knowledge does not have to be justified by any kind of social utility.

New Testament
Luke, Chapter 16
(circa 90 CE)

AFTER THE CITY OF JERUSALEM was destroyed by the Babylonians in 586 BCE, the region known as Judea was ruled, in succession, by the Babylonian, Persian, Greek, and Roman empires. By the year 30 CE, nearly a thousand years after the golden age of King David (the first ruler of a united Israel), Judea had become a province of Rome. Though the Roman authorities allowed local populations a high degree of religious autonomy, the Jews chafed under foreign rule. Spurred on by prophecies of a "Messiah" who would restore Israel's independence and former glory, a number of revolutionary sects arose in Judea during the first century of Roman rule, culminating in a massive, though ultimately unsuccessful, Jewish revolt in 66 CE. Into this environment, Jesus of Nazareth was born.

Very little about Jesus is known beyond the accounts in the New Testament. His followers clearly believed that he was the Messiah of Hebrew prophecy (the name "Christ" is simply a Greek rendering of the Hebrew word "Messiah"). Just as clearly, Jesus often clashed with the Jewish clergy of his day. The scriptural record contains numerous examples of Jesus's criticizing the priestly class in Jerusalem for focusing on the outward trappings of religious observance and ignoring the true nature of religion, which, for Jesus, was centered around personal devotion and charitable action.

Of the four Gospels, or narratives chronicling the life of Jesus Christ, the Gospel of Luke is the most detailed, and its accounts satisfy the requirements of objective history better than any other scriptural source. The Gospel of Luke also contains the fullest account anywhere of Jesus's parables. A parable is a brief, highly metaphorical narrative used to teach a principle or illustrate a point. In all, the New Testament contains accounts of some forty parables Jesus used to convey important theological points. Fully one-third of Jesus's words in the Synoptic (or biographical) Gospels (Matthew, Mark, and Luke; the Gospel of John, significantly different in form and content, was probably the last to be written) occur in the form of parables. Some of these parables—such as those of the Good Samaritan (Luke 10:30–37), the Lost Sheep (Matt. 18:12–14, Luke 15:3–7), and the Prodigal Son (Luke 15:11–32)—are now among the central metaphors of Western culture.

The following selections from chapter 16 of the Book of Luke present two parables relating to wealth and poverty. In the first, the Parable of the Unjust Steward, Jesus uses the example of a dishonest steward (or estate manager) to make a point about the moral uses of wealth. In the second, the Parable of the Rich Man and Lazarus, Jesus tells of a reversal of fortunes that typifies many of his parables and other teachings, which emphasize that material prosperity does not indicate God's favor; that people should seek heavenly, rather than earthly, rewards; and that wealth often presents a stumbling block on the way to salvation.

As a rhetorical device, the parable is related to arguments that use analogy and examples to support and develop a claim. While most such arguments draw on existing comparisons, however, the parable constructs its own example or analogy in the form of a narrative. The parables of Jesus are among the most famous examples of this rhetorical device in any culture.

1. AND HE SAID ALSO unto his disciples, There was a certain rich man, which had a steward; and the same was accused unto him that he had wasted his goods.

2. And he called him, and said unto him, How is it that I hear this of thee? give an account of thy stewardship; for thou mayest be no longer steward.[1]

3. Then the steward said within himself, What shall I do? for my lord taketh away from me the stewardship: I cannot dig; to beg I am ashamed.[2]

4. I am resolved what to do, that, when I am put out of the stewardship, they may receive me into their houses.

5. So he called every one of his lord's debtors unto him, and said unto the first, How much owest thou unto my lord?

6. And he said, An hundred measures of oil. And he said unto him, Take thy bill, and sit down quickly, and write fifty.

7. Then said he to another, And how much owest thou? And he said, An hundred measures of wheat. And he said unto him, Take thy bill, and write fourscore.

8. And the lord commended the unjust steward, because he had done wisely: for the children of this world are in their generation wiser than the children of light.[3]

9. And I say unto you, Make to yourselves friends of the mammon[4] of unrighteousness; that, when ye fail, they may receive you into everlasting habitations.

10. He that is faithful in that which is least is faithful also in much: and he that is unjust in the least is unjust also in much.

1. **Thou mayest be no longer steward:** The master is telling the steward (or estate manager) that he is going to be fired and must present an account of his management, thus giving him time to improve his situation.

2. **I cannot dig; to beg I am ashamed:** The steward is physically unfit for manual labor and reluctant to become a beggar.

3. **Children of light:** The meaning of this passage is that dishonest people (such as the steward) are often more shrewd and practical than honest, righteous people. Since the steward has not been honest, the master says, it is good that he was at least shrewd in his dishonesty.

4. **Mammon:** a Hebrew word meaning wealth or material goods. In this chapter, Jesus personifies "mammon" and presents it as a false god that competes with the true God for allegiance; hence, "Ye cannot serve God and mammon."

11. If therefore ye have not been faithful in the unrighteous mammon, who will commit to your trust the true riches?

12. And if ye have not been faithful in that which is another man's, who shall give you that which is your own? . . .

19. There was a certain rich man, which was clothed in purple and fine linen, and fared sumptuously every day:

20. And there was a certain beggar named Lazarus, which was laid at his gate, full of sores,

21. And desiring to be fed with the crumbs which fell from the rich man's table: moreover the dogs came and licked his sores.

22. And it came to pass, that the beggar died, and was carried by the angels into Abraham's bosom:[5] the rich man also died, and was buried;

23. And in hell he lift up his eyes, being in torments, and seeth Abraham afar off, and Lazarus in his bosom.

24. And he cried and said, Father Abraham, have mercy on me, and send Lazarus, that he may dip the tip of his finger in water, and cool my tongue; for I am tormented in this flame.

25. But Abraham said, Son, remember that thou in thy lifetime receivedst thy good things, and likewise Lazarus evil things: but now he is comforted, and thou art tormented.

26. And beside all this, between us and you there is a great gulf fixed: so that they which would pass from hence to you cannot; neither can they pass to us, that would come from thence.

27. Then he said, I pray thee therefore, father, that thou wouldest send him to my father's house:

28. For I have five brethren; that he may testify unto them, lest they also come into this place of torment.

29. Abraham saith unto him, They have Moses and the prophets; let them hear them.

30. And he said, Nay, father Abraham: but if one went unto them from the dead, they will repent.

31. And he said unto him, If they hear not Moses and the prophets, neither will they be persuaded, though one rose from the dead.

---

5. **Abraham's bosom:** heaven, paradise. Abraham was the first and greatest of the Hebrew patriarchs, and to be in his bosom meant to be close to him after death.

UNDERSTANDING THE TEXT

1. Why does Jesus illustrate his point with a servant's dishonest actions? Is the steward acting righteously or simply acting wisely? How do the two kinds of actions differ?

2. Why does the faithless servant partially forgive the debts of his master's debtors? Why does the master commend him for doing so? Are the servant's reasons for forgiving the debts the same ones for which Jesus praises him?

3. What ultimate point about material wealth is made in the Parable of the Unjust Steward? What uses of wealth does the parable condemn? What uses of wealth does it encourage? What "true riches" does Jesus refer to in verse 11?

4. In the Parable of the Rich Man and Lazarus, why does Lazarus end up in heaven? How does earthly lifestyle relate to eternal destination? According to these two parables, which is the more spiritually admirable and rewarding earthly condition: wealth or poverty?

5. What are the spiritual dangers of being wealthy, judging from Jesus's parables? Do you agree with the message that poverty is spiritually superior? Is it possible to be wealthy and be a good Christian (or even a good person)? How would one accomplish this?

6. How effectively do these parables argue by analogy (p. 602)? Where do Jesus's analogies illustrate his arguments effectively, and where do they become false analogies, employing insufficiently similar comparisons?

MAKING CONNECTIONS

1. Compare Jesus's portrayal of wealth with Gandhi's in "Economic and Moral Progress" (p. 332). What do Jesus and Gandhi say about the relationship between spiritual and moral "prosperity"?

2. How might some of the figures in Hogarth's *Gin Lane* (p. 320) be read as "parables" similar to those of Jesus in the New Testament? Could you imagine key stories in these characters' lives that would illustrate a moral principle?

3. Compare Jesus and Plato as storytellers. Does Plato use similar techniques to Jesus in "The Speech of Aristophanes" (p. 89)? What are the main differences between these two kinds of stories?

4. How might the Christian understanding of the evils of excess be reflected in the fiestas described by Octavio Paz in "The Day of the Dead" (p. 345), almost all of which celebrate specifically Christian themes or events?

WRITING ABOUT THE TEXT

1. Use a contemporary cultural setting to write a parable with the same message as the Parable of the Unjust Steward. Then write a similar parable that makes an opposite point, such as that money is more important than relationships.

2. The Parable of the Unjust Steward includes a very rare instance of Jesus's praising a person for dishonest actions. Discuss the possible reasons for this apparent incongruity.

3. Compare the teachings of the New Testament in Luke 16 and the *Tao te Ching* (p. 158) as they relate to material wealth.

William Hogarth
Gin Lane
(1751)

THOUGH A VISUAL ARTIST, the painter and engraver William Hogarth (1697–1764) was as important to the development of satire in England as were his literary contemporaries Jonathan Swift, Alexander Pope, and Henry Fielding. Many of Hogarth's most famous paintings occur in series with narrative contents, such as *The Harlot's Progress* (1731), *The Rake's Progress* (1735), and *Marriage à la Mode* (1743–45). In each series, between six and eight paintings, taken together, tell cohesive stories that issue strong warnings. Many of Hogarth's early series, or "progresses," were originally oil paintings, but he later re-created them as black-and-white engravings that could be mass produced, sold much more cheaply, and distributed much more widely than the paintings. Their wide dissemination dramatically increased Hogarth's audience and influence.

Hogarth created *Gin Lane* to support the Gin Act, which limited the sale of cheap gin. By the middle of the seventeenth century, gin had become one of the most destructive forces in urban England. Produced cheaply and sold for pennies, gin contributed to rampant alcoholism in England's cities, and was both a symptom and a cause of the extreme poverty and high rates of infant mortality that became the staples of urban life during Hogarth's lifetime. Previous attempts to limit the sale of gin had proved unsuccessful, and the Gin Act, which passed in the summer of 1751, sought to control consumption by doubling the tax on gin and forbidding distillers to sell it directly to the public.

In *Gin Lane*, Hogarth dramatizes the horrific poverty and deprivation that occur in places where cheap gin abounds. The scene emphasizes the effect of gin on children. In the center of the action, a baby falls while its drunken mother reaches for a pinch of snuff. Elsewhere, a child cries as its mother is placed into a coffin, a mother pours gin down the throat of her infant, and a drunken man marches down the street waving a baby impaled on a stick.

But Hogarth is doing more than commenting on the dangers of gin. He is also depicting the effects of poverty. Though Hogarth supported the Gin Act, he also understood that the root of the problem was poverty and that gin had become popular among the poor because it offered a false solution to—and, in the process, exacerbated—this very real problem. *Gin Lane*, which Hogarth originally sold for only a shilling per print, gave the middle and upper classes a rare glimpse into the reality of poverty. Generations of viewers have appreciated *Gin Lane* for reasons that transcend the original sociopolitical context that produced it. ❧

WILLIAM HOGARTH

Gin Lane, 1751 (engraving).

Bibliothèque Nationale, Paris, France / Lauros–Giraudon / Bridgeman Art Library

UNDERSTANDING THE TEXT

1. What is happening to the two figures in the foreground of William Hogarth's *Gin Lane*? What is the woman doing while her child falls to its death? What accounts for the man who appears to have starved to death?

2. How does the physical structure of the city reflect the moral structure of its inhabitants? Why is it significant that the only building *not* in disrepair is the pawnbroker's shop?

3. How are children generally treated in *Gin Lane*? What might Hogarth be suggesting by these portrayals?

4. Hogarth is famous for including in most of his engravings dogs and cats whose actions comment on the behavior of human beings. Where do you see examples of this device in *Gin Lane*?

5. How many images of death are in the picture? How many people are or appear to be dead? How can each of these deaths be traced directly to the consumption of gin?

MAKING CONNECTIONS

1. How might Octavio Paz (p. 345) interpret *Gin Lane*'s scenes of drunkenness and excess? How do the actions depicted in this engraving compare with the actions that he describes as part of fiestas?

2. Like Picasso's *Guernica* (p. 271), *Gin Lane* portrays intense violence and suffering. What specific similarities can you find between the two works? What accounts for these similarities?

3. How do *Gin Lane* and *Migrant Mother* (p. 341) differ in their portrayals of poverty? Pay special attention to the maternal depictions in both images.

4. How would you rate the rhetorical effectiveness of *Gin Lane*? Is it art with a message, like Picasso's *Guernica* (p. 271), or overt political propaganda, like the ad for China's One-Child Policy (p. 516)? How does art differ from propaganda?

WRITING ABOUT THE TEXT

1. In a few paragraphs, state, in your own words, the argument that Hogarth makes visually in *Gin Lane*.

2. Write an essay that proposes contemporary images to replace *Gin Lane*. What might symbolize poverty and urban decay in society today?

3. Select one of the characters depicted in *Gin Lane* and write a brief story of that person's life. You may use either the first- or the third-person point of view.

4. *Gin Lane* can be read as both a critique of the poor for drinking gin and a critique of the wealthy for ignoring the poor. Argue for one of these interpretations over the other. Support your argument with a close analysis of the image.

5. Choose a contemporary film, painting, photograph, or literary work that depicts poverty and urban decay. Compare this contemporary source with *Gin Lane*. How do the concerns, elements, and treatments differ? How are they similar?

Thomas Malthus
from *An Essay on the Principle of Population*
(1798)

BEFORE THE ENGLISH ECONOMIST Thomas Malthus (1766–1834) published "An Essay on the Principle of Population," most British economists and politicians believed that population increases were desirable, in that they supplied extra workers on farms and in factories and they led to elaborate family systems, which acted as security networks for the old and the unemployed. After the publication of this essay, chapter 2 of which is excerpted here, the concept of "overpopulation" entered the general European consciousness, and within a generation, population increases began to be seen as threats to, rather than harbingers of, prosperity.

Malthus was an unlikely messenger for the bad news that he bore. He belonged to a wealthy, intellectual family and attended Cambridge University, where he studied for the ministry; upon graduation, he became an Anglican pastor. Deeply religious, he vehemently opposed population-control measures such as abortion and contraception, which he viewed as sinful.

For Malthus, the problem of population could be reduced to a simple, abstract mathematical proposition: that human population, when left unchecked, increases geometrically, while the ability of a given society to produce food increases arithmetically. In practical terms, this means that every society in which the population increases will eventually produce more people than it can feed, thereby condemning a certain percentage of the population to live beneath the subsistence level. When this occurs, poverty becomes a check on population, as people are unable to support more children. This natural check disappears when the food supply catches up to the population level, and the cycle of growth and check begins anew. Malthus believed that while population and food production could increase indefinitely, they could not increase indefinitely at the same rate. Population will always win the race; therefore, some percentage of the human race will always live in poverty.

Most people in the early nineteenth century saw Malthus as a pessimist, and many condemned him for the matter-of-fact way that he dealt with these potentially emotional issues; legislators, however, paid attention to his ideas. In the 1830s, Malthusian principles were invoked by the British Parliament when it dramatically decreased government aid to the poor. Politicians argued that government aid allowed those who could not support children to have them anyway and increase the population, and therefore poverty, even further. Charles Dickens created the character Ebenezer Scrooge—who famously tells a solicitor that those who would rather die than go to a workhouse "had better do it, and decrease the surplus population"—as a satire of precisely this view. Malthus's writings also helped prompt the development of the

British Census, which began in 1801, and they proved a major influence on Charles Darwin's theory of natural selection. As population increases in the twentieth (and so far, the twenty-first) century have confirmed many of Malthus's assertions, his writings continue to influence public policy and social theory.

Malthus supports his claim with statistical data and other facts. All of the facts that he gives, though, were well known to his contemporaries. It is his ability to analyze these facts deductively and produce an inescapable conclusion that made Malthus's essay so compelling.

I SAID THAT POPULATION, when unchecked, increased in a geometrical ratio, and subsistence for man in an arithmetical ratio.[1]

Let us examine whether this position be just. I think it will be allowed, that no state has hitherto existed (at least that we have any account of) where the manners were so pure and simple, and the means of subsistence so abundant, that no check whatever has existed to early marriages, among the lower classes, from a fear of not providing well for their families, or among the higher classes, from a fear of lowering their condition in life. Consequently in no state that we have yet known has the power of population been left to exert itself with perfect freedom.

Whether the law of marriage be instituted or not, the dictate of nature and virtue seems to be an early attachment to one woman. Supposing a liberty of changing in the case of an unfortunate choice, this liberty would not affect population till it arose to a height greatly vicious;[2] and we are now supposing the existence of a society where vice is scarcely known.

In a state therefore of great equality and virtue, where pure and simple manners prevailed, and where the means of subsistence were so abundant that no part of the society could have any fears about providing amply for a family, the power of population being left to exert itself unchecked, the increase of the human species would evidently be much greater than any increase that has been hitherto known.

In the United States of America, where the means of subsistence have been more ample, the manners of the people more pure, and consequently the checks to early marriages fewer, than in any of the modern states of Europe, the population has been found to double itself in twenty-five years.

5

This ratio of increase, though short of the utmost power of population, yet as the result of actual experience, we will take as our rule, and say, that population, when

---

1. A **geometrical ratio** increases by doubling (1, 2, 4, 8, 16, 32, . . .) while an **arithmetical ratio** increases by simple addition (1, 2, 3, 4, 5, 6, . . .). Though both ratios can double from 1 to 2, simultaneously, the geometric ratio—even if it begins the process at a substantially lower number—will always outstrip the arithmetical ratio.

2. **Vicious:** For Malthus, "vicious" means simply "full of vice," rather than "extremely cruel." A conservative Anglican minister, Malthus believed that adultery, premarital sex, abortion, and contraception were sinful and, therefore, "vicious."

unchecked, goes on doubling itself every twenty-five years or increases in a geometrical ratio.

Let us now take any spot of earth, this Island[3] for instance, and see in what ratio the subsistence it affords can be supposed to increase. We will begin with it under its present state of cultivation.

If I allow that by the best possible policy, by breaking up more land and by great encouragements to agriculture, the produce of this Island may be doubled in the first twenty-five years, I think it will be allowing as much as any person can well demand.

In the next twenty-five years, it is impossible to suppose that the produce could be quadrupled. It would be contrary to all our knowledge of the qualities of land. The very utmost that we can conceive, is, that the increase in the second twenty-five years might equal the present produce. Let us then take this for our rule, though certainly far beyond the truth, and allow that, by great exertion, the whole produce of the Island might be increased every twenty-five years, by a quantity of subsistence equal to what it at present produces. The most enthusiastic speculator cannot suppose a greater increase than this. In a few centuries it would make every acre of land in the Island like a garden.

Yet this ratio of increase is evidently arithmetical.   10

It may be fairly said, therefore, that the means of subsistence increase in an arithmetical ratio. Let us now bring the effects of these two ratios together.

The population of the Island is computed to be about seven millions, and we will suppose the present produce equal to the support of such a number. In the first twenty-five years the population would be fourteen millions, and the food being also doubled, the means of subsistence would be equal to this increase. In the next twenty-five years the population would be twenty-eight millions, and the means of subsistence only equal to the support of twenty-one millions. In the next period, the population would be fifty-six millions, and the means of subsistence just sufficient for half that number. And at the conclusion of the first century the population would be one hundred and twelve millions and the means of subsistence only equal to the support of thirty-five millions, which would leave a population of seventy-seven millions totally unprovided for.

A great emigration necessarily implies unhappiness of some kind or other in the country that is deserted. For few persons will leave their families, connections, friends, and native land, to seek a settlement in untried foreign climes, without some strong subsisting causes of uneasiness where they are, or the hope of some great advantages in the place to which they are going.

But to make the argument more general and less interrupted by the partial views of emigration, let us take the whole earth, instead of one spot, and suppose that the restraints to population were universally removed. If the subsistence for man that

3. **This Island:** England.

the earth affords was to be increased every twenty-five years by a quantity equal to what the whole world at present produces, this would allow the power of production in the earth to be absolutely unlimited, and its ratio of increase much greater than we can conceive that any possible exertions of mankind could make it.

Taking the population of the world at any number, a thousand millions, for instance, the human species would increase in the ratio of—1, 2, 4, 8, 16, 32, 64, 128, 256, 512, etc. and subsistence as—1, 2, 3, 4, 5, 6, 7, 8, 9, 10, etc. In two centuries and a quarter, the population would be to the means of subsistence as 512 to 10: in three centuries as 4096 to 13, and in two thousand years the difference would be almost incalculable, though the produce in that time would have increased to an immense extent.

No limits whatever are placed to the productions of the earth; they may increase for ever and be greater than any assignable quantity, yet still the power of population being a power of a superior order, the increase of the human species can only be kept commensurate to the increase of the means of subsistence by the constant operation of the strong law of necessity acting as a check upon the greater power.

The effects of this check remain now to be considered.

Among plants and animals the view of the subject is simple. They are all impelled by a powerful instinct to the increase of their species, and this instinct is interrupted by no reasoning or doubts about providing for their offspring. Wherever therefore there is liberty, the power of increase is exerted, and the superabundant effects are repressed afterwards by want of room and nourishment, which is common to animals and plants, and among animals by becoming the prey of others.

The effects of this check on man are more complicated. Impelled to the increase of his species by an equally powerful instinct, reason interrupts his career and asks him whether he may not bring beings into the world for whom he cannot provide the means of subsistence. In a state of equality, this would be the simple question. In the present state of society, other considerations occur. Will he not lower his rank in life? Will he not subject himself to greater difficulties than he at present feels? Will he not be obliged to labour harder? and if he has a large family, will his utmost exertions enable him to support them? May he not see his offspring in rags and misery, and clamouring for bread that he cannot give them? And may he not be reduced to the grating necessity of forfeiting his independence, and of being obliged to the sparing hand of charity for support?

These considerations are calculated to prevent, and certainly do prevent, a very great number in all civilized nations from pursuing the dictate of nature in an early attachment to one woman. And this restraint almost necessarily, though not absolutely so, produces vice.[4] Yet in all societies, even those that are most vicious,

---

4. Malthus believed that young men and women were naturally disposed to form monogamous attachments and begin having children. However, the economic forces listed in the previous para- graph often hinder this process and lead to non-marital sexual activity, which Malthus equated with "vice."

the tendency to a virtuous attachment is so strong that there is a constant effort towards an increase of population. This constant effort as constantly tends to subject the lower classes of the society to distress and to prevent any great permanent amelioration of their condition.

The way in which these effects are produced seems to be this. We will suppose the means of subsistence in any country just equal to the easy support of its inhabitants. The constant effort towards population, which is found to act even in the most vicious societies, increases the number of people before the means of subsistence are increased. The food therefore which before supported seven millions must now be divided among seven millions and a half or eight millions. The poor consequently must live much worse, and many of them be reduced to severe distress. The number of labourers also being above the proportion of the work in the market, the price of labour must tend toward a decrease, while the price of provisions would at the same time tend to rise. The labourer therefore must work harder to earn the same as he did before. During this season of distress, the discouragements to marriage, and the difficulty of rearing a family are so great that population is at a stand. In the mean time the cheapness of labour, the plenty of labourers, and the necessity of an increased industry amongst them, encourage cultivators to employ more labour upon their land, to turn up fresh soil, and to manure and improve more completely what is already in tillage, till ultimately the means of subsistence become in the same proportion to the population as at the period from which we set out. The situation of the labourer being then again tolerably comfortable, the restraints to population are in some degree loosened, and the same retrograde and progressive movements with respect to happiness are repeated.

This sort of oscillation will not be remarked by superficial observers, and it may be difficult even for the most penetrating mind to calculate its periods. Yet that in all old states some such vibration does exist, though from various transverse[5] causes, in a much less marked, and in a much more irregular manner than I have described it, no reflecting man who considers the subject deeply can well doubt.

Many reasons occur why this oscillation has been less obvious, and less decidedly confirmed by experience, than might naturally be expected.

One principal reason is that the histories of mankind that we possess are histories only of the higher classes. We have but few accounts that can be depended upon of the manners and customs of that part of mankind where these retrograde and progressive movements chiefly take place.[6] A satisfactory history of this kind, on one people, and of one period, would require the constant and minute attention of an observing mind during a long life. Some of the objects of inquiry would be, in what

5. **Transverse:** connected like the beams of a cross.
6. **Retrograde and progressive:** back and forth. Malthus refers here to the fact that most of the periodic increases and decreases in the population of a society take place among its poorest members, who are the most sensitive to fluctuations in the food supply. Since most of recorded history concerns the upper and middle classes, we do not have a record of these population trends.

proportion to the number of adults was the number of marriages, to what extent vicious customs prevailed in consequence of the restraints upon matrimony, what was the comparative mortality among the children of the most distressed part of the community and those who lived rather more at their ease, what were the variations in the real price of labour, and what were the observable differences in the state of the lower classes of society with respect to ease and happiness, at different times during a certain period.

Such a history would tend greatly to elucidate the manner in which the constant 25 check upon population acts and would probably prove the existence of the retrograde and progressive movements that have been mentioned, though the times of their vibrations must necessarily be rendered irregular from the operation of many interrupting causes, such as the introduction or failure of certain manufacturers, a greater or less prevalent spirit of agricultural enterprise, years of plenty, or years of scarcity, wars and pestilence, poor laws, the invention of processes for shortening labour without the proportional extension of the market for the commodity, and, particularly, the difference between the nominal and real price of labour,[7] a circumstance which has perhaps more than any other contributed to conceal this oscillation from common view.

It very rarely happens that the nominal price of labour universally falls, but we well know that it frequently remains the same, while the nominal price of provisions has been gradually increasing. This is, in effect, a real fall in the price of labour, and during this period the condition of the lower orders of the community must gradually grow worse and worse. But the farmers and capitalists are growing rich from the real cheapness of labour. Their increased capitalists enable them to employ a greater number of men. Work therefore may be plentiful, and the price of labour would consequently rise. But the want of freedom in the market of labour, which occurs more or less in all communities, either from parish laws, or the more general cause of the facility of combination among the rich, and its difficulty among the poor, operates to prevent the price of labour from rising at the natural period, and keeps it down some time longer; perhaps till a year of scarcity, when the clamour is too loud and the necessity too apparent to be resisted.

The true cause of the advance in the price of labour is thus concealed, and the rich affect to grant it as an act of compassion and favour to the poor, in consideration of a year of scarcity, and, when plenty returns, indulge themselves in the most unreasonable of all complaints, that the price does not again fall, when a little rejection would shew them that it must have risen long before but from an unjust conspiracy of their own.

---

7. **Nominal and real price of labour:** The "nominal price," the actual wage paid to workers, differs from the "real price," which measures the buying power of a given wage by factoring in increases in the prices of goods. Comparisons of the nominal prices of goods or labor are almost meaningless over long periods of time, since the prices of almost everything else increase at the same time. Thus, economists usually use "real wages" as an index of prosperity.

But though the rich by unfair combinations contribute frequently to prolong a season of distress among the poor, yet no possible form of society could prevent the almost constant action of misery upon a great part of mankind, if in a state of inequality, and upon all, if all were equal.

The theory on which the truth of this position depends appears to me so extremely clear that I feel at a loss to conjecture what part of it can be denied.

That population cannot increase without the means of subsistence is a proposi-   30
tion so evident that it needs no illustration.

That population does invariably increase where there are the means of subsistence, the history of every people that have ever existed will abundantly prove.

And that the superior power of population cannot be checked without producing misery or vice, the ample portion of these too bitter ingredients in the cup of human life and the continuance of the physical causes that seem to have produced them bear too convincing a testimony.

UNDERSTANDING THE TEXT

1. What does Thomas Malthus mean when he notes that the human population grows in a "geometrical ratio" but resources grow in an "arithmetical ratio"? What problem does this imbalance eventually create?

2. What assertion does Malthus attempt to support by citing the rate of population increase in the United States? Do you find his use of evidence compelling? Why or why not?

3. Would it be possible, according to Malthusian theory, for the human population to continue to grow unchecked? What natural consequences check the animal and plant populations? What capability checks human populations?

4. Why have most population fluctuations throughout history not been recorded? What does Malthus believe that we would see if we could examine a more complete historical record of population trends?

5. What role do phenomena such as war, plague, and famine play in establishing an equilibrium between food and population?

6. According to Malthus's theory, what is the root cause of poverty? Can the problem of poverty ever be "solved," or is it an inherent feature of any imaginable configuration of society?

MAKING CONNECTIONS

1. Malthus lived at almost the same time as William Hogarth (p. 320) and saw many of the same scenes of urban poverty. However, for Malthus, the root of the problem was not gin, not even inequality, but excess population. What different ways of dealing with the problem of poverty come from these two perceptions of its cause?

2. Compare Malthus's essay with the twentieth-century Malthusian philosopher Garrett Hardin's essay "Lifeboat Ethics: The Case against Helping the Poor" (p. 357). How does Hardin's argument against providing food and other aid to underdeveloped countries follow from Malthus's theory?

3. Charles Darwin cited "An Essay on the Principle of Population" as a major influence on *The Origin of Species* (p. 405). What similarities between the two works can you detect? How might "natural selection" affect human overpopulation?

4. How does the ad for China's One-Child Policy (p. 516) invoke Malthusian rhetoric? Would Malthus have considered this ad useful?

WRITING ABOUT THE TEXT

1. Research world population growth since 1800, then evaluate Malthus's claim that human population grows geometrically. Conduct similar research to evaluate his claim that food supplies grow arithmetically.

2. Hogarth (p. 320) and Malthus both looked at England during the Industrial Revolution and tried to find the underlying cause of the poverty there. Write an essay outlining what you see as the root cause or causes of poverty within your own society.

3. Dispute Malthus's claim that poverty is an unsolvable problem. Use either historical examples or logical analysis to provide solutions to the problem even in a society with a high population.

4. Examine the connection between vice and poverty. Does poverty cause immoral behavior, or does immoral behavior cause poverty? How do economic factors influence definitions of "morality" and "vice"? Should the unequal distribution of wealth be considered "immoral"? Explain.

Mohandas K. Gandhi
Economic and Moral Progress
(1916)

THOUGH MOHANDAS KARAMCHAND GANDHI (1869–1948) never held a political or religious office, he was the most potent political force in modern India and a spiritual leader—known as "Mahatma," meaning "great soul"—to hundreds of millions of people around the world. His charismatic leadership, shrewd political instincts, and commitment to nonviolent civil disobedience created one of the most successful liberation movements in history and influenced subsequent civil rights movements in the United States, South Africa, Tibet, and Burma.

Gandhi was born in the Indian state of Gujarat, where his father was an important Indian official in the British-controlled government. After studying law in England, he joined an Indian company in South Africa, whose population then included many Indian immigrants. In South Africa, Gandhi confronted the legally sanctioned discrimination that would later develop into the doctrine of apartheid (Afrikaans for "separateness"). Between 1894 and 1914, he developed a philosophy of nonviolent resistance—for which he coined the term *satyagraha*, from the Sanskrit for "truth" and "persistence"—and trained his followers to allow themselves to be punished by the unjust government without using violence to retaliate. His methods were extremely successful, largely because they generated support for his cause around the world and forced the South African government to negotiate with him or face international condemnation.

In 1914, Gandhi returned to India with an international reputation as a skilled mediator and a powerful spokesman for justice. He was soon swept up in the Indian struggle for independence from Great Britain, which had occupied India as its colony since 1858. Using the techniques that he had developed in South Africa, Gandhi led boycotts against British goods, demonstrations against colonial authority, and highly public acts of civil disobedience against unjust laws of the British Empire. In one particularly successful campaign, he led his followers in a march to the coastal village of Dandi to make salt by hand, in direct defiance of the British salt monopoly. More than sixty thousand of Gandhi's followers were arrested, but the demonstrations focused so much world attention on India that the British government decided to negotiate with Gandhi for the release of all political prisoners in the country.

In 1947, the British government granted India its independence. As part of the agreement, India was divided into two countries: Pakistan, which would be Muslim, and India, which would be Hindu. Only a few months later, Gandhi was assassinated by a Hindu extremist who resented Gandhi for forcing the Indian government to make economic concessions to Pakistan.

Gandhi did not often write for publication. However, various collections of his letters, speeches, and newspaper articles have been published since his death, giving readers key insights into his motivations and character. The speech included here was originally given at the December 22, 1916, meeting of the Muir Central College Economics Society, in Allahabad, India, where Gandhi had been invited to address a group of scholars and students on the topic of "economic progress."

Because Gandhi's audience for these remarks included both Hindus and Christians, he argues from the authority of both religions' scriptural traditions. The majority of these references are to the New Testament—the sacred text of India's colonizers—suggesting a strong desire to appeal to Christians on their own rhetorical ground. ◗

WHEN I ACCEPTED Mr. Kapildeva Malaviya's[1] invitation to speak to you upon the subject of this evening, I was painfully conscious of my limitations. You are an economic society. You have chosen distinguished specialists for the subjects included in your syllabus for this year and the next. I seem to be the only speaker ill-fitted for the task set before him. Frankly and truly, I know very little of economics, as you naturally understand them. Only the other day, sitting at an evening meal, a civilian friend deluged me with a series of questions on my crankisms.[2] As he proceeded in this cross-examination, I being a willing victim, he found no difficulty in discovering my gross ignorance of the matters. I appeared to him to be handling with a cocksureness worthy only of a man who knows not that he knows not. To his horror and even indignation, I suppose, he found that I had not even read books on economics by such well-known authorities as Mill, Marshall, Adam Smith[3] and a host of such other authors. In despair, he ended by advising me to read these works before experimenting in matters economic at the expense of the public. He little knew that I was a sinner past redemption.

My experiments continue at the expense of trusting friends. For, there comes to us moments in life when about some things we need no proof from without. A little voice within us tells us, 'You are on the right track, move neither to your left nor right, but keep to the straight and narrow way.' With such help we march forward slowly indeed, but surely and steadily. That is my position. It may be satisfactory enough for me, but it can in no way answer the requirements of a society such as yours. Still it was no use my struggling against Mr. Kapildeva Malaviya. I knew that he was intent upon having me to engage your attention for one of your evenings. Perhaps you will treat my intrusion as a welcome diver-

---

1. **Mr. Kapildeva Malaviya's:** Pandit Madan Mohan Malaviya (1861–1946) was a well-known Indian scholar, journalist, and independence advocate and the founder of the Banaras Hindu University.

2. **Crankisms:** eccentricities.

3. **Mill, Marshall, Adam Smith:** John Stuart Mill (1806–1873), Alfred Marshall (1842–1924), and Adam Smith (1723–1790) were important British economists and social theorists.

sion from the trodden path. An occasional fast after a series of sumptuous feasts is often a necessity. And as with the body, so, I imagine, is the case with the reason. . . .

Before I take you to the field of my experiences and experiments, it is perhaps best to have a mutual understanding about the title of this evening's address: *Does economic progress clash with real progress?* By economic progress, I take it, we mean material advancement without limit and by real progress we mean moral progress, which again is the same thing as progress of the permanent element in us. The subject may therefore be stated thus: 'Does not moral progress increase in the same proportion as material progress?' I know that this is a wider proposition than the one before us. But I venture to think that we always mean the larger one even when we lay down the smaller. For we know enough of science to realise that there is no such thing as perfect rest or repose in this visible universe of ours. If therefore material progress does not clash with moral progress, it must necessarily advance the latter. Nor can we be satisfied with the clumsy way in which sometimes those who cannot defend the larger proposition put their case. They seem to be obsessed with the concrete case of thirty millions of India stated by the late Sir William Wilson Hunter[4] to be living on one meal a day. They say that before we can think or talk of their moral welfare, we must satisfy their daily wants. With these, they say, material progress spells moral progress. And then is taken a sudden jump: what is true of thirty millions is true of the universe. They forget that hard cases make bad law. I need hardly say to you how ludicrously absurd this deduction would be. No one has ever suggested that grinding pauperism can lead to anything else than moral degradation. Every human being has a right to live and therefore to find the wherewithal to feed himself and where necessary to clothe and house himself. But, for this very simple performance, we need no assistance from economists or their laws.

'Take no thought for the morrow'[5] is an injunction which finds an echo in almost all the religious scriptures of the world. In well-ordered society, the securing of one's livelihood should be and is found to be the easiest thing in the world. Indeed, the test of orderliness in a country is not the number of millionaires it owns, but the absence of starvation among its masses. The only statement that has to be examined is whether it can be laid down as a law of universal application that material advancement means moral progress.

4. **Sir William Wilson Hunter:** member (1840–1900) of the British civil service in India and the author of a number of popular books about India for Western audiences.

5. **'Take no thought for the morrow':** from Jesus' Sermon on the Mount: "Therefore take no thought, saying, What shall we eat? or, What shall we drink? or, Wherewithal shall we be clothed? (For after all these things do the Gentiles seek:) for your heavenly Father knoweth that ye have need of all these things. But seek ye first the kingdom of God, and his righteousness; and all these things shall be added unto you. Take therefore no thought for the morrow: for the morrow shall take thought for the things of itself. Sufficient unto the day is the evil thereof" (Matthew 6:31–34).

Now let us take a few illustrations. Rome suffered a moral fall when it attained   5
high material affluence. So did Egypt and so perhaps most countries of which we
have any historic record. The descendants, kinsmen of the royal and divine
Krishna, too, fell when they were rolling in riches. We do not deny to the Rockefellers and the Carnegies[6] possession of an ordinary measure of morality but we
gladly judge them indulgently. I mean that we do not even expect them to satisfy
the highest standard of morality. With them material gain has not necessarily
meant moral gain. In South Africa, where I had the privilege of associating with
thousands of our countrymen on most intimate terms, I observed almost invariably that the greater the possession of riches, the greater was their moral turpi-
tude. Our rich men, to say the least, did not advance the moral struggle of passive
resistance as did the poor. The rich men's sense of self-respect was not so much
injured as that of the poorest. If I were not afraid of treading on dangerous ground,
I would even come nearer home and show you that possession of riches has been
a hindrance to real growth. I venture to think that the scriptures of the world are
far safer and sounder treatises on laws of economics than many of the modern text-
books.

The question we are asking ourselves this evening is not a new one. It was
addressed to Jesus two thousand years ago. St. Mark has vividly described the scene.[7]
Jesus is in his solemn mood; he is earnest. He talks of eternity. He knows the world
about him. He is himself the greatest economist of his time. He succeeded in
economising time and space—he transcended them. It is to him at his best that one
comes running, kneels down, and asks: 'Good Master, what shall I do that I may
inherit eternal life?' And Jesus said unto him: 'Why callest thou me good? There is
none good but one, that is God. Thou knowest the commandments. Do not commit adultery, Do not kill, Do not steal, Do not bear false witness, Defraud not, Honour thy father and mother.' And he answered and said unto him: 'Master, all these
have I observed from my youth.' Then Jesus beholding him, loved him and said unto
him: 'One thing thou lackest. Go thy way, sell whatever thou hast and give to the
poor, and thou shalt have treasure in heaven—come take up the cross and follow
me.' And he was sad at that saying and went away grieved—for he had great possessions. And Jesus looked round about and said unto his disciples: 'How hardly shall
they that have riches enter into the kingdom of God.' And the disciples were astonished at his words. But Jesus answereth again and saith unto them: 'Children, how
hard it is for them that trust in riches to enter into the kingdom of God. It is eas-

6. **The Rockefellers and the Carnegies:** John
D. Rockefeller (1839–1937) and Andrew
Carnegie (1835–1919) were wealthy American
industrialists. **Krishna:** According to Hindu
scripture, Krishna is an incarnation of the god
Vishnu. He is Arjuna's chariot driver in the

Mahābhārata and speaks almost all of the text of
the *Bhagavad Gītā*.
7. The scriptural passages quoted in this paragraph and the next are from the tenth chapter
of the Gospel of Mark.

ier for a camel to go through the eye of a needle than for a rich man to enter into the kingdom of God!'

Here you have an eternal rule of life stated in the noblest words the English language is capable of producing. But the disciples nodded unbelief as we do even to this day. To him they said as we say today: 'But look how the law fails in practice. If we sell all and have nothing, we shall have nothing to eat. We must have money or we cannot even be reasonably moral.' So they state their case thus. 'And they were astonished out of measure saying among themselves: "Who then can be saved?"' And Jesus looking upon them said: 'With men it is impossible but not with God, for with God all things are possible.' Then Peter began to say unto him: 'Lo, we have left all, and have followed thee.' And Jesus answered and said: 'Verily I say unto you there is no man that has left house or brethren or sisters, or father or mother, or wife or children or lands for my sake and the Gospels, but he shall receive one hundred fold, now in this time houses and brethren and sisters and mothers and children and lands with persecutions and in the world to come eternal life. But many that are first shall be last and the last first.' You have here the result or reward, if you prefer the term, of following the law.

I have not taken the trouble of copying similar passages from the other non-Hindu scriptures and I will not insult you by quoting in support of the law stated by Jesus passages from the writings and sayings of our own sages, passages even stronger if possible than the Biblical extracts I have drawn your attention to. Perhaps the strongest of all the testimonies in favour of the affirmative answer to the question before us are the lives of the greatest teachers of the world. Jesus, Mahomed, Buddha, Nanak, Kabir, Chaitanya, Shankara, Dayanand, Ramkrishna[8] were men who exercised an immense influence over and moulded the character of thousands of men. The world is the richer for their having lived in it. And they were all men who deliberately embraced poverty as their lot.

I should not have laboured my point as I have done, if I did not believe that, in so far as we have made the modern materialistic craze our goal, in so far are we going downhill in the path of progress. I hold that economic progress in the sense I have put it is antagonistic to real progress. Hence the ancient ideal has been the limitation of activities promoting wealth. This does not put an end to all material ambition. We should still have, as we have always had, in our midst people who make the pursuit of wealth their aim in life. But we have always recognised that it is a fall from the ideal. It is a beautiful thing to know that the wealthiest among us have

8. **Nanak . . . Ramkrishna:** Guru Nanak (1469–1530) founded the Sikh religion in India. Kabir (1440–1518) was an Indian mystic whose teachings were important to Hindus and Muslims. Caitanya Mahaprabhu (1486–1534) was a devotee of Krishna and a social reformer in the Indian province of Bengal; his teachings form the basis for the International Society of Krishna Consciousness (Hare Krishna) in the West. Adi Shankara (eighth century CE) was a well-known Hindu teacher and philosopher. Dayananda Saraswati (1824–1883) was a Hindu reformer. Bhagavan Sri Ramakrishna Paramahamsa (1836–1886) was a well-known Hindu teacher.

often felt that to have remained voluntarily poor would have been a higher state for them. That you cannot serve God and Mammon[9] is an economic truth of the highest value. We have to make our choice. Western nations today are groaning under the heel of the monster-god of materialism. Their moral growth has become stunted. They measure their progress in £.s.d.[10] American wealth has become standard. She is the envy of the other nations. I have heard many of our countrymen say that we will gain American wealth but avoid its methods. I venture to suggest that such an attempt if it were made is foredoomed to failure.

We cannot be 'wise, temperate and furious'[11] in a moment. I would have our leaders teach us to be morally supreme in the world. This land of ours was once, we are told, the abode of the gods. It is not possible to conceive gods inhabiting a land which is made hideous by the smoke and the din of mill chimneys and factories and whose roadways are traversed by rushing engines dragging numerous cars crowded with men mostly who know not what they are after, who are often absent-minded, and whose tempers do not improve by being uncomfortably packed like sardines in boxes and finding themselves in the midst of utter strangers who would oust them if they could and whom they would in their turn oust similarly. I refer to these things because they are held to be symbolical of material progress. But they add not an atom to our happiness. This is what Wallace,[12] the great scientist, has said as his deliberate judgement.

10

> In the earliest records which have come down to us from the past, we find ample indications that general ethical considerations and conceptions, the accepted standard of morality, and the conduct resulting from these were in no degree inferior to those which prevail to-day.

In a series of chapters, he then proceeds to examine the position of the English nation under the advance in wealth it has made. He says:

> This rapid growth of wealth and increase of our power over nature put too great a strain upon our crude civilization, on our superficial Christianity, and it was accompanied by various forms of social immorality almost as amazing and unprecedented.

---

9. **Mammon:** a Hebrew word meaning wealth or material goods; Jesus' statement "Ye cannot serve God and mammon" occurs twice in the New Testament, in Matthew 6:24 and in Luke 16:13.
10. **£.s.d.:** the standard abbreviations for the three major British monetary units: pounds, shillings, pence.
11. **Wise, temperate, and furious:** a reference to William Shakespeare's *Macbeth*: "Who can be

wise, amazed, temp'rate and furious, / Loyal and neutral in a moment? No man" (2.3.105–06).
12. **Wallace:** Alfred Russel Wallace (1823–1913), a British naturalist who, along with Charles Darwin, articulated the principles of the theory of evolution by natural selection. The passages that Gandhi quotes are found in Wallace's 1913 book, *Social Environment and Moral Progress.*

He then shows how factories have risen on the corpses of men, women and children, how as the country has rapidly advanced in riches, it has gone down in morality. He shows this by dealing with insanitation, life-destroying trades, adulteration, bribery and gambling. He shows how, with the advance of wealth, justice has become immoral, deaths from alcoholism and suicide have increased, the average of premature births and congenital defects has increased, and prostitution has become an institution. He concludes his examination by these pregnant remarks:

> The proceedings of the divorce courts show other aspects of the result of wealth and leisure, while a friend who had been a good deal in London society assured me that both in country houses and in London various kinds of orgies were occasionally to be met with which would hardly have been surpassed in the period of the most dissolute emperors. Of war, too, I need say nothing. It has always been more or less chronic since the rise of the Roman Empire; but there is now undoubtedly a disinclination for war among all civilized peoples. Yet the vast burden of armaments, taken together with the most pious declarations in favour of peace, must be held to show an almost total absence of morality as a guiding principle among the governing classes.

Under the British aegis,[13] we have learnt much, but it is my firm belief that there is little to gain from Britain in intrinsic morality, that if we are not careful, we shall introduce all the vices that she has been a prey to, owing to the disease of materialism. We can profit by that connection only if we keep our civilization, and our morals, straight, i.e., if instead of boasting of the glorious past, we express the ancient moral glory in our own lives and let our lives bear witness to our past. Then we shall benefit her and ourselves. If we copy her because she provides us with rulers, both they and we shall suffer degradation. We need not be afraid of ideals or of reducing them to practice even to the uttermost. Ours will only then be a truly spiritual nation when we shall show more truth than gold, greater fearlessness than pomp of power and wealth, greater charity than love of self. If we will but clean our houses, our palaces and temples of the attributes of wealth and show in them the attributes of morality, we can offer battle to any combinations of hostile forces without having to carry the burden of a heavy militia. Let us seek first the kingdom of God[14] and

---

13. **Aegis:** technically, a shield or breastplate; more commonly, mentorship or guidance.
14. **Let us seek first the kingdom of God:** an allusion to Matthew 6:33: "But seek ye first the kingdom of God, and his righteousness; and all these things shall be added unto you."

His righteousness and the irrevocable promise is that everything will be added with us. These are real economics. May you and I treasure them and enforce them in our daily life.

UNDERSTANDING THE TEXT

1. What does Mohandas Gandhi mean by "economic progress"? What does he mean by "moral progress"? How are the two terms interrelated in this speech?

2. Though Gandhi was a Hindu speaking to a largely Hindu audience, his primary religious source for this speech is the New Testament. Why does he emphasize Christian Scriptures? What does this choice say about the ethos (pp. 608–10) he was trying to construct?

3. What is Gandhi's position on poverty? Does he suggest that moral development requires the renunciation of physical needs? Are extremely poor people morally superior to others? Are wealthy people morally inferior? Explain.

4. What does Gandhi see as "real progress"? Whom does he name as having furthered the real progress of humankind? What traits do these individuals share? What are the "real economics" that he refers to at the end of this speech?

MAKING CONNECTIONS

1. Compare Gandhi's position on the connection between wealth and morality with similar discussions in the New Testament (p. 315) and the writings of Mo Tzu (p. 308). How do these texts, taken together, support the idea of a universal (or at least widespread) religious approach to economics?

2. Would Muhammad Yunus (p. 369) support Gandhi's view that economic progress is at odds with moral progress? How might Gandhi respond to Yunus's attempts to use a key principle of capitalism (credit) to lift the poorest of the poor out of poverty?

3. Martin Luther King Jr. cited Gandhi as a major influence on his thinking and social activism. How might "Economic and Moral Progress" have informed "Letter from Birmingham City Jail" (p. 202)?

4. Does Gandhi's distinction between economic and moral progress rely on the same kind of distinction between illusion and reality found in the classic Buddhist text "The Precious Garland" (p. 110)? Explain.

WRITING ABOUT THE TEXT

1. Write your own response to the key question that Gandhi raises: What is the relationship between economic progress and moral progress?

2. Analyze "Economic and Moral Progress" from the perspective of "The Precious Garland" (p. 110). Are Gandhi's views consistent with Buddhist scripture?

3. Compare Gandhi's arguments about wealth and morality with those of Jesus in the sixteenth chapter of Luke (p. 315). How substantially do the views differ?

4. Refute Gandhi's claim by arguing that many people have been able to accomplish good things through their material wealth.

Dorothea Lange
Migrant Mother
(1936)

OF ALL THE IMAGES OF POVERTY and despair that came out of the Great Depression, none had more impact than Dorothea Lange's *Migrant Mother*. Lange (1895–1965) took this photograph while working for the federal government's Resettlement Administration—later called the Farm Security Administration—a Depression-era agency that attempted to combat rural poverty by purchasing land from subsistence farmers and resettling the farmers on larger tracts of land where they could work in large collectives under the supervision of government scientists. Between 1935 and 1944, the agency employed a number of photographers—including Lange—to create support for their mission by documenting the effects of poverty on sharecroppers, homesteaders, migrant farmers, and other rural victims of the Great Depression.

The photograph now commonly known as *Migrant Mother* is in the Library of Congress under the title "Destitute pea pickers in California. Mother of seven children. Age thirty-two. Nipomo, California." In 1960, Lange recounted her experience the day that the iconic photograph was taken:

> I saw and approached the hungry and desperate mother, as if drawn by a magnet. I do not remember how I explained my presence or my camera to her, but I do remember she asked me no questions. I made five exposures, working closer and closer from the same direction. I did not ask her name on her history. She told me her age, that she was thirty-two. She said that they had been living on frozen vegetables from the surrounding fields, and birds that the children killed. She had just sold the tires from her car to buy food. There she sat in that lean-to tent with her children huddled around her, and seemed to know that my pictures might help her, and so she helped me. There was a sort of equality about it.

For years, this was all that was known about the woman in the image. However, in 1978, a reporter named Emmett Corrigan found her living in a mobile home in Modesto, California. He was able to identify her as Florence Owens Thompson (1903–1983), a Cherokee woman who had moved with her husband from Oklahoma to California in 1922 and was later caught up in the economic hardships of the Depression. Thompson expressed frustration and anger that the picture that had made her face famous had never helped her or her family in any way. Five years later, however, when Americans learned that Thompson was dying of cancer and had no way to pay her medical bills, her family received more than $30,000 in contributions from those who had been moved by the photograph over the years.

DOROTHEA LANGE
Migrant Mother, 1936.
Library of Congress

UNDERSTANDING THE TEXT

1. What does the woman in Dorothea Lange's photograph appear to be looking at? What is she looking away from? What might the direction of her gaze communicate about her state of mind?

2. Why do you think the two older children in the picture have their faces turned away from the camera? What effect might the photographer herself have had on the picture?

3. From what is visible in the picture, what can you tell about the baby that the mother is holding?

4. Imagine that you saw this photograph without any knowledge of the title, the photographer, the cultural and historical context of the photo, or its subject. What would the photograph mean to you? What would you think the photographer was trying to say? How does knowing the context and other information about the photo change how you see it?

MAKING CONNECTIONS

1. Compare the mother in this picture with the mothers in *Gin Lane* (p. 320) and *Guernica* (p. 271). How does each mother respond to the misery of her family? What might account for the differences?

2. Compare the rhetorical use of the mother-child relationship in *Migrant Mother* and "Ad for Chinese Population Policy" (p. 516). Could Lange's photograph be classified as a type of propaganda? If so, what would be the photographer's main message?

3. What might Mohandas Gandhi (p. 332) or Garrett Hardin (p. 357) say upon seeing this image? How does it affirm or rebut the arguments that they make?

WRITING ABOUT THE TEXT

1. Write an essay in which you interpret *Migrant Mother* by carefully examining its formal elements, such as shading, lighting, balance, composition, and contrast. Explain how the formal elements of the image reinforce its theme.

2. Use *Migrant Mother*, "Ad for Chinese Population Policy" (p. 516), and *Igbo Mother and Child* (p. 129) as the basis for an essay about the use of maternal images in different cultures. Explain how certain conceptions of motherhood are vital to the power of these images and how they might be different if they depicted a father and a child.

3. Show *Migrant Mother* to friends, roommates, or family members who may not be familiar with the picture and ask them what they think it is about. Do not share the title or any information about the photo. Then write an essay in which you compare and contrast their responses. Why do you think they respond as they do?

4. Do research to find out when and where *Migrant Mother* was originally published and write an essay explaining the impact (or lack of impact) that it had on its original audience.

Octavio Paz
from *The Day of the Dead*
(1950)

FOR MUCH OF THE TWENTIETH CENTURY, Octavio Paz (1914–1998) was Mexico's most famous living poet and one of its most visible public figures. In addition to writing more than forty books—of poetry, essays, criticism, and political commentary—he served as Mexico's ambassador to India from 1962 until 1968. In 1990, he became the first Mexican—and only the fourth Latin American—to win the Nobel Prize for literature.

Paz's most famous prose work is *The Labyrinth of Solitude* (1950). In the nine essays that constitute this book, Paz sets for himself the daunting task of defining Mexican identity. To do this, he analyzes many different layers of Mexico's history, including Aztec myths, Catholic spiritual traditions, the Spanish conquest, French imperialism under Napoleon III, and American militarism in the nineteenth century and economic dominance in the twentieth century. Because the country has been subject to so many different conquests, occupations, and fragmentations, Paz argues, its national character is divided, lacking in confidence, and deeply suspicious.

The key to understanding Mexico is, for Paz, understanding the nature of its people's solitude. This solitude is based not in physical separation but in the inability to form emotional connections. The people who emerge from the pages of *The Labyrinth of Solitude* feel their country's history of poverty, betrayal, and vulnerability in the cores of their beings. "They act," he writes, "like persons who are wearing disguises, who are afraid of a stranger's look because it could strip them and leave them stark naked." *The Labyrinth of Solitude* seeks to understand this condition by looking at myths, customs, language, politics, history, and other representatives of what Paz calls "the psychology of a nation."

The following selection comes from the essay "The Day of the Dead," which deals with one of Mexico's most important holidays. In this selection, Paz attempts to explain the nature of great celebrations, or fiestas, in his country's cultural life. Paz begins with the observation that very poor villages often spend the majority of their collective wealth each year on one or two elaborate fiestas. He notes that elaborate celebrations are much more important to the poor than to the rich, but he also insists that their very nature is shrouded in ambiguity. They simultaneously celebrate life and death, order and chaos, love and hate, and joy and sorrow. Because of this ambiguity, Paz argues, these intensely communal celebrations also preserve the Mexican tradition of solitude.

Paz's purpose in this selection is to explain both the practice of the fiesta and the deep psychology behind this practice. In the process he advances a very subtle thesis about the connection between poverty and occasional excess. ◣

THE SOLITARY MEXICAN loves fiestas and public gatherings. Any occasion for getting together will serve, any pretext to stop the flow of time and commemorate men and events with festivals and ceremonies. We are a ritual people, and this characteristic enriches both our imaginations and our sensibilities, which are equally sharp and alert. The art of the fiesta has been debased almost everywhere else, but not in Mexico. There are few places in the world where it is possible to take part in a spectacle like our great religious fiestas with their violent primary colors, their bizarre costumes and dances, their fireworks and ceremonies, and their inexhaustible welter of surprises: the fruit, candy, toys and other objects sold on these days in the plazas and open-air markets.

Our calendar is crowded with fiestas. There are certain days when the whole country, from the most remote villages to the largest cities, prays, shouts, feasts, gets drunk and kills, in honor of the Virgin of Guadalupe or Benito Juárez.[1] Each year on the fifteenth of September, at eleven o'clock at night, we celebrate the fiesta of the *Grito*[2] in all the plazas of the Republic, and the excited crowds actually shout for a whole hour . . . the better, perhaps, to remain silent for the rest of the year. During the days before and after the twelfth of December,[3] time comes to a full stop, and instead of pushing us toward a deceptive tomorrow that is always beyond our reach, offers us a complete and perfect today of dancing and revelry, of communion with the most ancient and secret Mexico. Time is no longer succession, and becomes what it originally was and is: the present, in which past and future are reconciled.

But the fiestas which the Church and State provide for the country as a whole are not enough. The life of every city and village is ruled by a patron saint whose blessing is celebrated with devout regularity. Neighborhoods and trades also have their annual fiestas, their ceremonies and fairs. And each one of us—atheist, Catholic, or merely indifferent—has his own saint's day, which he observes every year. It is impossible to calculate how many fiestas we have and how much time and money we spend on them. I remember asking the mayor of a village near Mitla, several years ago, "What is the income of the village government?" "About 3,000 pesos a year. We are very poor. But the Governor and the Federal

---

The translator's footnotes have been omitted.

1. **The Virgin of Guadalupe or Benito Juárez:** The Virgin of Guadalupe, the patron saint of Mexico, is the form that the Virgin Mary purportedly took when she appeared to the Indian convert Juan Diego in 1531 and instructed him to build a church. Benito Juárez (1806–1872), the only Indian to serve as the president of Mexico, remains one of that country's greatest heroes. He led Mexico's famous victory over the French under Napoleon III, who attempted to install a puppet government under the "Emperor" Maximilian.

2. **The *Grito*:** *El Grito de Dolores* ("The Shout of Pain"), the sermon by Spanish priest Miguel Hidalgo that launched the Mexican Revolution by detailing Mexico's grievances against Spain. The date of this sermon, September 16, is celebrated as Independence Day in Mexico.

3. **The twelfth of December:** the Festival of the Virgin of Guadalupe.

Government always help us to meet our expenses." "And how are the 3,000 pesos spent?" "Mostly on fiestas, señor. We are a small village, but we have two patron saints."

This reply is not surprising. Our poverty can be measured by the frequency and luxuriousness of our holidays. Wealthy countries have very few: there is neither the time nor the desire for them, and they are not necessary. The people have other things to do, and when they amuse themselves they do so in small groups. The modern masses are agglomerations of solitary individuals. On great occasions in Paris or New York, when the populace gathers in the squares or stadiums, the absence of people, in the sense of *a* people, is remarkable: there are couples and small groups, but they never form a living community in which the individual is at once dissolved and redeemed. But how could a poor Mexican live without the two or three annual fiestas that make up for his poverty and misery? Fiestas are our only luxury. They replace, and are perhaps better than, the theater and vacations, Anglo-Saxon weekends and cocktail parties, the bourgeois reception, the Mediterranean café.

In all of these ceremonies—national or local, trade or family—the Mexican opens   5 out. They all give him a chance to reveal himself and to converse with God, country, friends or relations. During these days the silent Mexican whistles, shouts, sings, shoots off fireworks, discharges his pistol into the air. He discharges his soul. And his shout, like the rockets we love so much, ascends to the heavens, explodes into green, red, blue, and white lights, and falls dizzily to earth with a trail of golden sparks. This is the night when friends who have not exchanged more than the prescribed courtesies for months get drunk together, trade confidences, weep over the same troubles, discover that they are brothers, and sometimes, to prove it, kill each other. The night is full of songs and loud cries. The lover wakes up his sweetheart with an orchestra. There are jokes and conversations from balcony to balcony, sidewalk to sidewalk. Nobody talks quietly. Hats fly in the air. Laughter and curses ring like silver pesos. Guitars are brought out. Now and then, it is true, the happiness ends badly, in quarrels, insults, pistol shots, stabbings. But these too are part of the fiesta, for the Mexican does not seek amusement: he seeks to escape from himself, to leap over the wall of solitude that confines him during the rest of the year. All are possessed by violence and frenzy. Their souls explode like the colors and voices and emotions. Do they forget themselves and show their true faces? Nobody knows. The important thing is to go out, open a way, get drunk on noise, people, colors. Mexico is celebrating a fiesta. And this fiesta, shot through with lightning and delirium, is the brilliant reverse to our silence and apathy, our reticence and gloom.

According to the interpretation of French sociologists, the fiesta is an excess, an expense. By means of this squandering the community protects itself against the envy of the gods or of men. Sacrifices and offerings placate or buy off the gods and the patron saints. Wasting money and expending energy affirms the community's wealth in both. This luxury is a proof of health, a show of abundance and power.

Or a magic trap. For squandering is an effort to attract abundance by contagion. Money calls to money. When life is thrown away it increases; the orgy, which is sexual expenditure, is also a ceremony of regeneration; waste gives strength. New Year celebrations, in every culture, signify something beyond the mere observance of a date on the calendar. The day is a pause: time is stopped, is actually annihilated. The rites that celebrate its death are intended to provoke its rebirth, because they mark not only the end of an old year but also the beginning of a new. Everything attracts its opposite. The fiesta's function, then, is more utilitarian than we think: waste attracts or promotes wealth, and is an investment like any other, except that the returns on it cannot be measured or counted. What is sought is potency, life, health. In this sense the fiesta, like the gift and the offering, is one of the most ancient of economic forms.

This interpretation has always seemed to me to be incomplete. The fiesta is by nature sacred, literally or figuratively, and above all it is the advent of the unusual. It is governed by its own special rules, that set it apart from other days, and it has a logic, an ethic and even an economy that are often in conflict with everyday norms. It all occurs in an enchanted world: time is transformed to a mythical past or a total present; space, the scene of the fiesta, is turned into a gaily decorated world of its own; and the persons taking part cast off all human or social rank and become, for the moment, living images. And everything takes place as if it were not so, as if it were a dream. But whatever happens, our actions have a greater lightness, a different gravity. They take on other meanings and with them we contract new obligations. We throw down our burdens of time and reason.

In certain fiestas the very notion of order disappears. Chaos comes back and license rules. Anything is permitted: the customary hierarchies vanish, along with all social, sex, caste, and trade distinctions. Men disguise themselves as women, gentlemen as slaves, the poor as the rich. The army, the clergy, and the law are ridiculed. Obligatory sacrilege, ritual profanation is committed. Love becomes promiscuity. Sometimes the fiesta becomes a Black Mass.[4] Regulations, habits and customs are violated. Respectable people put away the dignified expressions and conservative clothes that isolate them, dress up in gaudy colors, hide behind a mask, and escape from themselves.

Therefore the fiesta is not only an excess, a ritual squandering of the goods painfully accumulated during the rest of the year; it is also a revolt, a sudden immersion in the formless, in pure being. By means of the fiesta society frees itself from the norms it has established. It ridicules its gods, its principles, and its laws: it denies its own self.

The fiesta is a revolution in the most literal sense of the word. In the confusion that it generates, society is dissolved, is drowned, insofar as it is an organism   10

---

4. **Black Mass:** a Satanic parody of the Christian Mass; according to legend, it culminates with a sexual orgy.

ruled according to certain laws and principles. But it drowns in itself, in its own original chaos or liberty. Everything is united: good and evil, day and night, the sacred and the profane. Everything merges, loses shape and individuality and returns to the primordial mass. The fiesta is a cosmic experiment, an experiment in disorder, reuniting contradictory elements and principles in order to bring about a renascence of life. Ritual death promotes a rebirth; vomiting increases the appetite; the orgy, sterile in itself, renews the fertility of the mother or of the earth. The fiesta is a return to a remote and undifferentiated state, prenatal or presocial. It is a return that is also a beginning, in accordance with the dialectic[5] that is inherent in social processes.

The group emerges purified and strengthened from this plunge into chaos. It has immersed itself in its own origins, in the womb from which it came. To express it in another way, the fiesta denies society as an organic system of differentiated forms and principles, but affirms it as a source of creative energy. It is a true "re-creation," the opposite of the "recreation" characterizing modern vacations, which do not entail any rites or ceremonies whatever and are as individualistic and sterile as the world that invented them.

Society communes with itself during the fiesta. Its members return to original chaos and freedom. Social structures break down and new relationships, unexpected rules, capricious hierarchies are created. In the general disorder everybody forgets himself and enters into otherwise forbidden situations and places. The bounds between audience and actors, officials and servants, are erased. Everybody takes part in the fiesta, everybody is caught up in its whirlwind. Whatever its mood, its character, its meaning, the fiesta is participation, and this trait distinguishes it from all other ceremonies and social phenomena. Lay or religious, orgy or saturnalia,[6] the fiesta is a social act based on the full participation of all its celebrants.

Thanks to the fiesta the Mexican opens out, participates, communes with his fellows and with the values that give meaning to his religious or political existence. And it is significant that a country as sorrowful as ours should have so many and such joyous fiestas. Their frequency, their brilliance and excitement, the enthusiasm with which we take part, all suggest that without them we would explode. They free us, if only momentarily, from the thwarted impulses, the inflammable desires that we carry within us. But the Mexican fiesta is not merely a return to an original state of formless and normless liberty: the Mexican is not seeking to return, but to escape from himself, to exceed himself. Our fiestas are explosions. Life and death, joy and sorrow, music and mere noise are united, not to re-create or recognize themselves, but to swallow each other up. There is nothing so joyous as a Mexican fiesta, but there is also nothing so sorrowful. Fiesta night is also a night of mourning.

---

5. **Dialectic:** the combined effect of two contradictory phenomena (p. 624).

6. **Saturnalia:** a riotous, unrestrained celebration, named after the ancient Roman festival of Saturn.

If we hide within ourselves in our daily lives, we discharge ourselves in the whirlwind of the fiesta. It is more than an opening out: we rend ourselves open. Everything—music, love, friendship—ends in tumult and violence. The frenzy of our festivals shows the extent to which our solitude closes us off from communication with the world. We are familiar with delirium, with songs and shouts, with the monologue . . . but not with the dialogue. Our fiestas, like our confidences, our loves, our attempts to reorder our society, are violent breaks with the old or the established. Each time we try to express ourselves we have to break with ourselves. And the fiesta is only one example, perhaps the most typical, of this violent break. It is not difficult to name others, equally revealing: our games, which are always a going to extremes, often mortal; our profligate spending, the reverse of our timid investments and business enterprises; our confessions. The somber Mexican, closed up in himself, suddenly explodes, tears open his breast and reveals himself, though not without a certain complacency, and not without a stopping place in the shameful or terrible mazes of his intimacy. We are not frank, but our sincerity can reach extremes that horrify a European. The explosive, dramatic, sometimes even suicidal manner in which we strip ourselves, surrender ourselves, is evidence that something inhibits and suffocates us. Something impedes us from being. And since we cannot or dare not confront our own selves, we resort to the fiesta. It fires us into the void; it is a drunken rapture that burns itself out, a pistol shot in the air, a skyrocket.

UNDERSTANDING THE TEXT

1. In what ways is a Mexican fiesta a form of ritual?

2. Why, according to Octavio Paz, do people in poor nations have a greater desire for elaborate celebrations than do people in wealthy nations?

3. Why do celebrations occasionally result in "quarrels, insults, pistol shots, stabbings"? What aspect of the fiesta encourages these extreme elements? Are they a natural outgrowth of the fiesta?

4. Why does Paz cite the opinion of French sociologists that the fiesta represents "an excess" designed to protect a community "against the envy of the gods"? Does he accept this theory? How does he incorporate it into his own ideas (p. 627)?

5. How do fiestas relate to the established social order in Mexico? Why does Paz call the fiesta a "revolution"? How might the fiesta's short duration relate to its revolutionary nature?

MAKING CONNECTIONS

1. How might Paz respond to Mo Tzu's assertion (p. 308) that expending resources on luxury activities simply increases the misery of the poor? Would Mo Tzu see anything "useful" in a fiesta?

2. How does Paz's view of the regulated lawlessness of the fiesta compare with other views of law and disobedience, such as Martin Luther King Jr.'s "Letter from Birmingham City Jail" (p. 202) or Aung San Suu Kyi's "In Quest of Democracy" (p. 219)? How might a brief period of controlled chaos be a way to preserve order?

3. How do the drunken revelers in Hogarth's *Gin Lane* (p. 320) compare with the celebrants Paz describes in this selection? What are their key differences?

WRITING ABOUT THE TEXT

1. In light of Paz's view of the fiesta, examine a party or cultural celebration you have attended. How does Paz's model work as a way to interpret your own experiences?

2. Write an essay criticizing or defending the mayor of a small town for spending all of the town's money on an elaborate celebration when many townspeople lack adequate food, clothing, and shelter.

3. Explore the connection between celebration and revolution. Research not only Mexican fiestas but also different kinds of carnivals, festivities, and other parties in which social orders and categories are, at least for a time, reversed or made unstable.

Lucy Lameck
Africans Are Not Poor
(1965)

Lucy Selina Lameck Somi (circa 1930–1992) was born in the Kilimanjaro region of British Tanganyika, a large territory of East Africa ceded to Britain by Germany after World War I. She attended British schools and studied to be a nurse, but as a young adult she instead became an activist in the Tanganyika African National Union (TANU), a nationalist party seeking independence from Great Britain. Lameck's mother was also a TANU activist, and the family was close to the party's leader, Julius Nyerere (1922–1999), who would later serve for more than twenty years as the president of the Republic of Tanzania.

In 1957, Lameck left Tanganyika to study economics and sociology at Oxford University in England and then international relations at Western Michigan University in the United States. When she returned to her homeland in 1961, she was elected to serve in the parliament of the newly independent nation of Tanganyika. In 1964, Tanganyika combined with the nearby island nation of Zanzibar to form the Republic of Tanzania. Lameck was initially named Parliamentary Undersecretary for Commerce and Cooperatives. In 1970, she became the country's secretary of health and social welfare.

The selection reprinted here is from a speech Lameck gave to the parliament of Tanzania on June 15, 1965, just one year after the creation of the nation and only five years after the end of British rule in the region. At the time, most of Lameck's parliamentary colleagues were lamenting the poverty in their nation and other newly independent African nations. Lameck, however, argues that this is the wrong vocabulary for talking about African problems. The resources of the African continent have made Western nations wealthy and, she argues, properly managed, they can make African nations wealthy as well. Rather than presenting themselves to the world as helpless victims, she argues, Africans should take control of their own destinies and develop uniquely African ways to generate and distribute wealth.

Lameck's rhetorical situation is particularly important because this selection is a speech delivered as part of a parliamentary debate—it is meant to persuade a particular audience at a particular point in time. Her primary strategy is to contest the underlying assumptions about poverty held by her audience and offer a new, less stigmatizing definition in its place. 🖎

Among the words we use when addressing the public, or in various councils, is the phrase that "we are poor people," that our country is still young, and that we Tanzanians are "still poor." This word has been worrying me for quite a long time because, Mr. Speaker, I don't agree at all that our country is poor and that Tanzanians are poor people. Our country today has value, it has riches, it has culture, it has people, it has agriculture, it has good land, it has animals, different types of livestock, minerals—and it is rumored that there are millions and millions of [tons of] coal, iron and other ores—which we have not yet managed to find the means to explore and exploit and process for our benefit. Hence, I don't agree at all that our country is poor and, indeed, when we use the word we only humiliate ourselves. Today, when I looked at the speech delivered by the Honorable Minister, and went over the financial figures for the period from 1960 that he was explaining to us—I can it see here, Honorable Mr. Speaker, I will read—I am sorry I don't have the Kiswahili[1] version, I have the English one—Mr. Minister says: "When we took over the government in 1960 the total budget under the colonial regime for that year was 19,000,000 pounds for recurrent [expenditure] and 6,000,000 pounds for development, making a total of 25,000,000 pounds. Today I am happy to say that the Nationalist Government has more than doubled the size of the country's budget. The total budget which I have presented amounts to a little over 36,000,000 pounds recurrent and 31,000,000 pounds development, a total of 67,000,000 pounds in one year." Honorable Mr. Speaker, in poor countries people walk [live] on the streets, they go without food and die of hunger, they have no farms, no houses; they have nothing. One could not use the language used by Mr. Minister here in reference to such people. In a one-year period we have been able to raise 67,000,000 pounds. Therefore, Mr. Speaker, we have to be a bit careful about the word "poverty," because we will condition the thinking of the people. Our growing schoolchildren, whom we would like to grow in an independent country, should be able to enter the army of the builders of our republic; if we still tell them every day that we are poor, we will be debasing ourselves and debasing our other foundations. What we lack—and this we have to accept—is that our situation is weak because right now we don't have enough experience and our revenue is erratic. The most important resource for us is knowledge: In our present circumstances, the government is directing its efforts towards attaining expertise in different fields, so that we may disentangle ourselves from this problematic situation, and use our new knowledge to explore the minerals, exploit our resources, expand our industries, and employ many workers, so that we may extricate ourselves from this despicable situation.

Mr. Speaker, I think the other thing that makes us feel very poor is the situation of the world in which we live. The world surrounding us is developing fast in the economic and scientific spheres: rockets are being sent into space, huge buildings are being erected, the condition of life is so different, there are many industries, etc. That is why we feel that we still have a long way to go, that we have yet to arrive. But I would like us to remember, whenever we compare ourselves to others, the methods used by them to build their countries' economies. The British, the Ameri-

---

1. **Kiswahili:** the Swahili language of Eastern Africa. *Kiswahili* is the Swahili word for *Swahili*.

cans, and others have built their countries from the sweat of other people. The British had many colonies in Africa and other lands; the Americans had several slaves who cultivated their cotton and other farms. The Negroes were, and are up to today, cheap labor. In these countries, the governments belonged to a few people, the rich people ran the governments. They used to get materials and other things from our countries. Yes, we are indeed far behind, it is true. We are many steps behind, but we must always remind ourselves of the basis and the means these fellows used to get where they now are. Let this be an objective and a warning to us, reminding us of our principles. Our objective in this country is to see to it that this country develops in general, right from the districts, towns, villages, and neighborhoods; that the living conditions in our country change step by step, village by village, and neighborhood by neighborhood. That being the case, we have to accept that one of our greatest responsibilities is to tighten our belts and do everything we can in order to increase the income of our country, so that our country can develop as fast as we are able to make it. At the same time, we have to remember that we have a great responsibility towards our republic, that of laying the foundations that conform to the needs and experience of Tanzanians themselves: economic, political, and developmental foundations for the people and the community which are homegrown and not stolen from foreign countries, but arise from and are in harmony with the Tanzanian people's experience and traditions.

Honorable Speaker . . . we are thankful that, when our Central Committee of TANU[2] met recently, it authorized the Father of the Nation [Prime Minister Nyerere] to appoint a special council or commission to deliberate and advise him on how we may formulate a policy based on African socialism. I very much welcome the idea, for indeed, it will help us overcome many economic problems. It will elaborate on what should be the basis of our socialism, how we should move forward, which of the things inherited from the colonial era are right, and which things in our traditions still have great value and should be preserved.

I think this council will greatly help us because there is a lot of misunderstanding, and I often ask myself about the African Socialism that we Tanzanians want to follow. Some few years ago, the republic tried to lay down a basis without a clear system and without a guidebook, like a Bible, that elaborates what African socialism is all about. It tried, as much as it could, to use advice and the existing foundations to adjust our institutions so as to have a policy which reflects the principles of our African political democracy. However, right now there is a great need to have a clear vision of the kind of future we want.

For at times, there is confusion. There is a lot of talk. Today it is declared that 5 big vehicles should be appropriated; tomorrow small cars are declared bad; the day

2. **TANU:** The Tanganyika African National Union, a nationalist political party founded by Julius Nyerere (1922–1999), who later became president of Tanzania.

after there will be this and that declaration. There is confused talk, so that we do not really know where we are going and what we want to be: Will there be motor-cars or not? Will there be farms or not? And if farms will be there, on what basis will they be run? What type of economy shall our country have? Will foreigners and the common people living here go on with the same type of life or will their lives be organized differently? Hence, Honorable Speaker, I welcome the council, which will be established by the Honorable Father of the Nation so that it may expound more on our political principles and chart out a good and clear way forward, so that we do not quarrel in future, or fumble and stumble every day as humans are wont.

UNDERSTANDING THE TEXT

1. Why does Lucy Lameck insist that it is incorrect to call Africans "poor"? What kinds of evidence does she use to support this claim?

2. What does Lameck mean when she says that using the word *poverty* will "condition the thinking of the people"?

3. What does Lameck see as the real problem affecting the Tanzanian people? How is this different from "poverty"?

4. How, according to Lameck, do comparisons with other nations make Africans perceive themselves as poor? Does it make sense to discuss poverty as a relative phenomenon? Or should there be a definition of poverty that does not take into account the wealth of other nations or other people? Explain.

5. What kinds of economic decisions does Lameck believe that the new nation needs to make? How does she feel that native values and perceptions should shape these decisions?

MAKING CONNECTIONS

1. Compare the economic conditions that Lameck describes with those described by Muhammad Yunus in "The Stool Makers of Jobra Village" (p. 369). Would the kinds of solutions that Yunus describes work in Lameck's society?

2. Compare Lameck's position as a member of parliament in post-colonial Tanzania with Desmond Tutu's position as a member of the Truth and Reconciliation Committee of post-apartheid South Africa (p. 227). Do you see any similarities in the ways that they approach their tasks? If so, what are they, and if not, what accounts for the differences?

3. How might Mohandas Gandhi (p. 332) evaluate Lameck's arguments about the need for Africans to develop and distribute wealth? Does Gandhi's experience with European colonialism appear to be similar to Lameck's? How so?

WRITING ABOUT THE TEXT

1. Examine the new definition of poverty that lies beneath Lameck's argument and, in a paragraph or two, explain how this definition is different from the usual one.

2. Write an essay in which you create your own definition of poverty and apply it to the economic situation that Lameck narrates in "Africans Are Not Poor." Be sure to discuss whether the definition should be comparative (i.e., define poverty as a standard of living below some other standard) or absolute (i.e., define poverty as the lack of certain things considered essential).

3. Examine the colonial experience that Lameck describes in relation to Lin Tse-hsü's experience in "A Letter to Queen Victoria" (p. 193). Are there similarities in the Chinese and African experiences with British imperialism and colonialism? Use research to support your arguments.

4. Use the Internet to locate a speech about poverty given in the U.S. Congress, the Canadian Parliament, or another Western government body. Compare the rhetorical style in this speech with that of Lucy Lameck in "Africans Are Not Poor." In what ways are the discussions of poverty similar? How might they be different?

Garrett Hardin
Lifeboat Ethics: The Case against Helping the Poor
(1974)

FOR THE LAST THREE DECADES of the twentieth century, Garrett Hardin (1915–2003), professor of human ecology at the University of California at Santa Barbara, was the most famous American representative of the neo-Malthusian school of thought. Using Thomas Malthus's basic formulation that population increases geometrically while resources increase arithmetically, Hardin insisted that it is ethically imperative for human beings to understand and respect the "carrying capacity" of the earth, and that failure to do so will invite human catastrophe on the largest scale.

In his famous 1968 essay, "The Tragedy of the Commons," Hardin uses a common grazing area, "the commons," as a metaphor for all nonproprietary resources. Because nobody owns a common pasture, everyone may use it for grazing cattle. When the population of cattle using the commons exceeds the commons' carrying capacity, it is in everybody's collective interest to decrease the number of cattle. However, since each individual has an interest in grazing as many cattle as possible on the commons, people will inevitably destroy the pasture by overgrazing it. The tragedy of the commons, then, is that what serves the best interests of everybody collectively usually does not serve the best interests of anybody specifically. Thus, individuals making hundreds of *rational* economic decisions about the use of a common resource will lead, inevitably, to the completely *irrational* destruction of that resource. The tragedy of the commons explains such phenomena as air and water pollution, overfishing, public parking problems, and, most of all, the overpopulation of the earth.

Hardin ended "The Tragedy of the Commons" by stating that "the only way we can preserve and nurture other and more precious freedoms is by relinquishing the freedom to breed." He believed that governments throughout the world should enact mandatory barriers and strong incentive programs to prevent population growth. In a follow-up essay, "Lifeboat Ethics: The Case against Helping the Poor," included here, Hardin argues that the wealthy societies of North America and Western Europe should refuse to subsidize population growth in less-developed countries by providing them with food and other necessities, and that comparatively wealthy nations should severely restrict immigration from poorer countries on the grounds that increased immigration makes local efforts at population control irrelevant to the carrying capacity of the land.

Though Hardin's solutions to the problem are harsh, so much so that they have never been enacted by Western governments, they are solidly rooted in the utilitarian ethic of providing the "greatest good for the greatest number of people." Like Malthus, Hardin believed that overpopulation was the primary cause of human misery in his lifetime and the greatest threat to Earth's future in the long term. Food banks, international aid programs, and unrestricted immigration do not solve this problem, he insisted; they merely allow the number of people who suffer from it to increase.

As the title of this essay implies, "Lifeboat Ethics" relies on a sustained analogy between the developed world and a lifeboat. Early in the essay, Hardin offers this analogy as a replacement for the more common analogy of "Spaceship Earth." Moral decisions aboard a lifeboat, he says, must be approached differently from moral decisions aboard a spaceship. The remainder of the essay explores the implications of this analogy as they apply to the world's scarce resources.

ENVIRONMENTALISTS USE THE METAPHOR of the earth as a "spaceship" in trying to persuade countries, industries and people to stop wasting and polluting our natural resources. Since we all share life on this planet, they argue, no single person or institution has the right to destroy, waste, or use more than a fair share of its resources.

But does everyone on earth have an equal right to an equal share of its resources? The spaceship metaphor can be dangerous when used by misguided idealists to justify suicidal policies for sharing our resources through uncontrolled immigration and foreign aid. In their enthusiastic but unrealistic generosity, they confuse the ethics of a spaceship with those of a lifeboat.

A true spaceship would have to be under the control of a captain, since no ship could possibly survive if its course were determined by committee. Spaceship Earth certainly has no captain; the United Nations is merely a toothless tiger, with little power to enforce any policy upon its bickering members.

If we divide the world crudely into rich nations and poor nations, two thirds of them are desperately poor, and only one third comparatively rich, with the United States the wealthiest of all. Metaphorically each rich nation can be seen as a lifeboat full of comparatively rich people. In the ocean outside each lifeboat swim the poor of the world, who would like to get in, or at least to share some of the wealth. What should the lifeboat passengers do?

First, we must recognize the limited capacity of any lifeboat. For example, a nation's   5
land has a limited capacity to support a population and as the current energy crisis has shown us, in some ways we have already exceeded the carrying capacity of our land.

Adrift in a Moral Sea

So here we sit, say 50 people in our lifeboat. To be generous, let us assume it has room for 10 more, making a total capacity of 60. Suppose the 50 of us in the lifeboat see 100 others swimming in the water outside, begging for admission to our boat or for handouts. We have several options: we may be tempted to try to live by the Christian ideal of being "our brother's keeper," or by the Marxist ideal of "to each according to his needs." Since the needs of all in the water are the same, and since they can all be seen as "our brothers," we could take them all into our boat, making a total of 150 in a boat designed for 60. The boat swamps, everyone drowns. Complete justice, complete catastrophe.

Since the boat has an unused excess capacity of 10 more passengers, we could admit just 10 more to it. But which 10 do we let in? How do we choose? Do we pick the best 10, "first come, first served"? And what do we say to the 90 we exclude? If we do let an extra 10 into our lifeboat, we will have lost our "safety factor," an engineering principle of critical importance. For example, if we don't leave room for excess capacity as a safety factor in our country's agriculture, a new plant disease or a bad change in the weather could have disastrous consequences.

Suppose we decide to preserve our small safety factor and admit no more to the lifeboat. Our survival is then possible although we shall have to be constantly on guard against boarding parties.

While this last solution clearly offers the only means of our survival, it is morally abhorrent to many people. Some say they feel guilty about their good luck. My reply is simple: "Get out and yield your place to others." This may solve the problem of the guilt-ridden person's conscience, but it does not change the ethics of the lifeboat. The needy person to whom the guilt-ridden person yields his place will not himself feel guilty about his good luck. If he did, he would not climb aboard. The net result of conscience-stricken people giving up their unjustly held seats is the elimination of that sort of conscience from the lifeboat.

This is the basic metaphor within which we must work out our solutions. Let us now enrich the image, step by step, with substantive additions from the real world, a world that must solve real and pressing problems of overpopulation and hunger. 10

The harsh ethics of the lifeboat become even harsher when we consider the reproductive differences between the rich nations and the poor nations. The people inside the lifeboats are doubling in numbers every 87 years; those swimming around outside are doubling, on the average, every 35 years, more than twice as fast as the rich. And since the world's resources are dwindling, the difference in prosperity between the rich and the poor can only increase.

As of 1973, the U.S. had a population of 210 million people, who were increasing by 0.8 percent per year. Outside our lifeboat, let us imagine another 210 million people (say the combined populations of Colombia, Ecuador, Venezuela, Morocco, Pakistan, Thailand and the Philippines) who are increasing at a rate of 3.3 percent per year. Put differently, the doubling time for this aggregate population is 21 years, compared to 87 years for the U.S.

The harsh ethics of the lifeboat become harsher when we consider the reproductive differences between rich and poor.

Multiplying the Rich and the Poor

Now suppose the U.S. agreed to pool its resources with those seven countries, with everyone receiving an equal share. Initially the ratio of Americans to non-Americans in this model would be one-to-one. But consider what the ratio would be after 87 years, by which time the Americans would have doubled to a population of 420 million. By then, doubling every 21 years, the other group would have swollen to 354 billion. Each American would have to share the available resources with more than eight people.

But, one could argue, this discussion assumes that current population trends will   15
continue, and they may not. Quite so. Most likely the rate of population increase will decline much faster in the U.S. than it will in the other countries, and there does not seem to be much we can do about it. In sharing with "each according to his needs," we must recognize that needs are determined by population size, which is determined by the rate of reproduction, which at present is regarded as a sovereign right of every nation, poor or not. This being so, the philanthropic load created by the sharing ethic of the spaceship can only increase.

The Tragedy of the Commons

The fundamental error of spaceship ethics, and the sharing it requires, is that it leads to what I call "the tragedy of the commons." Under a system of private property, the men who own property recognize their responsibility to care for it, for if they don't they will eventually suffer. A farmer, for instance, will allow no more cattle in a pasture than its carrying capacity justifies. If he overloads it, erosion sets in, weeds take over, and he loses the use of the pasture.

If a pasture becomes a commons open to all, the right of each to use it may not be matched by a corresponding responsibility to protect it. Asking everyone to use it with discretion will hardly do, for the considerate herdsman who refrains from overloading the commons suffers more than a selfish one who says his needs are greater. If everyone would restrain himself, all would be well; but it takes only one less than everyone to ruin a system of voluntary restraint. In a crowded world of less than perfect human beings, mutual ruin is inevitable if there are no controls. This is the tragedy of the commons.

One of the major tasks of education today should be the creation of such an acute awareness of the dangers of the commons that people will recognize its many varieties. For example, the air and water have become polluted because they are treated as commons. Further growth in the population or per-capita conversion of natural resources into pollutants will only make the problem worse. The same holds true for the fish of the oceans. Fishing fleets have nearly disappeared in many parts of the world, technological improvements in the art of fishing are hastening the day of complete ruin. Only the replacement of the system of the commons with a responsible system of control will save the land, air, water and oceanic fisheries.

The World Food Bank

In recent years there has been a push to create a new commons called a World Food Bank, an international depository of food reserves to which nations would contribute according to their abilities and from which they would draw according to their needs. This humanitarian proposal has received support from many liberal international groups, and from such prominent citizens as Margaret Mead,[1] U.N. Secretary General Kurt Waldheim, and Senators Edward Kennedy and George McGovern.

A world food bank appeals powerfully to our humanitarian impulses. But before we rush ahead with such a plan, let us recognize where the greatest political push comes from, lest we be disillusioned later. Our experience with the "Food for Peace program," or Public Law 480, gives us the answer. This program moved billions of dollars worth of U.S. surplus grain to food-short, population-long countries during the past two decades. But when P.L. 480 first became law, a headline in the business magazine *Forbes* revealed the real power behind it: "Feeding the World's Hungry Millions: How It Will Mean Billions for U.S. Business."

And indeed it did. In the years 1960 to 1970, U.S. taxpayers spent a total of $7.9 billion on the Food for Peace program. Between 1948 and 1970, they also paid an additional $50 billion for other economic-aid programs, some of which went for food and food-producing machinery and technology. Though all U.S. taxpayers were forced to contribute to the cost of P.L. 480 certain special interest groups gained handsomely under the program. Farmers did not have to contribute the grain; the Government or rather the taxpayers, bought it from them at full market prices. The increased demand raised prices of farm products generally. The manufacturers of farm machinery, fertilizers and pesticides benefited by the farmers' extra efforts to grow more food. Grain elevators profited from storing the surplus until it could be shipped. Railroads made money hauling it to ports, and shipping lines profited from carrying it overseas. The implementation of P.L. 480 required the creation of a vast Government bureaucracy, which then acquired its own vested interest in continuing the program regardless of its merits.

Extracting Dollars

Those who proposed and defended the Food for Peace program in public rarely mentioned its importance to any of these special interests. The public emphasis was always on its humanitarian effects. The combination of silent selfish interests and highly vocal humanitarian apologists made a powerful and successful lobby for extracting money from taxpayers. We can expect the same lobby to push now for the creation of a World Food Bank.

However great the potential benefit to selfish interests, it should not be a decisive argument against a truly humanitarian program. We must ask if such a program

1. See p. 274.

would actually do more good than harm, not only momentarily but also in the long run. Those who propose the food bank usually refer to a current "emergency" or "crisis" in terms of world food supply. But what is an emergency? Although they may be infrequent and sudden, everyone knows that emergencies will occur from time to time. A well-run family, company, organization or country prepares for the likelihood of accidents and emergencies. It expects them, it budgets for them, it saves for them.

Learning the Hard Way

What happens if some organizations or countries budget for accidents and others do not? If each country is solely responsible for its own well-being, poorly managed ones will suffer. But they can learn from experience. They may mend their ways, and learn to budget for infrequent but certain emergencies. For example, the weather varies from year to year, and periodic crop failures are certain. A wise and competent government saves out of the production of the good years in anticipation of bad years to come. Joseph taught this policy to Pharaoh in Egypt more than 2,000 years ago. Yet the great majority of the governments in the world today do not follow such a policy. They lack either the wisdom or the competence, or both. Should those nations that do manage to put something aside be forced to come to the rescue each time an emergency occurs among the poor nations?

"But it isn't their fault!" some kind-hearted liberals argue. "How can we blame the poor people who are caught in an emergency? Why must they suffer for the sins of their governments?" The concept of blame is simply not relevant here. The real question is, what are the operational consequences of establishing a world food bank? If it is open to every country every time a need develops, slovenly rulers will not be motivated to take Joseph's advice. Someone will always come to their aid. Some countries will deposit food in the world food bank, and others will withdraw it. There will be almost no overlap. As a result of such solutions to food shortage emergencies, the poor countries will not learn to mend their ways, and will suffer progressively greater emergencies as their populations grow.

Population Control the Crude Way

On the average poor countries undergo a 2.5 percent increase in population each year; rich countries, about 0.8 percent. Only rich countries have anything in the way of food reserves set aside, and even they do not have as much as they should. Poor countries have none. If poor countries received no food from the outside, the rate of their population growth would be periodically checked by crop failures and famines. But if they can always draw on a world food bank in time of need, their population can continue to grow unchecked, and so will their "need" for aid. In the short run, a world food bank may diminish that need, but in the long run it actually increases the need without limit.

Without some system of worldwide food sharing, the proportion of people in the rich and poor nations might eventually stabilize. The overpopulated poor countries would decrease in numbers, while the rich countries that had room for more people would increase. But with a well-meaning system of sharing, such as a world food bank, the growth differential between the rich and the poor countries will not only persist, it will increase. Because of the higher rate of population growth in the poor countries of the world, 88 percent of today's children are born poor, and only 12 percent rich. Year by year the ratio becomes worse, as the fast-reproducing poor outnumber the slow-reproducing rich.

A world food bank is thus a commons in disguise. People will have more motivation to draw from it than to add to any common store. The less provident and less able will multiply at the expense of the abler and more provident, bringing eventual ruin upon all who share in the commons. Besides, any system of "sharing" that amounts to foreign aid from the rich nations to the poor nations will carry the taint of charity, which will contribute little to the world peace so devoutly desired by those who support the idea of a world food bank.

As past U.S. foreign-aid programs have amply and depressingly demonstrated, international charity frequently inspires mistrust and antagonism rather than gratitude on the part of the recipient nation. . . .

Chinese Fish and Miracle Rice

The modern approach to foreign aid stresses the export of technology and advice, 30 rather than money and food. As an ancient Chinese proverb goes: "Give a man a fish and he will eat for a day; teach him how to fish and he will eat for the rest of his days." Acting on this advice, the Rockefeller and Ford Foundations have financed a number of programs for improving agriculture in the hungry nations. Known as the "Green Revolution," these programs have led to the development of "miracle rice" and "miracle wheat," new strains that offer bigger harvests and greater resistance to crop damage. Norman Borlaug, the Nobel Prize–winning agronomist who, supported by the Rockefeller Foundation, developed "miracle wheat," is one of the most prominent advocates of a world food bank.

Whether or not the Green Revolution can increase food production as much as its champions claim is a debatable but possibly irrelevant point. Those who support this well-intended humanitarian effort should first consider some of the fundamentals of human ecology. Ironically, one man who did was the late Alan Gregg, a vice president of the Rockefeller Foundation. Two decades ago he expressed strong doubts about the wisdom of such attempts to increase food production. He likened the growth and spread of humanity over the surface of the earth to the spread of cancer in the human body, remarking that "cancerous growths demand food; but, as far as I know, they have never been cured by getting it."

Overloading the Environment

Every human born constitutes a draft on all aspects of the environment: food, air, water, forests, beaches, wildlife, scenery and solitude. Food can, perhaps, be significantly increased to meet a growing demand. But what about clean beaches, unspoiled forests, and solitude? If we satisfy a growing population's need for food, we necessarily decrease its per capita supply of the other resources needed by men.

India, for example, now has a population of 600 million, which increases by 15 million each year. This population already puts a huge load on a relatively impoverished environment. The country's forests are now only a small fraction of what they were three centuries ago and floods and erosion continually destroy the insufficient farmland that remains. Every one of the 15 million new lives added to India's population puts an additional burden on the environment, and increases the economic and social costs of crowding. However humanitarian our intent, every Indian life saved through medical or nutritional assistance from abroad diminishes the quality of life for those who remain, and for subsequent generations. If rich countries make it possible, through foreign aid, for 600 million Indians to swell to 1.2 billion in a mere 28 years, as their current growth rate threatens, will future generations of Indians thank us for hastening the destruction of their environment? Will our good intentions be sufficient excuse for the consequences of our actions?

My final example of a commons in action is one for which the public has the least desire for rational discussion—immigration. Anyone who publicly questions the wisdom of current U.S. immigration policy is promptly charged with bigotry, prejudice, ethnocentrism, chauvinism, isolationism or selfishness. Rather than encounter such accusations, one would rather talk about other matters leaving immigration policy to wallow in the crosscurrents of special interests that take no account of the good of the whole, or the interests of posterity.

Perhaps we still feel guilty about things we said in the past. Two generations ago 35 the popular press frequently referred to Dagos, Wops, Polacks, Chinks and Krauts in articles about how America was being "overrun" by foreigners of supposedly inferior genetic stock. . . . But because the implied inferiority of foreigners was used then as justification for keeping them out, people now assume that restrictive policies could only be based on such misguided notions. There are other grounds.

A Nation of Immigrants

Just consider the numbers involved. Our Government acknowledges a net inflow of 400,000 immigrants a year. While we have no hard data on the extent of illegal entries, educated guesses put the figure at about 600,000 a year. Since the natural increase (excess of births over deaths) of the resident population now runs about 1.7 million per year, the yearly gain from immigration amounts to at least 19 percent of the total annual increase, and may be as much as 37 percent if we include the estimate for illegal immigrants. Considering the growing use of birth-control devices, the potential effect of education campaigns by such organizations as Planned Parenthood Federation of America and Zero Population Growth, and the influence of inflation and the housing shortage, the fertility rate of American women may decline so much that immigration could account for all the yearly increase in population. Should we not at least ask if that is what we want?

For the sake of those who worry about whether the "quality" of the average immigrant compares favorably with the quality of the average resident, let us assume that immigrants and native-born citizens are of exactly equal quality, however one defines that term. We will focus here only on quantity; and since our conclusions will depend on nothing else, all charges of bigotry and chauvinism become irrelevant.

Immigration vs. Food Supply

World food banks move food to the people, hastening the exhaustion of the environment of the poor countries. Unrestricted immigration, on the other hand, moves people to the food, thus speeding up the destruction of the environment of the rich countries. We can easily understand why poor people should want to make this latter transfer, but why should rich hosts encourage it?

As in the case of foreign-aid programs, immigration receives support from selfish interests and humanitarian impulses. The primary selfish interest in unimpeded immigration is the desire of employers for cheap labor, particularly in industries and trades that offer degrading work. In the past, one wave of foreigners after another was brought into the U.S. to work at wretched jobs for wretched wages. In recent years the Cubans, Puerto Ricans and Mexicans have had this dubious honor. The interests of the employers of cheap labor mesh well with the guilty silence of the country's liberal intelligentsia. White Anglo-Saxon Protestants are particularly reluctant to call for a closing of the doors to immigration for fear of being called bigots.

But not all countries have such reluctant leadership. Most educated Hawaiians, 40 for example, are keenly aware of the limits of their environment, particularly in terms of population growth. There is only so much room on the islands, and the islanders know it. To Hawaiians, immigrants from the other 49 states present as great a threat as those from other nations. At a recent meeting of Hawaiian government officials in Honolulu, I had the ironic delight of hearing a speaker, who like most of his audience was of Japanese ancestry, ask how the country might practically and constitutionally close its doors to further immigration. One member of the audience countered: "How can we shut the doors now? We have many friends and relatives in Japan that we'd like to bring here some day so that they can enjoy Hawaii too." The Japanese-American speaker smiled sympathetically and answered: "Yes, but we have children now, and someday we'll have grandchildren too. We can bring more people here from Japan only by giving away some of the land that we hope to pass on to our grandchildren some day. What right do we have to do that?"

At this point, I can hear U.S. liberals asking: "How can you justify slamming the door once you're inside? You say that immigrants should be kept out. But aren't we all immigrants, or the descendants of immigrants? If we insist on staying, must we not admit all others?" Our craving for intellectual order leads us to seek and prefer symmetrical rules and morals: a single rule for me and everybody else; the same rule yesterday, today and tomorrow. Justice, we feel, should not change with time and place.

We Americans of non-Indian ancestry can look upon ourselves as the descendants of thieves who are guilty morally, if not legally, of stealing this land from its Indian owners. Should we then give back the land to the now living American descendants of those Indians? However morally or logically sound this proposal may be, I, for one, am unwilling to live by it and I know no one else who is. Besides, the logical consequence would be absurd. Suppose that, intoxicated with a sense of pure justice, we should decide to turn our land over to the Indians. Since all our other wealth has also been derived from the land, wouldn't we be morally obliged to give that back to the Indians too?

Pure Justice vs. Reality

Clearly, the concept of pure justice produces an infinite regression to absurdity. Centuries ago, wise men invented statutes of limitations to justify the rejection of such pure justice, in the interest of preventing continual disorder. The law zealously defends property rights, but only relatively recent property rights. Drawing a line after an arbitrary time has elapsed may be unjust, but the alternatives are worse.

We are all the descendants of thieves, and the world's resources are inequitably distributed. But we must begin the journey to tomorrow from the point where we are today. We cannot remake the past. We cannot safely divide the wealth equitably among all peoples so long as people reproduce at different rates. To do so would guarantee that our grandchildren and everyone else's grandchildren would have only a ruined world to inhabit.

To be generous with one's own possessions is quite different from being generous 45 with those of posterity. We should call this point to the attention of those who, from a commendable love of justice and equality, would institute a system of the commons, either in the form of a world food bank, or of unrestricted immigration. We must convince them if we wish to save at least some parts of the world from environmental ruin.

Without a true world government to control reproduction and the use of available resources, the sharing ethic of the spaceship is impossible. For the foreseeable future, our survival demands that we govern our actions by the ethics of a lifeboat, harsh though they may be. Posterity will be satisfied with nothing less.

UNDERSTANDING THE TEXT

1. Why does Garrett Hardin use the lifeboat as his principal metaphor for the earth? How do "lifeboat ethics" differ from "spaceship ethics"? Does limited carrying capacity really make the earth comparable to a lifeboat? What might the global equivalent of a capsized lifeboat be?

2. Why does Hardin reject both the Christian and the Marxist formulations for helping the poor? (See the selection from the New Testament, p. 315). Is his argument entirely contrary to Christian principles?

3. How does Hardin's concept of "the tragedy of the commons" inform this essay? What kinds of "common resources" are compromised by population increases? In what way is the proposed World Food Bank a "commons"?

4. Why does Hardin believe that increasing food production by genetically altering plants and animals is not a good idea? What does he believe will be the result of increasing the world's food supply to support the current population at a subsistence level?

5. What resources other than food does Hardin believe people should consider when making decisions about population and immigration? Which of the things he lists are necessities and which are luxuries?

6. Why does Hardin believe that previous injustices—such as the European conquest of the Americas—are of no practical importance today? Do you agree?

7. What does Hardin see as the difference between absolute justice and the practical necessities of the real world? Does he see "pure justice" as desirable? What assumptions about morality and immorality does Hardin use as the basis for his ethical argument?

MAKING CONNECTIONS

1. How accurately does Hardin represent Malthus's arguments about population growth and human poverty (p. 324)?

2. How well does Hardin counter the arguments of Jesus (p. 315) and Gandhi (p. 332) about the need to help the poor? How do his arguments compare with those of his fellow utilitarian Mo Tzu (p. 308)?

3. To what extent is Hardin's argument a form of social Darwinism (see the excerpt from "Natural Selection," p. 405)? How would an environment governed by natural selection respond to unchecked population growth within a community?

WRITING ABOUT THE TEXT

1. Write an essay entitled "The Case for Helping the Poor" in which you rebut Hardin. As possible starting points for your essay, consider the positions of Jesus (p. 315) Gandhi (p. 332), and Muhammad Yunus (p. 369).

2. Respond positively or negatively to Hardin's view of immigration. Perhaps take the perspective of an immigrant hoping to enter a wealthy country or of a citizen opposed to that immigrant's entrance.

3. Opponents of population control often argue that the overwhelming catastrophe that Malthus predicted in 1798 and that Hardin predicted in 1974 has not occurred, despite populations having grown at about the expected rates. Write an essay in which you consider whether the facts invalidate Malthusian theory.

4. Using as much demographic data as possible, determine whether world overpopulation is a serious problem. If not, give evidence and support that it is not; if so, propose a solution.

Muhammad Yunus
The Stool Makers of Jobra Village
(1999)

MUHAMMAD YUNUS WAS BORN in British India, in the Bengali district of Chittagong, in 1940. As a boy, he witnessed the end of British rule in 1947, which resulted in the partition of the former British colony into the nations of India and Pakistan. Yunus's home province of East Bengal elected to join the Muslim nation of Pakistan, even though it was separated from the rest of Pakistan by more than 1,000 miles of territory belonging to India. Though East Bengal was plagued by chronic poverty, Yunus's father, a jeweler with nine children, earned enough money to provide a good education for his children. In 1957, Yunus entered the University of Dhaka in Dhaka, Bangladesh, where he earned both a bachelor's and a master's degree in economics.

In 1965, Yunus won a Fulbright scholarship to study in the United States. He earned a Ph.D. in economics from Vanderbilt University in 1971 and accepted a professorship at Middle Tennessee State University. But Yunus's academic career in the United States was cut short by events in his home country. In March 1971, East Bengal declared its independence from Pakistan, igniting civil war. Yunus immediately began coordinating the efforts of other Bengalis living in the United States to support the independence movement. India entered the war on the side of the Bengalis, and in December 1971, the Pakistani army officially surrendered. The nation of Bangladesh was born. Feeling that it was his patriotic duty to return to his new country, Yunus resigned his position at Middle Tennessee State and accepted a position as the head of the economics faculty at Chittagong University in the nation of Bangladesh.

In 1972, Bangladesh was one of the poorest countries in the world. The war for independence had devastated its infrastructure and left millions of people unable to support themselves. Harsh weather conditions and a famine in 1974 further devastated the population. On his frequent visits to a small village near his university, Yunus observed that most of the people he encountered had the skills necessary to lift themselves out of poverty by making useful items that could be sold at a local market. What they lacked was the capital necessary to purchase supplies, which meant that they had to deal with exploitive moneylenders or middlemen. Yunus believed that many of these people could escape poverty if they had access to credit in the amount of just a few U.S. dollars apiece.

This insight gave birth to the revolutionary concept of microcredit. Yunus theorized that small loans given directly to the poor could play a major role in eliminating poverty. To test this theory, he set up the Grameen Bank in 1976 as a research project. Grameen made small loans (usually about four or five U.S. dollars) to poor Bangladeshis at an interest rate of 20 percent. Loans were paid back with extremely small daily payments, and all borrowers were required to work in groups to support each other in repaying the loan. In the thirty years since its inception, the Grameen Bank has expanded to many times its original size. It is now owned almost entirely by its borrowers, 97 percent of whom are women, and has loaned out more than six billion U.S. dollars with more than 98 percent of loans paid back in full. In 2006, Muhammad Yunus and the Grameen Bank shared the Nobel Peace Prize for their work in combating poverty in the developing world.

Yunus makes his case by way of a simple, direct narrative about his experiences in a small Bangladeshi village. Throughout the narrative, he appeals to the reader's emotions, relying on us to feel both compassion for the poor workers who are trapped in a cycle of poverty and outrage at the banking system for being unwilling to take the simple steps necessary to address the problem. ◖

In 1976, I began visiting the poorest households in Jobra to see if I could help them directly in any way. There were three parts to the village: a Muslim, a Hindu, and a Buddhist section. When I visited the Buddhist section, I would often take one of my students, Dipal Chandra Barua, a native of the Buddhist section, along with me. Otherwise, a colleague, Professor H. I. Latifee, would usually accompany me. He knew most of the families and had a natural talent for making villagers feel at ease.

One day as Latifee and I were making our rounds in Jobra, we stopped at a run-down house with crumbling mud walls and a low thatched roof pocked with holes. We made our way through a crowd of scavenging chickens and beds of vegetables to the front of the house. A woman squatted on the dirt floor of the verandah, a half-finished bamboo stool gripped between her knees. Her fingers moved quickly, plaiting the stubborn strands of cane. She was totally absorbed in her work.

On hearing Latifee's call of greeting, she dropped her bamboo, sprang to her feet, and scurried into the house.

"Don't be frightened," Latifee called out. "We are not strangers. We teach up at the university. We are neighbors. We want to ask you a few questions, that is all."

Reassured by Latifee's gentle manner, she answered in a low voice, "There is   5 nobody home."

She meant there was no male at home. In Bangladesh, women are not supposed to talk to men who are not close relatives.

Children were running around naked in the yard. Neighbors peered out at us from their windows, wondering what we were doing.

In the Muslim sections of Jobra, we often had to talk to women through bamboo walls or curtains. The custom of *purdah* (literally, "curtain" or "veil") kept married

Muslim women in a state of virtual seclusion from the outside world. It was strictly observed in Chittagong District.

As I am a native Chittagonian and speak the local dialect, I would try to gain the confidence of Muslim women by chatting. Complimenting a mother on her baby was a natural way to put her at ease. I now picked up one of the naked children beside me, but he started to cry and rushed over to his mother. She let him climb into her arms.

"How many children do you have?" Latifee asked her.   10

"Three."

"He is very beautiful, this one," I said.

Slightly reassured, the mother came to the doorway, holding her baby. She was in her early twenties, thin, with dark skin and black eyes. She wore a red sari and had the tired eyes of a woman who labored every day from morning to night.

"What is your name?" I asked.

"Sufiya Begum."   15

"How old are you?"

"Twenty-one."

I did not use a pen and notepad, for that would have scared her off. Later, I only allowed my students to take notes on return visits.

"Do you own this bamboo?" I asked.

"Yes."   20

"How do you get it?"

"I buy it."

"How much does the bamboo cost you?"

"Five taka." At the time, this was about twenty-two cents.

"Do you have five taka?"   25

"No, I borrow it from the *paikars.*"

"The middlemen? What is your arrangement with them?"

"I must sell my bamboo stools back to them at the end of the day as repayment for my loan."

"How much do you sell a stool for?"   30

"Five taka and fifty poysha."

"So you make fifty poysha profit?"

She nodded. That came to a profit of just two cents.

"And could you borrow the cash from the moneylender and buy your own raw material?"

"Yes, but the moneylender would demand a lot. People who deal with them only get poorer."

"How much does the moneylender charge?"   35

"It depends. Sometimes he charges 10 percent per week. But I have one neighbor who is paying 10 percent per day."

"And that is all you earn from making these beautiful bamboo stools, fifty poysha?"
"Yes."

Sufiya did not want to waste any more time talking. I watched as she set to work again, her small brown hands plaiting the strands of bamboo as they had every day for months and years on end. This was her livelihood. She squatted barefoot on the hard mud. Her fingers were callused, her nails black with grime.

How would her children break the cycle of poverty she had started? How could they go to school when the income Sufiya earned was barely enough to feed her, let alone shelter her family and clothe them properly? It seemed hopeless to imagine that her babies would one day escape this misery.

Sufiya Begum earned two cents a day. It was this knowledge that shocked me. In my university courses, I theorized about sums in the millions of dollars, but here before my eyes the problems of life and death were posed in terms of pennies. Something was wrong. Why did my university courses not reflect the reality of Sufiya's life? I was angry, angry at myself, angry at my economics department and the thousands of intelligent professors who had not tried to address this problem and solve it. It seemed to me the existing economic system made it absolutely certain that Sufiya's income would be kept perpetually at such a low level that she would never save a penny and would never invest in expanding her economic base. Her children were condemned to live a life of penury, of hand-to-mouth survival, just as she had lived it before them, and as her parents did before her. I had never heard of anyone suffering for the lack of *twenty-two cents*. It seemed impossible to me, preposterous. Should I reach into my pocket and hand Sufiya the pittance she needed for capital? That would be so simple, so easy. I resisted the urge to give Sufiya the money she needed. She was not asking for charity. And giving one person twenty-two cents was not addressing the problem on any permanent basis.

Latifee and I drove back up the hill to my house. We took a stroll around my garden in the late-afternoon heat. I was trying to see Sufiya's problem from her point of view. She suffered because the cost of the bamboo was five taka. She did not have the cash necessary to buy her raw materials. As a result, she could survive only in a tight cycle—borrowing from the trader and selling back to him. Her life was a form of bonded labor, or slavery. The trader made certain that he paid Sufiya a price that barely covered the cost of the materials and was just enough to keep her alive. She could not break free of her exploitative relationship with him. To survive, she needed to keep working through the trader.

Usurious rates have become so standardized and socially acceptable in Third World countries that the borrower rarely realizes how oppressive a contract is. Exploitation comes in many guises. In rural Bangladesh, one *mound* (approximately 37 kilograms) of husked rice borrowed at the beginning of the planting season has to be repaid with two *maunds* at harvest time. When land is used as security, it is placed at the disposal of the creditor, who enjoys ownership rights over it until the total amount is repaid. In many cases, a formal document such as a *bawnanama* establishes the right of the creditor. According to the *bawnanama*, the creditor usually refuses to accept any partial payment of the loan. After the expiration of a certain period, it also allows the creditor to "buy" the land at a predetermined "price." Another form of security is the *dadan* system, in which traders advance loans against standing crops for purchase of the crops at predetermined prices that are below the market rate. Sufiya Begum was producing her bamboo stools under a *dadan* arrangement with a *paikar*.

In Bangladesh, the borrowing is sometimes made for specific and temporary purposes (to marry off a daughter, to bribe an official, to fight a court case), but sometimes it is necessary for physical survival—to purchase food or medication or to meet some emergency situation. In such cases, it is extremely difficult for the borrower to extricate himself or herself from the burden of the loan. Usually the borrower will have to borrow again just to repay the prior loan and will ultimately wind up in a cycle of poverty like Sufiya. It seemed to me that Sufiya's status as a bonded slave would only change if she could find that five taka for her bamboo. Credit could bring her that money. She could then sell her products in a free market and charge the full retail price to the consumer. She just needed twenty-two cents.

The next day I called in Maimuna Begum, a university student who collected 45 data for me, and asked her to help me make a list of people in Jobra, like Sufiya, who were dependent on traders. Within one week, we had a list prepared. It named forty-two people, who borrowed a total of 856 taka—less than 27 dollars.

"My God, my God. All this misery in all these families all for of the lack of twenty-seven dollars!" I exclaimed.

Maimuna stood there without saying a word. We were both sickened by the reality of it all.

My mind would not let this problem lie. I wanted to help these forty-two able-bodied, hard-working people. I kept going around and around the problem, like a dog worrying a bone. People like Sufiya were poor not because they were stupid or lazy. They worked all day long, doing complex physical tasks. They were poor because the financial institutions in the country did not help them widen their economic base. No formal financial structure was available to cater to the credit needs of the poor. This credit market, by default of the formal institutions, had been taken over by the local moneylenders. It was an efficient vehicle; it created a heavy rush of one-way traffic on the road to poverty. But if I could just lend the Jobra villagers the twenty-seven dollars, they could sell their products to anyone. They would then get the highest possible return for their labor and would not be limited by the usurious practices of the traders and moneylenders.

It was all so easy. I handed Maimuna the twenty-seven dollars and told her, "Here, lend this money to the forty-two villagers on our list. They can repay the traders what they owe them and sell their products at a good price."

"When should they repay you?" she asked. 50

"Whenever they can," I said. "Whenever it is advantageous for them to sell their products. They don't have to pay any interest. I am not in the money business."

Maimuna left, puzzled by this turn of events.

Usually when my head touches the pillow, I fall asleep within seconds, but that night sleep would not come. I lay in bed feeling ashamed that I was part of a society that could not provide twenty-seven dollars to forty-two skilled persons to make a living for themselves. It struck me that what I had done was drastically insufficient. If others needed capital, they could hardly chase down the head of an economics department. My response had been ad hoc and emotional. Now I needed to create an institutional answer that these people could rely on. What was required was an institution that would lend to those who had nothing. I decided to approach the local bank manager and request that his bank lend money to the poor. It seemed so simple, so straightforward. I fell asleep.

The next morning I climbed into my white Volkswagen beetle and drove to my local branch of the Janata Bank, a government bank and one of the largest in the country. Janata's university branch is located just beyond the gates of the campus on a stretch of road lined with tiny stores, stalls, and restaurants where local villagers sell students everything from betel nuts to warm meals, notebooks, and pens. It is here that the rickshaw drivers congregate when they are not ferrying students from their dormitories to their classrooms. The bank itself is housed in a single square room. Its two front windows are covered with bars and the walls are painted a dingy dark green. The room is filled with wooden tables and chairs. The manager, sitting in the back to the left, waved me over.

"What can I do for you, sir?" 55

The office boy brought us tea and cookies. I explained why I had come. "The last time I borrowed from you was to finance the Three Share Program in Jobra village.[1] Now I have a new proposal. I want you to lend money to the poor people in Jobra. The amount involved is very small. I have already done it myself. I have lent twenty-seven dollars to forty-two people. There will be many more poor people who will need money. They need this money to carry on their work, to buy raw materials and supplies."

"What kind of materials?" The bank officer looked puzzled, as if this were some sort of new game whose rules he was not familiar with. He let me speak out of common respect for a university head, but he was clearly confused.

"Well, some make bamboo stools. Others weave mats or drive rickshaws. If they borrow money from a bank at commercial rates, they will be able to sell their products on the open market and make a decent profit that would allow them to

---

1. **Three Share Farm:** a cooperative farming venture that Yunus led in Jobra Village in the winter of 1975.

live better lives. As it is now, they work as slaves and will never manage to get themselves out from under the heel of the wholesalers who lend them capital at usurious rates."

"Yes, I know about *mahajons* [moneylenders]," the manager replied.

"So I have come here today because I would like to ask you to lend money to these villagers." 60

The bank manager's jaw fell open, and he started to laugh. "I can't do that!"

"Why not?" I asked.

"Well," he sputtered, not knowing where to begin with his list of objections. "For one thing, the small amounts you say these villagers need to borrow will not even cover the cost of all the loan documents they would have to fill out. The bank is not going to waste its time on such a pittance."

"Why not?" I said. "To the poor this money is crucial for survival."

"These people are illiterate," he replied. "They cannot even fill out our loan forms." 65

"In Bangladesh, where 75 percent of the people do not read and write, filling out a form is a ridiculous requirement."

"Every single bank in the country has that rule."

"Well, that says something about our banks then, doesn't it?"

"Even when a person brings money and wants to put it in the bank, we ask him or her to write down how much she or he is putting in."

"Why?" 70

"What do you mean, 'Why?'"

"Well, why can't a bank just take money and issue a receipt saying, 'Received such and such amount of money from such and such a person?' Why can't the banker do it? Why must the depositors do it?"

"Well, how would you run a bank without people reading and writing?"

"Simple, the bank just issues a receipt for the amount of cash that the bank receives."

"What if the person wants to withdraw money?" 75

"I don't know . . . there must be a simple way. The borrower comes back with his or her deposit receipt, presents it to the cashier, and the cashier gives back the money. Whatever accounting the bank does is the bank's business."

The manager shook his head but did not answer this, as if he did not know where to begin.

"It seems to me your banking system is designed to be anti-illiterate," I countered.

Now the branch manager seemed irritated. "Professor, banking is not as simple as you think," he said.

"Maybe so, but I am also sure that banking is not as complicated as you make it out to be." 80

"Look, the simple truth is that a borrower at any other bank in any place in the world would have to fill out forms."

"Okay," I said, bowing to the obvious. "If I can get some of my student volunteers to fill out the form for the villagers, that should not be a problem."

"But you don't understand, we simply cannot lend to the destitute," said the branch manager.

"Why not?" I was trying to be polite. Our conversation had something surreal about it. The branch manager had a smile on his face as if to say he understood that I was pulling his leg. This whole interview was humorous, absurd really.

"They don't have any collateral," said the branch manager, expecting that this would put an end to our discussion.

"Why do you need collateral as long as you get the money back? That is what you really want, isn't it?"

"Yes, we want our money back," explained the manager. "But at the same time we need collateral. That is our guarantee."

"To me, it doesn't make sense. The poorest of the poor work twelve hours a day. They need to sell and earn income to eat. They have every reason to pay you back, just to take another loan and live another day! That is the best security you can have—their life."

The manager shook his head. "You are an idealist, Professor. You live with books and theories."

"But if you are certain that the money will be repaid, why do you need collateral?"

"That is our bank rule."

"So only those who have collateral can borrow?"

"Yes."

"It's a silly rule. It means only the rich can borrow."

"I don't make the rules, the bank does."

"Well, I think the rules should be changed."

"Anyway, we do not lend out money here."

"You don't?"

"No, we only take deposits from the faculty members and from the university."

"But don't banks make money by extending loans?"

"Only the head office makes loans. We are here to collect deposits from the university and its employees. Our loan to your Three Share Farm was an exception approved by our head office."

"You mean to say that if I came here and asked to borrow money, you would not lend it to me?"

"That is right." He laughed. It was evident the manager had not had such an entertaining afternoon in a long time.

"So when we teach in our classes that banks make loans to borrowers, that is a lie?"

"Well, you would have to go through the head office for a loan, and I don't know what they would do."

"Sounds like I need to talk to officials higher up."

"Yes, that would be a good idea."

As I finished my tea and got ready to leave, the branch manager said, "I know you'll not give up. But from what I know about banking, I can tell you for sure that this plan of yours will never take off."

A couple of days later, I arranged a meeting with Mr. R. A. Howladar, the regional manager of the Janata Bank, in his office in Chittagong. We had very much a repeat of the conversation I had with the Jobra bank manager, but Howladar did bring up the idea of a guarantor, a well-to-do person in the village who would be willing to act on behalf of the borrower. With the backing of a guarantor, the bank might consider granting a loan without collateral.

I considered the idea. It had obvious merit, but the drawbacks seemed insur- *110* mountable.

"I can't do that," I explained to Howladar. "What would prevent the guarantor from taking advantage of the person whose loan he was guaranteeing? He could end up a tyrant. He could end up treating that borrower as a slave."

There was a silence. It had become clear from my discussions with bankers in the past few days that I was not up against the Janata Bank per se but against the banking system in general.

"Why don't I become guarantor?" I asked.

"You?"

"Yes, you can accept me as guarantor for all the loans?" *115*

The regional manager smiled. "How much money are you talking about?"

To give myself a margin of error and room to expand, I answered, "Altogether probably 10,000 taka ($300), not more than that."

"Well," he fingered the papers on his desk. Behind him I could see a dusty stack of folders in old bindings. Lining the walls were piles of similar pale blue binders, rising in teetering stacks to the windows. The overhead fan created a breeze that played with the files. On his desk, the papers were in a state of permanent fluttering, awaiting his decision.

"Well," he said. "I would say we would be willing to accept you as guarantor up to that amount, but don't ask for more money."

"It's a deal." *120*

We shook hands. Then something occurred to me. "But if one of the borrowers does not repay, I will not step in to honor the defaulted loan."

The regional manager looked up at me uneasily, not certain why I was being so difficult.

"As guarantor, we could force you to pay."

"What would you do?"

"We could start legal proceedings against you." *125*

"Fine. I would like that."

He looked at me as if I were crazy. That was just what I wanted. I felt angry. I wanted to cause some panic in this unjust, archaic system. I wanted to be the stick in the wheels that would finally stop this infernal machine. I was a guarantor, maybe, but I would not guarantee.

"Professor Yunus, you know very well we would never sue a department head who has personally guaranteed the loan of a beggar. The bad publicity alone would off-set any money we might recover from you. Anyway, the loan is such a pittance it would not even pay for the legal fees, much less our administrative costs of recovering the money."

"Well, you are a bank, you must do your own cost-benefit analysis. But I will not pay if there is any default."

"You are making things difficult for me, Professor Yunus."   130

"I am sorry, but the bank is making things difficult for a lot of people—especially those who have nothing."

"I am trying to help, Professor."

"I understand. It is not you but banking rules I have a quarrel with."

After more such back and forth, Howladar concluded, "I will recommend your loan to the head office in Dhaka, and we will see what they say."

"But I thought you as regional officer had the authority to conclude this matter?"   135

"Yes, but this is far too unorthodox for me to approve. Authorization will have to come from the top."

It took six months of writing back and forth to get the loan formalized. Finally, in December 1976, I succeeded in taking out a loan from the Janata Bank and giving it to the poor of Jobra. All through 1977, I had to sign each and every loan request. Even when I was on a trip in Europe or the United States, the bank would cable or write to me for a signature rather than deal with any of the real borrowers in the village. I was the guarantor and as far as the bank officials were concerned I was the only one that counted. They did not want to deal with the poor who used their capital. And I made sure that the real borrowers, the ones I call the "banking untouchables," never had to suffer the indignity and demeaning harassment of actually going to a bank.

That was the beginning of it all. I never intended to become a moneylender. I had no intention of lending money to anyone. All I really wanted was to solve an immediate problem. Out of sheer frustration, I had questioned the most basic banking premise of collateral. I did not know if I was right. I had no idea what I was getting myself into. I was walking blind and learning as I went along. My work became a struggle to show that the financial untouchables are actually touchable, even huggable. To my great surprise, the repayment of loans by people who borrow without collateral has proven to be much better than those whose borrowings are secured by assets. Indeed, more than 98 percent of our loans are repaid. The poor know that this credit is their only opportunity to break out of poverty. They do not have any cushion whatsoever to fall back on. If they fall afoul of this one loan, they will have lost their one and only chance to get out of the rut.

UNDERSTANDING THE TEXT

1. What steps did Muhammad Yunus take to earn the trust of the villagers in Jobra? Why were these steps necessary?

2. What key conclusions did Yunus draw about the laborers that he met in Jobra? What was the primary reason that these people could not make a profit from their labor?

3. Why does Yunus resist the urge to give Sufiya Begum the small amount of money (twenty-two cents) she needs to purchase bamboo?

4. Why does Yunus try so hard to persuade local banks to loan money to the "poorest of the poor" in Jobra? Why does he eventually start a bank himself rather than seek charitable donations to ease the suffering of these people?

5. Why does Yunis agree to become a guarantor for loans to the villagers but, at the same time, refuse to pay back any loan that is defaulted on?

MAKING CONNECTIONS

1. Compare Yunus's view of poverty with that of Mohandas Gandhi in "Economic and Moral Progress" (p. 332). Does Yunus share Gandhi's view that Western-style capitalism is spiritually destructive? How do you know?

2. Do Yunus's experiences with the productive capabilities of the villagers confirm Lucy Lameck's view of poverty in developing countries in "Africans Are Not Poor" (p. 352)? Why or why not?

3. How does the poverty that Yunus describes compare with the poverty that William Hogarth depicts in *Gin Lane* (p. 320)?

4. Compare the interaction between Eastern and Western values in "The Stool Makes of Jobra Village" with that found in Aung San Suu Kyi's "In Quest of Democracy" (p. 219). How do Yunus's and Kyi's backgrounds affect their interactions with their native cultures?

WRITING ABOUT THE TEXT

1. In your own words, explain the problem that Yunus encounters in Jobra Village and the theory that he constructs to solve that problem. Pay special attention to the underlying assumptions of the banking system that he confronts.

2. Contrast Yunus's response to poverty with the one Octavio Paz describes in "The Day of the Dead" (p. 345). How are the experiences of the poor villages in these two readings shaped by the Bengali and Mexican cultures?

3. One of the basic philosophies of the Grameen Bank is that people should have access to credit so that they can make a living with the skills that they

already have. Other charities or government institutions have different anti-poverty philosophies, such as that people should be educated and trained for specific careers or that they should be given money or goods to alleviate their immediate needs. Research several anti-poverty initiatives, whether government or private sector, locate the philosophies at their core, and compare them, using your own criteria to determine their worth and effectiveness. Remember to document your sources.

6

SCIENCE AND NATURE

HOW CAN WE BEST UNDERSTAND THE NATURAL WORLD?

God does not play dice.
—*Albert Einstein*

DURING THE 1920s, the physicists Albert Einstein and Neils Bohr carried on a series of debates regarding the relatively new field of quantum mechanics. According to Bohr's theories, certain facts about the universe cannot be known at the same time. Even with the most advanced instruments, a certain amount of probability, rather than certainty, in our understanding of atomic and subatomic particles is inevitable. Einstein believed that a unifying set of laws must be governing all physical systems, from galaxies to atoms. He accepted that we do not know some things about the universe, but he could not accept that anything is inherently unknowable. Most scientists now agree that Bohr successfully defended quantum mechanics against Einstein's objections, and this model of particles' behavior—with all of its uncertainty, probability, and "fuzziness"—has gone on to be one of the most successful theories (in terms of experimental verification and ability to predict events) in the history of science.

Like many scientific arguments, the Bohr-Einstein debates were less about nature than about the frameworks that should be used to understand nature. Einstein's most famous statement during the debates, "God does not play dice," proceeded from a deeply held philosophical belief in the existence of fundamental physical laws beneath the apparent uncertainty of quantum theory. Bohr's purported response to Einstein, "Stop telling God what to do with his dice," proceeded from an equally deep commitment to the scientific principles of observation, experimentation, and hypothesis testing—all of which, as he saw it, confirmed the inherent uncertainty of some quantum operations.

The kind of science to which Bohr and Einstein devoted their lives—a science that draws conclusions based on observation and analysis—is a fairly recent invention. Until the sixteenth century in Europe, and much later in other places, science was considered a branch of philosophy. The first two readings in this chapter come from medieval philosophers who worked in the natural philosophy tradition. In the first of these, the Islamic thinker Averroës defends scientific and philosophical inquiry from those who would limit the study of the natural world to whatever can be learned from the scriptures. Revealed truth and philosophical reflection were, for Averroës, two different paths to the same eternal truths. The Jewish thinker Moses Maimonides took this argument a step further. Maimonides argued that a philosophical approach to the natural world could illuminate evidence of God's design that did not appear in the scriptures.

The European Enlightenment brought new tools for understanding the natural world, as the authority of both scripture and the ancient philosophers was supplanted by the scientific method. Two of the readings in this chapter exemplify how this scientific method changed history. The first, drawn from the fourth chapter of Charles Darwin's *Origin of Species*, offers a compelling hypothesis, supported by large amounts of experimental and observational evidence, that changed the way that humans see themselves and their place in the world. The second, drawn from Rachel Carson's *Silent Spring*—a foundational text of the modern environmental movement—is a scientific argument that initiated a popular groundswell and changed public policy. Two later readings amplify both the method that Darwin employs and the environmental concerns that Carson brings to the surface. "The Sacred Balance," by Canadian scientist David Suzuki, advances Carson's argument about pesticides into the ecosystem and argues that human beings have become intellectually detached from their environments in a way that threatens their ability to live full and purposeful lives. Al Gore's "The Climate Emergency" (the basis of the film *An Inconvenient Truth*) marshals evidence for the claim that, in at least one instance—the climate change caused by the proliferation of carbon dioxide in the atmosphere—our detachment from the environment may have catastrophic consequences for all life on earth.

A final reading here is from *The Quantum and the Lotus*, a relatively recent book about the intersections between Buddhism and quantum physics. The selection consists of a dialogue between Matthieu Ricard, a respected biologist who became a Buddhist monk in the foothills of the Himalayas, and Trinh Xuan Thuan, a Vietnamese Buddhist who became a respected astrophysicist at the University of Virginia. The dialogue between these two figures centers on the Buddhist notion of "interdependence"—a belief that has strong connections to the world of quantum mechanics advocated by Bohr and questioned by Einstein.

The themes of these readings are reinforced by four visual texts. The first, which is also the first selection in the chapter, is a representation of the universe as conceived by the ancient Greek scientist Ptolemy. The earth stood at the center of Ptolemy's universe, surrounded by more than a dozen concentric circles containing the planets and all of the stars—all of which rotated around the earth. This image is followed by a map of the world created by the eighth-century Spanish monk Beatus of Liébana, who built his image of the world around the tenets of medieval Christianity. The final image in the chapter gives a very different picture of the universe. This image, a photograph taken by the Hubble Space Telescope of a distant galaxy cluster called Abell 1689, contains perhaps a million million different stars, including the most distant (and therefore the oldest) object ever observed from Earth. In the middle of the chapter, a painting by Joseph Wright of Derby, painted during the Enlightenment, dramatizes the both the fear and wonder that accompanied the shift from the view of the natural world represented by Ptolemy and the view represented by the Hubble Space Telescope. From what source or sources can we learn the most about the natural world? What roles do religion and science play in understanding the natural world? Can we always trust the evidence of our senses? What constitutes "proof" in a discussion of principles too small, or too large, to form part of human experience? Does our understanding of the natural world ever pass from the realm of theoretical speculation and become true knowledge? Philosophers, religious leaders, and scientists have been asking these questions for a very long time, and like so many questions about the workings of the natural world, they are still debated today.

Cosmological Chart of the Ptolemaic Universe
(circa 150 CE)

CLAUDIUS PTOLEMAEUS, or Ptolemy (2nd century CE), was a Greek scientist who worked in Egypt at the height of the Roman Empire. Around 150 CE, he collected the astronomical knowledge of Greece, Babylon, Egypt, and Rome into a book, *The Great Treatise.* The Muslim scholars who rediscovered and translated this work in the tenth century CE gave it the Arabic name it is now known by: *Almagest.* In the *Almagest,* Ptolemy presented a model for the movement of the planets and the stars, an astronomical system that predominated for more than a millennium.

As in earlier versions of this model, the earth is the center of the universe, surrounded by a series of concentric, crystal spheres, each of which contains a different body or collection of celestial bodies. The sun is in one of these bodies, as is each planet that was known to the ancients. All the stars exist in a single sphere, far removed from the earth. Surrounding all the spheres is the *primum mobile,* or "prime mover," a sphere that contains no celestial bodies, but whose movement drives the motion of all the other spheres. Beyond this lies the *coelum empyreum,* or "highest heaven," the outermost sphere, which is not subject to the movement of the inner spheres.

Ptolemy had subjected the early geocentric (that is, Earth-centered) models to rigorous tests, observations, and calculations. While preserving their essential structure, he brought them into harmony with observable facts. The Ptolemaic model accurately predicted the motions of celestial bodies, and eminent scientists in both the Christian and the Islamic traditions considered it realistic. Because it appeared to confirm certain passages in the Bible that spoke of the motion of the sun and the stars, the model became Catholic Church doctrine.

Despite acknowledged problems with the Ptolemaic system, not until the works of the European astronomers Copernicus (1473–1543), Galileo (1564–1642), and Johannes Kepler (1571–1630) explained and accurately predicted celestial movement did heliocentrism, in which the planets revolve around the sun, replace geocentrism. Contrary to popular belief, Ptolemy and his contemporaries considered the possibility that the earth rotated around the sun. However, they understood that such movement would result in observable shifts in the position of the stars; since they did not observe these shifts, they rejected the idea. We know now that the stars are so far from the earth that their changes in position are nearly indetectable, although modern instruments have been able to measure them.

The diagram presented here was created by the Polish astronomer Johannes Hevelius (1611–1687) for his book *Selenographia* (1647). ◣

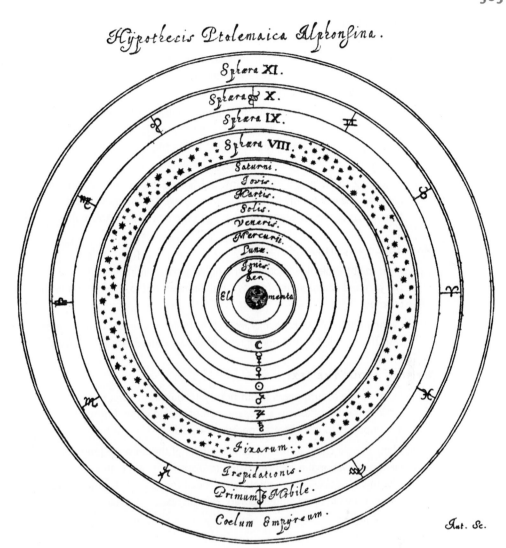

Cosmological chart of the Ptolemaic universe, circa 150 CE.
University of Cambridge / Trinity College Library

UNDERSTANDING THE TEXT

1. What does Ptolemy's placement of the earth at the center of the universe say about his conception of humanity? How were his governing assumptions related to the scientific knowledge of his time?

2. Though Ptolemy himself was neither Christian nor Muslim, his model was enthusiastically embraced by Christians and Muslims for more than a thousand years. For a time, Christian leaders excommunicated and even executed scientists who disagreed with the model. Why would this model have appealed to monotheists?

3. The sphere that Ptolemy calls the *primum mobile*, or "prime mover," contains no celestial bodies, but provides the motion for all the other spheres. Why might such a sphere be necessary within this model? Why do you think that, in later times, "the prime mover" became a reference to God?

4. According to Ptolemy's calculations, the "prime mover" rotated around the earth once every twenty-four hours. What would this suggest about the actual size of the stars and the planets in the rest of the Ptolemaic system?

MAKING CONNECTIONS

1. How might Ptolemy's model of the universe have influenced Averroës (p. 391) and Maimonides (p. 397) in their views of the role of God in the cosmos?

2. Compare the role of humanity implied in Ptolemy's model of the universe with that implied by the photograph of Galaxy Cluster Abell 1689 (p. 451).

WRITING ABOUT THE TEXT

1. Examine the assumptions about humanity, human nature, or the natural world implicit in Ptolemy's presentation of the universe. Compare these assumptions to ones that a contemporary scientist might hold.

2. Many people clung to the Ptolemaic model of the universe long after sufficient observational evidence existed to disprove it. Write an essay exploring why this model was so vigorously defended for so long. Compare this phenomenon with some contemporary equivalents.

Beatus of Liébana
The Beatus Map
(776 CE)

CARTOGRAPHY, THE MAKING OF MAPS, is one of the oldest activities recorded in human culture. Graphic reproductions of landscapes, terrains, and political boundaries have been discovered in nearly every human civilization. Even the Lascaux cave paintings, made by hunter-gatherers sometime near 14,000 BCE, contain an image that scholars now believe to be a celestial navigation map. The desire to create representations of our surroundings appears to be a universal human trait.

Most cartographers place a high value on accuracy, but no map can ever be entirely free of subjective judgments. The way a culture chooses to represent three-dimensional space in a two-dimensional medium says much about its perceptions and values. Perhaps no kind of map demonstrates this better than the medieval *mappa mundi*, or "map of the world." These medieval maps, which varied greatly in size and style, nonetheless all incorporated a number of distinctive elements unique to the medieval Christian European worldview.

One of the most famous surviving examples of the *mappi mundi* is the Beatus Map, so named because it was created by the Spanish monk and scholar Beatus of Liébana (circa 730–circa 800). The map was not designed to stand alone; rather, it was one of many illustrations in Beatus's manuscript *Commentary on the Apocalypse*, which was popular in European monasteries throughout the Middle Ages. Though the original manuscript has been lost, more than thirty copies survive, with composition dates ranging from the tenth through the sixteenth centuries.

The Beatus Map shows the earth as a flat disc surrounded by water on all sides. It does not use the now-standard orientation scheme that places north at the top and south at the bottom. The top of this map is east (*oriens*), with west at the bottom, north at the left, and south at the right. The earth is represented as a single land mass consisting of three continents: Asia in the east, Africa in the southwest, and Europe in the northwest. The continents are separated by a system of rivers and seas, and each is populated by well-known European place names such as Albania, Rome, and the southern French kingdom of Aquitaine.

Though many of the places depicted in the map may be familiar to modern readers, they are presented in locations and proportions that are utterly inconsistent with contemporary maps. But *mappae mundi* were not designed for geographic accuracy. Rather, this map reflects the world as it was understood by the medieval reading of the Bible, especially the Book of Genesis. The center of the world, in this view, is the holy city of Jerusalem. The three continents correspond to the traditional locations of the three sons of Noah: Ham in Africa, Shem in Europe, and Japheth in Asia. And at the top of the map, which represents the Far East, we find the site of the original Garden of Eden. 🖋

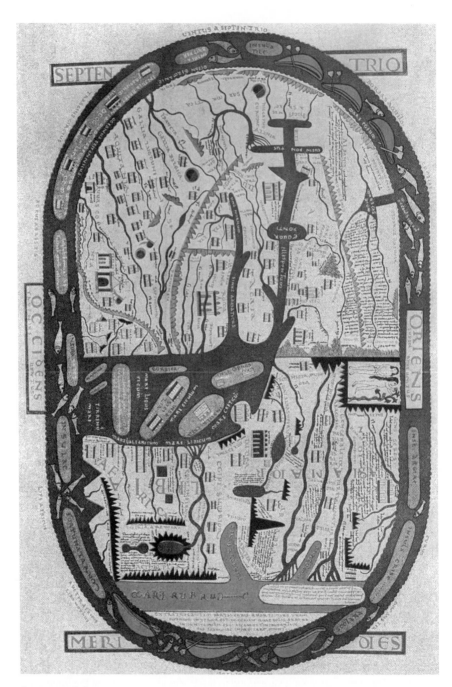

BEATUS OF LIÉBANA

The Beatus Map, 776 CE.

See p. C-5 in the color insert for a full-color reproduction of this image.

UNDERSTANDING THE TEXT

1. Though it is not correctly proportioned or historically accurate, and it cannot be used for either navigation or political demarcation, this image has traditionally been considered a "map." What qualities does it share with contemporary maps that you are familiar with? Do you think it should be called a "map"? Why or why not?

2. How does the map portray the earth's proportions of land and water? Do the proportions strike you as accurate? Why does so much of the center of the earth appear to be covered in water?

3. What locations depicted on the Beatus Map do you recognize? Why do you think that some place names—such as Rome, Egypt, Jerusalem, and the Garden of Eden—were included, while many others were not? What commonalities can you see among the included place names?

4. The Beatus Map was created long before the invention of the printing press. Each copy of the map was hand-drawn, and the book that accompanied it was hand-copied—both processes that required tremendous labor and skill. What about this map do you think justified the effort for the medieval scribes who copied it?

MAKING CONNECTIONS

1. Compare the Beatus Map with Ptolemy's cosmological chart of the universe (p. 384). How does each map incorporate the worldview of the society that produced it? What can you deduce about the two societies by analyzing the maps?

2. Compare the Beatus Map with the images from the *New England Primer* (p. 32). Both sets of images mix a secular purpose (mapping the world or teaching the alphabet) with a religious one (teaching some principle of Christian doctrine). How does each work its religious themes into its overall structure?

3. In what ways is the Beatus Map similar to the Papyrus of Ani (p. 154), which purports to give a guide to the underworld? Could this ancient Egyptian text also be considered a "map"? Explain.

WRITING ABOUT THE TEXT

1. Using the Beatus Map as an example, write an essay in which you define the word "map." Consider both the appearance and the practical value of both the Beatus Map and a contemporary map, and construct a definition that could account for them both.

2. Write an essay in which you compare the Beatus Map with *The Progress of an Aztec Warrior* (p. 265). What similar features do the two manuscript illus-

trations display? Look especially for similarities in purpose, and refer to specific elements of both images in your comparison.

3. Write an essay that explores the symbolism of the Beatus Map. Explain why the map mixes the medieval (Aquitaine, Gallia), the classical (Rome, Judea), and the biblical (the Garden of Eden)—even though these civilizations did not exist at the same time. Consider what symbolic or allegorical purpose might be served by such mixtures.

Averroës
from *On the Harmony of Religions and Philosophy*
(1190)

THE ISLAMIC SCHOLAR IBN RUSHD (1126–1198), known in the Christian world as Averroës, was born in Cordoba, Spain, when almost all of Spain was under Muslim control. From a young age, he was attracted to the mixture of classical philosophy and Islam that was put forth by philosophers such as al-Farabi (circa 870–circa 950 CE) and Avicenna (980–1037). One of the most important recurring themes in Averroës's work is that philosophy (including science) and religion can coexist. All truth is the same; logic, science, and the Quran are simply different paths to the same true principles.

Most of Averroës's fame in the West derives from his work on Aristotle. He translated many of Aristotle's treatises into Arabic and wrote lengthy commentaries on many more. He also developed a philosophical system that harmonized Aristotle's teachings with Islam's. Because Aristotle's powers of observation and analysis had led him to many of the same principles that would later be revealed in the Quran, Averroës thought it proper that the two bodies of thought be harmonized into one system.

By the time of Averroës's birth, the attack on Greek philosophy in al-Ghazālī's *The Incoherence of the Philosophers* had already begun to make Islamic thinkers shy away from the Greek philosophers who had been popular in Islamic intellectual circles since the eighth century. Averroës spent most of his career trying to stem the Muslim world's hostility to classical thought. To this end, he wrote a point-by-point rebuttal to *The Incoherence of the Philosophers* entitled *The Incoherence of the Incoherence*, as well as a number of other scholarly defenses of classical thought. The following selection comes from the introduction to his *On the Harmony of Religions and Philosophy*, which is devoted to demonstrating that Aristotelian reasoning can bolster Quranic concepts of natural and cosmic phenomena.

Though Averroës worked for nearly forty years to preserve a place for Greek philosophy in the world of Islamic thought, by the end of his life he clearly had lost the battle. Both he and his works fell into disrepute in Muslim Spain at the end of the twelfth century. He was banished from public life, and many of his works were destroyed and lost forever. Ironically, his most important legacy has been his impact on Christianity—a group of medieval Christian theologians, most notably Thomas Aquinas, were devoted readers of Averroës. Through his influence on medieval Christian thinkers, this great Muslim philosopher ensured that Aristotle's works were preserved, translated, and passed on to the West.

Averroës's rhetoric combines appeals to the authority of the Quran—obligatory for any writer in his society—with clear deductive arguments about the application of scriptural precedent to the study of the natural world.

W<small>E</small> MAINTAIN THAT THE BUSINESS of philosophy is nothing other than to look into creation and to ponder over it in order to be guided to the Creator—in other words, to look into the meaning of existence. For the knowledge of creation leads to the cognizance of the Creator, through the knowledge of the created. The more perfect becomes the knowledge of creation, the more perfect becomes the knowledge of the Creator. The Law encourages and exhorts us to observe creation. Thus, it is clear that this is to be taken either as a religious injunction or as something approved by the Law. But the Law urges us to observe creation by means of reason and demands the knowledge thereof through reason. This is evident from different verses of the Qur'an. For example, the Qur'an says: "Wherefore take example from them, you who have eyes" [Qur'an 49.2]. That is a clear indication of the necessity of using the reasoning faculty, or rather both reason and religion, in the interpretation of things. Again it says: "Or do they not contemplate the kingdom of heaven and earth and the things which God has created" [Qur'an 7.184]. This is in plain exhortation to encourage the use of observation of creation. And remember that one whom God especially distinguishes in this respect, Abraham, the prophet. For He says: "And this did we show unto Abraham: the kingdom of heaven and earth" [Qur'an 6.75]. Further, He says: "Do they not consider the camels, how they are created; and the heaven, how it is raised" [Qur'an 88.17]. Or, still again: "And (who) meditate on the creation of heaven and earth, saying, O Lord you have not created this in vain" [Qur'an 3.176]. There are many other verses on this subject: too numerous to be enumerated.

Now, it being established that the Law makes the observation and consideration of creation by reason obligatory—and consideration is nothing but to make explicit the implicit—this can only be done through reason. Thus we must look into creation with the reason. Moreover, it is obvious that the observation which the Law approves and encourages must be of the most perfect type, performed with the most perfect kind of reasoning. As the Law emphasizes the knowledge of God and His creation by inference, it is incumbent on any who wish to know God and His whole creation by inference, to learn the kinds of inference, their conditions and that which distinguishes philosophy from dialectic and exhortation from syllogism.[1] This is impossible unless one possesses knowledge beforehand of the various kinds of reasoning and learns to distinguish between reasoning and what is not reasoning. This cannot be done except one knows its different parts, that is, the different kinds of premises.[2]

Hence, for a believer in the Law and a follower of it, it is necessary to know these things before he begins to look into creation, for they are like instruments for observation. For, just as a student discovers by the study of the law, the necessity of knowledge of legal reasoning with all its kinds and distinctions, a student will find out by observing the creation the necessity of metaphysical reasoning. Indeed, he has a greater claim on it than the jurist. For if a jurist argues the necessity of legal reasoning from the saying of God: "Wherefore take example *from them* O you who have eyes" [Qur'an 59.2], a student of divinity has a better right to establish the same from it on behalf of metaphysical reasoning.

One cannot maintain that this kind of reasoning is an innovation in religion because it did not exist in the early days of Islam. For legal reasoning and its kinds are things which were invented also in later ages, and no one thinks they are innovations. Such should also be our attitude towards philosophical reasoning. . . . A large number of the followers of this religion confirm philosophical reasoning, all except a small worthless minority, who argue from religious ordinances. Now, as it is established that the Law makes the consideration of philosophical reasoning and its kinds as necessary as legal reasoning, if none of our predecessors has made an effort to enquire into it, we should begin to do it, and so help them, until the knowledge is complete. For if it is difficult or rather impossible for one person to acquaint himself single-handed with all things which it is necessary to know in legal matters, it is still more difficult in the case of philosophical reasoning. And, if before us, somebody has enquired into it, we should derive help from what he has said. It is quite immaterial whether that man is our co-religionist or not; for the instrument by which purification is perfected is not made uncertain in its usefulness by its being in the hands of one of our own party, or of a foreigner, if it possesses the attributes of truth. By these latter we mean those Ancients who investigated these things before the advent of Islam.

Now, such is the case. All that is wanted in an enquiry into philosophical reasoning has already been perfectly examined by the Ancients. All that is required of us is that we should go back to their books and see what they have said in this connection. If all that they say be true, we should accept it and if there be something wrong, we should be warned by it. Thus, when we have finished this kind of research we shall have acquired instruments by which we can observe the universe, and consider its general character. For so long as one does not know its general character one cannot know the created, and so long as he does not know the created, he cannot know its nature.

All things have been made and created. This is quite clear in itself, in the case of animals and plants, as God has said: "Verily the idols which you invoke, beside God, can never create a single fly, though they may all assemble for that purpose" [Qur'an 22.72]. We see an inorganic substance and then there is life in it. So we know for certain that there is an inventor and bestower of life, and He is God. Of

5

The translator has supplied bracketed Quran references.

1. **Syllogism:** an argument consisting of two premises and a conclusion (p. 597). Both terms are important to Aristotle's system of reasoning (p. 489). **Dialectic:** discussion, specifically philosophical discussion with truth, rather than persuasion, as its object.

2. Averroës's reasoning here is standard for pre–scientific revolution philosophy. Until a conceptual framework was created that emphasized observation and experimentation, it was generally assumed that the best way to discover the truth about the natural world was to begin with accepted premises and apply rigorous chains of deduction to produce new conclusions.

the heavens we know by their movements, which never become slackened, that they work for our benefit by divine solicitude, and are subordinate to our welfare. Such an appointed and subordinate object is always created for some purpose. The second principle is that for every created thing there is a creator. So it is right to say from the two foregoing principles that for every existent thing there is an inventor. There are many arguments, according to the number of the created things, which can be advanced to prove this premise. Thus, it is necessary for one who wants to know God as He ought to be known to acquaint himself with the essence of things, so that he may get information about the creation of all things. For who cannot understand the real substance and purpose of a thing, cannot understand the minor meaning of its creation. It is to this that God refers in the following verse: "Or do they not contemplate the heaven and the earth, and the things which God has created?" [Qur'an 7.184]. And so a man who would follow the purpose of philosophy in investigating the existence of things, that is, would try to know the cause which led to its creation. . . .

This method is the right path by which God has invited men to a knowledge of His existence, and informed them of it through the intelligence which He has implanted in their nature. The following verse refers to this fixed and innate nature of man, "And when the Lord drew forth their posterity from the loins of the sons of Adam, and took them witness against themselves, Am I not your Lord? They answered, Yes, we do bear witness" [Qur'an 7.171]. So it is incumbent for one who intends to obey God, and follow the injunction of His Prophet, that he should adopt this method, thus making himself one of those learned men who bear witness to the divinity of God, with His own witness, and that of His angels, as He says, "God has borne witness, that there is no God but He, and the angels, and those who are endowed with wisdom profess the same; who execute righteousness; there is no God but He; but Mighty, the Wise" [Qur'an 3.16]. Among the arguments for both of themselves is the praise which God refers to in the following verse, "Neither is there anything which does not celebrate his praise; but you understand not their celebration thereof" [Qur'an 17.46].

It is evident from the above arguments for the existence of God that they are dependent upon two categories of reasoning. It is also clear that both of these methods are meant for particular people; that is, the learned. Now as to the method for the masses. The difference between the two lies only in details. The masses cannot understand the . . . above-mentioned arguments but only what they can grasp by their senses; while the learned men can go further and learn by reasoning also, besides learning by sense. They have gone so far that a learned man has said, that the benefits the learned men derive from the knowledge of the members of human and animal body are a thousand and one. If this be so, then this is the method which is taught both by Law and by Nature. It is the method which was preached by the Prophet and the divine books. The learned men do not mention these two lines of reasoning to the masses, not because of their number, but because of a want of depth of learning on their part about the knowledge of a single thing only. The example of the common people, considering and pondering over the universe, is like a man who looks into a thing, the manufacture of which he does not know. For all that such a man can know about it is that it has been made, and that there must be a maker of it. But, on the other hand, the learned look into the universe, just as a man knowing the art[3] would do; try to understand the real purpose of it. So it is quite clear that their knowledge about the Maker, as the maker of the universe, would be far better than that of the man who only knows it as made. The atheists, who deny the Creator altogether, are like men who can see and feel the created things, but would not acknowledge any Creator for them, but would attribute all to chance alone, and that they come into being by themselves.

Now, then, if this is the method adopted by the Law, it may be asked: What is the way of proving the unity of God by means of the Law; that is, the knowledge of the religious formula that "there is no god, but God." The negation contained in it is an addition to the affirmative, which the formula contains, while the affirmative has already been proved. What is the purpose of this negation? We would say that the method, adopted by the Law, of denying divinity to all but God is according to the ordinance of God in the Qur'an . . .

If you look a little intently it will become clear to you, that in spite of the fact that the Law has not given illustration of those things for the common people, beyond which their imagination cannot go, it has also informed the learned men of the underlying meanings of those illustrations. So it is necessary to bear in mind the limits which the Law has set about the instruction of every class of men, and not to mix them together. For in this manner the purpose of the Law is multiplied. Hence it is that the Prophet has said, "We, the prophets, have been commanded to adapt ourselves to the conditions of the people, and address them according to their intelligence." He who tries to instruct all the people in the matter of religion, in one and the same way, is like a man who wants to make them alike in actions too, which is quite against apparent laws and reason.

UNDERSTANDING THE TEXT

1. According to Averroës, what is the Quran's position on scientific and philosophical inquiry? Why are Muslims allowed, even required, to seek after knowledge of the natural world?

2. What does Averroës see as the connection between legal reasoning and philosophical reasoning? Why does he believe that the Quran authorized the same kind of inquiry into the natural world that almost everyone believed it authorized into the study of the law?

3. **A man knowing the art:** someone who understands how a thing is made, as opposed to the "common people," who only know that a thing has been made.

3. What arguments against philosophical and scientific inquiry does Averroës anticipate? How does he counter each argument?

4. What two categories of reasoning does Averroës identify? What two classes of people does each category apply to? Does his reasoning here suggest that he believes philosophers to be superior to ordinary people?

MAKING CONNECTIONS

1. Compare Averroës's application of philosophy to Islam with Maimonides' merging of philosophy with Judaism (p. 397). Keep in mind that Averroës and Maimonides lived at roughly the same time and had access to many of the same materials.

2. How might Richard Feynman (p. 68) evaluate Averroës's argument in this passage? Does his text show evidence of the critical thinking that Feynman prizes?

3. How does Averroës's attempt to harmonize science and religion compare with that of Matthieu Ricard and Trinh Xuan Thuan in "The Universe in a Grain of Sand" (p. 435)?

WRITING ABOUT THE TEXT

1. Describe, in your own words, the relationship between science and religion. Consider the different ways that scientific knowledge and religious learning are represented today.

2. Examine the way that philosophers of different religions apply scientific and philosophical reasoning to their religious beliefs. Consider words by the Christian Thomas Aquinas (p. 260), the Muslim Averroës, the Jewish Moses Maimonides (p. 397), and the Buddhists Matthieu Ricard and Trinh Xuan Thuan (p. 435).

3. Evaluate Averroës's arguments as scientific statements. Do the points that he makes provide a good model of scientific reasoning, or is it best understood as philosophy?

Moses Maimonides
The Guide for the Perplexed
(circa 1200)

THE JEWISH SCHOLAR Moses Maimonides (1135–1204) ranks, along with the Christian Thomas Aquinas (1225–1274) and the Muslim Averroës (1126–1198), as one of the greatest medieval interpreters of Greek philosophy, particularly the works of Aristotle. Maimonides was born in the Spanish city of Córdoba when it was the capital of the Islamic Caliphate that ruled most of the Iberian Peninsula. Historically, the Jews in Spain had been less persecuted than those in other European cities, but when Spain was conquered by Berber Muslims from Africa in 1148, Spanish Jews were forced into exile. Maimonides and his family left Spain and settled in Morocco.

In Morocco, Maimonides studies at the University of Al-Qarawiyyin and became a prominent physician. He eventually settled in Egypt, where he became the physician to great sultan Saladin (1138–1193), who successfully recaptured Jerusalem from the European Christians who occupied it for nearly a hundred years after capturing it in 1099 at the end of the First Crusade. An educated man, Maimonides read the works of the great Islamic philosophers of his time and the works of the Ancient Greeks that these philosophers translated into Arabic. Following the lead of these Islamic scholars, who employed the tools of Greek philosophy to study questions important to Islam, Maimonides used the same set of tools to study Judaism.

Maimonides wrote in both Hebrew and Arabic and produced rabbinical commentary and treatises on medicine, law, and philosophy. His most famous work is *The Guide for the Perplexed*, a three-volume treatise written in the form of a letter to one of his pupils. The *Guide* uses the tools of analytical philosophy, such as the Aristotelian syllogism, to present a coherent and compelling Jewish interpretation of God, the cosmos, and the creation of the earth. Though originally written in Arabic, *The Guide for the Perplexed* was translated into Hebrew soon after its initial publication and became influential throughout both the Christian and Muslim worlds, in the Middle Ages and beyond.

The chapter excerpted here comes from the Second Book of the *Guide for the Perplexed*, which focuses on the creation of the universe. Maimonides, applying Aristotle's concepts of causality, argues that the universe is an effect whose existence can only be explained by a cause, and that this cause must be God. He argues not just that God's existence can be inferred from the existence of the universe, but also that the universe contains evidence of a clear and coherent design.

Maimonides' arguments in this section anticipate the proofs for God's existence given by later medieval and early modern philosophers as well as current controversies about the role of a some kind of "intelligent design" in the creation of the universe. He supports his claim by using deductive reasoning to create a chain of conclusions. 🖉

IT HAS BEEN SHOWN that according to Aristotle, and according to all that defend his theory, the Universe is inseparable from God;[1] He is the cause, and the Universe the effect; and this effect is a necessary one; and as it cannot be explained why or how God exists in this particular manner, namely, being One and incorporeal, so it cannot be asked concerning the whole Universe why or how it exists in this partic-ular way. For it is necessary that the whole, the cause as well as the effect, exist in this particular manner, it is impossible for them not to exist, or to be different from what they actually are. This leads to the conclusion that the nature of everything remains constant, that nothing changes its nature in any way, and that such a change is impossible in any existing thing. It would also follow that the Universe is not the result of design, choice, and desire; for if this were the case, they would have been non-existing before the design had been conceived.

We, however, hold that all things in the Universe are the result of design, and not merely of necessity; He who designed them may change them when He changes His design. But not every design is subject to change; for there are things which are impossible, and their nature cannot be altered, as will be explained. Here, in this chapter, I merely wish to show by arguments almost as forcible as real proofs, that the Universe gives evidence of design; but I will not fall into the error in which the Mutakallemim[2] have so much distinguished themselves, namely, of ignoring the existing nature of things or assuming the existence of atoms, or the successive cre-ation of accidents, or any of their propositions which I have tried to explain, and which are intended to establish the principle of Divine selection. You must not, how-ever, think that they understood the principle in the same sense as we do although they undoubtedly aimed at the same thing, and mentioned the same things which we also will mention, when they treated of Divine Selection. For they do not dis-tinguish between selection in the case of a plant to make it red and not white, or sweet and not bitter, and determination in the case of the heavens which gave them their peculiar geometrical form and did not give them a triangular or quadrilateral shape. The Mutakallemim established the principle of determination by means of their propositions, which have been enumerated above (Part I., chap. lxxiii.). I will establish their principle only as far as necessary, and only by philosophical proposi-tions based on the nature of things. But before I begin my argument, I will state the

1. **The Universe is inseparable from God:** Aristotle did not invoke God; he merely argued that effects must proceed from causes. **All that defend his theory** refers to the Islamic Aris-totelians whom Maimonides read, such as

Averroës, Avicenna (980–1037) and al-Farabi (872–950).

2. **Mutakallemim:** a group of Muslim philoso-phers who sought to prove religious ideas through philosophy.

following facts: Matter is common to things different from each other; there must be either one external cause which endows this matter partly with one property, partly with another, or there must be as many different causes as there are different forms of the matter common to all things. This is admitted by those who assume the Eternity of the Universe. . . .

Aristotle has proved that the difference of forms becomes evident by the difference of actions. Since, therefore, the motion of the elements is rectilinear,[3] and that of the spheres circular, we infer that the substances are different. This inference is supported by Natural Science. When we further notice that substances with rectilinear motion differ in their directions, that some move upward, some downward, and that substances which move in the same direction have different velocities, we infer that their forms must be different.

There is a phenomenon in the spheres[4] which more clearly shows the existence of voluntary determination; it cannot be explained otherwise than by assuming that some being designed it: this phenomenon is the existence of the stars. The fact that the sphere is constantly in motion, while the stars remain stationary, indicates that the substance of the stars is different from that of the spheres. Abu-nasr[5] has already mentioned the fact in his additions to the *Physics* of Aristotle. He says: "There is a difference between the stars and the spheres; for the spheres are transparent, the stars are opaque; and the cause of this is that there is a difference, however small it may be, between their substances and forms." So far Abu-nasr. But I do not say that there is a small difference, but a very great difference; because I do not infer it from the transparency of the spheres, but from their motions. I am convinced that there are three different kinds of substance, with three different forms, namely:—(1) Bodies which never move of their own accord; such are the bodies of the stars; (2) bodies which always move, such are the bodies of the spheres; (3) bodies which both move and rest, such are the elements. Now, I ask, what has united these two bodies, which, according to my opinion, differ very much from each other, though, according to Abu-nasr, only a little? Who has prepared the bodies for this union? In short, it would be strange that, without the existence of design, one of two different bodies should be joined to the other in such a manner that it is fixed to it in a certain place but does not combine with it. . . .

The best proof for design in the Universe I find in the different motions of the spheres, and in the fixed position of the stars in the spheres. For this reason you find all the prophets point to the spheres and stars when they want to prove that there must exist a Divine Being. Thus Abraham reflected on the stars, as is well known; Isaiah (xl. 26) exhorts to learn from them the existence of God, and says,

5

---

3. **Rectilinear:** movement along a straight line.
4. **Spheres:** the concentric circles surrounding the earth in the Ptolemaic model of the universe accepted in Maimonides' day (see p. 397). According to Maimonides' understanding of the universe, the stars inhabited these various spheres, which moved around the earth while the stars themselves remained stationary.
5. **Abu-Nasr:** alternative name for al-Farabi, an early Islamic Aristotelian.

"Lift up your eyes on high, and behold who hath created these things?" Jeremiah [calls God] "The Maker of the heavens"; Abraham calls Him "The God of the heavens" (Gen. xxiv. 7); [Moses], the chief of the Prophets, uses the phrase explained by us (Part I., chap. lxx.), "He who rideth on the heavens" (Deut. xxxiii. 26). The proof taken from the heavens is convincing; for the variety of things in the sublunary world, though their substance is one and the same, can be explained as the work of the influences of the spheres, or the result of the variety in the position of the substance in relation to the spheres, as has been shown by Aristotle. But who has determined the variety in the spheres and the stars, if not the Will of God?

Understanding the Text

1. In the first paragraph, what conclusion does Moses Maimonides draw from the works of Aristotle? Does he support this idea in the rest of the text or refute it?

2. What does Maimonides see as the difference between necessity and design? What does he mean by the statement, "we . . . hold that all things in the universe are the result of design, and not merely of necessity"?

3. According to Maimonides, what is the error of the Mutakallemim? How does his own position differ from theirs?

4. Why does Maimonides believe that the existence of the stars demonstrates that the universe was designed? What assumptions does he make about the stars and the "spheres" that they inhabit?

5. What does Maimonides see in the motion of the spheres that requires a divine creator? What about this motion represents "design" rather than "necessity"?

Making Connections

1. Why is Maimonides' argument dependent on the Ptolemaic model of the universe (p. 384)? How would his argument be different if he knew what we now know about the movement of the stars?

2. Does Maimonide use philosophy to examine the creation of the world in a way consistent with Averroës's view in "On the Harmony of Religions and Philosophy" (p. 391? How so? Would Averroës agree with his conclusions?

3. How might Maimonides' argument be reconfigured to account for the universe described by Trinh Xuan Thuan (p. 435) and shown by the Hubble Space Telescope (p. 451)? Is there an argument for design in this much larger universe? Explain.

WRITING ABOUT THE TEXT

1. Contrast Maimonides' view of a "universal designer" with Darwin's view of natural selection as a force that produces complexity through natural means. Could natural selection be said to be a "designer" in the sense that Maimonides favors?

2. Examine the modern arguments in favor of teaching "intelligent design" in schools and write an essay comparing these arguments with those that Maimonides makes in *The Guide for the Perplexed*. Could Maimonides be considered an early advocate of "intelligent design," or the belief that the universe is too complicated to have emerged by chance?

3. Compare Maimonides' conclusions to contemporary understandings of the universe. Can any part of his argument survive the transition from a Ptolemaic model of the universe (p. 384) to the Copernican model now accepted by scientists, in which the earth revolves around the sun?

Joseph Wright of Derby
An Experiment on a Bird in the Air Pump
(1768)

PERHAPS MORE THAN any other painter of his day, Joseph Wright (1734–1797) made science the subject of art. Born in the English town of Derby, Wright studied in London with the well-known painter Thomas Hudson (1701–1779) before returning to his native town and adopting its name as part of his official signature. His paintings often centered around scientific and industrial contraptions that were unfamiliar to his audience, such as the "orrey," or model solar system, which is the subject of his 1766 painting *A Philosopher Lecturing on the Orrey*. In his paintings, he often attempted to capture the transition from an unscientific worldview to a scientific one.

An Experiment on a Bird in the Air Pump is one of Joseph Wright of Derby's most famous paintings and one of the most recognizable artistic images of the scientific revolution. In the painting, a scientist is using an air pump to create a vacuum in a small glass container holding a bird, which, deprived of oxygen, is going into convulsions. The crowd gathered for the experiment displays a range of reactions, from horror to intense interest to complete indifference.

The experiment does not seem to serve any valid scientific purpose. Though even before this time air pumps had been used by the English physicist and chemist Robert Boyle (1627–1691) and others in important research, this experiment takes place not in a laboratory or another controlled environment that would allow it to yield useful data but in a private home, apparently for entertainment. The spectators are not students or colleagues of the scientist, and the exotic bird in the container—a cockatoo—is not well suited for this kind of experiment—it is far too rare and expensive to use as a research subject. The entire display seems designed as a scientific-themed sideshow with no real value for the production or dissemination of knowledge. Both the experiment and the reactions of the crowd work allegorically to capture a number of contradictory attitudes about science during the eighteenth century. 🖋

Joseph Wright of Derby
An Experiment on a Bird in the Air Pump, 1768 (oil on canvas).
National Gallery, London, UK / Bridgeman Art Library
See p. C-6 in the color insert for a full-color reproduction of this image.

Understanding the Text

1. How does each spectator project or represent a possible opinion about science?

2. Does the scientist seem more like an experimenter or a showman? What might Joseph Wright of Derby be suggesting about science through this figure?

3. Why does the painting focus on an act of cruelty that does not seem to have any scientific value?

4. How does the lighting of the picture function symbolically? What is the symbolic significance of the candle on the table?

5. Why is the servant lowering the curtain? How might this act figure into the symbolic drama?

6. What overall view of scientific experimentation, progress, and technology comes through in the painting?

MAKING CONNECTIONS

1. Compare the scientist in *An Experiment on a Bird in the Air Pump* with Liberty in *Liberty Leading the People* (p. 268). If both figures symbolize revolutions, one scientific and one political, could both paintings be considered "revolutionary"?

2. *An Experiment on a Bird in the Air Pump* dates from about the same time as Hogarth's *Gin Lane* (p. 320). Compare these works' treatments of the scientific and industrial revolutions and of those revolutions' effects on society.

3. Some people have criticized NASA's Hubble Space Telescope program for preferring high-interest, spectacular photographs to less interesting—but ultimately more important—scientific research (p. 451). Does this change make NASA comparable to the "experimenter" in this painting? Explain.

WRITING ABOUT THE TEXT

1. Using *An Experiment on a Bird in the Air Pump* as a model, choose a contemporary scientific discovery or new field of inquiry, such as cloning, genetic engineering, or virtual reality, and propose an allegorical artwork conveying that phenomenon and responses to it.

2. Translate the symbolism in *An Experiment on a Bird in the Air Pump*—the use of light and darkness, the figures, the allegorical significance—into words.

3. Consider *An Experiment on a Bird in the Air Pump* in terms of research involving the injury or death of animals. Is the acquisition of knowledge always worth the costs?

4. How might Wright's portrayal of the scientist as entertainer apply to contemporary scientists? Read and contrast media portraits of, for example, laboratory researchers and the authors of books that popularize scientific ideas. Does showmanship invalidate good science?

Charles Darwin
from *Natural Selection; or, the Survival of the Fittest*
(1859)

THOUGH CHARLES DARWIN (1809–1882) was one of the most famous naturalists in world history, he originally studied theology and medicine. After an unremarkable undergraduate career at Cambridge University, he took the job of ship's naturalist on the H.M.S. *Beagle*, a scientific survey vessel that from 1831 to 1836 charted navigable waters throughout South America, the Pacific Islands, and Australia. At some points on this journey, Darwin observed enormous variations in species in environments that were separated from each other by only a few miles. These variations inspired him to formulate a theory of how organisms might evolve through time to adapt to their environment.

Contrary to popular belief, Darwin did not originate the theory of evolution. Many scientists in Darwin's time accepted the idea that organisms evolved through gradual changes over time, but they did not understand the mechanism that produced those changes. Before Darwin, the most widely accepted theory was that of the French naturalist Jean-Baptiste Lamarck (1744–1829), who speculated that organisms acquired slight useful modifications during their lifetimes and passed them on to their offspring, resulting in gradual change over time.

Darwin, however, theorized that changes in a species resulted from a mechanism that he called "natural selection." Working from the understanding that variations exist in all species, Darwin reasoned that naturally occurring variations within species sometimes give an organism distinct advantages in the competition for resources. These advantages might help the organism find food or defend itself from predators, thus allowing it to survive long enough to reproduce; or they might help the organism attract a mate or disseminate its seeds. In either case, an organism with an advantageous variation will have more reproductive success, and that variation will eventually become a more prominent characteristic of the species.

Darwin was influenced by the work of Thomas Malthus, whose "Essay on the Principle of Population" argued that people tend to produce more offspring than local resources can support. He also benefited from the work of nineteenth-century geologists such as Sir Charles Lyell (1797–1875), who demonstrated that the earth was millions of times older than had previously been imagined. Darwin understood that his work would be opposed by those who believed that God created all the individual species of plants and animals—including human beings—and these concerns probably influenced his decision to delay the publication of his theories until more than twenty years after he formulated them. Though his book *The Origin of Species*—of which "Natural Selection" is chapter 4—encountered resistance on religious grounds when it was published, and continues to do so today in some places, the scientific community has accepted natural selection as the mechanism by which life on Earth adapts and changes.

Unlike the earlier writers in this chapter—who make deductive arguments about nature by beginning with general principles derived from religious or classical sources—Darwin's arguments are primarily inductive. He begins with specific observations about nature that have not been sufficiently explained in previous theories and then draws general principles from those observations to create a new explanation. 🖎

How will the struggle for existence . . . act in regard to variation? Can the principle of selection, which . . . is so potent in the hands of man, apply under nature? I think we shall see that it can act most efficiently. Let the endless number of slight variations and individual differences occurring in our domestic productions, and, in a lesser degree, in those under nature, be borne in mind; as well as the strength of the hereditary tendency. Under domestication, it may be truly said that the whole organisation becomes in some degree plastic. But the variability, which we almost universally meet with in our domestic productions, is not directly produced, as Hooker and Asa Gray[1] have well remarked, by man; he can neither originate varieties, nor prevent their occurrence; he can preserve and accumulate such as do occur. Unintentionally he exposes organic beings to new and changing conditions of life, and variability ensues; but similar changes of conditions might and do occur under nature. Let it also be borne in mind how infinitely complex and close-fitting are the mutual relations of all organic beings to each other and to their physical conditions of life; and consequently what infinitely varied diversities of structure might be of use to each being under changing conditions of life. Can it, then, be thought improbable, seeing that variations useful to man have undoubtedly occurred, that other variations useful in some way to each being in the great and complex battle of life, should occur in the course of many successive generations. If such do occur, can we doubt (remembering that many more individuals are born than can possibly survive) that individuals having any advantage, however slight, over others, would have the best chance of surviving and of procreating their kind? On the other hand, we may feel sure that any variation in the least degree injurious would be rigidly destroyed. This preservation of favourable individual differences and variations, and the destruction of those which are injurious, I have called Natural Selection, or the Survival of the Fittest. Variations neither useful nor injurious would not be affected by natural selec-

---

1. **Hooker and Asa Gray:** Sir Joseph Dalton Hooker (1817–1911) was an English botanist; Asa Gray (1810–1888) was an American botanist and a professor at Harvard University. Both were friends of Darwin and early champions of the theory of evolution by natural selection.

tion, and would be left either a fluctuating element, as perhaps we see in certain polymorphic species,[2] or would ultimately become fixed, owing to the nature of the organism and the nature of the conditions.

Several writers have misapprehended or objected to the term Natural Selection. Some have even imagined that natural selection induces variability, whereas it implies only the preservation of such variations as arise and are beneficial to the being under its conditions of life. No one objects to agriculturists speaking of the potent effects of man's selection; and in this case the individual differences given by nature, which man for some object selects, must of necessity first occur. Others have objected that the term selection implies conscious choice in the animals which become modified; and it had even been urged that, as plants have no volition, natural selection is not applicable to them! In the literal sense of the word, no doubt, natural selection is a false term; but who ever objected to chemists speaking of the elective affinities[3] of the various elements?—and yet an acid cannot strictly be said to elect the base with which it in preference combines. It has been said that I speak of natural selection as an active power or Deity; but who objects to an author speaking of the attraction of gravity as ruling the movements of the planets? Every one knows what is meant and is implied by such metaphorical expressions; and they are almost necessary for brevity. So again it is difficult to avoid personifying the word Nature; but I mean by Nature, only the aggregate action and product of many natural laws, and by laws the sequence of events as ascertained by us. With a little familiarity such superficial objections will be forgotten.

We shall best understand the probable course of natural selection by taking the case of a country undergoing some slight physical change, for instance, of climate. The proportional numbers of its inhabitants will almost immediately undergo a change, and some species will probably become extinct. We may conclude, from what we have seen of the intimate and complex manner in which the inhabitants of each country are bound together, that any change in the numerical proportions of the inhabitants, independently of the change of climate itself, would seriously affect the others. If the country were open on its borders, new forms would certainly immigrate, and this would likewise seriously disturb the relations of some of the former inhabitants. Let it be remembered how powerful the influence of a single introduced tree or mammal has been shown to be. But in the case of an island, or of a country partly surrounded by barriers, into which new and better adapted forms could not freely enter, we should then have places in the economy of nature which would

2. **Polymorphic species:** species in which an individual changes form during its lifetime, such as frogs and butterflies.
3. **Elective affinities:** a term from eighteenth- and early-nineteenth-century chemistry regarding chemical compounds that interacted with each other only in certain circumstances. Darwin's point is that, like this term, "natural selection" can be taken to attribute humanlike qualities to abstract nature, but in both cases the attribute of intentional selection or election is simply a metaphor.

assuredly be better filled up, if some of the original inhabitants were in some manner modified; for, had the area been open to immigration, these same places would have been seized on by intruders. In such cases, slight modifications, which in any way favoured the individuals of any species, by better adapting them to their altered conditions, would tend to be preserved; and natural selection would have free scope for the work of improvement.

We have good reason to believe . . . that changes in the conditions of life give a tendency to increased variability; and in the foregoing cases the conditions have changed, and this would manifestly be favourable to natural selection, by affording a better chance of the occurrence of profitable variations. Unless such occur, natural selection can do nothing. Under the term of "variations," it must never be forgotten that mere individual differences are included. As man can produce a great result with his domestic animals and plants by adding up in any given direction individual differences, so could natural selection, but far more easily from having incomparably longer time for action. Nor do I believe that any great physical change, as of climate, or any unusual degree of isolation to check immigration, is necessary in order that new and unoccupied places should be left, for natural selection to fill up by improving some of the varying inhabitants. For as all the inhabitants of each country are struggling together with nicely balanced forces, extremely slight modifications in the structure or habits of one species would often give it an advantage over others; and still further modifications of the same kind would often still further increase the advantage, as long as the species continued under the same conditions of life and profited by similar means of subsistence and defence. No country can be named in which all the native inhabitants are now so perfectly adapted to each other and to the physical conditions under which they live, that none of them could be still better adapted or improved; for in all countries, the natives have been so far conquered by naturalised productions, that they have allowed some foreigners to take firm possession of the land. And as foreigners have thus in every country beaten some of the natives, we may safely conclude that the natives might have been modified with advantage, so as to have better resisted the intruders.

As man can produce, and certainly has produced, a great result by his methodi- 5
cal and unconscious means of selection, what may not natural selection effect? Man can act only on external and visible characters: Nature, if I may be allowed to personify the natural preservation or survival of the fittest, cares nothing for appearances, except in so far as they are useful to any being. She can act on every internal organ, on every shade of constitutional difference, on the whole machinery of life. Man selects only for his own good: Nature only for that of the being which she tends. Every selected character is fully exercised by her, as is implied by the fact of their selection. Man keeps the natives of many climates in the same country; he seldom exercises each selected character in some peculiar and fitting manner; he feeds a long

and a short beaked pigeon on the same food; he does not exercise a long-backed or long-legged quadruped in any peculiar manner; he exposes sheep with long and short wool to the same climate. He does not allow the most vigorous males to struggle for the females. He does not rigidly destroy all inferior animals, but protects during each varying season, as far as lies in his power, all his productions. He often begins his selection by some half-monstrous form; or at least by some modification prominent enough to catch the eye or to be plainly useful to him. Under Nature, the slightest differences of structure or constitution may well turn the nicely balanced scale in the struggle for life, and so be preserved. How fleeting are the wishes and efforts of man! how short his time! and consequently how poor will be his results, compared with those accumulated by Nature during whole geological periods! Can we wonder, then, that Nature's productions should be far "truer" in character than man's productions; that they should be infinitely better adapted to the most complex conditions of life, and should plainly bear the stamp of far higher workmanship?

It may metaphorically be said that natural selection is daily and hourly scrutinising, throughout the world, the slightest variations; rejecting those that are bad, preserving and adding up all that are good; silently and insensibly working, *whenever and wherever opportunity offers*, at the improvement of each organic being in relation to its organic and inorganic conditions of life. We see nothing of these slow changes in progress, until the hand of time has marked the lapse of ages, and then so imperfect is our view into long-past geological ages, that we see only that the forms of life are now different from what they formerly were.

In order that any great amount of modification should be effected in a species, a variety when once formed must again, perhaps after a long interval of time, vary or present individual differences of the same favourable nature as before; and these must be again preserved, and so onwards step by step. Seeing that individual differences of the same kind perpetually recur, this can hardly be considered as an unwarrantable assumption. But whether it is true, we can judge only by seeing how far the hypothesis accords with and explains the general phenomena of nature. On the other hand, the ordinary belief that the amount of possible variation is a strictly limited quantity is likewise a simple assumption.

Although natural selection can act only through and for the good of each being, yet characters and structures, which we are apt to consider as of very trifling importance, may thus be acted on. When we see leaf-eating insects green, and bark-feeders mottled-grey; the alpine ptarmigan[4] white in winter, the red-grouse the colour of heather, we must believe that these tints are of service to these birds and insects in preserving them from danger. Grouse, if not destroyed at some period of

---

4. **Ptarmigan:** a bird, belonging to the grouse family, that lives mainly in cold climates; members of the species have various colors during most of the year, but all turn white during the winter, enabling them to blend in with snow.

their lives, would increase in countless numbers; they are known to suffer largely from birds of prey; and hawks are guided by eyesight to their prey—so much so, that on parts of the Continent persons are warned not to keep white pigeons, as being the most liable to destruction. Hence natural selection might be effective in giving the proper colour to each kind of grouse, and in keeping that colour, when once acquired, true and constant. Nor ought we to think that the occasional destruction of an animal of any particular colour would produce little effect: we should remember how essential it is in a flock of white sheep to destroy a lamb with the faintest trace of black. We have seen how the colour of the hogs, which feed on the "paint-root" in Virginia, determines whether they shall live or die.[5] In plants, the down on the fruit and the colour of the flesh are considered by botanists as characters of the most trifling importance; yet we hear from an excellent horticulturist, Downing,[6] that in the United States, smooth-skinned fruits suffer far more from a beetle, a Curculio,[7] than those with down; that purple plums suffer far more from a certain disease than yellow plums; whereas another disease attacks yellow-fleshed peaches far more than those with other coloured flesh. If, with all the aids of art, these slight differences make a great difference in cultivating the several varieties, assuredly, in a state of nature, where the trees would have to struggle with other trees, and with a host of enemies, such differences would effectually settle which variety, whether a smooth or downy, a yellow or purple fleshed fruit, should succeed.

In looking at many small points of difference between species, which, as far as our ignorance permits us to judge, seem quite unimportant, we must not forget that climate, food, &c., have no doubt produced some direct effect. It is also necessary to bear in mind that, owing to the law of correlation, when one part varies, and the variations are accumulated through natural selection, other modifications, often of the most unexpected nature, will ensue.

As we see that those variations which, under domestication, appear at any particular period of life, tend to reappear in the offspring at the same period;—for instance, in the shape, size, and flavour of the seeds of the many varieties of our culinary and agricultural plants; in the caterpillar and cocoon stages of the varieties of the silk-worm; in the eggs of poultry, and in the colour of the down of their chickens; in the horns of our sheep and cattle when nearly adult;—so in a state of nature natural selection will be enabled to act on and modify organic beings at any age, by the accumulation of variations profitable at that age, and by their

10

---

5. **Paint-root:** a plant that grows in marshy areas along the eastern coast of North America. According to some evidence with which Darwin was familiar, the plant is poisonous to pigs with light skin but edible by those with dark skin, causing most of the pigs in the regions where the plant grows to be dark.

6. **Downing:** Andrew Jackson Downing (1815–1852), American landscaper and horticulturalist.

7. **Curculio:** a type of snout beetle that causes significant damage in peach, plum, cherry, and apple orchards in the United States.

inheritance at a corresponding age. If it profit a plant to have its seeds more and more widely disseminated by the wind, I can see no greater difficulty in this being effected through natural selection, than in the cotton-planter increasing and improving by selection the down in the pods on his cotton-trees. Natural selection may modify and adapt the larva of an insect to a score of contingencies, wholly different from those which concern the mature insect; and these modifications may effect, through correlation, the structure of the adult. So, conversely, modifications in the adult may affect the structure of the larva; but in all cases natural selection will ensure that they shall not be injurious: for if they were so, the species would become extinct.

Natural selection will modify the structure of the young in relation to the parent, and of the parent in relation to the young. In social animals it will adapt the structure of each individual for the benefit of the whole community; if the community profits by the selected change. What natural selection cannot do, is to modify the structure of one species, without giving it any advantage, for the good of another species; and though statements to this effect may be found in works of natural history, I cannot find one case which will bear investigation. A structure used only once in an animal's life, if of high importance to it, might be modified to any extent by natural selection; for instance, the great jaws possessed by certain insects, used exclusively for opening the cocoon—or the hard tip to the beak of unhatched birds, used for breaking the egg. It has been asserted, that of the best short-beaked tumbler-pigeons a greater number perish in the egg than are able to get out of it; so that fanciers assist in the act of hatching. Now if nature had to make the beak of a full-grown pigeon very short for the bird's own advantage, the process of modification would be very slow, and there would be simultaneously the most rigorous selection of all the young birds within the egg, which had the most powerful and hardest beaks, for all with weak beaks would inevitably perish; or, more delicate and more easily broken shells might be selected, the thickness of the shell being known to vary like every other structure.

It may be well here to remark that with all beings there must be much fortuitous destruction, which can have little or no influence on the course of natural selection. For instance a vast number of eggs or seeds are annually devoured, and these could be modified through natural selection only if they varied in some manner which protected them from their enemies. Yet many of these eggs or seeds would perhaps, if not destroyed, have yielded individuals better adapted to their conditions of life than any of those which happened to survive. So again a vast number of mature animals and plants, whether or not they be the best adapted to their conditions, must be annually destroyed by accidental causes, which would not be in the least degree mitigated by certain changes of structure or constitution which would in other ways be beneficial to the species. But let the destruction of the adults be ever so heavy, if the number which can exist in any district be not wholly kept down by such causes,—or again let the destruction of eggs or seeds be so great that only a hundredth or a thousandth part are developed,—yet of those which do survive, the best adapted individuals, supposing that there is any variability in a favourable direction, will tend to propagate their kind in larger numbers than the less well adapted. If the numbers be wholly kept down by the causes just indicated, as will often have been the case, natural selection will be powerless in certain beneficial directions; but this is no valid objection to its efficiency at other times and in other ways; for we are far from having any reason to suppose that many species ever undergo modification and improvement at the same time in the same area.

Sexual Selection

Inasmuch as peculiarities often appear under domestication in one sex and become hereditarily attached to that sex, so no doubt it will be under nature. Thus it is rendered possible for the two sexes to be modified through natural selection in relation to different habits of life, as is sometimes the case, or for one sex to be modified in relation to the other sex, as commonly occurs. This leads me to say a few words on what I have called Sexual Selection. This form of selection depends, not on a struggle for existence in relation to other organic beings or to external conditions, but on a struggle between the individuals of one sex, generally the males, for the possession of the other sex. The result is not death to the unsuccessful competitor, but few or no offspring. Sexual selection is, therefore, less rigorous than natural selection. Generally, the most vigorous males, those which are best fitted for their places in nature, will leave most progeny. But in many cases, victory depends not so much on general vigor, as on having special weapons, confined to the male sex. A hornless stag or spurless cock would have a poor chance of leaving numerous offspring. Sexual selection, by always allowing the victor to breed, might surely give indomitable courage, length to the spur, and strength to the wing to strike in the spurred leg, in nearly the same manner as does the brutal cock-fighter by the careful selection of his best cocks. How low in the scale of nature the law of battle descends, I know not; male alligators have been described as fighting, bellowing, and whirling round, like Indians in a war-dance, for the possession of the females; male salmons have been observed fighting all day long; male stag-beetles sometimes bear wounds from the huge mandibles of other males; the males of certain hymenopterous insects have been frequently seen by that inimitable observer M. Fabre,[8] fighting for a particular female who sits by, an apparently unconcerned beholder of the struggle, and then retires with the conqueror. The war is, perhaps, severest between the males of polygamous animals, and these seem oftenest provided with special weapons. The males of carnivorous animals are already well armed; though to them and to others, special means of defence may be given through means of sexual selec-

---

8. **M. Fabre:** Jean-Henri Fabre (1823–1915), French botanist and etymologist. **Hymenopterous insects:** members of the hymenoptera order, which includes wasps, bees, and ants.

tion, as the mane of the lion, and the hooked jaw to the male salmon; for the shield may be as important for victory, as the sword or spear.

Amongst birds, the contest is often of a more peaceful character. All those who have attended to the subject, believe that there is the severest rivalry between the males of many species to attract, by singing, the females. The rock-thrush of Guiana, birds of paradise, and some others, congregate; and successive males display with the most elaborate care, and show off in the best manner, their gorgeous plumage; they likewise perform strange antics before the females, which, standing by as spectators, at last choose the most attractive partner. Those who have closely attended to birds in confinement well know that they often take individual preferences and dislikes: thus Sir R. Heron has described how a pied[9] peacock was eminently attractive to all his hen birds. I cannot here enter on the necessary details; but if man can in a short time give beauty and an elegant carriage to his bantams, according to his standard of beauty, I can see no good reason to doubt that female birds, by selecting, during thousands of generations, the most melodious or beautiful males according to their standard of beauty, might produce a marked effect. Some well-known laws, with respect to the plumage of male and female birds, in comparison with the plumage of the young, can partly be explained through the action of sexual selection on variations occurring at different ages, and transmitted to the males alone or to both sexes at corresponding ages; but I have not space here to enter on this subject.

Thus it is, as I believe, that when the males and females of any animal have the same general habits of life, but differ in structure, colour, or ornament, such differences have been mainly caused by sexual selection: that is, by individual males having had, in successive generations, some slight advantage over other males, in their weapons, means of defence, or charms, which they have transmitted to their male offspring alone. Yet, I would not wish to attribute all sexual differences to this agency: for we see in our domestic animals peculiarities arising and becoming attached to the male sex, which apparently have not been augmented through selection by man. The tuft of hair on the breast of the wild turkey-cock cannot be of any use, and it is doubtful whether it can be ornamental in the eyes of the female bird;—indeed, had the tuft appeared under domestication, it would have been called a monstrosity.

Illustrations of the Action of Natural Selection, or the Survival of the Fittest

In order to make it clear how, as I believe, natural selection acts, I must beg permission to give one or two imaginary illustrations. Let us take the case of a wolf, which preys on various animals, securing some by craft, some by strength, and some

9. **Pied:** spotted, patched. **Sir R. Heron:** Sir Robert Heron (1765–1854), an English politician with whom Darwin maintained a correspondence.

by fleetness; and let us suppose that the fleetest prey, a deer for instance, had from any change in the country increased in numbers, or that other prey had decreased in numbers, during that season of the year when the wolf was hardest pressed for food. Under such circumstances the swiftest and slimmest wolves would have the best chance of surviving and so be preserved or selected,—provided always that they retained strength to master their prey at this or some other period of the year, when they were compelled to prey on other animals. I can see no more reason to doubt that this would be the result, than that man should be able to improve the fleetness of his greyhounds by careful and methodical selection, or by that kind of unconscious selection which follows from each man trying to keep the best dogs without any thought of modifying the breed. I may add, that, according to Mr. Pierce, there are two varieties of the wolf inhabiting the Catskill Mountains, in the United States, one with a light greyhound-like form, which pursues deer, and the other more bulky, with shorter legs, which more frequently attacks the shepherd's flocks. . . .

It may be worth while to give another and more complex illustration of the action of natural selection. Certain plants excrete sweet juice, apparently for the sake of eliminating something injurious from the sap: this is effected, for instance, by glands at the base of the stipules in some Leguminosæ,[10] and at the backs of the leaves of the common laurel. This juice, though small in quantity, is greedily sought by insects; but their visits do not in any way benefit the plant. Now, let us suppose that the juice or nectar was excreted from the inside of the flowers of a certain number of plants of any species. Insects in seeking the nectar would get dusted with pollen, and would often transport it from one flower to another. The flowers of two distinct individuals of the same species would thus get crossed; and the act of crossing, as can be fully proved, gives rise to vigorous seedlings which consequently would have the best chance of flourishing and surviving. The plants which produced flowers with the largest glands or nectaries, excreting most nectar, would oftenest be visited by insects, and would oftenest be crossed; and so in the long-run would gain the upper hand and form a local variety. The flowers, also, which had their stamens and pistils[11] placed, in relation to the size and habits of the particular insects which visited them, so as to favour in any degree the transportal of the pollen, would likewise be favoured. We might have taken the case of insects visiting flowers for the sake of collecting pollen instead of nectar; and as pollen is formed for the sole purpose of fertilisation, its destruction appears to be a simple loss to the plant; yet if a little pollen were carried, at first occasionally and then habitually, by the pollen-devouring insects from

10. **Leguminosæ:** a family of plants that includes more than eighteen thousand species, the most well-known of which are beans, peas, soybeans, lentils, alfalfa, and clover. **Stipules:** small outgrowths on the base of a leaf.

11. **Stamens and pistils:** parts of the reproductive system of plants. The **stamen** is the male organ that produces pollen; the **pistil** is the female organ that receives pollen; the **anther** (below) is part of the stamen that contains the pollen.

flower to flower, and a cross thus effected, although nine-tenths of the pollen were destroyed it might still be a great gain to the plant to be thus robbed; and the individuals which produced more and more pollen, and had larger anthers, would be selected.

When our plant, by the above process long continued, had been rendered highly attractive to insects, they would, unintentionally on their part, regularly carry pollen from flower to flower; and that they do this effectually, I could easily show by many striking facts. I will give only one, as likewise illustrating one step in the separation of the sexes of plants. Some holly-trees bear only male flowers, which have four stamens producing a rather small quantity of pollen, and a rudimentary pistil: other holly-trees bear only female flowers; these have a full-sized pistil, and four stamens with shrivelled anthers, in which not a grain of pollen can be detected. Having found a female tree exactly sixty yards from a male tree, I put the stigmas of twenty flowers, taken from different branches, under the microscope, and on all, without exception, there were a few pollen-grains, and on some a profusion. As the wind had set for several days from the female to the male tree, the pollen could not thus have been carried. The weather had been cold and boisterous, and therefore not favourable to bees, nevertheless every female flower which I examined had been effectually fertilised by the bees, which had flown from tree to tree in search of nectar. But to return to our imaginary case: as soon as the plant had been rendered so highly attractive to insects that pollen was regularly carried from flower to flower, another process might commence. No naturalist doubts the advantage of what has been called the "physiological division of labour"; hence we may believe that it would be advantageous to a plant to produce stamens alone in one flower or on one whole plant, and pistils alone in another flower or on another plant. In plants under culture and placed under new conditions of life, sometimes the male organs and sometimes the female organs become more or less impotent; now if we suppose this to occur in ever so slight a degree under nature, then, as pollen is already carried regularly from flower to flower, and as a more complete separation of the sexes of our plant would be advantageous on the principle of the division of labour, individuals with this tendency more and more increased, would be continually favoured or selected, until at last a complete separation of the sexes might be effected. It would take up too much space to show the various steps, through dimorphism and other means, by which the separation of the sexes in plants of various kinds is apparently now in progress; but I may add that some of the species of holly in North America, are, according to Asa Gray, in an exactly intermediate condition, or, as he expresses it, are more or less diœciously polygamous.[12]

---

12. **Diœciously:** referring to a characteristic within plant species of having the male and female reproductive parts carried separately by different plants. **Dimorphism:** the existence of two distinctive forms within the same species.

Let us now turn to the nectar-feeding insects; we may suppose the plant, of which we have been slowly increasing the nectar by continued selection, to be a common plant; and that certain insects depended in main part on its nectar for food. I could give many facts showing how anxious bees are to save time: for instance, their habit of cutting holes and sucking the nectar at the bases of certain flowers, which, with a very little more trouble, they can enter by the mouth. Bearing such facts in mind, it may be believed that under certain circumstances individual differences in the curvature or length of the proboscis, &c., too slight to be appreciated by us, might profit a bee or other insect, so that certain individuals would be able to obtain their food more quickly than others; and thus the communities to which they belonged would flourish and throw off many swarms inheriting the same peculiarities. The tubes of the corolla of the common red and incarnate clovers (Trifolium pratense and incarnatum) do not on a hasty glance appear to differ in length; yet the hive-bee can easily suck the nectar out of the incarnate clover, but not out of the common red clover, which is visited by humble-bees alone; so that whole fields of red clover offer in vain an abundant supply of precious nectar to the hive-bee. That this nectar is much liked by the hive-bee is certain; for I have repeatedly seen, but only in the autumn, many hive-bees sucking the flowers through holes bitten in the base of the tube by humble-bees. The difference in the length of the corolla in the two kinds of clover, which determines the visits of the hive-bee, must be very trifling; for I have been assured that when red clover has been mown, the flowers of the second crop are somewhat smaller, and that these are visited by many hive-bees. I do not know whether this statement is accurate; nor whether another published statement can be trusted, namely, that the Ligurian bee which is generally considered a mere variety of the common hive-bee, and which freely crosses with it, is able to reach and suck the nectar of the red clover. Thus, in a country where this kind of clover abounded, it might be a great advantage to the hive-bee to have a slightly longer or differently constructed proboscis. On the other hand, as the fertility of this clover absolutely depends on bees visiting the flowers, if humble-bees were to become rare in any country, it might be a great advantage to the plant to have a shorter or more deeply divided corolla, so that the hive-bees should be enabled to suck its flowers. Thus I can understand how a flower and a bee might slowly become, either simultaneously or one after the other, modified and adapted to each other in the most perfect manner, by the continued preservation of all the individuals which presented slight deviations of structure mutually favourable to each other.

I am well aware that this doctrine of natural selection, exemplified in the above imaginary instances, is open to the same objections which were first urged against Sir Charles Lyell's[13] noble views on "the modern changes of the earth, as illustra- 20

13. **Sir Charles Lyell's:** English geologist (1797–1875), whose book *Principles of Geology* postulated that the earth was millions, rather than thousands, of years old. Lyell felt that great changes in the earth's structure resulted from natural forces acting gradually over long periods of time.

tive of geology"; but we now seldom hear the agencies which we see still at work, spoken of as trifling or insignificant, when used in explaining the excavation of the deepest valleys or the formation of long lines of inland cliffs. Natural selection acts only by the preservation and accumulation of small inherited modifications, each profitable to the preserved being; and as modern geology has almost banished such views as the excavation of a great valley by a single diluvial[14] wave, so will natural selection banish the belief of the continued creation of new organic beings, or of any great and sudden modification in their structure.

UNDERSTANDING THE TEXT

1. Why, according to Charles Darwin, is natural variation within species important to evolution? What would happen to a species if all of its members were born with uniform characteristics?

2. Why does Darwin believe that very slight advantages increase an organism's chances to survive? What other factors make this the case? Do you agree?

3. How would natural selection operate without any directive will? What would the selection process entail?

4. What does Darwin mean by "man selects only for his own good"? How does such selection support Darwin's theory?

5. What examples does Darwin give of characteristics that help organisms survive in specific environments? How might an advantage in one environment become a disadvantage in another environment?

6. What does Darwin mean by "sexual selection"? How does this process differ from the kinds of selection that he refers to earlier? Why does he say that it is "less rigorous than natural selection"?

7. What kinds of potential objections does Darwin refer to in the final paragraph of this selection? How do the objections that he expects to be raised against his work resemble those that were raised against Lyell's ideas?

8. Analyze Darwin's uses of evidence to prove his points. How effectively do his examples support his argument?

MAKING CONNECTIONS

1. Elsewhere, Darwin reports that Thomas Malthus's "Essay on the Principle of Population" (p. 324) started him thinking about natural selection. How does Darwin draw on Malthus's ideas, especially concerning the competition for resources?

---

14. **Diluvial:** relating to a flood. Darwin here alludes to the Christian belief that major geological changes in the earth can be attributed to the great flood described in the Book of Genesis.

2. How does Darwin's view of the natural world compare with Hobbes's view (p. 119) of the state of nature?

3. How does the concept of natural selection compare with Ruth Benedict's assertions (p. 132) about character traits and culture? In what sense are cultures and societies "environments" that shape their members through natural selection? At what point does such an analogy break down?

4. How is Garrett Hardin's argument in "Lifeboat Ethics" (p. 357) consistent with the theory of natural selection? What role does overpopulation play in the "survival of the fittest"?

Writing about the Text

1. Some nineteenth-century commentators argued that the poor are not well-adapted to survive, that perhaps their poverty is a result of their poor adaptation. Does the theory of natural selection support this interpretation? Or is a society's tendency to support its poorer members an evolutionary advantage, increasing that society's ability to survive? Consider such questions in an essay on poverty and Darwinian theory.

2. Compare Darwin's use of the word "nature" with its uses by Rachel Carson (p. 419), David Suzuki (p. 427), and Matthieu Ricerd and Trinh Xuan Thuan (p. 435). How do subtle differences in the definition of this word lead to very different kinds of arguments?

3. Research the current controversy over teaching evolution in public schools and write an essay outlining the arguments posed by the advocates of the theory of "intelligent design." Is this theory compatible with the theory of natural selection? Why or why not?

Rachel Carson
The Obligation to Endure
(1962)

BEFORE SHE TOOK UP the problem of chemical pesticides in *Silent Spring*, Rachel Carson (1907–1964) was already a respected scientist and a best-selling author. After earning a master's degree in zoology from Johns Hopkins University in 1932, she spent her early career as an aquatic biologist with the U.S. Bureau of Fisheries and its later incarnation as the Fish and Wildlife Service. In 1949, she rose to the position of chief editor of publications for the Fish and Wildlife Service and published three books about the ocean: *Under the Sea-Wind* (1941), *The Sea Around Us* (1951), and *The Edge of the Sea* (1955). The second of these books won the National Book Award and sold so many copies that Carson was able to give up her job and devote her time to writing.

With the publication of her most famous work, *Silent Spring*, Carson took on the unfamiliar role of social activist. The book began as a magazine article about the environmental impact of pesticides, especially of the compound dichlorodiphenyl-trichloroethane, better known as DDT. During and after World War II, DDT had been used throughout the world to control insects, remove disease threats, and increase food production. Carson traced the poisonous effects of DDT and other pesticides through the ecosystem, beginning with plants and insects and moving swiftly to fish, birds, wildlife, domestic animals, and finally to people, for whom, Carson argued, DDT was a carcinogen.

When the book was published, the chemical pesticide industry launched a major counterstrike aimed at discrediting Carson. Despite their attack, the book became a phenomenal best seller and caused millions of Americans to reevaluate their faith in technology, scientific progress, and the role of government in protecting their interests.

Carson died of breast cancer in 1964 before she could see the effect that her work had on the world. In 1972, largely because of *Silent Spring*, the Environmental Protection Agency banned the use of DDT. In 1980, Carson was posthumously awarded the Presidential Medal of Freedom. And in 1999, the Modern Library Editorial Board ranked *Silent Spring* as one of the most important nonfiction books of the twentieth century.

Carson's accomplishment in *Silent Spring*, chapter 2 of which follows, goes beyond exposing the dangers of pesticides. The portrait that she created of a deeply interconnected natural world, where changes to one species have far-reaching, unforeseen consequences for the entire ecological system, struck a deep chord with her readers and even changed their perception of nature. Today, many consider the publication of *Silent Spring* to mark the beginning of the modern environmental movement.

Carson's claim about the dangers of chemicals is primarily supported by facts and statistics. She links together a series of historical and scientific facts to focus readers' attention on the negative consequences of using chemicals that most people saw only in terms of their positive effect. 🖎

THE HISTORY OF LIFE on earth has been a history of interaction between living things and their surroundings. To a large extent, the physical form and the habits of the earth's vegetation and its animal life have been molded by the environment. Considering the whole span of earthly time, the opposite effect, in which life actually modifies its surroundings, has been relatively slight. Only within the moment of time represented by the present century has one species—man—acquired significant power to alter the nature of his world.

During the past quarter century this power has not only increased to one of disturbing magnitude but it has changed in character. The most alarming of all man's assaults upon the environment is the contamination of air, earth, rivers, and sea with dangerous and even lethal materials. This pollution is for the most part irrecoverable; the chain of evil it initiates not only in the world that must support life but in living tissues is for the most part irreversible. In this now universal contamination of the environment, chemicals are the sinister and little-recognized partners of radiation in changing the very nature of the world—the very nature of its life. Strontium 90, released through nuclear explosions into the air, comes to earth in rain or drifts down as fallout, lodges in soil, enters into the grass or corn or wheat grown there, and in time takes up its abode in the bones of a human being, there to remain until his death. Similarly, chemicals sprayed on croplands or forests or gardens lie long in soil, entering into living organisms, passing from one to another in a chain of poisoning and death. Or they pass mysteriously by underground streams until they emerge and, through the alchemy of air and sunlight, combine into new forms that kill vegetation, sicken cattle, and work unknown harm on those who drink from once pure wells. As Albert Schweitzer[1] has said, "Man can hardly even recognize the devils of his own creation."

It took hundreds of millions of years to produce the life that now inhabits the earth—eons of time in which that developing and evolving and diversifying life reached a state of adjustment and balance with its surroundings. The environment, rigorously shaping and directing the life it supported, contained elements that were

1. **Albert Schweitzer:** German-Alsatian theologian, philosopher, music scholar, and physician (1875–1965), who won the Nobel Peace Prize in 1952 for his lifelong devotion to providing medical services in Africa.

hostile as well as supporting. Certain rocks gave out dangerous radiation; even within the light of the sun, from which all life draws its energy, there were short-wave radiations with power to injure. Given time—time not in years but in millennia—life adjusts, and a balance has been reached. For time is the essential ingredient; but in the modern world there is no time.

The rapidity of change and the speed with which new situations are created follow the impetuous and heedless pace of man rather than the deliberate pace of nature. Radiation is no longer merely the background radiation of rocks, the bombardment of cosmic rays, the ultraviolet of the sun that have existed before there was any life on earth; radiation is now the unnatural creation of man's tampering with the atom. The chemicals to which life is asked to make its adjustment are no longer merely the calcium and silica and copper and all the rest of the minerals washed out of the rocks and carried in rivers to the sea; they are the synthetic creations of man's inventive mind, brewed in his laboratories, and having no counterparts in nature.

To adjust to these chemicals would require time on the scale that is nature's; it   5 would require not merely the years of a man's life but the life of generations. And even this, were it by some miracle possible, would be futile, for the new chemicals come from our laboratories in an endless stream; almost five hundred annually find their way into actual use in the United States alone. The figure is staggering and its implications are not easily grasped—500 new chemicals to which the bodies of men and animals are required somehow to adapt each year, chemicals totally outside the limits of biologic experience.

Among them are many that are used in man's war against nature. Since the mid-1940's over 200 basic chemicals have been created for use in killing insects, weeds, rodents, and other organisms described in the modern vernacular as "pests"; and they are sold under several thousand different brand names.

These sprays, dusts, and aerosols are now applied almost universally to farms, gardens, forests, and homes—nonselective chemicals that have the power to kill every insect, the "good" and the "bad," to still the song of birds and the leaping of fish in the streams, to coat the leaves with a deadly film, and to linger on in soil—all this though the intended target may be only a few weeds or insects. Can anyone believe it is possible to lay down such a barrage of poisons on the surface of the earth without making it unfit for all life? They should not be called "insecticides," but "biocides."

The whole process of spraying seems caught up in an endless spiral. Since DDT was released for civilian use, a process of escalation has been going on in which ever more toxic materials must be found. This has happened because insects, in a triumphant vindication of Darwin's principle of the survival of the fittest, have evolved super races immune to the particular insecticide used, hence a deadlier one has always to be developed—and then a deadlier one than that. It has happened also because, for reasons to be described later, destructive insects often undergo a "flareback," or resurgence, after spraying, in numbers greater than before. Thus the chemical war is never won, and all life is caught in its violent crossfire.

Along with the possibility of the extinction of mankind by nuclear war, the central problem of our age has therefore become the contamination of man's total environment with such substances of incredible potential for harm—substances that accumulate in the tissues of plants and animals and even penetrate the germ cells to shatter or alter the very material of heredity upon which the shape of the future depends.

Some would-be architects of our future look toward a time when it will be pos-   10
sible to alter the human germ plasm by design. But we may easily be doing so now by inadvertence, for many chemicals, like radiation, bring about gene mutations. It is ironic to think that man might determine his own future by something so seemingly trivial as the choice of an insect spray.

All this has been risked—for what? Future historians may well be amazed by our distorted sense of proportion. How could intelligent beings seek to control a few unwanted species by a method that contaminated the entire environment and brought the threat of disease and death even to their own kind? Yet this is precisely what we have done. We have done it, moreover, for reasons that collapse the moment we examine them. We are told that the enormous and expanding use of pesticides is necessary to maintain farm production. Yet is our real problem not one of *over-production*? Our farms, despite measures to remove acreages from production and to pay farmers *not* to produce, have yielded such a staggering excess of crops that the American taxpayer in 1962 is paying out more than one billion dollars a year as the total carrying cost of the surplus-food storage program. And is the situation helped when one branch of the Agriculture Department tries to reduce production while another states, as it did in 1958, "It is believed generally that reduction of crop acreages under provisions of the Soil Bank will stimulate interest in use of chemicals to obtain maximum production on the land retained in crops."

All this is not to say there is no insect problem and no need of control. I am saying, rather, that control must be geared to realities, not to mythical situations, and that the methods employed must be such that they do not destroy us along with the insects.

The problem whose attempted solution has brought such a train of disaster in its wake is an accompaniment of our modern way of life. Long before the age of man, insects inhabited the earth—a group of extraordinarily varied and adaptable beings. Over the course of time since man's advent, a small percentage of the more than half a million species of insects have come into conflict with human welfare in two principal ways: as competitors for the food supply and as carriers of human disease.

Disease-carrying insects become important where human beings are crowded together, especially under conditions where sanitation is poor, as in time of natural disaster or war or in situations of extreme poverty and deprivation. Then control of some sort becomes necessary. It is a sobering fact, however, as we shall presently see, that the method of massive chemical control has had only limited success, and also threatens to worsen the very conditions it is intended to curb.

Under primitive agricultural conditions the farmer had few insect problems. These arose with the intensification of agriculture—the devotion of immense acreages to a single crop. Such a system set the stage for explosive increases in specific insect populations. Single-crop farming does not take advantage of the principles by which nature works; it is agriculture as an engineer might conceive it to be. Nature has introduced great variety into the landscape, but man has displayed a passion for simplifying it. Thus he undoes the built-in checks and balances by which nature holds the species within bounds. One important natural check is a limit on the amount of suitable habitat for each species. Obviously then, an insect that lives on wheat can build up its population to much higher levels on a farm devoted to wheat than on one in which wheat is intermingled with other crops to which the insect is not adapted.

The same thing happens in other situations. A generation or more ago, the towns of large areas of the United States lined their streets with the noble elm tree. Now the beauty they hopefully created is threatened with complete destruction as disease sweeps through the elms, carried by a beetle that would have only limited chance to build up large populations and to spread from tree to tree if the elms were only occasional trees in a richly diversified planting.

Another factor in the modern insect problem is one that must be viewed against a background of geologic and human history: the spreading of thousands of different kinds of organisms from their native homes to invade new territories. This worldwide migration has been studied and graphically described by the British ecologist Charles Elton in his recent book *The Ecology of Invasions*. During the Cretaceous Period, some hundred million years ago, flooding seas cut many land bridges between continents and living things found themselves confined in what Elton calls "colossal separate nature reserves." There, isolated from others of their kind, they developed many new species. When some of the land masses were joined again, about 15 million years ago, these species began to move out into new territories—a movement that is not only still in progress but is now receiving considerable assistance from man.

The importation of plants is the primary agent in the modern spread of species, for animals have almost invariably gone along with the plants, quarantine being a comparatively recent and not completely effective innovation. The United States Office of Plant Introduction alone has introduced almost 200,000 species and varieties of plants from all over the world. Nearly half of the 180 or so major insect enemies of plants in the United States are accidental imports from abroad, and most of them have come as hitchhikers on plants.

In new territory, out of reach of the restraining hand of the natural enemies that kept down its numbers in its native land, an invading plant or animal is able to become enormously abundant. Thus it is no accident that our most troublesome insects are introduced species.

These invasions, both the naturally occurring and those dependent on human assistance, are likely to continue indefinitely. Quarantine and massive chemical campaigns are only extremely expensive ways of buying time. We are faced, according to Dr. Elton, "with a life-and-death need not just to find new technological means of suppressing this plant or that animal"; instead we need the basic knowledge of animal populations and their relations to their surroundings that will "promote an even balance and damp down the explosive power of outbreaks and new invasions." 20

Much of the necessary knowledge is now available but we do not use it. We train ecologists in our universities and even employ them in our governmental agencies but we seldom take their advice. We allow the chemical death rain to fall as though there were no alternative, whereas in fact there are many, and our ingenuity could soon discover many more if given opportunity.

Have we fallen into a mesmerized state that makes us accept as inevitable that which is inferior or detrimental, as though having lost the will or the vision to demand that which is good? Such thinking, in the words of the ecologist Paul Shepard, "idealizes life with only its head out of water, inches above the limits of toleration of the corruption of its own environment . . . Why should we tolerate a diet of weak poisons, a home in insipid surroundings, a circle of acquaintances who are not quite our enemies, the noise of motors with just enough relief to prevent insanity? Who would want to live in a world which is just not quite fatal?"

Yet such a world is pressed upon us. The crusade to create a chemically sterile, insect-free world seems to have engendered a fanatic zeal on the part of many specialists and most of the so-called control agencies. On every hand there is evidence that those engaged in spraying operations exercise a ruthless power. "The regulatory entomologists . . . function as prosecutor, judge and jury, tax assessor and collector and sheriff to enforce their own orders," said Connecticut entomologist Neely Turner. The most flagrant abuses go unchecked in both state and federal agencies.

It is not my contention that chemical insecticides must never be used. I do contend that we have put poisonous and biologically potent chemicals indiscriminately into the hands of persons largely or wholly ignorant of their potentials for harm. We have subjected enormous numbers of people to contact with these poisons, without their consent and often without their knowledge. If the Bill of Rights contains no guarantee that a citizen shall be secure against lethal poisons distributed either by private individuals or by public officials, it is surely only because our forefathers, despite their considerable wisdom and foresight, could conceive of no such problem.

I contend, furthermore, that we have allowed these chemicals to be used with lit- 25
tle or no advance investigation of their effect on soil, water, wildlife, and man himself. Future generations are unlikely to condone our lack of prudent concern for the
integrity of the natural world that supports all life.

There is still very limited awareness of the nature of the threat. This is an era of
specialists, each of whom sees his own problem and is unaware of or intolerant of
the larger frame into which it fits. It is also an era dominated by industry, in which
the right to make a dollar at whatever cost is seldom challenged. When the public
protests, confronted with some obvious evidence of damaging results of pesticide
applications, it is fed little tranquilizing pills of half truth. We urgently need an end
to these false assurances, to the sugar coating of unpalatable facts. It is the public
that is being asked to assume the risks that the insect controllers calculate. The public must decide whether it wishes to continue on the present road, and it can do so
only when in full possession of the facts. In the words of Jean Rostand,[2] "The obligation to endure gives us the right to know."

Understanding the Text

1. What "power" have human beings recently acquired that, according to
   Rachel Carson, makes the current time period unique in the history of life
   on Earth?

2. What does Carson mean by "in the modern world there is no time"?

3. What happens when insects adapt to pesticides in their environment? Could
   any pesticide, theoretically, not result in an increased tolerance for that pesticide among insects? Why or why not?

4. What arguments in favor of pesticide use does Carson anticipate? How does
   she build responses to these arguments into her treatment of the issues?

5. What role does single-crop farming play in the rise of insect populations?
   Why is it dangerous, in Carson's view, to limit diversity in specific natural
   areas?

6. Which of the dangers and mysteries of pesticide use does Carson object
   to most?

Making Connections

1. How do large increases in human populations create conditions in which
   insects and other forms of life must be controlled? How does Malthus anticipate these kinds of problems in his "Essay on the Principle of Population"
   (p. 324)?

2. **Jean Rostand:** French biologist and playwright (1894–1997).

2. Exactly how does Darwin's principle of natural selection (p. 405) explain insects' adaptation to pesticides?

3. How have Carson's views of nature influenced later environmental writers such as David Suzuki (p. 427) and Al Gore (p. 454)?

Writing about the Text

1. Conducting extra research as necessary, describe an environmental threat to the ecosystem in the area in which you live. How are the lives of insects, birds, fish, animals, and plants connected to each other, and how are they threatened?

2. Analyze Carson's use of evidence in this selection. What claims does she make, and how effectively does she support each one?

3. The international accord on pesticides reached in Stockholm, Sweden, in 2004 contains this "malaria exception" in its restriction of DDT:

> The Stockholm Convention on Persistent Organic Pollutants (POPs) recognizes that in some countries, especially those in sub-Saharan Africa, DDT remains an important tool in the war against malaria. Countries that ratify the Convention may continue using DDT for controlling mosquitoes that spread malaria. Thus, the Convention will not increase the likelihood that people will be infected with malaria.

Many environmental groups opposed this exception, but supporters argued that DDT had already prevented hundreds of millions of people from dying of malaria and that, if its use were entirely eliminated, the human costs in some of the world's poorest countries would be severe. Write an essay supporting or opposing this exception, based on the case against DDT that Carson outlines in "The Obligation to Endure."

David Suzuki
The Sacred Balance
(1997)

DAVID SUZUKI WAS BORN IN 1936 in Vancouver, British Columbia. His grand-parents had immigrated to Canada from Japan around the turn of the century. During World War II, Suzuki and his family, along with thousands of other Japan-ese-Canadians, were sent to an internment camp and, after the war, forced to move to another part of Canada. Suzuki graduated from Amherst College in Massachu-setts in 1958 and received a Ph.D. in zoology from the University of Chicago in 1961. From 1963 to 2001, he was a professor of genetics at the University of British Columbia.

Suzuki's early research in genetics was important and well received, but he owes his position as Canada's most famous scientist to his second career as a television personality. In the 1970s, he hosted several science-themed TV and radio shows with small followings. In 1979, he began hosting CBC Television's signature science show *The Nature of Things*. In the thirty years that Suzuki has been hosting this program, it has been broadcast in more than fifty countries and has won dozens of national and international awards. When the CBC asked its viewers in 2004 to name the great-est Canadians in history, Suzuki came in fifth place—and was the highest-rated living Canadian in the survey.

One of Canada's best-known environmental activists, Suzuki has championed con-servation, wilderness preservation, and, in recent years, has become increasingly con-cerned about global climate change. In 1990, he and his wife, Tara Cullis, founded the David Suzuki Foundation, a charitable organization that, according to its mission statement, "works through science and education to protect the diversity of nature and our quality of life, now and for the future."

Suzuki is also a prolific author who has written forty-three books on scientific and environmental topics. The text reprinted here is the preface to his bestselling book *The Sacred Balance* (1997). In it, Suzuki lays out the fundamental arguments of the book: that every aspect of nature has evolved to depend on every other aspect, that human beings do not stand outside of this circle of interdependence, that recent human activities have seriously disrupted the balance of the natural world, and that human beings, in order to live rich and full lives, must learn to respect and preserve the interdependent ecosystem that we all inhabit.

Suzuki uses a variety of different rhetorical strategies and appeals. He supports his ideas with many facts and examples; he uses inductive reasoning to draw con-clusions from observations and appeal to logic; and he emphasizes the grandeur of the natural world to appeal to his readers' emotions.

SUPPOSE THAT 200,000 YEARS AGO, biologists from another galaxy searching for life forms in other parts of the universe had discovered Earth and parked their space vehicle above the Rift Valley in Africa. They would have gazed upon vast grasslands filled with plants and animals, including a newly evolved species, *Homo sapiens*. It is highly unlikely that those extra-galactic exobiologists would have concentrated their attention on this young upright ape species in anticipation of its meteoric rise to preeminence a mere two hundred millennia later. After all, those early humans lived in small family groups that didn't rival the immense herds of wildebeest and antelope. In comparison with many other species, they weren't especially large, fast or strong, or gifted with sensory acuity. Those early humans possessed a survival trait that was invisible because it was locked within their skulls and only revealed through their behaviour. Their immense and complex brains endowed them with tremendous intelligence, conferring as well a vast capacity for memory, an insatiable curiosity and an astonishing creativity, abilities that catapulted their descendants into a position of dominance on the planet.

The eminent Nobel laureate François Jacob[1] suggests that the human brain has an inbuilt need for order. Chaos is terrifying to us because without an understanding of cause and effect, we have no possibility of controlling the cosmic forces impinging on our lives. Early humans recognized that there are patterns in nature that are predictable—the diurnal cycle,[2] the lunar cycle, the tides, the seasons, animal migration and plant succession. They were able to exploit these regularities for their own benefit and to avoid potential hazards. Over time, every human society evolved a culture that inculcated an understanding of its place on Earth and in the cosmos. The collective knowledge, beliefs, languages and songs of each society make up what anthropologists call a "world-view." In every world-view, there is an understanding that everything is connected to everything else, that nothing exists in isolation or alone. People have always understood that we are deeply embedded in and dependent upon the natural world.

In such a world of interconnectedness, it is understood that every action has consequences, and when we were part of that world, we had a responsibility to act properly to keep the world in order. Many of our rituals, songs, prayers and ceremonies were reaffirmations of our dependence on nature and our commitment to behave properly. That is how it has been for most of human existence all over the world.

From Naked Ape to Superspecies

But suddenly in the last century, *Homo sapiens* has undergone a radical transformation into a new kind of force that I call a "superspecies." For the first time in the

---

1. **François Jacob:** Nobel Prize–winning French biologist (b. 1920).

2. **Diurnal cycle:** the complete rotation of the earth on its axis that is accomplished in twenty-four hours, creating a single day.

3.8 billion years that life has existed on Earth, one species—humanity—is altering the biological, physical and chemical features of the planet on a geological scale. That shift to superspecies has occurred with explosive speed through the conjunction of a number of factors. One is population. It took all of human existence to reach a billion people in the early nineteenth century. A hundred years later, when I was born, in 1936, there were two billion people on Earth. In my lifetime, that doubling time has shrunk to its current twelve to thirteen years while the population has tripled. Thus, by virtue of our numbers alone, our species' "ecological footprint" on the planet has enlarged explosively.

We are now the most numerous mammalian species on the planet but unlike all   5 the others, our ecological impact has been greatly amplified by technology. Virtually all of modern technology has been developed within the past century, thereby escalating both the scale and the scope of our ability to exploit our surroundings. Resource exploitation is fuelled by an exploding consumer demand for products, and the fulfilment of that demand has become a critical component of economic growth. Hyperconsumption in the developed world serves as the model for people in developing countries now that globalization has rendered the entire world population a potential market. Taken together, human numbers, technology, consumption and a globalized economy have made us a new kind of force on the planet. Throughout our evolutionary past, we never had to worry about the collective impact of our entire species because our ecological footprint was so much lighter and nature was vast and endlessly self-renewing. Our new status of superspecies has been achieved so rapidly that we are only now becoming aware of a new level of collective responsibility, which reflects a dawning realization that taken all together, human activity is the main cause of the current decline in the biosphere's rich diversity and productivity that support all life on earth.

A Shattered World

As we have shifted status to a superspecies, our ancient understanding of the exquisite interconnectivity of all life has been shattered. We find it increasingly difficult to recognize the linkages that once gave us a sense of place and belonging. After all, we are flooded with food and goods that come from all parts of the world, so we scarcely notice that in the middle of winter we are still able to buy fresh strawberries and cherries. The constraints of locality and seasons are pushed aside by the global economy. Exacerbating the fragmentation of the world has been the stunning shift from predominant habitation in rural, village communities to population concentration in large cities. In big cities, it becomes easy to assume that we differ from all other species in that we create our own habitat and thereby escape the constraints of nature. Nature cleanses water, creates air, decomposes sewage, absorbs garbage, generates electricity and produces food, but in cities, these "ecosystem services" are assumed to be performed by the workings of the economy.

To make matters worse, as information both proliferates and shrinks to smaller and smaller bytes, the context, history and background needed to set new "facts" or events in place are lost and our world is broken up into disconnected bits and pieces. While we look to science to reveal the secrets of the cosmos, its primary methodology of reductionism focusses on parts of nature. And as the world around us is examined in pieces, the rhythms, patterns and cycles within which those pieces are integrated are lost and any insight we gain become illusions of understanding and mastery. Finally, as transnational corporations, politics and telecommunications move onto the global stage, the sense of the local is decimated.

This, then, is where we are at the beginning of the third millennium. With explosive speed, we have been transmogrified from a species like most others that live in balance with our surroundings into an unprecedented force, a superspecies. Like a foreign species that flourishes in a new environment, we have expanded beyond the capacity of our surroundings to support us. It is clear from the history of the past two centuries that the path we embarked on after the Industrial Revolution is leading us increasingly into conflict with the natural world. Despite forty years of experience in the environmental movement, we have not yet turned onto a different path.

The Growth of Environmentalism

Like millions of people around the world, I was galvanized in 1962 by Rachel Carson's eloquent call to action in her book *Silent Spring*.[3] We were swept up in what was to become the "environmental movement." In British Columbia, that meant protesting such things as the American testing of nuclear weapons at Amchitka in the Aleutian Islands (a protest that gave birth to Greenpeace in Vancouver), clear-cut logging throughout the province, proposed offshore drilling for oil, the planned dam at Site C on the Peace River, and air and water pollution from pulp mills. In my mind, the problem was that we were taking too much from the environment and putting too much waste back into it. From that perspective, the solution was to set limits on how much and what could be removed from the biosphere for human use and how much and what could be put back into our surroundings, then make sure to enforce the regulations. So in addition to protesting, marching and blockading, many of us were lobbying politicians to set aside more parks, to enact Clean Water and Clean Air legislation, to pass Endangered Species Acts and to establish the agencies to enforce the regulations.

But Carson's book itself offered evidence of the need for a deeper analysis, and the more involved I became, the clearer it became to me that my rather simple-minded approach wouldn't work because we were too ignorant to anticipate the

10

3. *Silent Spring*: groundbreaking book about the environment and the dangers posed to it by pesticides and other human inventions, by American science writer Rachel Carson (p. 419).

consequences of our activity and to set appropriate limits. Carson's book dealt with DDT. In the 1930s when Paul Mueller, working for the chemical company Geigy in Switzerland, discovered that DDT killed insects, the economic benefits of a chemical pesticide were immediately obvious. Trumpeting the imminent scientific conquest of insect pests and their associated diseases, Geigy patented the discovery and went on to make millions, and Mueller was awarded the Nobel prize in 1948. But years later, when bird watchers noted the decline of eagles and hawks, biologists investigated and discovered the hitherto unknown phenomenon of "biomagnification," whereby compounds become concentrated as they are ingested up the food chain. How could limits have been set on DDT in the early 1940s when we didn't even know about biomagnification as a biological process until birds began to disappear?

Similarly, CFCs[4] were hailed as a wonderful creation of chemistry. These complex molecules were chemically inert, so they didn't react with other compounds and thus made excellent fillers in aerosol cans to go along with substances such as deodorants. No one anticipated that because of their stability, CFCs would persist in the environment and drift into the upper atmosphere, where ultraviolet radiation would break off ozone-scavenging chlorine-free radicals. Most people had never heard of the ozone layer and certainly no one could have anticipated the long-term effects of CFCs, so how could the compounds have been regulated? I have absolutely no doubt that genetically modified organisms (GMOs) will also prove to have unexpected consequences despite the benefits vaunted by biotech companies. But if we don't know enough to anticipate the long-term consequences of human technological innovation, how can its impact be managed? For me as a scientist, this posed a terrible conundrum.

A Way Out

I gained an important insight to free me from this quandary in the late 1970s. As host of the long-running television series *The Nature of Things*, I proposed that we do a program on the battle over clear-cut logging in the Queen Charlotte Islands, off the coast of British Columbia. For thousands of years, the islands have been home to the Haida, who refer to their lands as Haida Gwaii. The forestry giant MacMillan Bloedel had been clear-cut logging huge areas of the islands for years, an activity that had generated increasingly vocal opposition. I flew to Haida Gwaii to interview loggers, forestry officials, government bureaucrats, environmentalists and natives. One of the people I interviewed was a young Haida artist named Guujaaw who had led the opposition to logging for years.

---

4. **CFCs:** chlorofluorocarbons, chemicals used in aerosol sprays that have been shown to deplete the ozone layer.

Unemployment was very high in the Haida communities, and logging generated desperately needed jobs for the Haida. So I asked Guujaaw why he opposed the logging. He replied that of course after the trees were all gone, Haida people would still be there, but added, "Then we'll be like everyone else. We won't be Haida anymore." It was a simple statement whose implications escaped me at the time. But on reflection I realized that he had given me a glimpse into a profoundly different way of seeing the world. Guujaaw's statement suggested that for his people, the trees, the birds, the fish, the water, the wind are all parts of Haida identity. Haida history and culture and the very meaning of why Haida are on earth reside in the land. Ever since that interview, I have been a student learning from encounters with indigenous people in many parts of the world. From Japan to Australia, Papua New Guinea, Borneo, the Kalahari, the Amazon and the Arctic, aboriginal people express that vital need to be connected to the land. They refer to Earth as their Mother, who they say gives birth to us.

Changing Our Perspective

In 1990, my wife, Tara Cullis, and I decided to establish an organization that would examine the root causes of ecological destruction so that we could seek alternatives to our current practices. We decided to draft a document that would express the foundation's world-view and perspective and could be offered to the Earth Summit in Rio de Janeiro in 1992. We called it a Declaration of Interdependence. Tara and I formulated a rough draft and asked for input from Guujaaw, ethnobiologist Wade Davis and the children's singer Raffi. When I was working on the first draft, I tried writing. "We are made up of molecules from the air, water and soil," but this sounded like a scientific treatise and didn't convey the simple truth of our relationship with Earth in an emotional way. After spending days pondering the lines, I suddenly thought, "We *are* the air, we *are* the water, we *are* the earth, we *are* the Sun."

With this realization, I also saw that environmentalists like me had been framing the issue improperly. There is no environment "out there" that is separate from us. We can't manage our impact on the environment if we *are* our surroundings. Indigenous people are absolutely correct: we are born of the earth and constructed from the four sacred elements of earth, air, fire and water. (Hindus list these four and add a fifth element, space.)

15

Once I had finally understood the truth of these ancient wisdoms, I also realized that we are intimately fused to our surroundings and the notion of separateness or isolation is an illusion. Through reading I came to understand that science reaffirms the profundity of these ancient truths over and over again. Looked at as biological beings, we are no more removed from nature than any other creature. Our animal nature dictates our essential needs: clean air, clean water, clean soil, clean energy. This led me to another insight, that these four "scared elements" are created, cleansed and renewed by the web of life itself. If there is to be a fifth sacred element, it is biodiversity itself. And whatever we do to these elements, we do directly to ourselves.

As I read further, I discovered the famed psychologist Abraham Maslow,[5] who pointed out that we have a nested series of needs. At the most basic level, we require the five sacred elements in order to live rich, full lives. But when those basic needs are met, a new set of necessities arises. We are social animals, and the most profound force shaping our humanity is love. And when that vital social need is fulfilled, then a new level of spiritual needs arises as an urgent priority. This is how I made the fundamental reexamination of our relationship with Earth that led to *The Sacred Balance*. In the five years since, I have yet to meet anyone who would dispute the reality and primacy of these fundamental needs. And everything in my reading and experiences since then has reaffirmed these basic needs. The challenge of this millennium is to recognize what we need to live rich, rewarding lives without undermining the very elements that ensure them.

UNDERSTANDING THE TEXT

1. Why does David Suzuki begin with the hypothetical example of an extraterrestrial visitor to earth 200,000 years ago? What is this device intended to convey? How effective do you find it?

2. What are the consequences of François Jacob's suggestion that the human brain desires order and is repelled by chaos? How has this need for order played a role in human history?

3. How, according to Suzuki, have technological advances in the last one hundred years affected the balance of nature? What does he mean when he writes that humans are a "superspecies"?

4. What kinds of political actions does Suzuki believe flow from the understanding of the human interconnectedness with nature? Do you agree with his assessment? Why or why not?

5. How has Suzuki's understanding of interdependence affected his views as an environmentalist? What does he see as the difference between an environmentalism that sees nature as something external and an environmentalism that sees nature as part of oneself?

MAKING CONNECTIONS

1. Why does Suzuki refer to Rachel Carson's *Silent Spring* (p. 419)? How does her message in "The Obligation to Endure" relate to Suzuki's argument?

---

5. **Abraham Maslow:** American psychologist (1908–1970) best known for his "hierarchy of needs," which Suzuki describes in this passage.

2. How have the population shifts described by Thomas Malthus (p. 324) and Garrett Hardin (p. 357) affected the balance of nature that Suzuki describes in this selection?

3. Compare Suzuki's view of humanity's effect on nature with Al Gore's view in "The Climate Emergency" (p. 454). Would Suzuki support Gore's argument that human activity can affect the global climate in potentially disastrous ways? Explain.

WRITING ABOUT THE TEXT

1. Identify Suzuki's claim in this essay and explain how his anecdotes, facts, and references to other texts all support this claim.

2. Compare Suzuki's view of interdependence with that of Matthieu Ricard in "The Universe in a Grain of Sand" (p. 435). Can Suzuki's argument be fairly described as a Buddhist one? Write an essay in which you outline the basic tenets of a Buddhist view of the universe, as described by Ricard, and explain how Suzuki's beliefs correspond with this view—or how they do not.

3. Think about your own experience of the interconnectedness of nature. Select a single experience you've had in the wilderness and write a personal essay in which you first narrate the story of your experience and then reflect on what it meant to you. If you haven't had a significant experience with wilderness, explain that fact and reflect on how it may have affected your worldview.

Matthieu Ricard and Trinh Xuan Thuan
The Universe in a Grain of Sand
(2001)

THE LIVES AND PROFESSIONS of Matthieu Ricard (b. 1946) and Trinh Xuan Thuan (b. 1948) form a remarkable intersection between East and West and between Buddhism and science. This intersection is all the more remarkable because their early years provided few clues to the directions these men's lives would take.

Ricard is the son of the well-known French philosopher Jean-François Revel (b. 1924). He was educated as a scientist and received a Ph.D. in biology at the prestigious Institute Pasteur in 1972, after working with the eminent biologists François Jacob (b. 1920) and Jacques Monod (1910–1976) on their Nobel Prize–winning genetic research. Soon after completing his doctoral dissertation, Ricard moved to India to become a full-time student of Buddhism. He was ordained a Buddhist monk in 1979 and is currently the official French translator for the Buddhist spiritual leader the Dalai Lama. In 1998, he and his father wrote *The Monk and the Philosopher*, a series of conversations about the intersections between Buddhism and Western philosophy.

Thuan was born in a Buddhist family in Hanoi, Vietnam. Because Vietnam was a French colony at the time, he studied in French schools before beginning his college education in Switzerland. In 1967, he transferred to the California Institute of Technology, which, at the time, was home to both the largest telescope and the foremost astrophysics program in the world. He received a Ph.D. in astrophysics from Caltech, and since 1976 he has been a professor of astronomy at the University of Virginia. In addition to a large body of scientific research, Thuan has published three books for general readers: *The Birth of the Universe* (1993), *The Secret Melody* (1994), and *Chaos and Harmony* (2000).

In 1997, Ricard and Thuan began a series of conversations about Buddhism and science that resulted in the book *The Quantum and the Lotus* (published in French in 2000; English translation, 2001). Like *The Monk and the Philosopher*, *The Quantum and the Lotus* is a dialogue—Ricard and Thuan pose questions to each other and answer them from their respective positions within Buddhism and science.

"The Universe in a Grain of Sand," chapter 4 of *The Quantum and the Lotus*, deals with interconnectedness. According to classical Buddhist thought, the independent existences of people and things are an illusion. In reality, human consciousness and all matter are connected to each other in a relationship of mutual dependence. The perception that we exist apart from other things and from other people causes us to desire things that we do not realize are already part of us. These desires produce suffering, and Buddhist practice aims to remove this suffering. However, simply eliminating desires is not enough—Buddhism also seeks to remove the illusions about nature that produce desires in the first place. In their conversation, Ricard and Thuan find similarities between the ancient Buddhist concept of interdependence and the modern scientific concept of nonseparability.

Both Ricard and Thuan bring their own perspectives and rhetorical styles to their discussion. But it is the juxtaposition of these perspectives that suggests a key idea of the text. The mere act of bringing these two worldviews together implies that they can learn from each other. Taken as a whole, "The Universe in a Grain of Sand" constructs an extended comparison of the scientific principles of quantum mechanics and the religious philosophy of Buddhism. 🖎

The Interdependence and Nonseparability of Phenomena

*T*HE CONCEPT OF INTERDEPENDENCE *lies at the heart of the Buddhist vision of the nature of reality, and has immense implications in Buddhism regarding how we should live our lives. This concept of interdependence is strikingly similar to the concept of nonseparability in quantum physics. Both concepts lead us to ask a question that is both simple and fundamental: Can a "thing," or a "phenomenon," exist autonomously? If not, in what way and to what degree are the universe's phenomena interconnected? If things do not exist per se, what conclusions must be drawn about life?*

THUAN: . . . Buddhism rejects the idea of a principle of creation,[1] as well as the radical notion of parallel universes—though it may accommodate the idea of multiple universes. To Buddhism, the extraordinary fine-tuning of the physical constants and the initial conditions that allowed the universe to create life and consciousness are explained by "the interdependence of phenomena." I think it's time to explain more about this idea.

MATTHIEU: To do so, we should first return to the concept of "relative truth." In Buddhism, the perception we have of distinct phenomena resulting from isolated causes and conditions is called "relative truth" or "delusion." Our daily experience makes us think that things have a real, objective independence, as though they existed all on their own and had intrinsic identities. But this way of seeing phenomena is just a mental construct. Even though this view of reality seems to be commonsense, it doesn't stand up to analysis.

Buddhism instead adopts the notion that all things exist only in relationship to others, the idea of mutual causality. An event can happen only because it's depend-

The authors' footnotes have been omitted.
1. Buddhists believe that the universe's underlying reality has always existed, so that speaking in terms of a "creation" or a "creator" is erroneous. Both terms imply a beginning and, before it, a time of nonexistence.

ent on other factors. Buddhism sees the world as a vast flow of events that are linked together and participate in one another. The way we perceive this flow crystallizes certain aspects of the nonseparable universe, thus creating an illusion that there are autonomous entities completely separate from us.

In one of his sermons, the Buddha described reality as a display of pearls— each pearl reflects all of the others, as well as the palace whose façade they decorate, and the entirety of the universe. This comes down to saying that all of reality is present in each of its parts. This image is a good illustration of interdependence, which states that no entity independent of the whole can exist anywhere in the universe.

T: This "flow of events" idea is similar to the view of reality that derives from modern cosmology. From the smallest atom up to the universe in its entirety, including the galaxies, stars, and humankind, everything is moving and evolving. Nothing is immutable.

M: Not only do things move, but we see them as "things" only because we are viewing them from a particular angle. We mustn't give the world properties that are merely appearances. Phenomena are simply events that happen in certain circumstances. Buddhism doesn't deny conventional truth—the sort that ordinary people perceive or the scientist detects. It doesn't contest the laws of cause and effect, or the laws of physics and mathematics. It quite simply affirms that, if we dig deep enough, there is a difference between the way we see the world and the way it really is, and the way it really is, we've discovered, is devoid of intrinsic existence.

T: So what has that true nature got to do with interdependence?

M: The word "interdependence" is a translation of the Sanskrit *pratitya samutpada*, which means "to be by co-emergence" and is usually translated as "dependent origination." The saying can be interpreted in two complementary ways. The first is "*this* arises because *that* is," which comes down to saying that things do exist in some way, but nothing exists on its own. The second is "*this*, having been produced, produces *that*," which means that nothing can be its own cause. Or we could say that everything is in some way interdependent with the world. We do not deny that phenomena really do occur, but we argue that they are "dependent," that they don't exist in an autonomous way. Any given thing in our world can appear only because it's connected, conditioned and in turn conditioning, co-present and co-operating in constant transformation. Their way of "being" is simply in relation to one another, never in and of themselves. We tend to cling to the notion that "things" must precede relationships. This is not the case here. The characteristics of phenomena are defined only through relationships.

Interdependence explains what Buddhism sees as the impermanence and emptiness of phenomena, and this emptiness is what we mean by the lack of "reality." The
seventh Dalai Lama[2] summarized this idea in a verse:

> *Understanding interdependence, we understand emptiness.*
> *Understanding emptiness, we understand interdependence.*
> *This is the view that lies in the middle,*
> *And which is beyond the terrifying cliffs of eternalism and nihilism.*[3]

Another way of defining the idea of interdependence is summarized by the term
tantra, which stands for a notion of continuity and "the fact that everything is part
of the whole, so that nothing can happen separately."

Ironically, though we might think that the idea of interdependence undermines
the notion of reality, in the Buddhist way of thinking, it is interdependence that
actually allows for reality to appear. Let's think about an entity that exists independently from all others. As an immutable and autonomous entity, it couldn't act
on anything, or be acted on itself. For phenomena to happen, interdependence is
required.

This argument refutes the idea of distinct particles that are supposed to constitute matter. What's more, this interdependence naturally includes consciousness.
The reality of any given object depends on a subject that is aware of that object.
This was what the physicist Erwin Schrödinger meant when he wrote: "Without
being aware of it, and without being rigorously systematic about it, we exclude the
subject of cognizance from the domain of nature that we endeavor to understand.
We step with our own person back into the part of an onlooker who does not belong
to the world, which by this very procedure becomes an objective world."

Finally, the most subtle aspect of interdependence, or "dependent origination,"
concerns what we call a phenomenon's "designation base" and its "designation." A
phenomenon's position, form, dimension, color, or any other of its apparent characteristics is merely one of its "designation bases." This designation is a mental construct that invests a phenomenon with a distinct reality. In our everyday experience,
when we see an object, we aren't struck by its nominal existence, but rather by its
true existence. If we analyze this "object" more closely, however, we discover that it
is produced by a large number of causes and conditions, and that we are incapable
of pinpointing an autonomous identity. Since we have experienced it, we can't say
that the phenomenon doesn't exist. But neither can we say that it corresponds to
an intrinsic reality. So we conclude that the object exists (thus avoiding a nihilistic

---

2. **Dalai Lama:** the spiritual leader of the largest
division of Tibetan Buddhism and, before the
Chinese invasion (1949), Tibet's head of state.
The seventh Dalai Lama was Kelzang Gyatso
(1708–1757).

3. **Nihilism:** the philosophical position that
rejects any basis for determining truth or value;
it holds that existence has no meaning or purpose. Ricard defines **eternalism** three paragraphs
below.

view), but that this existence is purely nominal, or conventional (thus also avoiding the opposite extreme of material realism, which is called "eternalism" in Buddhism). A phenomenon with no autonomous existence, but that is nevertheless not totally inexistent, can act and function according to causality and thus lead to positive or negative effects. This view of reality therefore allows us to anticipate the results of our actions and organize our relationship with the world. A Tibetan poem puts it this way:

> To say a thing is empty does not mean
> It cannot function—it means it lacks an absolute reality.
> To say a thing arises "in dependence" does not mean
> It has intrinsic being—it means it is illusion-like.
> If thus one's understanding is correct and certain
> Of what is meant by voidness and dependent origin,
> No need is there to add that voidness and appearance
> Occur together without contradiction in a single thing.

T: I find everything you've told me about interdependence striking. Science, too, has discovered that reality is nonseparable, or interdependent, both at the subatomic level and in the macrocosmic world. The conclusion that subatomic phenomena are interdependent was derived from a famous thought experiment conducted by Einstein and two of his Princeton colleagues, Boris Podolsky and Nathan Rosen, in 1935. It's called the EPR experiment, from the initials of their surnames.

To follow this experiment, you need to know that light (and matter, too) has a dual nature. The particles we call "photons" and "electrons," as well as all the other particles of matter, are Janus-faced. Sometimes they appear as particles, but they can also appear as waves. This is one of the strangest and most counterintuitive findings of quantum theory.[4] Even stranger is the finding that what makes the difference about whether a particle is in the wave or particle state is the role of an observer—if we try to observe the particle in its wave state, it becomes a particle. But if it is unobserved, it remains in the wave state.

Take the case of a photon. If it appears as a wave, then quantum physics says that it spreads out in all directions through space, like the ripples made by a pebble thrown into a pond. The photon in this state has no fixed location or trajectory. We can then say that the photon is present everywhere at the same time. Quantum mechanics states that when a photon is in this wave state, we can never predict where the

15

---

4. **Quantum theory:** or quantum mechanics, the dominant theory in physics dealing with atomic and subatomic particles. Unlike classical Newtonian physics, quantum mechanics accepts a certain amount of inevitable uncertainty in what can be known about the behavior of atomic and subatomic particles. This uncertainty, which is introduced by the very act of observing and trying to measure a phenomenon, is a principle of physics rather than simply the result of inadequate measuring devices. **Janus-faced:** two-sided.

photon will be at any given moment; all we can do is evaluate the probability of its being in a particular position. The chances might be 75 percent or 90 percent, but never 100 percent. Since Einstein was a committed determinist, he couldn't accept that the quantum world was ruled in this way by probability or chance. He argued famously that "God does not play dice," and stubbornly set about trying to find the weak link in quantum mechanics and its probabilistic interpretation of reality. That's why he came up with the EPR experiment.

The experiment goes like this: First imagine that you have constructed a measuring apparatus with which you can observe the behavior of particles of light, called photons. Now imagine a particle that disintegrates spontaneously into two photons, *a* and *b*. The law of symmetry dictates that they will always travel in opposite directions. If *a* goes northward, then we will detect *b* to the south. So far, so good. But we're forgetting the strangeness of quantum mechanics. Before being captured by the detector, if quantum mechanics is correct, *a* appears as a wave, not a particle. This wave wasn't localized, and there was a certain probability that *a* might be found in any given direction. It's only when it has been captured that *a* changes into a particle and "learns" that it's heading northward. But if *a* didn't "know" before being captured which direction it had taken, how could *b* have "guessed" what *a* was doing and ordered its behavior accordingly so that it could be captured at the same moment in the opposite direction? This is impossible, unless we admit that *a* can inform *b* instantaneously of the direction it has taken. But Einstein's cherished theory of relativity states that nothing can travel faster than light. The information about *a*'s location would need to travel faster than the speed of light in order to get to *b* in time, because, after all, *a* and *b* are both particles of light and are therefore traveling themselves at the speed of light. "God does not send telepathic signals," Einstein said, adding, "There can be no spooky action at a distance."

On the basis of these thought-experiment results, Einstein concluded that quantum mechanics didn't provide a complete description of reality. In his opinion, the idea that *a* could instantaneously inform *b* of its position was absurd: *a* must know which direction it was going to take, and tell *b* before they split up; *a* must then have an objective reality, independent of actual observation. Thus the probabilistic interpretation of quantum mechanics, which states that *a* could be going in any direction, must be wrong. Quantum uncertainty must hide a deeper, intrinsic determinism. Einstein thought that a particle's speed and position, which defined its trajectory, were *localized* on the particle without any observation being necessary. This is what was called "local realism." Quantum mechanics couldn't describe a particle's trajectory because it didn't take other "hidden variables" into account. And so it must be incomplete.

And yet Einstein was wrong. Eventually, physicists showed that exactly what Einstein thought couldn't happen in the EPR experiment did happen. Since its invention, quantum mechanics—and its probabilistic interpretation of reality—has never slipped up. It has always been confirmed by experiments and it still remains today the best theory that we have to describe the atomic and subatomic world.

M: When was the EPR effect confirmed experimentally?

T: EPR remained only a thought experiment for some time. No one knew how to carry it out physically. Then, in 1964, John Bell, an Irish physicist working at CERN, devised a mathematical theorem called "Bell's inequality," which would be capable of being verified experimentally if particles really did have hidden variables, as Einstein thought. This theorem at last allowed us to take the debate from the metaphysical plane to concrete experimentation. In 1982 the French physicist Alain Aspect, and his team at the University of Orsay, carried out a series of experiments on pairs of photons in order to test the EPR paradox. They found that Bell's inequality was violated without exception. Einstein had it wrong, and quantum mechanics was right. In Aspect's experiment, photons a and b were thirteen yards apart, yet b always "knew" instantaneously what a was doing, and reacted accordingly.

M: How do we know that this happens instantaneously, and that a light beam hasn't relayed the information from a to b?

T: Atomic clocks, connected to the detectors that capture a and b, allow us to gauge the moment of each photon's arrival extremely accurately. The difference between the two arrival times is less than a few tenths of a billionth of a second—it is probably zero, in fact, but existing atomic clocks don't allow us to measure periods of under 10^{-10} seconds. Now, in 10^{-10} seconds, light can travel only just over an inch—far less than the thirteen yards separating a and b. What is more, the result is the same if the distance between the two photons is increased. Even though light can definitely not have had the time to cross this distance and relay the necessary information, the behavior of a is always exactly correlated with that of b.

The latest experiment was carried out in 1998 in Geneva by Nicolas Gisin and his colleagues. They began by producing a pair of photons, one of which was then sent through a fiber-optic cable toward the north of the city, and the other toward the south. The two pieces of measuring equipment were over six miles apart. Once they arrived at the end of the cables, the two photons had to choose at random between two possible routes—one short, the other long. It was observed that they always made the same decision. On average, they chose the long route half the time, and the short route half the time, but the choices were always identical. The Swiss physicists were sure that the two photons couldn't communicate by means of light, because the difference between their response times was under three-tenths of a billionth of a second, and in that time light could have crossed just three and half inches of the six miles separating the two photons. Classic physics states that because they can't communicate, the choices of the two photons must be totally independent. But that is not what happens. They are always perfectly correlated. How can we explain why b immediately "knows" what a is doing? But this is paradoxical only if, like Einstein, we think that reality is cut up and localized in each photon. The problem goes away if we admit that a and b are part of a nonseparable reality, no matter how far apart they are. In that case, a doesn't need to send a signal to *b* because these two light particles (or, rather, phenomena that the detector sees as light particles) stay constantly in touch through some mysterious interaction. Wherever it happens to be, particle *b* continues to share the reality of particle *a*.

M: Even if the two particles were at opposite ends of the universe? 25

T: Yes. Quantum mechanics thus eliminates all idea of locality. It provides a holistic idea of space The notions of "here" and "there" become meaningless, because "here" is identical to "there." This is the definition of what physicists call "nonseparability."

M: This should have enormous repercussions on how physicists understand reality and our own ordinary perception of the world.

T: Indeed. Some physicists have had problems accepting the idea of a nonseparable reality and have tried to find a weak link in these experiments or in Bell's theorem. So far, they've all failed. Quantum mechanics has never been found to be wrong. So phenomena do seem "interdependent" at a subatomic level, to use the Buddhist term.

Another fascinating and famous experiment in physics shows that interdependence isn't limited to the world of particles, but applies also to the entire universe, or in other words that interdependence is true of the macrocosm as well as the microcosm. This is the experiment often referred to in short as Foucault's pendulum.

A French physicist, Léon Foucault, wanted to prove that the Earth rotates on its 30 axis. In 1851 he carried out a famous experiment that is reproduced today in displays in many of the world's science museums. He hung a pendulum from the roof of the Panthéon in Paris. Once in motion, this pendulum behaved in a strange way. As time passed, it always gradually changed the direction in which it was swinging. If it was set swinging in a north-south direction, after a few hours it was swinging east-west. From calculations, we know that if the pendulum were placed at either one of the poles, then it would turn completely around in twenty-four hours. But because of the latitude of Paris, Foucault's pendulum performed only part of a complete rotation each day.

Why did the direction change? Foucault answered by saying that the movement was illusory. In fact, the pendulum always swung in the same direction, and it was the Earth that turned. Once he'd proved that the Earth rotated, he let the matter drop. But Foucault's answer was incomplete, because a movement can be described only in comparison with a fixed reference point; absolute movement doesn't exist. Long before, Galileo[5] said that "movement is as nothing." He understood that it

5. **Galileo:** Italian astronomer and physicist (1564–1642), an early advocate of the heliocentric, or sun-centered, model of the universe.

exists only relative to something else. The earth must "turn" in relation to something that doesn't turn. But where to find this "something"? In order to test the immobility of a given reference point, a star for instance, we simply set the pendulum swinging in the star's direction. If the star is motionless, then the pendulum will always swing toward it. If the star moves, then the star will slowly shift away from the pendulum's swing.

Let's try the experiment with known celestial bodies, both near and far. If we point the pendulum toward the Sun, after a few weeks there is a clear shift of the Sun away from the pendulum's swing. After a couple of years, the same happens with the nearest stars, situated a few light-years away. The Andromeda galaxy, which is 2 million light-years away, moves away more slowly, but does shift. The time spent in line with the pendulum's swing grows longer and the shift away tends toward zero the greater the distance is. Only the most distant galaxies, situated at the edge of the known universe, billions of light-years away, do not drift away from the initial plane of the pendulum's swing.

The conclusion we must draw is extraordinary: Foucault's pendulum doesn't base its behavior on its local environment, but rather on the most distant galaxies, or, more accurately, on the entire universe, given that practically all visible matter is to be found in distant galaxies and not in nearby stars. Thus, what happens here on our Earth is decided by all the vast cosmos. What occurs on our tiny planet depends on all of the universe's structures.

Why does Foucault's pendulum behave like this? We don't know. Ernst Mach, the Austrian philosopher and physicist who gave his name to the unit of supersonic speed, thought it could be explained by a sort of omnipresence of matter and of its influence. In his opinion, an object's mass—that is to say, the amount of its inertia, or resistance to movement—comes from the influence of the entire universe. This is what is called Mach's principle. When we have trouble pushing a car, its resistance to being moved has been created by the whole universe. Mach never explained this mysterious universal influence in detail, which is different from gravity, and no one has managed to do so since. Just as the EPR experiment forces us to accept that interactions exist in the microcosm that are different from those described by known physics, Foucault's pendulum does the same for the macrocosm. Such interactions are not based on force or an exchange of energy, and they connect the entire universe. Each part contains the whole, and each part depends on all the other parts.

M: In Buddhist terms, that's a good definition of interdependence. It's not a question of proximity in time or space, or of the speed of communication and physical forces whose influence wanes over great distances. Phenomena are interdependent because they *coexist* in a global reality, which functions according to mutual causality. Phenomena are naturally simultaneous because one implies the presence of the other. We are back with "*this* can only be if *that* also exists; *this* can change only if

35

that also changes." Thus we arrive at an idea that everything must be connected to everything else. Relationships determine our reality, the conditions of our existence, particles and galaxies.

T: Such a vision of interdependence certainly agrees with the results of the experiments I've just mentioned. The EPR experiment, Foucault's pendulum, and Mach's inertia can't be explained by the four fundamental physical forces.[6] This is extremely disturbing for physicists.

M: I think that we have a good example here of the difference between the scientific approach and Buddhism. For most scientists, even if the global nature of phenomena has been demonstrated in rather a disturbing way, this is merely another piece of information, and no matter how intellectually stimulating it may be, it has little effect on their daily lives. For Buddhists, on the other hand, the repercussions of the interdependence of phenomena are far greater.

The notion of interdependence makes us question our basic perception of the world and then use this new perception again and again to lessen our attachments, our fears, and our aversions. An understanding of interdependence should demolish the wall of illusions that our minds have built up between "me" and "the other." It makes a nonsense of pride, jealousy, greed, and malice. If not only all inert things but also all living beings are connected, then we should feel deeply concerned about the happiness and suffering of others. The attempt to build our happiness on others' misery is not just amoral, it's also unrealistic. Feelings of universal love (which Buddhism defines as the desire for all beings to experience happiness and to know its cause) and of compassion (the desire for all beings to be freed of suffering and its causes) are the direct consequences of interdependence. Thus knowledge of interdependence leads to a process of inner transformation, which continues throughout the journey of spiritual enlightenment. For, if we don't put our knowledge into practice, we are like a deaf musician, or a swimmer who dies of thirst for fear of drowning if he drinks.

T: So the interdependence of phenomena equals universal responsibility. What a marvelous equation! It reminds me of what Einstein said: "A human being is part of a whole, called by us the 'Universe,' a part limited in time and space. He experiences himself, his thoughts and feelings, as something separated from the rest—a kind of optical delusion of his consciousness. This delusion is a kind of prison for us, restricting us to our personal desires and to affection for a few per-

6. **The four fundamental physical forces:** the four forces—strong nuclear force, electromagnetic force, weak nuclear force, and gravity— that physicists believe account for all observable physical interactions.

sons nearest us. Our task must be to free ourselves from this prison by widening our circles of compassion to embrace all living creatures and the whole of nature in its beauty."

In fact, the language of physics is currently incapable of expressing the global, holistic nature of reality. Some people even talk of another truth, a "veiled reality" in the words of the French physicist Bernard d'Espagnat.   40

M: This is an interesting idea, as long as we don't see this "veiled reality" as the ultimate solid reality hidden behind appearances. Doing so would just reify the world of phenomena once more. An important point we must keep in mind about interdependence is that it is not just a simple interaction between phenomena. Instead, it is the precondition for their appearance.

T: Heisenberg[7] expressed a similar idea when he wrote, "The world thus appears as a complicated tissue of events, in which connections of different kinds alternate or overlap or combine, and thereby determine the texture of the whole."

M: If, however, "veiled" means "illusory" or "inaccessible to concepts," then Buddhism would be in agreement with d'Espagnat.

T: I don't think d'Espagnat would call his "veiled reality" illusory. To his mind, it's a reality that escapes our perceptions and measuring apparatus. While I agree with you that interdependence must be the fundamental law, science can't describe it yet.

But even if scientists are having trouble grasping the fullness of interdependence, they are having no trouble finding a wide range of evidence for different kinds of interconnections in our world. For example, there is the cosmic interconnection of the Big Bang. We are all products of that primordial explosion. The hydrogen and helium atoms that make up 98 percent of the universe's ordinary matter were made during the first three minutes of its existence. The hydrogen in seawater and in our bodies all comes from that primordial soup. So we all have the same genealogy. As for the heavy elements that are needed for complexity and life, and which make up the other 2 percent of the universe's matter, they were produced by the nuclear alchemy in the center of the stars and the explosion of supernovas.

We are all made of stardust. As brothers of the wild beasts and cousins of the flowers in the fields, we all carry the history of the cosmos. Just by breathing, we are linked to all the other beings that have lived on the planet. For example, still today we are breathing in millions of atomic nuclei from the fire that burned Joan of Arc

7. **Heisenberg:** Werner Heisenberg (1901–1976), German physicist and a founder of quantum mechanics.

in 1431, and some of the molecules from Julius Caesar's dying breath. When a living organism dies and decays, its atoms are released back into the environment, and eventually become integrated into other organisms. Our bodies contain about a billion atoms that once belonged to the tree under which the Buddha attained enlightenment.

M: This also offers another way of looking at the EPR effect. Since all "particles"—whatever that might mean—were closely bound together in the singularity of the Big Bang (and perhaps during other Big Bangs), they must still be so now. Thus the natural condition for phenomena always has been and always will be global.

But in Buddhism, it isn't so much the molecular connections that matter—for they have little effect on our happiness or suffering—but rather the fact that all sentient beings, with whom we are *all* related through interdependence, wish to be happy and to escape suffering.

T: Yet another kind of interconnection discovered by science is that we're all linked together genetically. We all descend from *Homo habilis*, who appeared in Africa about 1,800,000 years ago, regardless of our race or skin color. As a child of the stars, humanity perhaps experienced a feeling of cosmic affiliation most intensely when we saw for the first time those stirring pictures from the space missions of our blue planet floating, so beautiful and yet so fragile, in the immense darkness of space. This global view reminds us that we are all responsible for our Earth and must save it from the ecological disaster that we're inflicting on it. William Blake[8] expressed the global nature of the cosmos beautifully in the following lines:

> To see a World in a Grain of Sand
> And a Heaven in a Wild Flower,
> Hold infinity in the palm of your hand
> And Eternity in an hour.

The entire universe is indeed contained in a grain of sand, because the explanation of the simplest phenomena brings in the history of the entire universe.

M: Those Blake lines remind me of one of the quatrains of a sutra by the Buddha: 50

> As in one atom,
> So in all atoms,
> All worlds enter therein—
> So inconceivable is it.

8. **William Blake:** English painter, poet, and engraver (1757–1827), best known for his books *Songs of Innocence* and *Songs of Experience*.

Buddhist writings also say that the Buddha knows at all times the nature and the multifariousness of the universe's phenomena, in both space and time, as clearly as if he were holding them in the palm of his hand, and that he can transform an instant into an eternity, or an eternity into an instant. I can't help wondering if William Blake had read these texts, or whether inspiration passed down over the ages! If you consider these thoughts carefully, then you will see that the Buddha's omniscience corresponds exactly to a global perception. There's no need to see the Buddha as a god. It's enough to know that enlightenment embraces everything and knows at each instant the number and the nature of things. It is this global view that permits omniscience. The Indian Buddhist philosopher and poet Asvaghosa wrote, "As a result of deep concentration, one realizes the oneness of the expanse of reality." On the other hand, fundamental ignorance results in fragmentation, and hence a limitation, of knowledge. We can perceive only certain aspects of reality, and fail to see its true nature.

T: The infinity of worlds makes me think of the other intelligent life-forms that probably exist in the cosmos. The observable universe contains several hundred billion galaxies, each having several hundred billion stars. If, like our sun, most of those stars have ten or so planets orbiting them, then we arrive at a total of several hundred billion trillion planets. It seems absurd that among such a huge number, our planet should be the only one to house conscious life. The existence of extraterrestrial civilizations raises interesting theological questions. For instance, Christianity says that God sent his Son, Jesus Christ, to Earth to save humankind. So are there a multitude of Jesus Christs visiting each planet that has conscious life in order to save the beings that have evolved there?

M: Buddhism talks of billions of different worlds, where different forms of beings live. It is said that most of these worlds have a Buddha who teaches the beings how to reach enlightenment. A Buddha doesn't save souls as one would throw a stone at a mountaintop. He gives them the means to identify the cause of their suffering and deliver themselves from it, and eventually to achieve the ultimate wisdom and bliss of enlightenment.

T: The Italian philosopher Giordano Bruno had already raised these questions at the end of the sixteenth century, when he suggested that the universe was infinite and contained an infinite number of worlds with an infinite variety of life-forms. He paid for such temerity with his life, for the Church condemned him to be burned at the stake four centuries ago, in 1600. It's fascinating to see that Buddhism was asking this sort of question more than two thousand years ago . . .

M: It is also said that on each blade of grass and each grain of dust, in each atom and in each pore of the Buddha's skin, there is an infinite number of worlds, but that it is not necessary for these worlds to shrink, or for the pores to grow larger. In other words, each element includes all of the others through interdependence without having to change its dimensions.

T: What a striking image! During our conversations I've greatly admired how Buddhism manages to use poetic images to express concepts that are often difficult, run against common sense, and can't be expressed in everyday language. According to Buddhism, does the world exist when it's not being perceived by a consciousness? 55

M: Of course, the world around us doesn't vanish when we are no longer conscious of it. But this is a false question because, to begin with, consciousness exists and is thus an active part of interdependence and, second, it would be impossible to imagine or describe what reality would be like if there were no consciousness. Thus, this position is neither nihilistic or idealistic, in that it doesn't deny conventional reality. But neither is it realistic or materialistic, given that a reality existing only by its own means is meaningless for us. This is what the Buddha calls the Middle Way. In the words of a Tibetan commentator:

> Two sticks which, when rubbed together, produce a fire, are themselves burned up in the blaze. Just so, the dense wood of all conceptual bearings of both existence and nonexistence will be totally consumed by the fires of wisdom of ascertaining that all phenomena lack true existence. To abide in that primal wisdom in which all concepts have subsided—this is indeed the Great Madhyamaka, the Great Middle Way, free from all assertions.

This is summed up by Nagarjuna[9] in these verses from his major work, *The Fundamental Treatise on the Middle Way*:

> The words "There is," means clinging to eternal substance,
> "There is not" connotes the view of nihilism.
> Thus in neither "is" nor "is not"
> Is the dwelling place of those who know.

In the *Sutra Requested by Sagaramati*, the Buddha said:

> The wise have understood interdependent origination,
> They do not rely on extremist views.
> They know that things have causes and conditions,
> And that nothing is without cause or condition.

---

9. **Nāgārjuna:** an Indian Buddhist philosopher (circa 150–250 CE) and founder of the Madhyamaka branch of Buddhism (p. 110).

And Nagarjuna went on:

> *That which arises dependent on something*
> *Is not in the least that thing,*
> *Neither is it different from it.*
> *Therefore it is neither permanent nor nothing.*

According to the Buddha, the ultimate nature of phenomena is thus a union between appearances and emptiness:

> *Know that all phenomena*
> *Are like reflections appearing*
> *In a very clear mirror,*
> *Devoid of inherent existence.*

UNDERSTANDING THE TEXT

1. According to Buddhist thought, what does "the interdependence of phenomena" mean? How does this idea relate to illusion? What is illusory about the way that we normally perceive the world?

2. How does the Buddhist notion of interdependence mirror certain ideas in the field of quantum mechanics? In what ways do subatomic particles behave interdependently? At what point does the analogy break down, so the two are not the same?

3. What did Einstein mean by "God does not play dice"? To what principle of quantum mechanics did he object?

4. Describe the EPR experiment. What point was Einstein trying to prove? How would this point, if true, refute the principle of quantum mechanics he disputed?

5. How does the experiment known as Foucault's Pendulum demonstrate the interdependent nature of matter? What conclusion did Foucault draw from his experiment? How did he miss the significance of his own most famous contribution to science?

6. What does the concept of infinity mean for Ricard and Thuan? How is it important to their respective worldviews?

MAKING CONNECTIONS

1. How does the Buddhist view of the interconnectedness of all life compare with Rachel Carson's understanding of the earth's ecosystem (p. 419)? How do these holistic views relate to environmentalism?

2. Compare Matthieu Ricard's quotation from Nāgārjuna with the selection from Nāgārjuna's "The Precious Garland" (p. 110). Do the two authors seem to have the same understanding of Buddhism? Explain.

3. Does Ricard use the term "interdependence" in the same way that David Suzuki uses it in "The Sacred Balance" (p. 427)? Are there any key differences in these two authors' approach to nature?

WRITING ABOUT THE TEXT

1. How clearly do Ricard and Trinh Xuan Thuan present their arguments, and how well do they illustrate their points? Focus on one or two major principles on which the two agree or disagree.

2. Compare the Buddhist view of nature with the Jewish view according to Moses Maimonides (p. 397) or the Muslim view according to Averroës (p. 391). Are there similarities in the way that all three approach the task of harmonizing religion and science? How might Ricard's training in modern science have changed his perceptions?

3. Use the two viewpoints in this reading as the foundation of an essay on science and religion. What fundamental differences between the religious and scientific worldviews do you detect?

Galaxy Cluster Abell 1689
(2002)

WHEN IT WAS FINALLY LAUNCHED into space in 1990, the Hubble Space Telescope—a collaborative effort between NASA and the European Space Agency—had already endured nearly a decade of delays, funding problems, and cancelled launch dates. And within weeks of the telescope's initial deployment, scientists realized that its main mirror had not been ground correctly and that the resulting images were far inferior to the quality that they had expected. In 1993, however, the crew of the space shuttle *Endeavor* carried out a ten-day servicing mission that added a second mirror that completely corrected the flaws of the first. Since then, the Hubble Space Telescope has returned some of the most detailed and spectacular images of the cosmos ever seen on Earth.

The Hubble image reprinted here was taken in June 2002, by an astronomical research team collaborating with NASA scientists. The image is of Galaxy Cluster Abell 1689, one of the most distant and massive objects in the known universe. This cluster of galaxies is more than 2.2 billion light years from Earth and contains more than 1 trillion stars. The gravitational pull of Abell 1689 is so great that it works as a magnifying glass for other galaxies located behind it, a phenomenon known as "gravitational lensing." In fact, some of the faintest points of light in the image are not part of Abell 1689; they are much more distant galaxies made visible to us only through a combination of Hubble's sophisticated technology and gravitational lensing.

In 2008, scientists determined that one of the objects made visible by this effect—a galaxy known as A1689-zD1, which can be seen very faintly in the image reproduced here—is nearly 13 billion light years away, the most distant object ever observed. Since the light from A1689-zD1 took 13 billion years to reach the earth, we are able to see it as it was at the beginning of the universe, just a few hundred million years (a very short time in the life of the universe) after the Big Bang. This kind of observation, made possible by the Hubble Space Telescope, has contributed significantly to our understanding of the universe. ✎

GALAXY CLUSTER ABELL 1689, 2002.
NASA, N. Benitez (JHU), T. Broadhurst (Racah Institute of Physics / The Hebrew University),
H. Ford (JHU), M. Clampin (STScI), G. Hartig (STScI), G. Illingworth (UCO / Lick Observa-
tory), the ACS Science Team and ESA
See p. C-7 in the color insert for a full-color reproduction of this image.

UNDERSTANDING THE TEXT

1. Estimate the number of stars and planets in this photograph. (Planets are not generally visible in the image, but think about how many *might* exist in such a vast area of space.) How many of these planets do you think might be capable of supporting life? What do you think is the likelihood that some of them contain intelligent life? Explain both the math behind your estimate and the reasoning behind your response.

2. Why do you think scientists find it valuable to examine distant galaxies such as those contained in this photograph? What might we learn from such studies?

3. How does the fact that this is a photograph make it different from a drawing or written description of what astronomers see through a telescope? Do you respond to this photo differently than you would to a written text or hand-drawn picture of the same subject? Does the fact that it is a photograph make it more reliable? Why or why not?

MAKING CONNECTIONS

1. Does anything in the photograph of Abell 1689 support or contradict the argument for an intelligently designed universe put forward by Maimonides in *The Guide for the Perplexed* (p. 397)? Explain.

2. David Suzuki (p. 427) and Matthieu Ricard (p. 435) both propose that everything in the universe is connected. Does the immensity of the universe displayed in this photograph affect how you feel about their ideas? How so?

3. How does looking at this image affect your understanding of the earth and its place in the universe? How is this different than the understanding that comes from looking at the cosmological chart of the Ptolemaic universe (p. 384)?

WRITING ABOUT THE TEXT

1. Compare the photograph of Abell 1689 with the image of the Ptolemaic model of the universe (p. 384). What might the differences between these images say about the different views of science in the societies that produced them?

2. NASA has been criticized for spending billions of dollars on equipment such as the Hubble and other long-distance space projects. Does the knowledge gained from the information these devices send back, like the image of Abell 1689, justify their cost? Why or why not? Write an essay in which you argue either that the space program deserves its costly budget or that the budget should be drastically reduced (or eliminated). Research NASA to learn about its goals, budget, and results, and include what you discover in your essay. Remember to document your sources.

Al Gore
The Climate Emergency
(2004)

ALBERT ARNOLD GORE JR. was born in 1948 in Washington, D.C., where his father was serving as a congressman from Tennessee. Four years later, Al Gore Sr. was elected to the Senate, and his family began splitting its time between Washington and the Gore family farm in Carthage, Tennessee. Gore graduated from Harvard University in 1969 and immediately enlisted in the Army, where his service included a five-month tour in Vietnam as a military journalist. When he returned from Vietnam in 1971, Gore studied at Vanderbilt University and worked as a journalist. In 1976, he was elected to the congressional seat once held by his father, and in 1984, he was elected to the Senate. He ran unsuccessfully for president in 1988; four years later, Bill Clinton selected him as his running mate in the 1992 presidential campaign. The Clinton-Gore ticket won the election, and for the next eight years Gore served as vice president of the United States.

In 2000, Gore ran as the Democratic nominee for president against the Republican nominee, George W. Bush, the son of former president George H. W. Bush. In the closest presidential election in American history, Gore won the popular vote but lost the electoral vote—but by such a narrow margin that after several weeks of recounts and ballot challenges in Florida, whose electoral votes would determine the results of the election, the election ended up being decided by the Supreme Court of the United States, which declared Bush the winner by a 5-4 vote.

After conceding the election, Gore moved away from national politics and became an activist for one of the causes he was most concerned about as a senator: the environment. In his first book, the 1992 best-seller *Earth in the Balance*, Gore had argued for a series of policy initiatives to address the ecological consequences of human actions over the past century. In 2004, Gore began speaking to audiences about global climate change, developing a lengthy slide presentation that marshaled an impressive amount of evidence to support his claim that human actions have caused sudden alterations to the global climate that could have catastrophic effects for the world. This slide-show presentation was the basis for the documentary *An Inconvenient Truth* (2007), which was a modest box-office hit and won two Academy Awards. Gore was awarded the 2007 Nobel Peace Prize for this efforts "to build up and disseminate greater knowledge about man-made climate change, and to lay the foundations for the measures that are needed to counteract such change."

The speech reprinted here, "The Climate Emergency," was given at Yale University in April 2004. It contains the basic argument that Gore expanded upon in *An*

Inconvenient Truth and the accompanying best-selling book of the same title. Gore supports his claim with facts and statistics and appeals to his audience's emotions. Both the facts and the emotional appeal benefit from his use of visuals—charts, graphs, photos—to supplement his speech.

I'M AL GORE. I used to be the next president of the United States. This has been an interesting period of my life. I wanted to start by inviting you to put yourselves in my shoes for a minute. It hasn't been easy, you know. For eight years I flew on Air Force II, and now I have to take off my shoes to get on an airplane.

Not long after Tipper[1] and I left the White House, we were driving from our home in Nashville to a small farm we have fifty mile east of Nashville. We were driving ourselves. I looked in the rear view mirror and all of a sudden it just hit me that there was no motorcade. Some of you may have heard of phantom limb pain.

It was mealtime, so we looked for a place to eat. We pulled off the interstate highway and finally found a Shoney's Restaurant, a low-cost, family restaurant chain. We walked in and sat down. The waitress came over and made a big commotion over Tipper. She took our order and then went to the couple in the booth next to us, and lowered her voice so much I had to really strain to hear what she was saying: "Yes, that's former Vice President Al Gore and his wife Tipper." And the man said, "He's come down a long way, hasn't he?"

The very next day, continuing a true story, I got on a plane and flew to Africa, to Nigeria, to the city of Lagos, to make a speech about energy. I began my speech by telling that story, that had just happened the day before back in Tennessee, and I told it pretty much the same way I just told it here. They laughed. Then I went on and gave my speech and went back to the airport and flew back toward the U.S. I fell asleep on the plane, and was awakened in the middle of the night when we were landing on the Azores Islands out in the middle of the Atlantic. They opened the door of the plane to let some fresh air in, and I looked out, and here came a man running across the runway waving a piece of paper saying "Call Washington, call Washington."

I thought—what in the world, in the middle of the night, in the middle of the Atlantic, what in the world could be wrong in Washington? And then I remembered it could be a bunch of things. But what it turned out to be was that my staff back in Washington was very, very upset. A wire service reporter in Lagos had written a story about my speech, and it had already been transmitted to the U.S. and printed all over the country. The story began: "Former Vice President Al Gore announced in Nigeria yesterday 'My wife Tipper and I opened a low-cost family restaurant named Shoney's and we are running it ourselves.'" Before I could get back

5

---

1. **Tipper:** Gore's wife, Tipper Gore (b. 1948).

to U.S. soil, the late-night comics Leno and Letterman had already started in on me. They had me in a big white chef's hat and Tipper was taking orders—"One more with fries!" Three days later I got a nice long handwritten letter from my friend Bill Clinton that said "Congratulations on the new restaurant, Al!" We like to celebrate each other's successes in life.

Anyway, it really is an honor to be here and to share some words about the climate issue. The title I chose for this speech is not a misprint. The phrase "climate emergency" is intended to convey what it conveys—that this is a crisis with an unusual sense of urgency attached to it, and we should see it as an emergency. The fact that we don't, or that most people don't, is part of what I want to cover here.

Climate Change: Impacts and Evidence

There is a very famous picture called Earth Rise. A young astronaut named William Anders took it on December 24, 1968. This mission, Apollo 7, was the first one to go around the moon. It went on Christmas Eve, and they had just been on the dark side of the moon, coming back around, seeing the earth for the first time. Anders— the rookie astronaut, without a big fancy camera—took this snapshot and it instantly became an icon. Many people believe that this one picture, Earth Rise, in many ways was responsible for the birth of the modern environmental movement. Less than two years after this picture was printed, the first Earth Day was organized. This picture became a powerful force in changing the way people thought about the earth and about the environment.

The environment is often felt to be relatively invulnerable because the earth is so big. People tend to assume that the earth is so big that we as human beings can't possibly have any impact on it. That is a mistake. The most vulnerable part of earth's environment is the atmosphere. It's astonishingly thin, as any image from space shows. The space is so small that we are able to fill it up with greenhouse gases, such as CO_2 [carbon dioxide] which form a thick blanket of gas surrounding the earth, trapping some of the sun's radiation. This process, called the "greenhouse effect," is what leads to increased global temperatures or what most refer to as climate change.

In Europe during the summer of 2003, we experienced an extreme heat wave that killed an estimated 20,000 people, and many predict such events will be much more commonplace as a result of increasing temperatures. The anomaly was extreme, particularly in France, with consequences that were well reported in the press. Year-to-year, decade-to-decade there's variation, but the overall upward trend worldwide since the American Civil War is really clear and really obvious, at least to me.

If you look at the glaciers around the world, you see that many are melting away. A friend of mine named Lonnie Thompson of Ohio State studies glaciers, and he reports that 15 to 20 years from now there will be no more snows of Kilimanjaro. This shrinking of glaciers is happening all around the world, including Latin Amer-

10

ica, China, and the U.S. In our own Glacier National Park, all of the glaciers are predicted to be gone within 15 to 20 years.

One of the remarkable things about glaciers is that they really could care less about politics. They either melt or freeze. Rhetoric has no impact on them whatsoever. A few years ago some hikers in the Alps between Austria and Italy were walking along and they ran across what looked like a 5,000-year-old man. Actually he was from 3,000 B.C., and you don't see that every day. The reason you don't is that the ice there hasn't melted for 5,000 years. Every mountain glacier in the entire world, with the exception of a few in Scandinavia that are affected by the Gulf Stream patterns, is melting rapidly.

Lonnie Thompson and his team of researchers don't just watch glaciers melt. They drill down into the glaciers and pull up columns of ice. Then they study the bubbles of air trapped in the ice, and they can do that year by year because every year there's a new layer. In Antarctica the layers are paper-thin and they stack up 400,000 years back. Ninety-five percent of all the fresh water in the world is locked up as ice in Antarctica. It's two miles high.

When Lonnie and his team drill down through Antarctica, they're able to get 400,000 years worth of ice. They can then look at the little bubbles of atmosphere and measure the CO_2 content, and they can also measure temperature by comparing the ratio of different oxygen isotopes. However that works, it's extremely accurate and not controversial. And here's what that record shows where carbon dioxide is concerned:

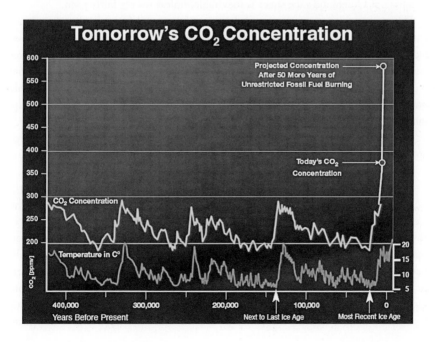

Now, there are two points here. The first is: Do those lines—the line for level of temperature and the line for concentration of CO_2—look like they go together to you? They do to me. The second point is: Here in New Haven, on the temperature line, the difference of approximately 15°C of average temperature is the difference between a nice day and having one mile of ice over your head. What has been happening lately is that the concentration of CO_2 is approaching 380 parts per million. So that's way, way above anything that has been sent for as far back as we can measure—400,000 years. And within fifty years it's going to approach 600 parts per million. So if a difference of approximately 200 parts per million of CO_2 on the cold side is a mile of ice over your head, what does that much difference represent on the warm side?

Or to state the question another way, is it perfectly sane and rational and reasonable to go ahead and do this? Or is it in fact crazy? It is crazy, but that is what the world is doing right now. And fifty years is not a long time. Unless we make decisions very soon, we will reach much higher levels. So, when I use the phrase *climate emergency*, I have partly in mind the fact that this is happening right now. And it carries with it, unless we do something, catastrophic consequences for all civilization. 15

In Antarctica you've heard about ice shelves the size of Rhode Island coming off and calving. There are actually a bunch of them in the Antarctic, and also in Greenland. Incidentally, there was a flurry of publicity on April 9th about a new study showing that if greenhouse gas emissions continue to rise at current rates the disappearance of Greenland's ice sheet is inevitable, unless we act fairly soon.

When ice melts in mountains and in Antarctica and Greenland—when land-based ice melts—it raises sea level. When you have rivers that are close to the ocean like the Thames River in London, the water level goes up, and it threatens the lower lying areas. London, in 1983, built barriers to protect the city against flooding from higher sea level and thus higher storm surges. These barriers had to be closed only once in 1983. Twenty years later, in 2003, they were closed 19 times. Again, the same pattern shows up wherever you look.

An area of Bangladesh is due to be flooded where ten million people live. A large area of Florida is due to be flooded. The Florida Keys are very much at risk. The Everglades are at risk.

Now the Arctic is very different from the Antarctic because, while the Antarctic is land surrounded by ocean, the Arctic is ocean surrounded by land. And the ice in the Arctic is floating on top of the ocean, so it doesn't get nearly as thick. Instead of two miles thick, it's only ten feet thick—that is, it used to be ten feet. Just in the last few decades it has melted quite a bit. I went up there twice in a submarine. They have these specially designed submarines where the wings rotate vertically so that they can cut through the ice. Ice in water, or thinner ice, melts more rapidly and leads to temperature increases because, as soon as little bit of ice melts, the water absorbs a lot more temperature. This effect is now happening to the entire

Arctic Ocean. The Arctic ice cap has thinned by 40 percent in the last 40 years. Let me repeat that. Listen to that number. The Arctic ice cap has thinned 40 percent in 40 years. Within 50 years it may be entirely gone.

That's a big problem because when the sun hits the ice cap, 95 percent of the energy bounces off like a big mirror. But when it hits the open ocean more than 90 percent is absorbed. So it's a phase change, it's not a gradual change. Ice is that way—the difference between 33F° and 31F° is not just two degrees. That puts more energy into the system and it changes the amount of evaporation off the oceans, so you get more rain and snow but it comes at different times and you get more soil 20

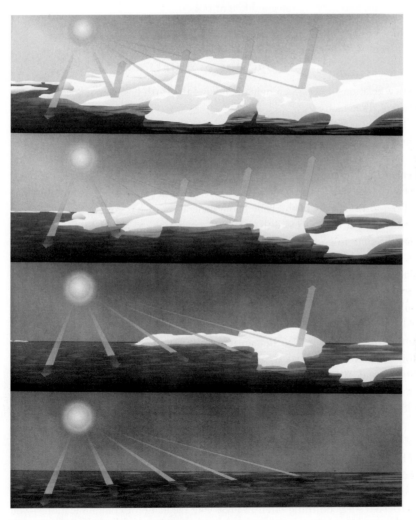

Effect of global warming on Arctic ice cap.

erosion as well. You get simultaneously more flooding and more droughts, which is really a bad thing. You get more precipitation in one-time storm events. More of it comes at one time in big storms.

The trend is very clear. What's behind it all? I've come to believe that global warming, the disappearance of the ocean fisheries, the destruction of the rain forests, the stratospheric ozone depletion problem, the extinction crisis, all of these are really symptoms of an underlying cause. The underlying cause is a collision between our civilization and the earth. The relationship between the human species and our planet has been completely changed. All of our culture, all of our literature, all of our history, everything we've learned, was premised on one relationship between the earth and us, and now we have a different one.

Three Leading Causes: Population Growth, Technology, and Our Way of Thinking

The new relationship between humankind and the earth has been caused by a confluence of three factors.

The first is population, which has been growing rapidly. The population crisis has actually been a success story in some ways. We've slowed it down, but the momentum of the population increases is readily incredible. Say the scientists are right and we emerged as a species 160,000 years ago. It took from that time, almost 160,000 years until the end of World War II, before we got to a population of 2 billion. Since I've been alive, as part of the baby boom generation, it has gone from 2 billion to 6.3 billion. So if it takes more than 10,000 generations to reach 2 billion and one human lifetime to go from 2 to 6, and if I live to the demographic average of the baby boom generation, it'll go close to 9 billion. That is one of the reasons why the relationship between our species and the earth is different now than ever before.

Some of the other global patterns, species loss for example, match the human population pattern. Most importantly, however, the increase in the population of developing nations is driving food demand, water demand, and energy demand, creating intense pressures on human resources. We are seeing a pattern of devastation and destruction that is simply driven by those factors. And it really is a political issue. We in the U.S. are responsible for more greenhouse gas emissions than Africa, South America, Central America, India, and China combined. The world average is way below where we are. Just to recap—this is 1,000 years of carbon emissions, CO_2 concentrations, and temperature. This is not rocket science. Those lines match up.

The second factor that changes the relationship between humans and the earth is technology. In many ways, it is more powerful and significant than the population explosion because new technologies have increased our power beyond imagination. That's a good thing often in areas like medicine or communications—you can fill in the blanks. There are all kinds of great things that represent progress. Even

25

cleaning up the environment with new technology. There are a lot of great things that have come out of this, but when we don't examine habits that have persisted for a long time, and then use the same habits with new technology and don't take into account the new power that we have, then the consequence can get away from us. One quick example: warfare was one thing with swords and bows and arrows and even muskets, but when nuclear weapons were created, the consequences of war were utterly transformed. So we had to think differently about war. And what happened? The cold war emerged and unfortunately the other kind didn't completely go away, but we're in the midst of rethinking that age-old habit of warfare. We just have to, because the new technologies make it unthinkable to continue as we were doing in the past.

Now think about that pattern: old habits, new technologies. Think about the subsistence that we have always drawn from the earth. The plow was a great advance, as was irrigation. But then we began to get more powerful with these tools. At the Aral Sea in Russia, something as simple as irrigation on a large scale led to the virtual disappearance of the fourth largest inland body of water in the world. We're changing the surface of the earth, and technology sometimes seems to dwarf our human scale. We now have to try to change this pattern.

The third factor is our way of thinking. We have to change our way of thinking. One illustration comes from the fact that, as I said earlier, we have these big assumptions that we don't question. I had a classmate in the sixth grade. Every time our geography teacher put a map of the world up he would mutter. Onetime, he got up his courage and pointed to the outline of South America and the outline of Africa and said, "Did they ever fit together?" And the teacher said "Of course not. That's the most ridiculous thing I've ever heard." In fact, until about the 1960s, the guy who talked about continental drift was thought to be a kook because he said that Africa and South America fit together. It turns out that they did, but the teacher in this story had an assumption in his mind. Continents are so big they obviously don't move, thereby illustrating the old philosopher's saying that "What gets us into trouble is not what we don't know. It's what we know for sure that just ain't so" (Yogi Berra). We know for sure that the earth is so big we can't have a big impact on it, but that's just not so.

You know this cliché, I'm sure: That a frog's nervous system is such that if it's dropped into a pot of boiling water it will jump right out because it perceives the contrast, but if it's put in a pot of tepid water which is slowly heated, it doesn't jump out unless it's rescued. Here's the deeper meaning of that cliché: the frog did perceive the sudden boiling water, but did not perceive the slow process.

Global warming seems to be gradual in the context of a human life, but it is actually fairly sudden. Another problem with our thinking is that there are people who are paid money by some coal companies and oil companies to go out and pretend that the science says something that it doesn't say. These are scientific camp followers who are willing to do things for money. And some of the very same individ-

POPULATION GROWTH THROUGHOUT HISTORY

First modern humans

| 160,000 BC | 100,000 BC | 10,000 BC | 7000 BC | 6000 BC | 5000 BC | 4000 BC |

Population Growth Throughout History

uals who are doing this now (i.e., trying to persuade people that global warming is not a problem) were some of the same people who took money from the tobacco companies after the Surgeon General's report came out warning of the dangers of smoking. The tobacco companies hired that scientific camp followers to go out and try to confuse the public into thinking that the science wasn't clear. They produced marketing campaigns like "More doctors smoke Camels." On a similar note, the Republican pollster Frank Luntz advised the White House that the issue of the environment is important, but the way to deal with it is to make the lack of scientific certainly a primary issue by finding people who are willing to say that it's confusing when it's really not.

There's another assumption that needs to be questioned. In contrast to the idea that the earth is so big that we can't have any impact on it, there are others who

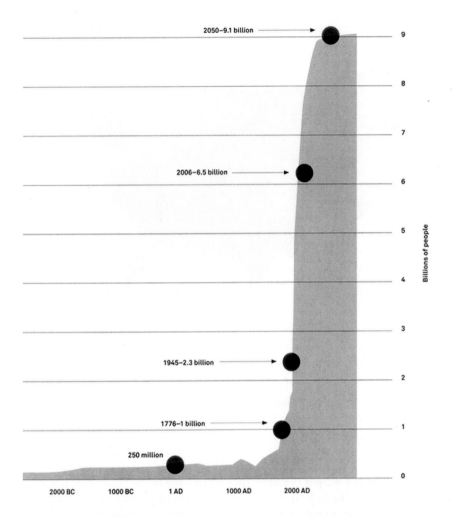

assume that the climate change problem is so big we can't solve it. I, however, believe that we can if we put our minds to it. We had a problem with the ozone hole, a big global problem that seemed too big to solve. In response, we had political leadership and the world passed a treaty outlawing chlorofluorocarbons, the chemicals that caused this problem.

The United States led the way, and we brought about a dramatic drop in CFCs and are now in the process of solving that problem. We now have the ability to buy hybrid cars like the Toyota Prius and the marketplace for new sources of energy is increasing dramatically. We're also seeing new efficiencies with energy savings. If we have political leadership and the collective political will to say it is important to solve this problem, we cannot only solve it, we can create more jobs, we can create higher incomes, a better way of life, and a higher quality of life by solving the problem.

2.3%
CANADA

30.3%*
UNITED STATES
*INCLUDES ALASKA AND HAWAII

3.8%
CENTRAL AMERICA
SOUTH AMERICA

CONTRIBUTIONS TO GLOBAL WARMING

■ United States ▨ Other industrialized nations ■ Developing nations

CONTRIBUTIONS TO GLOBAL WARMING
Source: U.S. Department of Energy, Energy Information Administration, Carbon Dioxide
Information Analysis Center

And finally, it's an issue of values. Back when I was in the Senate, the first President Bush was trying to fend off some of the attacks by myself and many others in Congress who were saying we have to solve this global warming problem. So they had a White House conference on global stewardship. One of their view graphs caught my attention. Their view of the global environmental crisis was represented by a scale with money, in the form of gold bars on one side, and on the other side of the scales was the entire planet. The point they were trying to make was that we have to find a balance between our monetary wealth and the well being of the entire planet. Boy, that's a tough one! It's a false choice—because you're not going to have much wealth if you lose the planet and there is wealth to be made in saving it. We have to get our perspective right.

Everything we have ever known—and Carl Sagan[2] made a beautiful long statement about this—all the wars, all the heartbreak, all the romance, every triumph,

2. **Carl Sagan:** American astronomer and writer (1934–1996).

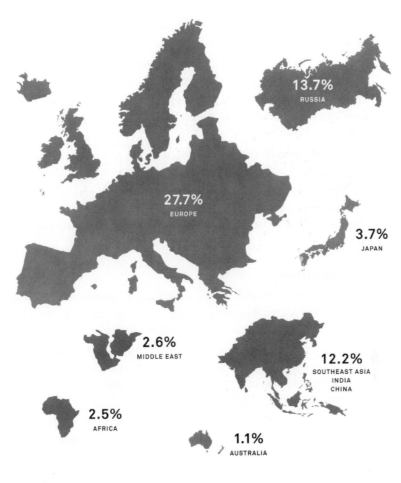

13.7%
RUSSIA

27.7%
EUROPE

3.7%
JAPAN

2.6%
MIDDLE EAST

12.2%
SOUTHEAST ASIA
INDIA
CHINA

2.5%
AFRICA

1.1%
AUSTRALIA

SOURCE: U.S. DEPARTMENT OF ENERGY, ENERGY INFORMATION ADMINISTRATION, CARBON DIOXIDE INFORMATION ANALYSIS CENTER   251

every mistake, everything we've ever known is contained in this small planet. If we keep the right perspective and keep our eyes on the prize, we *can* solve this problem, we *will* solve this problem, we *must* solve this problem. It really is up to you.

UNDERSTANDING THE TEXT

1. Why does Al Gore begin his speech with the anecdote about eating at Shoney's restaurant? How does his story about being misunderstood by a Nigerian audience relate to the overall topic of the speech?

2. Why does Gore insist on calling the climate situation an "emergency"? Why does he believe that people might think this title a mistake?

3. Why does Gore believe that people think the environment is invulnerable to human activity? What is the error in perspective that underlies this mistake?

4. What is the role of carbon dioxide (CO_2) in global warming? How does an increase of this gas in the atmosphere produce higher temperatures?

5. How do Gore's graphs and pictures add to the effectiveness of his argument? Would his speech be as persuasive if it did not have these visual arguments?

6. What is the connection between population growth and climate change? Why do some populations have a greater effect on climate change than others?

7. Why does Gore find it significant that the same people who give scientific testimony against the reality of climate change once worked for the tobacco industry? What larger point is Gore making about the reliability of scientific testimony?

MAKING CONNECTIONS

1. How does Gore's view of the global environment compare to that of David Suzuki in "The Sacred Balance" (p. 427)? Does Gore appeal to the same sense of interconnectedness that Suzuki does? Explain.

2. Can the global environment be considered a "commons" in Garrett Hardin's sense of the word (p. 357)? Could global climate change be attributed to what Hardin describes as a "tragedy of the commons"? Explain.

3. Are Gore's views of the effects of population comparable to those of Thomas Malthus in "Essay on the Principle of Population" (p. 324)? What elements does Gore add to the Malthusian equation, and why?

WRITING ABOUT THE TEXT

1. Compare "The Climate Emergency" to Rachel Carson's "The Obligation to Endure" (p. 419). What do the environmental issues of climate change and DDT have in common? In what ways do they differ? Write an essay in which you compare the issue of climate change as it is understood today and the issue of DDT as it was understood in the 1970s, when Carson wrote "The Obligation to Endure." Do research into the public response to both issues; remember to document your sources.

2. Conduct research into climate change and write a research essay in which you agree or disagree (or both) with what Gore says in "The Climate Emergency."

3. Watch the movie *An Inconvenient Truth*, which grew out of Gore's slide-show presentations, and write a letter to Gore in which you evaluate his skill as a public speaker. How persuasive do you find him and why? Give him specific examples of where he succeeds and fails, and offer suggestions for improvement.

7

LANGUAGE AND RHETORIC

HOW DO WE USE LANGUAGE TO
COMMUNICATE PERSUASIVELY?

> Rhetoric is useful . . . because things that are true and things that
> are just have a natural tendency to prevail over their opposites.
> —*Aristotle*

THE DISCIPLINE OF RHETORIC includes all the elements involved in using language persuasively. Rhetoricians study logic, style, audience awareness, methods of delivery, strategies for generating ideas, models of organization, and many other topics related to the creation of persuasive arguments. In short, rhetoric covers precisely the things that most college students learn about in composition classes. Indeed, most colleges and universities that offer advanced courses in writing and in teaching others to write do so in a program or department called Rhetoric and Composition.

The roots of rhetoric stretch back to the fifth century BCE in Athens, Greece. When the Athenians established the world's first democracy, which included an assembly that debated important issues and voted on them, they also created one of the world's first great markets for persuasive speaking. People were willing to pay large sums of money to be instructed in the art of writing and delivering persuasive speeches that could help them gain support for their ideas.

The traveling teachers who came into Athens to meet this new need were collectively known as the Sophists. Sophists taught their students how to win arguments, and they believed that a speech's success was measured by persuasiveness, rather than inherent justice or truthfulness. They found many willing students, but they also earned the enmity of another group of teachers—philosophers, such as Socrates and

Plato, who believed that seeking the truth was far more important than learning techniques of persuasion.

Very few of the Sophists' writings have survived, but several of Plato's major dialogues fictionally dramatize debates between Sophists and Socrates. In *Gorgias*, the most famous of these dialogues, Socrates challenges the most successful Sophist of his day; this chapter includes a selection from their debate in which Socrates compels Gorgias to admit that the study of rhetoric can only mimic genuine philosophy. The arguments against rhetoric that Plato outlines in this passage—that it produces no knowledge, that it shows contempt for truth, and that it dangerously forges actual ability—have followed the study of rhetoric for millennia and are answered, in different forms, by all the other readings in this chapter. An example of the kind of rhetoric that Plato despised is found in the first selection in the chapter, Pericles' "The Funeral Oration," which celebrates Athens and asks its citizens to make every sacrifice necessary to keep it free.

The first rebuttal to Plato, which remains one of the most influential, came from his own student Aristotle. In his treatise *Rhetoric*, Aristotle uses a Platonic argument to refute Plato's dismissal of rhetoric. "Rhetoric is useful," he argues, "because things that are true and things that are just have a natural tendency to prevail over their opposites." For Aristotle, truth is inherently superior and will always prevail in equal contests. Since those making bad arguments study rhetoric, Aristotle reasons, those who make good arguments must study it too; otherwise the contest will not be equal. Aristotle saw rhetoric as valuable far beyond its function in political deliberations, in judicial affairs, public celebrations, and community speeches. Understanding the basic principles of persuasion, he believed, was part of being an educated member of a society.

After these four ancient readings, the chapter speeds to the twentieth century, where the study of language and rhetoric has been vital to the emergence of modern culture and contemporary educational institutions. The first selection from the twentieth century, Gertrude Buck's "The Present Status of Rhetorical Theory," provides a stringent rebuttal to the Sophists and a partial defense of Plato's position in the *Gorgias*. Unlike Plato, however, Buck does not dismiss rhetoric entirely. Instead, she attempts to construct it as a tool for building social harmony. Following Buck's essay, Norman Rockwell's painting *Freedom of Speech* depicts a community meeting in a small American town. This image, which emphasizes the importance of speaking one's mind and listening respectfully to others, was part of one of the U.S. Treasury Department's most famous war bond drives during World War II. Another image, a poster commissioned by the government of the People's Republic of China to promote its One-Child Policy, emphasizes the happiness and stability that come with small families. Though these two paintings derived from very different kinds of government, they both used powerful rhetorical techniques to influence millions of people.

The chapter's four final readings come from writers whose cultures have often been marginalized by the way that others use language. In "Language and the Destiny of Man," Chinua Achebe, one of Africa's most respected writers, discusses the social benefits of language and the great potential for harm that comes with its abuse. In "Personal Reflections," American Indian writer N. Scott Momaday makes a similar point while emphasizing the way that Native American languages and oral traditions reflect a worldview essentially different from that of Americans of European descent. In "How to Tame a Wild Tongue," the well-known Chicana writer Gloria Anzaldúa argues that attempts to rob people of their native tongues correspond to attempts to rob them of their dignity and political rights. In her Nobel Prize acceptance speech, African American novelist Toni Morrison explains that with the great power of language comes an equally great responsibility for how we use it.

Language and rhetoric are integral parts of modern life. Most people today do not give speeches in great assemblies, but most write letters, memos, email, and, in college classes, essays and compositions. All of these acts are fundamentally rhetorical: they involve a writer, an audience, and an act of persuasion. What forms of persuasion are most effective? What moral responsibilities come with persuading other people to help you accomplish your goals? When does language become a tool of ignorance and oppression rather than of education and liberation? These questions have been with us since the days of the Athenian democracy, and they remain vital to the health of our society.

Pericles
The Funeral Oration
(431 BCE)

IN 431 BCE, war broke out between the two most powerful military alliances in the region of Greece: the Delian League, an alliance of Greek city-states led by Athens, and the Peloponnesian League, a similar alliance led by Sparta. The contrast between the two principal city-states could not have been greater. Athens was the world's only democracy. It had an elected assembly, a profitable export (olive oil), a powerful military, and a thriving culture. Sparta, on the other hand, was a rigidly controlled dictatorship in which all citizens were trained exclusively for war. The Peloponnesian War between these two city-states and their allies lasted from 431 to 404 BCE, ending with the total defeat of the Athenians and a profound reshaping of the Greek world.

The leader of Athens at the outbreak of the war was Pericles (495–429 BCE), who was a skilled orator, a dedicated patron of the arts, and a passionate defender of Athenian democracy. His rule is often seen as both a political and a cultural high point, a time in which the city produced such luminaries as the playwrights Aristophanes, Sophocles, Euripides, and Aeschylus and the philosopher Socrates. However, many historians also see Pericles as a primary instigator of the Peloponnesian War and the subsequent collapse of the Athenian Empire. Pericles is, therefore, remembered for both creating and helping to destroy the golden age of Athenian civilization.

Much of what historians know about this period comes from *History of the Peloponnesian War* by the Athenian general Thucydides (460–395 BCE). Thucydides was an eyewitness to the events that he chronicled, and most scholars believe that his account is essentially objective, though occasionally pro-Athenian. Along with his own narrative of the war and analysis of its causes, Thucydides included dozens of speeches by both Athenians and Spartans involved in the war. The most famous of these speeches is "The Funeral Oration of Pericles," which Pericles delivered at an annual ceremony to honor Athens's war dead. In this speech, Pericles departs from the traditional formula for such speeches. Rather than simply praising the dead, as was expected of such orations, Pericles praises the entire city of Athens, condemns its enemies, and makes the case for continuing the war.

One of the most intriguing speculations about the funeral oration is that it was written not by Pericles but by a woman named Aspasia of Miletus. Aspasia's exact status is the subject of much debate. She has been alternately labeled a prostitute, a mistress, and a wife to Pericles. But her influence upon him and his speeches has been commented on by, among others, Plato, Xenephon, Plutarch, and Cicero. In his dialogue "Menexenus" (circa 380 BCE), Plato includes a somewhat satirical version of the funeral oration that he attributes directly to Aspasia. The actual involvement of Aspasia in this speech, or in any of Pericles' speeches, is subject to much debate, but the philosophical tradition contains at least some reasonable speculation that the brains behind Athens's greatest statesman may have been a woman.

Pericles' speech provides a good example of the appeal to emotion. The primary emotion that he appeals to is patriotism, the love of one's country. Pericles introduces this topic early on and he uses the superiority of Athens as an organizing principle of the speech. 🖎

MOST OF THOSE WHO HAVE spoken before me on this occasion have praised the man who added this oration to our customs because it gives honor to those who have died in the wars; yet I would have thought it sufficient that those who have shown their mettle in action should also receive their honor in an action, as now you see they have, in this burial performed for them at public expense, so that the virtue of many does not depend on whether one person is believed to have spoken well or poorly.

It is a hard matter to speak in due measure when there is no firm consensus about the truth. A hearer who is favorable and knows what was done will perhaps think that a eulogy falls short of what he wants to hear and knows to be true; while an ignorant one will find some of the praise to be exaggerated, especially if he hears of anything beyond his own talent—because that would make him envious. Hearing another man praised is bearable only so long as the hearer thinks he could himself have done what he hears. But if a speaker goes beyond that, the hearer soon becomes envious and ceases to believe. Since our ancestors have thought it good, however, I too should follow the custom and endeavor to answer to the desires and opinions of every one of you, as far as I can.

I will begin with our ancestors, since it is both just and fitting that they be given the honor of remembrance at such a time. Because they have always lived in this land, they have so far always handed it down in liberty through their valor to successive generations up to now. They deserve praise; but our fathers deserve even more, for with great toil they acquired our present empire in addition to what they had received, and they delivered it in turn to the present generation. We ourselves who are here now in the prime of life have expanded most parts of the empire; and we have furnished the city with everything it needs to be self-sufficient both in peace and in war. The acts of war by which all this was attained, the valiant deeds of arms that we and our fathers performed against foreign or Greek invaders—these I will pass over, to avoid making a long speech on a subject with which you are well acquainted. But the customs that brought us to this point, the form of government and the way of life that have made our city great—these I shall disclose before I turn to praise the dead. I think these subjects are quite suitable for the occasion, and the whole gathering of citizens and guests will profit by hearing them discussed.

We have a form of government that does not try to imitate the laws of our neighboring states. We are more an example to others, than they to us. In name, it is called a democracy, because it is managed not for a few people, but for the majority. Still, although we have equality at law for everyone here in private disputes, we do not let our system of rotating public offices undermine our judgment of a candidate's virtue; and no one is held back by poverty or because his reputation is not well known, as long as he can do good service to the city. We are free and generous not only in our public activities as citizens, but also in our daily lives: there is no suspicion in our dealings with one another, and we are not offended by our neighbor for following his own pleasure. We do not cast on anyone the censorious looks that—though they are no punishment—are nevertheless painful. We live together without taking offense on private matters; and as for public affairs, we respect the law greatly and fear to violate it, since we are obedient to those in office at any time, and also to the laws—especially to those laws that were made to help people who have suffered an injustice, and to the unwritten laws that bring shame on their transgressors by the agreement of all.

Moreover, we have provided many ways to give our minds recreation from labor: 5
we have instituted regular contests and sacrifices throughout the year, while the attractive furnishings of our private homes give us daily delight and expel sadness. The greatness of our city has caused all things from all parts of the earth to be imported here, so that we enjoy the products of other nations with no less familiarity than we do our own.

Then, too, we differ from our enemies in preparing for war: we leave our city open to all; and we have never expelled strangers in order to prevent them from learning or seeing things that, if they were not hidden, might give an advantage to the enemy. We do not rely on secret preparation and deceit so much as on our own courage in action. And as for education, our enemies train to be men from early youth by rigorous exercise, while we live a more relaxed life and still take on dangers as great as they do.

The evidence for this is that the Lacedaemonians[1] do not invade our country by themselves, but with the aid of all their allies; when we invade our neighbors, however, we usually overcome them by ourselves without difficulty, even though we are fighting on hostile ground against people who are defending their own homes. Besides, no enemy has yet faced our whole force at once, because at the same time we are busy with our navy and sending men by land to many different places. But when our enemies run into part of our forces and get the better of them, they boast that they have beaten our whole force; and when they are defeated, they claim they were beaten by all of us. We are willing to go into danger with easy minds and natural courage rather than through rigorous training and laws,

---

1. **Lacedaemonians:** inhabitants of Laconia, a city-state on the southern coast of Greece.

and that gives us an advantage: we'll never weaken ourselves in advance by preparing for future troubles, but we'll turn out to be no less daring in action than those who are always training hard. In this, as in other things, our city is worthy of admiration.

We are lovers of nobility with restraint, and lovers of wisdom without any softening of character. We use wealth as an opportunity for action, rather than for boastful speeches. And as for poverty, we think there is no shame in confessing it; what is shameful is doing nothing to escape it. Moreover, the very men who take care of public affairs look after their own at the same time; and even those who are devoted to their own businesses know enough about the city's affairs. For we alone think that a man who does not take part in public affairs is good for nothing, while others only say he is "minding his own business." We are the ones who develop policy, or at least decide what is to be done; for we believe that what spoils action is not speeches, but going into action without first being instructed through speeches. In this too we excel over others: ours is the bravery of people who think through what they will take in hand, and discuss it thoroughly; with other men, ignorance makes them brave and thinking makes them cowards. But the people who most deserve to be judged tough-minded are those who know exactly what terrors or pleasures lie ahead, and are not turned away from danger by that knowledge. Again we are opposite to most men in matters of virtue:[2] we win our friends by doing them favors, rather than by accepting favors from them. A person who does a good turn is a more faithful friend: his goodwill towards the recipient preserves his feeling that he should do more; but the friendship of a person who has to return a good deed is dull and flat, because he knows he will be merely paying a debt—rather than doing a favor—when he shows his virtue in return. So that we alone do good to others not after calculating the profit, but fearlessly and in the confidence of our freedom.

In sum, I say that our city as a whole is a lesson for Greece, and that each of us presents himself as a self-sufficient individual, disposed to the widest possible diversity of actions, with every grace and great versatility. This is not merely a boast in words for the occasion, but the truth in fact, as the power of this city, which we have obtained by having this character, makes evident.

For Athens is the only power now that is greater than her fame when it comes   10 to the test. Only in the case of Athens can enemies never be upset over the quality of those who defeat them when they invade; only in our empire can subject states never complain that their rulers are unworthy. We are proving our power with strong evidence, and we are not without witnesses: we shall be the admiration of people

2. **Virtue:** *areté.* This traditionally involved doing good to one's friends and harm to one's enemies; that is why Pericles uses the concept here to introduce the topic of friendship among cities. [Translator's note]

now and in the future. We do not need Homer, or anyone else, to praise our power with words that bring delight for a moment, when the truth will refute his assumptions about what was done. For we have compelled all seas and all lands to be open to us by our daring; and we have set up eternal monuments on all sides, of our setbacks as well as of our accomplishments.

Such is the city for which these men fought valiantly and died, in the firm belief that it should never be destroyed, and for which every man of you who is left should be willing to endure distress.

That is why I have spoken at such length concerning the city in general, to show you that the stakes are not the same, between us and the enemy—for their city is not like ours in any way—and, at the same time, to bring evidence to back up the eulogy of these men for whom I speak.[3] The greatest part of their praise has already been delivered, for it was their virtues, and the virtues of men like them, that made what I praised in the city so beautiful. Not many Greeks have done deeds that are obviously equal to their own reputations, but these men have. The present end these men have met is, I think, either the first indication, or the final confirmation, of a life of virtue. And even those who were inferior in other ways deserve to have their faults overshadowed by their courageous deaths in war for the sake of their country. Their good actions have wiped out the memory of any wrong they have done, and they have produced more public good than private harm. None of them became a coward because he set a higher value on enjoying the wealth that he had; none of them put off the terrible day of his death in hopes that he might overcome his poverty and attain riches. Their longing to punish their enemies was stronger than this; and because they believed this to be the most honorable sort of danger, they chose to punish their enemies at this risk, and to let everything else go. The uncertainty of success they entrusted to hope; but for that which was before their eyes they decided to rely on themselves in action. They believed that this choice entailed resistance and suffering, rather than surrender and safety; they ran away from the word of shame, and stood up in action at risk of their lives. And so, in the one brief moment allotted them, at the peak of their fame and not in fear, they departed.

Such were these men, worthy of their country. And you who remain may pray for a safer fortune, but you must resolve to be no less daring in your intentions against the enemy. Do not weigh the good they have done on the basis of one speech. Any long-winded orator could tell you how much good lies in resisting our enemies; but you already know this. Look instead at the power our city shows in action every day, and so become lovers of Athens. When the power of the city seems great to you, consider then that this was purchased by valiant men who knew their duty and kept their honor in battle, by men who were resolved to contribute the most noble gift to their city: even if they should fail in their attempt, at least they would leave their fine character [*areté*] to the city. For in giving their lives

---

3. **These men for whom I speak:** the war dead being honored at the funeral.

for the common good, each man won praise for himself that will never grow old; and the monument that awaits them is the most splendid—not where they are buried, but where their glory is laid up to be remembered forever, whenever the time comes for speech or action. For to famous men, all the earth is a monument, and their virtues are attested not only by inscriptions on stone at home; but an unwritten record of the mind lives on for each of them, even in foreign lands, better than any gravestone.

Try to be like these men, therefore: realize that happiness lies in liberty, and liberty in valor, and do not hold back from the dangers of war. Miserable men, who have no hope of prosperity, do not have a just reason to be generous with their lives; no, it is rather those who face the danger of a complete reversal of fortune for whom defeat would make the biggest difference: they are the ones who should risk their lives. Any man of intelligence will hold that death, when it comes unperceived to a man at full strength and with hope for his country, is not so bitter as miserable defeat for a man grown soft.

That is why I offer you, who are here as parents of these men, consolation rather than a lament. You know your lives teem with all sorts of calamities, and that it is good fortune for anyone to draw a glorious end for his lot, as these men have done. While your lot was grief, theirs was a life that was happy as long as it lasted. I know it is a hard matter to dissuade you from sorrow, when you will often be reminded by the good fortune of others of the joys you once had; for sorrow is not for the want of a good never tasted, but for the loss of a good we have been used to having. Yet those of you who are of an age to have children may bear this loss in the hope of having more. On a personal level new children will help some of you forget those who are no more; while the city will gain doubly by this, in population and insecurity. It is not possible for people to give fair and just advice to the state, if they are not exposing their own children to the same danger when they advance a risky policy. As for you who are past having children, you are to think of the greater part of your life as pure profit, while the part that remains is short and its burden lightened by the glory of these men. For the love of honor is the one thing that never grows old, and useless old age takes delight not in gathering wealth (as some say), but in being honored.

As for you who are the children or the brothers of these men, I see that you will have considerable competition. Everyone is used to praising the dead, so that even extreme virtue will scarcely win you a reputation equal to theirs, but it will fall a little short. That is because people envy the living as competing with them, but they honor those who are not in their way, and their good will towards the dead is free of rivalry.

And now, since I must say something about feminine virtue, I shall express it in this brief admonition to you who are now widows: your glory is great if you do not fall beneath the natural condition of your sex, and if you have as little fame among men as is possible, whether for virtue or by way of reproach.

15

Thus I have delivered, according to custom, what was appropriate in a speech, while those men who are buried here have already been honored by their own actions. It remains to maintain their children at the expense of the city until they grow up. This benefit is the city's victory garland for them and for those they leave behind after such contests as these, because the city that gives the greatest rewards for virtue has the finest citizens.

So now, when everyone has mourned for his own, you may go.

UNDERSTANDING THE TEXT

1. Read the first three paragraphs of Pericles' speech and consider the way he frames the introduction. How does he introduce his major ideas? How effective is the introduction?

2. Why does Pericles spend so much time praising Athens, its form of government, and its culture? What does this suggest about his real motives in making this speech?

3. What difference does Pericles see between the way Athens prepares for war and the way its neighbors do? Why is this difference important to the speech?

4. Pericles tries throughout his speech to increase the hostility of his audience towards Sparta. Find several passages where he does this and explain the effect each would have on the audience and why.

5. How does Pericles distinguish himself from "long winded orates"? Why does he say so little about the men whose funeral he is speaking at?

6. What advice does Pericles give to women? Might anything in this passage confirm Plato's argument that it was Aspasia, a woman, who wrote the oration for Pericles to give? Explain.

MAKING CONNECTIONS

1. Both "The Funeral Oration" and the Nazi Party rally filmed in Leni Riefenstahl's *Triumph of the Will* (p. 199) were intended to honor soldiers killed in war. With this purpose in mind, what similarities can you find between the two texts?

2. Compare the way that Pericles treats war with the way that George Orwell does in "Pacifism and the War" (p. 282). Does Pericles treat the enemies of Athens the same way that Orwell treats the threat of fascism? Explain. Which argument do you find most persuasive? Why?

3. Does Pericles use rhetoric the same way that, according to Plato, dishonest Sophists such as Gorgias do (p. 478)? Is there anything in the text that suggests that Pericles might not believe what he is saying? Explain.

WRITING ABOUT THE TEXT

1. Write an essay in which you argue for or against the theory that Aspasia actually wrote "The Funeral Oration." Use passages from the text to support your claim.

2. How does Pericles appeal to emotion and logic in his argument? Write an essay in which you analyze his appeals to each, citing specific passages to support your analysis.

3. Write an essay in which you compare and contrast the assumptions about war in "The Funeral Oration" with those in *Guernica* (p. 271), *Liberty Leading the People* (p. 268), or "What Is a Just War?" (p. 293). Analyze each text to determine what it says about war, and use passages from the texts (or descriptions of the images) to support your claim.

4. Examine a twentieth-century speech by a political leader at a time of war and compare it to Pericles' funeral oration, delivered during the Peloponnesian War. Be sure to identify and account for both similarities and differences.

PLATO (circa 428–348 or 347 BCE), one of the greatest philosophers of the ancient world, came of age during an era of almost perpetual warfare. In 431 BCE, the Peloponnesian War, between his native Athens and the militaristic city-state of Sparta, began. The war lasted for twenty-seven years, during which time Plato grew up in an aristocratic family and became a disciple of the Greek philosopher Socrates. When the war ended in Athens's total defeat, the Athenian assembly tried and executed Socrates, who had been one of the war's strongest critics. Officially, Socrates was charged with impiety and corrupting the young, but Plato felt that his mentor had been executed because he had spent years engaging the city's people in conversations designed to unmask their foolishness and hypocrisy. Plato recorded Socrates' trial in his *Apology*.

The war and Socrates' execution affected Plato deeply; he saw both as fruits of Athens's unwise government, in which an assembly of ordinary men made decisions that affected the entire state. Masterminded by a few very persuasive speakers who managed to build consensus within the assembly, these events made Plato especially suspicious of the art of rhetoric, which, he felt, focused on persuasion at the expense of truth. He believed that important questions should be decided by wise leaders and not be subjected to public debate and popular vote.

For Plato, the figures that symbolized rhetoric's dangers were the Sophists, a group of teachers—most of them foreign—who had set up successful schools of rhetoric in Athens. Sophists often taught that the truth of a situation depended on one's perspective, that any argument could be effective if presented well, and that "winning" a debate was more important than discovering the truth. All of these views were anathema to Plato, who believed that the most important thing in life was to discover the truth.

The Sicilian rhetorician Gorgias (circa 483–376 BCE) was one of the most successful Sophists in Athens. His major discourse, *On Nature or the Non-Existent*, has not survived, but accounts indicate that it argued against the possibility of knowing, or communicating, anything. Although Plato's dialogue *Gorgias* is a debate between Socrates and Gorgias about the relative merits of philosophy and rhetoric, such a conversation probably never occurred; Plato often expressed his ideas through fictional dialogues that echoed the kind of persistent questioning for which Socrates was famous. This format is especially apt for the *Gorgias*, in which Plato focuses on the ultimate purpose of dialogue.

Plato's rhetorical strategy in *Gorgias*, as in most of his dialogues, is to place his own argument in Socrates' mouth while summarizing his opponent's argument in the person of Gorgias. This strategy can be very effective, but Plato has often been criticized for turning characters such as Gorgias into straw men for his own rhetorical ends.

WHAT ARE WE TO CALL YOU, and what is the art which you profess?

Gor. Rhetoric, Socrates, is my art.

Soc. Then I am to call you a rhetorician?   5

Gor. Yes, Socrates, and a good one too, if you would call me that which, in Homeric language, "I boast myself to be."

Soc. I should wish to do so.

Gor. Then pray do.

Soc. And are we to say that you are able to make other men rhetoricians?

Gor. Yes, that is exactly what I profess to make them, not only at Athens, but in all places.

Soc. And will you continue to ask and answer questions, Gorgias, as we are at present doing and reserve for another occasion the longer mode of speech which Polus[1] was attempting? Will you keep your promise, and answer shortly the questions which are asked of you?

Gor. Some answers, Socrates, are of necessity longer; but I will do my best to   10
make them as short as possible; for a part of my profession is that I can be as short as any one.

Soc. That is what is wanted, Gorgias; exhibit the shorter method now, and the longer one at some other time.

Gor. Well, I will; and you will certainly say, that you never heard a man use fewer words.

Soc. Very good then; as you profess to be a rhetorician, and a maker of rhetoricians, let me ask you, with what is rhetoric concerned: I might ask with what is weaving concerned, and you would reply (would you not?), with the making of garments?

Gor. Yes.

Soc. And music is concerned with the composition of melodies?   15

Gor. It is.

Soc. By Herè,[2] Gorgias, I admire the surpassing brevity of your answers.

Gor. Yes, Socrates, I do think myself good at that.

Soc. I am glad to hear it; answer me in like manner about rhetoric: with what is rhetoric concerned?

Gor. With discourse.   20

---

1. **Polus:** a student of Gorgias and a minor character in the *Gorgias*.

2. **Herè:** Hera, in Greek mythology the wife of Zeus and queen of the gods.

Soc. What sort of discourse, Gorgias?—such discourse as would teach the sick under what treatment they might get well?

Gor. No.

Soc. Then rhetoric does not treat of all kinds of discourse?

Gor. Certainly not.

Soc. And yet rhetoric makes men able to speak?   25

Gor. Yes.

Soc. And to understand that about which they speak?

Gor. Of course.

Soc. But does not the art of medicine, which we were just now mentioning, also make men able to understand and speak about the sick?   30

Gor. Certainly.

Soc. Then medicine also treats of discourse?

Gor. Yes.

Soc. Of discourse concerning diseases?

Gor. Just so.

Soc. And does not gymnastic[3] also treat of discourse concerning the good or evil   35 condition of the body?

Gor. Very true.

Soc. And the same, Gorgias, is true of the other arts:—all of them treat of discourse concerning the subjects with which they severally have to do.

Gor. Clearly.

Soc. Then why, if you call rhetoric the art which treats of discourse, and all the other arts treat of discourse, do you not call them arts of rhetoric?

Gor. Because, Socrates, the knowledge of the other arts has only to do with some   40 sort of external action, as of the hand; but there is no such action of the hand in rhetoric which works and takes effect only through the medium of discourse. And therefore I am justified in saying that rhetoric treats of discourse.

Soc. I am not sure whether I entirely understand you, but I dare say I shall soon know better; please to answer me a question:—you would allow that there are arts?

Gor. Yes.

Soc. As to the arts generally, they are for the most part concerned with doing, and require little or no speaking; in painting, and statuary, and many other arts, the work may proceed in silence; and of such arts I suppose you would say that they do not come within the province of rhetoric.

Gor. You perfectly conceive my meaning, Socrates.

Soc. But there are other arts which work wholly through the medium of language,   45 and require either no action or very little, as, for example, the arts of arithmetic, of calculation, of geometry, and of playing draughts; in some of these speech is pretty

---

3. **Gymnastic:** the general science of exercise and physical education.

nearly co-extensive with action, but in most of them the verbal element is greater—
they depend wholly on words for their efficacy and power: and I take your meaning
to be that rhetoric is an art of this latter sort?

Gor. Exactly.

Soc. And yet I do not believe that you really mean to call any of these arts rhetoric; although the precise expression which you used was, that rhetoric is an art
which works and takes effect only through the medium of discourse; and an adver-
sary who wished to be captious might say, "And so, Gorgias, you call arithmetic rhetoric." But I do not think that you really call arithmetic rhetoric any more than
geometry would be so called by you.

Gor. You are quite right, Socrates, in your apprehension of my meaning.

Soc. Well, then, let me now have the rest of my answer:—seeing that rhetoric is
one of those arts which works mainly by the use of words and there are other arts
which also use words tell me what is that quality in words with which rhetoric is
concerned:—Suppose that a person asks me about some of the arts which I was mentioning just now; he might say, "Socrates, what is arithmetic?" and I should reply to
him, as you replied to me, that arithmetic is one of those arts which take effect
through words. And then he would proceed to ask, "Words about what?" and I should
reply, Words about odd and even numbers, and how many there are of each. And
if he asked again, "What is the art of calculation?" I should say, That also is one of
the arts which is concerned wholly with words. And if he further said, "Concerned
with what?" I should say, like the clerks in the assembly, "as aforesaid" of arithmetic,
but with a difference, the difference being that the art of calculation considers not
only the quantities of odd and even numbers, but also their numerical relations to
themselves and to one another. And suppose, again, I were to say that astronomy is
only words—he would ask, "Words about what, Socrates?" and I should answer, that
astronomy tells us about the motions of the stars and sun and moon, and their relative swiftness.

Gor. You would be quite right, Socrates.   50

Soc. And now let us have from you, Gorgias, the truth about rhetoric: which you
would admit (would you not?) to be one of those arts which act always and fulfil all
their ends through the medium of words?

Gor. True.

Soc. Words which do what? I should ask. To what class of things do the words
which rhetoric uses relate?

Gor. To the greatest, Socrates, and the best of human things.

Soc. That again, Gorgias, is ambiguous; I am still in the dark: for which are the   55
greatest and best of human things? I dare say that you have heard men singing at
feasts the old drinking song, in which the singers enumerate the goods of life, first
health, beauty next, thirdly, as the writer of the song says, wealth honestly obtained.

Gor. Yes, I know the song; but what is your drift?

Soc. I mean to say, that the producers of those things which the author of the song praises, that is to say, the physician, the trainer, the money-maker, will at once come to you, and first the physician will say: "O Socrates, Gorgias is deceiving you, for my art is concerned with the greatest good of men and not his." And when I ask, Who are you? he will reply, "I am a physician." What do you mean? I shall say. Do you mean that your art produces the greatest good? "Certainly," he will answer, "for is not health the greatest good? What greater good can men have, Socrates?" And after him the trainer will come and say, "I too, Socrates, shall be greatly surprised if Gorgias can show more good of his art than I can show of mine." To him again I shall say, Who are you, honest friend, and what is your business? "I am a trainer," he will reply, "and my business is to make men beautiful and strong in body." When I have done with the trainer, there arrives the money-maker, and he, as I expect, will utterly despise them all. "Consider, Socrates," he will say, "whether Gorgias or any one else can produce any greater good than wealth." Well, you and I say to him, and are you a creator of wealth? "Yes," he replies. And who are you? "A money-maker." And do you consider wealth to be the greatest good of man? "Of course," will be his reply. And we shall rejoin: Yes; but our friend Gorgias contends that his art produces a greater good than yours. And then he will be sure to go on and asks, "What good? Let Gorgias answer." Now I want you, Gorgias, to imagine that this question is asked of you by them and by me; What is that which, as you say, is the greatest good of man, and of which you are the creator? Answer us.

Gor. That good, Socrates, which is truly the greatest, being that which gives to men freedom in their own persons, and to individuals the power of ruling over others in their several states.

Soc. And what would you consider this to be?

Gor. What is there greater than the word which persuades the judges in the courts, or the senators in the council, or the citizens in the assembly, or at any other political meeting?—if you have the power of uttering this word, you will have the physician your slave, and the trainer your slave, and the money-maker of whom you talk will be found to gather treasures, not for himself, but for you who are able to speak and to persuade the multitude.   60

Soc. Now I think, Gorgias, that you have very accurately explained what you conceive to be the art of rhetoric; and you mean to say, if I am not mistaken, that rhetoric is the artificer of persuasion, having this and no other business, and that this is her crown and end. Do you know any other effect of rhetoric over and above that of producing persuasion?

Gor. No: the definition seems to me very fair, Socrates; for persuasion is the chief end of rhetoric.

Soc. Then hear me, Gorgias, for I am quite sure that if there ever was a man who entered on the discussion of a matter from a pure love of knowing the truth, I am such a one, and I should say the same of you.

Gor. What is coming, Socrates?

Soc. I will tell you: I am very well aware that I do not know what, according to   65
you, is the exact nature, or what are the topics of that persuasion of which you speak,
and which is given by rhetoric; although I have a suspicion about both the one and
the other. And I am going to ask—what is this power of persuasion which is given
by rhetoric, and about what? But why, if I have a suspicion, do I ask instead of telling
you? Not for your sake, but in order that the argument may proceed in such a manner as is most likely to set forth the truth. And I would have you observe, that I am
right in asking this further question: If I asked, "What sort of a painter is Zeuxis?"[4]
and you said, "The painter of figures," should I not be right in asking, "What kind
of figures, and where do you find them?"

Gor. Certainly.

Soc. And the reason for asking this second question would be, that there are other
painters besides, who paint many other figures?

Gor. True.

Soc. But if there had been no one but Zeuxis who painted them, then you would
have answered very well?

Gor. Quite so.   70

Soc. Now I want to know about rhetoric in the same way;—is rhetoric the
only art which brings persuasion, or do other arts have the same effect? I mean
to say—Does he who teaches anything persuade men of that which he teaches
or not?

Gor. He persuades, Socrates,—there can be no mistake about that.

Soc. Again, if we take the arts of which we were just now speaking:—do not arithmetic and the arithmeticians teach us the properties of number?

Gor. Certainly.

Soc. And therefore persuade us of them?   75

Gor. Yes.

Soc. Then arithmetic as well as rhetoric is an artificer of persuasion?

Gor. Clearly.

Soc. And if any one asks us what sort of persuasion, and about what,—we shall
answer, persuasion which teaches the quantity of odd and even; and we shall be able
to show that all the other arts of which we were just now speaking are artificers of
persuasion, and of what sort, and about what.

Gor. Very true.   80

Soc. Then rhetoric is not the only artificer of persuasion?

Gor. True.

Soc. Seeing, then, that not only rhetoric works by persuasion, but that other arts
do the same, as in the case of the painter, a question has arisen which is a very fair
one: Of what persuasion is rhetoric the artificer, and about what?—is not that a fair
way of putting the question?

---

4. **Zeuxis:** a well-known painter from the Greek city of Ephesus.

Gor. I think so.

Soc. Then, if you approve the question, Gorgias, what is the answer? 85

Gor. I answer, Socrates, that rhetoric is the art of persuasion in courts of law and other assemblies, as I was just now saying, and about the just and unjust.

Soc. And that, Gorgias, was what I was suspecting to be your notion; yet I would not have you wonder if by-and-by I am found repeating a seemingly plain question; for I ask not in order to confute you, but as I was saying that the argument may proceed consecutively, and that we may not get the habit of anticipating and suspecting the meaning of one another's words; I would have you develop your own views in your own way, whatever may be your hypothesis.

Gor. I think that you are quite right, Socrates.

Soc. Then let me raise another question; there is such a thing as "having learned"?

Gor. Yes.

Soc. And there is also "having believed"? 90

Gor. Yes.

Soc. And is the "having learned" the same as "having believed," and are learning and belief the same things?

Gor. In my judgment, Socrates, they are not the same.[5]

Soc. And your judgment is right, as you may ascertain in this way:—If a person 95
were to say to you, "Is there, Gorgias, a false belief as well as a true?"—you would reply, if I am not mistaken, that there is.

Gor. Yes.

Soc. Well, but is there a false knowledge as well as a true?

Gor. No.

Soc. No, indeed; and this again proves that knowledge and belief differ.

Gor. Very true. 100

Soc. And yet those who have learned as well as those who have believed are persuaded?

Gor. Just so.

Soc. Shall we then assume two sorts of persuasion,—one which is the source of belief without knowledge, as the other is of knowledge?

Gor. By all means.

Soc. And which sort of persuasion does rhetoric create in courts of law and other 105
assemblies about the just and unjust, the sort of persuasion which gives belief without knowledge, or that which gives knowledge?

Gor. Clearly, Socrates, that which only gives belief.

Soc. Then rhetoric, as would appear, is the artificer of a persuasion which creates belief about the just and unjust, but gives no instruction about them?

Gor. True.

---

5. The historical Gorgias probably would not have conceded this point so easily, as he is said to have taught that nothing is ultimately knowable.

Soc. And the rhetorician does not instruct the courts of law or other assemblies about things just and unjust, but he creates belief about them; for no one can be supposed to instruct such a vast multitude about such high matters in a short time?

Gor. Certainly not.   110

Soc. Come, then, and let us see what we really mean about rhetoric; for I do not know what my own meaning is as yet. When the assembly meets to elect a physician or a shipwright or any other craftsman, will the rhetorician be taken into counsel? Surely not. For at every election he ought to be chosen who is most skilled; and, again, when walls have to be built or harbours or docks to be constructed, not the rhetorician but the master workman will advise; or when generals have to be chosen and an order of battle arranged, or a proposition taken, then the military will advise and not the rhetoricians: what do you say, Gorgias? Since you profess to be a rhetorician and a maker of rhetoricians, I cannot do better than learn the nature of your art from you. And here let me assure you that I have your interest in view as well as my own. For likely enough some one or other of the young men present might desire to become your pupil, and in fact I see some, and a good many too, who have this wish, but they would be too modest to question you. And therefore when you are interrogated by me, I would have you imagine that you are interrogated by them. "What is the use of coming to you, Gorgias?" they will say—"about what will you teach us to advise the state?—about the just and unjust only, or about those other things also which Socrates has just mentioned?" How will you answer them?

Gor. I like your way of leading us on, Socrates, and I will endeavour to reveal to you the whole nature of rhetoric. You must have heard, I think, that the docks and the walls of the Athenians and the plan of the harbour were devised in accordance with the counsels, partly of Themistocles, and partly of Pericles,[6] and not at the suggestion of the builders.

Soc. Such is the tradition, Gorgias, about Themistocles; and I myself heard the speech of Pericles when he advised us about the middle wall.

Gor. And you will observe, Socrates, that when a decision has to be given in such matters the rhetoricians are the advisers; they are the men who win their point.

Soc. I had that in my admiring mind, Gorgias, when I asked what is the nature   115
of rhetoric, which always appears to me, when I look at the matter in this way, to be a marvel of greatness.

Gor. A marvel, indeed, Socrates, if you only knew how rhetoric comprehends and holds under her sway all the inferior arts. Let me offer you a striking example of this. On several occasions I have been with my brother Herodicus or some other

---

6. **Pericles:** the leader of Athens (circa 495–429 BCE) during much of its golden age and a major proponent of the Peloponnesian War. **Themistocles:** the Athenian leader (circa 524–circa 460 BCE) who masterminded the naval victory over the Persian Empire, in 480 BCE, which established Athens as a regional power.

physician to see one of his patients, who would not allow the physician to give him medicine, or apply a knife or hot iron to him; and I have persuaded him to do for me what he would not do for the physician just by the use of rhetoric. And I say that if a rhetorician and a physician were to go to any city, and had there to argue in the Ecclesia[7] or any other assembly as to which of them should be elected state-physician, the physician would have no chance; but he who could speak would be chosen if he wished; and in a contest with a man of any other profession the rhetorician more than any one would have the power of getting himself chosen, for he can speak more persuasively to the multitude than any of them, and on any subject. Such is the nature and power of the art of rhetoric! And yet, Socrates, rhetoric should be used like any other competitive art, not against everybody—the rhetorician ought not to abuse his strength any more than a pugilist or pancratiast or other master of fence;[8] because he has powers which are more than a match either for friend or enemy, he ought not therefore to strike, stab, or slay his friends. Suppose a man to have been trained in the palestra[9] and to be a skilful boxer—he in the fulness of his strength goes and strikes his father or mother or one of his familiars or friends; but that is no reason why the trainers or fencing-masters should be held in detestation or banished from the city—surely not. For they taught their art for a good purpose, to be used against enemies and evil-doers, in self-defence not in aggression, and others have perverted their instructions, and turned to a bad use their own strength and skill. But not on this account are the teachers bad, neither is the art in fault, or bad in itself; I should rather say that those who make a bad use of the art are to blame. And the same argument holds good of rhetoric; for the rhetorician can speak against all men and upon any subject—in short, he can persuade the multitude better than any other man of anything which he pleases, but he should not therefore seek to defraud the physician or any other artist of his reputation merely because he has the power; he ought to use rhetoric fairly, as he would also use his athletic powers. And if after having become a rhetorician he makes a bad use of his strength and skill, his instructor surely ought not on that account to be held in detestation or banished. For he was intended by his teacher to make a good use of his instructions, but he abuses them. And therefore he is the person who ought to be held in detestation, banished, and put to death, and not his instructor.[10]

---

7. **Ecclesia:** the Athenian Assembly, which, in Plato's day, consisted of more than forty thousand citizens.

8. **Master of fence:** fencing master. **Pugilist or pancratiast:** Pugilists were the ancient equivalent of boxers; pancratiasts practiced *pankration*, a Greek martial art featured in the early Olympic games.

9. **Palestra:** a public training ground for wrestling and other athletic events.

10. Gorgias's defense of rhetoric here repeats the defense that the Athenian orator Isocrates (436–338 BCE) makes in his rhetorical tract *Antidosis*. Thus it was probably standard to argue that, as a tool, rhetoric was morally neutral and could be used for good or bad. Plato would not have been impressed by such a defense—he believed that something must be actively good to be morally justified.

Soc. You, Gorgias, like myself, have had great experience of disputations, and you must have observed, I think, that they do not always terminate in mutual edification, or in the definition by either party of the subjects which they are discussing; but disagreements are apt to arise—somebody says that another has not spoken truly or clearly; and then they get into a passion and begin to quarrel, both parties conceiving that their opponents are arguing from personal feeling only and jealousy of themselves, not from any interest in the question at issue. And sometimes they will go on abusing one another until the company at last are quite vexed at themselves for ever listening to such fellows. Why do I say this? Why, because I cannot help feeling that you are now saying what is not quite consistent or accordant with what you were saying at first about rhetoric. And I am afraid to point this out to you, lest you should think that I have some animosity against you, and that I speak, not for the sake of discovering the truth, but from jealousy of you. Now if you are one of my sort, I should like to cross-examine you, but if not I will let you alone. And what is my sort? you will ask. I am one of those who are very willing to be refuted if I say anything which is not true, and very willing to refute any one else who says what is not true, and quite as ready to be refuted as to refute; for I hold that this is the greater gain of the two, just as the gain is greater of being cured of a very great evil than of curing another. For I imagine that there is no evil which a man can endure so great as an erroneous opinion about the matters of which we are speaking; and if you claim to be one of my sort, let us have the discussion out, but if you would rather have done, no matter—let us make an end of it.

UNDERSTANDING THE TEXT

1. How does Gorgias initially define "rhetoric"? To what redefinition does Socrates lead him? Why does Socrates not simply state his redefinition—what does he gain by drawing it out of Gorgias?

2. What other subjects besides rhetoric does Socrates claim to be focused on persuasion? What is the difference between these subjects and rhetoric, according to the dialogue?

3. Explain the distinction that Socrates draws between "knowledge" and "belief." Which one is the province of rhetoric? Which, then, is the subject of philosophy? Do you agree with Socrates that all kinds of persuasion create either knowledge or belief? Why or why not?

4. What major defense of rhetoric does Gorgias offer? Do you agree with his reasoning? Why or why not?

5. Are the words that Plato puts into Gorgias's mouth strong enough to represent an actual argument? At which points is Gorgias's position at its strongest, and at which points is it at its weakest?

MAKING CONNECTIONS

1. Would Plato agree with Aristotle's assertion (p. 553) that good arguments naturally tend to prevail over bad ones? Would Plato agree with Aristotle's implicit assumption that rhetoric should be studied so that good arguments can compete on the same grounds as bad ones? Explain your answers.

2. In what ways does Plato see language as exercising a destructive power? Compare his perspective to the views of Chinua Achebe (p. 592) and Toni Morrison (p. 539) about the power of language.

3. Compare Plato's attack on Sophism with that of Gertrude Buck in "The Present Status of Rhetorical Theory" (p. 496). Are the two authors' points the same? Explain.

WRITING ABOUT THE TEXT

1. Use Socrates' arguments against rhetoric to analyze a television commercial or other advertisement. In what ways might the advertiser have focused on persuasion at the expense of truth? Does the advertisement seemed aimed at producing knowledge or belief?

2. Defend the teaching of rhetoric on the grounds that knowing how to be persuasive increases one's ability to do good. Perhaps draw on the examples of historical figures (Mohandas K. Gandhi or Martin Luther King Jr., for instance) who accomplished great things because of their ability to persuade others.

3. Analyze Plato's rhetorical use of the dialogue form. How does the format of a fictional debate affect the persuasiveness of Plato's argument? How might Plato reconcile his use of rhetoric with the opposition to rhetoric that he expresses in *Gorgias*?

Aristotle
from *Rhetoric*
(350 BCE)

THE PHILOSOPHER ARISTOTLE (384–322 BCE) began his career as a brilliant student in Plato's Academy. However, his views often clashed with those of Plato and of the other students, and after Plato's death (in 348 or 347 BCE), he left Athens and eventually became the private tutor of Prince Alexander of Macedon, later known as Alexander the Great. When he returned to Athens, in 355 BCE, Aristotle founded his own school, the Lyceum, where he taught philosophy, natural science, and rhetoric.

Contemporary references indicate that Aristotle composed as many as 150 treatises on a wide variety of subjects (however, many of these were probably detailed lecture notes taken by students at the Lyceum). The thirty surviving treatises cover such topics as logic, ethics, physics, metaphysics, politics, literature, and rhetoric and lay the foundations of Western reasoning. Unlike Plato, whose writings focused on the mind and the world of ideal forms, Aristotle focused on the tangible realities of the external world. Also, while Plato's arguments tended to be *prescriptive*, or to advocate positions and points of view, Aristotle's writings were mostly *descriptive*, describing, organizing, and classifying their subjects.

Plato's and Aristotle's distinct approaches to philosophy can be seen clearly in their different approaches to rhetoric. Plato's *Gorgias* is an argument about the value of rhetoric, which he condemns as an inferior and dangerous counterfeit of philosophy. Aristotle's *Rhetoric*, on the other hand, concerns the practice of rhetoric. In it, he classifies different kinds of arguments, appeals, and tools that can form the basis for persuasive arguments. Much like the Sophists, Aristotle acknowledges that rhetoric can be either helpful or harmful, depending on how it is used. Unlike the Sophists, however, he believes that rhetoric inherently favors moral and just arguments because "things that are true and things that are just have a natural tendency to prevail over their opposites."

The first two chapters of Aristotle's *Rhetoric* are excerpted here. In the first part of this excerpt, Aristotle gives an overview of and explains the usefulness of rhetoric. Rhetoric forms the counterpart of what he calls "dialectic"—while rhetoric is public speaking designed to persuade, dialectic is a more private philosophical dialogue designed to uncover the truth. In the second part of the excerpt, Aristotle establishes three categories of persuasive appeal: pathos (appeals to emotion), logos (appeals to logic and reasoning), and ethos (appeals based on the character of the speaker).

Aristotle's own rhetorical style highlights the deductive reasoning for which he was famous. Aristotle typically starts with a statement of general principle and then applies it to specific instances. He also spends a great deal of time dividing and classifying phenomena.

1

RHETORIC IS THE COUNTERPART of Dialectic.[1] Both alike are concerned with such things as come, more or less, within the general ken of all men and belong to no definite science. Accordingly all men make use, more or less, of both; for to a certain extent all men attempt to discuss statements and to maintain them, to defend themselves and to attack others. Ordinary people do this either at random or through practice and from acquired habit. Both ways being possible, the subject can plainly be handled systematically, for it is possible to inquire the reason why some speakers succeed through practice and others spontaneously; and every one will at once agree that such an inquiry is the function of an art.

Now, the framers of the current treatises on rhetoric[2] have constructed but a small portion of that art. The modes of persuasion are the only true constituents of the art: everything else is merely accessory. These writers, however, say nothing about enthymemes,[3] which are the substance of rhetorical persuasion, but deal mainly with non-essentials. The arousing of prejudice, pity, anger, and similar emotions has nothing to do with the essential facts, but is merely a personal appeal to the man who is judging the case. Consequently if the rules for trials which are now laid down in some states—especially in well-governed states—were applied everywhere, such people would have nothing to say. All men, no doubt, *think* that the laws should prescribe such rules, but some, as in the court of Areopagus,[4] give practical effect to their thoughts and forbid talk about non-essentials. This is sound law and custom. It is not right to pervert the judge by moving him to anger or envy or pity—one might as well warp a carpenter's rule before using it. Again, a litigant has clearly nothing to do but to show that the alleged fact is so or is not so, that it has or has not happened. As to whether a thing is important or unimportant, just or unjust, the judge must surely refuse to take his instructions from the litigants: he must decide for himself all such points as the law-giver has not already defined for him.

Now, it is of great moment that well-drawn laws should themselves define all the points they possibly can and leave as few as may be to the decision of the judges; and this for several reasons. First, to find one man, or a few men, who are sensible persons and capable of legislating and administering justice is easier than to find a large number. Next, laws are made after long consideration, whereas decisions in the courts are given at short notice, which makes it hard for those who try the case to

1. **Dialectic:** discussion, specifically philosophical discussion that aims to uncover truth rather than persuade. Aristotle's use of the term differs somewhat from Hegel's (see p. 624).

2. **Current treatises on rhetoric:** the works of Sophists such as Gorgias, Isocrates, and Protagoras.

3. **Enthymemes:** In Aristotle's terms, an "enthymeme" was the basic unit of an argument: a conclusion attached to a single supporting premise, with other premises merely implied. A rough modern equivalent is the "thesis statement."

4. **Areopagus:** Athens's "Hill of Ares," where murder trials were held in Aristotle's time.

satisfy the claims of justice and expediency. The weightiest reason of all is that the decision of the lawgiver is not particular but prospective and general, whereas members of the assembly and the jury find it *their* duty to decide on definite cases brought before them. They will often have allowed themselves to be so much influenced by feelings of friendship or hatred or self-interest that they lose any clear vision of the truth and have their judgement obscured by considerations of personal pleasure or pain. In general, then, the judge should, we say, be allowed to decide as few things as possible. But questions as to whether something has happened or has not happened, will be or will not be, is or is not, must of necessity be left to the judge, since the lawgiver cannot foresee them. If this is so, it is evident that any one who lays down rules about other matters, such as what must be the contents of the 'introduction' or the 'narration' or any of the other divisions of a speech, is theorizing about non-essentials as if they belonged to the art. The only question with which these writers here deal is how to put the judge into a given frame of mind. About the orator's proper modes of persuasion they have nothing to tell us; nothing, that is, about how to gain skill in enthymemes.

Hence it comes that, although the same systematic principles apply to political as to forensic oratory,[5] and although the former is a nobler business, and fitter for a citizen, than that which concerns the relations of private individuals, these authors say nothing about political oratory, but try, one and all, to write treatises on the way to plead in court. The reason for this is that in political oratory there is less inducement to talk about non-essentials. Political oratory is less given to unscrupulous practices than forensic, because it treats of wider issues. In a political debate the man who is forming a judgement is making a decision about his own vital interests. There is no need, therefore, to prove anything except that the facts are what the supporter of a measure maintains they are. In forensic oratory this is not enough; to conciliate the listener is what pays here. It is other people's affairs that are to be decided, so that the judges, intent on their own satisfaction and listening with partiality, surrender themselves to the disputants instead of judging between them. Hence in many places, as we have said already, irrelevant speaking is forbidden in the law-courts: in the public assembly those who have to form a judgement are themselves well able to guard against that.

It is clear, then, that rhetorical study, in its strict sense, is concerned with the modes of persuasion. Persuasion is clearly a sort of demonstration, since we are most   5 fully persuaded when we consider a thing to have been demonstrated. The orator's demonstration is an enthymeme, and this is, in general, the most effective of the modes of persuasion. The enthymeme is a sort of syllogism,[6] and the consideration of syllogisms of all kinds, without distinction, is the business of dialectic, either of dialectic as a whole or of one of its branches. It follows plainly, therefore, that he

---

5. **Forensic oratory:** arguments designed to establish facts from the past, especially as they relate to guilt or innocence in a criminal trial.

6. See p. 597.

who is best able to see how and from what elements a syllogism is produced will also be best skilled in the enthymeme, when he has further learnt what its subject-matter is and in what respects it differs from the syllogism of strict logic. The true and the approximately true are apprehended by the same faculty; it may also be noted that men have a sufficient natural instinct for what is true, and usually do arrive at the truth. Hence the man who makes a good guess at truth is likely to make a good guess at probabilities.

It has now been shown that the ordinary writers on rhetoric treat of non-essentials; it has also been shown why they have inclined more towards the forensic branch of oratory.

Rhetoric is useful (1) because things that are true and things that are just have a natural tendency to prevail over their opposites, so that if the decisions of judges are not what they ought to be, the defeat must be due to the speakers themselves, and they must be blamed accordingly. Moreover, (2) before some audiences not even the possession of the exactest knowledge will make it easy for what we say to produce conviction. For argument based on knowledge implies instruction, and there are people whom one cannot instruct. Here, then, we must use, as our modes of persuasion and argument, notions possessed by everybody, as we observed in the *Topics*[7] when dealing with the way to handle a popular audience. Further, (3) we must be able to employ persuasion, just as strict reasoning can be employed, on opposite sides of a question, not in order that we may in practice employ it in both ways (for we must not make people believe what is wrong), but in order that we may see clearly what the facts are, and that, if another man argues unfairly, we on our part may be able to confute him. No other of the arts draws opposite conclusions: dialectic and rhetoric alone do this. Both these arts draw opposite conclusions impartially. Nevertheless, the underlying facts do not lend themselves equally well to the contrary views. No; things that are true and things that are better are, by their nature, practically always easier to prove and easier to believe in. Again, (4) it is absurd to hold that a man ought to be ashamed of being unable to defend himself with his limbs, but not of being unable to defend himself with speech and reason, when the use of rational speech is more distinctive of a human being than the use of his limbs. And if it be objected that one who uses such power of speech unjustly might do great harm, *that* is a charge which may be made in common against all good things except virtue, and above all against the things that are most useful, as strength, health, wealth, generalship. A man can confer the greatest of benefits by a right use of these, and inflict the greatest of injuries by using them wrongly.

It is clear, then, that rhetoric is not bound up with a single definite class of subjects, but is as universal as dialectic; it is clear, also, that it is useful. It is clear, fur-

---

7. **Topics:** one of Aristotle's six known works on logic, which form a collective work called the *Organon*.

ther, that its function is not simply to succeed in persuading, but rather to discover the means of coming as near such success as the circumstances of each particular case allow. In this it resembles all other arts. For example, it is not the function of medicine simply to make a man quite healthy, but to put him as far as may be on the road to health; it is possible to give excellent treatment even to those who can never enjoy sound health. Furthermore, it is plain that it is the function of one and the same art to discern the real and the apparent means of persuasion, just as it is the function of dialectic to discern the real and the apparent syllogism. What makes a man a 'sophist' is not his faculty, but his moral purpose. In rhetoric, however, the term 'rhetorician' may describe either the speaker's knowledge of the art, or his moral purpose. In dialectic it is different: a man is a 'sophist' because he has a certain kind of moral purpose, a 'dialectician' in respect, not of his moral purpose, but of his faculty.

Let us now try to give some account of the systematic principles of Rhetoric itself—of the right method and means of succeeding in the object we set before us. We must make as it were a fresh start, and before going further define what rhetoric is.

2

Rhetoric may be defined as the faculty of observing in any given case the available   10
means of persuasion. This is not a function of any other art. Every other art can instruct or persuade about its own particular subject-matter; for instance, medicine about what is healthy and unhealthy, geometry about the properties of magnitudes, arithmetic about numbers, and the same is true of the other arts and sciences. But rhetoric we look upon as the power of observing the means of persuasion on almost any subject presented to us; and that is why we say that, in its technical character, it is not concerned with any special or definite class of subjects.

Of the modes of persuasion some belong strictly to the art of rhetoric and some do not. By the latter I mean such things as are not supplied by the speaker but are there are the outset—witnesses, evidence given under torture, written contracts, and so on. By the former I mean such as we can ourselves construct by means of the principles of rhetoric. The one kind has merely to be used, the other has to be invented.

Of the modes of persuasion furnished by the spoken word there are three kinds. The first kind depends on the personal character of the speaker; the second on putting the audience into a certain frame of mind; the third on the proof, or apparent proof, provided by the words of the speech itself. Persuasion is achieved by the speaker's personal character when the speech is so spoken as to make us think him credible. We believe good men more fully and more readily than others: this is true generally whatever the question is, and absolutely true where exact certainty is impossible and opinions are divided. This kind of persuasion, like the others, should be achieved by what the speaker says, not by what people think of his character before he begins to speak. It is not true, as some writers assume in their treatises on rhetoric, that the personal goodness revealed by the speaker contributes nothing to his power of persuasion; on the contrary, his character may almost be called the most effective means of persuasion he possesses. Secondly, persuasion may come through the hearers, when the speech stirs their emotions. Our judgements when we are pleased and friendly are not the same as when we are pained and hostile. It is towards producing these effects, as we maintain, that present-day writers on rhetoric direct the whole of their efforts. This subject shall be treated in detail when we come to speak of the emotions. Thirdly, persuasion is effected through the speech itself when we have proved a truth or an apparent truth by means of the persuasive arguments suitable to the case in question.

There are, then, these three means of effecting persuasion. The man who is to be in command of them must, it is clear, be able (1) to reason logically, (2) to understand human character and goodness in their various forms, and (3) to understand the emotions—that is, to name them and describe them, to know their causes and the way in which they are excited. It thus appears that rhetoric is an offshoot of dialectic and also of ethical studies. Ethical studies may fairly be called political; and for this reason rhetoric masquerades as political science, and the professors of it as political experts—sometimes from want of education, sometimes from ostentation, sometimes owing to other human failings. As a matter of fact, it is a branch of dialectic and similar to it, as we said at the outset. Neither rhetoric nor dialectic is the scientific study of any one separate subject: both are faculties for providing arguments. This is perhaps a sufficient account of their scope and of how they are related to each other.

UNDERSTANDING THE TEXT

1. What, according to Aristotle, is rhetoric's primary purpose?

2. What does Aristotle consider the hallmarks of "well-drawn laws"? Do you agree with this assertion? Why or why not?

3. How does Aristotle differentiate between a "Sophist" and a "rhetorician"? Can one employ rhetoric without being a Sophist?

4. What are Aristotle's three means of persuasion? What specific skills does each method require? Which method do you consider the most persuasive, and why?

MAKING CONNECTIONS

1. Compare Aristotle's defense of rhetoric with the one made by Gorgias in Plato's *Gorgias* (p. 478). Which of Gorgias's ideas does Aristotle echo? How does his position differ from Gorgias's?

2. Can you detect Aristotle's influence on the medieval philosophers who emulated him, such as Averroës (p. 391) and Moses Maimonides (p. 397)? Explain.

3. How might Gertrude Buck (p. 496) respond to Aristotle's assertion that the strongest arguments will always prevail? Cite passages from "The Present Status of Rhetorical Theory" in your reply.

4. How do Aristotle's views of the natural superiority of true arguments compare with the warnings given by N. Scott Momaday (p. 519) and Toni Morrison (p. 539) about the destructive power of speech?

WRITING ABOUT THE TEXT

1. Select a text that was written specifically to persuade—such as Martin Luther King Jr.'s "Letter from Birmingham City Jail" (p. 202) or Rachel Carson's "The Obligation to Endure" (p. 419)—and analyze its use of Aristotle's three means of persuasion. How effective are the text's appeals to logic, appeals to emotion, and appeals based on the character of the speaker?

2. Write an essay in which you agree or disagree with Aristotle's assertion that "things that are true and things that are just have a natural tendency to prevail over their opposites." In your experience, do morally sound, factually correct arguments generally prevail in public discourse?

3. Compare Aristotle's and Plato's (p. 478) views on rhetoric. What underlying assumptions might have contributed to their very different ideas about the art of persuasion?

Gertrude Buck
The Present Status of Rhetorical Theory
(1900)

GERTRUDE BUCK was born into a wealthy family in Kalamazoo, Michigan, in 1871. She attended the University of Michigan for both undergraduate and graduate studies and, in 1898, became the first woman to receive a Ph.D. in rhetoric from that institution. Buck taught at Vassar College, then a woman's school, from 1897 until her death in 1922. She was a widely published literary critic and is now recognized as one of the first modern feminist rhetoricians.

Buck wrote during a time when scholars were showing great interest in the rhetorical theories of ancient Greece. In the nineteenth century, as democratic governments began to take hold in the world for the first time since ancient Athens, scholars and speakers increasingly found models of rhetorical practice in the works of Plato, Aristotle, and the group of pre-Socratic rhetoricians known as "Sophists." Buck's strong critiques of the Sophists are based largely on those made by Plato nearly 2500 years earlier.

In the *Gorgias*, Plato mounts a stinging attack on Sophists and, in the process, dismisses rhetoric as an inferior branch of study designed to create the pretense of knowledge rather than knowledge itself, which was the special province of philosophy. While Buck makes these same arguments against the sophistic conception of rhetoric, she does not follow Plato in rejecting the art of rhetoric entirely. Nor does she entirely agree with Roman rhetorician Quintilian's view that a rhetorician must, by definition, be a "good man skilled at speaking." Rather, she divides rhetoric into two categories: the sophistic, which is manipulative and focuses on the needs of the speaker at the expense of the audience; and the Platonic, which is collaborative and focuses on the shared interests of the speaker and audience.

Buck's ultimate concern in "The Present Status of Rhetorical Theory" is with how we use language to facilitate interaction in a community. Rhetoric, she believed, can either magnify human selfishness by allowing some people to impose their agendas on others, or it can facilitate human community by encouraging us to overlook our differences and focus on the interests that we share.

Buck presents her argument through comparison and contrast, expounding on all of the differences between sophistic and Platonic rhetoric, with no effort to hide her preference for the latter.

Two opposing conceptions of the nature of discourse bequeathed to us from classic times still struggle for dominance in our modern rhetorical theory—the social conception of Plato and the anti-social conception of the Sophists.[1] The latter, though known to us only fragmentarily from allusions and quotations in later treatises, can be, in its essential outlines, easily reconstructed. According to the sophistic teaching, discourse was simply a process of persuading the hearer to a conclusion which the speaker, for any reason, desired him to accept. Analyzed further, this familiar definition discloses certain significant features.

First of all it conveys, though somewhat indirectly, a notion of the ultimate end of the process of discourse. Why should discourse take place at all? Why should the hearer be persuaded? Because, answers the definition, the speaker wishes to persuade him. And, to pursue the inquiry still further, the speaker wishes to persuade the hearer to a certain belief presumably because he recognizes some advantage to himself in doing so. We should conclude, therefore, from examination of the definition before us, that discourse is for the sake of the speaker.

Nor is this conclusion threatened by further investigation into the pre-Platonic philosophy of discourse. It is true that the practical precepts of the sophistic rhetoricians pay great deference to the hearer, even seeming, at first glance, to exalt him over the speaker. Every detail of the speech is to be sedulously "adapted" to the hearer. Nothing is to be done without reference to him. His tastes are to be studied, his prejudices regarded, his little jealousies and chagrins written down in a book—but all this, be it remembered, in order simply that he may the more completely be subjugated to the speaker's will. As the definition has previously suggested, the hearer's ultimate importance to discourse is of the slightest. To his interests the process of discourse is quite indifferent.

But not only does persuasion, according to the sophistic notion, fail to consider the interests of the hearer; frequently it even assails them. In fact, the sophistic precepts bristle with implications that the hearer's part in discourse is virtually to be spoiled. The hearer is to be persuaded for the sake of some advantage to the speaker. If his own advantage should chance to lie in the same direction with that of the speaker, the utmost that the process of discourse could do would be merely to point out this fact to the hearer. In such a case little persuasive art is demanded. It is rather when the interests of the hearer, if rightly understood by him, oppose his acceptance of the conclusion urged by the speaker that real rhetorical skill comes into play. Then is the speaker confronted by a task worthy of his training—that of making the acceptance of this conclusion, which is really inimical to the hearer's interests, seem to him advantageous. In plainest statement, the speaker must by finesse assail the hearer's interests for the sake of his own.

1. **Sophists:** teachers in ancient Greece such as Gorgias (p. 478) who set up schools and taught students the art of rhetoric in exchange for money.

This is a typical case of discourse, according to the sophistic conception. Its essen- 5
tially anti-social character appears both in its conscious purpose and in its unrecog-
nized issues. We have seen that the end it seeks is exclusively individual, sanctioned
only by that primitive ethical principle of the dominance of the strong. The speaker
through discourse secures his own advantage simply because he is able to do so. The
meaning of his action to the hearer or to society as a whole, is purely a moral question with which rhetoric is not directly concerned. There is, in the rhetorical theory of the sophists, no test for the process of discourse larger than the success of the
speaker in attaining his own end.

But further, the sophistic conception of discourse is anti-social in its outcome.
Instead of levelling conditions between the two parties to the act, as we are told is
the tendency in all true social functioning, discourse renders these conditions more
unequal than they were before it took place. The speaker, superior at the outset, by
virtue at least of a keener perception of the situation, through the process of discourse, comes still further to dominate the hearer. As in primitive warfare the stronger
of two tribal organizations subdues and eventually enslaves the weaker, so in discourse the initial advantage of the speaker returns to him with usury.

This anti-social character of the sophistic discourse, as seen both in its purpose
and in its outcome, may be finally traced to the fact that the process, as we have
analyzed it, just fails of achieving complete communication between speaker and
hearer. Some conclusion is, indeed, established in the mind of the hearer, but not
necessarily the conclusion which the speaker himself has reached upon this subject.
It may, in fact, oppose all his own experience and thought, and thus hold no organic
relation to his own mind. But wishing the hearer to believe it, he picks it up somewhere and proceeds to insert it into the hearer's mind.

This absence of a vital relationship between the normal activities of the speaker's
mind and the action by which he seeks to persuade the hearer, breaks the line of communication between the two persons concerned. Conditions at the ends of the circuit
cannot be equalized, as in true social functioning, because the current is thus interrupted.

This conception of the process of discourse might be graphically represented in
Figure 1.

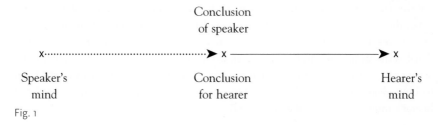

Conclusion
of speaker

x·····································➤ x ─────────────➤ x

Speaker's   Conclusion   Hearer's
mind   for hearer   mind

Fig. 1

The sophistic account of discourse, then, makes it a process essentially
individualistic, and thus socially irresponsible. It secures the advantage of the

speaker without regard to that of the hearer, or even in direct opposition to it. Because this conception leaves a gap in the chain of communication between the minds of speaker and hearer, it fails to equalize conditions between them. The speaker wins and the hearer loses continually. Discourse is purely predatory—a primitive aggression of the strong upon the weak. The art of rhetoric is the art of war.

Against this essentially crude and anti-social conception of discourse, Plato *10* seems to have raised the first articulate protest. Discourse is not an isolated phenomenon, he maintained, cut off from all relations to the world in which it occurs, and exempt from the universal laws of justice and right. The speaker has certain obligations, not perhaps directly to the hearer, but to the absolute truth of which he is but the mouthpiece, to the entire order of things which nowadays we are wont to call society. Discourse is, indeed, persuasion, but not persuasion to any belief the speaker pleases. Rather is it persuasion to the truth, knowledge of which, on the part of the hearer, ultimately advantages both himself and the speaker as well. The interests of both are equally furthered by legitimate discourse. In fact the interests of both are, when rightly understood, identical: hence there can be no antagonism between them.

In respect, then, to the advantage gained by each party to the act of discourse, speaker and hearer stand on a footing of at least approximate equality. In fact the ultimate end of discourse must be, from the Platonic premises, to establish equality between them. Before discourse takes place the speaker has a certain advantage over the hearer. He perceives a truth as yet hidden from the hearer, but necessary for him to know. Since the recognition of this truth on the part of the hearer must ultimately serve the speaker's interests as well, the speaker, through the act of discourse, communicates to the hearer his own vision. This done, the original inequality is removed, the interests of both speaker and hearer are furthered, and equilibrium is at this point restored to the social organism.

It is plain that the circuit of communication between speaker and hearer is in Plato's conception of discourse continuous. The speaker having himself come to a certain conclusion, does not set about establishing another in the hearer's mind, but simply transmits his own belief into the other's consciousness. The connection between the two minds is living and unbroken. The Platonic notion of the process of discourse may be thus illustratd as in Figure 2.

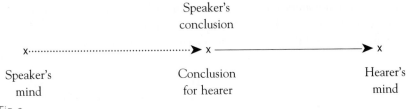

Fig. 2

Thus have been hastily reviewed the two opposing conceptions of discourse delivered to us by the earliest rhetoricians. The changes which they have suffered in the lapse of centuries are surprisingly slight. We find implicit in many of our modern text-books practically the same conception of discourse which was held by the pre-Platonic teachers of rhetoric—a conception which regards discourse as an act performed by the speaker upon the hearer for the advantage of the speaker alone. It is true that the present-day sophists include in the end of discourse not persuasion alone, but the production of any desired effect upon the hearer. This fact does not, however, modify fundamentally the nature of the process itself. The hearer (or reader as he has now become) is to be interested or amused, or reduced to tears, or overborne with a sense of the sublime, not indeed because the writer himself has previously been interested or amused and, in obedience to the primal social instinct, would communicate his experience to another, but because—well, because the writer wishes to produce this effect upon the reader. Thus wishing, and being able to gratify his desire, the act of discourse results—an act still individualistic and one-sided, serving no ends but those of the speaker himself. The effect to be produced upon the hearer, being wholly external to the experience of the speaker, leaves unjoined the old break between speaker and hearer in the process of communication. We have again, in but slightly altered guise, the sophistic conception of discourse.

But in spite of the persistence of this outworn conception in even some recent text-books, there are not wanting many evidences that the Platonic theory of discourse is at last coming home to the modern consciousness. It is doubtless true that the later social theory of rhetoric would not venture to define the end of discourse as that of declaring to another the absolute and universal truth. There may be two reasons for this. In the first place we are not now-a-days on such joyfully intimate terms with the absolute truth as was Plato. And, again, the practical value of even a little relative and perhaps temporary truth has become clearer to us—such truth as touches us through our personal experiences and observations. Yet it must be remembered that Plato himself allowed the subject-matter of discourse to be the speaker's own vision of the absolute truth, thus individualizing the abstraction until we cannot regard it as fundamentally alien from our modern conception of experience, in the largest sense of the word.

Granting this substantial identity, then, we have only to prove that Plato's idea of personal experience as the subject-matter of discourse is a real factor in modern rhetorical theory. For this no long argument is required. We find this idea theoretically expressed in rhetorical treatises even as far back as Quintilian, in the implied definition of discourse as self-expression, a conception recently popularized by such writers as Arnold and Pater.[2] This notion of discourse, neglecting that part of the

15

---

2. **Arnold and Pater:** Matthew Arnold (1822–1888) and Walter Pater (1839–1894), nineteenth-century British scholars and literary critics.

Quintilian: Marcus Fabius Quintilianus (circa 35–circa 100 CE), Roman scholar and orator.

process of communication by which an experience is set up in the mind of the writer, emphasized exclusively that segment which develops the experience of the writer into articulate form. Being thus incomplete as was the sophistic theory of discourse, it served only to supplement that by bringing out into clear consciousness the Platonic truth that the subject-matter of discourse has a direct relation to the mental processes of the writer.

On the practical side this truth has appeared in the comparatively recent decay of formal instruction in rhetoric, and the correlative growth of composition work in our schools. This practical study of composition, in so far as it deserved its name, displaced the writing of biographical essays, largely drawn from encyclopediac sources, and of treatises on abstract subjects far removed from any natural interests of the student who wrote. Both these lines of effort proving relatively profitless, the experiment was tried of drawing the material for writing directly from the every-day experience, observation and thinking of the student—an experiment whose results proved so successful that the practice has long been established in most of our schools. This is a piece of history so recent and so well known that it need not be dwelt upon. Its import, however, is worth noting. It means the practical, though perhaps unconscious, acceptance of Plato's principle that the subject-matter of discourse bears a vital relation to the mind of the speaker. And by virtue of this, it means the complete closing of the circuit of communication between speaker and hearer.

So far, then, the rising modern rhetorical theory agrees with the doctrine of Plato. It may, perhaps, differ from him in making discourse a process somewhat less self-conscious than he seems to have conceived it, arising from the speaker's primitive social instinct for sympathy, or (to put it more technically) for closer relations with his environment, rather than from any explicit desire to communicate his own vision of the truth to another. But this modification affects neither the nature of the process itself nor its ultimate outcome. Both the Platonic and the modern theory of discourse make it not an individualistic and isolate process for the advantage of the speaker alone, but a real communication between speaker and hearer, to the equal advantage of both, and thus a real function of the social organism.

This conception of discourse is rich in implications which Plato never saw, and which no modern has yet formulated. To this formulation, however, our practical teaching of English with all its psychological and sociological import, is daily bringing us nearer. It cannot be long before we shall recognize a modern theory of discourse as large in its outlines as Plato's and far better defined in its details; a theory which shall complete the social justification which rhetoric has so long been silently working out for itself.

UNDERSTANDING THE TEXT

1. What are the two opposing views of the nature of discourse that Gertrude Buck alludes to in the first paragraph? Which does she support?

2. According to Buck, how is sophistic rhetoric "anti-social"?

3. Why does Buck say that "the art of rhetoric is the art of war?" What definition of "war" does she base this statement on?

4. What is key difference between Figure 1 and Figure 2? How do these figures capture the two different kinds of rhetoric that Buck writes about?

5. How does Buck present the difference between Plato and modern rhetoricians on the question of absolute truth? What modifications does this require to Plato's original argument?

6. What, for Buck, is the ultimate goal of rhetoric? How does she compare this ultimate goal to the ultimate goal of Plato and the Sophists?

MAKING CONNECTIONS

1. Does Buck accurately present Plato's view of the Sophists as stated in the *Gorgias* (p. 478)? How does the transition from a dialogue, Plato's genre, to an essay, Buck's, affect the argument?

2. How does Buck's representation of sophistic rhetoric compare to Machiavelli's understanding of the way that a prince should tell the truth (p. 184)? Would she consider Machiavelli a Sophist? Explain.

3. How might Buck's analysis of rhetoric apply to propaganda such as Rockwell's *Freedom of Speech* (p. 503) or the "Ad for Chinese Population Policy" (p. 516)?

WRITING ABOUT THE TEXT

1. Use Buck's division between sophistic and Platonic rhetoric to analyze a recent political speech. Explain which of the two kinds of rhetoric the speaker employs.

2. Write a rebuttal to Buck from the perspective of a sophistic rhetorician. Argue that learning how to be persuasive is good in and of itself and does not need to be justified in any other way.

3. Analyze Buck's rhetorical theory from a feminist perspective. Explore how her view of language as a facilitator of community contrasts to the views of male rhetoricians and philosophers represented in this chapter.

Norman Rockwell
Freedom of Speech
(1943)

IN JANUARY 1941, President Franklin Roosevelt gave a speech to Congress in which he predicted that the United States would soon be drawn into the war that was engulfing the rest of the world. At the end of the speech, he articulated the "four freedoms" for which, he felt, the country must always stand: the freedom of speech, the freedom of worship, the freedom from want, and the freedom from fear. Roosevelt's words proved prophetic when, nearly a year later, Japanese planes attacked Pearl Harbor. In his 1942 State of the Union Address, Roosevelt once again emphasized both the four freedoms and America's willingness to fight for them.

Soon after the United States entered World War II, Roosevelt's four freedoms were translated into four paintings by the well-known American illustrator Norman Rockwell (1894–1978), who had been painting covers for the *Saturday Evening Post* for more than twenty-five years. A resident of Arlington, Vermont, Rockwell specialized in comic, heartwarming scenes of small-town American life. His renderings of the four freedoms soon became Rockwell's most famous paintings. They appeared initially in the *Saturday Evening Post*; later, the Treasury Department took Rockwell's originals to sixteen cities in a highly successful tour to raise money through the sale of war bonds. Though Rockwell's career as an artist lasted for another thirty-five years, these paintings remain, for many people, his most important works.

Freedom of Speech, the first of the *Four Freedoms* to appear in print, was published in the *Saturday Evening Post* on February 20, 1943. The scene, suggested to Rockwell by the experience of one of his neighbors, features a man standing and speaking in a public forum. The man is younger than most of his audience, and he is the only person in the room wearing working-class clothing rather than a business suit. Rather than dismissing the man, however, the members of the audience give him their full attention and listen respectfully as he presents an opinion that, the painting suggests (and Rockwell later confirmed), conflicts with their own opinions. Though it was created during one of the greatest global conflicts in world history, *Freedom of Speech* does not engage any of the major discussions of the day. Instead, it presents democracy working at a very basic level: at a public meeting in a small town in which everyone's opinion is considered worthy of being heard. 🖋

NORMAN ROCKWELL

Freedom of Speech, 1943 (oil on canvas).

© 1943 the Norman Rockwell Family Entities

See p. C-8 in the color insert for a full-color reproduction of this image.

UNDERSTANDING THE TEXT

1. What do the figures' styles of dress imply about their socioeconomic classes?

2. The man speaking has a booklet in his pocket, probably the same booklet that the man in the foreground is reading, which bears the title "An Annual Report of the Town." What do these details suggest about the discussion?

3. As many people have noted, Norman Rockwell appears to have intentionally exaggerated the size of the speaker's ears. What might this detail represent?

4. Critics often charge that Rockwell's paintings lack the depth and emotional complexity required of serious art. Do you agree? Is *Freedom of Speech* a work of art? Why or why not?

MAKING CONNECTIONS

1. Compare *Freedom of Speech* with Picasso's *Guernica* (p. 271), which is generally seen as great art, and with "Ad for Chinese Population Policy" (p. 516), which is generally considered propaganda. In which category would you place Rockwell's painting? How valid is the distinction between art and propaganda?

2. Analyze *Freedom of Speech* alongside Delacroix's *Liberty Leading the People* (p. 268) and Hogarth's *Gin Lane* (p. 320), two other works produced as part of specific political campaigns. In what ways are these three examples of visual rhetoric similar?

3. Research the Athenian Assembly or the Roman Senate and compare that body with the assembly presented in *Freedom of Speech*. How might the practice of rhetoric differ in each forum?

4. Does Rockwell appear to believe—as, for example, Gorgias (p. 478) did— that rhetorical training is necessary for the exercise of public discourse? Explain.

WRITING ABOUT THE TEXT

1. Examine the assumptions about rhetoric that underlie *Freedom of Speech*. Explain how Rockwell presents the role of free speech in a democratic society.

2. Search the Internet for the other three paintings in the *Four Freedoms* series— *Freedom of Worship*, *Freedom from Want*, and *Freedom from Fear*. Analyze each, focusing on what they say about values and about American society.

3. Compare *Freedom of Speech* with the still from *The Triumph of the Will* (p. 199). How does each of these World War II–era images reflect the political system of the culture that produced it? Does each accurately depict the values of its culture, or does it distort those values for rhetorical purposes?

Chinua Achebe
Language and the Destiny of Man
(1972)

THE EMINENT WRITER Chinua Achebe was born in 1930 in Ogidi, Nigeria. Achebe comes from the Igbo tribe, one of the three principal ethnic groups that the British government combined (along with many smaller groups) in 1960 to create the modern nation of Nigeria. Achebe's parents were devout Christians, and he was educated in British colonial schools and at the University College in Ibadan—at the time, part of the University of London—where he studied English literature. After graduation, Achebe worked briefly with the Nigerian Broadcasting Corporation, but when the Igbo region seceded from Nigeria and established the short-lived Republic of Biafra (1967–70), Achebe joined the new government and served as a diplomat. When the Biafran independence movement collapsed, Achebe devoted his efforts to writing and teaching literature.

Though he has had a distinguished career as both a novelist and an academic, Achebe's literary reputation rests largely on a single book that he wrote when he was only twenty-eight: *Things Fall Apart*, a narrative of Igbo tribal life before, during, and shortly after the British colonization of western Africa at the end of the nineteenth century. *Things Fall Apart* has been translated into fifty languages and is widely taught in both high schools and colleges throughout the world. By far the most widely read African novel written originally in English, it has been instrumental in introducing Western readers to an African culture that is neither falsely idealized nor filtered through unflattering colonial stereotypes.

Achebe's novels draw deeply on the stories of precolonial Igbo culture and on the tragic stories of colonial occupation and its aftermath. At the same time, his broad knowledge of the European literary tradition and of contemporary prose technique has made his novels highly accessible to readers throughout the world. Though he has often been called "the father of the African novel," Achebe vigorously rejects such honors. In Igbo culture, he explains, artists are not permitted to take credit for creative acts. They are the hands and the voice of an entire community, whose experiences they must represent and whose stories they must preserve.

"Language and the Destiny of Man" was first given as an address at Dartmouth College in 1972 and was subsequently published in Achebe's first collection of essays, *Morning Yet on Creation Day* (1975). In it, Achebe draws on myths from around the world—but especially from Africa—to discuss the importance of language in human society. Because language is a primary agent of social cohesion, Achebe argues, its corruption and abuse carry the potential for devastating consequences.

Achebe's rhetoric employs several kinds of inductive reasoning. He presents anthropological data and paraphrases the world's mythological and folk literature, and from this information he makes important generalizations about the role of language in human society. 🖋

In his long evolutionary history, man has scored few greater successes than his creation of human society. For it is on that primeval achievement that he has built those special qualities of mind and of behaviour which, in his own view at least, separate him from lower forms of life. If we sometimes tend to overlook this fact it is only because we have lived so long under the protective ambience of society that we have come to take its benefits for granted. Which, in a way, might be called the ultimate tribute; rather like the unspoken worship and thanksgiving which a man renders with every breath he draws. If it were different we would not be men but angels, incapable of boredom.

Unquestionably, language was crucial to the creation of society. There is no way in which human society could exist without speech. By society we do not, of course, mean the mechanical and mindless association of the beehive or the anthill which employs certain rudimentary forms of communication to achieve an unvarying, instinctual purpose, but a community where man "doomed to be free"—to use Joyce Cary's[1] remarkable phrase—is yet able to challenge that peculiar and perilous destiny with an even chance of wresting from it a purposeful, creative existence.

Speech too, like society itself, seems so natural that we rarely give much thought to it or contemplate man's circumstance before its invention. But we know that language is not inherent in man—the capacity for language, yes; but not language. Therefore, there must have been a time in the very distant past when our ancestors did not have it. Let us imagine a very simple incident in those days. A man strays into a rock shelter without knowing that another is there finishing a meal in the dark interior. The first hint our newcomer gets of this fact is a loose rock hurled at his head. In a different kind of situation which we shall call (with all kinds of guilty reservations) *human*, that confrontation might have been resolved less destructively by the simple question: What do you want? or even an angry: Get out of here!

Nobody is, of course, going to be so naïve as to claim for language the power to dispose of all, or even most, violence. After all, man is not less violent than other animals but more—apparently the only animal which consistently visits violence on its own kind. Yet in spite of this (or perhaps because of it) one does have a feeling that without language we should have long been extinct.

Many people following the fascinating progress of Dr. L. S. B. Leakey's[2] famous excavations in the Olduvai Gorge in Eastern Africa in the 1950s were shocked by   5

Some of the author's footnotes have been omitted.
1. **Joyce Cary's:** Irish author (1888–1957), whose 1939 novel *Mr. Johnson* is set in Nigeria.

2. **L. S. B. Leakey's:** Dr. Louis Leakey (1903–1972), British archeologist who worked primarily in Africa.

his claim that the so-called "pre-Zinjanthropus" child, the discovery of whose remains stirred many hearts and was one of the highlights of modern palaeontology, was probably murdered aged about twelve. Another excavator, Professor Raymond Dart, working further south, has collected much similar evidence of homicide in the caves of Transvaal.[3] But we should not have been surprised or shocked unless we had overlooked the psychological probability of the murder outside the Garden of Eden.[4]

Let us take a second and quite different kind of example. Let us imagine an infant crying. Its mother assumes that it is hungry and offers it food; but it refuses to eat and goes on crying. Is it wet? Does it have pain? If so, where? Has an ant crawled into its dress and bitten it? Does it want to sleep? etc., etc. Thus the mother, especially if she lacks experience (as more and more mothers tend to do), will grope from one impulse to another, from one possibility to its opposite, until she stumbles on the right one. Meanwhile the child suffers distress and she mental anguish. In other words, because of a child's inadequate vocabulary even its simplest needs cannot be quickly known and satisfied. From which rather silly example we can see, I hope, the value of language in facilitating the affairs and transactions of society by enabling its members to pass on their message quickly and exactly.

In small closely-knit societies such as we often call primitive the importance of language is seen in pristine clarity. For instance, in the creation myth of the Hebrews, God made the world by word of mouth; and in the Christian myth as recorded in St. John's Gospel the Word became God Himself.[5]

African societies in the past held similar notions about language and the potency of words. Writing about Igbo society in Nigeria, Igwe and Green had this to say:

> a speaker who could use language effectively and had a good command of idioms and proverbs was respected by his fellows and was often a leader in the community.[6]

From another part of Africa a Kenyan, Mugo Gatheru, in his autobiographical book gives even stronger testimony from his people: "among the Kikuyu those who speak well have always been honoured, and the very word chief means good talker."[7]

---

3. **Transvaal:** a province of South Africa from 1910 until 1994, when it was absorbed by other provinces.

4. Achebe refers here to Cain's murder of his brother Abel in Genesis 4:3–16.

5. The first verse of the Gospel of John in the King James Version of the Bible reads: "In the beginning was the Word, and the Word was with God, and the Word was God."

6. G. E. Igwe and M. M. Green, *Igbo Language Course*, Ibadan, Oxford University Press (Nigeria), 1967. [Author's note]

7. Mugo Gatheru, *A Child of Two Worlds*, London, Heinemann Educational Books, 1966, p. 40. [Author's note]

There is a remarkable creation myth among the Wapangwa people of Tanzania   10
which begins thus:

> The sky was large, white, and very clear. It was empty; there were no stars and
> no moon; only a tree stood in the air and there was wind. This tree fed on the
> atmosphere and ants lived on it. Wind, tree, ants, and atmosphere were con-
> trolled by the power of the Word, but the Word was not something that could
> be seen. It was a force that enabled one thing to create another.[8]

But although contemporary societies in Africa and elsewhere have moved away
from beliefs and attitudes which had invested language with such ritual qualities, we
can still find remains of the old dignity in certain places and circumstances. In his
famous autobiography, Camara Laye records the survival of such an attitude in the
Guinea of his boyhood, the strong impression that the traditional village could make
on the visitor from the town:

> In everything, I noticed a kind of dignity which was often lacking in town life
> . . . And if their minds seemed to work slower in the country, that was because
> they always spoke only after due reflection, and because speech itself was a
> most serious matter.[9]

And finally, from a totally different environment, these lines of a traditional
Eskimo poem, "Magic Words," from Jerome Rothenberg's excellent anthology,
Shaking the Pumpkin:

> That was the time when words were like magic
> The human mind had mysterious powers.
> A word spoken by chance
> might have strange consequences.
> It would suddenly come alive
> and what people wanted to happen could happen—
> all you had to do was say it.[10]

In small and self-sufficient societies, such as gave birth to these myths, the integrity
of language is safeguarded by the fact that what goes on in the community can easily be ascertained, understood and evaluated by all. The line between truth and falsehood thus tends to be sharp, and when a man addresses his fellows they know already

8. Ulli Beier (ed.), *The Origin of Life and Death*,
London, Heinemann Educational Books, 1966.
[Author's note]
9. Camara Laye, *The African Child*, London,
Fontana, 1959, p. 53. [Author's note]

10. Jerome Rothenberg (ed.), *Shaking the Pumpkin*, Garden City, N.Y., Doubleday, 1972, p. 45.
[Author's note]

what kind of person he is, whether (as Igbo people would put it) he is one with whose words something can be done; or else one who, if he tells you to stand, you know you must immediately flee!

But as society becomes larger and more complex we find that we can no longer be in command of all the facts but are obliged to take a good deal of what we hear on trust. We delegate to others the power to take certain decisions on our behalf, and they may not always be people we know or can vouch for. I shall return shortly to a consideration of this phenomenon. But first I shall consider a different, though related, problem—the pressure to which language is subjected by the mere fact that it can never change fast enough to deal with every new factor in the environment, to describe every new perception, every new detail in the ever-increasing complexity of the life of the community, to say nothing of the private perceptions and idiosyncrasies of particular speakers. T. S. Eliot comes readily to mind with those memorable lines from the *Four Quartets* in which he suggests to us the constant struggle, frustration and anguish which this situation imposes on a poet:

> Trying to learn to use words, and every attempt
> Is a wholly new start, and a different kind of failure . . .

Of course one might wonder whether this problem was a real one for ordinary people like ourselves or a peculiar species of self-flagellation by a high-strung devotee seeking through torment to become worthy of his deity. For when Eliot goes on to celebrate the "sentence that is right" his words do assume accents of holy intoxication:

> The common word exact without vulgarity,
> The formal word precise but not pedantic,
> The complete consort dancing together . . .

This curious mix of high purpose and carnival jollity may leave us a little puzzled, but there is no doubt whatever about Eliot's concern and solicitude for the integrity of words. And let us not imagine, even the most prosaic among us, that this concern and the stringent practice Eliot advocates are appropriate only to poets. For we all stand to lose when language is debased, just as every one of us is affected when the nation's currency is devalued; not just the Secretary to the Treasury or controllers of our banks.

Talking about Secretaries of the Treasury and devaluation, there was an amusing quotation by Professor Douglas Bush in an essay entitled "Polluting our Language" in the Spring 1972 issue of *The American Scholar*. The Secretary of the Treasury, John Connally, had said: "In the early sixties we were strong, we were virulent."[11] Clearly, that was only a slip, albeit of a kind that might interest Freudians. But it might not be entirely unfair to see a tendency to devaluation inherent in certain occupations!

We must now turn from considering the necessary struggle with language arising, as it were, from its very nature and the nature of the society it serves to the more ominous threat to its integrity brought about neither by its innate inadequacy nor yet by the incompetence and carelessness of its ordinary users, but rather engineered deliberately by those who will manipulate words for their own ends.

It has long been known that language, like any other human invention, can be abused, can be turned from its original purpose into something useless or even deadly. George Orwell,[12] who was very much concerned in his writings with this modern menace, reminds us that language can be used not only for expressing thought but for concealing thought or even preventing thought. I guess we are all too familiar with this—from the mild assault of the sales pitch which exhorts you: "Be progressive! Use ABC toothpaste!" or invites you to a "saving spree" in a department store; through the mystifications of learned people jealously guarding the precincts of their secret societies with such shibboleths[13] as: "Bilateral mastectomy was performed" instead of "Both breasts were removed"; to the politician who employs government prose to keep you in the dark about affairs on which your life or the lives of your children may depend or the official statistician who assures you that crime rates "are increasing at a decreasing rate of increase." I shall not waste your time about this well-known fact of modern life. But let me round off this aspect of the matter by quoting a little of the comment made by W. H. Auden[14] in an interview published by the *New York Times* (19 October 1971):

> As a poet—not as a citizen—there is only one political duty, and that is to defend one's language from corruption. And that is particularly serious now. It's being so quickly corrupted. When it is corrupted people lose faith in what they hear, and this leads to violence.

And leads also full circle to the caveman situation with which we began. And the heart of my purpose is to suggest that our remote ancestors who made and preserved language for us, who, you might say, crossed the first threshold from bes-

---

11. **Virulent:** medical term meaning "extremely harmful" or "malignant." Connally probably meant to say "virile."

12. **George Orwell:** pen name of the English author Eric Blair (1903–1950). Orwell's 1946 essay "Politics and the English Language" is a classic argument about the way that language can be intentionally perverted for political ends.

13. **Shibboleths:** words, phrases, or pronunciations that distinguish a person as a member of a specific group.

14. **W. H. Auden:** Wystan Hugh Auden (1907–1973), influential English poet who became an American citizen in 1946.

tiality to humanness, left us also adequate warning, wrapped in symbols, against its misuse.

Every people has a body of myths or sacred tales received from its antiquity. They are supernatural stories which man created to explain the problems and mysteries of life and death—his attempt to make sense of the bewildering complexity of existence. There is a proud, nomadic people, the Fulani, who inhabit the northern savannahs of Western Africa from Cameroon and Nigeria westwards to Mali and Senegal. They are very much attached to their cattle, whose milk is their staff of life. Here is a Fulani myth of creation from Mali:

> At the beginning there was a huge drop of milk.
> The Doondari came and he created the stone.
> Then the stone created iron;
> And iron created fire;
> And fire created water;
> And water created air.
>
> The Doondari descended the second time.
> And he took the five elements
> And he shaped them into man.
> But man was proud.
> Then Doondari created blindness and blindness defeated man.
> But when blindness became too proud,
> Doondari created sleep, and sleep defeated blindness;
> But when sleep became too proud,
> Doondari created worry, and worry defeated sleep;
> But when worry became too proud,
> Doondari created death, and death defeated worry.
>
> But when death became too proud,
> Doondari descended for the third time,
> And he came as Gueno, the eternal one
> And Gueno defeated death.[15]

You notice, don't you, how in the second section of that poem, after the creation of man, we have that phrase "became too proud" coming back again and again like the recurrence of a dominant beat in rhythmic music? Clearly the makers of that myth intended us not to miss it. So it was at the very heart of their purpose. *Man is destroyed by pride*. It is said over and over again; it is shouted like a message across vast distances until the man at the other end of the savannah has definitely got it,

15. Beir, op. cit. [Author's note]

despite the noise of rushing winds. Or if you prefer a modern metaphor, it is like making a long-distance call when the line is faulty or in bad weather. You shout your message and repeat it again and again just to make sure.

Claude Lévi-Strauss, the French structural anthropologist, has indeed sought to explain the repetitive factor in myth in this way, relating it to general information theory. Our forefathers and ancestors are seen in the role of *senders* of the message; and we, the novices of society, as *receivers*. The ancestors are sending us signals from the long history and experience of bygone days about the meaning of life, the qualities we should cultivate and the values that are important. Because they are so far away and because we are surrounded by the tumult and distractions of daily life they have to shout and repeat themselves not only in phrase after phrase but also in myth after myth, varying the form slightly now and again until the central message goes home.

If this interpretation is right then the Fulani myth of creation not only delivers a particular message on the danger of pride but also exemplifies beautifully the general intention and purpose of myths.

Let us now look at another short myth from the Igbo people in Nigeria which bears more directly on the question of language:

When death first entered the world, men sent a messenger to Chuku, asking him whether the dead could not be restored to life and sent back to their old homes. They chose the dog as their messenger.

The dog, however, did not go straight to Chuku, and dallied on the way. The toad had overheard the message, and as he wished to punish mankind, he overtook the dog and reached Chuku first. He said he had been sent by men to say that after death they had no desire at all to return to the world. Chuku declared that he would respect their wishes, and when the dog arrived with the true message he refused to alter his decision.

Thus although a human being may be born again, he cannot return with the same body and the same personality.[16]

It has been pointed out that there are more than seven hundred different versions   25
of this myth all over Africa. Thus, the element of repetition which we have seen in the form of a phrase recurring in time within one myth takes on the formidable power of spatial dispersion across a continent. Clearly the ancestral senders regard this particular signal as of desperate importance, hence its ubiquity and the profuse variations on its theme. Sometimes the messenger is the dog; sometimes the chameleon or the lizard, or some other animal. In some versions the message is garbled through the incompetence of the messenger, or through his calculated malice against men. In others, man in his impatience sends a second messenger to God, who in anger withdraws

16. Beir, op. cit. [Author's note]

the gift of immortality. But whatever variations in the detail the dominant theme remains: Men send a messenger to their Creator with a plea for immortality and He is disposed to grant their request. But something goes wrong with the message at the last moment. And this bounty which mankind has all but held in its grasp, this monumental gift that would have made man more like the gods, is snatched from him forever. And he knows that there is a way to hell even from the gates of heaven!

This, to my mind, is the great myth about language and the destiny of man. Its lesson should be clear to all. It is as though the ancestors who made language and knew from what bestiality its use rescued them are saying to us: Beware of interfering with its purpose! For when language is seriously interfered with, when it is disjoined from truth, be it from mere incompetence or worse, from malice, horrors can descend again on mankind.

UNDERSTANDING THE TEXT

1. According to Chinua Achebe, what is the relationship between language and society? How does human society, for Achebe, differ from the societies of anthills and beehives?

2. What significance does Achebe attach to anthropological evidence of homicides in precivilized cultures? What assertion does his evidence support?

3. Why does Achebe believe that myths and religious texts throughout the world have equated language with the creation of the world?

4. In what ways can language be manipulated and abused? What specific examples of this kind of abuse does Achebe mention? What damage can linguistic abuses lead to?

5. According to Achebe, how do a culture's myths communicate its values from one historical period to another? What ultimate message do myths communicate?

MAKING CONNECTIONS

1. Compare Achebe's view of the connection between language and violence with Toni Morrison's argument in her Nobel Prize acceptance lecture (p. 539).

2. In what sense might the development of language in human societies have been an evolutionary adaptation of the sort described by Charles Darwin in "Natural Selection" (p. 405)?

3. Compare Achebe's use of African folklore with N. Scott Momaday's use of Native American folklore in "Personal Reflections" (p. 519).

4. How does Achebe's implied "linguistic contract" compare with Hobbes's version of the "social contract" (p. 119)? What role does language play in preventing the "state of war" about which Hobbes was so concerned?

WRITING ABOUT THE TEXT

1. Drawing on Achebe's belief that myths have linguistic properties, examine a myth, folktale, or other common story that is important to your cultural heritage. What values does this narrative communicate?

2. Use Achebe's view of the disastrous effects of abusing language to analyze a political or commercial text that, in your opinion, misuses language. What are the social consequences of the misuse you see?

3. Write an essay comparing Achebe's views on language with Plato's views on truth (p. 478). In what sense does Plato's "truth" require purity of language?

Ad for Chinese Population Policy
(1980)

IN THE 1950S AND 1960S, the population of the People's Republic of China increased dramatically, from 540 million in 1949 to more than 850 million in 1970. Fearing that this population boom would produce an even larger increase when the new generation reached childbearing age—an increase that could lead to mass starvations, riots, and political instability—the Communist government of China began to implement measures to control the country's rate of population growth. In the 1970s, China began a government-sponsored advertising campaign encouraging couples to have children "later, spaced, and few." In 1979, the effort became more intense, as the government adopted a series of measures known collectively as the One-Child Policy, perhaps the most famous population control campaign in history.

Though the extent of the policy's effectiveness is the subject of much debate among scholars, most agree that it has substantially slowed the rate of population increase. Reliable estimates indicate that without the One-Child Policy, China, the world's most populous country, would have about three hundred million more people than it does today. However, the policy is not without critics. Government officials often take drastic measures to enforce it, including forced abortions, sterilizations, and fines on entire villages where unapproved births occur. Furthermore, since in Chinese culture male children are more highly valued than female children, some have charged that the policy has lead to sex-selective abortions and infanticide—both of which are illegal throughout China.

The poster reprinted here was created in 1980, during the early stages of the One-Child Policy. It depicts a man, a woman, and a child—the official government definition of a "perfect family"—wearing Western clothes. The man and the woman appear to be in their twenties or early thirties, older than the parents of a single infant would be in traditional Chinese culture. The child appears to be well fed and happy. Along the side appear the words "Few born, fine born; help revitalize China."

For the Communist government in China from the 1950s through the 1980s, posters such as this one provided an inexpensive solution to a tremendous rhetorical problem: how to influence the behavior of an extremely large population with a substantial illiteracy rate and only limited access to radio and television. Posters can be produced inexpensively and distributed quickly to even the poorest members of a society. Since a poster's argument can be carried through its visual elements, this medium can influence the extremely young and the illiterate. Thousands of different posters were mass-produced and distributed throughout China until the 1980s, when economic liberalization and increased access to broadcast made them obsolete. 🍃

少生优生振兴中华

Ad for Chinese population policy, 1980.
Courtesy of ISH, Stefan R. Landsberger Collection; www.lisg.nl/~landsberger

UNDERSTANDING THE TEXT

1. What characteristics of the couple does the poster emphasize? What characteristics of the child does it emphasize? What rhetorical points does it make in each case?

2. What does the background imply about the family?

3. How is it significant that the landscape would be "alien" to Chinese (and most other) people? How would the poster's message be different if the landscape were familiar or featured recognizable landmarks?

4. Does the poster achieve its rhetorical objective? Why or why not?

MAKING CONNECTIONS

1. Compare the Chinese propaganda poster with Hogarth's *Gin Lane* (p. 320) and Rockwell's *Freedom of Speech* (p. 503), which were also created with specific political objectives in mind. What elements do these works share?

2. How does the Chinese One-Child Policy, which this poster celebrates, fit into the overall theory of overpopulation articulated by Thomas Malthus (p. 309)?

3. How might a poster such as this fit in with the kind of population management suggested by Garrett Hardin in "Lifeboat Ethics" (p. 357)?

WRITING ABOUT THE TEXT

1. Write an essay about a practice in your community or culture that should be changed. What rhetoric and incentive programs would you combine to spread the message and effect the change? Would your plan constitute propaganda? Why or why not?

2. Write an essay on the rhetoric of propaganda, using this poster, the still from *The Triumph of the Will* (p. 199), and Rockwell's *Freedom of Speech* (p. 503) as the basis for an argument about what kinds of visual arguments change people's opinions and move them to action.

3. Research the Chinese One-Child Policy and write an essay evaluating its effectiveness. Focus specifically on the role of propaganda within the policy.

N. Scott Momaday
Personal Reflections
(1987)

NAVARRO SCOTT MOMADAY was born in 1934 on a Kiowa reservation near Lawton, Oklahoma. His father was a painter and his mother was an author of children's books. Both of his parents were also teachers at Indian reservation schools in Oklahoma and Arizona, and their son grew up with a solid understanding of the importance of education. Scott attended the University of New Mexico and Stanford University, where he obtained a Ph.D. in English literature in 1963. Throughout his career, he has held teaching positions at the University of California at Santa Barbara, the University of California at Berkeley, Stanford University, and the University of Arizona.

In 1969, Momaday published his first novel, *The House Made of Dawn*, which tells the story of a young Native American man who returns from World War II and must negotiate a tenuous path between the culture of the reservation that he grew up on and the larger American society that he is thrust into. *The House Made of Dawn* was awarded the Pulitzer Prize in 1969 and is widely seen as a breakthrough work that helped to establish Native American literature as an important cultural force in America—when contemporary critics speak of a "Native American Renaissance," they often trace its roots back to *The House Made of Dawn*. Momaday has published eleven books of fiction, drama, poetry, and criticism since winning the Pulitzer Prize. He is currently the poet laureate of Oklahoma, and in 2007 he was awarded the National Medal of the Arts.

The essay included here, "Personal Reflections," was originally written for the collection *The American Indian and the Problem of History*. Momaday was one of eighteen well-known scholars or writers invited to contribute a brief essay about the Native American view of time or the telling of history. Momaday's essay focuses on differences in the worldviews of Native Americans and Europeans and the ways that those differences are reflected in language and storytelling. Understanding these differences, Momaday believes, is necessary if the two cultures are ever to understand and appreciate each other's stories, cultures, or histories.

Momaday structures his essay as a comparison/contrast. He employs several different points of comparison to demonstrate that Native Americans and Europeans have fundamentally different ways of perceiving events in time and of using language to express their relationship to the natural world. 🖋

Y OU ASK ME TO identify and explain, within a brief space, what I consider to be the most crucial, most vital issue at work in the past five hundred years of North American Indian and white relations. That is a very tall order, of course, and a very serious matter. I should like to respond in a personal and a straightforward way.

I believe that there is a fundamental dichotomy at the center of these relations, past and present. The Indian and the white man perceive the world in different ways. I take it that this is an obvious fact and a foregone conclusion. But at the same time I am convinced that we do not understand the distinction entirely or even sufficiently. I myself do not understand it sufficiently, but I may be more acutely aware of it by virtue of my experience than are most. Let me qualify my point of view on the subject in order that my remarks might be taken within a certain frame of reference. I am an Indian. I was born into the Indian world, and I have lived a good part of my life in that world. That is worth something, and it is an indispensable consideration in the argument I wish to develop here. You may recall that Oliver La Farge,[1] in discussing his own, narrative point of view in the novel *Laughing Boy* (1929), drew a distinction between "the thing observed and the thing experienced" (1945:208). La Forge correctly thought of himself as an observer; his point of view was removed from the experience of which he wrote, and the distance of that remove was and is finally immeasurable. That is not to say that his powers of observation were in any way deficient—far from it; nor is it to say that *Laughing Boy* is less than a distinguished work of art. It is merely to remark the existence of intrinsic variables in man's perception of his universe, variables that are determined to some real extent on the basis of his genetic constitution. In the case of my own writing, where it centers upon Indian life, and especially upon an Indian way of looking at the world, I can say with some validity, I think, that I have written of "the thing experienced" as well as of "the thing observed." What this may or may not mean in terms of literary advantage is not a question that I wish to raise here, however. For the time being it is enough to establish that such a distinction is *prima facie*[2] real, and it bears importantly upon the matter under discussion.

What of the dichotomy that I have mentioned? How can we get at it? Let me suppose that my little daughter, Lore, who is not yet three, comes to me with the question, "Where does the sun live?" In my middle-aged and "educated" brain I consider the possibilities of reply. I begin to construct a formula like this: "Well, darling, as you can see, the sun lives in the sky." But already another perception, deeper

---

1. **Oliver La Farge:** American novelist (1901–1963) whose novel about Native American characters *Laughing Boy* (1929) won the Pulitzer Prize for Fiction.

2. ***Prima facie:*** "at first view." In legal terms, *prima facie* refers to a proposition supported by sufficient evidence that it can be presumed to be true until disproved.

in the blood, leads me to say, "The sun lives in the earth." I am aware that the first answer is more acceptable to the logic of my age than is the second, and it is more congenial to my learning. The sun is to be observed in the sky and not elsewhere. We are taught beyond any possibility of doubt that the sun and the earth are separated by an all but unimaginable distance. The word "live" we grant to the child as an indulgence, if we grant it at all; it is a metaphor, merely. We certainly do not mean to say that the sun is alive. We mean that, from our point of view the visible sun has its place in the heavens. And we take it for granted that we are speaking of dead matter. But the first answer is not true to my experience, my deepest, oldest experience, the memory in my blood.

For to the Indian child who asks the question, the parent replies, "The sun lives in the earth." The sun-watcher among the Rio Grande Pueblos, whose scared task it is to observe, each day, the very point of the sun's emergence on the skyline, knows in the depths of his being that the sun is alive and that it is indivisible with the earth, and he refers to the farthest eastern mesa as "the sun's house." The Jemez[3] word for home, *ketha'ame*, bears critical connotations of belonging. Should someone say to the sun, "Where are you going?" the sun would surely answer, "I am going home," and it is understood at once that home is the earth. All things are alive in this profound unity in which are all elements, all animals, all things. One of the most beautiful of Navajo prayers begins "*Tsegi yei!* House made of dawn. . . . " And my father remembered that, as a boy, he had watched with wonder and something like fear the old man Koi-khan-hole, "Dragonfly," stand in the first light, his arms outstretched and his painted face fixed on the east, and "pray the sun out of the ground." His voice, for he prayed aloud, struck at the great, misty silence of the Plains morning, entered into it, carried through it to the rising sun. His words made one of the sun and earth, one of himself and the boy who watched, one of the boy and generations to come. Even now, along an arc of time, that man appears to me, and his voice takes hold of me. There is no sunrise without Koi-khan-hole's prayer.

I want to indicate as best I can an American Indian attitude (for want of a better word) toward the whole as a whole. It is an attitude that involves the fullest accomplishment of belief. And I am talking neither about philosophy nor religion; I am talking about a spiritual sense so ancient as to be primordial, so pervasive as to be definitive—not an idea, but a perception on the far side of ideas, an act of understanding as original and originative as the Word. The dichotomy that most closely informs the history of Indian-white relations is realized in language, I believe.

Much has been said and written concerning the Indian's conception of time. Time is a wonderful abstraction; the only way in which we can account for apparent change in our world is by means of the concept of time. The language in which I write and

3. **Jemez:** also known as *Towa*, a language spoken by a small number of Pueblo Indians in northwestern New Mexico.

you read upon this page is predicated upon a familiar system of tenses—past, present, and future. In our Western understanding of time we involve the correlative of distance. The past is away in that direction, the future in that, and the present is just here, where I happen to be. But we speak of the passage of time; times come and go, the day will come. We remain in place and observe the flow of time, just as we sit at the cinema and watch, fascinated, as images fly before our eyes. The plane of time is shattered; it is composed of moments, *ad infinitum*, in perpetual motion.

"He loved melons. Always, when we went in the wagon to Carnegie, we stopped at a certain place, a place where there was a big tree. And we sat in the shade there and ate melons. I was little, but I remember. He loves melons, and he always stops at that place." When my father spoke to me of my grandfather, who died before I was born, he invariably slipped into the present tense. And this is a common thing in my experience of the Indian world. For the Indian there is something like an extended present. Time as motion is an illusion; indeed, time itself is an illusion. In the deepest sense, according to the native perception, there is only the dimension of timelessness, and in that dimension all things happen. The earth confirms this conviction in calendars of "geologic time." A few year ago Colin Fletcher[4] wrote a book in which he described his walk through the Grand Canyon. It was called significantly, *The Man Who Walked Through Time* (1967). In Fletcher's title we come as close as we can, perhaps, to one of the absolutes of the Indian world. If you stand on the edge of Monument Valley and look across space to the great monoliths that stand away in the silence, you will understand how it is that the mind of man can grasp the notion of eternity. At some point along the line of your sight there is an end of time, and you see beyond into timelessness.

as my eyes
search
the prairie
I feel the summer
in the spring

In this Chippewa song, time is reduced to a profound evanescence. We are given a stillness like that of the stars.

Yvor Winters,[5] who was my teacher and my friend, wrote in the introduction to his final work, *Forms of Discovery*, "Unless we understand the history which produced us, we are determined by that history; we may be determined in any event,

---

4. **Colin Fletcher:** British nature writer (1922–2007). His 1967 memoir *The Man Who Walked through Time* tells the story of his experience as the first person to backpack through the entire Grand Canyon in one continuous trek.

5. **Yvor Winters:** poet and literary critic (1900–1968) who taught at Stanford University when Momaday was a student there.

but the understanding gives us a chance" (1967:xix). It is a provocative, even com-pelling statement. And it is eminently wise. But, with respect to our present dis-cussion, there arises the question, How are we to understand the meaning of the word "history"?

In the summer of the centennial year, 1876, General George A. Custer and 265 men of the Seventh Cavalry were killed at the Battle of the Little Big Horn in Mon-tana. Rutherford B. Hayes and Samuel J. Tilden were nominated by their respective parties for the office of President of the United States. Colorado was admitted to the Union. The Chicago Daily News was founded, and the Dewey Decimal System was originated.

The summer of 1876 is indicated on the calendar of Set-t'an (a Kiowa) by the rude drawing of a medicine lodge, below which are the tracks of horses. This was the "Sun dance when Sun-boy's horses were stolen." During the dance, which was held that year at the fork of the Red River and Sweetwater Creek, all of Sun-boy's horses were stolen by a band of Mexicans. Following the dance a war party was sent in pursuit of the thieves, but the horses were not recovered. This is the single record of the summer of that year.

Set-t'an understood history in what can only seem to us extraordinary and incon-gruous terms. The summer of 1876 was in his mind forever to be identified with the theft of horses. You and I can marvel at that, but we cannot know what the loss of a horse meant to Set-t'an or to his people, whose culture is sometimes called the "horse" culture or the "centaur" culture. We can try to imagine; we can believe that Set-t'an was as deeply concerned to understand the history that produced him as any man can be. My friend Dee Brown[6] wrote in 1966 an estimable study of the year 1876, which he called *The Year of the Century*. Consider that, in some equation that we have yet to comprehend fully, Brown's book is more or less equal to a simple pic-tograph, the barest of line drawings, on a hide painting of the nineteenth century—or the wall of an ancient cave.

We could go on with such comparison as these, but this much will serve, I think, as a basis for the main point I wish to make. A good deal has been written about the inequities which inform the history of Indian-white relations in this country, by far the greater part of it from the point of view of the white man, of course. This is the point of view that has been—that can be—articulated in terms that are acceptable to American society as a whole, after all. One of the most perplexing ironies of Ameri-can history is the fact that the Indian has been effectively silenced by the intricacies of his own speech, as it were. Linguistic diversity has been a formidable barrier to Indian-white diplomacy. And underlying this diversity is again the central dichotomy, the matter of a difference in ways of seeing and making sense of the world around us.

10

6. **Dee Brown:** American historian and novel-ist (1908–2002) whose work *Bury My Heart at Wounded Knee* (1970) is a history of the inter-actions between Native American tribes and the U.S. government during the settling of the American West.

The American Indian has a highly developed oral tradition. It is in the nature of oral tradition that it remains relatively constant; languages are slow to change for the reason that they represent a greater investment on the part of society. One who has only an oral tradition thinks of language in this way: my words exist at the level of my voice. If I do not speak with care, my words are wasted. If I do not listen with care, words are lost. If I do not remember carefully, the very purpose of words is frustrated. This respect for words suggests an inherent morality in man's understanding and use of language. Moreover, that moral comprehension is everywhere evident in American Indian speech. On the other hand, the written tradition tends to encourage an indifference to language. That is to say, writing produces a false security where our attitudes toward language are concerned. We take liberties with words; we become blind to their sacred aspect.

> By virtue of the authority vested in me by section 465 of the Revised Statutes (25 U.S.C. #9 [section 9 of this title]) and as President of the United States, the Secretary of Interior is hereby designated and empowered to exercise, without the approval, ratification, or other action of the President or of any other officer of the United States, any and all authority conferred upon the United States by section 403 (a) of the Act of April 11, 1968, 82 Stat. 79 (25 U.S.C. #1323 (a) [subsec. (a) of this section]): provided, That acceptance of retrocession of all or any measure of civil or criminal jurisdiction, or both, by the Secretary hereunder shall be effected by publication in the *Federal Register* of a notice which shall specify the jurisdiction retroceded and the effective date of the retrocession: Provided further, That acceptance of such retrocession of criminal jurisdiction shall be effected only after consultation by the Secretary with the Attorney General.
>
> Executive Order No. 11435, 1968

> I have heard that you intend to settle us on a reservation near the mountains. I don't want to settle. I love to roam over the prairies. There I feel free and happy, but when we settle down we grow pale and die. I have laid aside my lance, bow, and shield, and yet I feel safe in your presence. I have told the truth. I have no little lies hid about me, but I don't know how it is with the commissioners. Are they as clear as I am?
>
> Satanta, Kiowa chief

The examples above speak for themselves. The one is couched in the legal diction of a special parlance, one that is far removed from our general experience of language. Its meaning is obscure; the words themselves seem to stand in the way of meaning. The other is in the plain style, a style that preserves, in its way, the power and beauty of language. In the historical relationship in question, the language of diplomacy has been determined by the considerations that have evolved into the style of the first of these examples. It is far removed from the American Indian oral tradition, far from the rhythms of oratory and storytelling and song.

The fundamental difference in ways of looking at the world, as those differences are reflected in the language of diplomacy, seem to me to constitute the most important issue in Indian-white relations in the past five hundred years.

15

UNDERSTANDING THE TEXT

1. What does N. Scott Momaday see as the core distinction in the way that Native Americans and whites see the world? How is this difference manifest in language?

2. How does Momaday use the distinction between "things observed" and "things experienced"? How does he position himself as an author working within this dichotomy?

3. According to Momaday, how does the answer to the child's question "where does the sun live?" illustrate the different perspectives of Native Americans and whites?

4. What does Momaday mean when he says that, for whites, the concept of time involves "the correlative of distance"? In what way does he believe that the Native American view of time is different?

5. What does the fact that the Native American tradition is largely oral say about Native American culture? How do oral stories and written stories affect their audiences differently?

MAKING CONNECTIONS

1. How does Momaday's understanding of the difference between the Native American and the white worldviews correspond to those of Kisautaq Leona Okakok in "Serving the Purpose of Education" (p. 76)? In what ways are they similar, and in what ways are they different?

2. How do Momaday's experiences negotiating Native American and European cultures correspond to Frederick Douglass's experiences as a slave learning to read and write (p. 46)?

3. Does learning about the ways that other cultures use language and tell stories qualify as "liberal learning" in John Henry Newman's sense of the term (p. 53)? What role does understanding other cultures play in a liberal education?

WRITING ABOUT THE TEXT

1. Compare Momaday's understanding of Native American language and story-telling traditions with Chinua Achebe's presentation of African languages and oral narratives in "Language and the Destiny of Man" (p. 506). Does the oral nature of each culture produce a similar philosophy of storytelling?

2. Evaluate Momaday's argument that written language produces "a false security where our attitudes toward language are concerned." How well does he support this claim with evidence? Identify areas where Momaday could strengthen his argument and suggest an approach or particular evidence that would be effective, or explain why his argument is already strong.

3. Write an essay that expresses, in your own words, the fundamental difference between the Native American and white views of time as presented by Momaday in "Personal Reflections." Do you believe that this distinction is valid? Why or why not?

Gloria Anzaldúa
How to Tame a Wild Tongue
(1987)

FOR THE MEXICAN-AMERICAN writer Gloria Anzaldúa (1942–2004), "borderlands" is a concept with many levels of meaning. Literally, it refers to the border between America and Mexico. But borderlands also exist wherever different cultures, languages, value systems, or sexual identities come into contact with each other. "Borderlands," she writes, "are physically present wherever two or more cultures edge each other, where people of different races occupy the same territory, where under, lower, middle and upper classes touch, where the space between two individuals shrinks with intimacy."

Anzaldúa spent most of her life positioned on the borderlands that became such an important image in her work. She was born and raised in the Rio Grande Valley of southern Texas. Most of the members of her family were farm laborers, and neither of her parents attended high school, but she excelled in school and became the first in her family to attend college. She received degrees from Pan American University and the University of Texas at Austin and, in 1972, went to work teaching the children of migrant families while, at the same time, editing several important volumes of essays by women of color. She taught English, women's studies, and cultural studies at Georgetown University, the University of Colorado, and the University of California at Santa Cruz. She published her most influential work, *Borderlands / La Frontera: The New Mestiza*, in 1987.

Borderlands of all kinds, Anzaldúa proposes, give birth to a category of person that she refers to as the *mestiza*, or "mixture." The *mestiza* exists between cultures, fully embracing—and fully embraced by—neither. For Anzaldúa, borderland culture must be considered distinct from and equal to the cultures that combine to produce it. *Borderlands / La Frontera* is a kind of mestiza, as Anzaldúa blends styles, genres, and even languages to produce a written text that cannot be reduced to single categories: it is at once English and Spanish, poetry and prose, narrative and analysis, academic and autobiographical.

The chapter included here, "How to Tame a Wild Tongue," deals specifically with the languages of the borderlands. Mestizos usually speak multiple languages; Anzaldúa's languages include not only Standard English and Standard Spanish but also various dialects that have emerged out of the collision of the two. Because language is a primary part of a person's identity, Anzaldúa insists, it is vital to validate all of the languages that people speak and claim as their own. In an academic context, this means allowing people to speak and write in their native tongues and trying to understand others by learning their languages rather than by forcing them to learn ours. To ignore the imperative need that people have to speak, write, and create in their native tongues, Anzaldúa claims, is an act of violence.

Rhetorically, Anzaldúa works toward a synthesis of two different positions: the view that Americans should all speak English and the view that all people of Mexican descent should speak Spanish. The Chicano/a language, like its speakers, is both a linguistic and an ideological synthesis. 🔖

W E'RE GOING TO HAVE to control your tongue," the dentist says, pulling out all the metal from my mouth. Silver bits plop and tinkle into the basin. My mouth is a motherlode.

The dentist is cleaning out my roots. I get a whiff of the stench when I gasp. "I can't cap that tooth yet, you're still draining," he says.

"We're going to have to do something about your tongue," I hear the anger rising in his voice. My tongue keeps pushing out the wads of cotton, pushing back the drills, the long thin needles. "I've never seen anything as strong or as stubborn," he says. And I think, how do you tame a wild tongue, train it to be quiet, how do you bridle and saddle it? How do you make it lie down?

> Who is to say that robbing a people of
> its language is less violent than war?
> —Ray Gwyn Smith[1]

I remember being caught speaking Spanish at recess—that was good for three licks on the knuckles with a sharp ruler. I remember being sent to the corner of the classroom for "talking back" to the Anglo teacher when all I was trying to do was tell her how to pronounce my name. "If you want to be American, speak 'American.' If you don't like it, go back to Mexico where you belong."

"I want you to speak English. *Pa' hallar buen trabajo tienes que saber hablar el inglés bien. Qué vale toda tu educación si todavía hablas inglés con un 'accent,'*"[2] my mother would say, mortified that I spoke English like a Mexican. At Pan American University, I, and all Chicano students were required to take two speech classes. Their purpose: to get rid of our accents.   5

Attacks on one's form of expression with the intent to censor are a violation of the First Amendment. *El Anglo con cara de inocente nos arrancó la lengua.* Wild tongues can't be tamed, they can only be cut out.

All notes are the author's unless otherwise indicated.

1. Ray Gwyn Smith, *Moorland Is Cold Country,* unpublished book.

2. At the author's request, all Spanish phrases in the text have been left untranslated. [Editor's note]

Overcoming the Tradition of Silence

Ahogadas, escupimos el oscuro.
Peleando con nuestra propia sombra
el silencio nos sepulta.

En boca cerrada no entran moscas. "Flies don't enter a closed mouth" is a saying I kept hearing when I was a child. *Ser habladora* was to be a gossip and a liar, to talk too much. *Muchachitas bien criadas,* well-bred girls don't answer back. *Es una falta de respeto* to talk back to one's mother or father. I remember one of the sins I'd recite to the priest in the confession box the few times I went to confession: talking back to my mother, *hablar pa' 'tras, repelar. Hocicona, repelona, chismosa,* having a big mouth, questioning, carrying tales are all signs of being *mal criada.* In my culture they are all words that are derogatory if applied to women—I've never heard them applied to men.

The first time I heard two women, a Puerto Rican and a Cuban, say the word "*nosotras,*" I was shocked. I had not known the word existed. Chicanas use *nosotros* whether we're male or female. We are robbed of our female being by the masculine plural. Language is a male discourse.

> And our tongues have become
> dry   the wilderness has
> dried out our tongues   and
> we have forgotten speech.
> —*Irena Klepfisz*[3]

Even our own people, other Spanish speakers *nos quieren poner candados en la boca.* They would hold us back with their bag of *reglas de academia.*

Oyé como ladra: el lenguaje de la frontera

Quien tiene boca se equivoca.
—*Mexican saying*

"*Pocho,* cultural traitor, you're speaking the oppressor's language by speaking   10
English, you're ruining the Spanish language," I have been accused by various Latinos and Latinas. Chicano Spanish is considered by the purist and by most Latinos deficient, a mutilation of Spanish.

---

3. Irena Klepfisz, "*Di rayze aheym* / The Journey Home," in *The Tribe of Dina: A Jewish Women's Anthology,* Melanie Kaye / Kantrowitz and Irena Klepfisz, eds. (Montpelier, VT: Sinister Wisdom Books, 1986), 49.

But Chicano Spanish is a border tongue which developed naturally. Change, *evolución, enriquecimiento de palabras nuevas por invención o adopción* have created variants of Chicano Spanish, *un nuevo lenguaje. Un lenguaje que corresponde a un modo de vivir.* Chicano Spanish is not incorrect, it is a living language.

For a people who are neither Spanish nor live in a country in which Spanish is the first language; for a people who live in a country in which English is the reigning tongue but who are not Anglo; for a people who cannot entirely identify with either standard (formal, Castillian) Spanish nor standard English, what recourse is left to them but to create their own language? A language which they can connect their identity to, one capable of communicating the realities and values true to themselves—a language with terms that are neither *español ni inglés*, but both. We speak a patois, a forked tongue, a variation of two languages.

Chicano Spanish sprang out of the Chicanos' need to identify ourselves as a distinct people. We needed a language with which we could communicate with ourselves, a secret language. For some of us, language is a homeland closer than the Southwest—for many Chicanos today live in the Midwest and the East. And because we are a complex, heterogeneous people, we speak many languages. Some of the languages we speak are:

1. Standard English

2. Working class and slang English

3. Standard Spanish

4. Standard Mexican Spanish

5. North Mexican Spanish dialect

6. Chicano Spanish (Texas, New Mexico, Arizona and California have regional variations)

7. Tex-Mex

8. *Pachuco* (called *caló*)

My "home" tongues are the languages I speak with my sister and brothers, with my friends. They are the last five listed, with 6 and 7 being closest to my heart. From school, the media and job situations, I've picked up standard and working class English. From Mamagrande Locha and from reading Spanish and Mexican literature, I've picked up Standard Spanish and Standard Mexican Spanish. From *los recién llegados*, Mexican immigrants, and *braceros*, I learned the North Mexican dialect. With Mexicans I'll try to speak either Standard Mexican Spanish or the North Mexican dialect. From my parents and Chicanos living in the Valley, I picked up Chicano Texas Spanish, and I speak it with my mom, younger brother (who married a Mexican and who rarely mixes Spanish with English), aunts and older relatives.

With Chicanas from *Nuevo México* or *Arizona* I will speak Chicano Spanish a lit-   15
tle, but often they don't understand what I'm saying. With most California Chicanas
I speak entirely in English (unless I forget). When I first moved to San Francisco,
I'd rattle off something in Spanish, unintentionally embarrassing them. Often it is
only with another Chicana *tejana* that I can talk freely.

Words distorted by English are known as anglicisms or *pochismos*. The *pocho* is an
anglicized Mexican or American of Mexican origin who speaks Spanish with an
accent characteristic of North Americans and who distorts and reconstructs the language according to the influence of English.[4] Tex-Mex, or Spanglish, comes most
naturally to me. I may switch back and forth from English to Spanish in the same
sentence or in the same word. With my sister and my brother Nune and with Chicano *tejano* contemporaries I speak in Tex-Mex.

From kids and people my own age I picked up *Pachuco*. *Pachuco* (the language of
the zoot suiters) is a language of rebellion, both against Standard Spanish and Standard English. It is a secret language. Adults of the culture and outsiders cannot understand it. It is made up of slang words from both English and Spanish. *Ruca* means
girl or woman, *vato* means guy or dude, *chale* means no, *simón* means yes, *churro* is
sure, talk is *periquiar*, *pigionear* means petting, *que gacho* means how nerdy, *ponte águila*
means watch out, death is called *la pelona*. Through lack of practice and not having
others who can speak it, I've lost most of the *Pachuco* tongue.

Chicano Spanish

Chicanos, after 250 years of Spanish/Anglo colonization have developed significant differences in the Spanish we speak. We collapse two adajcent vowels into a
single syllable and sometimes shift the stress in certain words such as *maíz/maiz*,
cohete/cuete. We leave out certain consonants when they appear between vowels:
lado/lao, *mojado/mojao*. Chicanos from South Texas pronounce *f* as *j* as in *jue* (*fue*).
Chicanos use "archaisms," words that are no longer in the Spanish language, words
that have been evolved out. We say *semos*, *truje*, *haiga*, *ansina*, and *naiden*. We retain
the "archaic" *j*, as in *jalar*, that derives from an earlier *h* (the French *halar* or the Ger-
manic *halon* which was lost to standard Spanish in the 16th century), but which is
still found in several regional dialects such as the one spoken in South Texas. (Due
to geography, Chicanos from the Valley of South Texas were cut off linguistically
from other Spanish speakers. We tend to use words that the Spaniards brought over
from Medieval Spain. The majority of the Spanish colonizers in Mexico and the
Southwest came from Extremadura—Hernán Cortés was one of them—and
Andalucía. Andalucians pronounce *ll* like a *y*, and their *d*'s tend to be absorbed by

---

4. R. C. Ortega, *Dialectología del Barrio*, trans. Hortencia S. Alwan (Los Angeles, CA: R. C. Ortega
Publisher & Bookseller, 1977), 132.

adjacent vowels: *tirado* becomes *tirao*. They brought *el lenguaje popular, dialectos y regionalismos*.[5])

Chicanos and other Spanish speakers also shift *ll* to *y* and *z* to *s*.[6] We leave out initial syllables, saying *tar* for *estar*, *toy* for *estoy*, *hora* for *ahora* (*cubanos* and *puertorriqueños* also leave out initial letters of some words). We also leave out the final syllable such as *pa* for *para*. The intervocalic *y*, the *ll* as in *tortilla, ella, botella*, gets replaced by *tortia* or *tortiya, ea, botea*. We add an additional syllable at the beginning of certain words: *atocar* for *tocar*, *agastar* for *gastar*. Sometimes we'll say *lavaste las vacijas*, other times *lavates* (substituting the *ates* verb endings for the *aste*).

We use anglicisms, words borrowed from English: *bola* from ball, *carpeta* from carpet, *máchina de lavar* (instead of *lavadora*) from washing machine. Tex-Mex argot, created by adding a Spanish sound at the beginning or end of an English word such as *cookiar* for cook, *watchar* for watch, *parkiar* for park, and *rapiar* for rape, is the result of the pressures on Spanish speakers to adapt to English.

We don't use the word *vosotros/as* or its accompanying verb form. We don't say *claro* (to mean yes), *imagínate*, or *me emociona*, unless we picked up Spanish from Latinas, out of a book or in a classroom. Other Spanish-speaking groups are going through the same, or similar, development in their Spanish.

20

Linguistic Terrorism

Desleguadas. Somos los del español deficiente. We are your linguistic nightmare, your linguistic aberration, your linguistic *mestisaje*, the subject of your *burla*. Because we speak with tongues of fire we are culturally crucified. Racially, culturally and linguistically *somos huérfanos*—we speak an orphan tongue.

Chicanas who grew up speaking Chicano Spanish have internalized the belief that we speak poor Spanish. It is illegitimate, a bastard language. And because we internalize how our language has been used against us by the dominant culture, we use our language differences against each other.

Chicana feminists often skirt around each other with suspicion and hesitation. For the longest time I couldn't figure it out. Then it dawned on me. To be close to another Chicana is like looking into the mirror. We are afraid of what we'll see there. *Pena.* Shame. Low estimation of self. In childhood we are told that our language is wrong. Repeated attacks on our native tongue diminish our sense of self. The attacks continue throughout our lives.

5. Eduardo Hernandéz-Chávez, Andrew D. Cohen, and Anthony F. Beltramo, El Lenguaje de los Chicanos: *Regional and Social Characteristics of Language Used by Mexican Americans* (Arlington, VA: Center for Applied Linguistics, 1975), 39.

6. Hernandéz-Chávez, xvii.

Chicanas feel uncomfortable talking in Spanish to Latinas, afraid of their censure. Their language was not outlawed in their countries. They had a whole lifetime of being immersed in their native tongue; generations, centuries in which Spanish was a first language, taught in school, heard on radio and TV, and read in the newspaper.

If a person, Chicana or Latina, has a low estimation of my native tongue, she also   25
has a low estimation of me. Often with *mexicanas y latinas* we'll speak English as a neutral language. Even among Chicanas, we tend to speak English at parties or conferences. Yet, at the same time, we're afraid the other will think we're *agringadas* because we don't speak Chicano Spanish. We oppress each other trying to out-Chicano each other, vying to be the "real" Chicanas, to speak like Chicanos. There is no one Chicano language just as there is no one Chicano experience. A monolingual Chicana whose first language is English or Spanish is just as much a Chicana as one who speaks several variants of Spanish. A Chicana from Michigan or Chicago or Detroit is just as much a Chicana as one from the Southwest. Chicano Spanish is as diverse linguistically as it is regionally.

By the end of this century, Spanish speakers will comprise the biggest minority group in the U.S., a country where students in high schools and colleges are encouraged to take French classes because French is considered more "cultured." But for a language to remain alive it must be used.[7] By the end of this century English, and not Spanish, will be the mother tongue of most Chicanos and Latinos.

So, if you want to really hurt me, talk badly about my language. Ethnic identity is twin skin to linguistic identity—I am my language. Until I can take pride in my language, I cannot take pride in myself. Until I can accept as legitimate Chicano Texas Spanish, Tex-Mex and all the other languages I speak, I cannot accept the legitimacy of myself. Until I am free to write bilingually and to switch codes without having always to translate, while I still have to speak English or Spanish when I would rather speak Spanglish, and as long as I have to accommodate the English speakers rather than having them accommodate me, my tongue will be illegitimate.

I will no longer be made to feel ashamed of existing. I will have my voice: Indian, Spanish, white. I will have my serpent's tongue—my woman's voice, my sexual voice, my poet's voice. I will overcome the tradition of silence.

> My fingers
> move sly against your palm
> Like women everywhere, we speak in code. . . .
> —Melanie Kaye/Kantrowitz[8]

7. Irena Klepfisz, "Secular Jewish Identity: Yidishkayt in America," in *The Tribe of Dina*, Kay/Kantrowitz and Klepfisz, eds., 43.

8. Melanie Kaye / Kantrowitz, "Sign," in *We Speak in Code: Poems and Other Writings* (Pittsburgh, PA: Motheroot Publications, Inc., 1980), 85.

"Vistas," corridos, y comida: My Native Tongue

In the 1960s, I read my first Chicano novel. It was *City of Night* by John Rechy, a gay Texan, son of a Scottish father and a Mexican mother. For days I walked around in stunned amazement that a Chicano could write and could get published. When I read *I Am Joaquín*[9] I was surprised to see a bilingual book by a Chicano in print. When I saw poetry written in Tex-Mex for the first time, a feeling of pure joy flashed through me. I felt like we really existed as a people. In 1971, when I started teaching High School English to Chicano students, I tried to supplement the required texts with works by Chicanos, only to be reprimanded and forbidden to do so by the principal. He claimed that I was supposed to each "American" and English literature. At the risk of being fired, I swore my students to secrecy and slipped in Chicano short stories, poems, a play. In graduate school, while working toward a Ph.D., I had to "argue" with one advisor after the other, semester after semester, before I was allowed to make Chicano literature an area of focus.

Even before I read books by Chicanos or Mexicans, it was the Mexican movies   30
I saw at the drive-in—the Thursday night special of $1.00 a carload—that gave me a sense of belonging. *"Vámonos a las vistas,"* my mother would call out and we'd all—grandmother, brothers, sister and cousins—squeeze into the car. We'd wolf down cheese and bologna white bread sandwiches while watching Pedro Infante in melodramatic tearjerkers like *Nosotros los pobres*, the first "real" Mexican movie (that was not an imitation of European movies). I remember seeing *Cuando los hijos se van* and surmising that all Mexican movies played up the love a mother has for her children and what ungrateful sons and daughters suffer when they are not devoted to their mothers. I remember the singing-type "westerns" of Jorge Negrete and Miquel Aceves Mejía. When watching Mexican movies, I felt a sense of homecoming as well as alienation. People who were to amount to something didn't go to Mexican movies, or *bailes* or tune their radios to *bolero*, *racherita*, and *corrido* music.

The whole time I was growing up, there was *norteño* music sometimes called North Mexican border music, or Tex-Mex music, or Chicano music, or *cantina* (bar) music. I grew up listening to *conjuntos*, three- or four-piece bands made up of folk musicians playing guitar, *bajo sexto*, drums and button accordion, which Chicanos had borrowed from the German immigrants who had come to Central Texas and Mexico to farm and build breweries. In the Rio Grande Valley, Steve Jordan and Little Joe Hernández were popular, and Flaco Jiménez was the accordian king. The rhythms of Tex-Mex music are those of the polka, also adapted from the Germans, who in turn had borrowed the polka from the Czechs and Bohemians.

9. Rodolfo Gonzales, *I Am Joaquín / Yo Soy Joaquín* (New York, NY: Bantam Books, 1972). It was first published in 1967.

I remember the hot, sultry evenings when *corridos*—songs of love and death on the Texas-Mexican borderlands—reverberated out of cheap amplifiers from the local *cantinas* and wafted in through my bedroom window.

Corridos first became widely used along the South Texas/Mexican border during the early conflict between Chicanos and Anglos. The *corridos* are usually about Mexican heroes who do valiant deeds against the Anglo oppressors. Pancho Villa's song, "*La cucaracha*," is the most famous one. *Corridos* of John F. Kennedy and his death are still very popular in the Valley. Older Chicanos remember Lydia Mendoza, one of the great border *corrido* singers who was called *la Gloria de Tejas*. Her "*El tango negro*," sung during the Great Depression, made her a singer of the people. The ever-present *corridos* narrated one hundred years of border history, bringing news of events as well as entertaining. These folk musicians and folk songs are our chief cultural mythmakers, and they made our hard lives seem bearable.

I grew up feeling ambivalent about our music. Country-western and rock-and-roll had more status. In the 50s and 60s, for the slightly educated and *agringado* Chicanos, there existed a sense of shame at being caught listening to our music. Yet I couldn't stop my feet from thumping to the music, could not stop humming the words, nor hide from myself the exhilaration I felt when I heard it.

There are more subtle ways that we internalize identification, especially in the forms 35
of images and emotions. For me food and certain smells are tied to my identity, to my homeland. Woodsmoke curling up to an immense blue sky; woodsmoke perfuming my grandmother's clothes, her skin. The stench of cow manure and the yellow patches on the ground; the crack of a .22 rifle and the reek of cordite. Homemade white cheese sizzling in a pan, melting inside a folded *tortilla*. My sister Hilda's hot, spicy *menudo*, *chile colorado* making it deep red, pieces of *panza* and hominy floating on top. My brother Carito barbequing *fajitas* in the backyard. Even now and 3,000 miles away, I can see my mother spicing the ground beef, pork and venison with *chile*. My mouth salivates at the thought of the hot steaming *tamales* I would be eating if I were home.

Si le pregunta a mi mamá, "¿Qué eres?"

> "Identity is the essential core of who
> we are as individuals, the conscious
> experience of the self inside."
> —*Kaufman*[10]

Nosotros los Chicanos straddle the borderlands. On one side of us, we are constantly exposed to the Spanish of the Mexicans, on the other side we hear the

10. Kaufman, Gershen. *Shame: The Power of Caring* (Cambridge, Mass.: Schenkman Books, Inc., 1980), 68.

Anglos' incessant clamoring so that we forget our language. Among ourselves we don't say *nosotros los americanos, o nosotros los españoles, o nosotros los hispanos.* We say *nosotros los mexicanos* (by *mexicanos* we do not mean citizens of Mexico; we do not mean a national identity, but a racial one). We distinguish between *mexicanos del otro lado* and *mexicanos de este lado.* Deep in our hearts we believe that being Mexican has nothing to do with which country one lives in. Being Mexican is a state of soul—not one of mind, not one of citizenship. Neither eagle nor serpent, but both. And like the ocean, neither animal respects borders.

> *Dime con quien andas y te diré quien eres.*
> (Tell me who your friends are and I'll tell you who you are.)
> —Mexican saying

Si le preguntas a mi mamá, "¿Qué eres?" te dirá, "Soy mexicana." My brothers and sister say the same. I sometimes will answer "*soy mexicana*" and at others will say "*soy Chicana*" o "*soy tejana.*" But I identified as "*Raza*" before I ever identified as "*mexicana*" or "*Chicana.*"

As a culture, we call ourselves Spanish when referring to ourselves as a linguistic group and when copping out. It is then that we forget out predominant Indian genes. We are 70–80% Indian.[11] We call ourselves Hispanic[12] or Spanish-American or Latin American or Latin when linking ourselves to other Spanish-speaking peoples of the Western hemisphere and when copping out. We call ourselves Mexican-American[13] to signify we are neither Mexican nor American, but more the noun "American" than the adjective "Mexican" (and when copping out).

Chicanos and other people of color suffer economically for not acculturating. This voluntary (yet forced) alienation makes for psychological conflict, a kind of dual identity—we don't identify with the Anglo-American cultural values and we don't totally identify with the Mexican cultural values. We are a synergy of two cultures with various degrees of Mexicanness or Angloness. I have so internalized the borderland conflict that sometimes I feel like one cancels out the other and we are zero, nothing, no one. *A veces no soy nada ni nadie. Pero hasta cuando no lo soy, lo soy.*

When not copping out, when we know we are more than nothing, we call our- 40
selves Mexican, referring to race and ancestry; *mestizo* when affirming both our Indian and Spanish (but we hardly ever own our Black ancestry); Chicano when referring to a politically aware people born and/or raised in the U.S.; *Raza* when referring to Chicanos; *tejanos* when we are Chicanos from Texas.

Chicanos did not know we were a people until 1965 when Ceasar Chavez and the farmworkers united and *I Am Joaquín* was published and *la Raza Unida* party was

11. Chávez, 88–90.
12. "Hispanic" is derived from *Hispanis* (*España*, a name given to the Iberian Peninsula in ancient times when it was a part of the Roman Empire) and is a term designated by the U.S. government to make it easier to handle us on paper.
13. The Treaty of Guadalupe Hidalgo created the Mexican-American in 1848.

Toni Morrison
Nobel Lecture
(1993)

TONI MORRISON was born in Lorain, Ohio, in 1931. She studied English at Howard University from 1949 to 1953, and in 1955 she received a master's degree in English from Cornell University with a thesis on the work of William Faulkner and Virginia Woolf—authors who would later influence her own work substantially. Morrison taught English at Texas Southern University and Howard University before moving to New York City in 1964 to work as an editor at Random House.

Morrison's first novel, *The Bluest Eye*, was published in 1970. Two huge critical successes followed: *Sula* (1975), which was nominated for a National Book Award, and *Song of Solomon* (1977), which won the National Book Critics Circle Award. Her biggest commercial and critical success, however, came in 1987 with *Beloved*, the haunting story of an escaped slave that won the Pulitzer Prize for Fiction. To date, over her thirty-year career, Morrison has published nine novels, several books of non-fiction, and many essays and works of literary criticism.

Morrison was awarded the Nobel Prize for Literature in 1993. In her acceptance speech, reprinted here, she explains her work as a writer within the context of a well-known African folklore about a wise woman who is confronted by two children wanting to know whether a bird that one of them holds in their hands is living or dead. Morrison weaves this story throughout her speech, constantly reinterpreting it in different frameworks to advance her argument. In all of her interpretations, the bird represents language, the old woman represents a writer, and the children represent the members of the culture that the writer addresses. The old woman's answer to the children, "It is in your hands," points out the great responsibility that we have to the language that has been entrusted to our care.

The folktale at the heart of Morrison's speech functions rhetorically much as the parables of Jesus do in the New Testament. The tale creates an analogy that serves as scaffolding for her observations. Morrison, though, repeatedly revises and reinterprets the meaning of her parable—and by doing so adds a new layer of meaning about the ambiguous nature of narrative itself. 🖋

"ONCE UPON A TIME there was an old woman. Blind but wise." Or was it an old man? A guru, perhaps. Or a griot soothing restless children. I have heard this story, or one exactly like it, in the lore of several cultures.

"Once upon a time there was an old woman. Blind. Wise."

In the version I know the woman is the daughter of slaves, black, American, and lives alone in a small house outside of town. Her reputation for wisdom is without peer and without question. Among her people she is both the law and its transgression. The honor she is paid and the awe in which she is held reach beyond her neighborhood to places far away; to the city where the intelligence of rural prophets is the source of much amusement.

One day the woman is visited by some young people who seem to be bent on disproving her clairvoyance and showing her up for the fraud they believe she is. Their plan is simple: they enter her house and ask the one question the answer to which rides solely on her differences from them, a difference they regard as a profound disability: her blindness. They stand before her, and one of them says, "Old woman, I hold in my hand a bird. Tell me whether it is living or dead."

She does not answer, and the question is repeated. "Is the bird I am holding living or dead?"

Still she doesn't answer. She is blind and cannot see her visitors, let alone what is in their hands. She does not know their color, gender or homeland. She only knows their motive.

The old woman's silence is so long, the young people have trouble holding their laughter.

Finally she speaks and her voice is soft but stern. "I don't know," she says. "I don't know whether the bird you are holding is dead or alive, but what I do know is that it is in your hands. It is in your hands."

Her answer can be taken to mean: if it is dead, you have either found it that way or you have killed it. If it is alive, you can still kill it. Whether it is to stay alive, it is your decision. Whatever the case, it is your responsibility.

For parading their power and her helplessness, the young visitors are reprimanded, told they are responsible not only for the act of mockery but also for the small bundle of life sacrificed to achieve its aims. The blind woman shifts attention away from assertions of power to the instrument through which that power is exercised.

Speculation on what (other than its own frail body) that bird-in-the-hand might signify has always been attractive to me, but especially so now thinking, as I have been, about the work I do that has brought me to this company. So I choose to read the bird as language and the woman as a practiced writer. She is worried about how the language she dreams in, given to her at birth, is handled, put into service, even withheld from her for certain nefarious purposes. Being a writer she thinks of language partly as a system, partly as a living thing over which one has control, but mostly as agency—as an act with consequences. So the question the children put to her: "Is it living or dead?" is not unreal because she thinks of language as susceptible to death, erasure; certainly imperiled and salvageable only by an effort of the will. She believes that if the bird in the hands of her visitors is dead the custodians are responsible for the corpse. For her a dead language is not only one no longer spoken or written, it is unyielding language content to admire its own paralysis. Like statist language,[1] censored and censoring. Ruthless in its policing duties, it has no desire or purpose other than maintaining the free range of its own narcotic narcissism, its own exclusivity and dominance. However moribund, it is not without effect for it actively thwarts the intellect, stalls conscience, suppresses human potential. Unreceptive to interrogation, it cannot form or tolerate new ideas, shape other thoughts, tell another story, fill baffling silences. Official language smitheryed[2] to sanction ignorance and preserve privilege is a suit of armor polished to shocking glitter, a husk from which the knight departed long ago. Yet there it is: dumb, predatory, sentimental. Exciting reverence in schoolchildren, providing shelter for despots, summoning false memories of stability, harmony among the public.

She is convinced that when language dies, out of carelessness, disuse, indifference and absence of esteem, or killed by fiat, not only she herself, but all users and makers are accountable for its demise. In her country children have bitten their tongues off and use bullets instead to iterate the voice of speechlessness, of disabled and disabling language, of language adults have abandoned altogether as a device for grappling with meaning, providing guidance, or expressing love. But she knows tongue-suicide is not only the choice of children. It is common among the infantile heads of state and power merchants whose evacuated language leaves them with no access to what is left of their human instincts for they speak only to those who obey, or in order to force obedience.

The systematic looting of language can be recognized by the tendency of its users to forgo its nuanced, complex, mid-wifery properties for menace and subjugation. Oppressive language does more than represent violence; it is violence; does more than represent the limits of knowledge; it limits knowledge. Whether it is obscuring state language or the faux-language of mindless media; whether it is the proud but calcified language of the academy or the commodity driven language of science; whether it is the malign language of law-without-ethics, or language designed for the estrangement of minorities, hiding its racist plunder in its literary cheek—it must be rejected, altered and exposed. It is the language that drinks blood, laps vulnerabilities, tucks its fascist boots under crinolines of respectability and patriotism as it moves relentlessly toward the bottom line and the bottomed-out mind. Sexist language, racist language, theistic language—all are typical of the policing languages of mastery, and cannot, do not permit new knowledge or encourage the mutual exchange of ideas.

The old woman is keenly aware that no intellectual mercenary, nor insatiable dictator, no paid-for politician or demagogue; no counterfeit journalist would be per-

---

1. **Statist language:** language produced by a government, with connotations of authoritarianism or propaganda.

2. **Smitheryed:** connected, as if in a blacksmith's forge.

suaded by her thoughts. There is and will be rousing language to keep citizens armed and arming; slaughtered and slaughtering in the malls, courthouses, post offices, playgrounds, bedrooms and boulevards; stirring, memorializing language to mask the pity and waste of needless death. There will be more diplomatic language to countenance rape, torture, assassination. There is and will be more seductive, mutant language designed to throttle women, to pack their throats like paté-producing geese with their own unsayable, transgressive words; there will be more of the language of surveillance disguised as research; of politics and history calculated to render the suffering of millions mute; language glamorized to thrill the dissatisfied and bereft into assaulting their neighbors; arrogant pseudo-empirical language crafted to lock creative people into cages of inferiority and hopelessness.

Underneath the eloquence, the glamor, the scholarly associations, however stirring or seductive, the heart of such language is languishing, or perhaps not beating at all—if the bird is already dead. 15

She has thought about what could have been the intellectual history of any discipline if it had not insisted upon, or been forced into, the waste of time and life that rationalizations for and representation of dominance required—lethal discourses of exclusion blocking access to cognition for both the excluder and the excluded.

The conventional wisdom of the Tower of Babel[3] story is that the collapse was a misfortune. That it was the distraction, or the weight of many languages that precipitated the tower's failed architecture. That one monolithic language would have expedited the building and heaven would have been reached. Whose heaven, she wonders? And what kind? Perhaps the achievement of Paradise was premature, a little hasty if no one could take the time to understand other languages, other views, other narratives period. Had they, the heaven they imagined might have been found at their feet. Complicated, demanding, yet, but a view of heaven as life; not heaven as post-life.

She would not want to leave her young visitors with the impression that language should be forced to stay alive merely to be. The vitality of language lies in its ability to limn the actual, imagined and possible lives of its speakers, readers, writers. Although its poise is sometimes in displacing experience it is not a substitute for it. It arcs toward the place where meaning may lie. When a President of the United States thought about the graveyard his country had become, and said, "The world will little note nor long remember what we say here. But it will never forget what they did here,"[4] his simple words are exhilarating in their life-sustaining properties because they refused to encapsulate the reality of 600,000 dead men in a cataclysmic race war. Refusing to monumentalize, disdaining the "final word," the precise "summing up", acknowledging their "poor power to add or detract," his words signal deference to the uncapturability of the life it mourns. It is the deference that moves her, that recognition that

3. **Tower of Babel:** In Genesis 11:1–9, the people of earth build a huge tower in the city of Babylon to try to reach God. As a punishment, God separates their single language into a mul-titude of languages, so that they cannot understand each other.
4. From Lincoln's Gettysburg Address.

language can never live up to life once and for all. Nor should it. Language can never "pin down" slavery, genocide, war. Nor should it yearn for the arrogance to be able to do so. Its force, its felicity is in its reach toward the ineffable.

Be it grand or slender, burrowing, blasting, or refusing to sanctify; whether it laughs out loud or is a cry without an alphabet, the choice word, the chosen silence, unmolested language surges toward knowledge, not its destruction. But who does not know of literature banned because it is interrogative; discredited because it is critical; erased because alternate? And how many are outraged by the thought of a self-ravaged tongue?

Word-work is sublime, she thinks, because it is generative; it makes meaning that   20
secures our difference, our human difference—the way in which we are like no other life.

We die. That may be the meaning of life. But we do language. That may be the measure of our lives.

"Once upon a time, . . ." visitors ask an old woman a question. Who are they, these children? What did they make of that encounter? What did they hear in those final words: "The bird is in your hands"? A sentence that gestures towards possibility or one that drops a latch? Perhaps what the children heard was "It's not my problem. I am old, female, black, blind. What wisdom I have now is in knowing I cannot help you. The future of language is yours."

They stand there. Suppose nothing was in their hands? Suppose the visit was only a ruse, a trick to get to be spoken to, taken seriously as they have not been before? A chance to interrupt, to violate the adult world, its miasma of discourse about them, for them, but never to them? Urgent questions are at stake, including the one they have asked: "Is the bird we hold living or dead?" Perhaps the question meant: "Could someone tell us what is life? What is death?" No trick at all; no silliness. A straightforward question worthy of the attention of a wise one. An old one. And if the old and wise who have lived life and faced death cannot describe either, who can?

But she does not; she keeps her secret; her good opinion of herself; her gnomic pronouncements; her art without commitment. She keeps her distance, enforces it and retreats into the singularity of isolation, in sophisticated, privileged space.

Nothing, no word follows her declaration of transfer. That silence is deep, deeper   25
than the meaning available in the words she has spoken. It shivers, this silence, and the children, annoyed, fill it with language invented on the spot.

"Is there no speech," they ask her, "no words you can give us that helps us break through your dossier of failures? Through the education you have just given us that is no education at all because we are paying close attention to what you have done as well as to what you have said? To the barrier you have erected between generosity and wisdom?

"We have no bird in our hands, living or dead. We have only you and our important question. Is the nothing in our hands something you could not bear to contemplate, to even guess? Don't you remember being young when language was magic without meaning? When what you could say, could not mean? When the invisible was what imagination strove to see? When questions and demands for answers burned so brightly you trembled with fury at not knowing?

"Do we have to begin consciousness with a battle heroines and heroes like you have already fought and lost leaving us with nothing in our hands except what you have imagined is there? Your answer is artful, but its artfulness embarrasses us and ought to embarrass you. Your answer is indecent in its self-congratulation. A made-for-television script that makes no sense if there is nothing in our hands.

"Why didn't you reach out, touch us with your soft fingers, delay the sound bite, the lesson, until you knew who we were? Did you so despise our trick, our modus operandi you could not see that we were baffled about how to get your attention? We are young. Unripe. We have heard all our short lives that we have to be responsible. What could that possibly mean in the catastrophe this world has become; where, as a poet said, "nothing needs to be exposed since it is already barefaced." Our inheritance is an affront. You want us to have your old, blank eyes and see only cruelty and mediocrity. Do you think we are stupid enough to perjure ourselves again and again with the fiction of nationhood? How dare you talk to us of duty when we stand waist deep in the toxin of your past?

"You trivialize us and trivialize the bird that is not in our hands. Is there no context for our lives? No song, no literature, no poem full of vitamins, no history connected to experience that you can pass along to help us start strong? You are an adult. The old one, the wise one. Stop thinking about saving your face. Think of our lives and tell us your particularized world. Make up a story. Narrative is radical, creating us at the very moment it is being created. We will not blame you if your reach exceeds your grasp; if love so ignites your words they go down in flames and nothing is left but their scald. Or if, with the reticence of a surgeon's hands, your words suture only the places where blood might flow. We know you can never do it properly—once and for all. Passion is never enough; neither is skill. But try. For our sake and yours forget your name in the street; tell us what the world has been to you in the dark places and in the light. Don't tell us what to believe, what to fear. Show us belief's wide skirt and the stitch that unravels fear's caul. You, old woman, blessed with blindness, can speak the language that tells us what only language can: how to see without pictures. Language alone protects us from the scariness of things with no names. Language alone is meditation.

"Tell us what it is to be a woman so that we may know what it is to be a man. What moves at the margin. What it is to have no home in this place. To be set adrift from the one you knew. What it is to live at the edge of towns that cannot bear your company.

"Tell us about ships turned away from shorelines at Easter, placenta in a field. Tell us about a wagonload of slaves, how they sang to softly their breath was indistinguishable from the falling snow. How they knew from the hunch of the nearest shoulder that

30

the next stop would be their last. How, with hands prayered in their sex, they thought of heat, then sun. Lifting their faces as though is was there for the taking. Turning as though there for the taking. They stop at an inn. The driver and his mate go in with the lamp leaving them humming in the dark. The horse's void steams into the snow beneath its hooves and its hiss and melt are the envy of the freezing slaves.

"The inn door opens: a girl and a boy step away from its light. They climb into the wagon bed. The boy will have a gun in three years, but now he carries a lamp and a jug of warm cider. They pass it from mouth to mouth. The girl offers bread, pieces of meat and something more: a glance into the eyes of the one she serves. One helping for each man, two for each woman. And a look. They look back. The next stop will be their last. But not this one. This one is warmed."

It's quiet again when the children finish speaking, until the woman breaks into the silence.

"Finally," she says, "I trust you now. I trust you with the bird that is not in your 35 hands because you have truly caught it. Look. How lovely it is, this thing we have done—together."

UNDERSTANDING THE TEXT

1. What is the moral of the story that Toni Morrison begins with? Why does she choose this particular story? Why does she stress that different regions of Africa have different versions of the story?

2. Morrison says that "children have bitten their tongues off and use bullets instead." In what ways might violence replace language as a way of dealing with others?

3. How, according to Morrison, can language be used to oppress and subjugate people? What other, more noble purposes of language does she suggest?

4. For Morrison, what is the difference between "living language" and "dead language"? How does this difference parallel the living or dead bird in the story that frames her speech?

5. Why does Morrison devote so much time at the end of her speech to the possibility that the children in her tale do not have a bird in their hand at all? How would this change the traditional moral of the story? What point about the possibilities of language does she make with this change?

MAKING CONNECTIONS

1. How does Morrison's use of African folktales compare with Chinua Achebe's in "Language and the Destiny of Man" (p. 506)? Both writers explore the power of language; what are the similarities and differences between the ideas in their texts?

2. Contrast Morrison's views on the abuse of language with those of N. Scott Momaday (p. 519) and Gloria Anzaldúa (p. 527). How might each of these authors' backgrounds have shaped their perceptions of language? Explain.

3. Would Frederick Douglass (p. 46) have agreed with Morrison's view that language can be used for violence and oppression? What are the characteristics of language used in these ways?

WRITING ABOUT THE TEXT

1. Write an essay in which you analyze the connection between language and violence. Refer to Morrison's text and to one other text in this chapter in your essay. You might also include anecdotes from your own life, facts, statistics, expert testimony, and other forms of evidence you can uncover during research.

2. Write an essay in which you analyze Morrison's use of an African folktale in this speech. Explain how this story functions as an introduction, a conclusion, and evidence for a claim, and evaluate its effectiveness in each role.

3. Listen to Morrison's speech online—it's available on the Nobel Prize website, nobelprize.org—and read it again carefully. Then, write an essay in which you explain how the experience of hearing the speech is different from the experience of reading it. In your essay, consider how these differences might be related to the differences between oral and written narrative that Morrison and others (such as Momaday, p. 519, and Achebe, p. 506) discuss.

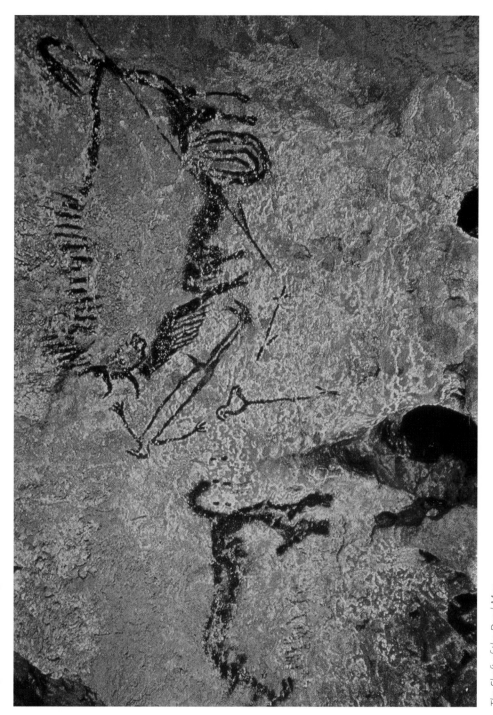

The Shaft of the Dead Man

Rock painting, Lascaux caves, Dordogne, France, 15,000–13,000 BCE.

Bridgeman Art Library

The Papyrus of Ani, circa 1250 BCE (painted papyrus)

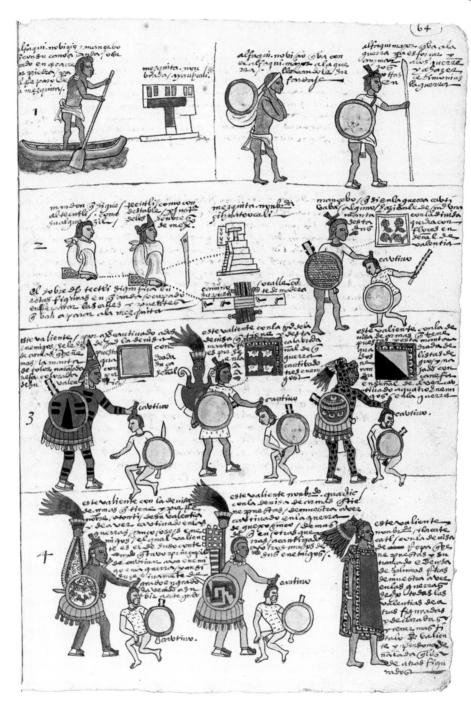

Progress of an Aztec Warrior, 1541.

Eugène Delacroix
Liberty Leading the People, 28 July 1830, 1830 (oil on canvas).
Louvre, Paris, France / Bridgeman Art Library

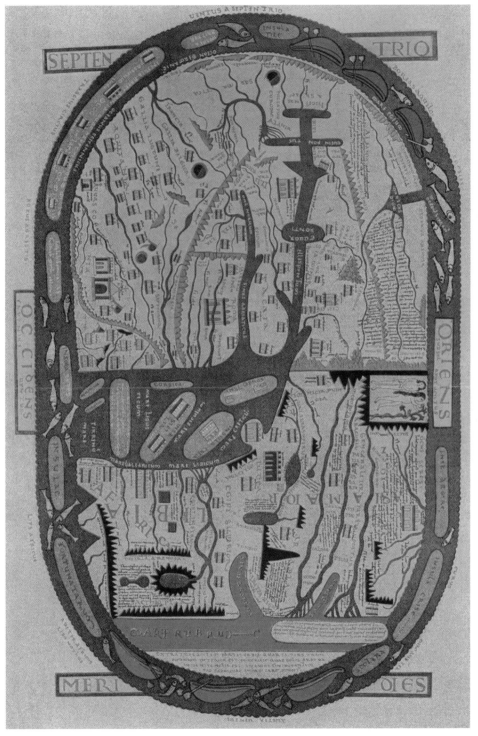

BEATUS OF LIÉBANA
The Beatus Map, 776 CE.

JOSEPH WRIGHT OF DERBY
An Experiment on a Bird in the Air Pump, 1768 (oil on canvas).
National Gallery, London, UK / Bridgeman Art Library

GALAXY CLUSTER ABELL 1689, 2002.
NASA, N. Benitez (JHU), T. Broadhurst (Racah Institute of Physics / The Hebrew University), H. Ford (JHU), M. Clampin (STScI), G. Hartig (STScI), G. Illingworth (UCO / Lick Observatory), the ACS Science Team and ESA

NORMAN ROCKWELL
Freedom of Speech, 1943 (oil on canvas).
© 1943 the Norman Rockwell Family Entities

PART 2

A Guide to Reading and Writing

8

Reading Ideas

READING CAN BE either passive or active. You read passively when, for example, you pick up a piece of writing and read it straight through, starting at the beginning, moving quickly through passages that do not interest you, and putting it aside, perhaps forever, when you have finished. Most people read passively most of the time—and with very good reason. Passive reading works perfectly well for getting the gist of a piece of writing. It allows for fairly simple information to be communicated, more or less intact, from the author to the reader. Passive reading works just fine for skimming a newspaper over breakfast, reading the day's mail, browsing the Web, or curling up in bed with an entertaining novel.

College-level reading, however, usually requires a more active approach. You should not expect to read challenging texts like the ones in this book the same way that you would read the back of a cereal box. No one can read difficult texts without some effort. People who read challenging texts successfully are not necessarily smarter than other people; they have simply mastered a set of strategies that allow them to get the most out of what they read.

This chapter will explore some of those active reading strategies, including **prereading**, **annotating**, **identifying patterns**, **reading visual texts**, **summarizing**, and **reading with a critical eye**. Mastering these skills will allow you to make your way through challenging material—and the texts in this book will give you plenty of practice.

PREREADING

Experienced readers rarely approach difficult texts without a pretty good idea of what they will find. This may sound odd, since the whole point of reading something is to find out what it says. But good readers know that reading is a process that begins long before they physically pass their eyes over the words on a page. **Prereading** encompasses all of the things that you do, before you start reading, to increase your capacity to understand the material. In many cases, taking just a few minutes to learn more about what you are about to read can dramatically increase your reading comprehension and retention.

Most college textbooks include a fair amount of editorial apparatus that has been designed to aid in the prereading process. The most obvious examples of this kind of apparatus in an anthology like this one are the chapter introductions and the introductions, or headnotes, to the individual readings. But footnotes, endnotes, study questions, and essay assignments also provide valuable clues to the themes and topics that the editors believe to be important. You might even first read the questions at the end of a reading—they will tell you some of the things to look for when you read the text.

Skimming a text is another good way to get a sense of what you are likely to find in it. A quick reading, in which you look at the beginning, some of the middle passages, and the end, can tell you a lot about the shape of the argument. People whose major reading experience is passive often find it unsettling to read the end of a work before reading the beginning. "Spoiling the ending" is the wrong way to read a mystery novel, to be sure, but it can be a very good way to read a complicated text. You might, for example, find a complicated text's major points summarized in neat little packages at the ends of essays or chapters. If you are struggling with what an author is saying, the end is just as good a place to start understanding it as the beginning. No rule says that you have to go in order.

The key to prereading is to use all of the resources available to you to understand a text *before* you start reading it. Your mind can focus on only so much while you read. Most likely, you try to construct a "big picture" while you read something. In the process, you often skip over important details because you lack a conceptual framework into which you can place these details. If you build the big picture before you start, you begin reading the text with a conceptual framework already in place. Then, when you encounter a new detail or a new bit of evidence in your reading, your mind will know what to do with it.

QUESTIONS FOR PREREADING

Here are some of the key questions that you should ask as you gather information in the prereading stage of the reading process:

Who is the author of the work?
The more information you have about an author, the better you will be able to anticipate the kinds of points that he or she will make. In reading a work like Aung San Suu Kyi's "In Quest of Democracy," for example, you can infer certain things about the argument before reading the text, once you know that the author is (1) the daughter of a famous Burmese political leader, (2) a Western-trained academic, (3) a devoted admirer of Mohandas K. Gandhi and Martin Luther King Jr., (4) the winner of a democratic national election that was invalidated by a military dictatorship, and (5) an outspoken advocate of democracy who is currently under house arrest in her own country. Knowing these key biographical facts—which are readily available in the selection introduction, on the back of any of her books, and on dozens of Web pages—allows you to begin reading "In Quest of Democracy" with a pretty good understanding of Aung San Suu Kyi's general argument, allowing you to focus on her specific claims and her support for those claims.

What was the work's original purpose?
None of the texts in this anthology were written for college students in need of things to write essays about. They all come from historical and rhetorical contexts that shaped both their meanings and their methods of presentation. Even very good readers can misread a text when they ignore the characteristics of the original intended audience. Take, for example, Mo Tzu's "Against Music." To modern readers, this essay might seem like a strict, old-fashioned argument against music. When it was written, however, music was a symbol of luxury, available only to the very wealthy, who enjoyed it at the expense of everybody else. In its original context, "Against Music" was therefore a radical attack on privilege and power.

What cultural factors might have influenced the author?
The further removed you are from an author's culture, the more difficult it can be to understand that author's work—even when the work's terminology does not seem especially difficult. When dealing with texts from very different cultures most modern readers will have to learn something about the conventions and concerns of these cultures before they can make sense of the texts. The basic argument of Mo Tzu's "Against Music"—that society should not support or allow the production of music—will make very little sense to contemporary readers who do not know that, in ancient China, music was an extremely expensive luxury available only to the most wealthy members of the aristocracy. Those who attempt to apply Mo Tzu's arguments to modern notions of music will miss the point entirely.

What are some of the author's major concerns?
Authors tend to have certain concerns that they address in many works, and knowing something about a particular author's concerns can often help you to interpret

his or her works. Knowing that Plato was perpetually concerned with the nature of reality, that Garrett Hardin wrote mostly about overpopulation, and that Gandhi consistently opposed British imperialism in India will help you understand the *Gorgias*, "Lifeboat Ethics: The Case against Helping the Poor," and "Economic and Moral Progress."

What larger conversation is this text part of?

A written text is part of a larger conversation, and reading a single text is often like listening to only one part of that conversation: you miss most of the questions that have been asked and points that are being responded to. Occasionally, this anthology will give you different texts from the same general historical conversation, such as the debate between Mencius and Hsün Tzu on the sense of human nature within Confucianism, or the opinions of Averroës and Maimonides on the connections between religion and science. More often, though, you will need to familiarize yourself with the terms of the discussion that surrounds a text you are preparing to read.

In anthologies, this kind of information might appear in the chapter introductions or in the headnotes or footnotes that accompany texts. You might also locate it quickly in a good encyclopedia or through a Web search. The effort required to learn as much as you can about a text before you start reading it will almost always pay off in increased understanding and increased retention—not to mention the time you will save by having to read the text only once to grasp its meaning.

PRACTICE PREREADING

Read the following passage from John Henry Newman's "Knowledge Its Own End." On your initial reading, do not do any prereading—just read it straight through and then summarize its key points.

I am asked what is the end of University Education, and of the Liberal or Philosophical Knowledge which I conceive it to impart: I answer, that what I have already said has been sufficient to show that it has a very tangible, real, and sufficient end, though the end cannot be divided from that knowledge itself. Knowledge is capable of being its own end. Such is the constitution of the human mind, that any kind of knowledge, if it be really such, is its own reward. And if this is true of all knowledge, it is true also of that special Philosophy, which I have made to consist in a comprehensive view of truth in all its branches, of the relations of science to science, of their mutual bearings, and their respective values. What the worth of such an acquirement is, compared with other objects which we seek,—wealth or power or honour or the conveniences and comforts of life, I do not profess her to discuss; but I would maintain, and mean to show, that it is an object, in its own nature so really and undeniably good, as to be the compensation of a great deal of thought in the compassing, and a great deal of trouble in the attaining.

Once you have read this passage without any prereading and summarized it, turn to the headnote for this reading (p. 53) and use the information in it to answer the following questions:

1. Who was John Henry Newman, and when did he write?
2. What was the original context of "Knowledge Its Own End"? What was Newman's position when he gave the lecture that would eventually become this essay?
3. How did Newman define the word "Catholic"? What did this definition have to do with his view of education?
4. What did Newman see as the difference between "useful knowledge" and "liberal knowledge"?

After you have answered these four questions, read and summarize the passage again, then compare your second summary to your first one. How has learning key facts about the text changed your ability to make sense of what you read?

ANNOTATING

After prereading to gather information about a text, your next step is to read the text closely. Your two most important tools will be a good dictionary and a pencil or a pen.

Reading with a dictionary at hand is extremely important, as it allows you to look up words that you do not know. This practice sounds obvious, but many people instead try to figure out the meanings of difficult words by their contexts. Sometimes, this strategy works; sometimes, it does not. But there is no reason to take the chance. If you do not understand a key term that an author uses, you are much less likely to understand the arguments in which the term is used. When you come across a word you don't know, you will want to check a good dictionary.

Your other important close reading tool is a pencil or a pen. As an active reader, you should write while you read. Taking notes on a computer or on a separate piece of paper is a good practice when reading a library book or one borrowed from someone else. Within your own book, **annotate** the text as you read by underlining key passages, writing comments in the margins, and recording insights as they come to you. Studies have shown that even if you never look again at the annotations that you make, the act of making them will increase the amount of information that you will recall in the future. Combining the act of writing with the act of reading helps you better understand the information that you read.

As you gain experience with active reading, you will discover annotation tricks and strategies that work for you. Different people annotate texts in different ways, depending on their learning styles and methods of recalling information. Here are a few things to keep in mind as you annotate difficult and unfamiliar texts:

Underline key points and any thesis statement

Whenever you encounter a single statement or part of a paragraph that summarizes one of the author's major arguments, underline it and write something in the margin that tells you that this is a key point. Once you determine that a certain statement summarizes a key part of the argument, you can use this statement as a reference point to see how that argument is supported. (For more on thesis statements, see p. 579.)

Note your insights

As you read a difficult idea, a certain part of your brain tries to forge connections between what you are reading and what you already know. This process can produce important insights while you are reading. However, if you do not record these insights, you may very well not remember them. Just the act of writing them in the margin helps to make them part of your long-term memory.

Respond to the author

Reading is always part of a dialogue with an author, and marginal notations are a good place to carry on that dialogue. If you strongly agree or disagree with something that you read, make a note of it. These notes will serve you well when it is time to develop your opinions in the form of an essay or in-class writing assignment.

Avoid the temptation to underline or comment too much

Like any good thing, annotating can be overdone. This overkill often defeats the purpose of annotating, since if everything is underlined it becomes impossible to distinguish what is important.

Here, using the same passage from "Knowledge Its Own End" that we used in the section on prereading, is an example of a moderate use of underlining that combines some of the strategies listed above.

*What is the
purpose of
education?*

I am asked what is (the end of University Education,) and of the (Liberal) or Philosophical Knowledge which I conceive it to impart: I answer, that what I have already said has been sufficient to show that it has a very tangible, real, and sufficient end, though the end cannot be divided from that knowledge itself. <u>Knowledge is capable of being its own end. Such is the constitution of the human mind, that any kind of knowledge, if it be really such, is its own reward.</u> And if this is true of all knowledge, it is true also of that special Philosophy, which I have made to consist in a comprehensive view of truth in all its branches, of the relations of science to science, of their mutual bearings, and their respective values. What the worth of such an acquirement is, compared with other objects which we seek,— wealth or power or honour or the conveniences and comforts of life, I do not profess here to discuss; but <u>I would maintain, and mean to show, that it is an object, in its own nature so really and undeniably good,</u> as to be the compensation of a great deal of thought in the compassing, and a great deal of trouble in the attaining.

Liberal knowledge = interdisciplinary "useless" knowledge

Thesis: Acquiring knowledge is good in and of itself

Knowledge is a good thing worth obtaining, even if it does not lead to other good things such as wealth or status

IDENTIFYING PATTERNS

Whenever you write, you use, consciously or unconsciously, some kind of organizational pattern. If you are writing about something that happened to you, your organizational pattern will likely be chronological (this happened, then this, and then this . . .); if you are describing a place, you will probably use a spatial order; and so on. When you are reading an unfamiliar text, it helps to try to figure out what kind of organizational pattern the author is using. This knowledge will help you anticipate arguments and conclusions and know where to look for them in the body of the text. Most good writing has characteristics of several different patterns, but often one pattern predominates, if not in an entire essay, at least in a particular passage. Here are some of the more common organizational patterns for written prose:

Chronological order

Historical texts, descriptions of events, personal narratives, and travelogues are often organized chronologically. The narrative begins at one point in time, then moves through the period described, with successive points in time forming the major organizational units of the text. Since the readings in *Reading the World* have been arranged chronologically, the chapter introductions generally use a straightforward chronological pattern to organize their main ideas.

Spatial order

While descriptions of events are often organized chronologically, descriptions of things and places are often organized spatially. Spatial organization can be used to describe everything from the nucleus of an atom to the known universe. When prose accompanies pictures, charts, graphs, or other graphic information, the text's content is oriented spatially to the visual information.

Classification

When an author wants to describe a number of different things—be they members of the beetle family, types of clouds, Greek philosophies, or (in the case of what you are reading right now) methods of organizing written information—he or she might create a classification system for the information and then present the information as a list. The list might be set off with bullets, headers, or other formatting information, or it might simply occur normally in the text, with nothing to indicate where the description of one item ends and another begins.

Claim/support

One of the most common organizational strategies of scientific and philosophical writing—including many selections in *Reading the World*—is to begin by stating a proposition (such as "human nature is evil" or "population grows exponentially while food supply grows arithmetically"), to continue by offering support for that proposition, and to conclude by restating the proposition and explaining its ramifications. This organizational pattern is also commonly used in college essays, with the "proposition" usually called the "thesis statement." (In college writing, though, the thesis statement will probably not look like the "thesis" of the five-paragraph essay model that you might have learned in high school. For more on thesis statements, see p. 579.) Once you have identified an essay as being organized in this fashion, you will have a pretty good idea where to look for the main point: it will probably be stated once in the first paragraph and once again near the end.

Problem/solution

Essays that make specific policy arguments—think of Al Gore's "The Climate Emergency" or Garrett Hardin's "Lifeboat Ethics: The Case against Helping the Poor"—are often organized from the top down: with the problems that need to be solved stated first, followed by the proposed solutions.

Statement/response

Another common organizational pattern of the readings in this book is statement/response. This strategy involves quoting or paraphrasing an argument (usually one that you oppose) in the beginning of the essay and then responding to that argument in the remainder of the essay. This form is usually used in texts that rebut other texts and in persuasive essays in which the author anticipates and responds to objections.

Cause/effect

One standard assumption of philosophy and science is that every effect proceeds from a cause. This movement from cause to effect is an important organizational strategy. Writers who organize their arguments along these lines can begin with the cause and move on to explain the effects—as Rachel Carson does, in "The Obligation to Endure," when she explains the chemical composition of DDT and then describes its effects on the environment. Many authors, however, present the effects first and then trace them back to a cause, as Al Gore does in "The Climate Emergency" when he presents the effects of global climate change and traces them back to changes in humanity's relationship to the earth.

Narrative

Stories, or narratives, are an important part of many different kinds of writing. The New Testament parables, the Buddhist *suttas*, African folktales, and the writings of great philosophers, ancient and modern, often rely on short narratives to make or illustrate points. In many of these texts, the narrative is followed immediately by an interpretation, in which the story becomes the basis for some conclusions or discussion.

Comparison/contrast

When an author is comparing two things—ideas, movements, people, etc.—he or she will often organize the text as an explicit comparison or contrast. Such an organizational pattern usually takes one of two forms. In the first of these forms, the author spends the first half of the essay discussing one subject of the comparison and the second half discussing the other. In the second variation, the author establishes several grounds for comparison and then goes back and forth between the things being compared. In *Reading the World*, perhaps the most straightforward example of this kind of organization is Matthieu Ricard and Trinh Xuan Thuan's "The Universe in a Grain of Sand," which compares and contrasts the perceptions of a Buddhist monk and of a quantum physicist.

READING VISUAL TEXTS

The word "text" does not apply only to written works. An oral narrative is a text, and so is a piece of music, a painting, a photograph, or a film. Works of all these types address audiences, advance ideas, make arguments, and require thoughtful strategies of reading and interpretation. In addition to its written texts, *Reading the World* includes a number of texts that present their ideas visually. These visual texts should be studied as seriously and interpreted as diligently as the written texts in the book.

Many of the strategies that we have already discussed apply just as much to visual texts as they do to written texts. Artists, like authors, have objectives, cultural contexts, and recurring concerns, and they respond to historical discussions and debates. You can ask the same "prereading" questions of a painting as of an essay. You can, however, use some additional reading strategies with visual texts. For an introduction to some of these strategies, look at the detail on p. 559 from William Hogarth's engraving *Gin Lane* (the full text of which appears on p. 320).

This detail shows two of the scenes in the foreground of the engraving. It is not difficult to understand Hogarth's message. Knowing only that the engraving is titled *Gin Lane*, you can infer that both of the major figures are intoxicated. One of them, a woman, is reaching for a pinch of snuff while her child falls from her breast and over a railing. The other figure is a man—holding a glass of gin in one hand and a bottle of gin in the other—who appears to be starving to death. Taken together, the two images present a fairly complete argument, which, if rendered in prose, would read something like: "Drinking gin is bad because it causes you to ignore your own health and the well-being of your family."

But there is much more to the text of the detail than this paraphrase suggests. As in most visual texts, the most important parts of the argument are made using visual elements, many of which cannot be translated into words without losing most of their rhetorical force. Some of the most important things to look for when "reading" a visual text are:

WILLIAM HOGARTH
Gin Lane, 1751 (engraving, detail).
Bibliothèque Nationale, Paris, France / Lauros–Giraudon / Bridgeman Art Library

Emotional appeals. Few images are as pitiable and emotionally charged as Hogarth's portrayal of a drunken mother allowing her infant child to fall from her exposed breasts to a certain death. The mother's oblivious lack of concern combines with the look of pure panic on the infant's face to produce a powerful emotional appeal in support of the otherwise bland argument that drinking gin is bad. Most people are extremely affected by emotional appeals, especially when those appeals are made visually. Most people can read many words about great suffering, misery, deprivation, and abuse without feeling the emotions that a single picture can convey.

Symbolism. The image of a baby at its mother's breast is a powerful symbol of motherhood and self-sacrifice in cultures throughout the world (see, for example,

Dorothea Lange's *Migrant Mother* on p. 341 or the Igbo statue on p. 129). By inverting this symbol, Hogarth taps into a very deep pool of cultural—and even cross-cultural—associations involving infants, mothers, and nursing. Many of the visual texts in this book feature similar kinds of symbolic representation: the swastikas decorating the tall banners in the still from *The Triumph of the Will* (p. 199), the gun and the French flag carried by Liberty in *Liberty Leading the People* (p. 268), and the light coming from the lamp in *An Experiment on a Bird in the Air Pump* (p. 402) all convey ideas through symbols whose physical forms only suggest their ultimate meaning.

Visual irony.   Hogarth was a master of visual irony, much of which requires very close reading of his art. For example, there is an obvious irony in the fact that the man in *Gin Lane* is starving to death while clutching a large quantity of gin, whose price could have purchased food instead. Only a very careful viewer will notice the irony, however, in the piece of paper in his basket. It reads "The downfall of Madam Gin," which is presumably the title of a broadside ballad, possibly one that he wrote himself, that he has been attempting to sell in the neighborhood—in order to get enough money to buy more gin.

Motifs.   If you look at the full version of *Gin Lane* (p. 320), you will see that the two images in this detail are part of larger motifs, or patterns of images that mirror and comment on each other. The "neglected child" motif is refigured in children and infants throughout the picture, including one who is being given a glass of gin instead of a milk bottle, one who is fighting with a dog for a bone, and one who is being carried through the street impaled on a skewer. The "suicide by gin" motif is just as prevalent and serves as the overall "big picture" motif of the engraving. The entire community is in the last stages of a painful death brought about by the ravages of gin.

Composition.   Any visual text includes compositional elements—line, perspective, color, use of space, etc.—that contribute to the work's meaning. In *Gin Lane*, for example, the mother and her infant are foregrounded and brightly lit so that the eye is immediately drawn to them, emphasizing their importance in Hogarth's argument. The dominant lines in the complete engraving—the top of the brick wall, the rooftop pole at the top right, the signpost on the building on the left, and the staircase and its railings—are at random angles to each other, emphasizing the unpredictability and topsy-turviness of a world dominated by gin.

All of these elements combine to form an overall impression. If the artist has arranged the elements well, the viewer will gain an overall sense of the text that can itself become a powerful persuasive element. Visual images can create impressions of, among other things, reverence, power, wonder, despair, peace, awe, and patriotism. The overall impression of *Gin Lane* is one of decay and hopelessness—both of which, according to the artist, should be attributed to gin consumption.

Visual texts convey just as much as written texts, but they do not make their meanings in quite the same ways. An essay on the evils of gin might give the reader an impression similar to that conveyed by *Gin Lane*, but it would use very different techniques to do so.

SUMMARIZING

If you really understand something that you have read, you should be able to summarize it in your own words. Often, teachers will assign essays that consist entirely or partially of summary as a way to evaluate your understanding of difficult material. In other kinds of essays, brief summaries of difficult information can give you a starting point for more sophisticated kinds of writing, such as analysis, synthesis, research, or critique. As part of active reading, summarizing helps you solidify your own understanding of a text and identify what you need to think about or analyze more closely.

A good **summary** need not relate every point that an author makes. It should, though, explain clearly and concisely the intent of the text being summarized, the major point or points that the author makes, and the major ways that those points are supported. A reader of your summary should feel that he or she has a pretty good idea of what the source you are summarizing is saying, even if that person has not read the original. Here are some suggestions to keep in mind as you create a summary:

Identify the main point
Even if the author does not come to the main point until the middle or the end of an essay, you should identify the main point immediately and put it at the beginning of your summary. Doing so will make clear early on what the text is about, and it will help you focus and organize the rest of your summary.

Identify support for the main point(s)
A summary does not always have to explain every specific bit of evidence that an author uses to support an argument (especially in very short summaries of very long works). It is important, however, for the summary to explain the kinds of evidence (analytical, experimental, statistical, deductive, etc.) that a text employs (see p. 595).

Quote from the text when appropriate
Good summaries often quote from the texts that they summarize, but they do so very selectively. The objective of a summary is to boil a large text down to its essential points. Similarly, quotations in a summary should include only a few words

here or there to get the point across, rather than large blocks of text that give complete arguments. Quote only when the author has stated something so eloquently that you cannot restate it, or when you want to emphasize the author's own words. Be sure to mark the quotation clearly, in quotation marks, and to cite the page number where the quotation is found.

Use your own words

When you summarize someone else's writing, make sure that you use your own structure as well as your own wording. A summary does not need to move chronologically through the text, relating points in the order that the author presents them. Because summarizing is an intellectual activity that you control, you should employ organizational strategies that fit your own needs, which may or may not mirror those of the author whose text you are summarizing.

READING WITH A CRITICAL EYE

To truly understand a text, you will often need to analyze its assumptions, discover its deeper arguments, and respond to those arguments with ones of your own. To do any of these things, you will need to read the text critically, in ways that require you to do more than simply understand what is being said on the surface.

Critical reading is difficult to define, as people in different disciplines use the term differently. In a literature class, "critical reading" may mean examining a literary work to find symbolic meanings beneath the surface, while in a history class it might mean evaluating the reliability of different sources used to reconstruct a historical event.

Perhaps the best way to define "critical reading" is through its opposite: uncritical reading. Those who read uncritically are likely to be persuaded by the loudest voices rather than the soundest arguments. Such readers tend to gravitate toward arguments that confirm their preconceived ideas, accepting such arguments without serious examination, and they usually reject opinions—and even well-documented facts—that challenge their beliefs. Uncritical readers can be very "critical" in the ordinary sense of the word, but they base their criticisms on how closely authors mirror their own points of view rather than on the texts' merits.

Critical readers, by contrast, approach all texts with a certain amount of skepticism, but they do not reject any argument without a fair hearing. They try to set aside their personal biases long enough to understand what they read. They seek to understand both texts and the contexts in which they are written, including, when appropriate, an author's use of symbolism, imagery, metaphor, and other figurative devices. Once they understand an argument on its own terms, critical readers evaluate its claims, its evidence, and its underlying assumptions both fairly and rigorously. They do not change their minds every time that they read something new, but neither do they refuse to consider a new idea because it disagrees with an opinion that they already hold. Learning to read critically is an important part of learning to think critically, which is one of the primary skills expected in higher education.

Learning to think and read critically is a lifelong process, but you can take concrete steps to develop the habit:

Think about your own perspective

The process of reading and thinking critically begins with the realization that you have your own perspective. Some aspects of your perspective come from your culture and the time in which you live; others may come from your family, your friends, and your own experience of the world. You cannot avoid this situation, nor should you try. Being situated in a culture, a time period, a society, and a family—and having opinions about things—is part of being human. You cannot eliminate your own beliefs, but you can be aware of them, understand where they come from, and take them into consideration when you read something with a perspective different from your own. You need not accept everything that you read—but you should realize when your own perspective might be getting in the way of understanding what a text is saying.

Understand the author's perspective

Just as readers have their own perspectives, so do authors. As a reader, you must approach a text with a balance of respect and skepticism, being open to an unfamiliar perspective while examining it with the same critical analysis that you apply to your own beliefs. You should approach every text that you read as having been shaped by cultural and individual perspectives, and you should realize that all such perspectives—your own and everybody else's—come with both insights and stumbling blocks of their own.

Determine how the argument works

All texts make arguments in the sense that they assert at least one point and support that point. Critical readers pay attention to how arguments work: what the main points are, what the supporting points are, and how different kinds of evidence are invoked to back up major and supporting points. You cannot evaluate a text's effectiveness until you understand the mechanics of its argument.

Evaluate the support for a claim

An author can support his or her claim in different ways, many of which will be covered in chapter 11. Some claims are supported by statistics, some by experimental data, some by logical analysis, and some simply by the force of the writer's or speaker's personality. There is no one right way to support all claims, but some kinds of evidence are more appropriate than others for certain kinds of claims.

Critical reading involves determining whether a text employs appropriate kinds of evidence for the kind of argument it is making.

Once you have determined the appropriateness of the kind of evidence that a text employs, you must still determine the strength of that evidence. For example, if statistical evidence is the best way to prove a certain point—such as Garrett Hardin's argument, in "Lifeboat Ethics: The Case against Helping the Poor," that the earth's population has exceeded its carrying capacity—you must evaluate the relevance and representativeness of the author's statistics. If drawing out general principles from historical examples is a good way to prove a particular point—such as Machiavelli's assertion, in *The Prince*, that it is better for a ruler to be feared than to be loved or Octavio Paz's assertion, in "The Day of the Dead," that Mexican identity is shaped by profound solitude—you must examine the relevance of the author's or authors' historical examples *and* the relevance of historical examples that have occurred since the texts were written. Both Thomas Malthus and Rachel Carson, for example, made arguments about what would happen in the future. Things that have happened since they wrote might confirm or refute the cases that they made.

Think about underlying assumptions

Most claims have stated points and underlying assumptions. The stated points are the ones that the author makes. The underlying assumptions are the premises that, though never stated, must be true for the argument to succeed. These unstated assumptions may be so obvious that the author does not feel the need to restate them; they may be assumptions that the author wishes to conceal from the audience; or they may be foundational beliefs so deeply engrained that the author does not recognize them. When you read, think about the assumptions beneath the author's claim. What needs to be true for the claim to be true? What would prevent the claim from being true? The chart below presents some assertions and the unstated assumptions that underlie them.

STATED ASSERTION	UNDERLYING ASSUMPTION(S)
The best way to derive truth about nature is through direct observation because primary evidence is better than secondary evidence.	Human senses give reliable information and do not deceive us.
Human nature is evil because people are inherently selfish and incapable of genuine concern for other people to the exclusion of self.	Focusing on one's self is evil, and focusing on other people, to the exclusion of one's self, is good.

Democracy is the best form of government because it guarantees the maximum amount of freedom for individuals.	Giving individuals a maximum amount of freedom is a good thing. / Individuals will not use their freedom in ways that destroy society and each other.
Helping those in need is important because we owe it to fellow human beings to eliminate as much suffering and misery as we can.	Helping those in need will relieve suffering and will not cause a greater amount of misery in the long term.
Higher education is a good thing because it helps people get good jobs and earn more money throughout their lives.	Earning more money is a good thing.

Of course, every assertion in this chart is debatable. The stated claims in the left-hand column, while very common, are not self-evidently true. Every one of them could be, and has been, disputed. However, even if you generally accept the stated claims in the left-hand column, their arguments absolutely depend on the unstated assumptions in the right-hand column. Each assumption can also be plausibly debated; and the rejection of any one would lead to the rejection of the corresponding argument in the left-hand column. Critical readers know how to delve beneath the stated assertions in a text and evaluate the assumptions that underlie those assertions.

9

GENERATING IDEAS

❧

MOST COLLEGE ESSAYS succeed or fail at the idea level. Good ideas are likely to produce good essays. A good idea contains within it the seeds of a good argument and an organized essay. Once you have hit upon a good idea, you will find that your essay is easier to organize, easier to write, and easier to revise.

Very few people simply "have" good ideas. The ability to generate good ideas—and good paper topics—is a skill that can be learned. This chapter will introduce some basic strategies—grouped under **considering expectations**, **exploring your topic**, and **achieving subtlety**—that you can use to move beyond your initial thoughts about a topic and generate worthwhile ideas to write about.

CONSIDERING EXPECTATIONS

Writing is an art, not a science. The writing process cannot be reduced to a precise set of formulas and equations that will produce "correct" essays in every class that requires writing. Different instructors have different preferences and grade written assignments differently. Sometimes, what works well for one instructor will not work at all for another.

Before you start thinking about a writing topic, then, make sure you understand what your instructor expects from you. If you do not meet these expectations, your ideas will not be judged "good"—even if they represent perfectly sound arguments that might be very successful in other contexts. Here are a few strategies that you can use to make sure that your essay ideas will meet your instructor's expectations:

Be sure you understand the assignment

The requirements of an assignment can be very general or very specific. In either case, you must gear your response to the terms of the assignment. Most assignments ask you to perform a certain writing task—to analyze, compare, describe, and so on. It is vital that you understand what this task entails. If you have any questions about the assignment, do not hesitate to ask your instructor to clarify it for you.

Agree/disagree. Assignments that ask you to agree or disagree will usually give you a proposition to consider. Sometimes, this proposition will be an entire reading, as in "Agree or disagree with George Orwell's points in 'Pacifism and the War.'" More often, the proposition will be a single statement or assertion, such as "In 'Pacifism and the War,' George Orwell states that a pacifist position during wartime is necessarily in favor of the enemy. Agree or disagree with this assertion."

A topic of this sort gives you the opportunity to state your opinion. When instructors assign topics such as this one, they are usually not looking for right or wrong answers. Nor do they want you to simply summarize Orwell's essay and state—at the beginning or the end of the essay—whether or not you approve. An assignment to agree or disagree is asking you to state and defend an opinion; it involves both an argument about what you believe *and* valid reasons for that argument. The quality of the reasons that you give, not your opinion, is the most important part of the assignment.

Analyze. "Analyze" is one of the most common directions in college-level writing assignments, but it can have many meanings. Generally speaking, to analyze something is to examine it by comparing how its parts relate to a whole or how certain causes produce an effect. In most (but not all) situations, a textual analysis should focus not on agreeing or disagreeing with the text but on showing how different parts of the text operate toward a particular end. An analysis of a literary text often looks at imagery, symbolism, and other kinds of figurative language. An analysis of an argumentative text usually requires you to look at the argument—to see what it claims and how persuasively it supports the claims.

Apply. One of the best ways to measure how well you understand an argument is to ask you to apply it to a new situation. Consider an assignment such as "Apply George Orwell's reasoning in 'Pacifism and the War' to America's actions in the war on terrorism." This assignment asks you to consider how the arguments advanced in the original essay—which in this case would include the assertion that refusing to fight an enemy is an act of support for that enemy rather than an act of neutrality—apply to America's actions in Afghanistan, in Iraq, and at home. There are, of course, several plausible ways to apply Orwell's argument to this situation. For example, you could argue that, according to Orwell's logic, one could not be a pacifist in the war on terror without being "objectively proterrorist." Or you could argue that, because terrorism is a criminal act rather than a military one, Orwell's argument allows for pacifism (objecting to a military solution to the problem) in the war on terror in a way that it did not allow for pacifism in World War II.

Claim/support. Many writing assignments involve some kind of claim/support structure, but some assignments specifically ask you to construct and support your own argument. In a college class, these assignments usually require you to develop fully your own opinions about things that you read, but they may or may not ask you to cite specific readings. Often, assignments for this kind of writing are phrased as questions: "Is human nature inherently good?" "Is it ever appropriate to disobey the law?" "When is war a justified response to aggression?" "Do people have a moral obligation to help the poor?" These highly debatable questions are all covered in this book, and, at some point, your instructor will probably require you to express and defend your opinions about issues such as these.

An argument about any issue consists of two parts: the claim and the support. You cannot simply make an assertion such as "Everybody has a moral obligation to help the poor" or "War is justified when people are defending their families." You also need to include a statement that gives a reason for your belief: "Everybody has a moral obligation to help the poor because morality is based on our responses to others" or "War is justified when people are defending their families because taking care of one's family is the most important duty that human beings have." The procedure for embedding a claim and a statement of support in a thesis statement is covered in depth in chapter 10 (p. 578).

Compare/contrast. Strictly speaking, "compare" means to show how things are alike, and "contrast" means to show how they are different. Sometimes, an assignment will ask you to "compare and contrast" two things, such as to "compare and contrast the views of Maimonides and Averröes on the possibility of reconciling faith and reason." Such an assignment asks you to explain similarities and differences in the two texts. Often, instructors simply use the term "compare" as a way to ask you to look for similarities and differences in two or more texts.

Describe. An assignment to describe something—whether that something is an argument, a painting, or your best friend—asks you to give its essential characteristics without evaluating or taking a position on those characteristics. Though perfect neutrality is rarely possible in a writing assignment (the act of choosing which characteristics to describe conveys an evaluation and a perspective), descriptive writing should present its subject objectively. For example, an assignment that asks you to "describe the situations that led to the emergence of Taoism and Confucianism in ancient China" is asking you to explain a set of historical facts, not to give your opinion about a pair of philosophies.

Respond. Many assignments ask you to respond to another text or to a specific argument in a text. Such assignments may or may not ask you to "agree or disagree" with the argument. They do, however, require something more than mere approval or disapproval. They require you to use the text that you are responding to as the basis for your own arguments or observations.

An assignment asking you to "respond to Machiavelli's assertion that it is better for a ruler to be feared than loved" is asking you to consider this argument and evaluate its appropriateness. Does this argument work better in some political systems than others? Does it rest on defensible assumptions about human nature? Which leaders might have agreed? Which ones might have disagreed? What would a government look like that completely accepted—or completely rejected—Machiavelli's advice? Each of these questions or their answers would be legitimate starting points for an essay asking you to "respond" to Machiavelli's argument.

Summarize/paraphrase. Some writing assignments ask you to summarize or paraphrase other texts. The two words do not mean exactly the same thing. A *summary* is a short encapsulation of a longer argument, cutting out all but the most important details; a *paraphrase* is a restatement of an argument in your own words, containing most of the original text's detail. A paraphrase of a three-page text should take about three pages, while a summary of such a text could consist of a few well-chosen sentences. When writing about other texts, do not summarize extensively or paraphrase unless you are asked to do so. If you merely summarize or paraphrase an argument that you have been asked to analyze or respond to, you will almost certainly fail to meet your instructor's expectations. (See also "Quoting, Paraphrasing, and Summarizing," p. 632.)

Get responses

To make sure that you have met your instructor's expectations for an assignment, get responses, both to your topic and to your early drafts. You might meet with your instructor to talk about your topic, or you might ask your instructor to comment on drafts. You might also seek out the tutoring resources at your school. Most colleges and universities have a writing center or other tutoring service that gives students free access to other students who have been trained in the process of peer tutoring.

Peer tutors can help writers with every stage of the writing process, not just with the finished product. A good peer tutor will be able to help you think critically about an assignment and brainstorm ideas and essay topics. Occasionally, a tutor will have the expertise to help in areas where you are weak. But sometimes, it just helps to have somebody to bounce ideas off of when you are trying to decide on an essay topic. A peer tutor can also read your essay and point out things that you might miss simply because you are too close to the writing process to view your essay objectively. If your college or university has a writing center, you have access to a tremendous resource for improving your writing, and smart students avail themselves of every opportunity that they have to improve their skills.

Consider your audience and purpose

Before you start writing, ask yourself who you are writing for and what you want to accomplish. The answers to these questions will help you present your ideas appropriately—in a class, this will help you meet your instructor's expectations; outside of school, it will help you effectively reach your intended readers. In both cases, considering your audience and purpose is essential.

Any time that you write for other people, you will be constrained by your audience's expectations. Novelists, journalists, corporate executives, screenwriters, Web designers, and even professors all know that the form, style, and content of their writing must meet certain expectations. "Good writing" in the absolute sense is virtually impossible to define, since writing always occurs in a context of stated or unstated expectations. An effective argument in one context might be totally ineffective in another. For example, the argument that providing beer in a college dining hall would make the dorms more attractive would probably be extremely successful with the student body, much less successful with faculty and administrators, and not successful at all with parents. Part of learning how to be a good writer is learning how to assess these expectations accurately and respond to them effectively.

Just as important as understanding your audience is understanding what you want to accomplish when you write. Different kinds of writing have different purposes. Writing can, among other things, inform, persuade, motivate, express, and entertain. Different purposes often require very different kinds of writing. An essay written to persuade your instructor of an argument will be very different from one designed to give an initial impression of a reading. If you begin with a solid understanding of what you want to accomplish when you write, you will be able to incorporate this purpose into every stage of the writing process.

EXPLORING YOUR TOPIC

The strategies listed below are all ways to help you generate ideas. Try them out and see which works best for you. Do not worry about coming up with the perfect topic right away; the process of generating ideas can help you think about different aspects and implications of the topic you finally choose, and you may end up using facets of other ideas in your writing.

Freewriting

The quickest, easiest, and most direct way to fill up an empty piece of paper or blank computer screen is just to start writing. Freewriting is an unconstrained writing exercise in which you simply write down whatever comes to your mind for a set period. The only rule is that you cannot stop writing. A freewriting exercise is designed to tap into the subconscious mind and pull out ideas that may be lurking beneath the surface. To complete such an exercise successfully, you need to override your mind's "editing function" and just write.

Here is a brief example of a freewriting session in response to an assignment to compare the view of liberal education in John Henry Newman's "Knowledge Its Own End" with that in Seneca's "On Liberal and Vocational Studies."

> OK, so I'm supposed to compare what John Henry Newman and Seneca said about education. Both of them talk a lot about liberal education and how it is not supposed to be useful for anything other than itself. When you read them, they sound a lot alike in this way, which is kind of weird since one of them lived in ancient Rome and the other one lived in England like a hundred years ago. Come to think of it, this is probably the biggest difference between them. Seneca lived in a very different kind of society than Newman lived in. Rome was an empire where people owned slaves and were divided into very distinct classes. Newman lived in an industrial country that was pretty much a democracy, at least at the end of his life. Maybe this is why Seneca thought that useful education was a bad thing, and only liberal education was worthwhile, while Newman just thought that they were different things. Most people in Newman's day couldn't afford not to think about how they would earn a living. I guess that's still true today.

This freewriting demonstration follows the usual pattern for such an exercise: it begins with a self-reflective discussion (here I am, doing what I am supposed to be doing), moves to some fairly surface observations about the texts (that both Seneca and Newman talk about liberal education) and then to a statement that, with a lot more refining, could be the basis of a very strong comparison paper: that Newman is more tolerant of practical education than Seneca because Newman lived in a democratic society.

Clustering

Clustering is a good strategy for processing information visually. It consists of drawing some kind of picture that represents the ideas that you are discussing and using that picture to show the relationship between a central, general idea and several more-focused, subordinate ideas. The easiest way to do this is with circles and lines, as in the following diagram, which responds to an assignment to "write a paper that uses Martin Luther King Jr.'s three categories of 'unjust law' to argue that a current law or type of law is unjust."

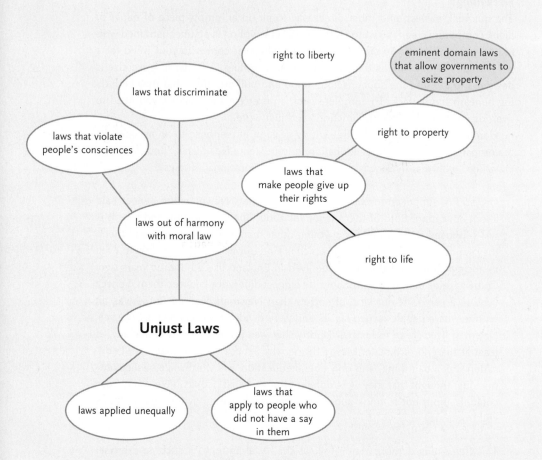

The goal of clustering here is to think of a current law that meets Martin Luther King Jr.'s classification of an unjust law, one that can then be the focus of the essay. Starting simply with "unjust laws," the writer branches out to come up with more-specific kinds of unjust laws. One kind of law, "laws that make people give up their rights," leads the writer to think about different rights, which then leads to the final essay topic: "eminent domain laws," which require people to give up their right to property. In clustering, every idea allows you to jot down several more ideas that are connected to it, so you can continue to refine and develop ideas with increasing layers of specificity. Once you reach an idea that seems workable, you can take it from your cluster and refine it further into an argumentative thesis statement.

Brainstorming

Like freewriting and clustering, brainstorming exercises are meant to get a lot of ideas down on paper without worrying—at least during the exercise—whether they will work for your essay assignment. A brainstorming session can be done alone or in a group, but the ground rules are the same: write down every idea that comes to you, do not try to evaluate the ideas as they come, do not worry about writing complete sentences, and move to the next idea quickly.

Now, imagine staying with the assignment to apply Martin Luther King Jr.'s criteria for unjust laws to a contemporary law and, instead of clustering different kinds of unjust laws, simply throwing out as many ideas as possible. A ten-minute brainstorming session might produce a list like this:

—Slavery
—Segregation laws
—Laws against gay marriage
—Laws that give police officers the right to collect information
—Affirmative action laws that treat minorities differently than others
—Prohibition
—Laws that keep women from voting
—Laws that allow countries to attack other countries
—Laws that make it illegal to practice your religion
—Laws against drugs
—Laws that won't let you drink when you are eighteen and can be drafted
  into the army
—Laws that make you wear a helmet or a seat belt
—Laws that don't let you go to the college you want to go to
—Eminent domain laws that allow governments to seize your property
—Laws that don't allow you to defend your house if someone breaks in
—Laws that treat rich people differently than poor people
—Laws that make people homeless
—Laws against people marrying people of other races

Not all the laws on this brainstormed list are suitable for the assignment; some are not current or are not current in the United States, some are too broad or ill-defined. But a third of these would work very well for the assignment with little or no modification. None of these ideas are thesis statements yet, but they are reasonably good examples of laws that fit the assignment and lend themselves well to good thesis statements and credible essays.

ACHIEVING SUBTLETY

Good writing goes beyond surface issues to explore the deeper meanings and implications of a topic. An argument or idea that digs beneath the surface, that goes beyond the obvious, might be usefully described as "subtle." In a college class, subtle ideas demonstrate to a teacher that you have really thought about an issue, struggled with its complexities, and learned something from an assignment. Once you have come up with a writing topic that meets all the specifications of an assignment, you need to develop and refine your topic to make sure it meets those standards of **subtlety**—to go beyond the obvious arguments, to do more than just say what you believe about a topic, to *learn* about the topic. This approach turns an acceptable or a good essay topic into a great one.

As you strive for this kind of deep, subtle analysis, keep the following suggestions in mind:

Go beyond your first ideas

The first ideas that will occur to you about a topic will often be the first ideas that occur to everybody else, making the resulting essay "average" by definition. Moreover, the first ideas that occur to you (and everybody else) are rarely very good. Consider an assignment, for example, in which you have been asked to compare the political philosophies of Christine de Pizan and Niccolò Machiavelli. The first thing that someone looking at these two philosophers will notice is that de Pizan is a woman and Machiavelli is a man. From there, many people will conclude that de Pizan's philosophy must be more "feminine" and Machiavelli's must be more "masculine." The gendered differences between these two authors, however, are by no means the most interesting or significant differences, and they would not lead to the most interesting essay.

Go beyond the standard positions

Issues that are regularly discussed in public forums tend to have easily recognizable "pro" and "con" positions. Sometimes, these standard positions are obvious, knee-jerk reactions to a topic; sometimes, they are well-constructed arguments that have simply been used too often. In most cases, you should steer your own arguments away from these standard arguments, since they are so well known that they will occur to everybody. Even if they are very good arguments, they are not *your* arguments, and they do not give you the opportunity to show what kinds of ideas you can come up with on your own.

If the assignment allows it, you might consider staying away entirely from issues that have been discussed so often that few new things are left to say about them. If you do write about such issues, however, approach them with subtlety and avoid the temptation to restate the usual lines of reasoning. Few readers will be persuaded by arguments that simply regurgitate standard lines of thinking.

Consider the following two arguments against legalized abortion, one of the most controversial and often-discussed issues in the modern political landscape:

Argument #1: "Abortion is murder. People who permit or perform abortions are taking innocent human lives, which is the definition of murder, and it doesn't matter how young each life is, since it is a life just the same. A child who has yet to be born is just as valuable as a child who has been born or an adult, so there is no reason why it should be acceptable to kill one if it is not acceptable to kill the other."

Argument #2: "The primary wrong-making feature of a killing is the loss to the victim of the value of its future. . . . The future of a standard fetus includes a set of experiences, projects, activities, and such which are identical with the futures of human beings and are identical with the futures of young children. Since the reason that it is sufficient to explain why it is wrong to kill human beings after the time of birth is a reason that also applies to fetuses, it follows that abortion is . . . seriously morally wrong." (Marquis, Don. "Why Abortion Is Immoral." *Journal of Philosophy* 87 [1990]: 262–77)

These passages are similar in many ways. Both assert that abortion is immoral because of its impact on a human life, and neither uses religious terms or clichés (see below). The first argument, however, simply strings together the standard, predictable arguments that one usually hears in discussions of abortion.

The second argument—which comes from a famous article by a philosophy professor—goes well beyond the standard arguments. It frames the issue in a way that most people have not considered and adds something new to a very familiar debate. This response is more intellectually challenging than the first and is much more likely to persuade someone who does not already hold an anti-abortion position. It is, in other words, a more subtle approach to the same basic argument.

Avoid clichés

A cliché is an argument, a phrase, a slogan, or a catchphrase that has been used so often that it no longer conveys its original thought. Sometimes a cliché is simply an overused comparison, such as "dead as a doornail" or "light as a feather," but arguments can also be clichéd. Consider statements such as "When guns are outlawed, only outlaws will have guns," "If you don't like abortion, don't have one," "Make love not war," or "America—love it or leave it." Whatever the original merits of these sentiments may have been, the arguments have become clichés that can be invoked by people who have never seriously considered the complicated issues that they raise.

In college writing, clichés often take the place of serious contemplation about an issue. Clichés discourage the development of new ideas. They tend to be short and memorable arguments with little support and inflexible conclusions, and they seem (and only seem) to make further thought unnecessary.

Construct a debatable position

For a claim to result in an interesting essay, it must be arguable. Consider, for example, the following claim and think of the essay that it would produce: "War kills innocent people." Most people would immediately agree that a lot of innocent people die in wars. Many people, however, would argue that sometimes war is necessary, even if it is bad. Others would disagree and say that war is always a bad thing, no matter how necessary it may seem. However, the claim that war kills innocent people would not result in an effective essay because it does not take a position that could be reasonably disputed. A better claim might be: "A commitment to pacifism on the part of world leaders is the only way to resolve difficult disputes without bloodshed," or "War is ineffective because it deals with the surface political problems that lead to disputes and not the ultimate problems that cause conflict in the first place."

Consider the implications of an argument

Most arguments have consequences and implications that are not directly stated but that can be clearly understood when read with a subtle, critical eye. When you develop your ideas, keep in mind what unstated assumptions (discussed in chapter 8, p. 564) they rest on and what their consequences might be. For example, if you are writing an essay about responses to poverty and you want to argue that the government should increase welfare to help lift people out of poverty, then you need to consider the implications of such an argument. One unstated assumption would be that people are poor because of their circumstances and not because of their behaviors—such as drug use or irresponsible spending—which cannot be controlled by welfare payments. Consider also the possible consequences of increasing welfare payments. Would more people go on welfare? Where would the additional money come from—higher taxes? Or would it be taken from the budgets for other social services, such as Medicare or Head Start (an early-childhood-development program)? Would it mean decreasing spending on other programs the government funds, like the National Institutes of Health or the National Endowment for the Arts? You need to consider as many aspects like these as possible in your writing. A subtle, persuasive argument addresses both the implications and the consequences of the claim.

This requirement also applies when you analyze or respond to another peron's ideas; an analysis or response that addresses unstated implications of an argument is far more effective than one that does not. Take, for example, Mo Tzu's essay "Against Music" (p. 308). Mo Tzu's stated argument is that music and the pageantry that accompanies it are harmful to society. Rather than focusing on this argument, a deeper reading would analyze the *reason* that Mo Tzu opposed music: music was a luxury that took resources away from society without adding anything to most people's lives. This reasoning has implications for many other things that required or require resources without benefiting the majority of people: past examples include the pyramids of Egypt, the Olympics of ancient Greece, the plays of Shakespeare's Globe Theatre, while present ones include art exhibits, country clubs, and celebrity weddings. A truly subtle analysis of Mo Tzu's argument would account for and examine the implications of his argument that go far beyond what is stated in the text.

Keep going until you have learned something

The reason that most instructors give writing assignments is that they believe, with good reason, that the act of writing can teach you something. If you take an assignment seriously, the experience of creating, developing, and structuring a set of ideas can teach you things that just going to class and reading a textbook cannot.

One way to judge whether you have generated a good idea is to consider seriously whether the idea has changed your outlook. Have you learned something that you did not know, considered something that you never have considered before, changed your opinion about a controversial issue, or learned to look at something in a different way? If you have accomplished any of these things, you most likely have produced a solid, fruitful writing topic.

10

STRUCTURING IDEAS

❧

GOOD IDEAS, EVEN WELL STATED, do not guarantee a good essay. Ideas, no matter how brilliant, must be organized effectively and presented intelligently so they can be understood by a reader. The previous two chapters focused on ways that you interact with both the ideas that you read and the ideas that you generate in response to your reading; both chapters dealt only with you and a text. This chapter will show you how to structure your ideas so that they can be read and appreciated by someone else.

Important structural elements of academic essays include **thesis statements**, **introductions**, **transitions**, and **conclusions**. This chapter will define these elements and offer techniques to help you use them effectively. Understanding these structural conventions will not only help you produce the kinds of essays that many of your instructors want to receive, it will also help you improve both your thinking and your writing.

In many ways, academic essays that adhere strictly to these guidelines are artificial creations rarely found outside the college classroom—and even in college classes, many teachers will expect you to move beyond these traditional academic writing techniques. But much can be said for the traditional thesis statement and the structural apparatus that supports it. Learning to use them properly can help you stay focused on a single idea and marshal evidence to support a claim, which are essential abilities for every kind of writing: academic, creative, or professional.

However, important as they are, mastering these techniques should not be your goal. They are designed simply to help you reach the ultimate goal of communicating your ideas to someone else. As the ancient Zen masters understood, the methods designed to lead people to enlightenment are not the same thing as enlightenment itself. As you progress as a student and a writer, keep your goal of communication separate from the techniques that you use to achieve it. Intelligent, thoughtful communication is more important than slavish devotion to technique, and these guidelines should be followed only to the extent that they help you reach that goal.

THESIS STATEMENTS

WHAT IS A THESIS?

People can mean two different things when they talk about a "thesis." On the one hand, a **thesis** is the basic argument that a particular piece of writing makes—the point that an author wants to get across. Most writers, in most circumstances, want to communicate something to an audience; therefore, most writing has a thesis. On the other hand, when writing instructors use the word "thesis," they are usually referring to a **thesis statement**, a single sentence that summarizes or encapsulates an essay's main argument. Thesis statements of this sort are not required of every kind of writing, nor are they always found in the works of the best professional writers. These writers have learned how to advance a thesis (in the first sense of the word) without creating a single sentence to sum up the argument.

However, composing a thesis statement can be a very useful exercise for developing an argument. It accomplishes several important tasks: 1) it helps you clarify exactly what you are trying to say, which makes the writing process smoother and easier; 2) it serves as a reference point that you can use to eliminate ideas that do not support the main point of the essay; and 3) it tells the reader what kinds of arguments to expect and forecasts what follows.

One common misconception is that a thesis statement should summarize an *essay* rather than an *argument*. The difference is crucial. A thesis statement designed to summarize an essay will usually try to provide a miniature outline and can very quickly become unwieldy. Consider the following example:

There are many differences between Seneca and John Henry Newman: Newman was religious and Seneca was not; Seneca lived in the ancient Roman Empire while Newman lived in Victorian England at a time when it was becoming a modern democracy; and Seneca believed that liberal education was the only good kind of education while Newman believed that both liberal and useful education had their place.

While this sentence may be a good one-sentence summary of a three-to-five-page essay, it does not make a good thesis statement because it does not make an argument. In attempting to summarize everything that the essay says, this sentence does not actually have a point. A better thesis statement would try to summarize less about the essay and more clearly state the major claim:

> Newman's view of liberal education is much less restrictive than Seneca's because the society in which Newman lived required most people to acquire enough useful knowledge to earn a living.

This sentence boils down all of the various ideas in the first example into a single, coherent, focused argument that can serve as the main point that the essay will make.

THE THESIS STATEMENT AS AN ARGUMENT

Any argument must have two elements: a claim and support for that claim. Because a thesis statement is always, at some level, an argument, it should also include these two elements. The following sentences would not make good thesis statements because they contain only a claim and do not support that claim:

> Gandhi had a better understanding of poverty than Malthus.

> True objectivity in science can never be achieved.

> Liberal general education is a good idea.

To turn these claims into arguments, and therefore thesis statements, you would have to add a "because clause" (which may or may not contain the word "because"), or a brief statement of support that gives the rationale for the claim:

> Gandhi's understanding of poverty, which takes into account the spiritual side of human nature, is better than that of Malthus, whose analysis is solely economic.

> True objectivity in science requires something that never can be achieved: the presence of a purely unbiased observer.

> Liberal general education is a good idea because it prepares people for a variety of different careers rather than for a single job.

REFINING YOUR THESIS STATEMENT

When you view the thesis statement as an argument, with both a claim and support for that claim, rather than as a summary, you can use it to test whether your essay's argument works. If the thesis statement is a weak argument, then the chances are very good that the essay is also weak. Keep refining your thesis statement until you are reasonably sure that it is a good argument, and then make sure your essay properly addresses the point of your thesis statement.

Revising a thesis statement is really the same thing as revising the *ideas* in your essay. Here are a few things to keep in mind as you revise a thesis statement:

Present an arguable claim

While this requirement is covered at greater length in the previous chapter (see "Construct a debatable position," p. 576), it is worth repeating that an essay topic—and therefore a thesis statement, which presents the essay topic—needs to be debatable. A thesis statement should present a claim that a reasonable person could disagree with.

Present a single, focused argument

An essay should have a single argument and a focused thesis statement. Unfortunately, the formula for a "five-paragraph essay," the first kind of essay most people learn to write, can often lead to three (or more) separate ideas that are linked together under a common heading. Consider this example:

> Christianity and Islam are similar to each other in their worship of a single God, their belief in a single holy book, and their strong belief in caring for the poor.

While this might appear at first glance to be a workable thesis statement, it actually offers three arguments instead of one—each similarity between Christianity and Islam could be the focus of an entire essay. Consider how this thesis statement could be broken into three more-specific thesis statements:

> Christianity and Islam are similar to each other because both assert the existence of a single, all-powerful deity who stands outside the natural world.

> The most important similarity between Christianity and Islam is that both religions' followers believe that God has spoken to them through a single book rather than through a long tradition of oral narratives.

> The moral codes of Christianity and Islam are nearly identical in that each religion preaches the spiritually destructive nature of material wealth and the importance of taking care of the poor.

Each of these thesis statements could produce an interesting, focused essay, and each would be more effective and interesting than the essay produced by the first example. This kind of streamlining does not mean that an argument cannot have subpoints, or that different paragraphs should not treat different parts of a general assertion. But you have a responsibility as a writer to make very clear how each assertion supports the main thesis.

Make sure your thesis is open enough to allow for further discussion
Consider the following thesis statement:

> Machiavelli's philosophy could never work because he advocates lying and liars always get caught.

A statement such as this would support only a single paragraph or two of argument after the introduction. The problem, of course, is not with the thesis statement but with the ideas in the essay—the author has not thought of enough to say. By considering how to make such a thesis stronger, you can figure out how to improve the quality of your ideas. Consider the following revision:

> While Machiavelli gave valuable advice to the princes and rulers of his own day, the modern notion of the separation of powers makes it unlikely that any leader of a modern democracy could practice these ideas today.

The writer of this thesis has thought more about what he or she wants to say than has the writer of the first thesis. This statement opens up many more possibilities for analysis, discussion, expansion, and examples of the phenomenon that the writer wants to discuss. This thesis, in fact, will serve as the basis for the full sample essay toward the end of this chapter.

Make sure your thesis can be reasonably supported in the assigned essay
While some theses are too focused to allow for further discussion, others are too expansive to be covered in a short essay. For example:

> Lao Tzu's philosophy in the *Tao te Ching* is so comprehensive that it encompasses every important aspect of what it means to be human.

This thesis might be defensible in a five-hundred-page book, but no writer could adequately defend such a sweeping statement in a three-to-five-page essay. Narrowing the thesis to a manageable assertion will vastly improve the essay. In the example above, choosing one aspect of human nature and exploring how it is treated in the *Tao te Ching* creates a much more focused thesis statement, which will lead to a much more manageable and interesting essay:

> In the *Tao te Ching*, Lao Tzu captures an important paradox of human nature: that inaction is often more productive than action.

The most important thing to remember when you are writing your thesis statement is that the claim that you make in it, and the support that you provide for that claim, set the parameters for the rest of your essay. You must be able to tie every assertion that you make in your essay back to the argument that you articulate in your thesis statement.

INTRODUCTIONS

The Introductory Paragraph

The introductory paragraph is where you make your first impression as a writer, and, just as they are in relationships, first impressions in reading are very difficult to overcome. This is why many experienced writers spend as much time on the first paragraph of an essay as they do on the rest of the essay. (The way that introductory paragraphs affect a writer's "ethos," or credibility, is covered in detail in chapter 11, p. 609.)

A good introductory paragraph should do three things:

Introduce the purpose of the essay and any important concepts

If your paper is about Wollstonecraft's and Okakok's views on education, your introduction should briefly introduce Wollstonecraft and Okakok and explain, in very basic terms, their views on education. Your goal in the introduction should not be to begin your argument outright, but to clarify all the concepts that you will use in your argument, so that when you use them in the body of your essay, the reader will be familiar with them.

Capture the reader's interest

The introduction should interest the reader in the rest of the essay. It needs to entice the reader to continue reading and convince him or her that something interesting is going to happen in the rest of the essay, that he or she will be educated or entertained or both. (Strategies for doing this are discussed below.)

Provide a platform for any thesis statement

Many writing instructors advise students to place the thesis statement somewhere in the first paragraph, often at or near the end. A thesis statement does not have to go in the introduction, but, if you do choose (or have been instructed) to place it there, it should flow naturally from the introduction. Even if you do not place your thesis statement there, the introduction needs to lay the groundwork for your essential argument, which is summarized in the thesis statement.

Strategies for Beginning

The strategies below, ways to begin an essay, can help make your introductory paragraph more effective. All the examples are based on the thesis statement on Machiavelli in the previous section (p. 582); the thesis statement is in bold in each example.

Give historical context

An introduction that offers a meaningful discussion of any key concepts can help to orient readers to your argument:

> In the early sixteenth century, a prince had absolute power over his state. When Machiavelli wrote *The Prince* in 1513, therefore, he set out to teach potential leaders how to best utilize the tyrannical power at their disposal. His advice was clear, concise, and very effective for its time; however, much has changed in the past five hundred years. Since the late eighteenth century—when in their new Constitution America's Founding Fathers experimented with a radical idea called the "separation of powers doctrine"—most of the industrialized democracies in the world have adopted some form of power sharing between their executive, legislative, and judicial branches of government. **While Machiavelli gave valuable advice to the princes and rulers of his day, the modern notion of the separation of powers makes it unlikely that any leader of a modern democracy could practice these ideas today.**

Build your introduction around a key definition

Many times, your essay will introduce, or even revolve around, a key definition that actually defines the argument that you are making. In such cases, it is often a good idea to organize your introduction around this definition:

> One of the most innovative features of the American Constitution is the doctrine known as the "separation of powers." According to this doctrine, the various forms of government authority—legislative, executive, and judicial—should never be concentrated in the same hands, and there should be a system of checks and balances to make sure that no single individual or group obtains enough power to exercise control as a dictator. Without the power of a dictatorship, American rulers have had a very difficult time heeding the advice of the Italian philosopher Niccolò Machiavelli, whose political theories are based on the notion of absolute power that he saw as necessary to the smooth running of a state. **While Machiavelli gave valuable advice to the princes and rulers of his day, the modern notion of the separation of powers makes it unlikely that any leader of a modern democracy could practice these ideas today.**

Lead directly into the thesis statement

One of the main purposes of the introduction is to set up the thesis statement. If you keep this in mind as you construct your introductory paragraph, you can often write it in such a way that nearly every sentence in it leads directly into the thesis, thus making for the kind of smooth transition that makes readers feel comfortable moving from your introduction to the body of your paper:

> The absolute power that princes had in Niccolò Machiavelli's time was not entirely a bad thing. In a feudal system of government, a strong ruler with great

power can be a good thing for a country, while a weak ruler can cause devastating problems. However, in a society that is no longer feudal, a leader with dictatorial power is no longer so desirable. When America's Founding Fathers wrote the Constitution, they realized this and included a requirement that federal powers be separated into difference branches of government; since the late eighteenth century, many other nations have adopted similar measures. **While Machiavelli gave valuable advice to the princes and rulers of his day, the modern notion of the separation of powers makes it unlikely that any leader of a modern democracy could practice these ideas today.**

Start with a question or a quote

A good quotation can hook readers into your essay by presenting them with something interesting to read right off the bat. Interesting questions addressed directly to the reader have much the same effect. If used skillfully, such an opening hook can be used as the basis for a very effective introductory paragraph. However, keep in mind that this approach can easily become a cliché; use quotes sparingly in your introduction, and only when they apply directly to your topic.

"Power tends to corrupt," wrote Lord Acton in 1887, "and absolute power corrupts absolutely." Acton's famous maxim is perhaps nowhere better demonstrated than in sixteenth-century Italy, where political power was the ultimate prize in a deadly game that often involved rebellion, assassination, treason, insurrection, and military conquest. When Niccolò Machiavelli wrote *The Prince* in 1513, he set out to tell political rulers exactly how to get the kind of absolute power that Acton warned of. In the America of today, however, people have learned well the lesson that Acton spent much of his life trying to teach. Since the founding of the American democracy, political power has been separated into three different areas—executive, legislative, and judicial—that are never allowed to fall into the same hands. **Thus, while Machiavelli gave valuable advice to the princes and rulers of his day, the modern notion of the separation of powers makes it unlikely that any leader of a modern democracy could practice these ideas today.**

Give a contextualizing example

If you are writing about something that may seem distant or be unfamiliar to your readers, consider starting with an example that might be more familiar. The example can then become a point of reference you can use throughout the paper to help explain more-difficult or distant concepts.

In 1974, Richard Nixon became the first president of the United States to resign from office. While it would be difficult to untangle the complicated web of conspiracy and deceit that brought Nixon to this position, most of the scandals known collectively as Watergate share a single motivation: Nixon wanted more power than the Constitution gave him. Being the chief executive officer of the nation was not enough; he also wanted to control legislation and judicial review and to have the power to gather his own intelligence about political enemies. For much of his career, Nixon was a perfect example of a political Machiavellian. However, in 1974 he became a perfect example of the reason that Machiavelli's approach is no longer valid. **While Machiavelli gave valuable advice to the princes and rulers of his day, the modern notion of the separation of powers makes it unlikely that any leader of a modern democracy could practice these ideas today.**

Avoid clichés

Such formulaic introductory phrases as "Throughout history . . . ," "Since the beginning of time . . . ," and "Webster's Dictionary defines . . . " have been used by so many students, in so many contexts, that they have lost whatever effectiveness they might ever have had as ways to introduce an argument.

TRANSITIONS

One of the most important things you can do to communicate your ideas to a reader is to provide transitions between all of the ideas and support that you use to prove your thesis. An effective transition shows how ideas connect and relate to each other; it also smooths the shift between one idea and another. There are three main kinds of transitions in academic writing:

Transitions within a paragraph.   An effective paragraph is organized logically, so that the information at the beginning of the paragraph leads logically to the information at the end of the paragraph. Each sentence in a paragraph should flow from the previous sentence and lead directly into the following one. Otherwise, readers become confused and alienated from your argument. Consider the following two paragraphs:

The ideas of Confucius have been responsible for one of the most important religions in the world: Confucianism. It would be more accurate to characterize Confucius as an "ethical philosopher" rather than as a "prophet" or a "religious figure." Confucius said nothing about the kinds of issues that religions usually deal with: divine beings, miracles, revelation, and the afterlife. He was concerned with constructing an ethical system that people could use to determine correct behavior in any situation.

The ideas of Confucius have been responsible for one of the most important religions in the world: Confucianism. **However**, Confucius himself said nothing about the kinds of issues that religions usually deal with: divine beings, miracles, revelation, and the afterlife. **Instead**, he was concerned with constructing an ethical system that people could use to determine correct behavior in any situation. It would, **therefore**, be more accurate to characterize Confucius as an "ethical philosopher" rather than as a "prophet" or a "religious figure."

Even though the ideas presented in the two paragraphs are identical, the second paragraph is much easier to read. There are two reasons for this. The first reason is structural: in the first example, the second sentence presents an unfamiliar claim (that Confucius should be considered a philosopher rather than a religious figure) that seems to contradict the claim in the first sentence (that the ideas of Confucius have been responsible for an important world religion). Such abrupt changes of thought tend to take readers by surprise. The second paragraph, by contrast, gives the evidence first and proceeds, step by step, to the conclusion, which, by the end of the paragraph, seems natural, logical, and even inevitable. Arranging ideas in a logical order helps you move smoothly from idea to idea.

The second reason that most readers would prefer the second paragraph is that it uses **transition words** such as "however," "instead," and "therefore" to show how ideas are related to each other within the paragraph. These transition words serve as cues that the reader can use to follow the writer's chain of reasoning and see logical relationships between different assertions. Good transition words should reflect the logical relationship between ideas that you are conveying. Some common transition words and phrases include:

ADDITION	COMPARISON
In addition to	Similarly
Also	In comparison
Furthermore	In the same way
Moreover	Compared to

CAUSATION	CONTRAST
Consequently	In contrast
Because of	By contrast
Thus	However
Therefore	Nevertheless
As a result of	Conversely
Hence	On the one hand
Then	On the other hand
	Instead

Transitions between paragraphs. A well-written paragraph generally centers on a single idea or claim. It is therefore extremely important to demonstrate how the information in one paragraph relates to the information in the next—otherwise, you end up with interchangeable paragraphs that make good points individually but do not add up to a coherent argument.

Transitions to the overall argument. It is not enough simply to show how the ideas in a paragraph relate to ideas in other paragraphs; you must also show how they relate to your overall argument—the argument encapsulated in your thesis statement. Each time you make a new claim, you should demonstrate how this new information relates to the overall thesis of the essay. A transition can link one claim to the thesis statement, and to the next claim.

For an example of the importance of these last two kinds of transitions, read the following sample essay carefully and try to determine how the ideas in it are connected to each other and to the overall thesis statement (which is the same thesis statement that we used when discussing introductions earlier in this chapter).

MACHIAVELLI: IDEAS WHOSE TIME HAS COME . . . AND GONE

In the early sixteenth century, a prince had absolute power over his state. When Machiavelli wrote *The Prince* in 1513, therefore, he set out to teach potential leaders how to best utilize the tyrannical power at their disposal. His advice was clear, concise, and very effective for its time; however, much has changed in the past five hundred years. Since the late eighteenth century—when in their new Constitution America's Founding Fathers experimented with a radical idea called the "separation of powers doctrine"—most of the industrialized democracies in the world have adopted some form of power sharing between their executive, legislative, and judicial branches of government. **While Machiavelli gave valuable advice to the princes and rulers of his own day, the modern notion of the separation of powers makes it unlikely that any leader of a modern democracy could practice these ideas today.**

Machiavelli argues that a leader must constantly prepare for war. While it is certainly true that a modern head of state must be concerned with the defense of the nation, it is no longer the case that he or she alone can make any final decisions about either war or preparation for war. Thus, when George W. Bush decided to send American troops to Iraq, he had to spend weeks lobbying Congress for permission to commit American troops to a foreign engagement and months attempting to raise the money to support them once they were there.

At the heart of Machiavelli's advice is the assumption that a prince is free to tax the people and spend their money as he or she sees fit. While this was true of all princes in Machiavelli's day, it is very rarely the case for leaders today. Executive officers, such as presidents, do not normally have the power to tax people or to spend their money—both of these powers now rest with legislative bodies, such as the House of Representatives and the Senate. During his first term, for example, President Bill Clinton attempted to violate one of Machiavelli's cardinal rules by taxing people heavily in order to finance a generous health care initiative.

Machiavelli's ideas would not work in most countries today. There are, of course, plenty of exceptions to this rule. Many twentieth-century political leaders managed to seize absolute power over their countries—from Hitler, Stalin, and Mussolini in the early part of the century to Pinochet, Mobutu, and Hussein in our time. These leaders have repeatedly shown that absolute power concentrated in a single person is not in the best interests of the state.

If you had trouble seeing the relationships between the main ideas in this paragraph, do not be alarmed. They are very difficult to see, because the essay does not have any transitions in it. It relies on the reader to be able to recognize the connections. The last three paragraphs in this essay are also completely interchangeable. If you were so inclined, you could take a pair of scissors and cut these paragraphs out, replace them in the essay in any order, and neither the flow nor the logic of the essay would suffer.

Now, read the same essay with all the transitions in place. You will notice that the transitions (in bold) account for about a third of the paper's total word count. Also notice that these transitions are not merely afterthoughts that are tacked on to each major idea, but are integral parts of the structure of each paragraph.

MACHIAVELLI: IDEAS WHOSE TIME HAS COME . . . AND GONE

In the early sixteenth century, a prince had absolute power over his state. When Machiavelli wrote *The Prince* in 1513, therefore, he set out to teach potential leaders how to best utilize the tyrannical power at their disposal. His advice was clear, concise, and very effective for its time; however, much has changed in the past five hundred years. Since the late eighteenth century—when in their new Constitution America's Founding Fathers experimented with a radical idea called the "separation of powers doctrine"—most of the industrialized democracies in the world have adopted some form of power sharing between their executive, legislative, and judicial branches of government. **While Machiavelli gave valuable advice to the princes and rulers of his day, the modern notion of the separation of powers makes it unlikely that any leader of a modern democracy could practice these ideas today.**

One of the most important aspects of the separation of powers doctrine is that it eliminates the ability of any president or prime minister to declare or prepare for war without the consent of a legislative body. Machiavelli argues that a leader must constantly prepare for war and study the art of armed conflict. While it is certainly true that a modern head of state must be concerned with the defense of the nation, it is no longer the case that he or she alone can make any final decisions about either war or preparation for war. **In nations that observe the separation of powers principle, both war and peacetime military expenditures have much more to do with budgetary committees than with presidential decrees.** Thus, when George W. Bush decided to send American troops to Iraq, he had to spend weeks lobbying Congress for permission to commit American troops to a foreign engagement and months attempting to raise the money to support them once they were there. **Machiavelli could not have imagined such a division of power in his own day and could hardly have been expected to anticipate it in his advice to princes.**

In addition to preventing leaders from going to war whenever they choose, the separation of powers principle also prevents leaders from taking Machiavelli's advice to avoid lavish expenses and to be content to be considered misers rather than spendthrifts (32–33). At the heart of this advice is the assumption that a prince is free to tax the people and spend their money as he or she sees fit. While this was true of all princes in Machiavelli's day, it is very rarely the case for leaders today. Executive officers, such as presidents, do not normally have the power to tax people or to spend their money—both of these powers now rest with legislative bodies, such as the House of Representatives and the Senate. During his first term, for example, President Bill Clinton attempted to violate one of Machiavelli's cardinal rules by taxing people heavily in order to finance a generous health care initiative. **He was prevented from doing this by a power that Machiavelli could not have understood: a legislative body that had to approve all new expenditures by the government.**

Our experiences with both war and taxation demonstrate that, even though some modern American presidents and European prime ministers have wanted to put Machiavelli's programs into effect, they have rarely had the concentration of power necessary to be completely Machiavellian. There are, of course, plenty of exceptions to this rule. Many twentieth-century political leaders managed to seize absolute power over their countries—from Hitler, Stalin, and Mussolini in the early part of the century to Pinochet, Mobutu, and Hussein in our time. These leaders have repeatedly shown that absolute power concentrated in a single person is not in the best interests of the state, **and their examples have caused countries all over the world to incorporate the separation of powers doctrine into their constitutions. This fact makes Machiavelli's advice increasingly less relevant to our day. Almost all of Machiavelli's advice assumed a leader with absolute power; wherever nations follow the doctrine of the separation of powers, such advice will be of little use to modern politicians.**

These transitions relate the various ideas in the paper both to each other and to the overall thesis of the essay: that Machiavelli's ideas would not work in a modern democracy because the separation of powers doctrine would prevent anyone from having the power that he ascribes to princes. Each paragraph extends this argument into some realm of contemporary politics and then explicitly explains how it relates back to the overall thesis. As a result, the entire essay comes across as a single, coherent argument about the contemporary relevance of Machiavelli's political theory.

CONCLUSIONS

Conclusions are important. They give readers a sense of closure and writers the opportunity to tie together various threads of argument into focused assertions or to demonstrate the significance of the cases that they have made in their essays. Consider the conclusion to the sample essay about Machiavelli (p. 588):

> Our experiences with both war and taxation demonstrate that, even though some modern American presidents and European prime ministers have wanted to put Machiavelli's programs into effect, they have rarely had the concentration of power necessary to be completely Machiavellian. There are, of course, plenty of exceptions to this rule. Many twentieth-century political leaders managed to seize absolute power over their countries—from Hitler, Stalin, and Mussolini in the early part of the century to Pinochet, Mobutu, and Hussein in our time. These leaders have repeatedly shown that absolute power concentrated in a single person is not in the best interests of the state, and their examples have caused countries all over the world to incorporate the separation of powers doctrine into their constitutions. This fact makes Machiavelli's advice increasingly less relevant to our day. Almost all of Machiavelli's advice assumed a leader with absolute power; wherever nations follow the doctrine of the separation of powers, such advice will be of little use to modern politicians.

This conclusion is designed to take the two major topics (war and taxation) and link them together as different manifestations of the same thing: the limitations imposed on national leaders by the separation of powers doctrine, an idea that goes hand in hand with the overall thesis. But it also has a secondary function, which is to anticipate and correct a potential weakness: the fact that not every government in the world today believes in the separation of powers, and that there are still dictators today who have the kind of absolute power that Machiavelli envisioned in *The Prince*. By bringing up some of these dictators, the writer demonstrates that he or she has considered this issue and that it does not disprove his or her thesis.

Though there are many ways to bring your essay to a close, below are a few strategies you can employ, along with examples of alternate conclusions to the sample paper that we have been working with:

Refer back to the introduction

If you started your essay with an introductory quotation, question, or historical situation, you can often return to your introduction as the basis for forming a conclusion. Consider the sample introduction on page 585 that begins with a discussion of Watergate as a way to discuss the separation of powers. Returning to the story of Nixon's resignation would be an excellent way to conclude an essay that began with such an introduction:

> In Machiavelli's society, leaders were often rebelled against, occasionally exiled, and, not infrequently, assassinated. But no Italian prince in the sixteenth century would ever have done what Richard Nixon was forced to do in 1974: resign and leave office because of a Supreme Court decision forcing him to turn over incriminating evidence to a congressional committee. Supreme Courts and congressional committees simply were not part of the world that Machiavelli inhabited. The fact that they have become such an important part of the world today, and that leaders in democratic countries are prevented from achieving the kind of power that Machiavelli assumed that a prince would have, makes it difficult to see his advice as relevant to American society in the twenty-first century.

Demonstrate the implications of your argument

Sometimes, you can reach the end of an essay only to discover that your argument has some major implications that you have not addressed. The conclusion can be a good place to show how the fairly focused argument that you have been making has broader and more general applications to other kinds of questions and arguments:

> Though America was founded with a separation of powers doctrine designed to prevent any individual from achieving the kind of power that Machiavelli attributed to princes, we have recently been in danger of forgetting what our Founding Fathers did. Recent presidents, from Lyndon Johnson to George W. Bush, have committed troops to long foreign engagements without ever receiving a declaration of war from Congress; congressional committees are famous for attaching spending bills to completely unrelated pieces of legislation; and, in 2000, the Supreme Court divided along partisan political lines to give the presidency of the United States to someone who had not been elected by a majority of the people. The writings of Niccolò Machiavelli do more than show us what life was like during a particularly violent period of the Italian Renaissance. They warn us what our lives will be like should we ever allow our leaders the power to act unilaterally and with impunity.

Close with a quotation

Just as a quotation can make a good hook for the beginning of an essay, so a quotation can provide an effective way to tie everything together at the end. Furthermore, a well-chosen quotation from someone that the reader recognizes can provide the sense of closure and completeness that should always characterize a concluding paragraph. Beware, however, of using a lengthy quote—another person's words should not make your argument for you but rather sum up what you have already effectively demonstrated:

> Americans often become annoyed at the inefficiency of our political system. Elections are long and drawn out, debates over important issues are held up by political maneuvering, and the courts, Congress, and the president are forever frustrating each other's plans. The media calls this "gridlock," but scholars of the Constitution call it "checks and balances"—and it is this very inefficiency that prevents rulers from being able to follow Machiavelli's advice completely. It is perhaps this element of democratic inefficiency that Winston Churchill had in mind when he reportedly said that "democracy is the worst form of government in the world with the single exception of all the others."

11

SUPPORTING IDEAS

🍂

THOUGH THE TWO TERMS are often used interchangeably, a claim is not the same thing as an argument. For a claim to become an argument, you need to provide some kind of support. You cannot offer support by simply magnifying the intensity of a claim. The claim that "pornography is extremely disgusting and horribly immoral" offers no more support (that is, no support at all) for its position than the simpler claim that "pornography is disgusting and immoral."

This chapter will show you how to support a claim and thus turn it into an argument. To begin with, you must understand how to provide appropriate evidence to support your claim. You must also understand the different ways that people can be persuaded by arguments. According to Aristotle, the three standard elements of persuasion are **logos (appeals to logic and reasoning)**, **pathos (appeals to emotion)**, and **ethos (appeals based on the speaker's character)**. All three elements often appear in the same text, and this chapter will examine how each can be used to support an argument.

SUPPORTING CLAIMS WITH EVIDENCE

Any time you make a claim, you have a responsibility to support it. Support can come in the form of facts, statistics, authorities, examples, or textual citation. The kind of support that you use depends on the claim that you make: for example, the claim that "affirmative action is not a useful educational policy because it has not increased minority graduation rates" would be best supported by statistical evidence, while the claim that "Mencius and Hsün Tzu held opposing views of human nature" would be best supported by quoting their writings (textual citation). When you think about ways to advance your claim, think about all the possible evidence that you can marshal in support of it.

Facts

Most claims benefit from the support of relevant, well-documented facts. Consider, for example, Charles Darwin's argument in *The Origin of Species*. To support his claim that evolution occurs by means of natural selection, Darwin combines several facts, including Charles Lyell's research showing that the earth is extremely old, Thomas Malthus's calculations about the growth rates of populations, and a summary of existing techniques to breed certain characteristics in livestock and domestic animals. Though these facts do not "prove" Darwin's principles, they create a context in which evolution by natural selection is possible and logical.

Sometimes the facts you need to support your claim are straightforward. A claim that "the benefits of organ donation outweigh any potential risks to the recipient" can be supported by facts about organ donation that are readily available in reference books or on the Web. (For more on finding and evaluating sources, see chapter 13, p. 628.) At times, however, other factors can complicate the level of support facts can offer. For example, different definitions of a key term can produce different perceptions of what is factual. The number of people living in poverty in the United States is much lower for those who define "poverty" as "living on the street" than for those who define it as "not owning a house and two cars." When using facts to support your claim, make sure they relate directly to your claim and are clearly defined.

Statistics

Statistics are facts that consist of numerical data. Statistical data can be harnessed in support of most claims about society, culture, or the collective facts of a given country or region. For these claims in particular, statistical evidence about birthrates, marriages, deaths, inheritances, lawsuits, and other matters of public record—the data of everyday life—can be extremely useful in making a historical argument that goes deeper than one based on political, military, and cultural leaders' documents, which usually do not reflect most people's lives. In arguments about contemporary societies, statistics can be found to support and refute arguments about race, gender, crime rates, education, employment, industry, income, political affiliation, public opinion, and dozens of other areas where collective behavior can be tracked and measured. An excellent source for many of these statistics in the United States is the *Statistical Abstract of the United States*, which is published each year by the Census Bureau and made available, free of charge, at www.census.gov.

Authorities

In areas where facts and statistics are unavailable or inconclusive, evidence can be gathered from those with an acknowledged expertise in the field. Though appealing to authority cannot prove a fact definitively—even experts make mistakes!—it can explain what is possible, what is likely, and what is impossible, all of which are extremely important in supporting claims. In many cultures, certain texts or authorities have such high status that their support will virtually guarantee many people's acceptance of a claim. The Bible, the Quran, the Buddha's teachings, and Confucius's words have all had this kind of authority in the cultures that have been built around them. However, these texts are not generally acceptable as authorities in modern academic arguments.

Examples

Examples drawn from history, fiction, personal experience, or even one's imagination can often be used to support a claim. Examples drawn from historical or current events are especially persuasive, as they add factual support. Consider how Margaret Mead uses examples in "Warfare: An Invention—Not a Biological Necessity" (p. 274). She begins by giving examples of "primitive" people who do not have a concept of organized warfare—the Lepchas and the Eskimos. Then, to illustrate the point that warfare does not come with increased social development, she gives examples of two equally undeveloped people—the Andamans and the Australian aborigines—who fight wars. Each time that she makes a claim about the development of warfare, she provides an example of a culture somewhere in the world that illustrates her point.

Textual Citation

Writing in response to other texts—such as the ones found in this book—often requires you to write interpretively, or to make claims about what texts mean. Interpretive writing requires you to find support for your claim within the source text. For example, if you claim that *The Treasure of the City of Ladies* gives a more accurate view of human nature than *The Prince* becuse it accounts for the human potential to do good, you will need to cite portions of de Pizan's text that refer to this potential. Conventions for documenting textual sources are discussed in depth in chapter 13 (p. 637).

LOGOS: APPEALS TO LOGIC AND REASON

What Aristotle called *logos*, or appealing to logic and reasoning, is an essential part of supporting an argument. While evidence provides the basis of an argument's support, how we apply logic to that evidence—that is, our reasoning—is part of what makes an argument persuasive.

According to classical theories of argument, our minds move in two different directions to reach conclusions. Sometimes, we reach a conclusion by applying a general fact that we know—or belief that we hold—to a specific situation. This is called **deductive reasoning**. Most people know, for example, that milk is more expensive at convenience stores than at grocery stores. When someone decides to save money by buying milk at a grocery store rather than at a convenience store, that person is reasoning deductively.

Inductive reasoning works in the opposite direction. We reason inductively when we use firsthand observations to form general conclusions. Sometimes, the process of induction is simply referred to as "generalizing." If, after buying milk at a certain grocery store three times and finding it spoiled each time, someone decided never to buy milk at that store again, that person would be reasoning inductively.

Most of us do not consciously decide to reason deductively or inductively to solve problems. Rather, we constantly employ both forms of reasoning at the same time. We gather facts and observations until we can use them to form general conclusions (inductive reasoning), and we use those general conclusions to make judgments about specific situations (deductive reasoning). When we do not have a good understanding of how deductive and inductive reasoning work, however, we can be more easily persuaded by arguments that are weak or misleading. This section will explain how both kinds of reasoning can support claims.

DEDUCTIVE REASONING

The basic unit of deductive reasoning is called a **syllogism**, which can be thought of as a kind of mathematical formula that works with words rather than numbers. In its most basic form, a syllogism contains two premises and a conclusion drawn from those premises:

Major premise (dealing with a category): All dogs have four legs.

Minor premise (dealing with an individual): Rover is a dog.

Conclusion: Rover has four legs.

The major premise asserts that all members of a category share a certain characteristic. In the example above, everyone who belongs to the category of "dogs" shares the characteristic of "four legs." However, the characteristic can apply to other categories, too—for example, cats also have four legs. If we were to represent the major premise above graphically, it would look like this:

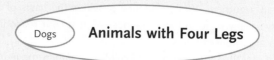

The three simple statements in the syllogism above do not include evidence that Rover is actually a dog; thus, we cannot be sure that the syllogism is true. We can say, though, that *if* all dogs have four legs *and* Rover is a dog, *then* Rover must have four legs. This is because the syllogism is **sound**, meaning that the premises lead infallibly to the conclusion. A syllogism can be completely true yet unsound. It can also be sound yet demonstrably untrue. Consider the following two arguments:

Major premise: Dogs have purple teeth and green fangs.

Minor premise: Rover is a dog.

Conclusion: Rover has purple teeth and green fangs. (Sound but untrue: the major premise is false.)

Major premise: Basketball players are tall.

Minor premise: Shaquille O'Neal is tall.

Conclusion: Shaquille O'Neal is a basketball player. (True but unsound: simply being tall does not make Shaquille O'Neal a basketball player; plenty of tall people are not basketball players.)

To see why the example above that uses basketball players and Shaquille O'Neal is unsound, consider how the major premise would look if represented graphically:

Because the category of "Basketball Players" is contained entirely within the characteristic of "Tall People," it is logical to assert that all basketball players are tall. It is also logical to assert that someone who is not tall cannot be a basketball player. However, since a large part of the circle representing "Tall People" lies outside the category "Basketball Players," it is not logical to assert that someone who is tall is also a basketball player. If we substitute a different name for "Shaquille O'Neal," it becomes clear why the syllogism is unsound:

Major premise: Basketball players are tall.

Minor premise: Barack Obama is tall.

Conclusion: Barack Obama is a basketball player. (Unsound and untrue)

The following syllogism would also be unsound, because it asserts that if an individual is not in the category named in the major premise (basketball players), he must not have the characteristic in the major premise (tallness):

Major premise: Basketball players are tall.

Minor premise: Barack Obama is not a basketball player.

Conclusion: Barack Obama is not tall. (Unsound and untrue)

To turn the original syllogism into a sound one that asserts that an individual fits the category of the major premise and therefore shares its characteristics, we would need to rewrite it like this:

Major premise: Basketball players are tall.

Minor premise: Shaquille O'Neal is a basketball player.

Conclusion: Shaquille O'Neal is tall. (Sound and true)

A sound syllogism can also assert that an individual who does not share the characteristic in the major premise (in this example, tallness) cannot be part of the category named in the major premise (in this example, basketball players):

Major premise: Basketball players are tall.

Minor premise: George Stephanopoulos is not tall.

Conclusion: George Stephanopoulos is not a basketball player. (Sound and true)

Understanding the structure of syllogisms can be helpful in understanding real-world claims. Consider the following hypothetical statement:

When America was attacked, those who sympathized with these attacks and wished our attackers well opposed going to war in Iraq. At the very moment that terrorists were hoping that we would not go to war, Senator Jones gave a speech on the Senate floor opposing the war. It is important that Americans understand that, in these crucial moments, Senator Jones's sympathies lay with the enemy.

Once we eliminate the political hyperbole in this statement, we are left with a fairly straightforward syllogism:

> Major premise: People who support terrorism opposed going to war in Iraq.
>
> Minor premise: Senator Jones opposed going to war in Iraq.
>
> Conclusion: Senator Jones supports terrorism.

Whether or not one considers the premises of this argument to be true, the conclusion is unsound: it states that because the minor premise asserts that an individual shares the characteristic in the major premise (opposing going to war), he must therefore belong to the category in the major premise (people who support terrorism).

When you examine an argument, such as the example above or the ones in this book, think critically about its logic and reasoning. If you were to state the argument in a syllogism, would the syllogism be sound? For example, consider this thesis statement offered earlier in the chapter: "Affirmative action is not a useful educational policy because it has not increased minority graduation rates." Arranged in a syllogism, it would look like this:

> Major premise: Useful educational policies increase graduation rates.
>
> Minor premise: Affirmative action has not increased minority graduation rates.
>
> Conclusion: Affirmative action is not a useful educational policy.

Since the minor premise claims that an individual (in this case, a specific instance of educational policy, affirmative action) does not share the characteristic in the major premise, the conclusion that it does not belong to the category in the major premise is sound—and, therefore, the argument is sound (which does not necessarily make it true). Applying this logic to your own arguments can help you ensure that your arguments are sound.

Inductive Reasoning

Inductive reasoning does not produce the kind of mathematical certainty that deductive reasoning does, but it can produce conclusions with a very high likelihood of being true. We engage in induction when we gather together bits of specific information and use our own knowledge and experience to make an observation about what must be true. Inductive reasoning uses observations and prior experiences, rather than syllogisms, to reach conclusions. Consider the following chains of observations:

Observation: John came to class late this morning.

Observation: John's hair was uncombed.

Prior experience: John is very fussy about his hair.

Conclusion: John overslept.

The reasoning process here is directly opposite to that used in deductive syllogisms. Rather than beginning with a general principle (people who comb their hair wake up on time), the chain of evidence begins with an observation and then combines it with other observations and past experience to arrive at a conclusion.

There are three basic kinds of inductive reasoning: **generalization**, **analogy**, and **statistical inference**.

Generalization

This is the most basic kind of inductive reasoning. You generalize whenever you make a general statement (all salesmen are pushy) based on observations (the last three salesmen who came to my door were pushy). When you use specific observations as the basis of a general conclusion, you are said to be making an **inductive leap**.

Generally speaking, the amount of support needed to justify an inductive leap is based on two things: the **plausibility** of the generalization and the **risk factor** involved in rejecting a generalization.

Implausible inductive leaps require more evidence than plausible ones do. More evidence is required, for example, to support the notion that a strange light in the sky is an invasion force from the planet Xacron than to support the notion that it is a low-flying plane. Since induction requires us to combine what we observe with prior experience, and most of us have more prior experience with low-flying planes than with extraterrestrial invaders, it will take more evidence of an alien invasion force to overcome our prior experience of low-flying planes.

An inductive leap is more easily justified—that is, you can supply less support for it—when rejecting it carries a great risk. Consider the following two arguments:

1. I drank milk last night and got a minor stomachache. I can probably conclude that the milk was a little bit sour, and I should probably not drink that milk again.

2. I ate a mushroom out of my backyard last night, and I went into violent fits of projectile vomiting and had to be rushed to the hospital to have my stomach pumped. I can probably conclude that the mushroom was poisonous, and I should probably not eat mushrooms from my backyard again.

Technically, the evidence for these two arguments is the same. They both generalize from a single instance, and they both reach conclusions that could be accounted for by other factors. However, most people would take the second argument much more seriously, simply because the consequences for not doing so are much more serious.

There are two common errors in generalization: **hasty generalization** and **exclusion**.

Hasty generalization. Inductive fallacies tend to be judgment calls—different people have different opinions about the line between correct and incorrect induction. You commit a hasty generalization, the fallacy most often associated with generalization, when you make an inductive leap that is not based on sufficient information. Another term for this is "jumping to conclusions." Look at the following three statements and try to determine which generalizations are valid and which are hasty.

1. General Widgets is a sexist company. It has over five thousand employees, and not a single one of them is female.
2. General Widgets is a sexist company. My friend Jane, who has a degree in computer science, applied for a job there, and it went to a man who majored in history.
3. General Widgets is a sexist company. My friend Jane applied there, and she didn't get the job.

Because different people can be convinced by different levels of evidence, it can be surprisingly difficult to identify a hasty generalization.

Exclusion. A second fallacy that is often associated with generalization, exclusion occurs when you omit an important piece of evidence from the chain of reasoning that is used as the basis for the conclusion. If I generalize that my milk is bad based on a minor stomachache and fail to take into account the seven hamburgers I ate after drinking the milk, I have excluded the hamburgers from the chain of reasoning and am guilty of exclusion, which can lead to an invalid conclusion.

Analogy
To make an argument using an analogy is to draw a conclusion about one thing based on its similarities to another thing. Consider, for example, the following argument against a hypothetical military action in the Philippines.

In the 1960s, America was drawn into a war in an Asian country, with a terrain largely comprising jungles, against enemies that we could not recognize and accompanied by friends that we could not count on. That war began slowly, by sending a few "advisors" to help survey the situation and offer military advice, and it became the greatest military disgrace that our country has ever known. We all know what happened in Vietnam. Do we really want a repeat performance in the Philippines?

An argument like this is perfectly valid. Analogies are useful in forming conclusions because, while the analogous situation differs somewhat from the situation being considered, they share common characteristics that are relevant to the argument. However, analogies are limited in their ability to prove a claim—that is, to provide clear, indisputable evidence that a claim is true. A well-constructed analogy can illustrate key points (such as the inability of modern militaries to contain rebellions based in jungle terrains), but they do not prove their points simply by being analogies. The most common error found in arguments that use analogies is the **false analogy**.

False analogy. A false analogy may compare two things that could be compared in a valid analogy, but in a false analogy the characteristics considered are irrelevant, inaccurate, or insufficient.

> **A valid analogy:** A war in the Philippines would be disastrous. Our soldiers had a terrible time fighting in the jungles in Vietnam, and the terrain around Manila is even worse.

> **A false analogy:** If we decide to attack the Philippines, we should probably do it in January. In 1991, we attacked Iraq in January, and look how well that turned out.

The first of these statements is a valid analogy: it takes an observation (we had a hard time fighting in the jungles of Vietnam), makes a generalization (it is hard to fight modern warfare in a jungle terrain), and then applies it to another instance (we would have a hard time fighting in the jungles of the Philippines). The second statement, however, is a false analogy; though it goes through the same process, it is based on irrelevant information (the time of year we attacked Iraq).

Statistical inference

We employ this third variety of inductive reasoning whenever we assume that something is true of a population as a whole because it is true of a certain portion of the population. Politicians and corporations spend millions of dollars a year gathering opinions from relatively small groups of people to form bases for statistical inferences, upon which they base most of their major decisions. Inductions based on statistics have proven to be extremely accurate as long as the sample sizes are large enough to avoid large margins of error. Political exit polls, for example, often predict results extremely accurately based on small voter samples, and the Nielsen ratings report the television viewing habits of over a hundred million households based on sample sizes of about a thousand American families. However, using statistical inference carries the risk of using an **unrepresentative sample**.

Unrepresentative sample. This is a statistical group that does not adequately represent the larger group that it is considered a part of. Any sample of opinions in America must take into account the differences in race, age, gender, religion, and geographic location that exist in this country. Thus, a sample of one thousand people chosen to represent all of these factors would tell us a great deal about the opinions of the electorate. A sample of one thousand white, thirty-year-old, Lutheran women from Nebraska would tell us nothing at all about the opinions of the electorate as a whole. Because samples must be representative to be accurate, it is a fallacy to rely on straw polls, informal surveys, and self-selecting questionnaires to gather statistical evidence.

LOGICAL FALLACIES

Rhetoricians have identified hundreds of different ways that reasoning can be used incorrectly. Understanding the most common of these fallacies can help you recognize where reasoning—your own and that of other people—goes astray. In this way, you can make your own writing more persuasive, and you can avoid being deceived by someone whose arguments are not logically sound.

Post hoc ergo propter hoc
The fallacy of *post hoc ergo propter hoc* (Latin, "before the fact therefore because of the fact") is committed whenever someone asserts or implies that because an event occurred before another event, the first event caused the second. This fallacy is often called simply the *post hoc* fallacy, and it is the abuse of reasoning that allows politicians to take credit for everything good that happened while they were in office—and for their opponents to blame them for everything bad that happened.

> Inflation tripled after Jimmy Carter was elected president. His policies must have been inflationary.

> Studies have conclusively proven that 83 percent of people who have died in automobile accidents last year ate ice cream within a month of their accidents. This figure strongly suggests that eating ice cream causes automobile accidents.

Ad hominem
The fallacy of *ad hominem* (Latin, "against the man") is the assertion that someone's argument or viewpoint should be discounted because of character flaws that have nothing to do with the issues at hand. This fallacy should not be confused

with simple name-calling, which is normally not an *ad hominem* fallacy as much as it is simply "being a jerk." Nor should the *ad hominem* fallacy be confused with a legitimate challenge to authority—if someone asserts a point based on his or her own authority, then it is very logical to call that authority into question.

> How can people believe the theory of evolution when it is a well-known fact that Darwin was a deadbeat?

> Rachel Carson's *Silent Spring* is the argument of a bitter woman who had an environmentalist ax to grind. There is no reason to limit DDT use on her account.

Straw man

The straw-man argument is named for a metaphor. The name invokes the image of a fight between a human opponent and a straw dummy dressed to look like a real opponent. When the straw man is knocked down, the human opponent claims victory. A straw-man argument is a summary of an opponent's position that is intentionally weak or easy to refute. By defeating an artificial, constructed version of someone else's argument, a speaker can claim victory, even though he or she has not really dealt with the points at issue.

> Those who want to adopt campus-wide codes against sexist, racist and homophobic speech believe that they can prevent such kinds of speech. As noble an idea as this is, realizing the idea is practically impossible. Prejudice, a basic component of human nature, will not be eliminated with the passage of new rules and laws. Those who would try to limit free speech on campus would curtail a vital part of the American Constitution in the name of a pipe dream.

> The problem with antipornography feminists is that they think sex is bad because men are evil. They tell us that any sexual relationship between a man and a woman will demean the woman and enforce the patriarchal hegemony of the man. This idea ignores the fact that a lot of men really do respect and care for women.

Dicto simpliciter

Dicto simpliciter (Latin, "I speak simply") is the illogical assumption that something that is good in general must therefore be good in a particular instance. Those who commit this fallacy are guilty of uncritically applying a general truism to a particular situation. Another word for *dicto simplicter* is "oversimplification."

> Milk is good for you, so everyone should drink milk.

> Exercise is good, so the college should require a physical education class every semester.

> It is good to date, so you should date me.

Bandwagoning

The fallacy of bandwagoning is the assertion that you should believe something or do something because everybody else believes it or does it. Bandwagoning works because most people have an innate desire to agree with others—we tend to see a kind of emotional security in doing and thinking as other people do and think. This fallacy is sometimes called *ad populum* (Latin, "appeal to the people").

> Don't be the last person on your street to buy a Clippermeister lawnmower—the only lawnmower that tells the neighbors that you care about the neighborhood as much as they do.

> The "pro-life" position is becoming increasingly difficult to maintain. A recent poll suggested that 85 percent of Americans favor some form of abortion.

False dilemma

The false dilemma, or false dichotomy, is a fallacy that presents two issues as if they are the only possible choices in a given situation. The rejection of one choice in such a situation requires the adoption of the second alternative. False dichotomies should be distinguished from true dichotomies. Sometimes, only two choices exist: everything in the world is either a dog or a nondog, but everything is not either a dog or a cat. In most situations, middle grounds or other options make it irresponsible to force a choice between two alternatives.

> If you are not for the war, you are against the troops. I support the war because I support our troops.

> I am pro-choice because to be otherwise would be antiwoman.

PATHOS: APPEALS TO EMOTION

Aristotle called his second element of persuasion *pathos*, or appeals to emotion. Most people are at least as governed by their emotions as they are by reason, and they are even more likely to be motivated to adopt an opinion or course of action when logical appeals are combined with appeals that work on an emotional level. Advertisers and political-message shapers have become extremely good at making these kinds of appeals—often to the point that they exclude logical arguments altogether and appeal only to emotions. They know that emotional appeals work. However, emotional appeals do not have to be manipulative; when used effectively and judiciously, they can help you connect with your reader or illustrate the emotional aspects of an issue.

Below are some of the most common kinds of emotional appeals. All of them can be used in manipulative ways, but they can also all be used in conjunction with other kinds of support to produce extremely compelling and effective arguments.

Sympathy

Most people are moved by the misfortunes of others. When we see victims of injustice, economic hardship, crime, war, or disaster, we sympathize and want to help. Appeals to sympathy or pity tend to be most persuasive when they describe the plights of individuals as well as giving facts, statistics, and an analysis of the large-scale phenomena. For example, in a piece of writing about poverty in less-developed countries, the story of a single child dying of starvation would provide a more effective emotional appeal than would a well-reasoned statistical analysis of childhood death rates in twenty-six nations, but the combination of the two would make for the best argument—it would appeal to both emotion and reason.

Fear

When people do not feel safe, or when they feel that their security (physical or economic) is in jeopardy, they become susceptible to appeals to fear. This is why automakers list safety as a major component of new cars and why politicians foreground their commitment to creating jobs and a healthy economy. An appeal to fear creates a sense of fear in the audience and connects its argument to resolving the fear. In the above example of automakers, emphasizing the safety of their cars both puts forth the possibility of being in an auto accident and offers the reassurance that if you buy one of their cars, you will be safe. Politicians who emphasize their commitment to creating new jobs and a healthy economy tap into fears of financial struggles and simultaneously offer the reassurance that if they are elected, they will put those fears to rest.

Anger

When writers appeal to anger, they frame an issue in a way that angers an audience and then use that anger to reinforce their claim. Usually, this means telling the audience something that they did not previously know and that, once known, elicits anger. For example, a common tactic in political campaigns is to reveal some fact about a politician's background or voting record that makes voters angry enough to vote for his or her opponent, whose campaign sponsored the ad.

Most people are moved to a sense of anger by injustice, unfairness, and cruelty. Making arguments by exposing unfairness can be an effective way to appeal to this sense of anger. Consider, for example, the following argument:

> Shopping at Cheap Stuff is immoral. In order to keep their prices low, they pay subminimum wages with no benefits, and they subject their employees to dangerous working conditions. They have been cited more times than any other corporation for unfair labor practices, and twelve employees during the past year have been killed on the job in unnecessary accidents. Cheap diapers just aren't worth supporting this corporation.

Belonging

Many successful arguments appeal to people's desire to be part of something larger than themselves. An obvious example of this kind of appeal is the appeal to patriotism, or the sense of belonging to a nation. People are often willing to risk their lives for what they believe to be their duty to their country. Appeals to belonging also connect claims to other groups: religious organizations, states, cities, schools, labor unions, fraternities, or other organizations with which people identify.

Successful appeals to belonging create a sense in the reader of being part of a larger group. This approach can be very similar to the fallacy of bandwagoning (p. 606). The difference is that an effective appeal does not offer itself as proof of a claim; it simply frames the argument in a way that creates a sense of belonging in the reader. Consider the following argument against censorship:

> The current efforts to censor language and content in popular music and television programs are fundamentally un-American. This nation was founded on ideas of freedom of speech and expression that were considered heretical in Europe but which became the fabric of the Constitution of the United States of America. This principle was enshrined in the First Amendment and is the reason that America has remained a great nation for two hundred years. Those who censor our entertainers destroy part of what makes America America.

The writer here is making an argument by appealing to the larger concept of "America" to which (we assume) the audience belongs. The appeal is grounded in the audience's desire to be part of this larger entity and the values that it espouses.

Pride/Vanity

Appeals to pride and vanity sometimes take the form of simple flattery, but they also include appeals to people's desire to be attractive, professional, and well-thought-of by their peers. As you might expect, this kind of appeal is common in advertising for clothing and cosmetics, as well as for alcohol and cars.

ETHOS: THE WRITER'S APPEAL

According to Aristotle, the most powerful element of persuasion is neither logos (logic) nor pathos (emotion), but the third element, ethos, which is also the most difficult of the three terms to define. Although the Greek word *ethos* is the root of our word "ethical," "ethos" does not quite mean "persuasion by appeals to ethics." Rather, it refers to the persuasion through the audience's perception of the speaker. At the heart of Aristotle's notion of ethos is the somewhat circular fact that most people are persuaded by arguments that are made by people that they find persuasive.

A writer's or speaker's ethos, then, is composed of everything that makes an audience consider him or her persuasive. You project a persuasive ethos when you communicate to your audience that you are the sort of person who should be believed: intelligent, well-qualified, and assertive, but also kind, moderate, and sympathetic to their points of view. The ethos of a speaker may include things like tone of voice, level of comfort in speaking, and physical attractiveness. The ethos of a writer may be harder to see, but it is no less important.

Reading someone's writing for the first time is like meeting someone new. We come to the text with certain expectations, which can be met, exceeded, or disappointed. In just a few minutes, we form an impression of the writer that, fair or not, colors the rest of our experience with the work and affects how persuaded we are by its argument. Here are a few things to consider as you work to create a good ethos in your writing:

Establish your credibility

In many kinds of writing, you can appropriately introduce yourself to an audience and explain why you are qualified to give the opinions you are about to give. For example, a very persuasive editorial on the problems faced by single mothers might begin with a paragraph such as this:

> Every time I hear some politician talk about the "single mother" problem, I cringe. To them, single motherhood is a problem to be solved; to me, it is a life to be lived. Five years ago, my husband died, leaving me with three daughters—twelve, nine, and four—to raise by myself. We were not rich, and my husband did not have life insurance. Since then, I have always had a job, sometimes two, and have at times paid more than half of my take-home pay in child care. And yes, I have also been on welfare—not because I am lazy or because I want the government to subsidize my "promiscuous lifestyle," but because I had no other way to feed and house my children.

The writer of this piece not only lays the groundwork for an argument about single mothers but also establishes that her own experience has qualified her to give an informed, thoughtful opinion.

Be generous to other points of view

People want to know that you respect them. When you are writing to a general audience—one in which every reader may have a different opinion on a given issue—be careful to avoid dismissing or disrespecting the people you are trying to persuade. Not only are people much more likely to be persuaded by someone who respects them, but writing that exhibits contempt for others often offends even those who share the opinion being expressed. Look at the following two paragraphs and determine which one projects a more persuasive ethos:

Example #1: There is something rotten in this country: fur. Can you imagine anything more inhumane and immoral than killing an animal just to wear its fur as an expensive coat? The prissy rich women and middle-class posers who participate in the fur trade are probably too dumb to realize that they are wearing the remains of a living creature that was killed just to make their pretentious coats fit with this year's fashion trends. If they do know they're contributing to the deaths of innocent animals, then they're just cruel, violent, shallow trend-followers who deserve to rot in jail. I hope that, someday, I'll see a fox wearing one of their sorry hides on its back.

Example #2: Society has come a long way since the days when people had to wear the skins of mammoths and saber-toothed tigers to keep warm during the cold winters. Now, synthetic materials can keep us much warmer than the skin of any animal. However, each year, forty million animals are killed to produce commercial fur. Many of these animals are still caught in the wild using painful traps. Millions of decent people who would never treat an animal with wanton cruelty unknowingly participate in just such cruelty when they buy coats, gloves, and other items of clothing made with animal fur.

In the first example, the writer displays contempt and anger for those who wear fur. In the second example, however, the writer makes a similar argument against wearing fur, but maintains a calm, respectful tone and offers those who do wear fur the benefit of the doubt.

Do not show off
Whatever your topic, it is important to show the reader that you know what you are talking about. Carefully research key concepts and make sure to point out relevant facts. But at the same time, avoid being overbearing. Beating people over the head with big words and unnecessary facts is rarely persuasive. The line between competence and arrogance is a fine one, but no distinction is more important to the construction of a persuasive ethos.

Make only claims that you can support
The best way to ruin a good case is to try to make it sound like a great case. If you have evidence to support the claim that affirmative action has had a minimal impact on minority graduate rates, then say so. Do not say "affirmative action has not helped a single person get through school" or "affirmative action has been completely useless over the last twenty years in regard to minority graduation rates." Sometimes, it can even be effective to understate your case a little bit in your introduction and let the evidence speak for itself, as in the following statement:

In the twenty years that affirmative action programs have been in effect at institutions of higher learning, their actual impact has been difficult to ascertain, but they do not appear to have been a decisive factor in minority graduation rates.

Proofread your writing carefully

When a piece of writing includes shifts in verb tense, sentence fragments, and careless errors in spelling, grammar, and punctuation, readers make certain assumptions about the writer. They assume that he or she is ignorant, careless, and uneducated. These assumptions may not be true, but they are nonetheless part of the ethos that the writer projects. Careful proofreading can eliminate basic grammatical errors that could seriously injure your ability to be persuasive.

ANTICIPATING COUNTERARGUMENTS

As you build support for your claims, try to anticipate the arguments that might be made against them. This will help you eliminate weaknesses in your argument that might prevent people from being persuaded by your claims. It will also demonstrate to your readers that you are aware of and have considered other positions.

To identify a counterargument, imagine that you were given an assignment to rebut your own argument. What weaknesses do you see that could become the basis for a rebuttal essay? If you know somebody else who can read what you have written with an objective eye and rebut it, ask that person to do so. Conducting research can also help you identify the kinds of arguments that have been made or are currently being made against the position that you are taking.

Once you have identified a counterargument, acknowledge it in your essay and respond to it directly. For example, if you are writing an essay about the importance of liberal education, one counterargument might be that colleges should teach useful job skills instead of a broad range of subjects. You could incorporate this into your essay by saying something like this:

> Some people may object to the argument that colleges and universities should focus on liberal education on the grounds that they would better serve students by providing them with the job skills they will need after college. However, there are plenty of ways that someone can learn how to weld or enter data into a spreadsheet—internships, part-time jobs, seminars, classes at a trade or vocational school. There is no other way to get the kind of liberal education that a university provides.

The best way to thwart a counterargument is to qualify your own claims—that is, to eliminate absolute claims from your essay, such as "every student can benefit from courses in philosophy" or "nobody learns everything that they need to know for a job in their undergraduate education." When you make claims such as these, they can be refuted with a single counterexample—for example, "the philosophy course I took never benefited me at all" or "as an undergraduate my sister learned everything she needed to know for her job." It is better to avoid such absolutes and say instead that "most students can benefit from courses in philosophy" or "as undergraduates the overwhelming majority of people do not learn everything they need to know for their jobs."

Finally, do not be afraid to cut out any claim that you cannot support. If you have several strong claims and one or two that are weaker or more difficult to support, cut the weakest claims so that they do not give people reasons to reject your entire argument.

12

SYNTHESIZING IDEAS

WHILE AN ISOLATED IDEA can occur to someone, more-interesting ideas—and, usually, changes in society, science, and scholastic thought—come from connecting several ideas. One name for this kind of connection is "synthesis." As the word *thesis* means a proposition, an argument, or a point of view, **synthesis** means a combination of different arguments, propositions, or points of view. One hallmark of an educated person is the ability to synthesize ideas from multiple sources to form his or her own opinions.

Synthesizing ideas requires you to use all of the skills discussed in other chapters of this guide. You must read and understand multiple sources and be able to summarize them quickly and efficiently; you must discover how to discuss different texts in ways that are meaningful without being clichéd; you must construct a claim—and in many cases a thesis statement—that asserts an interesting, arguable relationship between different ideas; and you must locate the evidence necessary to support that claim. This chapter will discuss some of the most common ways to synthesize ideas: **summarizing multiple sources, comparing and contrasting, finding themes and patterns,** and **synthesizing ideas to form your own argument.**

SUMMARIZING MULTIPLE SOURCES

Writers often need to summarize, as quickly as possible, what others have said before they can present their own thoughts on an issue. Most often, this kind of writing forms part of a response essay or a research essay.

Writing a literature review, or any other summary of multiple texts, is somewhat different from writing a summary of a single text. It simultaneously requires you to tighten your focus and to make connections between different texts. As you summarize multiple texts in your own writing, keep these suggestions in mind:

Be succinct and selective

The more you have to summarize, the less space you can devote to any one source. While a three-page summary of a single text will include quite a bit of detail about the main and supporting arguments, a three-page summary of ten texts can devote only a few sentences to each text. Choose the points that you want to include carefully, and make sure your wording is as concise as possible. Include only those elements of the text that relate to your overall purpose.

Construct a framework that leads to your ideas

Rather than simply stating the main idea of each text, construct a framework in which you can relate the ideas from multiple texts to each other, so that they all lead directly into your main idea. For example, imagine that you have been given an assignment to write your own definition of "human nature" based on the selections in this book by Thomas Hobbes, Ruth Benedict, and Edward O. Wilson. While simply summarizing each of these texts would adequately convey their major points, framing them so that they relate to each other makes the summary much more focused and concise, and allows you to synthesize them to form your own argument.

> Those who study human nature frequently focus on the interaction between human nature and culture, questioning how much our inherent nature forms our culture—and how much our culture can affect our basic nature. For Thomas Hobbes, human beings are inherently selfish and aggressive, but our own self-interest can compel us to form cooperative societies and develop cultures. Edward Wilson, working from a modern Darwinian framework unavailable to Hobbes, makes a very similar argument. According to Wilson, evolution-shaped attributes very similar to those that Hobbes perceived in human nature—such as the desire to mate and the urge to defend territory—determine the way that we interact with others in society, which forms the basis of culture.
>
> Ruth Benedict places a much stronger emphasis on the way that culture shapes human nature, but she also starts out with inherent (and presumably inherited) human characteristics. Like Hobbes and Wilson, Benedict believes that human beings across cultures have the same set of inherent traits. Unlike

the other two, however, Benedict focuses on the differences among human beings. According to Benedict, human beings in all cultures are born with the same spectrum of characteristics, but those characteristics are encouraged or discouraged to different extents by the cultures in which people live. This view is perfectly compatible with the views of both Hobbes and Wilson; it simply emphasizes the other half of the nature/culture equation.

The framework for this discussion revolves around a single question: how does each author view the interaction between human nature and culture? Once this question has been answered by the three authors whose works are summarized, the writer is free to propose his or her own answer to the question, thus synthesizing the ideas in the summary portion.

COMPARING AND CONTRASTING

One of the most common assignments in college courses is to compare or contrast different texts, concepts, or phenomena. (The format of this assignment is discussed in chapter 8, p. 558.) Technically, to *compare* things means to discuss how they are similar, while to *contrast* things means to show how they are different. However, in general usage, the term "compare" can be used for either operation. Though comparison/contrast assignments can cover almost any two things that have only the most general characteristics in common (Los Angeles and New York; Tom Cruise and Russell Crowe; ice cream and zucchini, etc.), most such assignments in college writing classes will be to compare or contrast different texts.

A comparison/contrast assignment involving texts (including visual texts such as paintings or photographs) requires you to make connections between two or more opinions, arguments, theories, or sets of facts. A good comparison/contrast essay, however, does more than just list similarities and differences—when done well, it can become a vehicle for generating a unique and creative synthesis of different ideas.

As with any writing assignment, the key to good comparison and contrast essays is to generate an interesting, subtle topic to write about. Look beyond surface similarities or differences and try to invent, rather than simply discover, a compelling basis for viewing two (or more) texts in relation to each other. Here are a few suggestions to keep in mind:

Choose a single point for comparison
Consider the following thesis statement:

Plato and Machiavelli are very different in their nationalities and their cultures; however, they are similar in the way that they present their ideas, in the emphasis that both place on knowledge, and in their belief that certain people are superior to others.

This kind of listing is appropriate for prewriting, but it lacks the focus and organization necessary for a good essay. Instead of simply listing similarities and differences, you need to create a framework in which the comparison makes sense. Doing so will often mean choosing a single area of similarity or difference and focusing entirely on that area, as in the following revision of the above statement:

> The crucial difference between Plato and Machiavelli is that Plato sees ultimate truth as existing beyond the material world while Machiavelli believes that material reality is the only truth that matters.

This framework, of course, cannot account for all the differences between Plato and Machiavelli, but it does not have to. A comparison/contrast paper does not need to be exhaustive nearly as much as it needs to be focused. By looking only at Plato's and Machiavelli's views of material reality, you will be able to develop a significant, interesting approach to reading the two texts together.

Do not try to compare everything

Any two things can be compared or contrasted in hundreds of different ways, most of which will not be relevant to your main point. Stick closely to the focus of that essay and be ruthless in cutting out details that do not support your primary claim.

Avoid stating the obvious

Many comparison/contrast assignments deal with pairs of things whose surface similarities or differences are easy to see. When this is the case, consider working against the obvious. Look for ways that clearly similar things are different or that clearly different things are the same. An apple is different from a monster truck, for example, in many ways—so many, in fact, that there is little value in pointing them out. If you can come up with a compelling argument, though, about how an apple is *like* a monster truck (perhaps that they have both become much bigger than they need to be to fulfill their natural functions), you will have a very interesting essay indeed.

The same principle applies when you are comparing ideas. Imagine that you have been asked to compare or contrast a pair of essays whose main points obviously contradict—such as Mencius's chapter on the inherent goodness of human nature and Hsün Tzu's rebuttal essay, "Man's Nature Is Evil." The essays clearly oppose each other, but they also share a number of assumptions about what kinds of behavior constitute "good" and "evil." Finding those assumptions and making them the basis of a comparison paper will be much more interesting than simply repeating the obvious fact that Mencius thought that people were good, while Hsün Tzu thought that they were bad.

Compare underlying assumptions

Beneath every claim is an assumption, a presumption that makes it possible for a claim to be true. The claim that "higher education is a good thing because it helps people get good jobs and earn more money throughout their lives" can be true only if earning more money is a good thing; it is the unstated assumption beneath the claim. (See chapter 8, p. 564, for more on this.) The most obvious—and therefore the least subtle—connections between two works will usually be found in what the authors explicitly state. More-sophisticated connections can be found in the underlying principles and premises that are necessary for an argument to make sense.

For example, consider this comparison, based on an underlying assumption shared by Plato's "Speech of Aristophanes" and David Suzuki's "The Sacred Balance":

> On the surface, David Suzuki's environmentalist essay "The Sacred Balance" seems to have little to do with Plato's tongue-in-cheek discourse on love, "The Speech of Aristophanes." While Suzuki argues for a renewed commitment to the earth and its ecological systems, Plato creates a metaphor for romantic attraction. Underneath these arguments, however, lies a shared view of human nature as limited, fractured, and in need of completion. Plato believes that we feel that something is missing because the other half of our true self has been missing since birth, and we must find it in another person in order to be complete. Suzuki, on the other hand, believes that the sense of emptiness we feel comes from our alienation from nature. Though Suzuki and Plato find different reasons for it, they both believe that humanity is incomplete, missing something crucial to its happiness.

Neither Plato nor Suzuki attempts to prove that people are incomplete; this assumption lies behind the arguments that both make. Keep in mind that an underlying assumption may not be referred to in a text. It is not a major point of an argument, but it is the underlying value or idea that makes the argument possible.

FINDING THEMES AND PATTERNS

Some ideas—particularly those featured in this book, such as the role of law and government and the essence of human nature—have been explored throughout history in societies that otherwise have little in common. Showing how these ideas influence one another and how they appear in different societies and different contexts throughout history can help you synthesize multiple arguments.

Show how ideas interact
One very important way to synthesize arguments is to demonstrate how ideas interact with each other. Ideas can influence other ideas in a number of different ways:

- One idea can be based directly on another idea. For example, Gertrude Buck's critique of sophistic rhetoric in "The Present Status of Rhetorical Theory" is drawn directly from Plato's critique of the Sophists in the *Gorgias*.

- An idea can be based indirectly on another idea. Garrett Hardin's "Lifeboat Ethics," for instance, draws much of its inspiration from Thomas Malthus's *Essay on the Principle of Population*.

- An idea can be influenced by a combination of other ideas. For example, Charles Darwin's *The Origin of Species* was influenced by Charles Lyell's *Principles of Geology*, which established that the earth was much older than people had previously thought, and Thomas Malthus's *Essay on the Principle of Population*, which showed how the competition for resources changed certain aspects of human society.

- An idea can be based on a general perception created by another influential text. For example, Edward Wilson's argument in "The Fitness of Human Nature" draws largely on the framework for understanding nature created by Charles Darwin.

- An idea can synthesize a number of other ideas. For example, Martin Luther King Jr.'s "Letter from Birmingham City Jail" cites the work of, among others, Jesus, Gandhi, Henry David Thoreau, and Thomas Aquinas.

- One idea can apply another idea to a new situation. For example, Matthieu Ricard's arguments in "The Universe in a Grain of Sand" apply the principles of Buddhism to the theory of quantum mechanics.

- An idea can be formulated as a rebuttal to another idea. For example, Hsün Tzu's "Man's Nature Is Evil" was written in direct rebuttal to Mencius's views in "Man's Nature Is Good."

- An idea can be formulated in general opposition to another system of thought. For example, George Orwell's "Pacifism and the War" opposes the entire ethical position of pacifism.

To demonstrate a pattern of influence among two or more texts, you must first establish that such influence is theoretically possible. You do not have to prove that one author knew another author's work directly. People can be very influenced by ideas whose sources they do not know. However, no idea has been universally influential at every moment in history. It would be difficult to assert, for example, that Plato was influenced by the Buddha's teachings, which were written down thousands of miles away in a culture that had no known contact with Plato's Athens. And it would be impossible to argue persuasively that Plato was influenced by the ideas of Paulo Friere, who lived and wrote more than two thousand years after Plato died.

Once the possibility of influence has been established, the case for influence must be made through very close readings of the relevant texts. Consider an assignment to explore the possible influences of Taoism on Sun Tzu's military theories in *The Art of War*. For the most part, Sun Tzu's ideas could not be further removed from Lao Tzu's. Lao Tzu was a pacifist who abhorred war and believed that it is wrong to try to force people to do anything. Sun Tzu was a military commander who believed that, with the right tools, it is always possible to impose one's will on another. However, both texts came out of China's Period of Warring States, and Lao Tzu's *Tao te Ching* is unquestionably the older of the two works. Under these circumstances, it is entirely possible that Sun Tzu's work was influenced by the *Tao te Ching*.

However, though this influence is possible, the fact that Sun Tzu does not directly quote or refer to Lao Tzu means that the case for influence must be made through close reading. To create a persuasive case for influence, begin by listing each text's main points:

TAO TE CHING	THE ART OF WAR
—Exertion is unnecessary.	**—The best way to win a battle is not to fight it.**
—Leaders should allow things to happen naturally.	
—Distinctions between people are counterproductive.	—An enemy should be taken intact, without destroying cities.
—Genuine power is achieved by allowing others to come to you.	—Understanding military strategy is important.
—The best way to govern people is not to govern them.	—Politicians should not interfere with generals.
—It is impossible to influence the course of events.	—Harmonious human relations are important to victory.
—War is senseless.	—Commanders should know themselves.
—Leaders should always follow "the Way."	—Commanders should know their enemies.

Lurking amid all of the different assertions in these two texts is one undeniable similarity: Sun Tzu, like Lao Tzu, believes that winning through inaction (that is, never having to fight) is superior to winning through action (that is, superior numbers or strategies). Given the prevalence of Taoist ideas during the time in which Sun Tzu wrote, this similarity is not likely coincidental; it is, rather, strong evidence of a pattern of influence.

Locate a larger theme

Another way to synthesize ideas is to show how a text fits into a larger theme, or "big idea." Many of the selections in this book attest to the fact that human beings struggling with similar questions often come up with similar—or at least partially similar—answers. Cultures and individuals with no connections to each other have arrived at strikingly similar responses to questions such as "Is human nature good or evil?", "Is war ever justified?", and "Do we have a responsibility to those less fortunate than ourselves?"

To see how individual ideas fit into larger themes or patterns, consider the following six images, all of which appear in this book:

- Dorothea Lange: *Migrant Mother* (p. 341)

- Igbo Mother and Child (p. 129)

- Pablo Picasso: *Guernica* (p. 271)

- William Hogarth: *Gin Lane* (p. 320)

- Joseph Wright of Derby: *An Experiment on a Bird in the Air Pump* (p. 402)

- Ad for Chinese Population Policy (p. 516)

The relationship between the first two works is easy to see: both consist almost entirely of a mother holding a child. Interestingly, though, each of the other four paintings also features a mother holding a child—though in extremely different circumstances. The following chart attempts to describe the mother-and-child theme of each work as it relates to the work's larger theme.

Work	Description of Mother-and-Child Scene	Overall Theme
Dorothea Lange: *Migrant Mother*	The mother holds a baby to her breast, shelters it from the camera and the squalor of the lean-to.	The determination of a mother to protect her children
Igbo Mother and Child	A contented mother nurses an infant; the mother's crown symbolizes strength and vitality.	The power of motherhood
Pablo Picasso: *Guernica*	An anguished mother holds the twisted body of a dead child.	The anguish of war
William Hogarth: *Gin Lane*	A drunken mother reaches for a dip of snuff while her infant child falls to its death.	The negative consequences of alcoholism

Joseph Wright of Derby: *An Experiment on a Bird in the Air Pump*	A terrified mother turns away from the experiment while holding her daughter, who looks on with a mix of terror and curiosity.	The mixed reaction to scientific progress during the Enlightenment
Ad for Chinese Population Policy	A happy, prosperous mother holds up an equally happy, prosperous child.	The happiness and prosperity produced by having only one child

As this chart shows, the connection between the works goes beyond simply the existence of a mother-and-child pair: in each case the relationship between the mother and the child reflects the argument of the overall work. In the painting about anguish, the mother is in anguish over the child; in the painting about alcoholism, the mother's alcoholism causes the child's death. A connection of this kind could lead to a very strong synthesis essay that could go beyond the six works here and draw conclusions about the overall theme of mothers and children in art. The introduction to such an essay might look like this:

MOTHERS AND CHILDREN IN ART

The bond between a mother and her children goes deeper than the patterns of any particular culture; the mother-child bond has a sound basis in evolution and forms one of the few truly universal elements of the human experience. For this reason, strong connections between mothers and children can be found in almost every human society, and depictions of mothers and children can be found in almost every kind of art. This does not mean, however, that the depictions are all the same. Different cultures value different things at different times, and artistic production usually follows along. However, because the connection between mothers and children is universally strong in human societies, artists from a variety of cultures have been able to use this connection as the basis for a variety of different arguments about the human condition.

SYNTHESIZING IDEAS TO FORM YOUR OWN ARGUMENT

One mark of an educated person is the ability to form ideas that draw upon other sources but that are neither slavish imitations of, nor uncritical reactions to, other people's opinions. This synthesis process lies at the very heart of critical analysis. Simply put, "synthesizing ideas to form your own argument" is the same thing as "thinking."

Synthesizing Ideas: A Model from Classical Rhetoric

When you encounter a new idea, you need not accept it as absolute truth *or* reject it out of hand. More-subtle, more-creative approaches exist between these two extremes. In their discussions of invention, ancient rhetoricians identified five different ways that an idea can affect a reader or a listener. One reaction from a reader or a listener is absolute and uncritical agreement, while another is complete disagreement. But, ancient rhetoricians recognized, most reactions fall somewhere in between. The other three cases, explored below, illustrate how your reaction to an idea can lead you to synthesize ideas to form your own.

You can simply become informed about an issue

Often, the process of coming up with your own idea requires nothing more than the knowledge that an issue exists and an understanding of the arguments that comprise it. Once you understand how an issue has been defined, you can apply your own experience to make informed judgments about it. It is often valuable to read other people's ideas simply to become informed about the issues that they discuss.

If, for example, you are one of the billions of people who do not understand much about quantum mechanics, you might not even be aware of the century-long debate about whether or not subatomic particles follow the normal laws of physics. A dialogue such as the one between Matthieu Ricard and Trinh Xuan Thuan in "The Universe in a Grain of Sand" is probably not going to convince anyone one way or another about this issue. However, it is enough to alert people without a scientific background to the existence of the issue and thereby pave the way for future discussions and arguments.

You can become convinced that an issue is important

Very often, people recognize an issue without really understanding its importance or its consequences. This was the case in 1798 when Thomas Malthus wrote *An Essay on the Principle of Population*. People at the time understood that populations were increasing, but they saw this as a good thing because it increased available labor and kept the price of goods down. Malthus, however, demonstrated with compelling arguments that increases in population would eventually outstrip increases in food supply and cause serious catastrophes for societies that did not control their growth rates.

Malthus's arguments awakened people to the dangers of unchecked population growth and opened a door for people to generate their own ideas about how best to deal with the problem. As it turns out, most modern thinkers who label themselves "Malthusian" advocate solutions to the problem of overpopulation that Malthus rejected—they have taken his ideas and synthesized them with other facts, policies, and values to create their own ideas. Malthus was a devout Anglican minister who believed that contraception was a sin and abortion an unspeakable evil. These beliefs, however, have not stopped Malthus's ideas from becoming the cornerstone of modern arguments favoring wide distribution of birth control and universal access to abortion. Those who hold such views are not being inconsistent; they are simply synthesizing Malthus's ideas about the importance of a problem with their own opinions of how best to solve it.

You can agree with only some points of an argument

Though writers often present their ideas as all-or-nothing propositions, you do not have to accept them as such. Most arguments are composed of different elements that often can be separated from each other and accepted on their own. It is perfectly valid, and occasionally quite sophisticated, to reject some elements of an argument and accept others as you work toward your own idea synthesis.

Look, for example, at the twelve qualities of the ideal ruler presented in al-Farabi's "Perfect Associations and Perfect Rulers":

1. freedom from physical defect
2. a good understanding of what people say
3. a good memory
4. intelligence
5. speaking ability
6. a fondness for learning
7. a fondness for truth
8. sexual restraint
9. a proud spirit and a fondness for honor
10. a lack of interest in worldly goods
11. a fondness for justice
12. strength of mind

Some of these, such as a fondness for truth and a fondness for justice, most people today would agree are requirements for a good ruler. Others, such as freedom from physical defect, would probably strike most people as unfair and irrelevant. Most of the rest of the items could be (and have been) subject to a great deal of debate by contemporary societies trying to identify the best potential leaders. Though al-Farabi saw these principles as part of the same ideology, most people today have embraced some of them and rejected others. You can do the same with any argument or idea, resulting in a synthesis that is both based on the ideas of others and yet uniquely your own.

Synthesizing Ideas: A Model from Philosophy

In the early part of the nineteenth century, the German philosopher Georg Wilhelm Friedrich Hegel (1770–1831) developed a system for synthesizing ideas that has become known as "Hegelian dialectic." Hegelian dialectic involves three steps, known to Hegel's students as the **thesis**, the **antithesis**, and the **synthesis**. In Hegel's sense of the word, a thesis is a proposition, an antithesis is an opposite proposition, and a synthesis is a third proposition that resolves the apparent contradiction between the two. Here is an example using the works of Mencius and Hsün Tzu that were discussed earlier in this chapter:

THESIS: Human nature is inherently good (Mencius).

ANTITHESIS: Human nature is inherently evil (Hsün Tzu).

SYNTHESIS: *Neither inherently good nor inherently evil, human nature is inherently self-interested, which can be "good" in some circumstances and "evil" in others.*

In the Hegelian model, the interplay between opposites, which is referred to as a "dialectic," occurs constantly, with each synthesis becoming a new thesis that provokes an antithesis and requires a new synthesis. For example, the "synthesis" statement above can become a new thesis:

THESIS: Human nature is self-interested.

ANTITHESIS: Human nature is altruistic.

SYNTHESIS: *There is no real opposition between selfishness and altruism, since human beings often perceive their own self-interest in helping others in their family and their society.*

And, of course, this synthesis can produce yet another trio of arguments:

THESIS: People help others because they perceive it to be in their own best interest.

ANTITHESIS: People often act altruistically when there is no hope of self-interest, as when soldiers sacrifice their lives to save others.

SYNTHESIS: *Even acts of suicidal altruism can be based on a form of self-interest, as when people who sacrifice their lives to help others derive pleasure from the knowledge that they are doing so.*

At this point, the exercise of resolving antitheses has led us to formulate an idea that is solidly based on the ideas of Mencius and Hsün Tzu without duplicating either of their opinions exactly. Any of the three "synthesis" propositions in this exercise could be refined to make an original and creative thesis. Taken together, they form the basis for the following sample paper, which also draws on ideas from Ruth Benedict and Thomas Hobbes to achieve a synthesis that does not completely accept or reject any of its source materials.

HUMAN NATURE, MORALITY, AND ALTRUISM: ARE PEOPLE GOOD, OR WHAT?

As Confucianism became more and more influential in ancient China, even the major Confucians could not agree on one key issue: is human nature essentially good or essentially evil? Mencius, the most influential Confucian besides Confucius himself, weighed in strongly on the side of inherent human virtue. His fellow Confucian, Hsün Tzu, believed the opposite—he felt that people are inherently evil. Though this same debate has been replicated in most of the great religions and philosophies of the world, the terms that it incorporates are problematic. *Human nature can be neither inherently good nor inherently evil, since "good" and "evil" are constructed differently by different cultures.*

In "The Individual and the Pattern of Culture," Ruth Benedict explains how different behaviors can be seen in different moral lights by different cultures. Eating a relative's dead body would be seen as a horribly evil act by someone in New York. Not eating a relative's dead body, on the other hand, would be seen as an unforgivable moral lapse in some parts of New Guinea. With these variations in what constitutes good and evil, it is impossible to ascribe either character trait to humanity in the abstract. The most that can be said is that human beings are inherently disposed or inherently not disposed to act according to the dictates of their home cultures.

One could argue with much more conviction, however, that human beings are inherently self-interested. In certain states, such as the Hobbesian "state of nature," this self-interest leads to a state of "war of all against all." However, Hobbes also states that human beings, recognizing their self-interest, come together and form societies and act—often altruistically—to preserve those societies. When this is the case, self-interest is at the heart of behavior that both Mencius and Hsün Tzu would undoubtedly have seen as "good." *There is, therefore, no real opposition between selfishness and altruism, since human beings often perceive their own self-interest in helping others in their family and their society.*

Yet there are some occasions—especially in times of war, plague, famine, or great oppression—in which people act altruistically when there is no possibility of this act working in their own favor. A young marine throwing himself on a hand grenade to save his companions, a mother giving the last bit of food to her family and starving to death, a political dissident taking on a totalitarian regime knowing that it will mean death—actions of these sorts can be documented in cultures throughout the world, and yet they do not seem to be accounted for by a theory of human nature as inherently selfish.

However, *even acts of suicidal altruism can be based on a form of self-interest, as when people who sacrifice their lives to help others derive pleasure from the knowledge that they are doing so.* Nothing is wrong with such a feeling. It would be foolish to suggest that people who derived pleasure in helping others were acting "selfishly" in the normal, pejorative sense of the word. It is reasonable, however, to assume that they would not act in this way unless they derived satisfaction from doing so—and satisfaction, even when earned through acts of great self-sacrifice, is "selfish" in the broadest sense of the word.

To return to the debate between Mencius and Hsün Tzu, it is fair to say that the two great Chinese thinkers used the terms "good" and "evil" when they really meant "selfish" and "unselfish." A close examination of human societies, however, supports the argument that no ironclad distinction exists between selfish and unselfish action, since both are, in some way or another, in the perceived self-interest of the people who act. The most that can be said about the "inherent" properties of human nature is that human nature is inherently self-interested—and that this is not necessarily a bad thing.

13

INCORPORATING IDEAS

❧

SINCE IDEAS BUILD on other ideas, writing *about* ideas often involves quoting, summarizing, paraphrasing, or otherwise referring to others' work. Such interconnection reflects thinking's collaborative nature which has always been at the heart of ideas that matter. Citing—that is, referring to—other people's ideas effectively and responsibly means observing certain rhetorical conventions and ethical standards. This chapter offers guidance on citing others' ideas, from **finding sources** to **evaluating sources,** from **quoting, paraphrasing, and summarizing** to **documenting sources.**

FINDING SOURCES

In recent years, the Internet has dramatically changed the way that research is conducted. With a few keystrokes, anyone can now find information that would have taken weeks, if not months, to locate before the advent of the World Wide Web. Thanks to the Web, people around the world now have instant access to research tools once available only to students at elite research institutions, such as specialized academic journals, large databases, census records, full-text books, and libraries' special collections.

As a writer, you need to know how to use the Web, but you cannot rely on it entirely. The Web is a good place for many kinds of research, but it is not the best place for *all* kinds of research. Many books and journals are available only in print, and many old and rare books—which are excellent primary sources—are still available only in special collections and rare-book rooms. Listed below are some of the research tools available to you.

LIBRARY SOURCES

Reference books

Most college libraries contain substantial reference sections, where you can find not only general works, such as encyclopedias, dictionaries, and almanacs, but also very specific reference works on most academic disciplines, such as the *Encyclopedia of American Politics*, the *Dictionary of Comparative Pathology and Experimental Biology*, or the *Encyclopedia of World Literature in the Twentieth Century*. Sources like these organize the major concepts and problems of the disciplines they cover and usually point toward other sources that you can use to get a deeper understanding of many relevant issues.

Library catalogs

Almost all college libraries now have their entire holdings indexed in electronic databases that can be searched with keywords relating to author, title, subject, and several other criteria. These databases allow you to find specific books and journals almost instantly and to browse through library holdings, including rare books and special collections.

Interlibrary loan

Most academic libraries will let you request books, articles, and other sources from other libraries through a procedure known as interlibrary loan. As the name indicates, an interlibrary loan allows you to have resources from another library collection delivered to your college library.

Electronic databases

Electronic databases such as *FirstSearch, EBSCOhost,* and *LexisNexis* package together the complete texts of thousands of newspapers, magazines, books, and journals and make them available to libraries on a subscription basis. The content of these databases can be accessed only by students and faculty at subscriber institutions.

Periodical indexes

Unlike databases, indexes do not offer the full texts of articles; instead, they offer lists of articles. Many fields have extensive indexes that list, in a searchable format, the thousands of articles published each year in specialized academic journals. A few of these indexes are the *MLA International Bibliography,* the *Social Sciences Index,* the *Humanities Index,* and the *General Science Index.* Periodical indexes are usually published in both print and electronic formats for the libraries that subscribe to them.

WEB SOURCES

Search engines

The hundreds of millions of pages of information on the Web can be searched through search engines such as Google, AltaVista, and Yahoo. Each search engine uses different strategies to find, rank, and display information, so try several ones when conducting a search. You can also use "meta" search engines such as Infocom and Dogpile to query several search engines at once. Google also offers several specialty search pages such as Google Scholar (http://scholar.google.com), for full-text academic articles, and Google News (http://news.google.com), which searches online news stories.

Dynamic databases

Not all information can be found through standard search engines. Some high-level research is stored on the Web in dynamic databases that create Web pages spontaneously when users enter queries. Such databases can be an excellent source for public archives, library holdings, business records, and some government documents. The Complete Planet (http://aip.completeplanet.com) is a search engine that specializes in these dynamic databases.

Government documents

The U.S. government makes hundreds of thousands of pages of data available on the Web every year. Useful government documents include the CIA's *World Fact Book,* which gives key data on nearly every country in the world, the Bureau of Labor Statistics' *Occupational Outlook Handbook,* which describes thousands of careers and forecasts the outlook for employment, and the U.S. Census Bureau's

Statistical Abstract of the United States (see p. 596), which reports statistics on nearly every aspect of American life. The Government Printing Office maintains a general catalog of its online publications at http://catalog.gpo.gov/F, and they can also be searched through Google's special "Uncle Sam" search page at www.google.com/ig/usgov.

EVALUATING SOURCES

The huge amount of material available on the World Wide Web comes with a price. Just as we have access to much more good information now than we did twenty years ago, we have access to even more bad information. The publication process at one time acted as a gateway (albeit an imperfect one) that prevented large amounts of useless information from being distributed widely. Most college and university libraries employed even-more-stringent safeguards against bad information by carefully selecting the materials they added to their collections. When students conducted research in these libraries, they could feel a certain amount of confidence that the materials they found had been vetted by agents, editors, publishers, bibliographers, librarians, and faculty members to enforce certain minimum standards of accuracy, integrity, and consistency.

As more and more academic research is done on the Web, these safeguards have begun to disappear. In many ways, this new freedom is a good thing, since it means that your access to information is no longer constrained by somebody else's definition of what is appropriate. But it also means that you cannot rely on other people to evaluate the information that you find. The responsibility for this evaluation now belongs almost entirely to you.

A Web site maintained by Dr. Tom Way of Villanova University offers an example of how online sources can be untrustworthy. The site, www.dhmo.org, appears to be an environmental action Web site devoted to alerting people to the dangers of dihydrogen monoxide (DHMO), a hazardous chemical, responsible for thousands of deaths every year, that the government has declared safe for industrial and even residential use. When it first appeared, the DHMO Web site caused a stir among some environmental and civic groups, several of which passed resolutions condemning the chemical's use—even though, as anyone with a background in chemistry knows, dihydrogen monoxide is simply the chemical name for water (H_2O). These environmental and civic organizations were taken in by the professional appearance of the DHMO Web site, to the extent that they neglected to think critically about the information it presented.

All external sources—not just those that you find on the Web—should be evaluated critically and rigorously. You are responsible for any information that you cite. If it is false or misleading, you will bear the consequences of including it in your work. Here are a few suggestions that you should keep in mind when you are finding and evaluating sources for inclusion in an essay.

Never rely on just one kind of source

The World Wide Web is a tremendous source for excellent research material, but it is not the only source, nor does it contain valuable material on every topic. Academic libraries still spend millions of dollars a year on print-based materials, such as books and journals, that contain valuable information not available anywhere else. At the same time, some research information is available only on the Web, and the sheer number of documents available there make it an essential resource. A good research strategy for most topics will include information in books, journals, electronic databases, Web archives, and publicly accessible Web sites. Good research means going wherever there is good information to be found.

Start with material that has already been evaluated

Whether you are working with print sources or electronic ones, begin with information that has already been evaluated by a professional academic librarian. Such an evaluation is not an absolute guarantee of quality, but it is worthwhile to take advantage of trained professionals in evaluating large amounts of information. All of the books in a college or university library have gone through such an evaluation, as have the electronic databases that college libraries subscribe to. These databases usually contain academic journals, reference materials, and even the full texts of books that have been reviewed by editors and librarians and found to be appropriate for academic research.

A number of excellent Web sites are maintained by scholars and professional librarians, who carefully evaluate Web sources before linking to them. Among the most widely used sites of this nature are:

Librarians' Internet Index
http://lii.org/

The Internet Public Library
www.ipl.org/

Infomine
http://infomine.ucr.edu/

Starting Points for Internet Research (Purdue University)
http://owl.english.purdue.edu/internet/tools/research.html

Research the source of your information

The less familiar you are with a source of information, the more you should research the source before trusting the material it includes. This advice is true for all sources, but especially for those that you find on the Web, where the bar for publication is low and the likelihood of inaccuracy is high. Often, groups whose main purpose is political advocacy present their Web sites and publications as unbiased research centers or public interest concerns. The best place to research a Web site is on the Web itself. A quick Google search on the term "DHMO," for example, yields several sites that discuss the satirical nature of the original site (p. 646). If you encounter a site run by an unfamiliar association, group, or individual, performing a Web search on that group will help you make an informed judgment about the reliability of the information that they offer.

Whether your source is on the Web or in print, consider its author, date of publication, and publisher (or, in the case of Web material, the site where it originally appeared). Is the author affiliated with any organizations? Was the article published or written recently? If not, is the information it offers out of date? Who is the publisher—a government organization, a private business, a special interest group? Does the publisher have a vested interest in the information being presented? All these factors can affect the reliability of your source.

Another good way to check a source—print or electronic—is simply to examine it very carefully. For Web sources, this often means reading other pages on the same site. If you encounter a site that seems to give good information about legalizing drugs, but you discover on another page that the same group or author is concerned about alien abductions, you would do well to treat the information about drug legalization with suspicion. The same principle applies to print sources. If you discover an article in a magazine or journal that you have never heard of, read the rest of the periodical. The other articles may well give you important clues to the overall purposes and biases of the article that you have found.

Cross-check facts

As a general rule, you should be able to verify a fact in additional sources. If you cannot, it may be not a fact at all but a piece of propaganda or misinformation in disguise. If you come upon a fact that does not sound plausible, from a source that you have no reason to consider credible, keep researching until you can verify the claim with at least one other source.

QUOTING, PARAPHRASING, AND SUMMARIZING

Support for a claim can come from facts, statistics, authorities, examples, or textual citations. Any of these may be quoted, paraphrased, or summarized from another source to support your argument. Quoting your source material is the best choice when the original wording is so eloquent or focused that something would be lost in rewording it. If you do not need to retain the wording of a passage but need to retain its details, paraphrasing is your best option. If you want only to highlight the most important details of a passage, summarize. (See chapter 11, p. 595, for more on supporting a claim.)

You must document the source of any material you cite (for documentation guidelines, see p. 639), and you must clearly indicate any wording that is not your own by enclosing it in quotation marks. Remember that paraphrases and summaries must use your own wording and sentence structure.

Here are a few suggestions for working with quotations, paraphrases, and summaries. More-specific suggestions on each kind of citation follow.

Maintain control of your own argument

You must always control the structure, organization, and content of your argument. You can use quotations, paraphrases, and summaries to set up, illustrate, establish, or support your own argument, but you should not allow quotations, paraphrases, and summaries to speak for you. Ultimately, your audience will be evaluating the strength of *your* argument, not those of your sources.

Introduce the context for a citation

Let your readers know where your citation originated—who said or wrote it, why he or she is an authority, where the citation can be found. Establishing that context clarifies the importance of the citation for the reader and, more often than not, will make the cited material more interesting and persuasive.

> **Awkward:** Princes cannot always be moral. "And you have to understand this, that a prince, especially a new one, cannot observe all those things for which men are esteemed, being often forced, in order to maintain the state, to act contrary to faith, friendship, humanity, and religion" (Machiavelli 136)

> **Revised:** Machiavelli writes that, while leaders should try to be moral when possible, they are often required by circumstances to act in ways that are contrary to "faith, friendship, humanity, and religion" (Machiavelli 136).

Select signal verbs carefully

As their name indicates, signal verbs signal to the reader that you are about to quote, paraphrase, or summarize from another source. The common signal verbs "say" and "think" (as in, "Machiavelli says that a leader 'cannot observe all those things for which men are esteemed'") are neutral, but other signal verbs can indicate how you, the writer, feel about the citation, or they can suggest the tone of the original text. The signal verb "claim" can indicate that you are skeptical about the source's belief; "argue" can indicate that the person being cited was emphatic. Select signal verbs carefully, and keep in mind the connotations they will have for your reader.

Two common styles for undergraduate writing are the Modern Language Association (MLA) style and the American Psychological Association (APA) style, and each style dictates different verb tenses for signal verbs. In MLA style, use the present tense to refer to a quotation, paraphrase, or summary: "In 'Serving the Purpose of Education,' Kisautaq Leona Okakok **compares** the Inupiaq idea of education with the Western model that children encounter in public schools (p. 76)." However, if your focus is on the author rather than the writing, use the past tense: "The great Italian political theorist Niccolò Machiavelli **believed** that leaders were 'often forced, in order to maintain the state, to act contrary to faith, friendship, humanity, and religion' (136)." In APA style, use the past tense to refer to a quotation, paraphrase, or summary: "In 'Origin of Species' Darwin **challenged** many of his culture's beliefs about the origins of life."

Quoting

Select quotes carefully

Select a few quotations that express important points within your argument. Make sure that every word of quoted material is relevant to your argument—quotations that are unnecessarily long distract the reader from *your* ideas.

Maintain control of the verb tense and sentence structure

If you quote someone else's words within your writing, you need to control the verb tense and sentence structure of your writing while still using the exact words of your source. Pay close attention to the verb tenses, subject-verb agreement, and noun-pronoun agreement when you incorporate a quote into your writing. If you need to, rewrite your sentence or use ellipses or brackets to alter the quotation.

> **Awkward:** Machiavelli believed about princes, "and you have to understand this, that a prince, especially a new one, cannot observe all those things for which men are esteemed" (136).

> **Revised:** Machiavelli did not believe that rulers should be immoral simply for the sake of immorality, but he did believe that practically minded political leaders did not have the luxury of observing "all those things for which men are esteemed" (136).

Use block quotes sparingly

A long quotation—in MLA style, four or more lines; in APA style, forty or more words—should be set off in a block, indented from the main body of the text. Block quotations are a good strategy for analyzing long passages from a text or for citing passages that are difficult to summarize and extremely important for your argument. However, you should use this strategy sparingly. Employ blocks of quoted text only when the material is extremely important and there is no better way to incorporate it into your essay.

If you use a block quotation, introduce it clearly and then present the quotation indented (in MLA style, it should be ten spaces from the left margin; in APA style, five spaces). Here is an example of how a block quotation looks within an essay:

One of Machiavelli's most controversial points is that leaders must be willing to act in immoral ways when doing so will preserve the stability of their government:

> A prince, especially a new one, cannot observe all those things for which men are esteemed, being often forced, in order to maintain the state, to

act contrary to faith, friendship, humanity, and religion. Therefore it is necessary for him to have a mind ready to turn itself accordingly as the winds and variations of fortune force it, yet, as I have said above, not to diverge from the good if he can avoid doing so, but, if compelled, then to know how to set about it. (136)

Use ellipses (. . .) and brackets ([ ]) to indicate changes in a quotation

Occasionally, you will be able to create a very poignant short quote by using just the beginning phrases and ending phrases from a long paragraph. Or you might find that a word or two in the middle of a sentence would confuse your reader by referencing material in a section of the text that you are not quoting. In instances such as these, you may use ellipsis marks (. . .) to indicate the omission of words in quoted material.

If you need to change the text of a quotation, use brackets ([ ]) to indicate the altered text. You most commonly will use brackets to change the verb tense to make the quoted material compatible with your own syntax, so that you can use the quote in the middle of your sentence. Adding a phrase in brackets can also allow you to clarify a confusing term or substitute a noun for a pronoun.

For example, the extended block quote above from Machiavelli's *The Prince* could be effectively altered within an essay like this:

Machiavelli argued that it was "necessary for [a prince] to have a mind ready to turn itself accordingly as the winds and variations of fortune force it . . . not to diverge from the good if he can avoid doing so, but, if compelled, then to know how to set about it" (136).

Ellipses and brackets are acceptable when used to shorten or focus an argument or to clarify meaning, but they should never be used to change an author's intent. For example, take John F. Kennedy's famous statement, "Ask not what your country can do for you; ask what you can do for your country." In certain circumstances, it would be acceptable to shorten this quotation to "Ask . . . what you can do for your country." However, it would never be appropriate to render it "Ask . . . what your country can do for you." This would change the meaning of the quotation and misrepresent the author's intent.

PARAPHRASING

Indicate source

Whenever you use someone else's ideas, you need to credit them—even if the wording is entirely your own (as it must be in a paraphrase). For guidelines on documenting your sources in MLA and APA styles, see p. 640.

Use your own words and your own sentence structure

By definition, a paraphrase must be in your own words and your own structure. One common way of trying to get around this rule is the "half-baked paraphrase," which attempts to use slightly different words to reproduce the ideas in a source. The first paragraph below comes from Margaret Mead's essay "Warfare: An Invention—Not a Biological Necessity"; the second is an example of a half-baked paraphrase of the same passage:

> **Source:** Warfare is just an invention known to the majority of human societies by which they permit their young men either to accumulate prestige or avenge their honor or acquire loot or wives or slaves or sago lands or cattle or appease the blood lust of their gods or the restless souls of the recently dead. It is just an invention, older and more widespread than the jury system, but none the less an invention. (279)

> **Unacceptable paraphrase:** According to Margaret Mead, war is only a discovery that most human cultures have in common, one that enables them to allow their youth to acquire honor or revenge or to get money, women, servants, property, or livestock or to placate their deities' desire for blood or the souls of those who have died recently. War is simply a discovery, one that has been around longer than trial by jury, but still a discovery. (279)

The second paragraph is far too close in sentence structure and wording to be a true paraphrase; the writer has not really used his own words. Here is an example of a true paraphrase of the same passage:

> **True paraphrase:** Margaret Mead argues persuasively that warfare is not an inevitable product of human nature. Rather, it was invented in most (not all) societies as an economic or religious tool, to permit young men in that society to become wealthy or worship appropriately. Although it is older and more common than many other inventions, like the jury system, it too was created for a purpose. (279)

Enclose in quotation marks any wording that is not your own

If you find in writing a paraphrase that you want to use wording from the original source, make sure that you enclose it in quotation marks. It should be clearly distinguished from your own wording and be properly documented. (See p. 639 for information on how to document sources.)

SUMMARIZING

Include only main ideas

Unlike quotations or paraphrases, summaries should not include details. Instead, summaries highlight the aspects of a source that are most important or most relevant to your argument. Keep your summaries short and focused, trim away any extraneous detail, and concentrate on what's most important. See, for example, how the following passage uses summaries to highlight and compare the main ideas from two texts:

> Even liberal modern philosophers cannot agree with each other about our moral responsibility to the poor. On the one hand, in "Two Principles of Justice," John Rawls insists that a basic understanding of fairness requires us to distribute our resources in a way that everybody would see as fair if they viewed it from a neutral perspective (354). Garrett Hardin, on the other hand, believed that giving food, money, or other resources to poor people, especially those in less developed countries, is actually an immoral action. In "Lifeboat Ethics: The Case against Helping the Poor," Hardin argues that the earth's carrying capacity is limited and that it is unfair to allow people to exceed this capacity by having more children than the planet can support—thus placing everyone in danger (360).

Use your own words

Like a paraphrase, a summary by definition must be in your own words. Avoid using words and phrases similar to those in the source.

Indicate the source

Whenever you use or cite someone else's ideas, you need to credit them—even if the wording is entirely your own. For guidelines on documenting your sources in MLA and APA styles, see p. 640.

DOCUMENTING SOURCES

Whenever you use another's ideas or refer to a source in your writing, you need to provide documentation—identifying information—for your source. The information you need to provide depends on the documentation style you are using (see p. 639), but all styles require that you provide (at least) the author, title, publisher, year of publication, and page number. (This information varies, of course, if you are referring to an Internet publication, magazine, government document, or other nonbook source.)

Plagiarism is any use of another person's idea without proper documentation. Plagiarism is an act of academic dishonesty that can have serious repercussions. At most colleges and universities, students who turn in plagiarized work risk, at a minimum, failing the course in which the plagiarism occurs. At many schools, additional punishments can include probation, suspension, loss of privileges, or permanent expulsion.

The long-term risks of plagiarism never outweigh the potential short-term benefits. The act could, quite literally, follow you for the rest of your life. But an even stronger reason exists to avoid plagiarism: it is a fundamentally illogical act. By coming to college, you are sacrificing both your time and, in all likelihood, a significant amount of money to get an education. When you turn in plagiarized work, you deprive yourself of the education that you are making real sacrifices to obtain.

The term "plagiarism," however, also covers many actions that are not intentionally dishonest. Even if it is accidental, documenting quotations, paraphrases, or summaries incorrectly or not at all is plagiarism, as is using another's idea without proper attribution. You must give proper credit and attribution for all of the following:

Words and phrases quoted directly from a source
Any time that you use words directly from another source, you must use *both* quotation marks *and* a proper source documentation. This requirement holds even if the direct quotation is only a single sentence or a few words. In some styles, indented block quotations do not require actual quotation marks because the spacing acts as a quotation marker. However, even in these cases, full and accurate documentation is absolutely essential.

Ideas you have summarized or paraphrased from a source
It is plagiarism to summarize, paraphrase, or just use someone's ideas without attributing those ideas to their source. For examples of paraphrases and summaries, see pp. 636–37.

In the example from "Warfare: An Invention—Not a Biological Necessity" on p. 636, it would have been dishonest for the writer of the paraphrase to take credit in any way for the basic idea of Mead's essay: that warfare is an invention that spread from culture to culture rather than an inherent element of the human condition. Any idea that you borrow from another source must be attributed to that source, even if all the writing is your own.

Facts that are not considered common knowledge
In the middle of "Warfare: An Invention—Not a Biological Necessity," Margaret Mead writes that the Andaman pygmies living in the Bay of Bengal had a knowledge of organized warfare long before they ever encountered Europeans or other more technologically sophisticated societies. Even if you use this fact in another context (say in an essay about the organization of pygmy tribes), you must still cite Mead as the basis for this information, because it is not what scholars call "common knowledge."

In this context, "common knowledge" refers to the kind of information that is generally known or that is easily available in reference works. For example, the facts that the Andaman Islands are in the Bay of Bengal and that the native inhabitants of these islands are pygmies can be readily found in reference books and on Web sites, making them part of the pool of general knowledge. You would not need to cite Mead (or anyone else) as your source for these facts.

Approaches or organizational strategies borrowed from a source

Creating interesting, subtle frameworks for discussing ideas is one of a writer's most important skills. If, in searching for such a framework, you borrow from some-one else's work, you must acknowledge it. Imagine, for example, that, in searching for a way to compare Machiavelli's *The Prince* and de Pizan's *Treasure of the City of Ladies*," you came across a Web site comparing them as "political theories," "cultural theories," and "theories of history." If you used these three categories in your own essay, you would need to acknowledge the Web site as your source—even if your actual comparisons did not borrow at all from the original source.

Anyone who has helped you develop your ideas

Whenever you collaborate with other people on your writing, make sure you give them proper credit. (Keep in mind that your instructor might not allow collabora-tion of any kind, in which case the ideas that you come up with must be entirely your own.) Contributions from other students, professors, colleagues, friends, and family should be acknowledged either in the body of the text or in a footnote or an endnote that explicitly gives credit where it is due. A note such as "Thanks to Dr. Mary Johnson of the Department of Psychology for her contribution to my understanding of Freud's concept of the ego" can be placed either at the end of an essay or at the place in the essay where the relevant discussion occurs.

DOCUMENTATION STYLES

Different academic disciplines use several different styles to document sources. Two common styles for undergraduate writing are the Modern Language Associ-ation (MLA) style and the American Psychological Association (APA) style.

The Modern Language Association (MLA) format

This style originated for the discussion of literature and is currently used in many humanities disciplines. MLA format places a minimal amount of information in an in-text citation and puts full bibliographical citations at the end on a Works Cited page.

The American Psychological Association (APA) format

APA style is used in most social sciences, including education, nursing, and social work. In-text citations in the APA style give a publication date as well as a name, with full bibliographic information provided on a References page.

Before writing an essay, determine which style your instructor prefers and refer to an official style guide for detailed instructions on using that style. The follow-ing table gives brief guidelines in MLA and APA styles for some of the most com-mon documentation tasks. This table is not a replacement for the style manuals, which provide much more detail on different kinds of documentation.

Modern Language Association Style Guide (MLA)

Seventh Edition, 2009

In-Text Citations

When you cite another source in your own writing, place enough information in parentheses for the reader to locate the source on your Works Cited page. If you have already identified your source, put the page number in parentheses immediately after the citation. Place the parentheses after the closing quotation marks but before the period:

> Brazilian educator Paulo Freire has argued that contemporary models of education have become "lifeless and petrified" (63).

If you're citing a source that doesn't have page numbers, such as a Web site, include the paragraph or section number in parentheses:

> Freire also founded the Paulo Freire Institute; according to its Web site, it "seeks to bring together scholars, activists, and teachers inspired by Freire's pedagogy to foster the advancement and 'reinvention' of Freirian educational theories" (par. 2).

Quotations that run for more than four lines should be set off in blocks, without quotation marks. In the block-quote format, the parenthetical citation comes after the period:

> Paulo Freire describes the kind of learning environment that results when teachers are expected to be simply depositors of information:
> Education thus becomes an act of depositing, in which the students are the depositories and the teacher is the depositor. Instead of communicating, the teacher issues communiqués and makes deposits which the students patiently receive, memorize, and repeat. (64)

American Psychological Association Style Guide (APA)

Sixth Edition, 2009

In-Text Citations

When you summarize the contents of an article, document the source by placing the date immediately after the author's name:

> Freire (1970) critiques the replication of oppressive power dynamics in the classroom.

If you quote in an essay, APA guidelines require the date immediately after the citation and the page number at the end of the quotation. This is also true if you paraphrase a passage or cite a fact that can be found on a specific page:

> Freire (1970) labels the current standard pedagogy in most classrooms as the "banking model of education" (p. 64).

> Freire (1970) asserts that education is most able to be library when it poses problems rather than trying to transfer information (p. 64).

In APA articles, it is not unusual to have two sources by the same author (since someone working on a given topic in the social sciences will often contribute to several papers as part of an overall study). If the texts are from the same year, use lowercase letters to distinguish between different articles:

> Freire (1970b) insists that educators who desire to be revolutionary must begin with the classroom environment that they create.

If your text does not contain enough information to identify a source that you are citing, give the name, date, and, if necessary, page number of that source in the parenthetical citation:

Even teachers who are committed to liberation often ignore the power dynamics of their own classrooms (Freire, 1970, p. 65).

If you need to quote more than 40 words, set the quotation off in a block. For block quotes, indent five spaces from the left margin and type the quoted text without quotation marks:

Freire (1970) explains how oppressive ideologies can translate into classroom practices:

> In the banking concept of education, knowledge is a gift bestowed by those who consider themselves knowledgeable upon those whom they consider to know nothing. Projecting an absolute ignorance onto others, a characteristic of the ideology of oppression, negates education and knowledge as processes of injury (p. 64).

If you are citing a source that does not have a page number—such as a Web page—include instead the number of the paragraph that the information comes from, using either the ¶ symbol or the abbreviation "para."

O'Malley (1997) points out that many teachers who use Black Vernacular English in their classrooms do so to "heighten children's awareness of the differences between AAVE and standard English and enhance their ability to speak the standard with fewer errors" (para. 5).

If a paragraph does not give enough information to identify a citation, then include the author's name parenthetically:

Liberation pedagogy asserts that teachers must do more than simply present information that is "disconnected from the totality that engendered them" (Freire 65).

If you have two works by the same author, add a word or phrase from the title to identify the work:

Freire lists ten distinct contrasts between the "banking model" and the "liberation model" of education ("Pedagogy" 63–66).

Bibliographical Citations

Full bibliographical citations are given at the end of an essay on a separate page titled "Works Cited." The Works Cited page lists sources alphabetically by author, or, if an author is unavailable, by title. When an author is listed multiple times, the listings are arranged alphabetically by title. Below are the formats for some of the most common kinds of citations that you will need to do on your Works Cited page.

Bibliographical Citations

Full bibliographical citations are given at the end of an essay on a separate page titled "References." The References page lists works alphabetically by author, or, if an author is unavailable, by title. When an author is listed multiple times, the listings are arranged by date. Below are the formats for some of the most common kinds of citations that you will need to do on your References page.

KIND OF CITATION	MLA FORMAT	APA FORMAT
Single-Author Book	Elshtain, Jean Bethke. *Just War against Terror: The Burden of American Power in a Violent World.* New York: Basic, 2003. Print.	Elshtain, J. B. (2003). *Just war against terror: The burden of American power in a violent world.* New York: Basic Books.
Multiple-Author Book (Fewer than Four Authors)	Malless, Stanley, and Jeffrey McQuain. *Coined by God: Words and Phrases That First Appear in the English Translations of the Bible.* New York: Norton, 2003. Print.	Malless, S., & McQuain, J. (2003). *Coined by God: Words and phrases that first appear in the English translations of the Bible.* New York: Norton.
Work in an Anthology	Achebe, Chinua. "Language and the Destiny of Man." *Reading the World: Ideas That Matter.* 2nd ed. Ed. Michael Austin. New York: Norton, 2010. 592–99. Print.	Achebe, C. (2010). Language and the destiny of man. In M. Austin (Ed.), *Reading the world: Ideas that matter* (pp. 506–15). New York: Norton. (Original work published 1972)
Single-Author Journal Article (Paginated by Volume)	Weinberger, Jerry. "Pious Princes and Red-Hot Lovers: The Politics of Shakespeare's *Romeo and Juliet.*" *Journal of Politics* 65 (2003): 370–75. Print.	Weinberger, J. (2003). Pious princes and red-hot lovers: The politics of Shakespeare's *Romeo and Juliet. Journal of Politics, 65,* 370–375.
Multiple-Author Journal Article (Paginated by Issue)	Weaver, Constance, Carol McNally, and Sharon Moerman. "To Grammar or Not to Grammar: That Is Not the Question!" *Voices from the Middle* 8.3 (2001): 17–33. Print.	Weaver, C., McNally, C., & Moerman, S. (2001). To grammar or not to grammar: That is *not* the question! *Voices from the Middle, 8*(3), 17–33.

Scholarly Edition	Austen, Jane. *Sense and Sensibility.* Ed. Claudia Johnson. New York: Norton, 2001. Print.	Austen J. (2001). *Sense and sensibility* (C. Johnson, Ed.). New York: Norton.
Magazine Article—Monthly	Zahi, Hawass. "Egypt's Forgotten Treasures." *National Geographic* Jan. 2003: 74–87. Print.	Zahi, H. (2003, January). Egypt's forgotten treasures. *National Geographic, 203,* 74–87.
Magazine Article—Weekly	Samuelson, Robert J. "The Changing Face of Poverty." *Newsweek* 18 Oct. 2004: 50. Print.	Samuelson, R. J. (2004, October 18). The changing face of poverty. *Newsweek, 144,* 50.
Newspaper Article	Farenthold, David. "Town Shaken by Lobster Theft." *Washington Post* 9 Oct. 2005: A3. Print.	Farenthold, D. (2005, October 9). Town shaken by lobster theft. *The Washington Post,* p. A3.
Article from an Electronic Database	Moore, Kathleen D. "The Truth of the Barnacles: Rachel Carson and the Moral Significance of Wonder." *Environmental Ethics* 27.3 (Fall 2005): 265–77. *Academic Search Premier.* Web. 9 Oct. 2005	Moore, K. D. (2005). The truth of the barnacles: Rachel Carson and the moral significance of wonder. *Environmental Ethics, 27*(3). 265–277. Retrieved from Academic Search Premier database.
Work That Appears Only Online	Nasr, Seyyed Hossein. "The Meaning and Concept of Philosophy in Islam." *Islamic Philosophy Online.* Ed. Muhammed Hozien. Islamic Philosophy Online, Inc., 5 May 2007. Web. 23 Apr. 2009.	Nasr, S. H. (2007, May 5). The meaning and concept of philosophy in Islam. Retrieved April 23, 2009, from http://www.muslimphilosophy.com/ip/nasr-ip1.htm
Online Work also Online	Gross, Daniel. "The Quitter Economy." *Slate.* Slate, 24 Jan. 2009. Web. 26 April 2009.	Gross, D. (2009, 24 January). The quitter economy. *Slate.* Retrieved from http://www.slate.com/id/2209617
Online Work also in Print	Dowd, Maureen. "Sacred Cruelties." *New York Times,* 7 April 2002. Web. 9 Oct. 2005.	Dowd, M. (2002, April 7). Sacred cruelties [Electronic version]. *New York Times,* p. A3o.

Sample Documented Essay (MLA Format)

Clarissa Porter

Professor Croft

English 101, Section 10

February 13, 2010

Human Nature in Mencius and Hsün Tzu

Mencius and Hsün Tzu were both Chinese scholars living during the Period of Warring States. They were both self-professed Confucians, and they both believed that rites and rituals were necessary in order to perfect human beings. Both Mencius and Hsün Tzu gave a lot of thought to questions of human nature, but, as many writers and scholars have pointed out, they came to very different conclusions. Mencius believed that human beings were inherently good, and that they only act in evil ways when their natural goodness is perverted. Hsün Tzu, on the other hand, believed that human nature is inherently evil and must be corrected by strict religious observances. These differences, however, have often been exaggerated. Mencius and Hsün Tzu have certain theoretical differences about the abstract concept of human nature, but their view of what humans should do is nearly identical.

The differences between Mencius and Hsün Tzu have been the subject of substantial commentary. In *China's Imperial Past,* for example, Charles O. Hucker asserts that

Porter 2

Whereas Mencius's conception of the essential goodness of human nature has led some specialists to characterize him as a tenderhearted idealist, it is universally agreed that the last great Confucian thinker of the formative age, Hsün Tzu, was an unsentimental, ruthlessly tough-minded rationalist. His characteristic intellectual approach was "Humbug! Let's consider the facts." (82)

Hucker's characterization here is backed up by the authors themselves. Mencius argues that "human nature is inherently good, just like water inherently flows downhill. There is no such thing as a person who isn't good, just as there's no water that doesn't flow downhill" (95). Hsün Tzu directly contradicts this. "Mencius," Hsün Tzu says, "states that man's nature is good, and that all evil arises because he loses his original nature. Such a view, I believe, is erroneous" (102). Even the title of Hsün Tzu's essay, "Man's Nature Is Evil," betrays his fundamental difference with Mencius.

The difference between the two Confucian scholars is fundamental, but is it important? Some scholars believe that the differences between them stem from different views of morality but that, in the words of David E. Soles, "they are in substantial agreement as to the empirical facts of human nature" (123). Soles believes that the differences between Mencius and Hsün Tzu are real, but that these differences are not the result of the two considering sets of facts about human behavior. Both philosophers acknowledge that human beings sometimes act morally and sometimes immorally. They differ drastically in what they see as the root cause for this behavior—Mencius believes that people are immoral when they deny their natures and

Hsün Tzu believes that they are immoral when they do not. Amazingly, though, these differences do not result in any practical differences in the behavior that they recommend.

Like Confucius, Hsün Tzu believes that we must all shape our characters through an elaborate series of purifying rituals. These rituals, he believes, turn inherently evil people into moral beings:

> Mencius states that man is capable of learning because his nature is good, but I say that this is wrong. It indicates that he has not really understood man's nature nor distinguished properly between the basic nature and conscious activity. The nature is that which is given by Heaven; you cannot learn it, you cannot acquire it by effort. Ritual principles, on the other hand, are created by sages; you can learn to apply them, you can work to bring them to completion. That part of man which cannot be learned or acquired by effort is called the nature; that part of him which can be acquired by learning and brought to completion by effort is called conscious activity.
>
> This is the difference between nature and conscious activity. (95)

Conscious activity is just as important to Mencius, who, according to the online edition of the *Stanford Encyclopedia*, "regarded the transformative power of a cultivated person as the ideal basis for government. In addition, he spelled out more explicitly the idea that order in society depends on proper attitudes within the family, which in turn depends on cultivating oneself." Mencius believed that people should engage in ritual self-cultivation through the very same Confucian rituals advocated by Hsün Tzu.

Porter 4

For Hsün Tzu, Confucian rituals are necessary to change human nature into some-thing good. For Mencius, they are necessary to cultivate raw human nature, which is already good, into the polished attributes of a gentleman. Their philosophical views could not be farther apart, but in the end, the behavioral norms that they expound are very similar, and their dedication to Confucian rituals is identical. Their enmity is limited to the realm of the abstract. In practice, they would have us do the same things, albeit for very different reasons.

Porter 5

Works Cited

Hsün Tzu. "Man's Nature Is Evil." *Reading the World: Ideas That Matter.* 2nd ed. Ed. Michael Austin. New York: Norton, 2009. 100–09. Print.

Hucker, Charles O. *China's Imperial Past: An Introduction to Chinese History and Culture.* Stanford, CA: Stanford UP, 1975. Print.

Mencius. "Man's Nature Is Good." *Reading the World: Ideas That Matter.* 2nd ed. Ed. Michael Austin. New York: Norton, 2009. 94–99. Print.

Shun, Kwong Loi. "Mencius." 2004. *Stanford Encyclopedia of Philosophy.* Web. 11 Feb. 2009.

Soles, David E. "The Nature and Grounds of Xunzi's Disagreement with Mencius." *Asian Philosophy* 9.2 (1999): 123–33. Print.

14

REVISING AND EDITING

W RITING IS NOT A *product* but a *process*—a draft can always be revised, reshaped, reformed, and improved. Once you've finished a draft of an essay, it's best to put it aside for a day or two and then approach it with a fresh eye—a "re-vision."

Revising a draft often means reimagining it from the ground up. During revision you'll want to **rethink** the basic ideas of your essay and **rewrite** the text as needed. You may revisit several stages of the writing process, perhaps doing more research, revising your thesis, and reorganizing your draft. Just as a renovated building often looks nothing like it did before renovations, it is not uncommon for writers to find that, after two or three revisions, almost nothing remains of the drafts that they started with.

Once you've completed rethinking and rewriting—a process you may go through several times—it's time to **edit**. This is the time to correct errors in spelling, punctuation, and grammar, and check for other mechanical issues.

In the following pages are guidelines and suggestions for the revision process—for rethinking, rewriting, and editing your essays.

RETHINKING

Give yourself plenty of time

Good writing takes time. You cannot create and revise multiple drafts the night before an essay is due. In fact, one of the most important parts of the writing process is leaving a draft alone for a day or two so you can come back to it with a fresh perspective. Your best essays will be the ones that you start well in advance of their due date and keep thinking about until they are done. This does not necessarily mean that you must spend more time on a paper than do those who procrastinate until the very end. Six hours spread over a week will almost always produce a better paper than six hours spent the night before it is due.

Ask other people to read your draft and provide feedback

The very act of writing suggests an audience, and, to be sure, your instructor will generally be the final audience for your efforts. But it is usually a good idea to get feedback on a draft during the revision process. A friend, a classmate, or a writing tutor can let you know if you have effectively translated your ideas into written words—and even if the ideas were worth translating in the first place.

Reread the assignment and make sure that you have followed it correctly

Good writing, as discussed in chapter 9, meets the expectations of its audience. When the audience is a teacher who has given you an assignment, you must make absolutely certain that you have followed the instructions as closely as possible. Refer to the assignment guidelines when you have finished a draft and again when you're revising—just to make sure that, in the process of crafting your essay, you have not strayed away from the assignment or failed to answer a critical question asked by the instructor.

Identify your thesis and consider how each part of the essay supports it

The writing process is also often a discovery process. We discover new ideas and perspectives in the process of writing about them. This is one of the main reasons that revision is so important. It's not unusual to discover what you are trying to say while you are writing your first draft. If you find that, by the end of your draft, you're focusing on a different thesis from the one you started with, you'll want to revise your original thesis statement or revise other parts of your essay. In either case, make sure that your entire essay, all your evidence, develops and supports the same thesis—and make sure that that thesis is clearly indicated.

Don't be afraid to throw out ideas that don't work

One of the hardest things for any writer to do is to cut out words, sentences, or whole paragraphs that he or she has spent a substantial amount of time creating. After we labor over a piece of writing, we feel an ownership of, and even a responsibility to, the words that we have brought into being. But nobody has good ideas all of the time, and even good ideas can be inappropriate if they don't support the thesis. When you revise, you must be willing to cut anything that does not work. If you decide that an idea is not worth pursuing, or that it doesn't support or develop your thesis, you must cut ruthlessly—even if it means scrapping the entire paper and starting over from scratch.

REWRITING

Make sure that your introduction and conclusion are consistent with each other

In the same way that ideas can drift away from the thesis during the course of writing a paper, conclusions can drift away from introductions. Use the revision process as an opportunity to revisit these two crucial paragraphs and make sure that they are working together. You might revise your introduction so that it anticipates your conclusion or revise your conclusion so that it refers to or extends your introduction—just make sure that they tie your essay together. This will encourage readers to view your essay as a self-contained, coherent argument.

Make sure that you have clear transitions between all major ideas

Transitions between ideas are an important part of orienting a reader to your paper (see p. 586). However, they can also be difficult to include in a first draft, since you are so often discovering ideas through the process of writing. You should therefore check the beginning and end of each paragraph and revise as needed to include transitions that move readers gracefully and seamlessly from one idea to the next.

Read sentences out loud to see how they sound

Reading sentences out loud can help you detect awkward constructions that are hard to see in written text. Although the written word can be more stilted and less fluid than speech—we often speak in sentence fragments and slang terms that we would never put in a formal essay—the "ear test" can uncover awkward sentence constructions and confusing syntax that might otherwise be masked by the elevated formality of the written word.

Look for ways to eliminate useless words and phrases

It's easy to fall into the trap of using more words than are needed to convey an idea, especially in a first draft. But fewer words often means clearer, more straightforward, and more elegant prose. If you look carefully at your first draft, you will probably find it full of "deadwood": "there is" or "there are" at the beginnings of sentences, wordy constructions such as "because of the fact that" (rather than simply "because"), and unnecessary additions and qualifications of all kinds. As you rewrite, look for ways to eliminate extra words that do not contribute to your meaning. Style guides such as Strunk and White's classic *Elements of Style* or other books your instructor may recommend can help you learn to spot deadwood and write active, powerful sentences.

Pay attention to your ethos

As we discussed in chapter 11, readers usually judge writers by the ethos (p. 608)—the overall persona—projected in a piece of writing. During the revision process, pay special attention to the ethos that you are projecting. This is the time to make sure that you do not antagonize readers by sounding arrogant or uncompromising, that you do not lose their confidence by sounding tentative or apologetic, and that you do not jeopardize your credibility by including incorrect information.

EDITING

Make sure that you have documented every source

Because of your high number of plagiarism cases that most colleges face each year, documentation errors tend to be punished more severely than other kinds of errors. As we saw in chapter 13, the line between accidentally omitting a certain and plagiarizing a paper is very thin. As you prepare your final draft for submission, make sure that you have properly documented every outside source that you used in any way.

Refer to a handbook or other source for grammar and usage questions

Many instructors require or recommend a handbook for composition courses. Handbooks contain a wealth of information about grammar rules, punctuation conventions, documentation styles, and other nuts-and-bolts elements of writing. If your instructor has chosen a specific handbook, use it faithfully. If not, select one in your library or bookstore and become familiar enough with it to use it when revising your papers. You do not need to know every rule and convention by heart, but you will need to know how to look them up when you need them.

Read your entire essay out loud to catch any errors you might have missed

Just as reading sentences out loud can help you catch awkward passages, reading an entire essay out loud, carefully and slowly, can help you see missing words, extra characters, spelling errors not caught by spellcheckers, and other problems with your paper that can result from carelessness.

REVISING AND EDITING CHECKLIST

During the revision process, keep the following questions in mind.

IDEAS

- Have you met the guidelines for the assignment? (See "Considering Expectations," p. 567.)
- Have you generated an idea that is original enough to make an impact on the reader? (See "Achieving Subtlety," p. 574.)
- Is the idea sufficiently focused?

STRUCTURE

- Is there an arguable, well-written thesis? (See "Thesis Statements," p. 579.)
- Does the introductory paragraph set up the thesis and define key terms in the essay? (See "Introductions," p. 583.)
- Are there solid, well-constructed transitions between all major ideas? (See "Transitions," p. 586.)
- Does the concluding paragraph tie together major arguments in the essay and bring the whole to a definite conclusion? (See "Conclusions," p. 591.)

ARGUMENT

- Have you considered how your audience will respond to your arguments? How have you appealed to your audience? (See "Considering Expectations," p. 567, and "Supporting Ideas," p. 594.)
- Have you constructed a persuasive ethos? Is it reasonable and knowledgeable? (See "Ethos: The Writer's Appeal," p. 608.)
- Are all of your major claims supported with appropriate evidence? (See "Supporting Claims with Evidence," p. 595.)
- Do all of the supporting arguments in the essay support the main thesis? That is, are they relevant and focused? (See "Supporting Ideas," p. 594.)

CORRECTNESS

- Have you integrated all quotations, paraphrases, and summaries smoothly into your own writing? (See "Quoting, Paraphrasing, and Summarizing," p. 632.)

- Have you properly documented all outside sources according to the style guide required by the assignment? (See "Documenting Sources," p. 637.)

- Have you read your essay out loud to check for awkward phrasing and to catch errors that you might miss reading silently?

- Have you proofread carefully and corrected any errors in grammar, spelling, or punctuation?

PERMISSIONS
ACKNOWLEDGMENTS

Viking Penguin, a division of Penguin Group (USA) Inc. In the United Kingdom, reproduced by permission of Penguin Books Ltd.

Lucy Lameck: "Africans Are Not Poor" by Lucy Lameck, translated by Saifu Kiango and M. M. Mulokozi from *Women Writing Africa: The Eastern Region*, edited by Amandina Lihamba, Fulata L. Moyo, M. M. Mulokozi, Naomi L. Shitemi, and Saïda Yahya-Othman. Reprinted by permission of the Feminist Press at CUNY.

Margaret Mead: "Warfare: An Invention—Not a Biological Necessity" by Margaret Mead (*Asia*, Vol. 40, No. 8, August 1940, pp. 402–05), courtesy of the Institute for Intercultural Studies, Inc., New York.

Mencius: Copyright © 1999 by David Hinton from *Mencius*. Reprinted by permission of Counterpoint.

N. Scott Momaday: "Personal Reflections" from *The American Indian and the Problem of History*, edited by Calvin Martin. By permission of Oxford University Press, Inc.

Toni Morrison: "Nobel Lecture" by Toni Morrison. Copyright © 1993 The Nobel Foundation.

Nāgārjuna: We have made diligent efforts to contact the copyright holder to obtain permission to reprint these sections. If you have information that would help us, please write to W. W. Norton & Company, Inc., 500 Fifth Avenue, New York, NY 10110.

Kenzaburo Oe: From *Hiroshima Notes* by Kenzaburo Oe, translated by David L. Swain and Toshi Yonezawa. Copyright © 1965 by Kenzaburo Oe. Translation copyright © 1981 by David L. Swain and Toshi Yonezawa. Used by permission of Grove/Atlantic, Inc. *Hiroshima Notes* by Kenzaburo Oe is published in the United Kingdom by Marion Boyars Publishers (London 1997).

Kisautaq Leona Okakok: Excerpted with permission from Kisautaq Leona Okakok, "Serving the Purpose of Education," *Harvard Educational Review* 59.4 (November 1989): 405–22. Copyright © by the President and Fellows of Harvard College. All rights reserved. For more information, please visit www.harvardeducationalreview.org.

George Orwell: "Pacifism and the War" from *The Collected Essays, Journalism and Letters of George Orwell, Volume II: My Country Right or Left, 1940–1943*, copyright © 1968 by Sonia Brownell Orwell and renewed 1996 by Mark Hamilton, reprinted by permission of Houghton Mifflin Harcourt Publishing Company. In the United Kingdom and Canada, reprinted by permission of Bill Hamilton as the Literary Executor of the Estate of the Late Sonia Brownell Orwell and Secker & Warburg Ltd.

INDEX